RIGHT
AND
REASON

RIGHT
AND
REASON
ETHICS IN THEORY AND PRACTICE

Austin Fagothey, S. J.

Professor of Philosophy, University of Santa Clara,
Santa Clara, California

Sixth edition

The C. V. Mosby Company

Saint Louis   1976

Imprimi potest: Richard P. Vaughan, S.J., Provincial
Nihil obstat: Lyman A. Fenn, S.S., S.T.D., Censor Librorum
Imprimatur: ✠ Joseph T. McGucken, S.T.D., Archbishop of San Francisco
June 23, 1975

SIXTH EDITION

Library of Congress Cataloging in Publication Data

Fagothey, Austin, 1901-1975.
   Right and reason: ethics in theory and practice.

   Bibliography: p.
   Includes index.
   1. Ethics. I. Title.
BJ1025.F18   1976   170   75-33045
ISBN 0-8016-1545-3

VH/VH/VH 9 8 7 6 5 4 3 2 1

IN MEMORIAM

Father Austin Fagothey completed his revisions for this sixth edition of *Right and Reason* just two weeks before he died of cancer on May 29, 1975. Throughout the course of the spring, he knew he was dying, but he did not stop. He maintained his careful concern for his students and his scholarly work until the end. This was the hallmark of the man. He spent forty years in the classroom, many of those years devoted to teaching ethics. *Right and Reason* is the fruit of many of those years spent in dialogue with his students about moral issues. He demanded rigorous thinking of himself and made that same demand of his students. Generous with his time and always ready to help them, he was an inspiration both to his students and to the faculty at the University of Santa Clara.

Santa Clara will not be the same without Austin Fagothey; it is certainly richer for the time he spent here, teaching and working in such an outstanding way. All of us who knew him—faculty, students, and graduates—remember him with fondness and respect. Students throughout the country have had the benefit of his thinking about moral matters. In the posthumous publication of this sixth edition of *Right and Reason,* I hope many more students will yet meet in spirit Austin Fagothey, the man and moral philosopher, and be inspired to think rigorously about morals and formulate their own set of moral convictions to guide their life and personal growth.

Milton Gonsalves, S.J.
University of Santa Clara
Santa Clara, California

PREFACE
to the fifth edition

There has been more change in student attitudes during the last few years than were visible over many previous decades. The teacher, especially if he is over thirty, has a hard time "keeping with it." If he gives up the effort, he loses his students, having not only fewer bodies to talk at but still fewer minds receptive to what he thinks might be wisdom. If he turns his class over wholly to dialogue among the students, he finds that they soon become bored with the exchange of their own ignorance and resent going out with little more than they came in with. The teacher himself will have to help in closing the generation gap and he should find it an exhilarating if sometimes frustrating experience.

Since the counterculture of youth has not yet produced anything resembling a philosophy, whatever ethics it has is extremely formless. Besides the emphasis on love, honesty, openness, and freedom, the chief characteristic noticeable seems to be a great uprising in pure subjectivism, in the idea that each one must develop his own ethics which will be tailored to fit his own unique and individual life style. Such an ethical theory, if it can be called one, is limited to the statement just made; after that each one is on his own. Morals, as one student put it, are decided by "gut" reaction and not by thought. Not all express the new romanticism so baldly, and those who are willing to do any thinking may still be brought to see that not all lives, not even all the freest lives, are equally beautiful. Besides, many young people are more conservative than some of their elders but they will have to live with their contemporaries. A look at all sides, and especially at the other side, is needed even to appreciate one's own position.

The present fifth edition of this book has been updated toward meeting the new attitude. More than half of it has been completely rewritten. Some students persist in seeing dogmatism or indoctrination in the most bland and noncommittal remarks. The approach to each problem has been revised to avoid giving as far as possible any appearance of grounds for such a suspicion, while performing at the same time the difficult feat of saying something. But I will not relinquish my freedom to sum up an investigation and express my convictions, with which both teacher and student are free to disagree. Thus most questions are treated by giving an equal number of arguments on each side, after which some ways of sifting out the truth are suggested. Traditional views are not omitted, but they are countered with current criticisms.

The first half of the book has been reorganized around ten major theories covering the whole spectrum of ethical positions. Students no longer come to ethics with a background of logic, epistemology, metaphysics, and history of philosophy. No procedure can overcome that disadvantage, but the approach adopted here has been found to offset it somewhat. Law and duty, distasteful concepts to some members of the younger generation, cannot be omitted from a study of ethics, but appeal to them has been toned down in favor of an emphasis on the dignity of the human person. Former sections on situation, freedom, love, sex, and protest have been expanded into a full chapter on each.

The teaching aids that were features of former editions have been retained in this: the use of ordinary language rather than technical vocabulary, quotations from classical and modern philosophers, summaries at the end of each chapter, reading lists encouraging the student to go to the sources, provocative questions to stimulate class discussion, and an updated bibliography and index. To these have been added a separate paperback publication, *Anthology of Right*

and Reason, containing a wide selection of readings for class use and designed to accompany this text. They go well together, but each can be used independently.

My haphazard bookkeeping methods make it impossible for me, even if space permitted, to acknowledge by name all those who have helped me in this work. I here thank them collectively, together with my teaching colleagues and students, all of whom have been a constant source of encouragement.

Austin Fagothey, S.J.

ACKNOWLEDGMENTS

Grateful acknowledgment is hereby made to the various authors and publishers who kindly granted permission to quote from the following works:

To the Oxford University Press and the Clarendon Press for permission to quote from *The Dialogues of Plato,* translated by B. Jowett; from *The Works of Aristotle Translated Into English,* edited by W. D. Ross; from Epicurus' *Letter to Menoeceus,* translated by Cyril Bailey; from J. B. Scott, *Classics of International law; Selections From Three Works of Francisco Suarez;* and from Hegel's *Philosophy of Right,* translated by T. M. Knox.

To Random House for permission to quote from *Basic Writings of St. Thomas Aquinas,* edited by Anton C. Pegis (quotations from *The Summa Theologica,* I-II, qq. 6-114, are from this source); and from E. A. Burtt, *The English Philosophers From Bacon to Mill.*

To Benziger Brothers for permission to quote from *The Summa Theologica of St. Thomas Aquinas,* translated by Fathers of the English Dominican Province (quotations from *The Summa Theologica,* I-II, qq. 1-5, 21, II-II, and III suppl., are from this source).

To Professor Lewis W. Beck and the University of Chicago Press for permission to quote from L. W. Beck, *Kant: Critique of Practical Reason and Other Writings in Moral Philosophy.*

To Houghton Mifflin Company for permission to quote from Benjamin Rand, *The Classical Moralists.*

To Charles Scribner's Sons for permission to quote from *The Range of Reason* by Jacques Maritain.

To T. & T. Clark, Edinburgh, for permission to quote from St. Augustine's *The City of God,* translated by Marcus Dods; and from Kant's *Philosophy of Law,* translated by W. Hastie.

To George Allen & Unwin, London, for permission to quote from Bertrand Russell, *Mysticism and Logic.*

To Charles H. Kerr & Company for permission to quote from their edition of Karl Marx's *Capital.*

To the Fordham University Press for permission to quote from St. Robert Bellarmine, *De Laicis, or the Treatise on Civil Government,* translated by K. Murphy; and from Le Buffe and Hayes, *Jurisprudence.*

To Victor Gollancz, Ltd., and Dover Publications, Inc. (publishers of the American edition), for permission to quote from *Language, Truth and Logic* by A. J. Ayer.

To the Philosophical Library for permission to quote from Jean-Paul Sartre, *Existentialism,* translated by Bernard Frechtman.

To the Journal Press for permission to quote from "Anthropology and the Abnormal" by Ruth Benedict, *Journal of General Psychology,* vol. 10, pp. 59-82, 1934.

CONTENTS

Chapter 1

ETHICS

ORIGIN OF ETHICS

The good life and how to live it must always have been the subject of human speculation. In all his varied actions man sees that not just any way of doing them will lead to success but that there is a right way and a wrong way. It must have been early in human history that man saw that this question could be asked of life as a whole: Is there a right and a wrong way of *living*, of gathering all these acts into the spending of a life? Is there a pattern, a model, an ideal of the good life? If so, where can one find it and how stringent is the demand that one follow it?

We have no record of any such primitive speculations, but in the dawn of history we find that man had already asked these questions and given some sort of answer to them. In fact, we find rather complex codes of conduct already existing and embedded in the customs of the tribe. This was prescientific knowledge, subject to all the errors and whimsies of nonscientific thinking, but out of material suggested by these primitive codes of conduct an awakened intelligence could fashion a science of the good life.

The transition from nonscientific to scientific knowledge began, in our Western culture, with the Greeks. By the sixth century before Christ they had reduced primitive speculations to some sort of order or system, and integrated them into the general body of wisdom called *philosophy*.

After a brilliant period of speculation on the structure of the universe, they began in the days of the Sophists and of Socrates to turn their insatiable curiosity on themselves, on human life and society. Nothing was too sacred for their penetrating scrutiny. As seafarers and colonizers they had come into close contact with various surrounding peoples and were struck by the variety of customs, laws, and institutions that prevailed. They began to ask themselves whether their own were really so superior, and, if so, why. In time their study led to an examination of all human conduct, and this part of philosophy they called *ethics*.

Ethics comes from *ēthos*, the lengthened form of *ĕthos*. Both words mean *custom*, but *ēthos* denotes a more fixed type of custom and is often used to mean a man's character. The Latin word for custom is *mos;* its plural, *mores*, is the equivalent of the Greek *ēthos*. From *mores* we derive the words *moral* and *morality*. Ethics is also called moral philosophy.

By derivation of the word, then, ethics is the study of human customs. Some are mere conventions, such as table manners, modes of dress, forms of speech, and expressions of courtesy. These are fads and fashions, varying in different parts of the world and at different times, and we feel that we can change them as we please. They are *manners*, not morals. There are other customs that seem more fundamental, such as telling the truth, paying our debts, honoring our parents, and respecting the

1

lives and property of others. We judge that such conduct is not only customary but *right*, that to deviate from it would be *wrong*, and that it results not from arbitrary whim but from some abiding principle in man's own being. These are *morals*, and it is with these alone that ethics deals. Hence ethics is the study of *right* and *wrong*, of *good* and *evil*, in human conduct.

PROBLEM

Is any such study possible? Philosophy would not be what it is if it merely took for granted that life has a meaning or purpose and that there is a kind of life that can be called the good life. All philosophy begins as skeptical in the sense that it asks questions, but it remains skeptical only if, after investigation, it decides that no answers can be found. There have been confirmed skeptics in all ages who swept away all knowledge including that of morals, but this skepticism was not directed more at ethics than at everything else. Our concern here is with some recent theories that have challenged the position of ethics in particular. Ethics deals with value judgments, and the validity of all value judgments has been questioned. Some have dismissed them as mere expressions of personal preference and subjective attitude, about which any scientifically objective study becomes an exercise in futility.

Since there is no point in trying to study what might turn out to be inherently incapable of being studied, the very possibility of ethics as a serious intellectual discipline should be our first question. Before attempting a solution, we should see first the commonly held answer in order to know what is being criticized, then the recent objections to it with the substitutes offered, and lastly an intermediate position that would accept ethics as a science but would merge it with other sciences in such a way that it would lose its identity and autonomy. We will consider the following points:

1. What is ethics as commonly understood?
2. What of the emotive theory and allied views?
3. Is a purely philosophical ethics possible?
4. Can any resolution of the problem be suggested?

ETHICS AS COMMONLY UNDERSTOOD

SUBJECT MATTER AND POINT OF VIEW

Ethics as the history of philosophy portrays it has for its purpose the interpretation of this fact of human life: the acknowledgment of right and wrong in human conduct. We find in the human race taken generally a tendency to judge that there are three kinds of acts:

1. Those that a man ought to do
2. Those that he ought not to do
3. Those that he may either do or not do

At this point in our study we do not yet determine whether this judgment is correct or mistaken; we simply note that it is a fact of experience that men do judge in this way. So important are these judgments considered that men will regulate their whole lives in accordance with them and will even sacrifice life itself rather than diverge from them. We apply these judgments not only to our own conduct but to the conduct of others; we punish people and even put them to death for doing what we think they ought not to do, or for not doing what we think they ought to do. The man who does whatever he wants, with no regard for what he *ought*, is outlawed from society and hunted down like a wild beast.

This fact, that men do make judgments of right and wrong, is the basic fact of experience from which ethics takes its start. Philosophy, as an interpretation of human life, cannot afford to overlook a fact of such significance but must investigate it and determine all that it entails. If men are correct in distinguishing right from wrong, we need to know why and on what grounds this judgment is justified. If men are mistaken in distinguishing right from wrong, we also want to know why, and how such wholesale error can be accounted for. Without prejudging the case in either way, ethics is a necessary study with a large and legitimate field of inquiry.

Every distinct branch of learning must have a subject matter that it studies from a more or less definite aspect or point of view. The subject matter of ethics is human conduct, those actions which a man performs consciously and willfully, and for which he is held accountable. The aspect or point of view from which ethics studies human conduct is that of its rightness or wrongness, its *oughtness*, if we may manufacture a noun corresponding to the ethical verb *ought*, which is the real verb in every ethical judgment. Ethics is not interested in what a man *does*, except to compare it with what he *ought* to do. We call those actions right which a man ought to do, and those actions wrong which a man ought not to do. Ethical writers of almost all shades of opinion agree that the investigation of the *ought* is the distinctive feature of ethics, the one that separates it from every other study.

RELATION TO OTHER STUDIES

Besides its relation to the other branches of philosophy, of which it forms a part, ethics is also related to the other human and social sciences. These all have the same broad subject matter, but ethics differs from them by its distinctive point of view.

Anthropology and ethics both deal with human customs on various levels of culture and civilization. Anthropology studies the origin and development of human customs, without passing any judgment on their moral rightness or wrongness, but it is this rightness or wrongness alone that interests ethics. Anthropology testifies to the existence of moral notions, however strange, among primitive tribes; ethics borrows such data from anthropology but goes on to criticize the moral value of these concepts and customs.

Psychology and ethics both deal with human behavior, with the abilities and acts of man. Psychology studies how man actually does behave, ethics how he ought to behave. Sanity and sanctity, a well-adjusted personality and a morally good character, despite an incidental relationship between them, are essentially different things; so, too, are their opposites, madness and sin, psychic eccentricity and moral depravity. What motivates a man to a deed, good or bad, is different from the goodness or badness of the deed he does. Ethics is dependent on psychology for much information on how the human mind works, but it always passes on from how man does act to how he ought to act.

Sociology, economics, and *political science* study man's social life, and so also does ethics, but the same difference of viewpoint remains. These three sciences deal with man's actual social, economic, and political institutions—what they are and how they function; ethics determines what they ought to be in terms of human rights and duties. A hard and fast line between these three sciences, and between them and ethics, would render all four studies impractical. The endeavor to remedy the social, economic, and political ills of mankind involves an application of ethics to these three fields. Such a combination is sometimes called *social, economic,* or *political philosophy*. But ethics, precisely as ethics, always preserves its distinctive point of view, the *ought*.

The *study of law* is closely related to ethics. Yet, though both deal with the *ought*, the civil law and the moral law do not always perfectly correspond. The study of civil law deals only with external acts and positive legality, ethics with internal acts of the will and the tribunal of conscience. There is a difference between crime and sin, legal immunity and moral worth, outward respectability and true virtue of soul. A mingling of ethics and the civil law on a wider field gives us the *philosophy of law,* the study of how laws *ought* to be framed and interpreted, a study some writers call *jurisprudence.*

ETHICS AS SCIENCE AND ART

The view has been expressed that ethics may be an interesting study but can never be a science. The scientific world is still largely under the spell of that nineteenth-century mode of thinking originated by Auguste Comte and known as *positivism,* which eliminates all metaphysics from philosophy and restricts scientific knowledge to facts and relations between facts. According to this view, the scientific method is one of exact mathematical measurement, but virtue and vice can never be measured in this way; science proceeds by prediction based on hypothesis and followed by experimental verification, but human conduct, especially if regarded as free, is too unpredictable; science deals with facts and the laws governing them, but ethics only with opinions on what ought to be and never wholly is; science engages in the hardheaded pursuit of wresting from nature her secrets, but ethics is lost in a nebulous quest for ever-beckoning yet ever-escaping ideals and aspirations.

The difficulty is partly semantic and depends on one's definition of science. If science is so defined as to apply to the physical and experimental sciences only, then ethics will not be a science. Aristotle had some inkling of this ambiguity when he warned that ethics cannot be an exact science and that we must look for no more precision than the subject admits.* But, though not an exact science, ethics can be called a science in a broad and philosophical use of the term. The word *science* in the sense of any body of systematized knowledge is still in current use, and ethics is surely this. The definition of science as the *certain knowledge of things in their causes* is traditional among philosophers; ethics preeminently fulfills this definition, for it studies the purpose or final cause of human life, the principles and laws governing the use of means to this end, and, like any science, tries to establish its conclusions with demonstrative thoroughness. Like every other science, including the physical, ethics will have its disputed points, but these will be shown to revolve around a solid core of established truth. Nor is it right for one group of scientists to rule out of court the legitimate subject matter of another science; there is need of a science of the *ought,* for the almost universal acknowledgment of some *ought* is itself a fact demanding explanation quite as insistently as the physical universe.

Is not ethics an *art,* the art of good living, rather than a science? It is both. As a science it discovers, explains, and demonstrates the rules of right conduct. As an art, in a very broad sense of this term, it applies these rules to the conduct of an individual man and results in the good life actually lived. A good life is indeed a work of art. It is obvious, however, that the art of ethics must be practiced by each person for himself, as the shaper of his destiny and the sculptor of his soul; ethics as a subject taught and studied can only give him the principles, and thus comes under the heading of science.

Sciences are either theoretical or practical: theoretical, if their purpose is the mere contemplation of truth; practical, if they are also directed to action. Since

*Aristotle, *Nicomachean Ethics,* bk. I, ch. 3 1094b 12, 25.

ethics is directed to enable a man to act and live rightly, it is a *practical* science, standing somewhere between a purely theoretical science and its corresponding art.

ETHICS AND METAETHICS

The distinction between ethics as a science and ethics as an art should be clear enough, for it is one thing to be a student of morals and another thing to live a moral life. Though ethics as a whole is a practical science, it is possible to distinguish in it its more emphatically practical aspect and the theoretical principles on which this practice rests. Accordingly, current terminology distinguishes between *normative ethics,* or the setting up of a code of rules for moral living, and *metaethics,* or the critical examination of the concepts, judgments, and reasoning processes used in ethics. In common with other names of sciences containing the Greek preposition *meta* (beyond), metaethics is ethics' own reflection on itself, where ethics, passing beyond itself and turning back to take a critical look at itself, judges its own worth as a science. It is necessary for ethics thus to become introspective and self-conscious. If ethics is the study of human conduct and if the construction of a body of ethics is a piece of human endeavor, the science of ethics itself should be ethical. This it could not be unless it were truthful, with its principles grounded in ascertainable knowledge and its conclusions validly and logically drawn. Hence metaethics tends to concern itself with logic and language, since these are the means by which ethical knowledge is developed and expressed.

For our purpose it would be too artificial to maintain a consistent separation between these two phases of ethics, between a first level and a second level of ethical discourse, between ethics talking about human conduct and ethics talking about itself. We shall try to justify ethical

concepts, principles, and conclusions as we come to them. Our reason for introducing this distinction here is that some modern ethicians have confined their studies almost wholly to metaethics, and others have used metaethics to invalidate all normative ethics. This threat we must cope with, and thus we come to our second main topic: recent objections against ethics as commonly understood.

POSSIBILITY OF A SCIENCE OF ETHICS

THE EMOTIVE THEORY

David Hume ends his *Inquiry Concerning Human Understanding* with this rhetorical outburst:

> Morals and criticism are not so properly objects of the understanding as of taste and sentiment. . . . When we run over libraries, persuaded of these principles, what havoc must we make? If we take in our hand any volume—of divinity or school metaphysics, for instance—let us ask, *Does it contain any abstract reasoning concerning quantity or number?* No. *Does it contain any experimental reasoning concerning matter of fact and existence?* No. Commit it then to the flames, for it can contain nothing but sophistry and illusion.°

Hume's seeds of discontent lay fallow until the rise of *positivism* under Auguste Comte, whose chief objection was to metaphysics rather than to ethics. Out of the general positivistic attitude arose the modern school of *logical positivism,* beginning with the Vienna Circle in the early 1920s but spreading rapidly to England and the United States, where empiricism and pragmatism had prepared for it a congenial home. The movement has now nearly disappeared, being succeeded by the school of *analytic philosophy,* which continues the same attitude in a more conciliatory form. It will suit our purpose better to look at

---

°Hume, *An Inquiry Concerning Human Understanding* (Indianapolis, The Bobbs-Merrill Co., Inc., 1955), p. 173.

the older logical positivism, which represents this position in its uncompromising purity.

Beginning with an understandable revulsion from the abstract and apparently meaningless jargon of many metaphysicians, among whom Hegel was a chief offender, the logical positivists analyze the meaning of propositions. By their criteria they find only two kinds of meaningful statements: those which are statements of identity and those which can be verified by experience. Identity statements are tautologies, true but impractical; their domain is that of pure logic and pure mathematics. Only verifiable statements of facts can contribute to the advancement of scientific knowledge. Metaphysical assertions do not belong to either class and must be discarded as neither true nor false, but meaningless. What about value judgments? They also are neither tautologies nor statements of fact, but are normative, laying down rules, expressing the *ought*. Thus they are not cognitive but emotive. They are wishes, exhortations, or commands, but not genuine propositions. Only the grammatical form is indicative; they are veiled optatives and imperatives. A. J. Ayer expresses this view with particular clarity and bluntness:

Fundamental ethical concepts are unanalyzable, inasmuch as there is no criterion by which we can test the validity of the judgments in which they occur. . . . The reason why they are unanalyzable is that they are mere pseudo-concepts. The presence of an ethical symbol in a proposition adds nothing to its factual content. Thus if I say to someone, "You acted wrongly in stealing that money," I am not stating anything more than if I had simply said, "You stole that money." In adding that this action is wrong I am not making any further statement about it. I am simply evincing my moral disapproval of it. It is as if I had said, "You stole that money," in peculiar tone of horror, or written it with the addition of some special exclamation marks. . . .

If now I generalize my previous statement and say, "Stealing money is wrong," I produce a sentence which has no factual meaning—that is, expresses no proposition which can be either true or false. . . .

In every case in which one would commonly be said to be making an ethical judgment, the function of the relevant ethical word is purely "emotive." It is used to express feelings about certain objects, but not to make any assertion about them.

It is worth mentioning that ethical terms do not serve only to express feeling. They are calculated also to arouse feeling, and so to stimulate action.[*]

The last part of this view, that ethical judgments are used to influence action in others, is developed by C. L. Stevenson,[†] who lays stress on ethical disagreements and makes extensive use of the persuasive definition. He objects to calling ethical judgments meaningless or neither true nor false, but thinks that their only truth is in the descriptive part, that the speaker has such or such an attitude, not in the emotive part, that this attitude is branded good or bad, right or wrong. The latter part alone is the concern of ethics, which is therefore only a way of persuading others to agree with me or at least to tolerate my view.

The emotive theory has some persuasive arguments:

1. Philosophers, though by no means the only offenders, have engaged in much abstract and apparently meaningless jargon. They can be dazzled with words, which often appear to represent some thing, but which actually refer to nothing but other word clusters equally detached from reality. Ethical as well as other statements can suffer from this disease.

2. The analysis of every statement, both in itself and in its connection with other statements, is a needed corrective for man's tendency to disguise emptiness of thought with beguiling verbal masks. Clear language, significant reference, and rigorous logic are important in all fields of knowledge. Ethical writing has been notoriously lacking in them.

3. *True* and *false* as predicates signify nothing but only add emphasis. "It is true

---

[*]Ayer, *Language, Truth and Logic*, pp. 107-108.
[†]Stevenson, *Ethics and Language*.

that it is raining" = "It is raining." The words "It is true" add nothing to the meaning, since every sentence is presumed to be meant as true. The words *good* and *bad, right* and *wrong* are predicated in the same way, though with different emotional overtones. These adjectives refer to no definable or ostensible characteristics in things, but only describe our attitude to them.

4. The grammatical form of ethical words and statements deceives us into thinking that they must represent things or properties of things, since we use the same form of sentence to express facts and values. It is the business of logic to cut through the illusions of common speech. Not all grammatical sentences are logical propositions; ethical statements are but veiled imperatives.

5. If we rebel against calling value judgments nonsignificant, we should acknowledge more than one variety of significance. Value judgments are emotionally significant, prescriptive of action in ourselves and others, not cognitively significant, as enlarging our knowledge of things as they are. Only the latter kind of significance is appropriate to a science.

6. The basic concepts of ethics turn out to be unanalyzable and indefinable. At least, ethicians do not agree on definitions or even on the possibility of definition. If this is so, there is no way of fixing the meaning of such a concept so that it will be the same through all stages of an argument. A conclusion drawn from statements containing them can only be suspect. This may be satisfactory for persuasion but cannot pretend to scientific cogency.

These arguments may not be the only ones that the emotivists can supply, but they are typical of their approach. The following are offered as counterarguments:

1. That philosophers and others have engaged in too much verbal juggling is rightly deplored but does not rule out the many valid statements they have made.

Emotivists, too, can be deceived by words. The decisive argument against them is that the emotive theory itself is neither a statement of identity nor verifiable by experience, and therefore falls by its own criterion.

2. Though every statement should be subjected to rigorous analysis, it is illogical to apply the criteria for one area of study to another where they do not fit. Empirical statements are not rejected because they are not mathematical, nor are mathematical statements because they are not empirical. Why, then, should ethical statements be rejected because they are neither of these but have their distinctive subject matter and criteria? If there is no place for them in any classification of meaningful statements, that only shows the classification to be incomplete.

3. The statement "X is good" cannot be analyzed into "I approve of X" without a distorting shift from the objective to the subjective mode of speech, a difference of meaning and not merely of grammar. "X is good" means "X is worthy of approval" and gives reasons for "I approve of X." A statement about X is not a statement about me but about something else distinct from me, even though I can have an attitude toward it. Reasons for approval or disapproval have cognitive content and can be true or false.

4. The attempt to reduce ethical judgments to wishes, exhortations, or commands is unsuccessful. Part of the meaning, and precisely the ethical part, is lost. For example, I can command you to do something and want the command obeyed, knowing all the time that I ought not to issue such a command and you ought not to obey it. This implied knowledge is the ethical judgment here, and it is opposed to the command. Is the ethical judgment only a hidden wish to be disobeyed? But this is exactly what I do not wish, though I judge my conduct and yours to be immoral.

5. To reduce ethical judgments to mere emotional expressions of approval, such as clapping or hissing, is equally unsuccessful. There is a difference between actual approval and right approval. The first is a statement of psychological fact: I do approve. Now I can go on to approve or disapprove of my approval, to judge that my approval was right or wrong. This is the ethical judgment, and it is no less capable of being true or false than the factual judgment.

6. All basic concepts are unanalyzable and indefinable. A verbal substitute, such as is found in the dictionary, does not tell what the thing really is. To demand that everything be defined is to make all knowledge impossible, including the kinds of knowledge the logical positivists accept. Great care must be taken in arguments containing indefinables, but the arguments are not necessarily invalidated by having indefinables in them. In this, ethics is no worse off than other disciplines.

POSTEMOTIVISTS

Recognition that logical positivism had gone too far led to its abandonment. What was good about it is preserved in the succeeding school of *analytic philosophy*. In ethics, while carrying on the stringent analysis of ethical language, it makes some attempts at introducing cognitive validity. We can only touch on a few of the more popular writers. R. M. Hare[*] distinguishes descriptive and prescriptive words and endeavors to build up within our existing logic a logic of imperatives, in which some cognitive meaning accompanies the evaluative meaning. P. H. Nowell-Smith[†] advocates a new logic based on G- or gerundive words that indicate a *pro* attitude, the substitution of logical oddness

for logical contradiction, and an endorsement theory of truth by which a proposition is true not because it squares with the facts but because I side with it, for each man must answer for himself what moral principles he will have. Stephen Toulmin[*] and Kurt Baier[†] are examples of the "good reasons" school of ethics, according to which there must be reasons for thinking an action worthy of approval, and these reasons furnish the cognitive element in ethics; we can show the consistency of these reasons, determine their relative weight, and see how our conduct squares with the principles we have adopted on our own or have taken from society.

We can learn a great deal from these efforts, but they still leave us outside the proper domain of ethics. Their only interest is to determine how we may speak and reason logically about ethics if we have already accepted some basic ethical commitments. They do not tell us what the ethical life is, nor do they even establish that there is an ethical life. We shall have to drink wisdom from deeper waters.

A PURELY PHILOSOPHICAL ETHICS

Whereas logical positivists and many linguistic analysts consider a science of ethics well-nigh impossible, others consider it unnecessary. All the religions of the world are concerned with morals and take on the task of showing men how to be good. Theology, the intellectual study of religion, investigates the moral aspect as well as the other phases of religion and should therefore make any purely philosophical study of morals redundant. So it is said.

The Christian religion, which is too conspicuous a fact of our society to be overlooked, is especially rich in moral teach-

---

[*]Hare, *The Language of Morals, Freedom and Reason*.
[†]Nowell-Smith, *Ethics*.

[*]Toulmin, *An Examination of the Place of Reason in Ethics*.
[†]Baier, *The Moral Point of View*.

ing, and its theology has developed an elaborate code of morality. Catholics use the term *moral theology* for that branch of theology whose business it is to examine the whole field of morals from the standpoint of the Catholic faith. Protestants tend to focus on *Christian ethics,* which is not ethics as a purely philosophical study but the treatment of morals from a post-Reformation view of the Christian revelation.

Does the Christian need a double study of morals, one from a purely philosophical standpoint and another from that of the Christian revelation? One could answer that the two viewpoints are supplementary: ethics is the study of morals from pure reason, and moral theology or Christian ethics is the same thing as known from revealed sources. This distinction is basic and valid, but it does not wholly solve the problem.

According to the theory of total depravity, still accepted in a toned-down form by some Protestant groups, man has been so entirely corrupted by original sin that man's reason is quite incapable of acting as a guide to the good life, and man's corrupted nature cannot serve as a norm of morality or as the basis of a natural law. Even those who do not wish to go so far are profoundly distrustful of human nature. Such a view does seem to make any purely philosophical ethics futile, and those who hold it are constrained to develop a Christian ethics based on God's saving revelation and redemption.

The Catholic view of original sin's effect on human nature is less drastic, and so admits a distinction between philosophical ethics and moral theology. But another difficulty arises. In theoretical studies such as metaphysics, epistemology, philosophical anthropology, and natural theology, we can adequately distinguish between reason and faith, between the natural and the supernatural, because of the abstract character of such studies. But ethics is a practical science dealing with man as he

concretely is and actually lives, and according to Catholic belief man is and lives in the supernatural order as one fallen and redeemed. A purely natural ethics would be valid only for a hypothetical man who never existed.

This view is open to several interpretations depending on what relation one holds to obtain between nature and grace. Jacques Maritain* holds that philosophical ethics is necessarily subordinated to moral theology for its completion and correction, and that therefore philosophical ethics cannot be an autonomous science. Its subordination is not only one of infraposition, as a science of lesser dignity, but also one of subalternation, as unavoidably leading to falsehood unless guided and corrected by the higher science of moral theology.

Not all will agree with this view. There are those who insist that philosophical ethics can achieve its own purpose by its own methods independently of divine revelation, and that the principles it uses and the conclusions it draws are true for man as he concretely exists and actually lives his life in the world today, even though it does not give man the whole truth and is open to supplementation by knowledge of a higher order. Between these two there need be no conflict, since the supernatural does not destroy the natural but rather continues and extends it. Besides, a practical science must look at the existential situation. There are millions who have not had the benefit of the Christian revelation, do not know that they actually live in the supernatural order of redemption, do not perceive the working of divine grace within them, and must trust entirely to their unaided natural powers to construct for themselves an ethical way of living. It seems monstrous to say that they have the obligation to live morally, as all men have, but

---

*Maritain, *Essay on Christian Philosophy,* pp. 38-43, 61-100; *Science and Wisdom,* pp. 107-127.

cannot find out what the moral life is or how to live it.

Thus there is no need to assume a necessary incompatibility between a Christian moral theology and an ethics autonomous in itself as a philosophical study. Ethics, although a purely natural and rational study, does not deny things outside its sphere but merely abstracts from them. Ethics cannot enter the field of theology or use its material. That leaves ethical knowledge incomplete, but all other sciences are incomplete inasmuch as none of them embraces all truth. To be incomplete is not to be false. As far as error is concerned, whatever corrections ethics may receive from moral theology are accidental rather than essential, as due to man's hasty and fallible use of his reason rather than to an inherent defect in human reason itself.

SUGGESTED RESOLUTION OF THE PROBLEM

Ethics has weathered many storms in its 2500 year history. It is reasonable to expect that it will survive the two attempts to discredit it that are described here: the reduction of it to logic and language analysis, and the absorption of it into religion and theology.

To avoid the first pitfall, ethics needs a firm grounding in metaphysics and epistemology. A formal study of these two subjects is not necessary for the reading of this book, but at least the student must bring to his study something more than the positivistic attitude that only the experimentally verifiable can be admitted as real. Whether the *ought* can be derived from the *is* is a question we take up later, but whether it can or not, the *ought* must be acknowledged as an existing feature of our world and something that can be grasped by man's mind. If new studies are needed to show how ethical statements can be fitted into the logic we now have, or if a new logic must be developed to cope

with them, by all means let us forward this task. But we should not eliminate an important part of human experience because we have not yet learned to think about it correctly, but rather learn to think in new and better ways about the experience we certainly do have. Logical positivism is primarily an epistemology that drastically reduces the scope of man's knowledge by eliminating all metaphysics, and with metaphysics the only possible basis for ethics. However, since logical positivism cannot establish itself, there is no reason that ethics should have to be approached from this narrow standpoint.

The relation of ethics to religion is part of the long history of the relations between faith and reason. The difficulty is not so much from the side of reason, which began to speculate long before the advent of the Christian faith into history, but rather of the Christian faith's interpretation of itself and its view of the nature of man. If it can recognize that faith and grace are gifts that enhance rather than suppress the natural goodness of God's creature man, there should be no insoluble conflict between the two. Then philosophical ethics will be a valuable study of what human reason can show to be the good life for man. Ethics, from its side, is not entitled to the arrogance it has sometimes shown and should acknowledge its openness to knowledge derivable from a higher source. It does not thereby become a dependent science but adequately preserves its autonomy within its own sphere, outside of which it should have no pretensions.

SUMMARY

Ethics originated in speculation on the good life and was systematized into a part of philosophy by the Greeks, who called it ethics from their word for custom. But it deals only with customs involving the idea of right and wrong, with *morals*.

10

As traditionally conceived, the purpose of ethics is to study a fact of experience, that men distinguish right from wrong and have a feeling for the *ought*. The *subject matter* of ethics is human conduct; its *point of view* is that of rightness and wrongness, of *oughtness*.

Ethics is related to all the human and social sciences but is always distinguished from them by its unique point of view, the *ought*.

If ethics is called a *science*, it is not in the sense of the experimental sciences but in the sense of the philosophical sciences. Ethics is a *practical* and *normative* science. It is also an art to be put in practice in one's own life. Only the science can be taught.

Today we distinguish *normative ethics*, a code of rules for moral living, from *meta-ethics*, a criticism of the language and concepts used in ethical discourse. An adequate study needs both, but they need not always be kept separate.

The *emotive theory*, stemming from *logical positivism*, holds that value judgments, including those of ethics, are noncognitive. They are neither identity statements nor verifiable by experience. They are only disguised wishes, exhortations, or commands. We are misled by grammatical structure into thinking that they are propositions that can be true or false. Nonemotivists reject this view as based on too narrow an epistemology and an inadequate theory of meaning. Later *linguistic analysts* are more conciliatory but limit themselves almost wholly to examining ethical language.

Some think that the study of morals so belongs to religion that no purely philosophical ethics is possible. It must be either Christian ethics or moral theology. Man, redeemed from original sin, now lives in the order of divine grace, and no purely natural life is possible for him. A philosophical ethics would deal with a hypothetical man who never existed. Others do not deny this but abstract from it, insisting that a study can be made of man's morals in the natural order. Ethics is incomplete, as all studies are, but that does not prevent it from being an autonomous science.

QUESTIONS FOR DISCUSSION

1 Do we merely assume that the ought is a legitimate object of study? Is there any sense in which we can say that the ought really exists? What sort of being does the ought have, if it has any?

2 Are normative sciences really sciences? Do they offer knowledge or only prescribe action? Are rules for acting a kind of knowledge or only an expression of wish or will?

3 Could an ethics be built up without any presuppositions? In that case where would you start and where would you go from there?

4 Is it true that man has made wonderful scientific advances but hardly any ethical advances? Has the study of ethics been futile because it has not actually made men live better? Should it not make men live better if it is a practical science?

5 Is ethics superseded by religion? How can a Christian, who believes that man actually lives in the supernatural order of faith, study man as if he lived merely in the natural order of philosophy?

READINGS

Aristotle's preface to his *Nicomachean Ethics*, bk. I, ch. 1-3, is the best start. There are many translations and editions. Aristotle's *Ethics* and *Politics* are continuous, forming one large treatise on human living.

St. Thomas, *Commentary on Aristotle's Ethics and Politics,* follows Aristotle section by section; each subsequent reference to Aristotle's *Ethics* or *Politics* can be understood to include a reference to St. Thomas' *Commentary.*

On the emotive theory two books are indispensable: A. J. Ayer, *Language, Truth and Logic;* and C. L. Stevenson, *Ethics and Language.* Criticisms of the emotive theory are found in A. C. Ewing, *Ethics,* ch. 7; J. D. Mabbott, *Introduction to Ethics,* ch. 8-9; and W. H. Werkmeister, *Theories of Ethics.* See also Stuart Hampshire, *Thought and Action;* R. M. Hare, *The Language of Morals;* P. H. Nowell-Smith, *Ethics;* and Stephen Toulmin, *Examination of the Place of Reason in Ethics.*

Henry Margenau, *Ethics and Science,* argues that ethics can be quite scientific.

Jacques Maritain, *Essay on Christian Philosophy,* pp. 38-43, and 61-100, and his *Science and Wisdom,* pp. 107-127, contain his discussion of the relations between ethics and moral theology. Martin D'Arcy expresses a different view in Ruth Nanda Anshen (ed.), *Moral Principles of Action,* ch. 24. An exposition from a Protestant viewpoint can be found in Paul Lehmann, *Ethics in a Christian Context.*

D. J. B. Hawkins, *Man and Morals,* has an original starting point.

Austin Fagothey, *Right and Reason—an Anthology,* a book of readings designed to accompany this text, contains Aristotle's *Nicomachean Ethics,* bk. I, ch. 1-3; and Ayer's *Language, Truth and Logic,* most of ch. 6.

12

CHAPTER 2

CONDUCT

PROBLEM

There are no good or bad babies, but there are good and bad men. How does the change come about? Obviously by the lives, the conduct, the actions of the persons in question. Man has no moral character to begin with, but builds up one for himself by the way he lives. Before we can determine what moral goodness or badness is, and how it gets into the acts one performs and from them into the man himself, we should look at man's conduct, in which moral goodness or badness can dwell. What sort of acts can a man do? Are all sorts of acts capable of becoming morally good or bad, or only some of them? If only some, what are these acts and what differentiates them from the rest? We can portion out our inquiry as follows:

1. What is human conduct?
2. How is human conduct under our control?
3. Can man control only his will or also his outward acts?
4. What qualities of the human act have ethical import?
5. How is responsibility entailed in the human act?

HUMAN ACTS

Man's actions taken collectively make up his behavior or conduct. *Behavior* is more of a psychological word and is applied even to animals, whereas *conduct* has an ethical meaning and is exclusively human.

We distinguish between the parts of our body we can control and those we cannot control, between those we can move more or less as we want and those which move in spite of us, between the striped, or voluntary, muscles and the smooth, or involuntary, muscles. The words *voluntary* and *involuntary* are interesting here because they are ethical rather than biological words and refer to the fact that certain actions are or are not subject to our will. In ethics we are not concerned with the muscles we use but with the actions we choose to do with or without them, and especially with the governing factor in us, whatever it may be, that we call the *will*. For the moment we can speak of the will as our ability to control ourselves, to be masters of ourselves, to do what we want to do rather than have it forced on us, so that as a result we are held responsible for what we do. Two main things that would prevent our acts from being voluntary, from being willed by us, are ignorance and compulsion, and therefore a voluntary act is said to be knowingly or deliberately willed. We do not say yet whether it must also be free, and for the present we may overlook the hint of freedom in the following classic statement:

Of actions done by man those alone are properly called human which are proper to man as man. Now man differs from irrational animals in this that he is master of his actions. Wherefore those actions alone are properly called human of which man is master. Now man is master of his actions through his reason and will, whence too

13

the free will is defined as the faculty of will and reason. Therefore those actions are properly called human which proceed from a deliberate will. And if any other actions are found in man, they can be called actions of a man, but not properly human actions, since they are not proper to man as man.*

From the foregoing we see that ethics establishes its subject matter by distinguishing two main kinds of acts:

1. *Voluntary acts* or *human acts:* those of which man is master, which he consciously controls and deliberately wills, and for which he is held responsible. These constitute human conduct and form the subject matter of ethics.

2. *Involuntary acts* or *acts of a man:* those which a man happens to perform but of which he is not master, which he does not consciously control or deliberately will, and for which he is not held responsible. Such are acts done in infancy, sleep, delirium, insanity, or fits of distraction. They do not constitute human conduct and have no ethical significance.

Note carefully that the distinction here is not between acts of the rational order and those of the sentient or vegetative order. It is true that rational acts, such as thinking and willing, are proper to man in the sense that he alone can do them, whereas sentient and vegetative acts, such as eating, sleeping, walking, and growing, are actions that man has in common with other beings. This is how psychology classifies them to understand human nature; ethics, however, tries to explain human *conduct,* and its whole question is whether man is master of his acts or not, be they of the rational, sentient, or vegetative order.

Man is the only creature in this world who can think, but if his thoughts simply run along by association without his conscious direction and control, such thoughts are only *acts of a man,* not *human acts,* even though they are of the rational order. On the other hand, eating and sleeping are

by their nature merely animal acts that man does in common with brutes, but they become *human acts* if the man does them knowingly and willingly. To put food in the mouth while in a distracted state of mind is an *act of a man,* but to determine deliberately to eat this food is a *human act.* To be overcome by drowsiness and fall asleep is an *act of a man,* but to go to bed intentionally for the purpose of sleeping is a *human act.* Hence, though it is impossible to have a *human act* unless it is guided by intellect and will, the act itself so guided can be of any sort. In other words, a human act can be either physical or mental in nature provided it is deliberately willed.

PSYCHOLOGICAL BACKGROUND

What goes on in me when I make an act of choice? The numerous studies made by psychologists on this subject, valuable as they may be in themselves, are generally of little help to the ethician, since they do not fix the exact point at which an act of a man may turn into a human act and thus pass from being ethically indifferent to being ethically significant. An exception must be made of St. Thomas,* whose lengthy exposition is inspired by Aristotle† but is carried much beyond him. We can give but the briefest digest of it:

A human act is the result of an interplay of man's intellect and will, or, to put it in more modern language, of his cognitive and his conative tendencies. Man knows and wants. His ability to know beyond the senuous is intellect; his ability to want what he thus knows and to seek it is will. Strictly speaking, intellect and will do not do any act at all; they are but abilities by which the whole man, the *person,* acts. Such abilities are not independent

---

*St. Thomas, *Summa Theologica,* I-II, q. 1, a. 1.

*St. Thomas, *Summa Theologica,* I-II, qq. 6-17.
†Aristotle, *Nicomachean Ethics,* bk. III, ch. 1-5; bk. VI, ch. 2, 5, 9-11.

agents,* little persons within the larger human person and doing things inside him on their own, nor are they geared like the wheels and levers of a machine. It would be absurd to take the following description too mechanically. It is an interplay of functions, for to know and to want are not the same kind of doing, though done by the selfsame person, who is the only doer in the whole process. If we speak of the intellect or will as doing anything, we are speaking in a loose way to mean that the *man,* the *person,* does them with his intellect or will.

For a man to act he must first be attracted by some good. When he perceives something as good, there arises in him a liking for it. If he sees that it is not only good in itself but also good for him, his liking becomes a desire or *wish.* A wish may remain ineffectual, but if he further understands the good as possible of attainment, this intellectual insight moves his will to an act of spontaneous *intention* or tendency toward the good, a stretching forth to gain the object without yet counting the cost in effort and loss of other goods. He now turns his intellect to the task of weighing the reasons for and against the carrying out of this intention and the various sets of means by which it might be accomplished. This act of the intellect is called counsel or *deliberation,* whose outcome is to arrive at one of two practical judgments: "This is to be done here and now," or "This is not to be done here and now." The matter has now been laid out for his decision. He now knows thoroughly what to do and the reasons why. The stage is set for his verdict, the supreme act of expression of his being as a self-directed person. He accepts one or the other of these alternative practical judgments of the intellect by a decision of his will, his act of commitment. The practical judgment immediately preceding his decision and expressing the alternative chosen is the *last practical judgment.* The yielding to one alternative rather than the other, after deliberation, is the deliberate act of the will. It has two moments: taken absolutely, as a yielding to the attraction of the object and an acquiescence in the judgment of the intellect, it is called *consent;* taken comparatively, as a preference of one alternative over the other, it is called *choice.* Then by the act of *command,* a guiding act of the intellect, he directs his will in the *use* of the means to carry his decision into execution. Finally, there come the perception that the end is attained and its *enjoyment.*

In all there are six acts of the will. Three are about the end: *wish, intention,* and *enjoyment.* Three are about the mean: *choice, consent,* and *use.* Each act of the will is preceded by an act of the intellect, the most important of which is *deliberation.**

	INTELLECT	WILL
End	{ Perception of the good { Judgment of attainability	Wish Intention
Means	{ Deliberation { Last practical judgment	Consent Choice
Execution	{ Command { Perception of attainment	Use Enjoyment

In the accompanying scheme the word *intention* is taken in a technical sense. The intention that precedes deliberation can mean only the spontaneous movement of the will toward embracing a perceived good. It is entirely outside our control whether we shall feel such an attraction and the preliminary stirring of desire. Recognition of this attraction in us starts off the process of deliberation, a kind of debate with ourselves whether to yield to it or to resist it. If yielded to by consent after deliberation, the intention persists

---

*Like the "ghost in the machine" of Gilbert Ryle, *The Concept of Mind,* ch. 1.

*St. Thomas, *Summa Theologica,* I-II, qq. 8 and 13, preamble.

until the execution of the act. Then we say that the act was done with *deliberate intent*, and the act is a human act. The initial intention before deliberation and consent is not a human act but only a spontaneous tendency.

Deliberation itself is not a human act unless we reflect on it and initiate a secondary deliberation. We spontaneously begin to weigh motives for and against our contemplated course of action without recognizing that we are doing so. But if our attention is turned to the fact that we are deliberating, the question arises whether we should continue our deliberation or break it off. If we decide to continue, our act of deliberating becomes a human act, but the original point at issue is not yet a human act because we have not yet consented to *it* but have consented only to deliberate about it. Such reflections on our own acts can become quite complex.

Deliberation consists of a series of practical judgments for and against the contemplated course of action. The last practical judgment is not distinct from the deliberation but is simply that one among all these judgments that the will consents to and accepts. Likewise *consent* and *choice* are not two distinct acts, but the consent to one alternative is the choice of it over its opposite, and vice versa. Only in a case where no two alternatives are offered could there be consent without choice. It is obvious that there cannot be choice without consent.

There is no need to consider each of the aforementioned stages as a distinct act; they blend together in the most confusing fashion and are much more complicated than can be described conveniently. We must, however, always distinguish the indeliberate from the deliberate acts of the will, that is, the act that preceded from the act that follows deliberation. The most important part of the process is *consent*, for it is this which makes the act ours in the sense that it is chargeable to us. Up to that point it was not a *human act;* afterward it is.

It may seem strange that in the foregoing exposition so much stress is put on the cognitive and conative aspects of man's nature, and so little on the third aspect, the affective, the realm of the feelings and emotions. The reason for doing so is that the feelings are an important part of human life and enter strongly into any act of decision, so much so that there are people whose lives are led almost wholly on the emotional plane. The question is: how much are they masters of their acts? A human act can be accompanied by very strong emotions, but for it to be a human act the emotions must be under the person's control. Insofar as they are not, the act is to that extent not a human act and the agent is a victim of internal forces he does not govern. Emotions are much concerned in the deliberative process, strengthening the reasons for or against, and they also exert great pressure on the will to consent or refuse consent. Thus they act within the process and affect the other two stages without forming a distinct category on the same level. We are dealing here, not with the way a person is tossed about by internal storms, but with the making of a rational decision by a self-controlled person in a period of calm. We all have some such moments, and only then are we fit to entrust ourselves with the working out of a major decision.

COMMANDED ACTS

We think of the will as the controlling factor in us, but we never accomplish anything by merely willing it. By the will we decide to walk, but the will cannot do the walking; it commands the legs to carry out the decision. By the will we decide to think, but the will cannot do the thinking; it commands the intellect to turn its attention to this thought rather than that. The will can command itself, as when it decides to reach a decision now or to put it off until later. The will can command, then, both external bodily acts and internal mental acts. I decide to study, and this decision is the act of the will itself. I take out my book, turn to the lesson, bend my eyes on the page; these are external bodily acts commanded by the will. I focus my mind on the matter, understand what I am reading, and fix it in my memory; these are internal mental acts commanded by the will. Thus study is a mixed act involving the use of the eyes in reading and of the intellect in understanding, both under command of the will.

Which of these acts is the *human act?* It might seem that only the internal act of the will itself is the *human act*. In the strictest sense this is true, for it is in the will that choice and consent reside and give an act its specifically human character. Hence if a man decides to do something with clear consent of his will but is prevented by circumstances from carrying out his decision, he is responsible for this consent. Thus a man can be guilty of murder in intent although he never gets the chance to carry it out.

Commanded acts share in the consent of the will that commands them. Man is held responsible for all that he controls through his will, both for the internal acts of the will itself and for the acts of other abilities that the will commands. Both are human acts, but the former are so in a stricter sense.

VOLUNTARINESS

After this brief survey of the psychological background of the *human act*, we must take a more intense look at that property which characterizes it from the ethical standpoint, the property of voluntariness.

It should be evident that there can be no voluntariness without knowledge. We cannot seek what we do not know. There can be no decision of the will unless enlightened by the intellect, whose business it is to perceive the good, to propose it to the will as something desirable, and to pass judgment on the suitability of the means to be used in its attainment. The work of the intellect is especially apparent in the process of deliberation, where the motives for and against cannot be weighed unless they are known. There must also be advertence to what one is about, a focusing of attention on the acts being done so that a man is conscious or aware of his acts. Advertence is impossible without a certain amount of reflection, by which the mind turns back and looks at itself acting. The person both knows that he knows and knows that he wills.

Advertence and reflection occur in varying degrees, thereby affecting the human character of the act. An act is a *human* act only insofar as it is known. Any part or circumstance of the act that the doer does not advert to is not attributable to him. This works both ways: a man who willfully kills another without knowing that the victim is his father commits murder but not patricide; a man who steals money not knowing that it is counterfeit is morally guilty of theft, though he gets no profit out of it.

To have a human act, it is not sufficient that it be guided by knowledge; it must also be *willed*. It is this union of knowledge and will which makes an act voluntary. After much groping about, Aristotle suggests the following definition:

> Since that which is done under compulsion or by reason of ignorance is involuntary, the voluntary would seem to be that of which the moving principle is in the agent himself, he being aware of the particular circumstances of the action.[*]

Aristotle, recognizing that sensation is knowledge and that sense-appetite is an inner principle of action, thus grants voluntariness to acts done by children and

---

[*]Aristotle, *Nicomachean Ethics*, bk. III, ch. 1, 1111a 22.

animals. St. Thomas points out that animals' actions can be called voluntary only in an analogous and participated sense (like our modern use of the term *animal intelligence*), and that the voluntary agent must know not merely the circumstances of the act but the end to which it leads. He puts his definition in these terms:

It is of the nature of a voluntary act that its principle be within the agent, together with some knowledge of the end.*

Throughout his whole discussion it is evident that the inner principle referred to is the will. Hence his definition may be amended thus: *A voluntary act is one that proceeds from the will with a knowledge of the end.*

Voluntariness is one of our simplest and most familiar notions. We should not take the impression that there is anything recondite or mysterious about it. A voluntary act is simply a *willed act,* one in which the agent knows what he is about to do and wills to do it. The difficulty is that some of the words we commonly use to indicate this kind of act have certain connotations we do not wish to stress. We say that a person acts willingly, willfully, intentionally, deliberately, or voluntarily; these words all mean the same in the present context. To act willingly one does not have to act gladly and eagerly; to act willfully it is not necessary to be wayward or obstinate; to act intentionally does not require that one act vigorously or ostentatiously; to act deliberately there is no need of acting slowly and painstakingly; to act voluntarily it is not necessary to volunteer or freely offer oneself for some work. The English words often have these shades of meaning, but we use them simply in the sense that a person *knowingly wills* what he does.

A voluntary act, as the product of a man's own will guided by his own reason,

*St. Thomas, *Summa Theologica,* I-II, q. 6, a. 2; but his main discussion of this matter is in a. 1.

is the actual exercise of his mastership over his conduct. Though the act is done and finished, it is still referable to its master as *his act.* The basic explanation of why it was done rather than not done is that *he willed it,* and thus it remains forever related to him. This relation we express by the words *responsibility* and *imputability.* They express the same relation between the agent and his act, but they look at the relation from different sides: we say that the agent is responsible, answerable, accountable for his act and that the act is imputable, chargeable, attributable to the agent. To determine the degree of a person's responsibility for an act is the same as to determine how far the act was voluntary on his part.

Besides the relation between the agent and his act, there may be a further relation of both to reward or punishment. An act is a transitory thing, lasting only so long as it is being done, but rewards and punishments are not always given immediately on the doing of a deed. A murderer kills his victim and is apprehended years later; we feel justified in punishing him now, though his evil act lasted only a moment. A soldier receives a medal for bravery long after the battle is over; we feel that, though his deed is only a memory, something of it remains in him and calls for a reward. Some kind of moral entity must be produced in the doer by his deed to connect him with the reward or punishment to come. This property or essential consequence of a human act is called *merit.* To merit something is to earn it, to deserve it, to be entitled to it as payment, or to be liable to it as punishment.

Responsibility and merit are thus two important consequences of voluntariness.

FREE WILL AND DETERMINISM

It may seem that we have settled the question of free will, for is not a voluntary act the same as a free act? No, the problem is not that simple. Freedom adds to voluntariness the possibility of choice, of two or more eligible alternatives, at least the alternatives of acting or not acting. Whatever one deliberately and willfully does is voluntary, whereas for freedom it is commonly thought that one must have been able at the moment to have chosen otherwise. In our description of the voluntary act we left open the relation between the last practical judgment and the consent. If the last practical judgment does not determine the will but becomes the last in the series of practical judgments merely by the fact that the will consents to it and thus cuts off deliberation, then we have free will. But if the last practical judgment is determined to be the last in the series by some cause other than the will itself and thus necessitates the will to embrace it, then we have determinism.

Full study of this problem belongs to philosophical anthropology, but we must see enough of it for our purpose. We can begin by eliminating some forms of determinism that are incompatible with freedom and responsibility in an ethical sense.

1. *Fatalism* supposes that each man's future is prescribed for him by some outside power called fate, whether it be an impersonal force or the decrees of the gods, whether it overpower man's will or use man's free choices as the very means of reaching its inexorable goal. Man is surely not accountable for events that he struggles in vain to prevent.

2. Not very different from fatalism is *theological determinism* based on God's omniscience, the view that, if God knows everything, he knows the future, including the so-called free choices of man, so that a man's whole future is inevitably laid out for him. Theologians and metaphysicians have wrestled with this problem for ages, but most recognize that it arises from too anthropomorphic an interpretation of God's knowledge, from the mistaken idea that knowledge produces its object instead of merely discovering it, from the difficulty of imagining a timeless knowledge portraying time-bound events, and from a confusion between predestination and predetermination. Predestination merely means that God accepts and ratifies his created universe with all that is in it, including human free choices and their consequences. Predetermination means that God causes human beings to choose the way they do, thus interfering with their freedom. Theological determinism interprets predestination as predetermination. Its difficulty concerns our idea of God rather than our idea of man.

3. Another form of determinism incompatible with free will is often called *hard determinism*. It appeals to the rigid causality apparent in the physical universe. Though it recognizes a distinction in concept between causation, determination, unavoidability, and predictability, in practice it makes all four of them imply one another. Not only must every effect (anything that happens) have a determinate cause (which may be a complex of many causal factors), but every cause must produce a single determinate and therefore predictable effect. The physical sciences are committed by their subject matter to this type of predictability. To admit freedom is to admit an element of randomness in the universe and to put the highly successful scientific method in jeopardy. What we call free choice in man is therefore nothing more than our own ignorance. We cannot predict our own or others' future behavior because we do not know all the elements entering into the situation. We cannot help engaging in the process of deliberation, but the decision we reach is determined by the stronger set of motives like the pull of a vector system. There is never any possible proof that we could have acted otherwise, since this is precisely what never did and never will take place. The criminal's life of crime is predetermined for him by his inheritance and

environment, and he is not responsible for what he does, though society is predetermined to hold him guilty and to punish him, using punishment for its corrective and deterrent values as part of the general predetermining environment. Determinists cannot help being determinists nor libertarians being libertarians. Both are predetermined to exhort to the good life, and the hearers are predetermined to accept or to refuse the exhortation according as they have been conditioned. Thus ethics itself becomes an empty game we have to play toward an already fixed score.

4. The absolute opposite of this hard determinism is *indeterminism*, the view that man is a partial exception to the rigid determinism that occurs in nature. It admits that the law of causality may apply to everything else in nature, thus agreeing with the meaning of causality as accepted by the hard determinists, but insists that such causality does not apply to man's free choices. There is no cause for man's free acts. They are uncaused acts, events that simply happen without being brought about by anything. Some appeal to Heisenberg's Principle of Indeterminacy to show that randomness in the universe is compatible with science. Let us remark here that this principle has nothing at all to do with free will, much less with any ethical considerations, and should not be brought into the argument. Indeterminism is a desperate remedy against an unacceptable hard determinism, but it gets into insoluble difficulties. An uncaused act might perhaps be called free in some sense, but it could not be free as the result of a free choice, for if the free choice were the cause of the act, the act would not be uncaused. It could not be the kind of act for which one would be morally responsible, for, if the act is uncaused, the doer of the act did not cause it and is therefore not accountable for it.

Besides these untenable views, there remain only two worth consideration.

5. *Soft determinism* is an effort to rec-oncile freedom with determinism. This it does by shaving down both concepts until the apparent incompatibility between them becomes unnoticeable. It admits that man is a free agent in the sense that he is often free from outside compulsion and is unhindered in doing what he chooses, but he is determined in the sense that he cannot choose to act against his character. He must submit to the greater attraction, and that is why one who knows him well can reasonably predict what he will do. However, his character is not wholly forced on him, but he himself helped to shape it by his previous choices, so that he freely made himself the kind of person he is. Since he is responsible for the kind of character he now has, he is responsible for the choice he now makes according to his character. Thus his every choice is caused, not by something outside him, but by the kind of being he is, which he chose to become by all his previous choices. This view, it is thought, avoids the folly of indeterminism, which admits causeless acts, and the rigidity of hard determinism, which makes all responsibility a baseless fiction.

Despite the conciliatory tone of soft determinism, many libertarians are not happy with it. What is the use, they say, of freedom to do what one chooses if one is not free to choose as one wants? What is the value of freedom from external compulsion if one is subject to an irresistible thrust of one's already formed character? In neither case can one at the present moment do otherwise than he is doing. The opposite may be both logically and physically possible, but it is not psychologically possible. It is no help to say that one's character, which determines one's present act, has been freely molded by the person's former free choices, for each of these so-called former free choices was determined by the state of one's character at that previous moment, and so on back to the beginning in childhood, when no deliberate free choices were possible. Thus the critics of soft determinism grant that it allows a kind of freedom, freedom from external compulsion, but that is not the kind of freedom meant by free choice or free will. They also grant that in this theory there can be a kind of responsibility, for no one else but the person himself can be blamed or praised for the act that is determined by that person's character shaped by his own former acts, but this is only the kind of responsibility one has to repair the damage he has caused in an accident he could not have avoided. Such an accident could hardly be called freely chosen. Like many compromises, this theory succeeds in fusing the two elements only by destroying what is worthwhile in each of them.

6. The theory called *self-determinism* is an alternate mediating proposal that does not work by compromise. It insists on the fact that nothing can happen without a cause, and therefore man's free acts are definitely *caused* acts. But it rejects the claim that all causes necessarily produce only one determined effect. There are necessary causes and free causes, and man when acting as a free agent is a free cause. When man chooses, the choice is not made by something else either outside or inside the man but is the act of the man himself. This is what it means to be a *person*. He is the cause of his acts, but within limits he freely decides what acts he will be the cause of. An act of free choice requires motives, which are conditions making choice possible, and motives on both sides, for and against the contemplated course of action. But, say the self-determinists, though the man is strongly influenced by the motives and deliberates between them, he is not necessitated by them either way; he himself makes the decision. Should it be said that he must be necessitated by the subjectively stronger set of motives, those which made the greater appeal at the time, we ask how they became subjectively stronger. The man himself made them so by freely attending to them, dwelling on

them, and building them up within him as part of a consciously controlled deliberation. The main point that self-determinism stresses is that in an act of free choice there is not something else in the person that chooses for him, but it is the person himself who makes his own choice. It is precisely in the ability of a person to do this that the dignity or worth of personality consists. An act so chosen as the free expression of one's personality obviously entails the kind of responsibility in which ethics is chiefly interested.

It is clear that self-determinism, more than any of the other theories, is compatible with an ethics of moral responsibility. In this view every voluntary act is free, with one exception: if all the motives are on one side and there is no motive for the opposite, the act could be voluntary, since it would be knowingly willed, but not free, since there is no possibility of refusal. Does this ever happen? Only if one were directly confronted with the absolutely perfect good. Since this does not happen in the normal choices faced in everyday life, voluntariness and freedom can be taken as coextensive, though slightly different, concepts.

As a final word on soft determinism, we should observe that, though open to serious criticism, it does leave room for freedom and responsibility of a type. By holding that man is at least remotely responsible for the development of his character, from which his acts flow, it accepts conclusions on which an ethical system can be based, even if it commits flaws of logic in arriving at those conclusions. Ethics is chiefly interested, not in how a man arrives at an acceptance of freedom and responsibility, but in the fact that he does accept them. We see no reason, however, for taking an inferior theory when a better one is at hand. Our future discussions will proceed on the basis of self-determinism, and the reader who holds other views can make the proper adjustments, either by an act of free choice or in accordance with the way he has been conditioned.

SUMMARY

What precisely is conduct? It consists of *human acts.* In contrast to mere *acts of a man, human acts* are those of which man is master by consciously controlling and deliberately willing them.

The *human act* is the result of a complex psychological process involving wish, intention, deliberation, choice, consent, use, and enjoyment. The decisive point is the *consent* of the will after the deliberation of the intellect. It is here that the person yields to the attractiveness of the object and commits himself to it.

Commanded acts, acts of faculties commanded by the will, share in the consent of the will and are also considered *human acts* in a borrowed sense.

Voluntariness is the chief characteristic of a human act. It means that the act is really willed, that it proceeds from the will with a knowledge of the end. It supposes that the agent knows what he is doing and wills to do it. *Knowledge* points out the end and the means to it, guides deliberation, and provides advertence and reflection, without which there can be no consent of the will.

Some main consequences of voluntariness are *responsibility* in the agent, *imputability* in the act, and *merit* in both.

Free will versus *determinism* is a metaphysical question but important for ethics. *Fatalism* and *theological determinism* have little appeal today. *Hard determinism* makes man's every act rigidly conform to the law of causality operative in the physical universe and reduces free choice to an illusion. *Indeterminism,* the opposite extreme, explains free choice by exempting man's free acts from all causal influence. *Soft determinism* compromises by admitting that man is free from outer compulsion but necessarily follows the bent of his character; he is determined not physically but psychologically. *Self-determinism* admits that man's free acts are caused, but caused by the person himself as a self-governing agent, so that he could have acted otherwise and freely chose not to do so.

One's answer to the free-will problem will color his interpretation of responsibility.

QUESTIONS FOR DISCUSSION

1 Must the whole description of the psychological background of a human act as given in the text be accepted to separate the human act from an act of a man? What elements are absolutely essential?

2 Is there any meaning to responsibility for one's act if that act is conceived as not free? Does the fact that the responsibility cannot be placed on anybody or anything outside you make you responsible?

3 Your inheritance and conditioning, your makeup and environment, determined for you the choice you actually made; they made it impossible for you to have made any other choice, but they did not make the choice. You made the choice and are therefore responsible. What do you think of this argument of the psychological determinists?

4 Would acting as described in the third question be voluntary because it comes from an internal principle with knowledge of the end? Should everything that goes on in the will be called voluntary, whether deliberate or indeliberate?

5 Are there some people with no sense of morality at all, psychopathic personalities immune to all perception of right and wrong, who could make other choices intelligently and freely but could make no moral choices?

READINGS

Aristotle, *Nicomachean Ethics*, bk. III, ch. 1-5, treats of voluntariness; he is feeling his way toward clarifying the concept. We have tried to reduce to a small space what St. Thomas says in the *Summa Theologica*, I-II, qq. 6, 8, 11-17. In q. 9 he discusses what moves (motivates) the will, and in q. 10 he shows that the will is not moved of necessity (not necessitated). This follows up what he had said in pt. I, qq. 82 and 83, on free will. Walter Farrell, *Companion to the Summa*, four volumes, is a readable popularization of St. Thomas' *Summa Theologica*, following St. Thomas' order. We need not refer to it again, since the appropriate place is easily found.

Etienne Gilson, *Moral Values and Moral Life*, ch. 2, and his *The Christian Philosophy of St. Thomas Aquinas*, pp. 251-256; Vernon Bourke, *Ethics*, ch. 3; and George Klubertanz, *Philosophy of Human Nature*, ch. 10, all give excellent summaries of the process of decision and the making of a human act.

For presentations of divergent viewpoints on free will see Sidney Hook, *Determinism and Freedom in the Age of Modern Science*, Bernard Berofsky, *Free Will and Determinism*, and Willard F. Enteman, *The Problem of Free Will*, three anthologies containing many well-known articles. See also William James, "The Dilemma of Determinism," in *The Will to Believe*, pp. 145-183; Jean-Paul Sartre, *Being and Nothingness*, pt. IV, ch. 1, §111; John Hospers, *Human Conduct*, ch. 10; C. A. Campbell, *On Selfhood and Godhood*, lecture 9, and *In Defense of Free Will*; P. H. Nowell-Smith, *Ethics*, ch. 20; Moritz Schlick, *Problems of Ethics*, pp. 143-158; Yves Simon, *Freedom of Choice*; and R. L. Franklin, *Freewill and Determinism*.

Austin Fagothey, *Right and Reason—an Anthology*, contains Aristotle's *Nicomachean Ethics*, bk. III, ch. 1-5; and Eric D'Arcy's *Human Acts*, pp. 2-26.

CHAPTER 3

RESPONSIBILITY

PROBLEM

From the acts man performs we have separated out those over which man has control. We have fixed the point of control in the consent of the will, prepared for by the deliberation of the intellect. If the consent can be thrown to either alternative, for or against, the person himself is the cause of his own decision and is therefore responsible for the act chosen. There is no other reason why this act was done rather than not done except that the man himself, by the choice of his will under the guiding light of his intellect, made that act to *be*. The act is *his* insofar as *he* did it.

Is a man equally responsible for all his human acts? Not all knowledge is equally clear, nor does the will consent always with equal decisiveness. What proceeds from the will may be closely or remotely connected with the will-act itself and may share in its voluntariness in varying degrees. We must therefore see the factors that enhance or limit a man's responsibility by increasing or diminishing his control, making the act more or less *human*, more or less *his*. The following points come up for discussion:

1. What are the main kinds of voluntariness?
2. What destroys or weakens our responsibility?
3. Are unwanted but foreseen consequences voluntary?
4. When may one permit foreseen evil consequences?

5. Must we avoid contributing to others' moral harm?

LEVELS OF WILLING AND NOT WILLING

There is a difference between *not willing* to do something and willing *not to do* something. In the first case there is no act of the will and therefore no voluntariness. In the second case there is an act of the will, an act of deliberate omission or refusal, and this is quite voluntary. Hence voluntariness can be positive or negative, according as we will to do something or to omit something, and both of these kinds of voluntariness are different from a state of nonvoluntariness, which is an absence of willing. Some writers reserve the word *involuntary* for what happens against our will and use *nonvoluntary* for what we have no attitude toward, but this usage is not consistently observed.

The state of not *willing* is often psychologically impossible to maintain. We *do not will* so long as the doing of an act does not even cross our mind. When we think of it, and especially after we have reflected on it and deliberated about it, we must do either of two things: take it or leave it, will to do it or will not to do it. One course is as voluntary as the other. Negative voluntariness is not the same as no voluntariness, just as a negative number is not the same as zero.

For my act to be voluntary I must knowingly will it. But must my mind be focused on the act at the very moment I am doing it? Can I be responsible for an act done in a state of complete distraction? For any responsibility to remain, must a previous decision to act still influence my behavior, or may it have entirely ceased its influence? Can I be responsible for something which I never did will but presumably would have willed if I ever thought of it?

To answer such questions, it is customary to distinguish four levels of intention with which an act is performed, representing a progressive diminution of voluntariness.

An *actual* intention is one that a person is conscious of at the moment he performs the intended action. The person pays attention not merely to what he is doing but also to the fact that he is here and now willing it.

A *virtual* intention is one that was once made and continues to influence the act now being done, but it is not present in the person's consciousness at the moment of performing the act. Thus a man walks to a definite destination; his intention was actual on starting out but soon becomes virtual as his mind drifts onto other subjects while he takes the right turns and arrives at where he wanted to go. What he willed was the whole series of acts that would bring him there, but he need not be thinking of his destination every step of the way. After his first decision, the subsequent acts could be carried out while his mind is completely distracted from its original purpose.

A *habitual* intention is one that was once made and not retracted, but it does not influence the performance of the intended act. Though called habitual, it does not imply any habit; it is an intention that was once *had* and is still had only in the sense that it was never revoked, for no psychic remnant of it need remain in the mind. A man fully resolves to kill his enemy but is prevented by circumstances from carrying out his intent, though he

never revokes it; later, while hunting, he shoots at what he thinks is an animal but finds that he has accidentally shot his enemy.

An *interpretative* intention is one that has not been made but presumably would have been made if the person were aware of the circumstances. If the literal application of a law would cause more harm than good, one might interpret the mind of the lawgiver and relax the law in this particular case. If a repentant thief cannot return stolen goods because he cannot discover the owner, he may give them to the poor on the presumption that this would be the will of the owner in the present circumstances.

For an act to be voluntary an actual intention is not necessary, but a virtual one suffices. The habitual and interpretative intentions have much less importance. They indicate that the person's will (either once actually had or merely presumed) is objectively carried out, but not by the person's own voluntary act. A habitual intention, however, is sufficient for the fulfillment of certain kinds of obligations; for example, if I give you a gift, completely forgetting that I already owe you the money in payment of a debt, the debt is satisfied.

MODIFIERS OF RESPONSIBILITY

Voluntariness is *full* or *perfect* if the agent has full knowledge and full consent. It is *diminished* or *imperfect* if there is something wanting in the agent's knowledge or consent or both, provided he has both in some degree. If either the knowledge were wholly lacking or the consent were wholly lacking, there could be no voluntariness at all. The question now arises: What renders voluntariness imperfect, reducing the specifically human character of the act and making the agent less responsible? Since we are not interested here in the strength of the will-act but in the agent's self-control, we shall call them *modifiers of responsibility.* There are five main ones:

1. Ignorance, affecting the knowledge
2. Passion, affecting the consent of the will
3. Fear, opposing to the will a contrary wish
4. Force, actual use of physical compulsion.
5. Habit, a tendency acquired by repetition

IGNORANCE

Lack of knowledge exists in varying degrees. The term *ignorant* is applied only to persons and not to things incapable of knowledge. One capable of knowledge but lacking it may or may not have an obligation to have such knowledge. Neither a sea captain nor a doctor needs to know music or archaeology; such merely negative ignorance has no ethical import. The case would be different if the sea captain piloted a ship without knowing navigation or if the doctor tried to practice without knowing medicine; ignorance in these instances is a privation of knowledge that ought to be present. Ignorance may exist without error but is implied in all error; one who mistakes Smith for Jones does not know either man.

Ignorance either can or cannot be overcome. Ignorance that can be overcome by acquiring the requisite knowledge is called *vincible ignorance.* Ignorance that cannot be overcome because the requisite knowledge cannot be acquired is called *invincible ignorance.* A person can be invincibly ignorant for one of two reasons: either he does not realize his state of ignorance, so that it does not cross his mind that there is any knowledge to be acquired; or he does realize his ignorance, but his efforts to obtain the knowledge are of no avail. Ignorance should be taken relatively to the person: Can this man obtain the information with a reasonable amount of effort, such as a normally prudent and sincere

man would feel obliged to use in the circumstances and in time for the decision he must make?

The culpability of vincible ignorance depends on the amount of effort put forth to dispel it, and the amount of effort called for depends on the importance of the matter and the obligation of the agent to possess such knowledge. One who makes a little effort, but not enough, shows some goodwill but insufficient perseverance. One may know that the knowledge can be obtained but is too lazy or careless to search for it. One may doubt whether the knowledge can be obtained, and after a little effort may hastily but wrongly judge that it cannot. One may make no effort at all, either with full knowledge that the ignorance is vincible, or not caring whether it is or not. One may deliberately avoid knowledge in order to plead ignorance as an excuse, such as refusing to read notices or dodging those who might inform him; this sort of pretense is called *affected* or *studied* ignorance.

1. *Invincible ignorance destroys responsibility.* Knowledge is requisite for voluntariness, and in the case of invincible ignorance this knowledge is not obtainable. Therefore what is done in invincible ignorance is not voluntary. A man who passes on counterfeit money, not suspecting that it is counterfeit, does no wrong. His act of *paying* is voluntary, but not his paying *in worthless money.*

2. *Vincible ignorance does not destroy responsibility, but lessens it.* The person knows that he is ignorant and that he can gain the knowledge. By deliberately failing to make sufficient effort he allows himself to remain in ignorance, and the effects that follow from this ignorance are indirectly voluntary or voluntary in cause, as will be explained more fully under that heading. By willing to remain in ignorance, the person is responsible for the consequences he foresees will or may follow from that ignorance. A surgeon, knowing

that he has not sufficient knowledge for a difficult operation that can be postponed, performs it anyway and kills the patient; though he did not want the patient to die, he deliberately exposed him to serious and unnecessary danger and is responsible for the death. However, though he recognizes his ignorance, he is not sure of its effects. He is less guilty than one who would deliberately plan to kill a man in this way.

3. *Affected ignorance in a way lessens, in a way increases, responsibility.* It lessens it, as does all lack of knowledge, since the person does not see clearly the full import of what he is doing. It increases it if the person intends to use the ignorance as an excuse; the removal of the risk of punishment is an added motive for the will; he is not only willing the act but also willing the ignorance as a means of facilitating the act.

PASSION

The idea we want here is that of any very strong motion of the sensitive appetite. It is difficult to find the precise word for it. *Lust* and *concupiscence,* used by the older writers, have become too narrow. *Feeling* is too weak; *emotion* is stronger but not strong enough. *Passion* seems to suit best, though it is not perfect, for it puts too much stress on two emotions, anger and love, and we mean them all.

We shall not enter into a psychological discussion of the passions—their nature, number, and varieties. We are interested only in the effect of the passions on a human act. Passions may make us will a thing more strongly, but with less self-control. Passion certainly increases the force of the will-act, but this is more of a psychological than an ethical consideration. The man who has less self-control has less responsibility, and his act is that much less a *human act.*

The passions may arise spontaneously before the will has acted. When an object is presented to the senses, the sensitive appetite is stirred up almost automatically and reacts by sudden feelings of joy, anger, hatred, grief, shame, pity, disgust, and the like. These emotions, if felt very strongly, are what we mean by the passions. They often occur in us without our will or against our will. Passion of this kind is called *antecedent,* because it comes before the will can act.

We can also intentionally stir up our passions by brooding on the objects that arouse them. We can actually make ourselves angry by vividly rehearsing insults in our imagination, or frightened by the hair-raising details of a horror story, or sad by an exaggerated indulgence in self-pity. Passion thus deliberately aroused is called *consequent,* because it comes after the choice of our will. Antecedent passion is but an *act of a man,* but consequent passion is a *human act.* Antecedent passion becomes consequent when it is recognized for what it is and then is deliberately retained or fostered.

1. *Antecedent passion may destroy responsibility.* If the passion is so sudden or violent as wholly to prevent the use of reason, it makes deliberation impossible, and the act performed under its influence is neither free nor voluntary. Experience shows that complete loss of control sometimes happens, though rarely.

2. *Antecedent passion does not usually destroy responsibility but lessens it.* In most cases a man even while upset by passion remains master of his acts. Enough knowledge and consent remain for his act to be both voluntary and free, and he is held responsible for it. Calm intellectual deliberation is more difficult, the motives on each side cannot be weighed with perfect impartiality, the will is predisposed more strongly toward one side than the other, and its freedom of action is hampered. Hence an act done with passion, when free, is less free than one done with cool premeditation and no disturbing influences. The act may be more voluntary

in the sense of a greater onrush of the will, but it is less so in the sense of self-control and moral responsibility dependent on calm judgment.

3. *Consequent passion does not lessen responsibility but may increase it.* The state of passion is deliberately aroused or fostered and is therefore voluntary in itself. The act resulting from the passion is voluntary either in itself or in its cause. A man intentionally broods over an insult in order to nerve himself for an act of revenge; he is using the passion as a means and the revenge as an end, and both are voluntary in themselves. A man who does not want to kill foresees that his continual brooding over his wrongs will get him into such a state of frenzy that he will kill; yet he deliberately continues to nurse his anger, and as a result becomes insane with rage and kills his enemy. His state of passion is voluntary in itself, but his act of killing is voluntary in cause.

FEAR

Fear is the apprehension of impending evil. It can be an emotion, a disturbance of the sensitive appetite, when it appears as a sudden fright-producing reflex or as an impulsive act of avoidance. In this sense fear is one of the passions and follows the rules on the passions. There is also an intellectual fear, comprising an understanding of a threatened evil and a movement of the will to avoid this evil by rationally devised means. This kind of fear may have no emotional component. Thus a man may coldly decide to steal because he is afraid of poverty, to lie because he is afraid of disgrace, to murder because he is afraid of blackmail. This is the kind of fear we mean as a separate modifier of responsibility.

In estimating its effect on responsibility, fear must be taken relatively to the person and his circumstances. What would produce a slight fear in one person may produce grave fear in another; some are naturally cautious whereas others are bold, and some have little aversion to a condition that others would find intolerable. A lesser evil that threatens us now may produce more fear than a greater evil still far off.

Fear is a modifier of responsibility only when we act *from* fear as a motive for acting and not merely *with* fear as an accompaniment of our act. A soldier deserting his post in battle through cowardice is motivated by fear; if he stays at his post despite the danger, he may have just as much fear, but he does not let it influence his conduct.

1. *Fear does not destroy responsibility.* It is true that the emotional type of fear can throw a person into such a panic that he loses all self-control; then it follows the rules on the passions. But the intellectual type of fear we are dealing with does not produce such an effect. The person calmly looks about for an escape from the threatened evil and makes a deliberate choice. He could choose to face the evil but prefers to yield to his fear instead of resisting it, and therefore wills what he does. This conduct is prudent when there is no obligation to resist.

2. *Fear lessens responsibility.* An act motivated by fear is one that we will, but would not will except for the fear we experience. This admixture of reluctance weakens the consent of the will, leaving us with a divided mind and a hankering for the other alternative, thus lessening our self-control.

If a person's decision is clear-cut and straightforward, so that he acts without any regret or reluctance, his act is voluntary, and the alternative he did not choose is involuntary. But when he acts regretfully and reluctantly, when he chooses something he would rather not be obliged to do, there is a conflict between his *will* and his *wish.* His will is what he deliberately chooses; his wish is what he would like if circumstances permitted. The time-honored example is that of the sea captain who throws his cargo overboard to save his ship in a storm. The act contains both a voluntary and an involuntary aspect: voluntary in the sense that he does it deliberately and intentionally with sufficient knowledge and consent, for he could refuse and try to weather out the storm or even let his ship sink; involuntary in the sense that he would rather not have to do this and, if there were no storm, certainly would not do it. Thus he *wills* to jettison his cargo, *wishing* that he did not need to do so. Despite the contrary wish, or *velleity*, the captain is held responsible for this act of jettisoning the cargo but not as responsible as he would be were there no contrary wish present. The contrary wish itself is involuntary, since it was not willed or consented to, and does not constitute human conduct.

Acts done under *duress* and *intimidation* have fear as a motive. These acts are extorted under threat of evil to be inflicted by another human will. Unless the person becomes so emotionally upset as to become temporarily insane, a matter of passion rather than of intellectual fear, acts done under duress and intimidation are responsible acts, for the person could have refused and taken the consequences. Contracts unjustly extorted through fear can be nullified by positive law, not necessarily because the parties are irresponsible but because the common good requires that extortion be made unprofitable.

FORCE

Force, violence, or compulsion is external physical power making one do something against his will. In common language, one who yields to a threat of violence is said to be *forced*, yet this is not really force but *fear*, and the person's voluntariness is to be judged by the rules on fear. As a distinct modifier of responsibility, *force* must be understood in its strictest sense as no mere threat but the *actual use of physical might*. If I hand over my money to a thug because he thrusts a gun at me, that is fear; if he physically overpowers me while he rifles my pockets, that is force.

Force in this physical sense cannot reach the will directly, for it touches only external acts and not the internal act of the will itself, in which voluntariness resides. We can continue to will the opposite, no matter how violently we are forced to do the act. Hence the act we are forced to do is involuntary, so long as the force is resisted. Somebody else may have the physical strength to make us *do* something, but he cannot make us *will* it.

The act a violent aggressor is trying to make us do may or may not be evil in itself. If it is not, we may yield to it and comply with his demands; our rights are outraged and injustice is done against us, but we ourselves are not doing wrong, only saving ourselves further harm. One who is kidnapped need not struggle (and this is true of one acting from fear as well as force), for there is no moral wrong in merely going off to another place. But in a case such as rape, where consent would involve moral wrong, resistance is required.

How much resistance? At least internal resistance, which consists in withholding the consent of the will, and passive external resistance, which consists in noncooperation with the aggressor. Active external resistance, which consists in positively fighting the aggressor, is also necessary when without it the withholding of consent would be too difficult to maintain, but not when it would be useless and there is no danger of consent.

The victim of force has no responsibility if he does not consent. If he consents reluctantly, he has reduced responsibility because of his contrary wish. If he actually wants to do what he is being forced to do and only pretends to resist, he is not truly a victim of force and has full responsibility.

HABIT

The nature and kinds of habit will be discussed in the chapter on habit; here we are interested only in the way habit may affect our responsibility for an act. For our present purpose we may define a habit as a constant way of acting obtained by repetition of the same act. When a habit has been acquired, the actions follow from it spontaneously and almost automatically, so that deliberate guidance becomes unnecessary.

1. We may set out *deliberately to acquire* a habit, as when we try to learn how to play a game or how to pick pockets. Then the habit is voluntary in itself, and the acts resulting from it are either voluntary in themselves if performed with the intention of acquiring the habit, or at least voluntary in cause if they are the unintended but foreseen consequences of the habit.

2. We may not intend to acquire a habit for its own sake but *voluntarily* perform acts that we know are *habit-forming,* as when a person takes up smoking or narcotics. Here the acts done are voluntary in themselves, and the forming of the habit is voluntary in cause, since we know that we cannot do habit-forming acts without getting the habit. After the habit has been acquired, acts unintentionally following from it are also voluntary in cause.

3. We may discover that we have *unintentionally* acquired a habit, either because we did not realize that we had done the same thing in the same way so often, or because it did not occur to us that such actions were habit-forming. Most of our habits of speech and gesture are of this type. In this case we are not responsible for the existence of the habit or for the acts that unintentionally follow from it, so long as we remain ignorant that we have the habit. A rather gross lack of reflectiveness may cause this condition to remain a long time.

In whatever way we may have acquired the habit, as soon as we fully recognize our condition we face the choice of either keeping the habit or trying to get rid of it. In either case a new act of the will is called for; the act of getting and the act of keeping are two separate acts, and each may be voluntary.

If we decide to *let the habit remain,* our possession of the habit now becomes voluntary in itself, and the acts that unintentionally follow from the habit are voluntary in cause. The habit, however acquired, is now deliberately kept, and we are responsible both for the habit itself and for its effects.

If we decide to *get rid of the habit,* as we are obliged to do if the habit is bad, we are now the victim of two opposite pulls, the voluntary decision of our will to suppress the habit and the involuntary persistence of the habit itself. Long-standing habits of a certain type are not overcome in a day and, when our vigilance is relaxed, will inadvertently spring out into the corresponding act. Success in this struggle is bought only by constant watchfulness and effort. If we let down the guards, we shall soon find ourselves drifting back to the old familiar way. Our responsibility for such acts depends on the amount of advertence at the moment when the act is performed and also on the amount of effort expended to get rid of the habit. Here, just as in the dispelling of vincible ignorance, we are obliged to put in an amount of effort proportional to the importance of the matter. Depending on these factors and on our sincerity, we may have full responsibility for acts done from habit, or some, or even none.

ADDITIONAL MODIFIERS

To these five modifiers of responsibility it is possible to add others, such a sleepiness, sickness, pain, alcohol, drugs, and other conditions that reduce awareness and self-control. They are very important, but since they produce their effect on voluntariness by involving one or more of the five modifiers already discussed, no new rules or principles are required.

Abnormal mental states will, of course, seriously affect the capacity of a person to perform human acts. The lighter neuroses will probably only lessen voluntariness, whereas the deeper psychoses may destroy it entirely. The mentally ill may have complete self-control at times or along certain lines, and none or little at other times or in other forms of behavior. A kleptomaniac may be a very rational person except when under the spell of this particular compulsion; these acts are involuntary but not the other acts the person performs. Each case is different and must be judged by itself.

The same principles seem applicable also to the refined methods of physical, mental, and social torture used for political purposes, beginning with "brainwashing" and aiming at total "thought control." It is said that in such a long, drawn-out process everyone has his breaking point. If so, the victim has full responsibility at the start, suffers a gradual diminution of it as the inhuman routine continues, and after the breaking point, if there really is one, he ceases to be a responsible person. He need not be reduced to actual insanity. It is sufficient that he cannot control his moral judgments or the actions resulting from them. Whether he has any moral responsibility left only the victim himself really knows, though a psychologist could make a good inference. What we have said applies to the victim. The perpetrator of this horror stands guilty of his own barbarity and of all its foreseen consequences.

Nothing has been said about the unconscious, about the drives, complexes, and motivations sunk beneath the threshold of our awareness, which are such powerful influences affecting our behavior. They are indeed of the greatest moment in the development of our personality and have much to do with our ethical life, especially with our moral principles and attitudes. They may explain why some have such a keen, and others such a blunted, sense of moral values, and why there seem to be moral psychopaths. Since such urges are unconscious, however, they exist in us involuntarily and do not enter into the performance of a human act. They are much like habits inadvertently developed. We cannot be responsible for them until we recognize them, and by that time they have been dredged up from the unconscious to a conscious condition. Then we are faced with the problem of what we shall choose to do about them. They may supply the actual motivation of acts we attribute to other motives, but since we choose the act as we see it, we are responsible for the act as seen and chosen, and not for the hidden motives from which it may really stem. The question of the unconscious is therefore extraneous to our present topic, which is *moral* responsibility. Thus again we see the difference between psychology and ethics.

THE INDIRECT VOLUNTARY

There is a difference between the way in which the act itself is voluntary and the way in which its consequences are voluntary. That is *voluntary in itself,* or *directly voluntary,* which is the thing willed, whether it be willed as an end or as means to an end. That is *voluntary in cause,* or *indirectly voluntary,* which is the unintended but foreseen consequence of something else that is voluntary in itself; the agent does not will this consequence either as end or as means but sees that he cannot get something else without getting it; he wills the cause of which this is a necessary effect. Thus one who throws a bomb at a king to assassinate him, knowing that he will kill the king's attendants also, directly wills the throwing of the bomb (as means), also directly wills the death of the king (as end), and indirectly wills the death of the attendants (as consequence) though their death gives him no profit. But a consequence that is neither intended nor foreseen is involuntary, such as the death of one who unexpectedly rushes up to the king after the bomb has left the thrower's hand.

The assassin just described is morally responsible for all the deaths he foresaw would result from his act, whether he wanted them or not. There is no moral problem here because the act is all bad. Good or indifferent acts also may have bad effects that can be foreseen. How responsible are we for them? Must we always refuse to do a good act if we foresee that it will or can have a bad consequence?

Though we have not yet established the existence of moral good and evil, much less separated out the factors from which these moral qualities arise, for our present purpose we can take them on the common-sense level on which we began our study: that in the judgment of mankind some acts are good, others are bad, and still others are indifferent. Our business here and now is to determine how responsible one is for the consequences of one's acts, whatever their moral quality, and our examples are mere commonsense illustrations.

If we were obliged to avoid every act that will have an evil consequence, life would soon become unlivable. One who accepts a job when jobs are scarce cuts someone else out of a livelihood, a doctor who tends the sick during a plague exposes himself to catching the disease, a lawyer who must present this bit of evidence to win his case may put an innocent person under suspicion, or a teacher who gives a competent examination knows that some will probably fail. We seem to be caught on the horns of a dilemma: either human life cannot be lived as it actually is, or we are compelled to do evil and to do it voluntarily.

We find the solution to the dilemma in the principle of the *indirect voluntary,* com-

monly known as the principle of *double effect,* one of the most useful ethical principles. It is based on the fact that evil must never be *voluntary in itself,* must never be willed either as end or as means, for then it is the direct object of the will-act and necessarily renders the act evil. Nor may evil ever be *voluntary in cause,* as a foreseen but unwanted consequence, unless it can somehow be reduced to an incidental and unavoidable by-product or side effect in the achievement of some good the person is rightfully seeking.

Though I am never allowed to will evil, I am not always bound to prevent the existence of evil. Just as I may tolerate the existence of evils in the world at large, since I could not cure them without bringing other evils on myself or my neighbor, so I may sometimes tolerate evil consequences from my own actions, if to abstain from such actions would bring a proportionate evil on myself or others. Sometimes I cannot will a good without at the same time permitting the existence of an evil which in the very nature of things is inseparably bound up with the good I will. But I must not do so indiscriminately. Sometimes I am bound to prevent evil, and in these cases it would be wrong for me to permit it. How can we determine these cases?

The *principle of double effect* says that it is morally allowable to perform an act that has a bad effect under the following conditions:

1. *The act to be done must be good in itself or at least indifferent.* This is evident, for if the act is evil of itself, evil would be chosen directly, either as an end or as a means to an end, and there could be no question of merely permitting or tolerating it.

2. *The good intended must not be obtained by means of the evil effect.* The evil must be only an incidental by-product and not an actual factor in the accomplishment of the good. If the act has two effects,

one good and the other bad, the good effect must not be accomplished by means of the bad, for then the evil would be directly voluntary as a means. We may never do evil in order that good may come of it. A good end does not justify the use of bad means. Hence the good effect must follow as immediately and directly from the original act as the evil effect. It is sometimes said that the evil must not come before the good, but this may be misunderstood. It is not a question of time but of causality; the good must not come *through* or *by means of* the evil.

3. *The evil effect must not be intended for itself but only permitted.* The bad effect may be of its own nature merely a by-product of the act performed, but if the agent wants this bad effect, he makes it directly voluntary by willing it. An evil intention is not to be presumed without evidence.

4. *There must be a proportionately grave reason for permitting the evil effect.* Though we are not always obliged to prevent evil, we are obliged to prevent a serious evil by a small sacrifice of our own good. Hence some proportion between the good and evil is required. How to estimate the proportion may be difficult in practice. For the present we can say that the good and the evil should be at least nearly equivalent. If the good is slight and the evil great, the evil could be called incidental only in a technical sense, and the obligation to avoid it would be overwhelming. Also, if there is any other way of getting the good effect without the bad effect, this other way must be taken; otherwise there is no proportionate reason for permitting the evil.

The act is not morally allowable unless all four conditions are fulfilled. If any one of them is not satisfied, even though the other three are, the act is morally wrong. There is no question here of telling people that in the conditions specified they can go ahead and do wrong. Rather, it is a way

of showing that the action in question is not wrong. The bad effect spoken of is a physical evil of some kind, which includes exposure to temptation. The double-effect principle expresses the conditions under which it is not morally evil to permit a physical evil to happen.

An example will help to illustrate the application of the principle. A passerby dashes into a burning building to save a child trapped there, though he may be severely burned and even lose his life. We recognize his deed as heroic, but its justification is found in the principle of double effect:

1. The act itself apart from its consequences is merely an act of entering a building. It is surely an indifferent act and allowable.

2. It has two effects: one good (saving the child) and the other bad (burning or even death to the rescuer). However, he does not save the child by means of dying or being burned but by means of reaching the child and carrying it or throwing it to safety. If he can do so without harm to himself, so much the better. The good effect is accomplished rather in spite of, than by means of, the bad effect, which is thus made only an incidental accompaniment in the rescue of the child.

3. If the rescuer were using this chance as an excuse for suicide, he would spoil the act by this bad intention, but there is no need for presuming any such intention.

4. There is a sufficient proportion: a life for a life. To enter a burning building to rescue some trifling possession could not be morally justified.

A few more cases will show how one or another of these four conditions can be violated:

1. An employee embezzles money to aid his sick child, hoping to pay it back later. Here the act itself of embezzlement (taking money belonging to another and falsifying the accounts) is not good or indifferent but wrong, and it cannot be justified by

any good intentions or good effects that might follow. He must try to raise the money in some other way. The first condition is violated, and the evil is *voluntary in itself*.

2. A man living with an alcoholic rich uncle stocks the house with liquor, knowing that he will inherit a fortune when the uncle has drunk himself to death. The act of stocking the house with liquor is indifferent in itself. It has two effects, bad for the uncle by occasioning his death, and good for the heir by bringing him his inheritance sooner. But the money cannot be inherited except through the uncle's death. The good effect (obtaining the money sooner) is accomplished by means of the bad effect (the uncle's death), and thus the second condition is violated.

3. A political boss distributes money to poor people to get them to vote for an unworthy candidate. Here the giving of money to the poor is a good act. The good effect (relieving poverty) is not accomplished by means of the bad effect (electing an unworthy candidate) but rather the other way round, the bad effect through the good. The third condition is violated because the evil effect, the election of the unworthy candidate, is directly intended as an end.

4. The owner of a private plane has his pilot fly him through exceedingly dangerous weather to complete a business deal that will net him a small profit. To fly a plane is an indifferent act; the danger has to do with the possible effect rather than with the act itself. The good effect (completing the business deal) is not obtained by means of the bad effect (possible loss of life). The bad effect is not intended for its own sake, for neither wants to die. The fourth condition can easily be violated here, for there does not seem to be a sufficient proportion between the risk to their lives and the rather slight financial advantage to be gained. There is always a risk in flying, and financial advantage can be great enough to justify it, but the present case supposes an excessive risk.

Though the foregoing examples show how the principle of double effect can be violated, many of the ordinary actions of life find their justification in a correct application of the principle. Thus people may take dangerous occupations to earn a livelihood, firemen and policemen can risk their lives to save others, a surgeon can operate even though he may cause pain, a man can vindicate his honor even though other people's reputations suffer from his disclosures, or the people may be subjected to great sacrifices to defend their country. If a man were obliged to avoid every deed to which evil could be incidental, he could do so little that he might as well stop living.

RESPONSIBILITY FOR THE ACTS OF OTHERS

Only the person who knowingly and willingly does an act can be responsible for it. In this sense no one can be responsible for the acts of another person. Each one is responsible for his own acts insofar as he knowingly and willingly intends to permit them to affect another person as incentives to good or evil. The ways in which we can help our neighbor to good are so numerous that it would be impossible to list them. It will be useful here, since we have just discussed the double-effect principle, to consider two ways in which we must try to avoid doing moral harm to other people, and how far this avoidance is possible.

OCCASION OF EVIL

The word *scandal* originally meant a stumbling block, and metaphorically something we trip on and fall over in our moral career. Now the word has lost its force and means only shocking conduct and juicy gossip. To regain the old meaning we shall call it *occasion of evil*. It is any word or deed tending to lead, entice, or allure another person into wrongdoing. It may be only *given,* or only *taken,* or both *given and taken,* so that the moral fault may be on either side or on both.

We *give* occasion of evil to another *directly* if we intend his evil act as an end or as a means. To intend it as an end would signify a truly diabolical hatred. The usual motive for inducing others to evil is to use it as a means to one's own profit, as do those who make their living by providing lewd entertainment.

We *give* occasion of evil to another *indirectly* if we do not intend the other person's evil act either as end or as means but foresee it as a consequence of something else we do. Care for our neighbor's moral welfare obliges us to avoid even this as far as possible, but life would be intolerably difficult if we had to avoid all actions in which others might find temptation. Here the principle of double effect applies: the act we do must not be wrong in itself though we foresee it will be a temptation to another, the good effect we intend must not be accomplished by means of the other's evil act, we must not want but only permit the other's temptation, and there must be a proportionate reason for permitting it.

Occasion of evil is *taken but not given* when someone with peculiar subjective dispositions is led to evil by another person's innocent words or deeds. It may be due to the taker's *malice,* and then is wholly his fault. Or it may be due to the taker's *weakness,* to his ignorance, youth, inexperience, prejudices, untamed passions, or unconquered habits. Love of our fellow man requires us to avoid words and actions, otherwise harmless, that might be a source of moral danger to the innocent or the weak. People should be more circumspect in their behavior before children, should not tantalize beyond endurance those who have trouble controlling their tempers, should not offer liquor to inveterate or re-

formed drunkards. But sometimes such situations cannot be avoided, and it is here that the principle of double effect comes into play. There is no obligation, at serious inconvenience to oneself or to the public, to abolish everything that might entice the weak or innocent, though all reasonable precautions should be taken. It would be absurd to close all theaters, taverns, and amusements that are conducted in a generally respectable fashion simply because some people with abnormal weaknesses find them seductive. When the young, innocent, or prejudiced are unavoidably exposed to temptation, precautionary instruction is usually the best remedy.

COOPERATION IN EVIL

Cooperation in another's evil deed may occur by joining him in the actual performance of the act or by supplying him with the means for performing it. If two men plan a robbery, one may hold the gun while the other relieves the victim of his valuables, or one may lend the other a gun to enable him to carry out the robbery alone. In either case one not only helps another to do evil but also joins in his evil intention. This is known as *formal* cooperation. It cannot be justified under any circumstances because the evil is directly willed.

A lesser variety of cooperation occurs when, without approving another's wrongdoing, one helps him perform his evil act by an action of one's own that is not of its nature evil. Thus an employee is forced by robbers to open up the safe, or the driver of a car is compelled by gangsters to drive them to the scene of intended murder. This is known as *material* cooperation. There is nothing wrong in what I do or in what I intend, but there is the bad circumstance that my otherwise innocent act aids others in their wrongdoing. Consequently, if there is a proportionately grave reason for permitting this evil circumstance, material cooperation can be justified by the principle of double effect. Since the act I do is not wrong in itself, and I do not use the other's evil deed as a means to any end of my own, and I have no wrong intention, the only remaining difficulty is that of the proportion. This proportion must be estimated by the following:

1. The amount of evil my cooperation helps others to do
2. The amount of evil that will happen to me if I refuse to cooperate
3. The closeness of my cooperative act to the other's evil act

The first two points are only common sense and are formally justified later by the principles on a conflict of rights. My duty to my fellowman does not oblige me to suffer an injury greater than or equal to that which I am trying to ward off from him, but it does oblige me to suffer a small loss to prevent a great loss from happening to another, and it may even oblige me to sacrifice my life to prevent a huge public calamity. The third point, however, needs some further explanation.

Cooperation may be *proximate* or *remote,* depending on how close it comes to the actual evil deed of the principal agent. For example, a man who writes an immoral book does an act evil in itself; publishers who accept and edit such a book are formal cooperators; typesetters, proofreaders, and others who prepare the actual text are proximate material cooperators; those who merely run the presses, bind the books, and prepare them for delivery are remote material cooperators. The heads of bookselling firms that stock such books are formal cooperators, hired clerks who sell them are proximate material cooperators, secretaries who handle the business correspondence concerning them are remote material cooperators. The more proximate the cooperation, the greater the proportionate reason required to make material cooperation allowable.

If no one else could be substituted to help in the evil act, I have a greater responsibility because I can actually prevent the act from happening, and I should have a proportionately greater reason. Also, greater reason is required to justify cooperation in persons who have an *explicit* duty to prevent that particular kind of evil from happening. This would occur in a soldier forced to cooperate with the enemy, a policeman with criminals, a watchman with burglars, a customs officer with smugglers.

The forms that cooperation can take are too numerous to mention, for it is possible to cooperate with almost any external act, at least by encouragement and support. Hired workers, because they engage their services to a company whose policy they do not determine, are particularly open to the danger of material cooperation. One should not keep a job with a company that continually and habitually does a morally objectionable business. If it does so only occasionally, employees need not be disturbed so long as their material cooperation is kept remote, but if they find that proximate material cooperation is demanded of them fairly frequently, they should have a grave reason for continuing in their job and should meanwhile make an earnest effort to obtain other work.

SUMMARY

Voluntariness is *positive* if one wills to do something; *negative* if one wills to omit something; *none* if one does not will. Intention is *actual* if now present to consciousness; *virtual* if unconsciously continuing to influence the act; *habitual* if once made, never retracted, and not now influencing the act; *interpretative* if it would have been made had the agent ever thought of it.

Voluntariness is *perfect* if there is full knowledge and full consent; *imperfect* if there is some flaw in one or both.

Ignorance is lack of knowledge in one

capable of it. Invincible ignorance cannot be overcome and destroys responsibility. Vincible ignorance can be overcome and does not destroy, though it lessens, responsibility.

Passion is any strong emotion. *Antecedent* passion, arising spontaneously, lessens responsibility and may, though rarely, destroy it. *Consequent* passion, deliberately aroused or fostered, does not lessen responsibility but may even increase it.

Fear is the apprehension of impending evil. Fear affects voluntariness only when it is the motive for acting. It does not destroy responsibility but lessens it because of the contrary wish mingled with our actual will.

Force is actual external physical power making us act against our will. The act is involuntary if we withhold consent.

Habit is a constant way of acting through repetition of the same act. The acquisition of a habit may be voluntary in itself, voluntary in cause, or involuntary. One who finds he has acquired a habit must choose either to keep it or get rid of it. Responsibility for habitual acts depends on the amount of advertence and on the effort to get rid of the habit.

An act is voluntary *in itself*, also called *directly* voluntary, if willed either as end or as means; it is voluntary *in cause*, also called *indirectly* voluntary, if it is the unintended but foreseen consequence of something else that is voluntary in itself. Unforeseen consequences are involuntary.

To try to avoid every act from which some bad effect might follow would make life impossible. We are never allowed to will evil but are not always bound to prevent the existence of evil.

The *principle of double effect* summarizes the conditions under which we may perform an act from which we foresee that a bad consequence will follow:

1. The act must be good or indifferent in itself.
2. The good must not be obtained by means of the evil.
3. The evil must not be intended for itself.
4. There must be a sufficient proportion.

All four conditions must be fulfilled. Violation of any one makes the evil directly willed, not merely permitted as an incidental by-product.

We can be responsible for another's misdeed by inciting him to it or helping him in it.

An *occasion of evil* is a word or deed leading another to wrongdoing. To intend the other's evil act as means or as end is always wrong. To permit it only as an indirect consequence is allowed when the principle of double effect is satisfied.

Cooperation in evil is helping another to do wrong by joining him in the act or by supplying him with the means. It is *formal* if we intend the evil, and *material* if without intending the evil we actually assist in its performance by an act of our own that is not of its nature evil. The former is always wrong; the latter is allowable when the principle of double effect is satisfied. We must consider not only the balance of evil to ourselves and to others but also how close our cooperation comes to the evil. Strong reasons are needed to justify *proximate* material cooperation; lesser reasons suffice for *remote* material cooperation.

QUESTIONS FOR DISCUSSION

1 What is the proof for the doubt-effect principle? Does it need proof? By means of such moral hair-splitting would it not be pos-

sible to justify almost anything? Yet, how does one who rejects this principle solve such cases?

2 One under strong emotion is incapable of judging his responsibility. Afterward the passion is not there to be examined, and memory is treacherous. How can one determine the degree of voluntariness in such cases?

3 Why is only a proportionate effort required in getting rid of a bad habit? Is not anything less than an all-out effort a partial pampering of the bad habit?

4 Has modern psychology, especially depth psychology, unearthed any new modifiers of responsibility? From the moral standpoint, is the person's conduct to be judged by various unconscious motivations that a psychologist can detect, or from what was consciously in his mind when he consented to the act?

5 How far can one living under a totalitarian government and disapproving of much of their policy cooperate with that government? May he take their education, serve in their army, fight in their wars, write ideological propaganda, or accept an official decision-making position?

READINGS

Plato in the *Laws*, bk. IX, talks about voluntary and involuntary crimes. In the *Lesser Hippias*, a work of doubtful genuineness, he discusses the question whether it is worse to do wrong voluntarily or involuntarily; the argument is inconclusive but illuminates the question.

Aristotle, *Ethics*, bk. III, ch. 1-5, makes the first serious study of voluntariness.

Read, St. Thomas, *Summa Theologica*, I-II, q. 6, on voluntariness; q. 76, on ignorance; q. 77, on passion; q. 78, on malice and habit. In I-II, qq. 22-48, St. Thomas gives a lengthy treatment of the passions. This matter is summarized in Étienne Gilson, *Moral Values and Moral Life*, ch. 4, and in his *Christian Philosophy of St. Thomas Aquinas*, pp. 282-286. One of the first express uses of the double-effect principle is found in St. Thomas' *Summa Theologica*, II-II, q. 64, a. 7, where he deals with self-defense.

Read Albert Jonsen, *Responsibility in Modern Religious Ethics*, especially ch. 1, 3, and 5. See also Nicolai Hartmann, *Ethics*, vol. III, ch. 13; H. Richard Niebuhr, *The Responsible Self*; Moira Roberts, *Responsibility and Practical Freedom*.

William James, *Principles of Psychology*, ch. 4, presents his famous essay on habits, which is well worth reading and can be inserted in any philosophical background. Arthur Koestler's *Darkness at Noon* and George Orwell's *1984* are novels dealing with the systematic breakdown of personality and responsibility; one can examine them in the light of the principles we have given.

Austin Fagothey, *Right and Reason—an Anthology*, contains Albert Jonsen's *Responsibility in Modern Religious Ethics*, pp. 35-70, and part of William James' chapter on habit from his *Principles of Psychology*, ch. 4.

CHAPTER 4

CONSCIENCE

PROBLEM

How far an individual man is responsible for his acts he alone knows. Others judge him, but they can see only the externals. A man knows when he has been misjudged by others, and can know it only by comparing their judgment with his own and passing a final judgment on both these judgments. This form of reflective knowledge, of awareness of his own responsibility, is sometimes confused with conscience but is more properly a form of *consciousness.*

A man judges not only whether and how far he is responsible for his acts but also whether these acts are good or bad. As was said in the beginning, ethics rests on a fact of experience: men's conviction that some acts are right and ought to be done, that others are wrong and ought not to be be done, and that still others are indifferent and may either be done or not. Whether such judgments are correct or not is another question, but the fact is that men do make them. The power to do so is called *conscience.*

Since we have been dealing so far with such subjective aspects of the human act as voluntariness and responsibility, and since morality first presents itself to our experience as a personal reflective judgment on our acts long before we have identified the principles on which such judgments should rest, it will be convenient to continue with the subjective aspects

of morality before passing to the objective. All men, no matter what their system of morals might be, make judgments of conscience and agree that they make them. It is when we try to find an objective basis for conscience and its judgments that ethical systems begin to diverge. But beyond all ethical systems and common to them all is the requirement that a man be true to himself and that he follow the good as he sees it, that is, that he follow his conscience. We have the following points to discuss:

1. What is morality?
2. What is conscience?
3. How is the judgment of conscience formed?
4. Must we always follow the dictate of conscience?
5. May we act with a doubtful conscience?
6. How can doubts of conscience be solved?

MEANING OF MORALITY

Morality is the quality in human acts by which we call them right or wrong, good or evil. It is a common term covering the goodness or badness of a human act without specifying which of the two is meant. The opposite of *moral* is properly *unmoral* or *nonmoral*, terms which indicate that the act has no moral significance at all, that it is simply unrelated to morals. The word *amoral* is

39

also used in this sense but is more often applied to persons deficient in moral concern or responsibility. Since the word *immoral* means morally bad, it indicates an act that has a definite moral quality (a bad one). When clearly opposed to *immoral,* the term *moral* means morally good. Thus *moral* and *unmoral* are contradictory, for everything either has or has not some reference to morals; *moral* and *immoral* are contrary, marking the extremes of good and bad within the field of morals while excluding the morally neutral or irrelevant.

In judging the morality of a human act, we may take into consideration the subjective peculiarities of the agent and look at the act as conditioned by his knowledge and consent, background, training, prejudices, emotional stability, and other personal traits. We ask whether this individual person did right or wrong in this particular case, whether this particular act was good or bad *for him.* Morality so considered is *subjective* morality and is determined by whether the act agrees or disagrees with the agent's own conscience.

We may also abstract from such subjective conditions, which, though always present in any individual act, can be known directly only by the personal conscience of the doer. We can simply look at the kind of act performed and at the outward circumstances apparent to any observer. We ask not whether this individual is excused from responsibility for the act because of his ignorance or passion or any other modifier of responsibility, but whether *any* normal person with full command of his faculties is allowed deliberately to will that kind of act. We are judging the objective nature of the act done, not the subjective state of the doer. Morality so considered is *objective* morality.

If we ask, "Is murder wrong?" "Is truthfulness right?" we are asking about objective morality. If we ask, "Did this man fully realize what he was doing when he killed that man?" "Did this man intend to tell the truth when he blurted out that remark?" we are asking about subjective morality.

Morality in its completeness includes both its subjective and its objective aspects. It is futile to ask which is more important. Unless acts have a rightness or wrongness of their own with which the judgment of conscience should be in agreement, anybody's judgment is as good as anybody else's, and ethics becomes a mere listing of opinions. Ethics as a study stresses objective morality. But each one has his own life to live, must account for his deeds as he saw them, and is rated good or bad on his sincerity in following his conscience even if his moral judgments have been objectively incorrect. In this sense subjective morality is paramount.

MEANING OF CONSCIENCE

In the popular mind conscience is often thought of as an "inner voice," sometimes as the "voice of God," telling us what to do or avoid, but this is metaphor. If conscience speaks with a voice, it is our own. Doubtless, most people do experience a reaction of the subconscious based on their childhood environment and training, a tendency to approve or disapprove of things for which approval or disapproval was shown in childhood. Such latent prepossessions will often give correct moral estimates if one has been brought up well. A result of such early psychological experiences may be a vague, unidentifiable feeling, a sense of unease and even of "guilt" in departing from the established pattern, even when the feeling is recognized as unreasonable. This is not what is meant by conscience in the traditional sense. It is not identified with Freud's "super-ego," though they are somewhat related.

Conscience is not a special faculty distinct from the intellect. Otherwise our judgment about the rightness or wrongness of our individual acts would be nonintellectual, nonrational, the product of some blind instinct. Conduct of this kind would be unworthy of one whose chief characteristic is intelligence. Conscience is only the intellect itself in a special function, the function of judging the rightness or wrongness of our own individual acts.

Conscience is a function of the practical intellect. It does not deal with theoretical questions of right and wrong in general, such as "Why is lying wrong?" "Why must justice be done?" but with the practical question: "What ought I to do here and now in this concrete situation?" "If I do this act I am thinking of, will I be lying, will I be unjust?" It is the same practical intellect by which I judge what to do or avoid in other affairs of life: how shall I run my business, invest my money, protect my health, design my house, plant my farm, raise my family? Like other human judgments, conscience can go wrong, can form false moral judgments. As a man can make mistakes in these other spheres of human activity, so he can make mistakes in personal conduct. In making any such practical judgment, however, man has no guide other than his intellect.

Conscience may therefore be defined as the practical judgment of reason on an individual act as good and to be performed, or as evil and to be avoided. The term *conscience* is applied to the following:

1. The intellect as the ability to form judgments about right and wrong individual acts
2. The process of reasoning that the intellect goes through to reach such a judgment
3. The judgment itself, which is the conclusion of this reasoning process

The reasoning process involved in arriving at a judgment of conscience is the same as in any logical deductive argument, though we rarely spell the steps out for ourselves. Deductive reasoning supposes a major premise or general principle, a minor premise or application of the principle to a particular case, and a conclusion necessarily following from the two premises. Since it is not the business of conscience to form the general principles but only to apply them, and since the conclusion is about a single instance here and now, the procedure has to be deductive.

The major premise employed in forming the judgment of conscience is a general moral principle. Medieval writers use the word *synderesis* to mean the habit of general moral principles, the habit of possessing such principles formed in mind and ready for use as the basis of one's conduct. What the broad metaphysical principles of contradiction, sufficient reason, causality, and the like are to theoretical reasoning, the principles of synderesis, such as "Do good and avoid evil," "Respect the rights of others," and "Do as you would be done by," are to practical moral reasoning. The major premise may be either a principle of synderesis or a conclusion derived from it but held by the individual as a general rule of conduct. The minor premise brings the particular act here and now to be done under the scope of the general principle enunciated in the major. The conclusion logically following is the judgment of conscience itself.

EXAMPLES:

Lies are not allowed.
This explanation of my conduct is a lie.
This explanation of my conduct is not allowed.

Dangerous mistakes must be corrected.
The mistake I just made is a dangerous one.
The mistake I just made must be corrected.

What belongs to no one may be kept.
This object I just picked up belongs to no one.
This object I just picked up may be kept.

We often draw the conclusions of conscience so quickly that we are not aware of their syllogistic form, but if we reflect on the process of reasoning that we have gone through, we readily see its syllogistic nature. It usually takes the shortened form of an enthymeme: "Should I say this? No; that would be a lie"; "Must I correct this mistake? Yes; it may hurt someone"; "May I keep this? Of course; no one else owns it." Some of the principles involved (the major premises) may be so simple that we have never expressly formulated them, though we have been acting on them for years.

KINDS OF CONSCIENCE

Conscience may be a guide to future actions, prompting us to do them or avoid them, or a judge of our past actions, the source of our self-approval or remorse. The former is called *antecedent* conscience, the latter *consequent* conscience. For the purpose of ethics, antecedent conscience is more important. Its acts are chiefly four: commanding or forbidding, when the act must either be done or avoided; persuading or permitting, when there is question of the better or worse course without a strict obligation.

Since the judgment of conscience is the judgment of the intellect and the intellect can err, either by adopting false premises or by drawing an illogical conclusion, conscience can be correct or erroneous. A *correct* conscience judges as good what is really good, and as evil what is really evil. Here subjective and objective morality correspond. An *erroneous* conscience judges as good what is really evil, or as evil what is really good. All error involves ignorance, because a person cannot make a false judgment in his mind unless he lacks knowledge of the truth. This ignorance involved in error is either vincible or invincible ignorance, and so we speak of error, too, as being vincible or invincible. Hence we have a *vincibly erroneous* conscience if the error can be overcome and the judgment corrected, or an *invincibly erroneous* conscience if the error cannot be overcome and the judgment cannot be corrected, at least by means any normally prudent man would be expected to use.

Conscience may also be certain or doubtful. A *certain* conscience judges without fearing that the opposite may be true. A *doubtful* conscience either hesitates to make any judgment at all or does make a judgment but with misgiving that the opposite may be true. If it makes no judgment, the intellect remains in suspense because it sees either no motives or equal motives on both sides. If the intellect judges with fear of the opposite, it assents to one side, but its judgment is only a probable opinion. There are varying degrees of probability, running all the way from slight suspicion to the fringes of certainty.

The fact that people differ in their sensitivity to moral values gives habitual characteristics to their judgments of conscience. We call consciences *strict* or *lax*, tender or tough, fine or blunt, delicate or gross, according as they are inclined to perceive or overlook moral values. A *perplexed* conscience belongs to one who cannot make up his mind and remains in a state of indecisive anguish, especially if he thinks that he will be doing wrong whichever alternative he chooses. A *scrupulous* conscience torments its owner by rehearsing over and over again doubts that were once settled, finding new sources of guilt in old deeds that were best forgotten, striving for a kind of certainty about one's state of soul that is beyond our power in this life. Scrupulosity can be a serious form of spiritual self-torture, mounting to neurotic anxiety, that is more of a psychological than an ethical condition. The person needs to learn, not the distinction between right and wrong, which he may know very well, but how to stop worrying over groundless fears, how to end his ceaseless self-examination and face life in a more confident spirit.

FOLLOWING THE JUDGMENT OF CONSCIENCE

Having seen what conscience is and the main forms it takes, we must now discuss our responsibility in following what conscience approves or disapproves. There are two chief rules, each of which involves a problem:

1. Always obey a certain conscience.
2. Never act with a doubtful conscience.

ALWAYS OBEY A CERTAIN CONSCIENCE

Notice the difference in meaning between a certain and a correct conscience. The term *correct* describes the objective truth of the person's judgment, that his conscience represents the real state of things. The term *certain* describes the subjective state of the person judging, how firmly he holds to his assent, how thoroughly he has excluded fear of the opposite. The kind of certainty meant here is a subjective certainty, which can exist along with objective error. Hence there are two possibilities:

1. A certain and correct conscience
2. A certain but erroneous conscience

1. *A certain and correct conscience* offers no difficulty, and our obligation is clear. The person judges what conduct is required of him here and now. His judgment is correct, and he is certain of its correctness.

What degree of certainty is required? It is sufficient that the conscience be *prudentially certain*. Prudential certainty is not absolute but relative. It excludes all *prudent* fear that the opposite may be true, but it does not rule out imprudent fears based on bare possibilities. The reasons are strong enough to satisfy a normally prudent man in an important matter, so that he feels safe in practice though there is a theoretical chance of his being wrong. He has taken every reasonable precaution but cannot guarantee against rare contingencies and freaks of nature. When there is question of action, of something to be done here and now, but often involving future consequences some of which are

dependent on the wills of other people, the absolute possibility of error cannot be wholly excluded; but it can be so reduced that no prudent man free from neurotic anxiety would be deterred from acting through fear of it. Thus a prudent man, having investigated the case, can say that he is *certain* that this business venture is safe, that this criminal is guilty, that this employee is honest. Prudential certainty, since it excludes all reasonable fear of error, is much more than high probability, which does not exclude such reasonable fear. One may, of course, define certainty so strictly as to make it mean absolute certainty only; but such a one is quarreling over words and must find another term to indicate what we have been describing in common language.

2. What happens when one has an *erroneous conscience?* If the error is *vincible*, it must be corrected. The person knows that he may be wrong, is able to correct the possible error, and is obliged to do so before acting. How can any conscience become vincibly erroneous? A man may merely have a probable opinion that he neglects to verify, though able to do so, or he may once have judged certainly yet erroneously, and now begins to doubt whether his judgment was correct. As long as he did not realize his error, his conscience was invincibly erroneous; the error has become vincible only because he is no longer subjectively certain and has begun to doubt. A vincibly erroneous conscience is therefore a name for a conscience that was either doubtful from the beginning or else was once subjectively certain but erroneous, and has now become a doubtful conscience. A certain but vincibly erroneous conscience is impossible, for how could one correct an error that he feels certain does not exist? Thus if the conscience is vincibly erroneous, it must be doubtful.

If the error is *invincible*, the conscience can be certain. Here we seem to have a dilemma. On the one hand, it does not seem right that a person should be obliged to follow an erroneous judgment; on the other hand, he does not know that he is in error and has no means of correcting it. We solve the apparent dilemma by remembering that conscience is a subjective guide to conduct, that invincible error and ignorance are unavoidable, that any wrong which occurs is not done voluntarily and hence is not chargeable to the agent. A person acting with an invincibly erroneous conscience may do something that is objectively wrong, but since he does not recognize it as such, it is not subjectively wrong. The person is free of moral responsibility by the invincible ignorance bound up in his error.

Hence a certain conscience must be obeyed, not only when it is correct, but even when it is invincibly erroneous. Conscience is the only guide a man has for the performance of concrete actions here and now, but an invincibly erroneous conscience cannot be distinguished from a correct conscience. Therefore if one were not obliged to follow a certain but invincibly erroneous conscience, we should be forced to the absurd conclusion that one would not be obliged to follow a certain and correct conscience.

The will depends on the intellect to present the good to it. Whether the intellect's judgment is correct or not, the will-act is good if it consents to the good presented by the intellect, and it is bad if it consents to what the intellect judges evil. If a man is firmly convinced that his action is right, he is choosing the good as far as he can; if he is firmly convinced that his action is wrong, he is choosing what he thinks to be evil, whether it really is so or not. He is not responsible for the error, but he is for his choice.

NEVER ACT WITH A DOUBTFUL CONSCIENCE

The man who is acting with a certain but invincibly erroneous conscience is avoiding moral evil as far as he can. It is not his fault that his judgment is mistaken, and he has no reason for believing that it is mistaken. The same cannot be said of one who acts with a *doubtful* conscience. He has reason for believing that his intended act may be wrong, yet he is willing to go ahead and perform it anyway. True, he is not certain that he will do wrong, but he will not take the means to avoid this probable wrongdoing. The man has no care for right or wrong, and if his act turns out to be objectively right, this is only accidental. Therefore one must never act with a doubtful conscience.

What, then, should a person with a doubtful conscience do? His first obligation is to try to solve the doubt. He must reason over the matter to see whether he can arrive at a certain conclusion. He must inquire and seek advice, even of experts if the matter is important enough. He must investigate the facts in the problem and make certain of them, if possible. He must use all the means that normally prudent people are accustomed to use, in proportion to the importance of the problem. Before deciding on an important course of action, business and professional men take a great deal of trouble to investigate a case, to secure all the data, to seek expert advice, besides thinking over the matter carefully themselves. The same seriousness is demanded in moral affairs.

What if the doubt cannot be solved? It may happen that the required information cannot be obtained because the facts are not recorded or the records are lost or the law remains obscure or the opinions of the learned differ or the matter does not admit of delay for further research. If one should never act with a doubtful conscience, what can one in doubt do? It may seem that the answer is easy: do nothing. But often this approach will not help, for omissions can be voluntary, and the doubt may concern precisely the question of whether we are allowed to refrain from acting in this case.

The answer to the difficulty is that every doubtful conscience can in actual practice be turned into a certain conscience, that no one need ever remain in doubt about what he must do. If the *direct method* of inquiry and investigation described has been used and proved fruitless, we then have recourse to the *indirect method* of forming our conscience by the use of reflex principles. Note that we are not offered a choice between using the direct or the indirect method. We *must* use the direct method *first*. Only when the direct method yields no result may we go on to the indirect method.

FORMING ONE'S CONSCIENCE

The doubting person who has exhausted the direct method without obtaining the knowledge has a double doubt:
1. What is the actual truth on the matter in hand?
2. What is one obliged to do in such a situation?

The first question is the *theoretical* or *speculative* doubt, and it cannot be answered because the direct method was used and failed to yield results. The second is the *practical* or *operative* doubt, and this question alone we claim can be answered in every instance.

Though many doubts are invincible theoretically, every doubt is vincible practically. A person can become certain of what he is obliged to do, how he is expected to act, what conduct is required of him, while remaining in a state of unsolved theoretical doubt. Thus, though the rightness or wrongness of the action is not settled in the abstract, this man becomes prudentially certain of what he in these actual circumstances is obliged or allowed to do, and therefore he acts with a certain conscience. That is, he finds out the kind of conduct that is *certainly* right for a *doubting* person. This process of solving a practical doubt without touching the theoretical doubt is called *forming one's conscience*.

The process of forming one's conscience is accomplished by the use of *reflex principles,* so called because the mind uses them while reflecting on the state of doubt and ignorance in which it now finds itself. There are only two possible courses: "play it safe" and "take the easy way." Since these are almost always opposite courses of action, may we take whichever we please in any case? No. On when to use one and when to use the other rests the formation of a correct conscience.

THE MORALLY SAFER COURSE

By the *morally* safer course is meant the one that more surely preserves moral goodness, more certainly avoids wrongdoing. Often it is physically more dangerous. Sometimes neither alternative appears morally safer, but the obligation on each side seems equal; then we may do either.

One is always *allowed* to choose the morally safer course. If a man is certainly not obliged to act but doubts whether he is allowed to act, the morally safer course is to omit the act; thus if I doubt whether this money is justly mine, I can simply refuse it. If a man is certainly allowed to act but doubts whether he is obliged to act, the morally safer course is to do the act; thus if I doubt whether I have paid a bill, I can offer the money and risk paying it twice.

Sometimes we are *obliged* to follow the morally safer course. We must do so when there is an end certainly to be obtained to the best of our power, and our doubt merely concerns the effectiveness of the means to be used for this purpose. Here the undoubted obligation to attain the end implies the obligation to use certainly effective means. A doctor may not use a doubtful remedy on his patient when he has a sure one at hand. A lawyer may not choose to defend his client with weak arguments when he has strong ones to present. A hunter may not fire into the bushes if he doubts whether the moving object is a man or an animal. A merchant may not pay a certainly existing debt with probably counterfeit coin or advertise probably damaged articles as first class goods. Such cases deal solely with *matters of fact*. The person's obligation is certain, and he must use means that will certainly fulfill it.

There are other cases in which the *obligation itself* is the thing in doubt. Here we have a very different question. The morally safer course, though always allowable, is often costly and inconvenient, sometimes heroic. Out of a desire to do the better thing we often follow it without question, but if we were obliged to follow it in *all* cases of doubt, life would become intolerably difficult. To be safe morally, we should have to yield every doubtful claim to others, who have no better right, and thus become victims of every sharper and swindler whose conscience is less delicate than ours. Such difficulties are avoided by the use of the second reflex principle: a doubtful obligation does not bind.

A DOUBTFUL OBLIGATION

The principle that *a doubtful obligation does not bind* is applicable only when I doubt whether I am bound by an obligation, when my doubt of conscience concerns the *lawfulness or unlawfulness,* the allowableness or forbiddenness, of an act I am thinking of doing. It applies to the moral law as well as to human laws. I may use this principle in both the following situations:

1. I doubt whether such an obligation exists or is valid.
2. I doubt how to interpret the obligation, whether it applies to my case.

For example: I may doubt whether the game laws forbid me to shoot deer on my farm, whether the fruit on my neighbor's tree hanging over my fence belongs to him or to me, whether I am sick enough to be excused from going to work today,

whether the damage I caused was purely accidental or due to my own carelessness. It is true that there are contained here questions of fact that cannot be settled, but they all bring up questions of lawfulness or permissibility of action: Am I allowed to shoot the deer, to pick the fruit, to stay home from work, to refuse to pay for the damage? Does any law exist, applicable to my case, which certainly forbids me? If the direct method fails to prove any, then I am morally justified in doing these things on the principle that *a doubtful obligation does not bind.*

The reason behind this principle is that promulgation is essential to law, and a doubtful law is not sufficiently promulgated, for it is not sufficiently made known to the person about to act here and now. Law imposes obligation, which is usually burdensome, and he who would impose an obligation or restrict the liberty of another must prove his right to do so. A man is presumed free until it becomes certain that he is restrained, and therefore a doubtfully existing restraint or law loses its binding force.

Be careful to distinguish these cases from those which fall under the other principle. If the obligation itself is the thing in doubt, I am not obliged. If the obligation is certain and only the means of carrying it out are doubtful, I may not use doubtful means if certain ones are available. I may not roll boulders down a hill in the mere hope that they may not hit anyone on the road below, but I may cart off boulders from property that is only probably mine. I may not leave poisoned food about on the chance that no one will care to eat it, but I may manufacture clearly labeled poison if such manufacture is only probably forbidden by law. In the first instances there is no doubt about the obligation: I am not allowed unnecessarily to jeopardize human life. It may happen that no harm results, but the acts are certainly dangerous, and *the morally safer course must be chosen.* In the second instances the law itself of not seizing others' property or of not manufacturing certain products is of doubtful application to my case, and I may take advantage of the doubt in my favor, for *a doubtful obligation does not bind.*

How doubtful does the law or duty have to be to lose its binding force? Must the existence or application of the law or duty be more doubtful than its nonexistence or nonapplication, or equally so, or will any doubt suffice to exempt one from the obligation? Such questions were hotly debated during the seventeenth and eighteenth centuries, more by moral theologians than by philosophical ethicians. The view that survived as the most tenable in theory and the only one workable in practice is called *probabilism.* It does not require a weighing of probabilities on either side of the case but merely requires that it be *solidly probable* that a law or duty does not exist or does not apply to my case for me to be free from its obligation. Solid probability means that the reasons against the obligation's existence or application are not frivolous or fictitious but valid and weighty, even though they may be less so than the reasons in favor of the obligation. No proposition can be certain if there are valid and weighty reasons against it. If it is not certain, it is doubtful, and if it is doubtful, it does not bind. To list all the reasons on both sides and weigh their relative merits is often a hopeless task, baffling the best experts. The average man has neither time nor knowledge nor ability for such a comparison. In practice, decisions must be made promptly and yet be made with a certain conscience. The theory of probabilism enables one to do so.

CONCLUSION

The whole matter of forming one's conscience may seem to involve a great deal of subtlety, as if we were whittling down moral obligation to its lowest terms. Is this not contrary to straightforward simplicity and sincerity? In answer, the first thing to note is that one can always follow the morally safer course. But in ethics we are studying not only what is the better, nobler, and more heroic thing to do, but also exactly what a man is strictly obliged to do. A generous man will not haggle over good works, but an enlightened man will want to know when he is doing a strict duty and when he is being generous.

Accurate moral discrimination is particularly necessary in judging the conduct of others. In our personal lives we may be willing to waive our strict rights and to go beyond the call of duty, but we have no business imposing on others an obligation to do so. The borderline between right and wrong is difficult to determine. It is foolish to skirt it too closely, but we are not allowed to accuse another man of wrongdoing if he has not done wrong. This is why we had to detail these principles so carefully.

SUMMARY

Morality means the rightness or wrongness of human acts. It is *objective* or *subjective,* according as it overlooks the personal peculiarities of the doer of the act or takes them into consideration. The norm of subjective morality is conscience.

Conscience is not a special faculty but a function of the practical intellect, which judges the concrete act of an individual person as morally good or evil. The reasoning used by the intellect is a deductive syllogism, the major premise being an accepted moral principle, the minor an application of the principle to the case at hand, the conclusion the judgment of conscience.

Antecedent conscience is a guide to future acts, *consequent* conscience a judge of past acts. A *correct* conscience judges good as good and evil as evil; an *erroneous* conscience judges good as evil or evil as good. A *certain* conscience judges without fear of the opposite; a *doubtful* conscience either makes no judgment or judges with fear of the opposite. Conscience is *strict* or *lax* according as it tends to perceive or overlook moral values.

Always obey a certain conscience even when invincibly erroneous. A *certain and correct* conscience is the clear and proper perception of one's moral duty. Prudential certainty, the exclusion of any *prudent* fear of the opposite, is all that can be expected in moral matters. A *certain but erroneous* conscience must also be followed because the agent cannot distinguish it from a correct conscience and has no other guide; the act is subjectively right even if objectively wrong.

Never act with a doubtful conscience. To do so is to be willing to perform an act whether it is wrong or not, refusing to take the means to avoid evil.

A person in doubt must first use the *direct method* of inquiry and investigation to dispel the doubt. If this method yields no results, the *indirect method* of forming one's conscience may be used, which consists in solving not the *theoretical doubt* (what is the actual truth?) but only the *practical doubt* (how should a doubting person act in this case?). The practical doubt can always be solved by using one or two reflex principles:

1. *The morally safer course is preferable.* This course is always allowable but is often costly. It *must* be used if the case concerns not the existence or application of an obligation but the effectiveness of means used to an end that must certainly be attained.

2. *A doubtful obligation does not bind.* This principle may be used only when there is question of the obligation itself, when either the existence or application of an obligation is in doubt. A doubtful law is not sufficiently promulgated and hence has no binding force, for promulgation is essential to law.

Probabilism holds that to bind, an obligation must be certain, and no obligation can be certain if there are solidly probable reasons against it, no matter how strong the probability for it may be. It is practically impossible to weigh the degrees of probability on each side; probabilism makes such a comparison unnecessary.

The purpose of this practical study of conscience is not to whittle down moral obligation but to help us make accurate moral discriminations.

QUESTIONS FOR DISCUSSION

1 To what extent does the term *conscience* as defined and explained here correspond with the term *conscience* as understood in common speech today?

2 Should a man not make himself more certain of his moral conduct than of any other type of activity he engages in? Why, then, would prudential certainty suffice for a judgment of conscience?

3 No number of probabilities ever adds up to a certainty. How, then, can a person by the use of probabilities or a system of probabilism render himself certain of the kind of conduct required of him?

4 People who have never heard of the method of forming a conscience must nevertheless solve their doubts of conscience and do

it without such help. Are not philosophers just trying to make life more complex than it need be?

5 Does this whole chapter present a legalistic view of morals, a living according to laws and rules that shrivels up all generous spontaneity in one's commitment to the right and the good?

READINGS

St. Thomas, *Summa Theologica*, I, q. 79, aa. 12-13, on synderesis and conscience; I-II, q. 19, aa. 5-6, on an erroneous conscience. *De Veritate*, translated into English under the title *Truth*, vol. II, q. 16, on synderesis, and q. 17 on conscience. The matter of this chapter was not very thoroughly developed in St. Thomas' time, although what he says contains the germ of future speculations.

Cardinal Newman's treatment in his *Grammar of Assent*, pp. 105-112, is well worth reading.

Eric D'Arcy, *Conscience and Its Right to Freedom*, is recommended as a whole; Parts I and II are pertinent here.

John Donnelly and Leonard Lyons (editors), *Conscience*, presents a philosophical analysis of conscience by contemporary authors. Freud's contention that the phenomenon of moral conscience is explained by his theory of the superego is examined, pp. 85-114.

A modern personalist approach to the subject is found in Ignace Lepp, *The Authentic Morality*, and in Louis Monden, *Sin, Liberty, and Law*. The treatment in both is psychological and somewhat theological, but they put it in the language of present-day phenomenological and existential philosophy.

Martin Heidegger has a long treatment of conscience in *Being and Time* from his own point of view.

The writings of psychoanalysts and behavioral scientists on conscience have little to say on its ethical aspect.

Austin Fagothey, *Right and Reason—an Anthology*, contains Eric D'Arcy's *Conscience and Its Right to Freedom*, pp. 3-19, 49-71.

CHAPTER 5

GOOD

PROBLEM

The individual man relies on his own consciousness to determine the degree of his responsibility for his acts, and on his own conscience to judge the good or evil, the rightness or wrongness, of these acts as done by him in concrete circumstances. There is no more ultimate court of appeal in this world than the testimony of conscience. But subjective morality alone is insufficient. If it were all we had, there would be as many judges of morality as there are persons, and sincerity would be the same as truth in moral matters. Conscience can be erroneous as well as correct; error can be vincible as well as invincible. When objective truth is attainable, conscience cannot rest satisfied with a subjective opinion that it knows may be false. Our next endeavor, therefore, must be to find whether there is an objective morality with which the judgment of conscience should be in agreement, and, if so, what that morality is. Henceforth the whole of our study will be devoted to this pursuit. We begin by asking:

1. Is the good definable?
2. Is the good an end to be sought?
3. Are we obliged to seek the good?
4. Is the good a value simply in itself?
5. What distinguishes moral values from other values?

DEFINABILITY OF GOOD

What is the good? How do we define goodness? It seems that we must settle this question at the outset, for if we do not know what *good* means, how will we recognize it when we come across it? On the other hand, no one has succeeded in giving a good definition of *good*. In fact, would not a good definition of *good* require that one already know *good* before defining it? And, if so, why define it?

The question of the definability of good was made acute around the turn of the century by George Edward Moore.* His reasoning is that all definition is analysis of a concept into its components, that good is a simple concept unanalyzable into anything simpler, and that therefore the concept of good is indefinable. We can, of course, point to certain properties in objects because of which we call these objects good, but that does not tell us what is good about these properties or why it is good to have them. In a sense we can define *the* good, the object which is good, but not the predicate *good* itself. That we cannot define good does not mean that we cannot know what it is. Not all knowledge is by definition. We cannot define yellow but can only point to yellow objects; the wavelength of the light tells us nothing about the look of the color we see. To try to define good in terms of something else that is not good is not to define it but to lose it. The reduction of good, the simplest of ethical ideas, to something nonethical involves what Moore calls the *naturalistic fallacy,* as if good

---

*G. E. Moore, *Principia Ethica,* ch. 1; also reprinted separately as "The Indefinability of Good."

were a sort of natural property that some things possess and others lack. Good is just good, irreducible, unanalyzable, and indefinable.

One might criticize this argument by pointing out that the dictionary contains a definition of good and that rules for the use of the word *good* in language can be formulated. Linguistic analysts spend much time at this task, but Moore anticipated them by noting that the subject matter of ethics is the concept of good itself and not correctness in speaking about it. Others solve the problem of the definability of good by actually defining it, for example, as pleasure, desirability, evolution, life according to nature, and similar concepts. We shall have to examine these claims, but they are examples of precisely what Moore means by the naturalistic fallacy. Another objection is that, if good cannot be defined, it will have to be known by some sort of direct intuition. This Moore admits, despite the unpopularity of intuitionism. How much intuition, if any, must be admitted in ethics is a question we will discuss later.

Whether or not good is indefinable in principle, we have to begin our study of it without a definition, since we could achieve one only by committing ourselves in advance to a philosophy we have not yet examined. Even without a definition much has been written about the good. The ancients developed one of its most fruitful aspects, the good as end, and we may as well begin with this traditional approach.

THE GOOD AS END

Aristotle begins his *Ethics* with the statement: "The good is that at which all things aim."* This is not to be taken as a definition of the good, but only as a recognition of the relationship between *good* and *end*. An end he declares to be "That

for the sake of which a thing is done,"* and locates it among his four causes. For him all change is a process whereby some given underlying substrate (the matter) acquires a new specification or determination (the form) through the action of an efficient operator (the agent) moved to act by the attraction of some good (the end). Such a view of the universe with its constant changes supposes *teleology*, or purposiveness, a directed world in which all things have an aim, as opposed to the *mechanistic* theory that all changes come about by chance. A directed world needs a principle of direction, and the name for it is *nature*. Each being is so structured that it acts only along certain definite lines. The nature is not some kind of driver, whether outside or inside the being, not something distinct from the being which acts, but its very self. It is the *essence* of each being considered as the principle or source of its activity. Direction supposes not only a nature, a moving principle to make a thing go, but also a target toward which to move. So nature and end are correlative terms. Natural activity is teleological activity.

Man also has a nature, the source of the inner dynamism of his being, making it *natural* for man to seek the good as his *end*. That the nature of a being structures it to act along definite lines is not a bar to freedom. Some beings have a free nature, are built to act freely, and it is natural to them to guide themselves to their end by free choice. Others lack freedom and automatically run along the tracks their nature has laid. In either case they tend to ends.

Every end is a good and every good is an end. An end would not be sought unless it were somehow good for the seeker, and the good by being sought is the end or purpose of the seeker's striving. No activity is possible except for the attainment

---

*Aristotle, *Nicomachean Ethics,* bk. I, ch. 1, 1094a 3.

*Aristotle, *Physics,* bk. II, ch. 3, 194b 33; *Metaphysics,* bk. V, ch. 2, 1013a 33.

of some end, for the sake of some good. This is the *principle of finality* or *teleology*, which St. Thomas explains as follows:

> Every agent of necessity acts for an end. For if in a number of causes ordained to one another the first be removed, the others must of necessity be removed also. Now the first of all causes is the final cause. The reason of which is that matter does not receive form save in so far as it is moved by an agent; for nothing reduces itself from potentiality to act. But an agent does not move except out of intention for an end. For if the agent were not determinate to some particular effect, it would not do one thing rather than another: consequently in order that it produce a determinate effect, it must of necessity be determined to some certain one, which has the nature of an end.*

In other words, before it acts, a being with potentiality for acting is in an indeterminate condition, and can either act or not act, act in this way or in that way. No action will ever take place unless something removes this indetermination, stirs the being to act, and points its action in a certain direction. Hence the principle of finality, "every agent acts for an end," is implicit in the concepts of potency and act, and in the whole notion of causality. If every agent acts for an end, the human agent certainly does so.

The foregoing description is based on Aristotle, who gave to teleology its classical expression. But our interest is in man. Whatever one may think of teleology in the world at large, no sane man can deny that human beings act for ends. Even one who tried to prove that they do not would have this as his end in view. Failure to adapt one's conduct to rational ends is the accepted sign of mental derangement. The very admission, therefore, that there are such things as rational human acts is an admission that human beings do act for ends.

The question arises: If all things, including man, inevitably seek an end that is also the good, how can any act fail to be good, how can human conduct go wrong? The good as end, as perfective, as good *for,* has various meanings among which we must sort out the moral good.

The thesis of the metaphysician, that "every being is good," refers only to *ontological* or *metaphysical* goodness. It means only that every being, by the very fact that it is a being, has some goodness about it and is good for something, contributing in some way to the harmony and perfection of the universe. Every being also has a certain amount of *physical* goodness, which consists in a completeness of parts and competence of activity. Though some things are physically defective, they are good insofar as they have being, defective insofar as they lack being. From the fact that every being is good for *something,* however, it does not follow that every being is good for *everything.* What is good for one thing may not be good for another, and what is good for a thing under these circumstances or from this aspect may not be good for the same thing under different conditions or from another standpoint. Metaphysics considers the good in its broadest scope and so can find good in everything in some way; ethics considers the good in the limited line of voluntary and responsible human conduct and often finds this line strangely warped. The murderer levels his gun and fells his victim. It is a good shot but an evil deed. As a piece of marksmanship it is admirable, but as an act of human conduct it is damnable. There is some good in all things, but it need not be the ethical or *moral* good.

Because not everything is good for everything, it is up to man's judgment to determine what things are good *for him.* Human judgments are open to error, and therefore he may mistake the *apparent* good for the *true* good. Unless a thing at least appears to be good we could not seek it at all, for it could make no appeal to our appetites; but we can easily confuse what is good for something else with what is good for us, or

---

*St. Thomas, *Summa Theologica*, I-II, q. 1, a. 2; see also *Summa Contra Gentiles*, bk. III, ch. 2, 3, 16.

what would be good for us in other circumstances with what is good for us here and now. If some lesser good makes impossible the attainment of the absolutely necessary good, then this lesser good is not the true good for us. The moral good must always be the true good.

Thus there are degrees of goodness. We may seek a good not for its own sake but as a means to some further good; it is desirable only because it leads to something more desirable. This is the *useful* or *instrumental* good, and it is good only in a qualified and analogous sense; such are all tools and instruments. We may seek a good for the satisfaction or enjoyment it gives without considering whether it will be beneficial to our whole being; it delights us now and may be harmless, but it offers us no guarantee that it may not hurt us in the long run and unfit us for the greater good. This is the *pleasant* good, and it attracts us most vividly. Lastly, we may seek a good because it contributes toward the perfection of our being as a whole, because it fits a man as such. This is the *befitting* good, the upright and honorable, the noble and righteous, and it is good in the fullest sense. It is not only good for us, as the term *befitting* implies, but good in itself as an independent value apart from its effect on others; under this aspect it is called the *intrinsic* good. The moral good, while it may also be useful and pleasant, is always and necessarily the befitting good.

This analysis of the kinds of good shows that human conduct must always be directed toward the good in some sense, but that this is not always the moral good. To make it the moral good is life's purpose and our responsibility.

THE GOOD AS OUGHT

The good, we have just seen, is our constant quest. We are not born possessors of it but are born seekers of it. Our existence is a passage from capacity to fulfill-ment, from potentiality to actuality, from perfectibility to perfection. Our emptiness clamors to be filled, and whatever satisfies our hunger is called a good. Thus the good appears to us as an end.

But what obliges us to engage in this quest? As an end the good is attractive and invites us to itself. It calls for being, it deserves to be, it should be realized, it ought to exist. But the bare recognition that a thing ought to be does not of itself imply that I am the one who should make it be. We say that a work of art ought to be, in the sense that it is a noble conception worthy of production and it would be a shame not to bring it to light; yet no particular artist is strictly obliged to create it. We tell a man that he ought to invest his money in this enterprise, that it ought to bring him a better return than he can hope for from any other investments; yet no one thinks of this ought as a strict obligation.

Here we see two different senses of the *ought*, which the good always implies, the nonmoral and the moral ought. Every good except the moral good is optional, but the moral good is necessary. There is no getting away from the demands of morality, from the requirement of living a good life and thus being a good man.

This obligatory character of the moral good is what impresses itself on those who see ethics chiefly in terms of duty. It is not so much the loveliness of the good that invites them as the stern voice of duty that calls them. Often the choice is between a moral good and some other kind of good, and the other kind of good seems at the moment by far the more attractive. If we consider the good merely as an object of desire, as an end to be sought, the apparent good can beckon with alluring smiles while the true good gravely points to the harder path. Yet one is obliged. to follow the true good and not the merely apparent good.

What is the nature of this moral *ought*

that commands with such authority? It is a kind of necessity that is unique and irreducible to any other. It is not a logical necessity based on the impossibility of thinking contradictions. It is not a metaphysical necessity stemming from the identity of being with itself: what is, is. It is not a physical necessity, a *must* that compels us from without, destroying our freedom. Nor is it a biological or a psychological necessity, an internal impossibility of acting differently built into our nature, likewise destroying our freedom. It is a *moral* necessity, that of the *ought,* guiding us in what we recognize as the proper use of our freedom. It is a freedom that is a necessity and a necessity that is a freedom. The requirement is absolute, and thus it is a necessity, but it can also be refused, though to our loss, and thus it is a freedom.

Moral necessity affects me, the acting subject, but it comes from the object, the kind of act I the subject am performing. The act in its real being is something contingent that may or may not be, but in its ideal being as held up to my reason and will for deliberation and choice, it assumes a practical necessity demanding decision. The demand is absolute. Bad use of artistic, economic, scientific, and other particular abilities is penalized by failure, not by fault, because I had no obligation to pursue these endeavors and hence no absolute obligation to succeed in them. But I cannot help being a man and absolutely have to succeed as a man. If I am a failure at it, it is my fault because the failure was willfully chosen. I do not become bad in a certain line, but become a *bad man.* Everything I do expresses my personality in some way, but the use of my freedom is the actual exertion of my unique personality as constituting my inmost self.

Take the case of a man offered a huge fortune for one act of murdering his best friend. Minimize the dangers and enhance the advantages as much as possible. Make the act absolutely foolproof. Yet it *ought not* to be done. Why not?

1. Eliminate the *legal* sanction. Suppose that the man is not only certain of not being caught but also finds some loophole by which he does not even break any existing civil law and could not be prosecuted for any crime. Yet he sees himself a murderer and cannot approve his act.

2. Eliminate the *social* sanction. Since no one will know, there is no one's disapproval to be feared. Yet he deserves that disapproval even if he does not receive it. How different when social sanctions are not deserved! We do not blame ourselves when we are innocent but blame society for condemning us unjustly.

3. Eliminate the *psychological* sanction. The feelings of depression, disgust, and shame, the inability to eat or sleep with the twinge of remorse and guilt, may disturb him, but others can be immune to such feelings, and even in him they can come from other sources. The moral element remains. If somehow the guilty *feelings* could be removed so that he no longer felt any psychological disturbance over his deed, still in all sincerity he would judge his act wrong and would *know* that he is guilty, despite the absence of feelings.

4. Eliminate the *religious* sanction. Were God not to punish it and were we certain that he would not, even in this absurd hypothesis the act ought not to be done. The doer might feel glad to escape but would know that he did not deserve to escape. The act is of the kind that God ought to condemn, and we would be disappointed in him if he did not. We would begin to question God's justice, so that God himself would no longer measure up to the ideal. This is perhaps the clearest indication of the absoluteness of the moral order.

5. What remains is the *moral* sanction. It is intrinsic to the very act itself, identical with the deliberate choice of the will,

the relationship between the doer and his deed.

In despising the moral good I despise myself. According as I accept or reject the moral good, I rise or fall in my own worth as a man. The moral good provides the scale by which I necessarily rate myself, unavoidably judge myself. This judgment is not merely a subjective opinion but an objective estimate of my true worth in the scheme of things. This rise or fall is not something optional; I am not allowed to fall. It is not a question of whether I am interested in my own betterment; I am not allowed not to be. It is not a disjunctive necessity: Do this or take the consequences. It is simply: Do this. I am not allowed to expose myself to the consequences of not doing it. In fact, whatever consequences there are must themselves be judged by this moral criterion, and ultimate consequences must contain their own moral worth.

Some writers* prefer to express this *ought* aspect by the terms *right* and *wrong* rather than *good* and *bad*. It is true that the first pair have a more obligatory flavor than the second, but it is impossible to get people to use such simple terms with consistency, especially if they are taken as indefinables. We can use them as synonyms and rely on the context to make them clear.

According as we emphasize the good as end or the good as ought, we have two main varieties of ethics: the teleological† and the deontological.‡ An unfortunate opposition between these two views has infected the whole study, as if one must opt either for an ethics of ends and consequences or for an ethics of law and obligation, in a word, for an ethics of happiness or for an ethics of duty. Is it possible to transcend such a dichotomy and to show that these two aspects are not opposed but supplementary? Should not the good be done for its own sake, purely and simply because it is good, independently of what consequences it may lead to or what authority may impose it as a duty? This may appear from a third and fairly modern approach to the good, the axiological,* the consideration of the good as value.

THE GOOD AS VALUE
VALUE IN GENERAL

The term *value* or *worth* seems to have its origin in economics, but long before the rise of axiology as a formal study it was applied analogously to other aspects of life. There is no more agreement on the definition of value than there is on the definition of good, but in practice we all know what a value is, and our discussion can begin on this commonsense level.

One thing appeals to us in some way, whereas something else does not. What appeals may supply a need, satisfy a desire, arouse an interest, stimulate an emotion, provoke a response, motivate a deed, or merely draw an approval. The existence of subjective values—valuations or evaluations or value judgments, as some prefer to call them—is a matter of experience. We do make value judgments, whether these judgments are justified or not, and whether they have any real content to them or not. Some of these judgments are noncomparative, in which we merely express our approval or disapproval; others are comparative, and by putting them in order we can construct a scale of values. A full scale would be too complex for anyone to complete, but we all have some constant preferences that represent known points on our scale.

*Ross, *The Right and the Good*.
†From the Greek *telos*, end.
‡From the Greek participle *deon* of the verb *dei*, it ought.

*From the Greek *axios*, worthy.

Some general characteristics of value immediately appear.

1. Values are *bipolar,* with a positive and a negative pole: pleasant, painful; easy, difficult; strong, weak; rich, poor; beautiful, ugly; true, false; good, bad. The positive pole is the one preferred; the negative pole is better not called a value at all but a disvalue.

2. Values are *not homogeneous* but of many kinds, some quite unrelated, and this is why the construction of a complete scale of values is so difficult; there are too many crosscuts.

3. Values *transcend facts* in the sense that nothing ever wholly comes up to our expectations; even if anything should, it only shows that our expectations were pitched too low and we want something further.

4. Values, though not wholly realizable, *clamor for realization.* They should exist, they deserve to be, even if we have no way of bringing them into existence.

EXISTENCE OF VALUE

Do values really exist or do they belong wholly to the domain of thought? Do we call a thing valuable because it possesses some real property in itself or because we clothe it with a value by our attitude toward it? The subjectivist philosopher, to be consistent, must adopt the latter view. But even objectivist philosophers, who in their general epistemology admit the existence of real being that is there independently of our thinking, can be subjectivist on the question of value. Things exist, they say, but whatever value they have is conferred on them by us; there is objective being, but no objective value. What evidence is there on this question?

That there are values is evident from the fact that we have preferences. That some values are wholly subjective is attested by the arbitrariness of some preferences. The thing has no intrinsic worth,

at least for us, but we give it a value because of our peculiar prejudices, our psychological conditioning, our unaccountable tastes and fancies. Social as well as personal values can be subjective. Polls, popular vote, and other forms of opinion gathering are only a summary of the personal values of individuals and do not prove that there is an objective basis for the widespread preference.

Other values are subjective in nature, but their lack of complete arbitrariness shows that they have some objective basis. Many values, such as the value of paper money, of credit, of reputation, of academic degrees, or of artistic masterpieces, are created by human convention. That these conventions are not wholly subjective is seen in the fact that, if they have no backing in reality, they are considered fraudulent and their value vanishes.

Besides both of these varieties of subjective value, we find others that we can properly call objective. Not that any value can be so absolutely objective that it does not contain a subjective component. All values have relation to a valuer; they are values for somebody. When we call a value objective, we do not deny this relation to a valuing subject but assert the existence of an objective reason for this relation in the valued object. There is something about the thing that makes it suitable for this person, so that his preference is not arbitrary. Thus a person's taste in foods is subjective and arbitrary, but his need for food in general is objective and rooted in his biological requirements.

How extensive objective values are can be seen from a partial list of them. That life is a value and death a disvalue, health a value and sickness a disvalue, pleasure a value and pain a disvalue, prosperity a value and poverty a disvalue, beauty a value and ugliness a disvalue, intelligence a value and stupidity a disvalue—carry the list as far as you want—is too evident to need comment. The reason is not merely the fact that most people prefer one to the other, but its congruence or incongruence with the kind of beings we are.

How do we come to recognize these values? Some derivative values can be arrived at by logical reasoning from other values, but the primary values, usually the most general or abstract, are not reasoned. They simply present themselves. We feel the attraction of the good. When we ask ourselves why the thing is attractive to us, either we find that there is no reason but our own psychological conditioning or the passing fads of the group, and these values we label subjective; or we find an objective reason in a real suitability of the thing to ourselves, a suitability that we do not create but find already existing, and these values we call objective.

The difficulty can be raised that all values are only abstractions and therefore subjective because they exist only in the mind that conceives them. This objection rests on the epistemological theory of *nominalism,* which underlies most forms of empiricism and positivism. Nominalism admits no basis in reality for abstractions and universal ideas but considers them as mere names that facilitate our way of speaking. Hence it is not surprising that nominalists have trouble with value, which is an abstract concept and a universal idea. The difficulty here is not with values but with nominalism, which is an inadequate epistemological theory. None but extreme Platonists wish to give to abstractions independent existence as real things, and thus abstractions exist formally as such only in the mind. Most abstractions, however, are not formed arbitrarily and therefore have their basis or foundation in the way things really are. Those who admit a realistic basis to universal ideas will accord the same realism to values, that is, to those values we called objective. As there is no universal without a knower to make the abstraction, so there is no value without a valuer to do the valuing. Values, like other universals, are drawn from the data of experience and have their concrete fulfillment in existing persons, things, and actions. It is a fact that we evaluate goods to buy, persons to employ, students to reward, candidates to vote for, and friends to live with. We do so because we see some objective qualities in them that make them deserving.

The foregoing is meant to be introductory to the question of moral values. Are there moral values distinct from other values such as those we have been describing, and are these moral values objective?

MORAL VALUES

The common estimate of mankind separates moral values from other values. We say that a man is a good scholar, athlete, businessman, politician, scientist, artist, soldier, worker, speaker, entertainer, companion, and yet that he is not a good man. We say that someone else is a failure at some or perhaps even all of these, and yet that he is a good man. On what do we base such judgments? Why do we separate out this last value? Because we recognize that it is distinct from the others and more fundamental, more valuable than the other values

Moral values are understood to be those that *make a man good purely and simply as a man.* They are not external objects that, though they may help a man to become the kind of being he ought to be, are not the man himself. Nor are they qualities or attributes of the man himself but outside his control, such as having good health or long life or family status or bodily beauty or mental acumen or artistic talent or a magnetic personality. These are all values, but no one can command them. Moral values are personal, not only because a person has them, but because they are the expression of each one's unique personality in the innermost center of its being, as shown in the act of choice. Moral values, therefore, reside both in the acts a man chooses to do and in the results of those acts on the character of the man. There are morally good or bad human acts and morally good or bad men.

A shark attacks one of two swimmers at the beach. The other comes to his rescue and, braving the danger, wards off the shark and brings the wounded companion to shore. We feel pity for the one who was bitten but pass no moral judgment on him. He did not act but was acted on. Toward the rescuer our attitude is quite different. His swimming may have been awkward, his lifesaving technique faulty, his approach to the shark unscientific, his act unseen and unpublicized, and the whole venture useless because the victim died. Even one whose feelings are not aroused to admiration cannot help judging the act to be fine and noble and worthy of approval. It has no value but one, and that is its *moral* value. Suppose an opposite case. The shark attacks both swimmers. To save himself, one of them deliberately kicks his companion into the path of the shark's mouth, thus gaining time to scramble onshore while the shark is occupied with its morsel. As an act of self-saving it has value, for it was done quickly, efficiently, cleverly, and resourcefully. But we cannot approve. The only excuse for such an act would be instinct or panic. As a willful, deliberate act it merits condemnation.

Two husbands have wives afflicted with a lingering and incapacitating disease. Both families are alike: five children, moderate income, no hope of remedy. One husband does his best to be both father and mother to the children, works overtime to pay for his wife's care, and spends what time he can with her to brighten her days. The other man decides that he has had enough, deserts wife and children, gets work in a distant city under an assumed name, and is not heard of again. Our emotional attitude toward the wives and children is one of congratulations in one case and compassion in the other, but they are only passive figures in the case. Toward the husbands also our emotional reactions differ, but there is a remaining element beyond all emotion. By our intellectual judgment we have to approve of the first husband and disapprove of the second. It is not a question of consequences. Suppose that the deserted dependents are better taken care of by public charity than the husband could have done for them. Still we must condemn his action as morally wrong. The moral value and disvalue remain in these two cases as irreducible elements.

Examples of this type could be multiplied indefinitely. But these are sufficient for our purpose: to isolate the characteristics of moral value as distinct from any other value.

1. Moral value can exist only in a *free* being and his *voluntary* or *human* acts. By willing moral good a man becomes good. It cannot happen accidentally. It makes no difference whether the act is successful or not. It is done intelligently in the sense that the agent knows what he is doing and wills to do it, but it need not be brilliantly planned and executed.

2. Moral value is *universal* in the sense that what holds for one holds for all in the same conditions. The reason is that it shows the worth of a man *as a man*. Even when no one else could duplicate one man's circumstances, all would approve of his action as the right thing to do in the case, whether they would have the strength to do it or not.

3. Moral value is *self-justifying*. Thus at least it appears on the surface, though we shall have to delve deeper into it later. We suspect that any further justification of moral value will be found to be part of the moral order itself and not some extrinsic reason. Even the truth must be pursued morally, though it be the truth about morals.

4. Moral value has a *preeminence* over every other value. A moral value can be

compared only with another moral value. If a moral value conflicts with another type of value, this other must take a subordinate place. We think that a man simply must be true to himself as a man, no matter how much else he might lose in the effort.

5. Moral value implies *obligation*. We just discussed this in our section on the good as ought and will say more on it later. Man may disregard all other values, and we shall call him foolish, stupid, clumsy, crude, dull, ignorant, impractical, and many other names, but we can still retain respect for him as a man. Not so if he loses his moral integrity.

THE MORAL IDEAL

The foregoing discussion brings out the fact that we do form for ourselves an ideal of human conduct and an ideal of manhood. These are not two ideals, for a man's conduct is his life. It is only good conduct that can make a good man, and a man is called good because his past acts show him to be the kind of man from whom good acts are expected.

We find it impossible not to form such an ideal, since it is implied in every moral judgment, and we do make moral judgments. The word *ideal* should not be understood here as some romantic fancy, a knight in shining armor, some sort of superman with unearthly powers, the kind of being that could not happen in real life. What we use in moral judgment is not an imaginative ideal nor an esthetic ideal, but a *moral* ideal. It is true that no one ever perfectly lives up to it, but it must mean the ideal he *could* live up to because he *ought* to. The ideal as an ideal does not exist in reality, but it is not subjective in the sense of being arbitrary. It is constructed by taking the various kinds of acts that experience shows us men perform, dropping from them all discordant notes, supplying all omissions, and heightening the whole to the limit

of human ability. The man whose acts are all of this type is our ideal of the moral man.

As the artist has an ideal of the perfectly proportioned human body, as the scholar has an ideal of the perfectly intelligent human mind—and, being human, these are not beyond the possibility of realization—so we all have an ideal of the perfectly living human being. So far as a man approaches this ideal, he has moral value and is good. So far as he admits into his life that which degrades this ideal, he has moral disvalue and is bad.

The notion of the good as expressed here is that of the intrinsic, or perfect, good as opposed to the instrumental, or perfective, good. The ideal is good, not as leading to something else, not as a means useful to something further, but in itself. It has value because it has what it ought to have to be itself in the fullest expression of itself. This is the good in the highest sense, for what is good for another ultimately supposes something for which others are good, and this last must be good in itself.

This conception of the good, especially this latter part dealing with the moral ideal, derives from Plato. The unacceptability of his interpretation of ideals should not prejudice us against what is true in his thought. We need not accept his theory of a direct vision of the ideal as Ideas or Forms recalled from a former life in which we saw them more clearly. Our concepts, including our concept of the ideal good, can be manufactured by the process of abstraction and intellectual refinement from the data of experience. How we do this and what standards we use in judging our moral ideas and ideals will be our occupation throughout the next chapter.

CONCLUSION

We have looked at the good under three aspects: as value, as ought, and as end.

A more learned way of saying it is that we have seen axiological, deontological, and teleological ethics. The good as *value* stresses the intrinsic good, the perfect good, that which is good in itself irrespective of any goodness it may have for anything else. This must be the most fundamental aspect of the good. The good as *ought* stresses the fact that each thing ought to be as perfect as it can be, that the ideal is not merely something to be contemplated but to be put into act, and that this demand is laid on a free being in the form of moral obligation. The good as *end* emphasizes the obligation of any being, if it is not yet perfect, to strive toward perfection as its end and to seek other goods as means to this end. These are not three kinds of good, but three ways of looking at the same good. The absolute good is the ultimate *end* that *ought* to be sought because of its supreme *value*.

SUMMARY

The good had best be taken as a primary notion, irreducible and indefinable. It can be considered as end, as ought, and as value.

As *end*, the good is that at which all things aim. An end is that for the sake of which a thing is done. Every good is an end, and every end is a good. A means is good insofar as it leads to the end.

All human conduct is for an end and a good, according to the principle of finality: "Every agent acts for an end." Since no agent can produce an undetermined effect, something must determine the agent to act rather than not, to produce this effect rather than that; what removes this indetermination is the end. A free agent determines his own end.

The good may be *ontological*, the good of mere being; or *physical*, the good of completeness; or *moral*, the good of right living, of rightly directing free conduct to its due end. The *true* good really *is* good;

the *apparent* good only seems so. The *useful* good leads to something else that is good; the *pleasant* good satisfies a particular appetite; the *befitting* good perfects the whole man as such. Though every being is ontologically good and has some physical goodness, not every being is always morally good. The moral good is always the true good and the befitting good.

As *ought*, the moral good is seen not as optional but as necessary. This necessity is of a unique kind called *moral* necessity, not a *must* but an *ought*, not physically compelling but morally demanding, leaving us able but not allowed to refuse. It is a man's absolute obligation to succeed *as a man* because he is a man. Hence it is derived from man's value as a being and as a person.

As *value,* the good displays its deepest meaning. Value or worth is a term used for anything that appeals to us in any way. At least subjective values exist, for we do make value judgments and have preferences. Values are bipolar, heterogeneous, idealized, yet calling for realization.

Some values may be purely subjective, but others are *objective*. We cannot be wholly arbitrary about them. As ideals they exist in the mind but are formed by the mind's abstractive power from the data of experience.

Moral values are those which make a man good simply as a man. They can exist only in a *free* being and in voluntary acts, are *universal* since they pertain to man as man, are *self-justifying* and independent of other values, are *preeminent* over every other value, and imply *obligation*.

It is impossible not to form a scale of values in which there is some top value or highest good. In such a scale, moral value claims the highest place. The ideal human life ideally lived is the *moral ideal*.

QUESTIONS FOR DISCUSSION

1 Is the good a simple experience or an intellectual intuition or a concept or a redundant expression? Are things good only because of the way I feel toward them, or do I feel a certain way toward them because of what they are?

2 Is the principle of finality a self-evident proposition, so that what appears to be an argument is merely an explanation or unfolding of the proposition's meaning?

3 Can we accept teleology in human action without accepting teleology in the universe at large? If so, why bring in the larger teleology? Does it strengthen or weaken the argument?

4 Is objective value necessary for the study of ethics? Does the mere nonarbitrariness of values prove their objectivity? Do values become less arbitrary the more abstract they are, and more arbitrary the more concrete they become?

5 Do you find from your own experience that you actually do have a moral ideal? Is it possible not to have one? Would people of different cultures have the same moral ideal? Would different moral ideals contain any common elements?

READINGS

Read Aristotle's *Nicomachean Ethics*, bk. I, ch. 1-6. Henry Veatch, *Rational Man*, gives a modern interpretation of Aristotle's *Ethics*.

Our present chapter is an adaptation of St. Thomas' *Summa Theologica*, I-II, q. 1, and his alternative presentation of the same matter in the *Summa Contra Gentiles*, bk. III, ch. 1-3, 16, 22, and 24. Some of St. Thomas' illustrations are drawn from antiquated physics and astronomy; they are not essential to his argument and can be judiciously bypassed. St. Thomas' metaphysical development of the good is found in the *Summa Theologica*, I, q. 5.

The following modern writers have matter pertinent to this chapter: Étienne Gilson, *Moral Values and Moral Life*, pp. 15-26; Mortimer Adler, *A Dialectic of Morals*, pp. 74-97; William R. O'Connor, *The Eternal Quest*, ch. 5-6; and Leo Ward, *Values and Reality*, ch. 1-4.

A study of the good is found in A. C. Ewing, *The Definition of the Good*, and in W. D. Ross, *The Right and the Good* and *Foundations of Ethics*. Ross makes obligation a characteristic of the right rather than of the good, as he defines them. G. E. Moore's essays on "The Indefinability of the Good" and "The Naturalistic Fallacy," the first two chapters of his *Principia Ethica*, are the source of much modern philosophizing on the ethical good. G. H. von Wright, *The Varieties of Goodness*, examines all the meanings of good.

A classical work on value theory is Ralph Barton Perry, *General Theory of Value*, supplemented by his later work, *Realms of Value*; John Dewey, *Theory of Valuation*; Nicolai Hartmann, *Ethics*, vol. I, sec. V, and vol. II; C. I. Lewis, *Analysis of Knowledge and Valuation*; and Stephen Pepper, *Sources of Value*, present value theory from various philosophical backgrounds. Ray Lepley edits two symposia, *Value, a Cooperative Inquiry*, and *The Language of Value*, by contemporary American philosophers on value theory, treated more from a behavioral than from an ethical standpoint. A. H. Maslow, *Toward a Psychology of Being*, pt. V, has a psychological-moral treatment of values.

Dietrich von Hildebrand, *Christian Ethics*, centers his whole book on values, treated in an original and somewhat Augustinian manner. See especially ch. 5-19.

Austin Fagothey, *Right and Reason—an Anthology*, contains most of G. F. Moore's *Principia Ethica*, ch. 1.

CHAPTER 6

PLEASURE

PROBLEM

The good life might accidentally happen to someone, but the chances are strongly against it. Even if a person were in ideal circumstances, it is possible for him so to misuse his opportunities that there results a life of failure and frustration. Philosophy, as organized human wisdom, is supposed to show a man how to avoid falling into any such unhappy state and to give him positive help toward making his life as satisfactory as can be.

In the search for something that might make life satisfactory, the most obvious candidate is pleasure. No one objects to enjoying himself, though not all will find their enjoyment in the same thing. One who enjoys nothing is in a sad condition indeed, except those abnormal persons who paradoxically enjoy being miserable, and they at least seem to enjoy that. So there is a place for pleasure in the good life. Many think that it is the only element in the good life, and this view expressed philosophically is called *hedonism,* from the Greek word for pleasure.

Hedonism assumes two chief forms, according to whose pleasure is sought. Egoistic hedonism concentrates on the personal pleasure of the individual. Altruistic hedonism seeks the pleasure of others; if it embraces that of the whole human race, it is often called universalistic hedonism. We shall follow general practice in reserving the word *hedonism* for the egoistic

variety and calling the altruistic and universalistic variety *utilitarianism.*

We consider the following questions:
1. What are the reasons for and against egoistic hedonism?
2. What are the reasons for and against altruistic hedonism or utilitarianism?
3. What is the proper place of pleasure in the good life?

HEDONISM

Hedonism is one of the oldest, simplest, and most earthly of ethical theories. It has persisted throughout all ages, and many people who have never consciously formulated for themselves any philosophy of life live according to its principles.

We find hedonism first proposed by Aristippus, leader of the Cyrenaic school, who identified happiness with pleasure. He held that pleasure results from gentle motion, and pain from rough motion. Anything is good which produces pleasure, and that is best which produces the most vivid and intense pleasure. Virtue is useful as restraining us from excessive passion, which is rough motion and unpleasant.

Hedonism was refined by Epicurus, who joined it to the physical theories of Democritus. It is the ethics most consistent with mechanistic materialism. For Epicurus the end of life is not intense pleasure, but an abiding peace of mind, a state of cheerful tranquility. Above all we must avoid fear of the gods and fear of death. Intellectual pleasures are better because they are more lasting, but we cannot do without sense pleasures. The wise man so regulates his life as to get into it the greatest amount of pleasure and the least amount of pain. Moderation is counseled to enable one to enjoy future pleasures. We must learn to restrict our desires within the bounds in which we think we can satisfy them. That is good which will increase our pleasure or our general peace of mind, and anything which decreases it is bad.

> We call pleasure the beginning and end of the blessed life. For we recognize pleasure as the first good innate in us, and from pleasure we begin every act of choice and avoidance, and to pleasure we return again, using the feeling as the standard by which we judge every good. And since pleasure is the first good and natural to us, for this very reason we do not choose every pleasure, but sometimes we pass over many pleasures, when greater discomfort accrues to us as the result of them. . . . Every pleasure then because of its natural kinship to us is good, yet not every pleasure is to be chosen: even as every pain also is an evil, yet not all are always of a nature to be avoided. Yet by a scale of comparison and by the consideration of advantages and disadvantages we must form our judgment on all these matters. . . . When, therefore, we maintain that pleasure is the end, we do not mean the pleasures of profligates and those that consist in sensuality . . . but freedom from pain in the body and from trouble in the mind.[°]

Thomas Hobbes would hardly be classed as an Epicurean, but he does subscribe to a hedonistic view with a strong strain of egoism. He thinks that nothing is by itself good or evil, but that these are names we give to what we desire or detest. We desire what will give us pleasure, either of body or mind, and we detest what gives us displeasure.[†] He does not think that the tranquility lauded by the Epicureans is possible in this struggling world, but the formation of the political state is our only means of controlling the struggle and making life bearable. Society is formed not for the benefit of other people or of mankind as such but for the peace and safety of each particular person looking out primarily for himself.

Though Jeremy Bentham did not limit his hedonism to the egoistic type and is commonly regarded as the founder of utilitarianism, his statement of the hedonistic principle is classic:

> Nature has placed mankind under the governance of two sovereign masters, *pain* and *pleasure*. It is for them alone to point out what we ought to do, as to determine what we shall do. On the one hand the standard of right and wrong, on the other the chain of causes and effects, are fastened to their throne. They govern us in all we do, in all we say, in all we think: every effort we can make to throw off our subjection will serve but to demonstrate and confirm it. In words a man may pretend to abjure their empire: but in reality he will remain subject to it all the while. The *principle of utility* recognizes this subjection, and assumes it for the foundation of that system, the object of which is to rear the fabric of felicity by the hands of reason and law.[°]

In Bentham we have hedonism with the egoistic aspect toned down. In our day several varieties of egoism have appeared with the pleasure aspect de-emphasized. Robert Olson[†] argues for a naturalistic pursuit of both personal and social well-being, in which rational self-interest is the supreme moral criterion, and health, friendship, contentment, and pleasure are the chief goods. Ayn Rand[‡] carries self-interest still further and makes a virtue of selfishness. The ultimate value is man's survival, without which there would be no men to have other values, and each one is responsible for working out for himself the means to survival. This must be done by reason, not by whim. She is confident that individual codes of values, if rationally con-

---

[°]Epicurus' "Letter to Menoeceus" in Diogenes Laertius' *Lives and Opinions of Eminent Philosophers*, bk. X, 27. Whether the letter is genuine or not, it is a good summary of Epicurean thought.
[†]Hobbes, *Leviathan*, bk. I, ch. 6.

[°]Bentham, *Introduction to the Principles of Morals and Legislation*, beginning.
[†]Olson, *The Morality of Self-Interest*.
[‡]Rand, *The Virtue of Selfishness*.

structed, will not conflict, for we deal with one another as traders, giving value for value. No sacrifice for another's sake is ever necessary, for the compromises we must make are in our own self-interest. Thus an economic system of laissez-faire capitalism and a hands-off policy by government are essential. Each working egotistically but rationally for his own interest will automatically bring about the best interest of all.

These samples of the hedonistic view are sufficient for our purpose. We may sum up their case as follows:

1. Rather than try to prove by argument their basic assumption, that everything we do is for pleasure, hedonists point to it as an evident fact. Why should a man do anything except to fulfill a desire, and what is a desire if not for something I want, and why should I want anything unless it affords me some satisfaction? Some think that we cannot act except for pleasure, or for the avoidance of pain, which is a kind of negative pleasure. Others do not insist on the impossibility of acting otherwise but state that we do not act otherwise. Others will admit that we do often act otherwise, but we ought not, for to deprive ourselves of pleasure is an unwise wasting of life's opportunities.

2. Few hedonists would limit man to sense pleasures alone. By including pleasures of intellect, imagination, and emotion, hedonists have no difficulty in explaining why men readily forego sense pleasure for the fulfillment of duty, because they acknowledge the satisfaction we experience in a duty well done. There is something intellectually satisfying in a harmonious life, even if it costs us something to live it. Self-sacrifice for others, if we want to call it that, stimulates our imagination, especially when we imaginatively put ourselves in another's place. Even heroism under the most tragic circumstances can be so emotionally appealing that we choose it rather than live in ignoble comfort.

3. Willingness to curb our appetites for the common good of society is explained by the fact that we ourselves are members of that society and share in this common good. Thus there is always a self-regarding interest in what seems to be the most altruistic behavior. Why not frankly admit it, instead of trying to disguise it under a puritanical hypocrisy? Even love has its self-regarding aspect and is unfulfilled unless it is returned.

4. Those who seek a reward in a next life are likewise motivated by hedonism. They are willing to wait longer for the enjoyment they hope for, but it is this expectation of future· happiness that motivates them to endure their present sufferings. Christianity has thus been called "egoism with a spyglass." The bliss of heaven is made appealing by fostering the belief that it will exceed anything we can now imagine, and its secure possession forever is worth a temporary price.

Nonhedonists are unable to take pleasure in these arguments because they find them unconvincing:

1. Mere statement of the hedonistic principle does not make it true. That many people pursue pleasure all the time and that all of us pursue it some of the time can be readily granted, but there are too many glaring exceptions for it to be a universal rule. Though I cannot willfully act except for something I want in some sense of the word *want*, and achieving it will be a satisfaction of that want, yet it does not follow that the want and the satisfaction must be of the type properly called *pleasure*. That we always act for pleasure can be refuted by deliberately refusing a pleasure; if we are told that we did it for the pleasure of showing our opponent wrong, then pleasure is made to mean any kind of acting; to hold that we always do what we do is hardly distinctive of hedonism.

2. Duty, generosity, self-sacrifice, and heroism have their attendant satisfaction; otherwise they could not be motives for acting. But to call every such satisfaction by the name of pleasure is a misuse of words. On what is the mind fixed, the duty itself or the pleasure attending it, the person helped or the glow felt in helping him, the sacrifice made or the joy in making it, the heroic act or the emotional uplift in dying nobly? It seems here that the accompanying pleasure can be absent and, even when it is present, it is too paltry to be the main motive. Even if it were uppermost, what constitutes the act a *moral* act—the fact that it is an act of duty, generosity, self-sacrifice, or heroism, or the fact that I enjoy it? If only the latter, wisdom dictates that I should pick less painful enjoyments.

3. The good of society does redound to the good of the individual. But what happens when the good of society does not redound to the good of *this* individual, as when he is called on to make the supreme sacrifice for the benefit of others? Hedonism requires that he cooperate with society only so far as he can share in its benefits. Enlightened self-interest has its place, but is society possible on these terms? To use society for one's own benefit alone seems to be the source from which most of the ills of society spring. And though there is a self-regarding aspect in all love, hedonists are not logical unless they make it the only aspect.

4. To live the moral life *exclusively* for the sake of pleasurable rewards, even in the life to come, would be a form of hedonism. There is surely nothing wrong in hoping for the happiness of heaven, just as there is nothing wrong in seeking legitimate pleasure on earth; hedonism occurs only when pleasure is made the exclusive end. The true hedonist would not do good or avoid evil unless he were rewarded for it. In his mind there is no good or evil except in the reward. Thus he makes himself, the one to be rewarded, the last end and the highest good. Most believers in a future life also believe that this would be the surest way of losing the reward.

UTILITARIANISM

The extension of hedonism beyond the pleasure of the individual to the pleasure of the group, and then to the pleasure of all mankind, is called *utilitarianism.* Jeremy Bentham[*] starts, as we have seen, with the idea that pleasure and pain are the only motives governing mankind, and goes on to show that personal pleasure and pain are dependent on the general happiness and prosperity of the whole community. Therefore in framing a hedonistic calculus, the calculation of pleasures and pains inseparable from any hedonistic system, we must consider, among the other criteria of intensity, duration, certainty, propinquity, fecundity, and purity, also the *extent* of pleasure and pain, the number of people affected by our policy of conduct. The moral goodness of an act is to be judged by its *utility* in promoting the common welfare of all as well as the personal advantage of each. The aim of human life is expressed in the *Greatest Happiness Principle:* "The greatest happiness of the greatest number." However, since Bentham wishes to promote the interests of the community at large chiefly because doing so will redound to oneself as a member of that community, his system is still more egoistic than altruistic.

In John Stuart Mill utilitarianism reached its full development. He recognized its strong roots in hedonism:

> The creed which accepts as the foundation of morals, *utility,* or the *greatest happiness principle,* holds that actions are right in proportion as they tend to promote happiness, wrong as they tend to produce the reverse of happiness. By happiness is

---

[*]Bentham, *Introduction to the Principles of Morals and Legislation,* ch. 1-4.

intended pleasure, and the absence of pain; by unhappiness, pain, and the privation of pleasure.°

Whereas Bentham thought that units of pleasure and pain can be calculated arithmetically and that ethics can be made into an exact science, Mill recognized that pleasures differ in *quality* as well as in quantity, that there are higher and lower pleasures, so that a lesser amount of a higher pleasure is better than a greater amount of a lower pleasure, the determination to be made by a man of culture who can experience both.

It is better to be a human being dissatisfied than a pig satisfied; better to be Socrates dissatisfied than a fool satisfied.†

An existence as free from pain and as rich in enjoyments as possible, both in quantity and quality, to be secured to all mankind, is the end of human action and the standard of morality. His proof is often quoted in logic books as an example of a fallacy, since "desirable" does not mean able to be desired but worthy of being desired:

The only proof capable of being given that an object is visible, is that people actually see it. The only proof that a sound is audible, is that people hear it: and so of the other sources of our experience. In like manner, I apprehend, the sole evidence it is possible to produce that anything is desirable, is that people do actually desire it. . . . No reason can be given why the general happiness is desirable except that each person, so far as he believes it to be attainable, desires his own happiness. This, however, being a fact, we have not only all the proof which the case admits of, but all which it is possible to require, that happiness is a good: that each person's happiness is a good to that person, and the general happiness, therefore, a good to the aggregate of all persons.‡

He goes on to show that virtue, far from being opposed to happiness, is one of the elements that make up happiness: the feeling of self-satisfaction in contributing to the common welfare even at personal expense.

Utilitarianism was given a new turn by Henry Sidgwick,° who united it with intuitionism. He has done us the service of putting utilitarianism to a most searching scholarly examination but can find no unassailable proofs for it. The greatest happiness principle is not an empirical induction, as Mill thought. The only way to save it as an ethical principle is to make it a rational intuition, like the axioms of mathematics. Sidgwick was convinced that there is no practical incompatibility between utilitarianism and intuitionism, though he could find no positive theory to explain their union.

G. E. Moore† combines utilitarianism and intuitionism in a different way. He calls his theory *ideal utilitarianism*. All actions are to be judged by their consequences, that is, their usefulness in producing the ideal good for mankind, which includes but is not limited to pleasure, and is an irreducible and indefinable nonnaturalistic property cognizable by us in some intuitive way.

Much is made today of a distinction between *act* utilitarianism and *rule* utilitarianism.‡ The former asks which act has the greatest utility, the latter which rule has. For the act-utilitarian "telling the truth" may be a good general rule, but one should tell a lie if in this particular case the general good would certainly be advanced more thereby. For the rule-utilitarian "telling the truth" may be found to be so necessary a rule for the general good that no exception may be allowed, that one ought to observe it even in cases in which it may be fraught with adverse results; the permission of exceptions would in

---

°Mill, *Utilitarianism*, ch. 2.
†*Ibid.*
‡*Op. cit.*, ch. 4.

°Sidgwick, *The Methods of Ethics*. Summarized and criticized in C. D. Broad, *Five Types of Ethical Theory*, ch. 6.
†Moore, *Principia Ethica*.
‡See Frankena, *Ethics*, pp. 30-35, for a lucid summary.

the long run have more disastrous consequences than all the particular advantages that could be gained from breaking the rule. Both, however, are forms of utilitarianism, for neither the acts nor the rules have any value in themselves apart from the consequences to which they lead. The same critique can be used, with proper reservations, of both.

Since utilitarianism has always had trouble with its own logic, it can perhaps make out the best case for itself by pointing out its own useful consequences:

1. Utilitarianism seeks a happiness in which all will be happy rather than only the fortunate few. The individual sacrifice required for this contribution to the general good is a small enough price to pay for the happiness of so many. Individual pleasure tends to restrict itself, for no one should feel happy knowing that his happiness is bought by others' misery.

2. As a wise combination of egoism and altruism, utilitarianism is an expression of the kind of life most of us lead. It recognizes that man is social, that we are all in this enterprise of life together, and that like passengers in a boat the safety of each is tied up with the safety of all. Avoidable pain should be eliminated. Unavoidable pain can be made tolerable by ensuring that no one has to bear more than his share. Thus utilitarianism is a great stimulus to social improvement, for it takes man's egoistic tendencies and harnesses them to social needs, since each sees his own happiness integrated in that of the group.

3. Those charged with the public welfare can hardly use any other than utilitarian principles, since they must seek the common good and at the same time protect individual rights. Utilitarianism gives each person the right to seek his own pleasure and limits him only when he would encroach on another's equal right. Utilitarianism thus seeks the greatest amount of individual liberty compatible with the greatest amount of public liberty.

4. Utilitarianism eliminates the grossness of egoistic hedonism by a qualitative discrimination of pleasures, and thus makes a place for culture, taste, and beauty in human life. It relies greatly on education as a means of enabling more people to appreciate the higher pleasures, and on economic and social reform as a way of bringing the better life within their grasp.

5. Utilitarianism is contrary neither to virtue nor to religion. It demands the social virtues needed for community living and restrains only those few whose fanatical or distorted interpretation of virtue might issue in antisocial acts. The principle of utility itself encourages the religious believer to store up for himself treasures in heaven, if he is convinced of a future life, and prohibits only the forceful imposition of such a belief on others, as destructive of freedom and incapable anyway of producing internal conviction.

For these and other reasons we see that there is a great deal of truth to utilitarianism, for in any system of ethics one must consider the consequences of one's actions, and social consequences are important. When the question is merely one of public welfare, and the means suggested to achieve it are all moral as determined by some other standard, then those means should be chosen which will best promote the public welfare, as far as enlightened foresight can determine it. But it will not function as the basic, and certainly not as the only, standard of morality. Among others, there are the following criticisms:

1. Egoistic hedonism is at least logical in proposing that, if pleasure is the highest good, each man should seek as much of it as he can get. But why should a man forego his own pleasure for the sake of others? If he enjoys sacrificing himself for others, that is still egoistic hedonism and not utilitarianism. If he feels that such sacrifice is some kind of duty, then the duty will have to be established by a firmer argument than a

mere announcement of the greatest happiness principle.

2. How is the pleasure of the group, and especially of all humanity, to be determined? Hardly by vote. Thus the common pleasure will be decided by each person according to what it pleases him to think the common pleasure should be. We are back to egoistic hedonism. Also, how far into the future must we look? The greatest happiness of the greatest number must include, not only the present generation, but all future generations. Any action taken now may have an indefinitely long train of consequences, and there is nothing in utilitarianism to limit us to immediately foreseeable consequences.

3. One of the simplest ways of eliminating pain from the world is to eliminate the sufferers. Infanticide for defective children, painless execution for hardened criminals, and euthanasia for the incurably sick would surely minimize pain throughout the world and increase the general level of happiness over unhappiness. How, apart from some intolerable despotism, could such a program be carried out? Utilitarians in general would repudiate any such drastic measures as immoral, but then they are using some other standard of morality than the utilitarian one.

4. The altruistic component in utilitarianism is not justified by the system. Unless there is something in the other person that makes him worthy of the sacrifices I am called on to make for him, I am losing my personal pleasure in vain. If we say that it is the dignity of the human person, then that dignity is measured by some other standard than utility, especially if he contributes nothing to my good or to the common good. The only kind of love utilitarianism can admit is a love based on usefulness, which is so poor a kind of love as hardly to deserve the name.

5. Virtue and religion can have only a peripheral place in utilitarianism. Virtue is recommended, not because it is virtue, but only because it has useful consequences.

The possibility of a future life is tolerated as a harmless eccentricity, for the only morally good acts acknowledged in the theory are those which maximize the pleasures of this life, and there is no way of knowing an act's worth for a future life without using some other criterion. Utilitarianism remains typical of the bourgeois ideal of middle-class comfort and reduces to that level all aspirations toward nobility and heroism.

THE PLACE OF PLEASURE IN THE GOOD LIFE

The attempt to make pleasure, either of the individual or of the group, the main purpose of life and the standard of morality results in failure. That does not mean that pleasure is not important in human experience or that it has no ethical significance. If the extreme of hedonism is to make pleasure everything, the opposite extreme, which we may call the puritanical spirit, is to consider pleasure bad, as if there were something not only frivolous but defiling about it. The proper attitude must be somewhere between these extremes.*

There is no sense in trying to define pleasure. We know what it is by experiencing it, and there is no doubt about the experience. Attempted definitions are merely verbal, substituting one term for another. Psychologists have written extensively on pleasure, but what they say has little ethical import, except for the *hedonistic paradox*—the fact that intense mental concentration on the pleasure one is now experiencing rather than on the pleasurable object causes the pleasure to disappear. This confirms the following analysis.

We have no special faculty of pleasure. We cannot just simply *enjoy*. We enjoy *this* or *that*, which means that we enjoy doing something or experiencing some-

---

* Plato and Aristotle give us a very balanced analysis for their day. See Plato, *Philebus;* Aristotle, *Nicomachean Ethics,* bk. VII, ch. 11-14; bk. X, ch. 1-5.

thing. The doing or experiencing must occur by the use of some ability we possess, the main purpose of which is something else besides enjoyment. The fact that we distinguish between sensuous and intellectual pleasure shows that pleasure is an accompaniment of the use of other powers, of either the sensuous or the intellectual order.

It has been suggested that electrical stimulation of an area of the brain might give us pure pleasure without any other accompanying activity. Even so, this could hardly be called normal life, and few people could afford to spend most of their time at it. The only thing immoral about such stimulation, if it is possible, would be that people might be tempted to overdo it and substitute it for real living.

Since, in the process of normal living, no one of our abilities has as its purpose pleasure and nothing else, pleasure is but the accompaniment of the normal exercise of abilities that exist for the accomplishment of some other purpose. We eat primarily to keep ourselves alive, though eating is also pleasant. We have eyes to perceive what we need and to guide our movements, though many sights also give delight. Sex is the biological means for the reproduction of the race, though it also has its pleasure. Intellect enables us to live a civilized life, and there is also satisfaction in a problem successfully solved. The same can be said of our other abilities. Pleasure finds its place in the scheme of things by alluring a person to exercise a natural function that is otherwise beneficial to the individual or the race. We might not take the trouble to eat unless we felt hunger and food had a taste. We keep our eyes open because we enjoy looking. People would not shoulder the responsibilities of matrimony were it not for the pleasures of married life. We would give up hard thinking if we did not find problems an attractive challenge.

It would be a mistake to think of pleasure merely as a means to an end. This is what it is objectively, in the way external nature is constructed, and man also uses pleasure as a means when he offers it to others as an incentive. But pleasure considered subjectively, as a personal experience of the enjoyer, is sought for its own sake and is its own end. It is foolish to ask a man why he wants enjoyment. He wants it because he enjoys it.

Failure to distinguish these two aspects of pleasure, the subjective and the objective, lies behind the two extreme attitudes we have mentioned. It is not possible to reduce pleasure to a mere means, at least for the person enjoying it, and he cannot help seeking it for its own sake, since that is the kind of thing it is. In this respect one may agree with the view* that pleasure taken precisely as pleasure is always good and never bad. If a pleasure can ever be called bad, it is not because the pleasing object is pleasant but because it has other features connected with it that are harmful or unworthy, such as violating others' rights or stunting one's personality. Thus there is nothing wrong in seeking pleasure for its own sake, since it cannot be sought otherwise, but it must be done within proper measure. It is when men so center on the subjective aspect of pleasure to the exclusion of the objective, by making pleasure the only end or the chief end in life, that they thereby exclude the end for which pleasure is adapted by nature as a means. By acting thus they contradict their own nature and make themselves incapable of fulfilling the purpose for which they exist. So pleasure is an end and a good, but it is not the last end and the highest good, though there could hardly be a last end or a highest good unaccompanied by a corresponding degree of pleasure.

Also, we must not forget the partial character of pleasure compared with the all-embracing nature of happiness. The pleasures of this life are not attainable by

*Hinted at by Aristotle, *Nicomachean Ethics,* bk. VII, ch. 13; bk. X, ch. 5.

all men at all times. To have some pleasures we must forego others. Pleasure is
not lasting, for none of our faculties can
stand ceaseless exercise. Too much indulgence makes pleasure cloying and often
brings with it its own punishment. Old
age diminishes the possibility of pleasure,
and death ends it. Hence, though there is
nothing wrong with legitimate pleasure,
it cannot fully satisfy.

Altruistic pleasure, though on a higher
plane than egoistic, is also unsatisfying.
The joy we feel in kindness, in giving gifts,
in helping others, in relieving distress, in
social uplift, in works of charity and benevolence, is among the purest and best
we can experience. The many who devote
their lives to these activities are worthy
of praise, but again, not all have the time
and means for such works, the joy taken
in them is often marred by ingratitude, and
many schemes for the betterment of mankind grind to a halt in disillusionment. The
philanthropist is by all means to be encouraged, but he had better keep his mind
on those he is helping and not expect too
much personal satisfaction. Besides, there is
something incoherent in the altruistic ideal
unbuttressed by other aims. If we exist for
the sake of other men, then what are the
other men for? If everybody exists for the
sake of everbody else, then, when the process is brought round full circle, what is all
humanity for?

This last is the question that egoism
and altruism, hedonism and utilitarianism,
indeed all other forms of naturalistic humanism, remain unable to answer. Despite
many useful contributions to the study of
human life, pleasure ethics must be set aside
in favor of a better philosophy, if any such
can be found.

SUMMARY

Hedonism picks egoistic pleasure as
man's highest good. It need not be the
pleasure of the moment or sensuous pleasure only, but can be a wise blend of enjoyments spread out over one's probable
lifetime.

Arguments *for:* We do in fact seek
pleasure and shun pain, even duty affords
a kind of intellectual satisfaction, altruistic
behavior has a self-regarding aspect, and
those who seek a reward in the next world
expect to enjoy it.

Arguments *against:* We often refuse
pleasure for higher motives, satisfaction in
doing one's duty is not the same as pleasure, enlightened self-interest is not our
only motive, and those who would not do
good unless it were rewarded are unworthy
of the reward.

Utilitarianism prefers the altruistic pleasure of seeking the greatest happiness of
the greatest number, and measures the
morality of an act by its utility in promoting the common welfare.

Arguments *for:* It seeks others' happiness
as well as one's own, it recognizes man's
social needs, it curbs man's selfish greed,
it accepts qualitative differences in pleasures, and it is open both to virtue and to
religion.

Arguments *against:* It gives no reason
why one should consider others, it cannot determine what makes for the general happiness, it should logically eliminate sufferers, it has no place for real
love, and it makes the noblest acts not
good in themselves but only useful
means.

Conclusion. Pleasure fails as the highest
good; yet it is a very important good. It
is a stimulus that nature uses to allure us
to the proper use of our abilities. It is also
a subjective experience sought for its own
sake. There is nothing wrong in seeking
pleasure for itself, so long as it is kept
within proper bounds and not too much is
expected of it. A puritanical attitude toward
pleasure is not praiseworthy. Pleasure is *a*
good, but not *the* good.

QUESTIONS FOR DISCUSSION

1 If pleasure is taken in a broad enough sense, it is the same as the good, for what is the good of a good one does not enjoy? Since no one else can enjoy my enjoyment, I must seek it myself.

2 What of the view that when life is difficult and survival is threatened, survival is the supreme value; but when survival is assured and life is easy, pleasure takes over as the supreme value?

3 The only reality to society is in the persons composing it. Society is not for itself but for persons. In any conflict between social and personal enjoyment, the personal should prevail. Does this prove egoism?

4 Must not political and social legislation use utilitarian criteria? If man is essentially a social being, should not social and thus utilitarian criteria govern the whole of man's life?

5 Altruists think that the good of others should always be preferred to one's own good and that a life of self-sacrifice is the noblest life. What are the reasons for and against such a view?

READINGS

Read Plato's *Philebus,* the dialogue on pleasure, and the part of the *Gorgias,* §492-500, where Plato argues that pleasure is not *the* good; and Aristotle's two sections on pleasure in the *Nicomachean Ethics,* bk. VII, ch. 11-14, and bk. X, ch. 1-5.

Lucretius' poem *De Rerum Natura* (On the Nature of Things) proclaims the philosophy of Epicurus. Cicero discusses Epicureanism together with other ancient philosophies in his *Tusculan Disputations* and other philosophical writings. Diogenes Laertius' *Lives and Opinions of Eminent Philosophers* gives a summary of Epicureanism, with some notice of the Cyrenaics.

Read Hobbes, *Leviathan,* pt. I, ch. 6, 11; Robert Olson, *The Morality of Self-Interest;* and Ayn Rand, *The Virtue of Selfishness,* for varieties of egoism.

Jeremy Bentham, *Introduction to the Principles of Morals and Legislation,* ch. 1-5; and John Stuart Mill, *Utilitarianism,* offer the classic exposition of utilitarianism.

Many books and articles give detailed criticisms of hedonism and utilitarianism, among them G. E. Moore, *Principia Ethica.*

John Rawls, "Two Concepts of Rules," in *Philosophical Review,* vol. 64, no. 2 (1955), reprinted in various collections, distinguishes act and rule utilitarianism.

Austin Fagothey, *Right and Reason—an Anthology,* contains Aristotle's *Nicomachean Ethics,* bk. VII, ch. 11-14; bk. X, ch. 1-5; Epicurus' *Letter to Menoeceus;* Bentham's *Introduction to the Principles of Morals and Legislation,* ch. 1, 4; and Mill's *Utilitarianism,* ch. 2, 4.

CHAPTER 7

CONVENTION

PROBLEM

Despite the large part that pleasure plays in life and despite the moral acceptability of many of the pleasures we may enjoy, pleasure itself cannot be the standard of moral good and evil. It affords no reason why we are morally bound to do some things we find unpleasant and to refrain from other things we are strongly attracted to. The ought is not always what we like, either as individuals or as a group. If the ought does not come from our likes and dislikes, where does it come from?

The later utilitarians had already gone beyond pleasure as that which constitutes the good of society. If we pursue the topic along these lines and provisionally take the good of society as the goal toward which we should strive in moral living, the next question would be: Who is to decide what that good is? The simplest answer is to let society itself decide what is good for it. The history of the human race is the history of man's constant quest for self-improvement. With long and often painful experience various groups of human beings have organized themselves for the pursuit of their common good and have embodied the results in their various laws and customs. They have not all arrived at the same formula for their common happiness, but each individual must live in the group, tribe, city, or nation to which he belongs, and must adapt himself to its way of living. Why not say, then, that morality is that which the group decrees and which it en-

forces by the strong sanctions of social approval and disapproval? Thus morality would not be something that man finds already existing in the world, but something that he created in order to make living possible, something artificial and fictitious in itself but a historical fact avoidable only by the outlaw and outcast. Morality would be reducible to the conventions of society, whether those conventions be enacted into law or informally recognized as approved customary behavior. We shall discuss the following points:

1. What is the meaning of conventional and natural morality?
2. Does all morality come from the civil law?
3. Does all morality come from custom and social pressure?
4. What is the place of convention in morals?

CONVENTIONAL AND NATURAL MORALITY

To set the question, we must define two important kinds of morality. An act that is neither good nor bad of its own very nature but becomes so only because it is commanded or forbidden by some law or custom is said to have *conventional* or *extrinsic* morality. An act that is good or bad of its own very nature independently of any command or prohibition is said to have *natural* or *intrinsic* morality. Note that both are varieties of objective morality, since they do not ask about the state of the doer's conscience but about what makes that kind of act, whoever does it, right or wrong.

That conventional morality exists in evident, for no one can deny the existence of laws, such as the laws of the state or the unwritten law of custom, which issue abundant commands and prohibitions, rendering good or bad many actions that would otherwise be morally indifferent. Hence the question is not one of choosing between conventional and natural morality, but whether *besides* conventional morality there is *also* natural morality. To sum up the question:

1. Are all acts good only because they are commanded, bad only because they are forbidden?
2. Or are some acts commanded because they are good, forbidden because they are bad in themselves?

To accept the first alternative is to say that all morality is determined by convention, that it is the result of some human will commanding or forbidding certain kinds of acts, that it is not based on something intrinsic in the human act itself or in the nature of man. Thus it makes all morality a creation of human society. The theory takes two main forms, according as the convention or decision to consider some acts right and others wrong is the result of the following:

1. The laws of the state—*social contract theories*
2. The customs of men—*social pressure theories*

SOCIAL CONTRACT THEORIES

Some think that no act is wrong unless there is a law against it, and the only law they acknowledge is the civil law. Where the arm of the law cannot reach, anything goes. Morality is thus the product of civilized life, which necessarily entails political organization. Morality is made the same as legality. This popular conception has had few philosophical defenders, but there are two of great influence.

Thomas Hobbes and probably Jean Jacques Rousseau maintain that before man organized himself into a political community there was no right and wrong. The state itself is not a natural society but the result of the social contract, a purely conventional agreement whereby men give up part of their natural rights (liberty to do anything they please) in order to preserve the rest. Once civil society is formed, it commands and forbids certain actions for the common good, and this is the beginning of right and wrong. Therefore no acts are right or wrong of their very nature but only because commanded or forbidden by the political state.

Hobbes and Rousseau differ greatly in their views on the state of nature, on the form of the social contract, on the mode of transferring rights, and on the seat of sovereignty, but these views belong rather to their theories on the state. Here we are interested only in the fact that they deny natural or intrinsic morality. One may wonder what value morals can have if they are merely arbitrary conventions of man, but Hobbes and Rousseau both insist on the validity of morality once the state has been established.

A few key passages will show Hobbes' view:

During the time men live without a common power to keep them all in awe, they are in that condition which is called war; and such a war as is of every man against every man. . . .

To this war of every man against every man, this also is consequent: *that nothing can be unjust.* The notions of right and wrong, justice and injustice, have there no place. Where there is no common power, there is no law; where no law, no injustice. Force and fraud are in war the two cardinal virtues. . . . It is consequent also to the same condition, that there be no propriety,° no dominion, no *mine* and *thine* distinct; but only that to be every man's that he can get; and for so long as he can keep it. . . .†

Where no covenant hath preceded, there hath

°*Propriety* here is but the old form of the word *property.*
†Hobbes, *Leviathan,* ch. 13.

no right been transferred, and every man has a right to everything and consequently, no action can be unjust. . . . Before the names of just and unjust can have place, there must be some coercive power, to compel men equally to the performance of their covenants, by the terror of some punishment greater than the benefit they expect by the breach of their covenant . . . and such power there is none before the erection of a commonwealth.*

It may be unfair to class Rousseau with Hobbes. Rousseau seems rather to think that man in his primitive state of innocence naturally did what is right without the formulation of any moral rules. Whatever his general theory, he lays himself open to the charge of conventionalism by the opening words of his *Social Contract:*

> Man is born free, and everywhere he is in chains. Many a one believes himself the master of others, and yet he is a greater slave than they. How has this change come about? I do not know. What can render it legitimate? I believe that I can settle this question. . . . The social order is a sacred right which serves as a foundation for all others. This right, however, does not come from nature. It is therefore based on conventions. The question is to know what these conventions are. . . . †
>
> Since no man has any natural authority over his fellow-man, and since force is not the source of right, conventions remain as the basis of all lawful authority among men. . . .‡
>
> The passage from the state of nature to the civil state produces in man a very remarkable change, by substituting in his conduct justice for instinct, and by giving his actions the moral quality they previously lacked.§

All readily admit that the state can pass laws on indifferent matters and make them binding under moral obligation. As guardian of public order and safety, the state decrees that we shall drive on the right side of the road, though either side might have been chosen. This law does not change the intrinsic nature of the road,

but it does make a deliberate act of driving on the wrong side unsafe, antisocial, and to that extent immoral. Thus the state gives extrinsic morality to an act intrinsically indifferent.

Can all acts be of this kind? There are some acts the state cannot command and others the state cannot forbid. No state could survive that commanded murder, theft, perjury, and treason, or that forbade kindliness, honesty, truthfulness, and loyalty. Such actions were good or bad before there was any state. They are not good or bad because the laws of the state command or forbid them, but the state is obliged to command or forbid them because they are good or bad in themselves.

SOCIAL PRESSURE THEORIES

The theory that morality is mere custom has always been widespread since the days of the Sophists and Skeptics of ancient Greece. Some give legitimacy to the custom after it has been introduced, whereas others advocate its abolition. One who wishes to do away with morality must adopt some such theory to explain how men ever became deceived into thinking that right and wrong exist.

Some think that morality was imposed on men by clever and influential persons to keep the common people in subjection: by the force of public opinion and the weight of tradition the ordinary man accepts the moral code and wears the chains forged for him; only a few bold spirits assert and achieve freedom. This is the philosophy of the world's moral rebels. Bernard de Mandeville* gives the idea expression but thinks it a providential arrangement.

The opinion of Friedrich Nietzsche† is

Op. cit., ch. 15.
†Rousseau, *Social Contract,* bk. I, ch. 1.
‡*Op. cit.,* bk. I, ch. 4.
§*Op. cit.,* bk. I, ch. 8.

*Mandeville, *Enquiry into the Origin of Moral Virtue.*
†Nietzsche, *Genealogy of Morals, Beyond Good and Evil,* and other works.

not very different. In the beginning there were no good and bad, only the strong and the weak. The strong, with their masculine virtues of power, cunning, and ruthlessness, despised the weak, with their feminine virtues of patience, obedience, and kindliness; and the weak feared the strong. Each class admired its own qualities and condemned the opposite; thus arose the distinction between master morality and slave morality. By weight of numbers, assisted by the influence of Christianity, slave morality triumphed. This outcome was a disaster. The common herd does not count, and it is the duty of society to produce an aristocracy of "Supermen," who will be the embodiment of the masculine virtues and will restore the master morality. The "Superman" will be beyond all good and evil, a law to himself.

Karl Marx and Friedrich Engels* with their communist followers hold the materialistic conception of history, according to which moral, political, artistic, social, and philosophical ideas are determined by the economic conditions of society; each age, people, and class forms its ideas to suit its own peculiar economic situations; the economic changes to be brought about by the downfall of capitalism will require the formation of a new morality to supplant the present outmoded "bourgeois" morality.

Social evolutionists, of whom Herbert Spencer† is typical, trace the first beginning of moral ideas in animals. As man gradually evolved from a brutish condition, these moral ideas underwent a parallel evolution. Ways of acting that were found profitable developed into primitive tribal customs, which with the progress of civilization were gradually purified into our present system of morals. This will give way to a still higher system as the evolutionary process continues.

Positivism, founded by Auguste Comte,* is a general philosophical attitude holding that metaphysics is useless and that philosophy is limited to the facts and laws discovered by the *positive* or experimental sciences. The last science to become positive is the science of society, for which Comte invented the name *sociology*. Ethics is a part of sociology, for moral customs grew out of social customs and fluctuate with changes in society.

John Dewey† reduces morals to customs, folkways, and established collective habits, but he admits that they so form the texture of our lives that there is no escaping from them. More will be said of his ethical relativism later.

All such views received new cogency from a nonphilosophical source, the rise of cultural anthropology and Freudian psychology. These studies are not necessarily committed to a definite ethical view, but in the hands of some have been used to bolster the social pressure theory of moral obligation. Tribal tabus, however artificial and fictitious they may seem, often serve a purpose in the culture in which they flourish, though advanced peoples have outgrown them. Civilized mores are merely a lingering remnant of the same thing in a more advanced style. Both have the same obligatory force: social pressure. It is easier to conform than to push against the demands of the crowd, and what is really only expediency becomes invested with an aura of duty.

---

*Marx and Engels, *Communist Manifesto.*
†Spencer, *Principles of Ethics,* of which the *Data of Ethics,* sometimes published separately, forms the first part.

*Comte, *Cours de philosophie positive.* A convenient exposition of his philosophy in English is Harriet Martineau's *Positivist Philosophy of Auguste Comte.* Positivism in general and logical positivism are named from the positive or experimental sciences, whereas moral positivism and legal positivism are named from positive law as opposed to natural law. The two meanings of positivism are not related, except incidentally.
†Dewey, *Human Nature and Conduct,* pt. I, sec. V.

We recognize that morality differs in every society, and is a convenient term for socially approved habits. Mankind has always preferred to say, "It is morally good," rather than, "It is habitual," and the fact of this preference is matter enough for a critical science of ethics. But historically the two phrases are synonymous.[*]

While some thus reduce ethics to anthropology, others make it a form of psychology, so that the sense of moral obligation is identified with submerged psychic feelings of guilt. The person vaguely feels bound but is unable to account for this inner sense of obligation until his early life is dredged up from the depths of the unconscious, and the feelings of guilt are seen as stemming from repressed infantile encounters with social, especially parental, disapproval. Doubtless, anthropological and psychological facts have strongly influenced the development of ethics. Whether they are the total explanation is another question.

All the foregoing opinions are but samples of this type of theory. They agree in reducing morality to social pressure and differ in their way of trying to account for the existence and influence of social pressure. They all deny that there is any intrinsic morality, that there is any basis in the nature of things for the distinction men commonly make between right and wrong. To assess this view we must see what is meant by custom.

WHAT IS CUSTOM?

Custom arises by repetition of the same kind of act in the same way. It is the external result of habit. Why do men repeat acts? Because the first time they did a certain act they found it pleasant or useful, and they want to obtain the same good again. In the beginning men do not repeat

acts merely because they have done them once or twice before, but for the sake of some advantage. Until the custom has been formed, custom itself is not the source of action. Customs and traditions have their value as passing on to future generations in ready-made form the profitable experiences of our elders. As historical connections with the past, as the cement of cultural continuity, they are the mainstay of every civilization.

Custom can also act as a drawback. Over a long period of time circumstances may radically change, and acts that were formerly advantageous may now in the new conditions become useless or even harmful; yet men by force of habit continue to perform them without reflecting on why they do so. Thus men continue to observe certain rites and ceremonies long after they have forgotten their meaning. Traditions can so pile up that a whole people will persist in doing a thing in a wasteful or illogical manner, even after they recognize its absurdity, because they find it easier to conform to prejudice than to try to make men abandon familiar patterns of behavior. Our clumsy calendar, our irregular English spelling, and our uncomfortable formal dress are instances.

As we noted in the very beginning of ethics, there are two kinds of customs: *manners,* which are mere customs in the sense that they are repeated solely because they have been done before, and *morals,* which are customary patterns of behavior but are based on something deeper in man than arbitrary usage. Manners can be changed by lapse of time, by powerful authority, by continual propaganda, and by popular reeducation. This change may be difficult to accomplish, but history shows that even the most deeply lodged traditions, if they are mere traditions, can be broken. This is not true of all customs, not of the kind called *morals,* for there are:

1. Some customs that cannot be abolished and

---

[*]Ruth Benedict, "The Concept of the Normal," taken from Mandelbaum, Gramlich, Anderson, and Schneewind, *Philosophic Problems,* ed. 2, p. 596.

2. Some kinds of acts that can never be made customary

SOME CUSTOMS NEVER ABOLISHED

Eating and breathing are customs, but men cannot be reeducated to do without them. Conversation and exchange of ideas are customs, but only a fool would try to prohibit them. Music and artistic expression are customs, but there is no prospect of ever eradicating them wholly from any people. The reason is that, though customary, they are not mere customs but are founded on man's physical, mental, and emotional needs.

These instances are drawn from outside the field of morality, but the same conclusion holds true of man's moral life. It is customary for men to respect the lives and property of others in peacetime, to love their children, to pay their debts, to tell the truth, to be faithful to their friends, to fulfill their promises, to help others in distress. But these are not mere customs. If they were, they could be abolished and the opposite customs introduced. Not only would men refuse to accept the opposite customs, but there would be an end to human life and society. There would be no property, no children, no commerce, no talking, no friends, no promises, and no man would live to maturity, much less produce a second generation. Here we are using only a few obvious examples and not trying to set up a full code of morality. We say only that some customs cannot be abolished, and the reader can take what examples he wishes.

We may call such acts customs in the broad sense of something done over and over again, but they are not mere customs in the sense that the only reason they are done is that they have been done before. They represent the way man must live if he is to have a human life at all. Therefore such acts are good, not because they are customary, but because of their very nature. They are good in themselves, and were so before they became customary.

SOME ACTS NEVER CUSTOMARY

We cannot make it customary for man to walk down the street shooting people indiscriminately, for witnesses in a lawcourt to lie, for soldiers to desert in battle, for hosts to poison their guests, for every man to slander his neighbor's character and run off with his neighbor's wife. There must be some reason why such acts could not be established as customary. It is because such acts are evil in themselves and of their very nature. They are destructive of the fundamental capacities and requirements of man, and hence of human nature itself.

Of course, there are men who do these things, but that is not the point. The point is that this kind of conduct is branded as wrong, and we are trying to find out why. Such conduct must ever be the exception, not the rule; the isolated instance, not the practice of the group; a blot on humanity, not the accepted ideal. If it becomes too widespread, it threatens the very existence of the society within which it grows. In our tolerance of human behavior, customary or otherwise, there is a limit beyond which, if we are to survive, we cannot go. There is a vast difference between antisocial conduct which people view with an amused or annoyed forbearance and the life of the outlaw, whom society is forced for its own protection to hunt down like a beast. This latter kind of conduct can never become so prevalent as to be the accepted custom of the race, and even if it should, nothing could make it moral. Morality, therefore, is based on something deeper than custom.

We do not deny that some evil customs may be adopted even by a whole people or nation, but history shows that no block of humanity can thus deteriorate without paying the price. Nations as well as individuals can be guilty of immoral conduct and can become outlaws from the family of nations. We are experiencing in the world today the results of international immorality, and the lesson to be drawn from it is this: You can't live that way!

PLACE OF CONVENTION IN MORALS

In the earliest stages of human development, both of the individual and of the race, probably little discrimination is made between physical and moral necessity, between legality and morality. As the child grows up and as primitive people arrive by self-examination at a more sophisticated attitude, the confusion disappears and the distinction is recognized. Compulsion from without is seen to be not the same as obligation from within. There is a difference between what I *must* do or suffer the penalty and what I *ought* to do whether there is a penalty or not.

Thus a person emancipates himself from sole dependence on social and political pressure, from the laws and customs of the tribe or city or nation with their sanctions, and recognizes those ways of life that are proper to a man as a man. He is still a member of the group and strongly influenced by its approval, but he has grown critical of it and has found some norm for his criticism. Even those who attack all moral obligation do so in the name of sincerity, authenticity, and freedom, as liberating man from the weight of superstition, prejudice, and conformity. Thus they attack existing moral values and obligations for the sake of other moral values and obligations, rejecting the socially accepted code for one of their own making. Since we are not saying here what the correct moral values are but only that there are *some*, we could hardly find a better instance of the impossibility of reducing moral obligation to social approval than in those who criticize society itself in the name of morals. Nor is total social rebellion necessary to perceive this. No mature person is wholly satisfied with his society.

Where his approval does not correspond with its approval, he is using some standard other than political or social convention.

CONCLUSIONS

There are some actions that are right or wrong merely because someone in authority has commanded or forbidden them. These actions are determined by positive law. The state has the right to forbid some actions not otherwise wrong for the sake of good order, and human customs may sometimes have the force of law.

There are other actions so good of their very nature that no human law or custom could make them bad, as well as actions so bad of their very nature that no human law or custom could make them good. Besides, no human law or custom can make acts that are good or bad in themselves become indifferent acts, but they can, by command or prohibition, make acts that are indifferent in themselves become extrinsically good or bad.

It must be insisted that diversity of opinion on morals does not affect the present question. However much opinions may differ, there is a common denominator of moral action among men, and the arguments are drawn from this alone. Men may dispute whether this particular act is murder, theft, lying, or adultery, but there is no dispute that all sane men condemn murder, theft, lying, and adultery in general, and recognize that such acts cannot be made the standard of good conduct by any law or custom. If not, there must be some reason why not, and this can be found only in the very nature of such acts.

We may tie all these strands together in one argument. If all morality were conventional, all actions would be right or wrong because commanded or forbidden, approved or disapproved, either by the state or by society, by law or by custom. But some actions are such that the command or prohibition, the approval or disapproval of the state and its laws, of society and its customs, could not be otherwise, for any other mode of behavior would be destructive of the state, society, and humanity itself. Therefore not all morality is conventional, but there is also a natural morality.

SUMMARY

Is all morality conventional, or is some morality natural?

Many hold the theory that all morality is conventional, resulting from the command or prohibition of the state and its laws or from the approval or disapproval of society and its customs, but that there are no acts good or bad of their very nature. The theory takes two forms:

1. *Social contract theories.* Hobbes and Rousseau say that there was no morality before the formation of the state, and that morality now consists in obedience or disobedience to the civil laws. The argument against this theory is that the state can give conventional morality to indifferent acts, but no state can be completely arbitrary in its laws; there are acts every state must command and other acts every state must forbid, because human life itself demands it; these acts were moral or immoral before there was any state.

2. *Social pressure theories.* These theories are held by philosophers as widely separated as Spencer and Nietzsche, Comte and Marx. Custom can attain the force of law and give conventional morality to indifferent acts, but not all morality can be based on custom, for some customs cannot be abolished, and some kinds of acts can never be made customary. The only reason is that these acts are good or bad independently of any custom, and custom is not the source of all morality.

Such theories fail to distinguish the *must* from the *ought*, compulsion from without and obligation from within. Why obey the law or custom? Force and fear are physical, not moral necessity.

Conclusion. Some acts have only a conventional morality; of themselves indifferent, they become good or bad only because someone in authority has commanded or forbidden them. There are other acts that have natural morality; they are good or bad of their very nature, and no human law or custom, no form of social approval or disapproval, can make them otherwise.

QUESTIONS FOR DISCUSSION

1 If man is social by nature, is not natural morality manifested to man by the mores of his social milieu, so that whatever the group dictates is natural morality for him?

2 Is it a fair statement of the social pressure theory to say that, because social approval accompanies good conduct and social disapproval accompanies bad conduct, good conduct and bad conduct are reducible to social approval and disapproval only?

3 The statement has been made that no common code of conduct could be approved by the United Nations because customs differ too widely. Does this show that morality is only convention, and morals are only mores?

4 Does the argument of this chapter do anything more than call at-

tention to the impossibility of making certain acts moral or immoral by law or by social approval? How is such impossibility proved? By trying it? Has anyone tried? How many trials would be necessary?

5 Is a person forced into having two kinds of morality, a natural morality for his private life and a conventional morality for his social and political life? For whatever we think of custom or convention, we will be punished for not observing it.

READINGS

Plato's *Gorgias*, §481 to the end, and *Republic*, bk. I, §338, to bk. II, §368, are pertinent to the subject. Also Cicero, *De Legibus* (On Laws), bk. I, xiv-xvi.

St. Thomas has one short chapter on the subject in the *Summa Contra Gentiles,* bk. III, ch. 129, and some background material in the *Summa Theologica,* I-II, q. 18, a. 1. Natural morality was taken for granted in his day and is not given extended treatment.

Read Hobbes' *Leviathan,* bk. I; Rousseau's *Social Contract,* bk. I; Nietzsche's *Genealogy of Morals* and *Beyond Good and Evil;* Spencer's *Data of Ethics;* Dewey's *Human Nature and Conduct,* pt. I, sec. V.

Austin Fagothey, *Right and Reason—an Anthology,* contains Hobbes' *Leviathan,* parts of ch. 13-15, 17; Rousseau's *Social Contract,* bk. I, ch. 1-6, 8; and Marx and Engels' *Communist Manifesto.*

CHAPTER 8

CONSEQUENCES

PROBLEM

The common mark of the ethical theories we have seen so far is that they are all forms of relativism. To these we may now add the variety of relativism called *pragmatism* because of its stress on the practical, on what works, on results or consequences. Pragmatism is closely associated with utilitarianism, the main difference being that pragmatism is an epistemological theory, holding the *true* to be that which works, so that the truth of propositions is to be tested by their consequences in producing more satisfaction for the individual or the group; whereas utilitarianism is an ethical theory, holding the *good* to be that which works, so that moral goodness is judged by its consequences for society in obtaining the greatest happiness of the greatest number. When there is question of the truth about the good, the two theories fairly coincide.

Utilitarianism is bound up with the pleasure principle because of its historical roots in hedonism. The later utilitarians, however, went beyond the narrow view of restricting consequences to pleasurable ones only, and included the overriding value of consequences generally beneficial to mankind, pleasurable or not. Such a broader view is pragmatism.

Ethical relativism means that there is nothing good or bad absolutely, but that all morality is relative to the individual or to the society to which one belongs. Utilitarianism and pragmatism, and also conventionalism in its way, talk about consequences.

Consequences *to whom?* What may have good consequences to one person may be disastrous to another, what may work in one part of the world or in one age may not in another, what may be beneficial to one form of society or culture may be harmful in another. Hence, relativists say, there is no common morality for the whole human race throughout all history, but we must be content with a morality relative to our time and place.

None of these ways of thinking need be regarded as subjectivism. They do not say that any act is moral merely because I think it moral, that I construct my own code of morals out of my own subjective whim. Rather, they are seeking the objective good, what is really beneficial to the individual or to society. Individuals and societies really differ, and so do their wants and needs. Hence for them ethics is not arbitrary, though is it not uniform.

Conventionalism is a form of relativism, but there are other forms of relativism that are not conventionalism. Pragmatism, for instance, would not be happy with a wholly extrinsic morality. It does not consider an act good or bad because commanded or forbidden by someone in authority, but rather tries to find what it is that authority ought to command or forbid. It is highly critical of existing society and recommends getting rid of outworn customs. Pragmatism is one of the strongest foes of traditionalism and is constantly calling for new social experiments to discover more beneficial ways of living. Society is constantly evolving, and the ways of the past may no longer serve the present or the future.

Relativism in the form of pragmatism is chiefly concerned with the ends or purposes of human living. It rejects any absolute good, any supreme purpose in life. In answering the question, "Has life any meaning?" it says yes, if you are willing to restrict yourself to relatively limited and immediate objectives that can differ for different times and places; but it says no, if you are asking for one absolutely ultimate end and supreme good for all men. This latter would be an absolute, the kind of thing relativism rejects.

Having thus set the stage, we may proceed to our questions:

1. Is it possible to have no aim in life?
2. Is man limited to short-range, relative ends?
3. Are there reasons for an absolutely last end?
4. Can the relative and the absolute be reconciled?

OPPORTUNISM

The problem of the meaning or purpose of life gradually grows on one. At first the child's life lies on the animal plane with no intellectually understood goals. As its reason unfolds, the child begins to see some short-term objectives and plans for them with a rudimentary use of means and ends. But to every normal person the time must come when the problem of life's meaning becomes acutely insistent, the irrationality of haphazard living grows glaringly evident, and the former excuse of ignorance and immaturity vanishes before the clear light of developed reason. From then on an intelligent organization of life is imperative.

While this development is going on, the child is not left to drift aimlessly. So long as it cannot steer itself, it is steered by others. It is born into a family and is meant by nature to accept parental direction, to be guided by the rules of the society it cannot yet criticize, and to rely on the primitive ob-servations it can form from its growing stock of experience. Eventually it will have to go through some process of self-searching and reflection in order to arrive at a reasoned plan of life with consciously formed aims.

As one can arrive at physical maturity without mental maturity, so one can attain to both without moral maturity. The unconsciously adopted philosophy of the child can be rationalized and protracted into adulthood. We call this widely practiced way of life *moral opportunism*. It is not merely a willingness to use opportunities as they arise and to adapt to sudden wind-falls of fortune, a useful trait for anybody, but rather it is a refusal to have any principles. It is a contentment to live on a day-to-day or a year-to-year basis, looking only to the immediate prospect and letting the far future take care of itself. It is a deliberate intention to remain open and uncommitted. Not so much a reasoned conviction as an attitude of intellectual and moral sloth, it merits the Socratic rebuff, "The unexamined life is not worth living."*

One may indeed consciously choose to float with the tide rather than set a course, to shun any fixed program so as to be free to reshape life as the main chance offers, and above all to avoid encumbrance by embarrassing principles and responsibilities. This is the life of the moral tramp or ethical hobo, a form of life that can be chosen quite deliberately. He who takes to it does not avoid having a goal in life; he mistakenly takes wandering itself for life's chief aim by the very fact that he seeks nothing beyond. One may aim at aimlessness, rationally choose to live irrationally, but such conduct must be branded as unworthy of a man. As the vagrant is an economic anomaly and a social liability, so is the opportunist an ethical misfit and a human failure. Since no one has yet written a philosophical defense of the ethics of laziness, we pass on to more promising prospects.

*Plato, *Apology*, §38.

RELATIVISM AND PRAGMATISM

For the opportunist, there is too much trouble in finding out life's meaning if it has one. For the relativist, especially of the pragmatist type, life can be somewhat meaningful in retrospect and in immediate prospect, but its total and ultimate meaning is undiscoverable by us now and unnecessary for relatively successful living.

John Dewey's* form of pragmatism, which he calls *instrumentalism*, is ethical relativism with a strong evolutionary bent. Thinking, he says, is functional, instrumental to action, not done for the sake of finding truth but of making life more satisfactory. A value is whatever a man finds satisfaction in doing in this world of experience. An ethical question arises when a man must choose between values. The good is always the better; an evil is only a rejected good. Selection is made by considering one's capacities, satisfactions, and the demands of the social situation, and by taking that which embodies the most foreseen possibilities of future satisfaction. A want arises only when a need is felt, that is, in a particular situation. Only felt wants demand satisfaction, and a satisfied want automatically creates a new want. When we have finished one stage, we experimentally cast about for means to the next stage in the ongoing process. Evolution is continuity of change, readjustment, and redirection. Each stage is a new experimental adventure, which includes the setting of new goals as well as the choice of new means. Thus there is no need of an absolutely fixed goal to give meaning to human life.

The general case for a relativistic pragmatism of this type can be argued in the following way:

1. Acute sensitivity to our limitations and to the folly of being ambitious beyond our known possibilities should cause us to re-

*Dewey, *Human Nature and Conduct*, pt. IV, I; *The Quest for Certainty*, ch. 10.

ject all absolutes. If such an assertion seems too absolute, it can be softened into the observation that no supreme purpose for man has yet been identified with certainty. We do not see far enough into the future to be able to make assertions about it with absolute confidence and thus cannot put before us an absolute goal without serious danger of deception and disillusionment. We have had to correct too many overconfident philosophers of the past. Intellectual humility requires that we lower our sights and probe cautiously into the unknown.

2. There is no need of absolutes to keep us from drifting with the tide, like the opportunist, not caring where. The shorter-range goals that experience puts before us are a sufficient guide toward improving our own condition and working earnestly toward universal betterment. Like a sailor in a fog, we steer in what seems the most likely direction at the moment, with a memory for the course we have traveled and with our eyes open for any clearing ahead. We have to be ready for continual readjustment and change of course.

3. We work chiefly by the trial-and-error method, experimenting with the data at hand. Absolutes have been used to rule out certain possible fields of experimentation until some bold innovator defied the tabu and was thus able immeasurably to expand our mental horizon. As man progressively adapts himself to a constantly changing environment, he finds his theories on morals, though lagging far behind, gradually changing into more enlightened and humane judgments on human behavior. These have rarely been set as fixed goals to be achieved but were usually the practical result of wise experimentation.

4. To many the very idea of an absolutely last end or ultimate goal appears too rigid and stifling. What would we do when we had reached such an end? Would there be no further growth or progress? How could there be if the last is the absolutely last in the sense that there is nothing fur-

ther? Such stagnation holds no hope for anyone. Without novelty the adventure of existence would lose all its zest. There is more joy in the excitement of the chase than in bagging the quarry, and when the journey is interesting it is better to travel than to arrive.

5. According to Dewey's theory of the *continuity of means-ends*,* as there is no means that is not a means to an end, so there is no end that is not a means to a further end. The chain of means and ends is thus necessarily indefinite in length, and the notion of an absolutely last end is essentially incoherent. Anything like an ultimate fixed goal is both impossible as breaking off the continuity of means-ends, and undesirable as curtailing the flexibility and freedom of human progress.

These samples of argumentation should make the theory clear enough. Nonrelativists are ready with replies:

1. It is well to remind philosophers of intellectual humility and the limitations of the human mind, but should we be so humble as to refuse to look at the truth when it stares at us? Genuine humility shows itself in the acceptance of the evident truth more than in refusal to submit to evidence. If the real motive is intellectual fear of being deceived or disillusioned, and if there is no further reason why the relativist adopts his relativism, he makes this a last end and an absolute, whether he cares to call it so or not. Thus a proximate end is lifted to the status of an ultimate end without deserving the honor.

2. Life does require continual adjustments, not of ends, however, but of means. We must be ready to alter our course only if there is some port for which we are making and some reason for trying to arrive there, but there is no sense in cruising about a foggy sea on a voyage to nowhere. How do we know we are bettering our condition unless there is some fixed standard of good-

ness by which we can measure our approach to it?

3. The trial-and-error method is the normal way of experiment when we are searching for means to a known end. If there is no end, why make the trial and how tell success from error? The pragmatists are correct in criticizing those who set up their pet notions as absolutes not to be questioned and thus block off possible avenues of fruitful experimentation, but the fact that it is possible to adopt false absolutes does not prove that there are none. Relativism is likewise open to abuse. Logically it reduces to Protagoras'* view that only that is true which the perceiver perceives here and now and only as long as he perceives it. No science is possible on these skeptical terms.

4. Why must a last end or goal of life be something static that would freeze all further growth instead of a condition of perpetually assured growth? Here imagination can play one false. The fulfillment of the human person would have to be something corresponding to the nature of man, not some stifling suppression of it. If death is the end of all, as many relativists are willing to accept relatively, it is the most static and rigid of all last ends, nothingness. There the excitement of the chase has ended, and all along there never was a quarry to bag.

5. There is no proof for Dewey's theory of the continuity of means-ends. There is nothing in the nature of an end that must necessarily make it a means to a further end. Perhaps only felt wants demand satisfaction, but it is false to assume that wants arise only in an immediate situation. To find some answer to the riddle of life and to seek some meaning or purpose in existence as a whole is an unquenchable want felt in every human being, and to try to satisfy it has been the business of philosophy from the beginning. An ethics that strives to answer it but fails can be respected for its effort, but it is hard

---

*Dewey, *Theory of Valuation.*

*Plato, *Theaetetus,* §152 ff.

to excuse an ethics that dismisses it as nugatory.

ABSOLUTELY LAST END

Those who are not satisfied with relativism have the burden of proving the impossibility of an endless series of means and ends. Some are willing to take this as self-evident: if there must be an end or purpose for each one of the parts, there must also be one for the whole; it is nonsensical to think that, whereas each single thing in life is seen to have a meaning, no meaning can be found for the whole of life which these acts are meant to constitute. Others consider the matter important enough to be put into a formal argument. One of the best has been proposed by St. Thomas. A review of some simple definitions is helpful in understanding it.

A thing is intended either for its own sake or for the sake of something else. The former is an *end,* the latter a *means.* A means always supposes an end; it is called a means precisely because it lies in a mean, or middle, position between the agent and the end, and its use brings the agent to the end. The same thing may be both means and end in different respects, for it may be sought both for its own sake and for the sake of something further. This is called an *intermediate* end, and there may be a long series of such intermediate ends, as when we want A in order to get B, B in order to get C, C in order to get D, and so on.

That which is sought for its own sake and not for the sake of anything further is what is meant by a *last end* or *ultimate end.* It closes the series of means and ends. It may be a last end only in a relative sense, meaning that it closes a particular series but that the whole series is directed to some further end; thus the reception of an academic degree terminates one's education, but education itself has the further purpose of fitting one for life. In the full sense of the word, the last end means the *absolutely last end,*

which is directed to no further end at all, but to it everything else is directed. Since the end and the good are identified, a being's absolutely last end must also be its highest good.

In a series of means and ends we must distinguish the order of *intention* from the order of *execution.* The first thing that comes to mind (the order of intention) is the end, and the means are chosen with a view to accomplishing the end; but in the actual carrying out of the work (the order of execution) the means must be used first, and the last thing that is obtained is the end. This is the key to the argument, for whatever may be thought of the possibility of an infinite series in other matters, an infinite series of means and ends is quite impossible; thus there must be an *absolutely last end* to which the whole of human life is directed.

That which is first in the order of intention is the principle as it were moving the appetite; consequently if you remove this principle there will be nothing to move the appetite. On the other hand, the principle in execution is that wherein operation has its beginning; and if this principle be taken away no one will begin to work. Now the principle in the intention is the last end; while the principle in execution is the first of the things which are ordained to the end. Consequently on neither side is it possible to go on to infinity; since, if there were no last end, nothing would be desired nor would any action have its term nor would the intention of the agent be at rest; while, if there is no first thing among those that are ordained to the end, none would begin to work at anything and counsel would have no term but would continue indefinitely.[*]

When a man uses A to get B, B to get C, C to get D, he must (unless he is acting at random and irrationally) first desire D, and then find out that to get D he needs C, to get C he needs B, to get B he needs A. Thus his planning (intention) is in inverse order to his acting (execution). That which is first in intention is last in execu-

---

[*]St. Thomas, *Summa Theologica,* I-II, q. 1, a. 4.

tion, and vice versa. Thus the steps are as follows, starting with D:

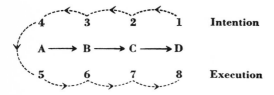

They are first planned out in the mind and then transferred to execution. If the planning went on forever, nothing would ever be done, for in rational action the execution cannot begin until the planning is complete. There must then be a point A (the proximate means) at which planning ends and execution begins. This closes the series on one side, but to arrive at point A in the planning, it was also necessary to begin somewhere. Neither A nor B nor C is wanted for itself. Unless there is some point D which is wanted for itself, neither A nor B nor C would be thought of, and no plan would be formed. Hence there must be some point D (the last end) which starts the whole process going. This closes the series on the other side. Hence in any intelligent procedure apart from fitful and random behavior, one must already have the last end in mind before beginning the first act. Man therefore not only acts for an end but for a last end.

But, one might say, this argument merely proves that there must be some end that is the last in a series, a relatively last end, not that there must be an absolutely last end to which all series of means and ends are directed and beyond which there can be nothing further. To this objection it is answered that the necessary logic of the argument carries it to all series of means and ends, and to all series of series. The very same reason which requires that a single series of means lead to an end requires that any series of series lead to an ultimate series, the last member of which is the absolutely last end, since neither a single means nor a series of means nor a series of series of means, no matter how far extended, would be chosen except for the sake of some end to which they all lead.

Another objection is that this argument proves too much and therefore nothing. A child would have to fix upon its last end and formulate a whole plan of life before it could even perform its first act, a supposition that flouts all experience. The answer is that what we described was the *rational* activity of a *mature* person, the use of means to end as directed by intellect in adult human behavior. The child comes only gradually to an understanding of life's purpose and is at first restricted to relative ends, but sometime between adolescence and maturity he must decide on the purpose of life as a whole or, as happens with the opportunist, find the question decided for him by default. In either case he is responsible, whether it be for choosing as he did or for choosing not to choose.

Does this mean that, once a person has chosen such a supreme goal in life, he is forever stuck with it? It seems that he should be, if it is an absolute; if he can change it, does that not show that it was merely provisional and relative? No. Even in the choosing of an absolutely ultimate goal, human error is possible. The possibility of error about the goal does not make the goal itself any less absolute, nor does the person commit himself to it only tentatively or provisionally. Certainty does not exclude the possibility but only the prudent fear of error; otherwise one could be certain of hardly anything. A man can commit himself wholeheartedly to a definite goal that he has chosen on mature reflection and thus be quite certain, without thereby closing his mind to all future knowledge. Succeeding periods of self-examination can bring greater maturity and enlightenment. If further experience and reflection show that he has made a mistake, he will correct the error and reform his decision. One can never be so stuck with an erroneous goal in life that the error cannot be corrected. On the other hand, no one should be afraid of being stuck with the truth, so to speak. The truth does cling to anyone who has found it, and that was why he sought it.

Supposing that there is an absolutely ultimate end for man, is there any reason it must be one and the same for all men? To grant various ultimate ends to different individuals and groups and historical eras might satisfy the claims of some cultural relativists. It is difficult to answer this question without determining just what the absolutely last end of man is, and we have not yet laid all the groundwork. For the moment we can say that, whereas subordinate ends may differ, the absolutely last end for man, whatever it is, would have to be something that is proper to *man as man,* and therefore would not be something different for various persons, races, classes, epochs, or cultures. Men differ subjectively in their judgments on what constitutes the ultimate goal of life, but we are dealing with the objective truth these judgments are groping to discover and express. Nor is each person faced with a number of possible last ends among which he might choose. He did not choose to be a man but finds himself one, like it or not. Only one last end or highest good is offered to us as men. We may take it or leave it, but we have no more option for a substitute than we have for becoming something other than human.

THE RELATIVE AND
THE ABSOLUTE

The controversy between relativists and absolutists involves the whole of one's metaphysical outlook. We cannot take up this larger issue but must restrict ourselves to the way in which these two attitudes affect our subject, ethics.

Much can be said in favor of relativism, especially if one be content to accept a relative form of relativism. The relativist who denies all absolutes contradicts himself by holding at least one absolute: the proposition that everything is relative. If absolutely everything is relative, then relativity itself becomes the absolute, and the distinction between relativity and absoluteness disappears. If only relatively everything is relative, then the absoluteness of relativity could be diluted only by the introduction of some nonrelative element, some absolute. Relativism does not go wrong by the admission of relativity but by the exclusion of any absolute to which all relatives could be relative.

Certainly there is no thing which is not related to some other thing, in fact, to all other things. Knowledge and truth are relations; the mere fact that we know a thing establishes a relation between it and us. Desire and goodness are relations; that a thing is good for us merely expresses a kind of relation it has to us. In the present chapter we said much about means and ends; these terms make no sense except in relation to each other. This last pair is useful to illustrate the fact that not all relatives are equally relative. There is less relativity in ends than in means. The means, taken precisely as means, exist wholly for the sake of the ends they serve, whereas the ends do not exist for the sake of the means that lead to them. The end, besides its relative aspect toward the means, has also an independent and absolute aspect.

This may give us our key to the solution. Relative and absolute are not things but ways of looking at things. If we look at the way a thing is toward something else, we stress its relative aspect; if we consider it merely as it is in itself, without denying but only disregarding its bearing on others, we stress its absolute aspect. In this way the same thing can be both absolute and relative at once, though not in the same respect. The saying, then, that everything is relative is true in the sense that everything has a relative aspect; false, in the sense that nothing has any absolute aspect.

When we speak of an absolutely last end, we do not mean that this end has no relation to us. It is absolute because there is no further end, relative because it is *our* end, one that *we* must achieve. To put before us an endless series of ends implies that, when all is said and done, there is no end to which we are related, and this is to make an absolute of ourselves. Some relativists may wish to do this and are merely saying so in a disguised fashion. We shall take up later the question of whether we can be our own absolutely last end.

In ethics, everything else but the absolutely last end is relative, and even this, as we just said, is relative to us, though not relative to a further end. All the means of living the moral life are relative to the end of moral living and thus to the person whose life it is. Only a few propositions in ethics will be announced absolutely, and these will turn out to be variants of a single proposition of such transcending generality that no more all-embracing proposition could be found to which it might be subordinated.

Pragmatism affords a very important secondary criterion of morality, for many acts are indifferent in themselves but become good or bad because of their consequences. Remove or modify these consequences and the acts change their moral significance. The difficulty with pragmatism is its insistence that every act is of this type and its failure to provide any moral criterion for judging the consequences except by further and further consequences forever.

These remarks have been made to show the importance of the relative and the pragmatic in ethics. They also have been made to show that the relative is inherently unintelligible except in terms of some absolute, and that the pragmatic must be judged in terms of some theory by which good and bad consequences can be discerned.

SUMMARY

Ethical *relativism* holds that there is nothing good or bad absolutely, but all morality is relative to the individual or to society.

Opportunism refuses to have a goal in life so as to remain open and uncommitted. But this aimlessness is itself an aim.

Pragmatism is a relativism that judges the moral value of acts by their consequences, not limiting itself, as utilitarianism does, to pleasurable ones. Dewey's *instrumentalism* is a form of pragmatism that admits proximate goals but no ultimate goal for human life, according to his theory of the continuity of means-ends.

Reasons *for:* We have been disillusioned too often, must be ready for continual readjustments, work by trial-and-error, find an absolute goal too rigid and stifling, and must be open for future progress.

Reasons *against:* We are not wholly deceived, use trial-and-error and make readjustments only to a known end, see no reason why an ultimate end must be static, and fail to see how progress is progress if it goes nowhere.

That all human conduct is for a last end and a highest good is argued thus: There cannot be an infinite series of means and ends, since ends are known before means can be chosen toward them, but the means must be used first before the end is achieved; intention and execution being thus in inverse order, the last end is the first thing desired and the last attained; if there is no last end, nothing is desired and no activity can be started.

The relative is intelligible only if there is some absolute to which all relatives are relative. Even an absolutely last end is relative to us but not relative to any further end. If everything is judged on its consequences, and these on their consequences, and so on, there is really no criterion of consequences or of anything.

QUESTIONS FOR DISCUSSION

1 Ethics is said to be a practical science. How otherwise can the practicality of ethics be determined than by seeing whether it works out in practice? Is not this precisely the claim of pragmatism?

2 Life is always an unfinished affair. One goes as far as possible in the allotted time, which is unequal and relative to each person. No absolute goal but only a relative goal is possible in this, the human condition.

3 Much of morality is relative to the times: clothes, reading, theater, dancing. What our ancestors banned we accept as normal. Some see in the new ways a return to paganism, others a liberation from puritanical tabus. Is this true of all morality? Why only of some?

4 Relativism and pragmatism are open to the future. Absolutism and rationalism are closed within an absolute rational system. Which offers more scope for man's freedom? Which offers a goal worth using one's freedom for?

5 Would a relativist be convinced by the argument given for a last end? What is the aim of philosophical argument: to convert other people to accept your view or to establish truth for yourself and anyone else willing to see? Or is it both? Or something else?

READINGS

Plato in the *Protagoras* and the *Theaetetus* discusses the relativity of knowledge without limiting it to ethical knowledge.

St. Thomas' arguments on man's last end are in the *Summa Theologica*, I-II, q. 1, aa. 1-2, 4-7; and *Summa Contra Gentiles*, bk. III, ch. 2-3.

William James argues against absolutes in his *Pragmatism*. For John Dewey's thought see *Human Nature and Conduct, The Quest for Certainty*, and *Reconstruction in Philosophy*. Eliseo Vivas, *The Moral Life and the Ethical Life*, ch. 6-8, is strongly critical of Dewey.

Edward Westermarck's two books, *The Origin and Development of the Moral Ideas* and *Ethical Relativity*, are classical statements of relativism. See also Moritz Schlick, *Problems of Ethics*, ch. 5; two articles from the *Journal of Philosophy:* Paul Taylor, "Social Science and Ethical Relativism," LV, 1 (1958); and Carl Wellman, "The Ethical Implications of Cultural Relativity," LX, 7 (1963).

Austin Fagothey, *Right and Reason—an Anthology*, contains a selection from John Dewey's *Theory of Valuation*.

CHAPTER 9

INTUITION

PROBLEM

All the ethical theories discussed so far imply some norm or standard of morality. They not only proclaim the fact that morality exists but also that there is some way of distinguishing the good from the evil, the right from the wrong. Ethical theories do not differ greatly in the actual codes of morality they adopt. The list of approved and disapproved acts, despite some glaring exceptions, is in general much the same. Where they differ most is in their reasons for the approval or disapproval, in the principles on which they base their judgment about morality, that is to say, in the norm or standard by which they judge morality.

This agreement about the facts and disagreement about the reasons is explained, say some moralists, by the hypothesis that we just know directly what is right and what is wrong. They think that we have a feel, a sense, an instinct, whatever one wants to call it, that immediately manifests to us what is good and what is evil in the moral sphere, and this is basically the same in all of us. It is when we come to explanations, to study, reasoning, and proof, that we begin to diverge in our views because we now are committing ourselves to some particular ethical theory.

The view that moral knowledge is direct, immediate, or intuitive, though out of favor with philosophers today, has always had a popular appeal. It gives one a sense of infallibility without having to give any reasons, for all moral problems are solved by placing them before the scrutiny of the internal moral faculty, which then delivers its oracular verdict. That this would be an easy solution to our moral difficulties is hardly an argument against it, and we cannot afford to pass it by unexamined. We have the following questions:

1. What is meant by a norm or standard of morality?
2. What are the reasons for and against a special moral faculty?
3. Is there intuition without a special faculty?
4. How is our first moral knowledge obtained?
5. How much truth, if any, is there in intuitionism?

MEANING OF A NORM

A norm is a rule, standard, or measure; it is something fixed with which we can compare something else whose nature, size, or qualities we doubt. Thus a norm of *morality* will be a rule, standard, or measure by which we can gauge the morality of an act, its goodness or badness. It will be something with which an act must positively agree to be morally good, with which it must positively disagree to be morally bad, and toward which it must be neutral to be morally indifferent.

A norm may be proximate or ultimate. To find out whether a space is a yard long, we apply a yardstick to it. But how do the markers of yardsticks determine what a true yard is? They measure their yardsticks by some officially recognized yard beyond which there is no appeal, such as the metal yard bar kept in London or a definite mathematical fraction of the metal meter bar kept in Paris. In general, a *proximate* or *derived* norm is one directly applicable to the thing to be measured and is here at hand ready for use; an *ultimate* or *original* norm is the last reason why the proximate norm is what it is. Theoretically, the same thing can fulfill the functions of both ultimate and proximate norms. It is possible to carry a thing to London or Paris and measure it by the metal bar there, but in practice this is inconvenient, and it is usual to have two concrete embodiments of the same abstract measure, one for practical use and one for ultimate reference.

That there must be some norm of morality is evident, if one admits the existence of morality at all. It would be nonsensical to suppose that one is expected to do the good and avoid the evil while being unable to distinguish one class of acts from the other. There must be a proximate norm, for otherwise the measure would be useless, inapplicable to individual concrete acts, which are the only kind that can actually exist. There must be an ultimate norm, for otherwise there would be nothing to guarantee the validity of the proximate norm.

THE MORAL SENSE THEORY

That the perception of moral good and evil is the work of some faculty distinct from the intellect or reason was held by a group of British moralists in the late seventeenth and throughout the eighteenth century. This special faculty they called the *moral instinct* or *moral intuition* or *moral sense*.

1. Shaftesbury,* who was much taken up with speculations on the beautiful, recognized that besides its other forms there is also moral beauty, that a moral life is really a beautiful life. The sense of beauty he considered a special faculty of the mind, and when applied to moral beauty it becomes the moral sense. Moral beauty consists in a proper balancing of public and private affections, of selfish and social impulses, resulting in a well-rounded and harmonious life. This theory is called *moral aestheticism.*

2. Francis Hutcheson* developed Shaftesbury's views by separating the moral sense from the aesthetic sense, giving to the former the specific function of distinguishing right from wrong. Joseph Butler† took the rather obvious step of identifying the moral sense with conscience, which he seems to consider a faculty distinct from the intellect. Thomas Reid, representative of the Scottish School of Common Sense philosophy, sums up the *moral sense theory* as follows:

> The abstract notion of moral good and ill would be of no use to direct our life, if we had not the power of applying it to particular actions, and determining what is morally good, and what is morally ill.
>
> Some philosophers, with whom I agree, ascribe this to an original power or faculty in man, which they call the *Moral Sense*, the *Moral Faculty*, *Conscience*. . . .
>
> In its dignity it is, without doubt, far superior to every other power of the mind; but there is this analogy between it and the external senses, that, as by them we have not only the original conceptions of the various qualities of bodies, but the original judgment that this body has such a quality, that such another; so by our moral faculty, we have both the original conceptions of right and wrong in conduct, of merit and demerit, and the original judgments that this conduct is right, that is wrong; that this character has worth, that demerit.‡

---

*Hutcheson, *Inquiry into the Original of Our Ideas of Beauty and Virtue,* Treatise II, sec. I.
†Butler, *Fifteen Sermons upon Human Nature,* Sermons II and III.
‡Reid, *Essays on the Active Powers of Man.* Essay III, pt. III, ch. 6.

---

*Shaftesbury (Anthony Ashley Cooper, third Earl of Shaftesbury), *Characteristics of Men, Manners, Opinions, and Times,* bk. I, pt. II, §3; bk. II, pt. I, §1.

3. Adam Smith, the economist, approaches ethics from the standpoint of psychological analysis. The moral faculty or conscience is an instinctive sentiment of sympathy, which he explains in a novel way:

> We either approve or disapprove of our own conduct, according as we feel that, when we place ourselves in the situation of another man, and view it, as it were, with his eyes, and from his station, we either can or cannot enter into and sympathize with the sentiments and motives which influence it. . . .
>
> When I endeavor to examine my own conduct, when I endeavor to pass sentence upon it, and either to approve or condemn it, it is evident that, in all such cases, I divide myself, as it were, into two persons; and that I, the examiner and judge, represent a different character from that other I, the person whose conduct is examined into and judged of.*

These theories all demand some faculty distinct from the intellect to judge of right and wrong, either making this its sole function or identifying it with the aesthetic sense or with conscience or with the sentiment of sympathy. David Hume,† though not interested in any special faculty, agrees with Smith in reducing morality to feeling, especially to the sentiment of humanity, benevolence, or sympathy, and insists that moral distinctions are not derived from reason. The moral intuitionism of Ralph Cudworth‡ and Samuel Clarke§ belongs in the same class of opinions, for though they make the intellect the faculty of judging right from wrong, they have it do so, not by any process of reasoning, but by an immediate intellectual intuition of the eternal fitness of things, which is an expression of the Divine Ideas.

Critics of these views reject any need for a special moral faculty distinct from the intellect. Moral judgments are not of an essentially different nature from other judgments. To understand is the function of the intellect. Any faculty other than the intellect would not understand why certain actions are good or bad. To make any such other faculty the norm would lower man's moral life to the instinctive and brutish. Why should we expect man to use his reason in the fields of science, business, law, and politics but not in the realm of morals and in the goal of life itself? In particular:

1. To identify the moral sense with the aesthetic sense solves no problem, for we need no special faculty for the perception of the beautiful. It is true that there is moral beauty, that virtue is beautiful and vice is ugly, but this judgment comes from intellectual reflection and not from immediate perception. It is not always their goodness that attracts us to good people, and we often have a sneaking admiration for splendid vices.

2. Conscience is the norm of subjective, not of objective, morality. It is not a special faculty but only the name for the intellect in its judgment of the morality of a particular concrete act here and now. The judgment of conscience is the conclusion of a syllogism arrived at by a process of intellectual reasoning. Conscience criticizes our actions according to the norms we have but does not set up those norms.

3. Sentiments, even the noblest, such as sympathy, cannot be a reliable guide to right and wrong. They are constantly varying, depending on our physical condition and emotional mood. The same act would be good or bad, according to one's feelings. Even if acts be classified by the feelings they commonly evoke rather than by the passing feeling of the moment, some objective reason must be assigned why they commonly evoke such feelings, and this objective reason will be the norm.

---

*Smith, *Theory of Moral Sentiments,* pt. III, ch. 1.
†Hume, *Treatise on Human Nature,* bk. III; also *Inquiry Concerning the Principles of Morals.*
‡Cudworth, *Treatise Concerning Eternal and Immutable Morality,* bk. IV, ch. 6.
§Clarke, *Discourse upon Natural Religion,* I.

INTUITIONISM IN GENERAL

The postulating of a special faculty for the perception of right and wrong has now become almost obsolete together with the general trend away from faculty psychology. It is still quite possible, however, to hold for some direct, immediate, intuitive knowledge of morality without attributing such knowledge to any special faculty. The following are some general reasons for moral intuitionism.

1. Any well-meaning person seems to have an immediate sense of what is right and what is wrong. Many who have had hardly any opportunity for moral instruction do nevertheless have a basic moral awareness. The great value of moral instruction is to settle doubtful details, to supply one with cogent reasons, and to bring consistency into one's moral beliefs, but all this is not necessary for the first formation of those beliefs.

2. Men had moral ideas and convictions long before philosophers developed a formal study of ethics. This prephilosophical knowledge of right and wrong was not reasoned out and logically criticized. It was therefore a spontaneous knowledge occurring to the mind without consciously directed reasoning, and hence it must come from some intuitive or insightful activity of the mind in recognizing the right and the wrong and discriminating between them.

3. Our reasoning on moral matters, when we do use it, is subsequent and confirmatory to an initial direct perception of rightness and wrongness. We first see that the course of action is right or wrong, as the case may be, and then look for reasons. If our reasoning leads to an answer contradictory to our spontaneous moral judgment, we tend to let the reasoning go and stick to our simple moral intuition, which we consider a surer guide than our elaborate arguments, whose very elaborateness can arouse a suspicion of rationalization.

4. Our reasoning can go wrong on moral matters as easily as on other matters. Though invincible ignorance excuses, we cannot allow it to govern so large a share of our lives that our moral responsibility is on the verge of vanishing. We must have some way of deciding basic moral issues. That we cannot do so by reasoning, studying, and philosophizing is evident from the many contradictory schools of ethical thought. Therefore we have to rely on some kind of moral instinct, insight, or intuition, which can act as a sure guide.

On the other hand there are serious difficulties against any form of intuitionism:

1. The word *intuition* has fallen on bad days and stirs up so much misunderstanding that it can hardly be used. Intuition is Latin for insight, a looking in, and therefore a very appropriate word for the direct activity of the intellect in grasping self-evident truths. But it has become associated with hunches, wild guesses, irrational inspirations, clairvoyance, and other fancies so lacking in scientific respectability as to give utterly the wrong impression. It should be clear that guesses and hunches are of no more value in the ethical sphere than in any other sphere.

2. We have no inborn set of moral rules with which we might compare our acts to see whether they are moral or not. There is no evidence for the existence of any innate ideas in the mind of man, including ethical ideas. All our knowledge comes from experience, and our moral ideas are likewise derived from experience. We do not have any faculty, not even conscience, that automatically flashes a warning signal as soon as we think of doing something wrong. If conscience seems to act in this way, it is nothing but habit, by which we have become accustomed through training to avoid actions of a certain kind and to judge them to be wrong. Such habitual action is quite different from instinctive action, and such judgments need not be intuitive.

3. An appeal to intuition has the disadvantage of being immune to objective

criticism. One claims that he sees it, and no one can prove that he does not; another claims that he does not see it, and no one can prove that he does. The two claims are not contradictory, for each reports only his own experience. Such intuitive knowledge, if it exists, can be of benefit only to the possessor and cannot be used to convince anyone else. Unless most people testify to having the same intuition (as does happen, for example, regarding sense experience), this sort of private knowledge lacks the universal character of scientific knowledge. Since there is no common agreement on moral intuitions, an appeal to intuition in morals can result only in subjectivism, each one following his own personal moral code revealed to him by his own personal insights.

4. Those who find that they do not experience moral intuitions are either left without any ethics while obliged to live ethically, or are obliged to develop an ethical theory on other grounds. They have to judge both their own ethical theory and the intuitionist theory on some other basis than intuition, which by hypothesis they themselves do not possess. The intuitionists, however, must either appeal to intuition to establish the truth of their own theory, thus convincing only themselves, or they must abandon intuition and resort to rational argument when it comes to establishing their theory. Either way shows the weakness of the method.

Despite these and similar criticisms of an intuitionist ethics, we can still ask whether it is possible to remove all intuition from ethics. Certainly we shall remove intuition in the sense of hunches and guesses, in the sense of a special faculty for the perception of morals, and also in the sense of a direct apprehension of moral rules immediately applicable to particular actions. These illegitimate uses of intuition have tended to ruin the whole concept.

However, there remains a legitimate use. Not all knowledge can be derived from previous knowledge. There must be some original knowledge, some primitive experience, some immediate apprehension from which derived knowledge can originate. Thus not all knowledge can be the result of a reasoning process. Premises are proved by previous premises and these by others still more previous, but the process cannot go on forever or nothing will ever be proved. Somewhere one must come to direct experience (and this is intuition in the original meaning of the term) or to some principle that cannot be proved and needs no proof because it is self-evident.*

In ethics there are two particular areas in which we must appeal to such direct and underived knowledge: one is the kind of knowledge of morals man had before developing a scientific ethics, and the other is the first or basic moral principle on which scientific ethics rests. In other words, the development of ethics in history must have been preceded by an era in which man had ethical ideas that were not the result of reasoned proof, and even after he has developed a scientific ethics he still has logically to trace it back to some immediately known and underived principles. The first of these principles is called connatural knowledge, our next topic.

CONNATURAL KNOWLEDGE

A person need not have studied ethics to know right from wrong. Ethics makes a formal and sophisticated investigation into the moral notions we already have, confirming or correcting our more primitive knowledge. How did we obtain this primitive knowledge, and how accurate is it? A child of today will receive it from his parents, teachers, and companions, and from religious instruction, social custom, and civil law. But how did they get it? Furthermore, the child turned youth will begin to criticize

---

*See Aristotle, *Posterior Analytics,* bk. II, ch. 19; *Metaphysics,* bk. IV, ch. 4

what has been told him, thus showing some source of knowledge besides tradition.

This primitive way of knowing is often called *knowledge by inclination* or *by connaturality;* it is connatural in the sense that it comes with our nature.* It is not innate but is easily picked up just by the experience of living. It is a self-awareness that reveals our own natures to ourselves, a direct perception of the powers we possess, of their clamor for exercise, and of the appropriate objects on which they are to be exercised. We do not have to reason the matter out to know what our eyes and hands and legs are for, what our minds and wills are for. We use them without question, knowing without argument that it is right to use them. Men sought food before they studied the science of nutrition, reproduced without benefit of genetics, trained their children before child psychology, formed families and cities without sociology, spoke without linguistics, claimed their due without law courts, and lived moral lives without a formal study of ethics.

This knowledge is an act not of the intellect alone but of the intellect plus the affections and appetites, the emotions and the will. It is nonlogical, nondiscursive knowledge, nonconceptual in its lack of clearly defined concepts, rational in the sense that it is done by the reason or intellect, and nonrational in the sense that it is not argumentative or demonstrative or scientific. In it the head consults the heart.

It is through connaturality that moral consciousness attains a kind of knowing—inexpressible in words and notions—of the deepest dispositions—longings, fears, hopes or despairs, primeval loves and options—involved in the night of the subjectivity. When a man makes a free decision, he takes into account not only all that he possesses of moral science and factual information, and which is manifested to him in concepts and notions, but also all the secret elements of evaluation which depend on what he is, and which are known to him through inclination, through his own actual propensities and his own virtues, if he has any.*

We began our study of ethics with the recognition of a fact, that men do have a sense of right and wrong, that they do make moral judgments. Our study would be incomplete if we made no effort to isolate the kind of knowledge that accounts for this fact. We should not be disturbed at being unable to describe it more clearly, for it is the nature of prescientific knowledge to be obscure, unformulated, and unreflective. When we reflect on it, conceptualize it, define its terms, catalogue its contents, pose its problems, and prove its theorems, it ceases to be connatural knowledge and becomes moral philosophy or ethics. Connatural knowledge is not immune from error and needs the criticism, correction, and development ethics can give it. In practical living the two continue side by side, for a reflective study does not eliminate the very thing it is studying.

Is this connatural knowledge intuitive? Since it is nonlogical, nondiscursive, nonargumentative, it can be called intuitive in the best sense of that misused term, in the sense of a directly perceptive and insightful experience. Notice that it makes no claim to infallibility, that it offers itself for critical examination, that it is quite willing to step down and yield to rationally investigated knowledge. Yet it is through this connatural knowledge that man first recognizes moral value and forms his moral ideal, that he has his first glimmering of moral obligation and his first thoughts of law, that he begins organizing his life purposively for the attainment of a meaningful end.

THE FIRST MORAL PRINCIPLE

The second area in ethics in which a direct, insightful, or intuitive knowledge is unavoidable is that of first principles, from

---

*St. Thomas, *Summa Theologica*, I-II, q. 94, a. 2; II-II, q. 45, a. 2.

*Maritain, *The Range of Reason*, ch. 3, p. 26.

which all other moral principles and directing norms are logically derived. Even a philosophically developed and fully sophisticated theory of morals will have to rest on some basic bedrock that accounts for itself and requires no further support beneath it. Ethics is not the kind of subject that can be based on a postulational system, logically drawing consistent conclusions from unverified assumptions, so that the whole theory achieves only a hypothetical truth. Ethics deals with real life, with the way a man must regulate his conduct in the actual world of experience, and since he cannot go through the experience of life again, failure in the enterprise is irremediable disaster. Hence he must have some way of knowing with certainty the basic principles from which all the rest of his ethical knowledge is derived.

One of the continually controverted questions is whether the *ought* can be derived from the *is*. If it can, then it could be said that ethics needs no self-evident principles, since its basic principle can be derived from other sciences, and ultimately from metaphysics, which is preeminently the science of being as being, of the *is*. Since Hume* emphatically stated the impossibility of deriving the *ought* from the *is*, mainly on the obvious ground that you cannot get an *ought* in the conclusion when there was none in the premises, many have considered the question settled. Some analysts, however, have resurrected the problem and find it a stimulating linguistic exercise.†

Hume and Thomas Aquinas have little in common in their general philosophical

outlook; yet they seem to agree, though for different reasons, on the underivability of the *ought* from the *is*. On first principles St. Thomas says:

> That which falls first under apprehension is *being*, the understanding of which is included in all things whatsoever a man apprehends. Therefore the first indemonstrable principle is that *the same thing cannot be affirmed and denied at the same time*, which is based on the notion of *being* and *not-being*: and on this principle all others are based, as is stated in *Metaphysics* iv.* Now as *being* is the first thing that falls under the apprehension absolutely, so *good* is the first thing that falls under the apprehension of the practical reason, which is directed to action (since every agent acts for an end, which has the nature of good). Consequently, the first principle in the practical reason is one founded on the nature of good, namely, that *good is that which all things seek after*. Hence this is the first precept of law, that *good is to be done and promoted, and evil is to be avoided*. All other precepts of the natural law are based upon this; so that all the things which the practical reason naturally apprehends as man's good belong to the natural law under the form of things to be done or avoided.†

It is clear that St. Thomas is speaking in terms of natural law, a subject we are not yet ready to discuss, but what he says about the first principle of morals can be understood independently of the conclusions that can be drawn from it and whether they assume the form of law or not. Before any law is possible there is logically presupposed such a thing as obligation, by which the subjects of the law are morally enjoined to keep it, and an infinite series of laws and obligations would solve nothing. Thus the first principle of the moral life, which can be stated in various ways: "Do good and avoid evil," "Lead a life of virtue," "Be the kind of man you ought to be," "To yourself be true," is not so much a precept of the natural law as a first principle and presupposition of all moral living. One may ask intelligently,

---

*Hume, *Treatise of Human Nature*, bk. III, pt. I, section 1, end.

†See for example Searle, John R., "How to Derive 'Ought' from 'Is,' " *Philosophical Review*, vol. 73, 1964, pp. 43-58. The author argues ingeniously from the *fact* of making a promise to the *obligation* of keeping it, but one may ask whether the *ought* is not already surreptitiously contained in the meaning of the word *promise*.

---

*Aristotle, *Metaphysics*, bk. IV, ch. 3, 1005b 29.

†St. Thomas, *Summa Theologica*, I-II, q. 94, a. 2.

"Why should I be moral?" but not, "Should I be moral?" just as in metaphysics one may ask, "What am I?" but there is no point in arguing the question, "Am I?"

To conclude this discussion, we may note that we have the following options:

1. We may admit moral intuition, with or without a special faculty for it, to which we can appeal for obtaining immediate insight into the moral quality of each particular act. There is no objective evidence for any such intuition.

2. We may deny moral intuition altogether. In this way we get rid of unverifiable subjective claims but are unable to explain the historically primitive and logically underived knowledge from which our moral reasoning can proceed.

3. We may reduce moral intuition to its narrowest scope, admitting it only where we cannot do without it. Intuition is thus confined to the intellect's grasp of self-evident truths and first indemonstrable principles.

The first two alternatives beget such unresolvable difficulties that any other alternative is preferable. The third option remains as the only tenable one. It does not give us a whole philosophy of intuitive ethics any more than a list of axioms gives us a geometry or stargazing gives us an astronomy. It only supplies us with the beginnings from which a science of ethics must be developed by further exercise of our intelligence.

SUMMARY

A *norm of morality* is a standard to which we can compare human acts to determine their goodness or badness. A *proximate* norm is immediately applicable to the acts; an *ultimate* norm guarantees the validity of the proximate norm. There must be some norm of morality, or else one would be obliged to do good and avoid evil without being able to distinguish them.

The *moral sense theory* appeals to a faculty distinct from the intellect for judging right from wrong. Most ethicians see no need for such a faculty; it would make moral conduct nonrational and unworthy of an intelligent human being.

Intuitionism in general holds that man has direct, immediate, or intuitive knowledge of morality, with or without a special faculty.

Reasons *for:* People can tell right from wrong without giving reasons, know right and wrong without studying ethics, use reasoning to confirm their spontaneous judgments, and reject arguments that contradict their basic moral beliefs.

Reasons *against:* Intuition is too vague a word to be of much use, we have no innate moral ideas or principles, intuition would be a purely subjective experience and scientifically useless, and the intuitionist can convince no one but himself.

There is a legitimate use for *intuition* in the sense of an intellectual acceptance of self-evident truths.

Connatural knowledge is the name for prescientific knowledge that is neither innate nor instinctive but comes from the use of our natural inclinations. It is knowledge in the intellect, but it is unformulated, unreflective, nonconceptual, and nondiscursive, because it has not been clearly defined and argued out. Ethics is the endeavor to formulate, criticize, correct, develop, and prove these primitive moral judgments.

If the first moral principle, such as "Do good and avoid evil," is not intuitively known, it must be derived from some other knowledge. It is debated whether the *ought* can be derived from the *is*, but so far no one seems to have done it convincingly. Thus for all practical purposes we must take the first moral principle as intuitively known and self-evident.

QUESTIONS FOR DISCUSSION

1 The search for ethical norms is futile. Since each school of ethical thought proposes a different norm, what is needed is a norm for ethical norms. But such a norm would itself be an ethical norm, and so on forever. What do you think of this argument?

2 If one denies primitive moral intuition, where does one begin? If you begin with sense experience, is not this a form of intuition? If you begin with reasoning, how do you know the first principles from which reasoning starts?

3 Those who deny special faculties in man introduce the same thing under other names: abilities, capacities, functions, powers, drives, and so on. Moral knowledge is a special kind of knowledge. Why not a special faculty for it?

4 Is it possible to argue from "is" to "ought"? Can "ought" be found in the conclusion if it is not in the premises? If "ought" must be in the premises, how does one arrive at the primitive "ought" on which other "oughts" logically depend? Is it a mere intuition?

5 Can you actually prove that there is such a thing as connatural knowledge? If it is nonscientific and nonphilosophical, it is not strictly ethical knowledge. But is it not moral knowledge? And are not "moral" and "ethical" the same? What is the difference, if any?

READINGS

The eighteenth-century British moralists and their main works are mentioned in the footnotes to the text. Selections can be found in convenient form in L. A. Selby-Bigge, *The British Moralists;* D. D. Raphael, *British Moralists;* Benjamin Rand, *The Classical Moralists;* and other collections.

Evaluation of Spinoza, Butler, Hume, Kant, and Sidgwick, all of whom contain some intuitionism, is found in C. D. Broad's *Five Types of Ethical Theory.*

W. D. Ross, *The Right and the Good* and *Foundations of Ethics;* A. C. Ewing, *Ethics,* ch. 1 and 7; and H. A. Prichard, *Moral Obligation,* advocate a limited intuitionism.

W. D. Hudson, *The Is/Ought Question,* has whole book of modern articles on both sides this vexed problem.

On connatural knowledge read St. Thomas, *Summa Theologica,* I-II, q. 94, a. 2; II-II, q. 4 a. 2. Also read Jacques Maritain's explanatio of it in *The Range of Reason,* ch. 3.

Austin Fagothey, *Right and Reason—an Anthol gy,* contains St. Thomas' *Summa Theologic* I-II, q. 94, a. 2; Maritain, *The Range of Rea son,* ch. 3; and H. A. Prichard's essay, "Do Moral Philosophy Rest on a Mistake," ch. 1 his *Moral Obligation.*

CHAPTER 10

REASON

PROBLEM

If we have no sense or instinct that immediately points out to us what is right and what is wrong, and if we cannot trust our feelings or emotions to render a reliable judgment, what can we use as a norm of morality? The immediate intellectual apprehension of the first moral principle, "Do good and avoid evil," can indeed be the bedrock of all thinking about morals, but it cannot be a norm, for it gives no further indication of just what is the good and just what is the evil.

One source still left to us is the proper use of human reason. This looks promising. We should not be surprised to find that moral knowledge is developed in the same way as all other knowledge and its truth established in the same way as all other truth. What have we been using all along in our evaluation of various ethical theories but the judgment of reason? Reason should be able not only to judge the value of ethical theories but also to judge the moral value of the actions the theories are constructed to explain.

That the good life is the life of reason, a life of intelligently controlled energy directing the thrust of our being, a life of rationally chosen means conducive to a rationally apprehended end, was a commonplace among the Greek philosophers. For Plato the man in whom the rational is predominant is the philosopher, capable of ruling a state because he is capable of ruling himself. For Aristotle the intellectual virtue of prudence or practical wisdom dictates the midpoint between excess and defect, and thus acts as the norm regulating the practice of the other virtues in which the moral life consists. The Stoics call reason the *hegemonikon*, or ruling power, by which a man conforms himself to the law of nature, frees himself from being a plaything of his feelings, and lives the life of a wise man. Even the Epicureans think that the pursuit of pleasure must be conducted in a rational way if it is to lead to any sort of tolerable life. In succeeding ages reason has played an honored part in nearly all theories of ethics.

The problem arises from the fact that human reason, though a trustworthy instrument in itself, is not immune from abuse. The philosopher has the task, not only of determining as exactly as possible the critical sensitivity of his instrument, but also of learning how to use it so that it actually does yield the desired results. When and how can reason go wrong and, if it does, what is the corrective? We have the following questions:

1. When is human reason right?
2. How does right reason act as an ethical norm?
3. How is right reason applied to human nature?
4. How practical is right reason as a norm?

MEANING OF RIGHT REASON

Human reason does not function in a vacuum but needs some data to go on, some findings from which the reasoning process can take its start. It derives them from experience, and in the ethical field not only from examination of our own conduct but also from the observation of human life around us and the actions we see men performing. Certain patterns in human behavior begin to emerge, and we group men's actions into various classes according to their common traits. We ask ourselves why we group them the way we do and state our reasons in the form of principles, expressing in general terms the characteristics that acts must have to deserve inclusion in one group rather than another. We turn to an examination of the principles themselves, rejecting some as inadequate, correcting others, and accepting those which can survive the scrutiny. We then attempt the task of ordering the accepted principles into a scheme or system that will give intelligibility to the whole.

The *inductive* use of reason is this finding of general principles in the particular human actions observed. It defines and compares concepts, and states and establishes rules, organizing both into wider and wider formulations, and more and more comprehensive generalizations, until it finally subsumes the whole under the universal embrace of the good. It sees, not only that they can be organized in this way, but also that their intelligibility demands that they be so organized, since they are logically interdependent. The *deductive* use of reason applies these principles to new specific acts a man is thinking of doing, pointing out to him why this mode of conduct is good or bad because of the relationship it has to him as a human being and to those among whom he must live. All this is an endeavor to *understand* what is good or bad about one's conduct, and why. Understanding, as we should expect, is done by the understanding, other names for which are intellect and reason.

The goal of reason in thus trying to work out a systematization of ethics would be a luminously intelligible concatenation of moral concepts and principles from the most general down to the most particular hierarchically grading the whole ethical life. Reason, being what it is, would delight in such an arrangement, just as it delights in a mathematical problem elegantly and brilliantly solved. The prospect looks chilling. Who would want to live in such a structural framework of icy logic? We need have no fear. The matter is far too complex and the human being too full of surprises for us ever to work out a complete system of human living. We will never be able to give man a rule book listing the goodness or badness of every possible form of human act, so that all he need do is look it up.

Reason and the rational have assumed a connotation today that need not be associated with these words. Perhaps the computer world in which we are beginning to live is responsible for our thinking of reason as behaving in a cold, impersonal, unfeeling, and loveless manner. We tend to forget that human reason is not something separate from man and functioning on its own. Rather it is part of man, the most distinctively human part of him. Since the feelings and emotions and sensibilities are also part of man, he would be a very unreasonable man who would fail to integrate them into whatever program he is devising for himself. Thus the reasonable man, if he is truly reasonable, is the total man.

But in man's totality a certain preeminence is given to reason because of its critical ability. The various other parts or aspects or features of man, important as they may be, are incapable of sitting in judgment on themselves. Reason judges not only itself but also the other aspects of man, and, what is particularly important, the various relations between all these constituents of man. An inability to construct a completely ordered system of ethical principles expressing the full gamut of moral values is not due to reason's incompetence or to the matter's unintelligibility but to the slow pace of man's intellectual growth. Meanwhile reason has explored and ordered a fairly large part of the field and guides us through some very difficult terrain. Thus it functions as a norm.

But how sure a norm? How are we to know when reason is right? Reason has to be its own critic. To determine when reason is right and when it is wrong, there is nothing else to appeal to but reason itself. Knowledge can be known only by knowledge reflecting on itself. By reason we discover truth and by the same reason we are capable of error, just as by the will we seek the good and by the same will we can do evil by seeking the merely apparent good. The will seeks anything that reason proposes to it as good; the will needs a norm but cannot be one. Reason needs a norm and must also be one; it can find none but itself. How can this paradox be resolved?

We distinguish two uses of reason: reason rationally exercised, consistent with itself, and faithful to its own law and function; and reason irrationally exercised, contradicting itself, enthralled by a law foreign to it, and functioning to its own destruction. Reason used to plot a crime, for instance, is reason used irrationally, for only the means are rational and not the end; reason thwarts itself by its own cleverness in rationally arranging parts into an irrational whole. When reason is enslaved to serve irrational ends and when it is free to be fully itself, reason alone can know.

RIGHT REASON AS A NORM

Does human reason have any guidelines for determining when it is right and when it is not? Since making such a determination is part of reason's own critical function, it will have to find the guidelines within itself. Let us see how reason works out an ethical judgment.

1. Any moral choice is preceded by deliberation, a weighing of the reasons for and against the contemplated course of action. These reasons are expressed in judgments, practical judgments that are directive of action. They present the good to the will for its acceptance, the arguments in its favor, the strength of the moral obligation involved, the general moral principle of which this act is an instance, and therefore the reasonableness of choosing this form of action. Such a process issues in a *dictate* of the practical reason, taking the form: I ought (or ought not) to do this act. Thus the first checkup on the rightness of reason consists in making sure that this particular action does verify in itself a moral principle that I already hold.

2. There is as yet no guarantee that the moral principles I hold are correct. The next point in reason's examination of itself is to see why I hold these principles. Except for my earliest actions, based on my parents' or others' principles rather than my own, my moral principles are habitual possessions. A habit is necessary, for, when the moment of decision has arrived, it is too late to examine the rationality of my moral principles; I must now have them ready for use. The habitual possession of rationally and correctly derived principles is sometimes called right reason, and the man who lives according to them is both upright and reasonable. Such a habit of right reason lies between *synderesis*, or the habit of first moral principles, and the habit or virtue of prudence, which applies principles to individual acts. But my moral principles are not necessarily correct from the mere fact that I happen to hold them. A periodic checking up on them is needed, especially in times of calm self-examination or when they are challenged. Since habits can be bad as well as good, wrong as well as right, they must be examined and certified before they can be cleared as *right* reason.

3. Habit is said to be second nature. If we want to find out whether habits are good or bad, we should compare them

with the nature they are supposed to enhance, especially so when the nature in question is rational and we are dealing with right reason. Reason, reflecting on the human nature of which it is a part, sees the congruity of some actions and the incongruity of other actions with that nature, pronouncing the former good and the latter bad. Conformity of action with nature is the rule all over the universe. Since man is a natural being within the scope of total nature, man's actions are good if they conform to his nature, bad if they go counter to it. But this is only a test of ordinary natural goodness, rating man as an efficiently performing animal of a definite type. In a determination of moral goodness, something more than mere nature must be considered. Many of man's actions are natural in the sense that he feels the prompting of nature to perform them; yet they are immoral because unfitting for a rational and free being. Thus human nature, if it is to be a norm of *morality,* is not to be taken merely as one nature among other natures, one type of being among other types, explaining how man *does* in fact behave in his own characteristically human way, as psychology and the social sciences study him. No, a norm of morality must exhibit how he *ought* to behave, for morality deals with the *ought.* Thus the emphasis here is not on human nature *as nature,* nor even on human nature *as human* in a general way, but on human nature *as rational and free,* the attributes he shares with no other nature on earth. These two connected attributes make morality possible, the first discerning the good and the second pursuing it. Nature in man does not work automatically, infallibly leading man in the right direction, but supplies him with intellect and will, with rationality and freedom, by which he can govern himself with responsibility for what he does. It is this which makes a man a *person* and explains why only a person has morality.

4. It is characteristic of reason to direct to an end. Aimless or random conduct is called *irrational,* even when a man performs it. Can we then say that reason is right when it clearly and certainly points out to a man those actions which will lead him to his final goal and those which will hinder him from it, labeling the first good and the second bad? Surely reason is right when it does this. But we continue to ask: Why should this be so? Is the act good because it leads to the end, or does it lead to the end because it is good? Is the moral good merely instrumental to some final good, or is the final good itself included within the moral good? Only the second alternative is acceptable. Reason can perceive the inner dynamism of the human being, his abilities and capacities craving fulfillment, and the suitability of certain acts and objects to contribute to the human being's fulfillment of his being. But the good as instrumental, as perfective as completing natural tendencies, appeal only to the nature *as nature* and does not specify the moral good as such. The end itself must be a good if it is good to strive for it. Thus right reason judges not only the means to good living but good living itself, not only what brings about fulfillment but also why fulfillment should be good for being and why this being deserves fulfillment.

5. We have been gradually pushing ourselves back into the realm of the self-evident. If something is good, not because it leads to something else but because it is good in itself, its goodness will shine out of itself into the eye of reason, which must necessarily acknowledge the evident truth it beholds. Some values are seen to be nobler in intrinsic worth, more inclusive in scope, more compatible with other values and more productive of order and harmony in man himself and in his relations with the universe. Reason sees that such values must have a higher place in any rationally co-

structed order of things, and that any effort to arrange them otherwise can be done only by flying in the face of reason and willfully acting irrationally. Only if reason were to say to itself: I see clearly that this is the higher value in the objective order of things and this other value is subordinate to it, but I am going to overturn this order and subject the higher value to the lower—only if reason were to act in this way could it fail to be right. Obviously it cannot thus deny its own truth under its own power, but it is not the only power in man. Reason can not only be disregarded, in which case it may be right but not used, but it also can be interfered with, can be enslaved by prejudice and passion and willfulness, can abdicate its leading position and thus deny its own value in the scheme of things. Then reason is not right. Nothing else can correct it but reason itself. This is what was meant by saying that reason is right when it is faithful to its own law. Then it declares that whatever is inconsistent with the ideal good or would prevent its realization must be rejected as not a true good, and whatever harmonizes with the ideal good and promotes its realization is the true good. The true good in the sphere of human conduct is the moral good.

Thus the norm of morality is found in right reason—but it must be taken in its full scope. No one of the five aspects just mentioned is to be taken in isolation, but they must all be fitted together. Then we can know that reason is right. In the deliberation preceding an act:

1. We advert to the *dictate* of practical reason pointing out the right path.
2. We check it against our *habitually* possessed code of rationally derived moral principles.
3. We examine the principles and recognize that they express the logical consequence of the kind of *nature* we have.

4. We see that the act we are contemplating will bring us to the attainment of the *end* to which our inner dynamism is driving us.
5. We perceive the end itself as not merely a good for us but as verifying in itself the *ideal* of the moral good.

HUMAN NATURE TAKEN COMPLETELY

We determine the useful or the pleasant good by noting its suitability to some partial aspect or particular craving of man. It may suit him in one way and harm him in another, but we are dealing here with the moral good, the befitting good, which must be good simply and without qualification. Hence right reason must look to the whole man, to human nature taken adequately or completely.

1. *Human nature must be taken with all its parts.* These comprise his metaphysical aspects (animality and rationality), his physical components (body and soul), and all the integral parts (members and faculties) that happen to be present in any individual man. Man is obliged to manage his complex nature and keep these parts working in harmony.

Man by nature is an animal and must live like an animal. He must take care of his body and minister to its needs. He must not ambition to live like an angel or a disembodied spirit. Man's nature is such that he could not live in this way, and to try to do so would not befit him. Man's bodily needs are so vivid and insistent that there is little temptation in this direction, but an exaggerated or fanatical asceticism is not suitable to man.

Man by nature is no mere animal, but a rational animal, and he must also live as a rational being. The life of a brute is not suitable to a man. The rational and the nonrational sides of man must be kept in harmony or there is rebellion in the very nature of man. When a conflict arises, as happens often enough, then the rational must prevail. If reason is dethroned, the life of a mere animal takes the place of that of a rational animal, and the man remains a man in nature but becomes a beast in conduct.

2. *Human nature must be taken with all its relations.* There must be not only inner harmony between the parts and abilities that make up man himself but also outer harmony between man and his surroundings. Man is not a solitary being but a part of the universe; he must fit himself into the total scheme of creation and occupy the place destined for him by the kind of nature he has. There are three essential relations and a number of accidental relations that may arise from circumstances or the fulfillment of certain conditions, such as marriage, parenthood, profession, employment, and the like. We need consider here the essential relations only, which make man:

1. A contingent being, regarding God
2. A social being, regarding his fellowman
3. A possessive being, regarding the goods of the earth

Toward what is above man, human nature is *contingent*. One who acknowledges the existence of God must recognize his dependence on God, from whom he derives his being. To arrogate absolute independence to himself is to refuse to accept his position as a creature and thus to go against his created nature.

Toward beings on the same level, human nature is social. Man is born into the society of the family and is made for companionship with his fellowman, on whom he is dependent to supply his needs and develop his abilities. Hence what promotes a well-functioning social life among men is good for man; what tends to disrupt human society and to hinder this mutual helpfulness and cooperation is bad for man.

Toward things beneath man, human nature is *possessive*. By his very nature man needs the use of material things: food, water, air, sunlight for the maintenance of life itself, and so many other less necessary goods for the development of his abilities and the living of a decent and cultured life, to which his rationality entitles him.

To sum up: That conduct is morally good which right reason shows to be befitting a rational animal, with all his components, created by God, living with his fellowman, and supporting himself on the products of this earth. That conduct is morally bad which right reason shows to be unbefitting such a being. In any conflict between the rational and the animal appetites, the rational must prevail. In any conflict between the three essential relations, the relation to God comes first, to fellowman second, to the goods of this world third. This hierarchy is arranged according to the intrinsic worth and excellence of these two main parts of man and of these three orders of beings.

Man is no exception to the general rule that every being must act according to its nature. But if man is no exception to the rule and we do not set up a norm of goodness for other beings, why do we do so for man? Because man is rational and free, whereas other beings in this world are not. Nonfree beings must act as their nature prescribes for them, and thus they necessarily fulfill their purpose in the universe. Man alone, being free, can act either according to his nature or against his nature. In all things the nature of the being is the norm of its activity. Since nonfree beings must necessarily act naturally, in them the norm is automatically applied and need not be definitely expressed. Since man ought to act naturally but can act unnaturally by abuse of his freedom, he needs rational formulation and conscious application of the norm of morality in his conduct.

PRACTICALITY OF THE NORM

How practical is such a norm? Is it actually usable by men trying to guide their moral lives and capable of direct application to definite human acts? There are the following affirmative reasons:

1. The norm must be such that from it the same rules of morality can be derived for all men. By its nature a standard must be applicable to all the objects of a class. To say that each person has his own standard of conduct is the same as saying that there is no standard at all. Human nature is common to all men, and the rules derived from it by the exercise of right reason will be applicable to all human beings.

2. The norm must be such that from it all the rules of morality can be derived. Otherwise it would not be the complete norm, but it plus something else would be the norm. Man, the doer of the act, is taken with all his parts, so that the act must be befitting to him as a whole, and the relations connect him with every possible object on which or toward which he can act, or that can in any way circumstance or condition the act. Human reason with its reflective power can embrace the totality of man's parts and relations.

3. The norm must be immutable yet flexible enough to admit of varying applications according to circumstances. If the norm is not immutable, it is really no standard; yet it will be useless if it is not applicable to every possible circumstance of human conduct, for this is what it is supposed to measure. Hence the norm must be flexible but not elastic, like a tape measure that is fixed in length but can conform to any surface. Human nature is immutable in essentials but accidentally variable, specifically the same but individually diversified, and human reason with its abstractive power can separate the essential from the accidental.

4. The norm must be constantly present and manifest to all men. Human acts entail responsibility and, if man could perform them without being able to find the norm of morality, he would be responsible for conduct the morality of which he could not determine. He must therefore, whenever he is confronted with a rational choice, always be able to compare his conduct with the norm. But the only thing always present to a man in all possible circumstances is his own rational human nature. Wrecked on a desert island, he still has the norm of morality with him.

No other conceivable standard has these qualifications. An external object distinct from man could be lost or left behind and not be available when needed. Something internal to man but only accidental to him would not be present in all men, though all must live morally. Something essential to man but only a part of his essence could not measure conduct suitable to the other parts of man's essence. Therefore it must be the whole of man's essence or nature.

The norm of morality is not only a standard, or measure, but also a director and guide. In this last function the concept of norm leads into that of law.

SUMMARY

The moral life is above all an intelligent life. Intellect or reason has an honored place in all traditional ethics because it is our critical ability, passing judgment on itself and everything else. But since reason can fall into error, it must be *right reason*.

How do we know when reason is right? Reason itself must be the judge. Reason is right when it is rationally exercised, consistent with itself, faithful to its own law. As a norm, right reason is a dictate of practical reason formulated by rational human nature directing itself to rational ends by using its habit of moral principles developed through the active pursuit of the ideal for man as rational and free.

Right reason is concerned with human nature taken completely in all its parts and relations.

Parts
- Metaphysical:
  - animality and rationality
- Physical:
  - body and soul
- Integral:
  - members and faculties

Relations
- Created:
  - toward God
- Social:
  - toward fellowman
- Possessive:
  - toward the goods of the earth

Argument for right reason as the norm of morality: Everything is intended to act according to its nature, since a nature is the essence of a thing as the inner directing principle of its activity. Reason is part of a rational nature and is the directing principle of free beings. Reason can criticize itself and know when it is right. Hence *right reason examining human nature taken completely in all its parts and relations* is held to be the norm of morality.

That this is a proximate and practical norm follows from the inability of anything else to fulfill the functions essential to a norm:

1. It gives the same rules of morality to all men.
2. It gives all the rules of morality to each man.
3. It is immutable yet applicable to all cases.
4. It is always present and manifest to all men.

QUESTIONS FOR DISCUSSION

1 Reason is found to be right when judged right by right reason. How is it possible to avoid begging the question in such a statement?

2 To make right reason the norm of morality is to require man to measure every act he is about to do by the rule of reason. How does this square with the ease, naturalness, and spontaneity that should characterize a free person?

3 Is an act good because it leads to the end, or does it lead to the end because it is good? Is morality merely a means to man's end? If not, can there be morality independently of man's end?

4 What is the relationship between the norm of morality and the moral ideal? Are they the same or different? Can there be one without the other? Are they coordinate or is one derived from the other?

5 What is the relationship between right reason and human nature? Does each imply the other? Which of the two terms seems preferable as expressing the norm of morality? Would it be better to speak of the human person than of human nature in this context?

READINGS

All of Plato's writings emphasize the role of reason in governing man's normal life. It is the whole theme of his *Republic*.

Aristotle's *Nicomachean Ethics,* bk. VI, deals with the intellectual virtues and the special impact of prudence on morals.

Marcus Aurelius' *Meditations* and Epictetus' *Discourses* stress the reigning position of reason in the Stoic ethical theory.

The concepts of *reason* and *nature* run throughout the whole Aristotelian-Thomistic philosophy. See the *Summa Theologica,* I-II, q. 19, aa. 3-4; q. 21, a. 1; q. 59, a. 5; q. 71, aa. 1-2; and the *Summa Contra Gentiles,* bk. III, ch. 129. Read Michael Cronin, *Science of Ethics,* vol. I, ch. 5; also Leo Ward, *Values and Reality,* ch. 11, and *Christian Ethics,* ch. 6-8.

Stephen Toulmin, *An Examination into the Place of Reason in Ethics,* and Kurt Baier, *The Moral Point of View,* take a new viewpoint on reason's place in ethics. The latter is an example of the "good reasons" school of moral thinking.

Austin Fagothey, *Right and Reason—an Anthology,* contains a number of passages from Aristotle, St. Thomas, and Kant, all of which are pertinent to this chapter.

CHAPTER 11

LAW

PROBLEM

Those who give a large place to reason in the determination of morality usually hold that right reason expresses itself in the form of law. Since there is question of practical reason directing action, the judgment of reason assumes the form of a command prescribing or forbidding a certain kind of conduct, and this is what is commonly understood as a law. A law is closely related to a norm or standard, the main difference being that a norm appeals to the intellect, enabling it to distinguish one thing from another, whereas a law imposes an obligation on the will to conform to the standard. Since norm and law are not contradictory but supplementary, it is not necessary always to keep a sharp distinction between them.

Law is a highly controversial topic in morals today. Some will not hear of the word. It is bad enough, they say, to have to endure laws in the state as a necessary evil needed to restrain the refractory and uncooperative elements in society, but let us hear nothing about laws governing our moral life. Surely the good life should appeal to us without any form of coercion, and how is it possible to coerce a moral life, whose dwelling place is in the interior of each man's soul?

We are faced with a difficult problem. Shall we throw away a good word because it has come to be perversely misunderstood, or engage in the task of educating people in the proper understanding of what law really is? If the word law had irretrievably picked up such disastrous connotations as to be beyond rehabilitation, we should drop it and use other expressions, but the case does not seem that desperate, and we would lose too much. The word *law* is so fixed in the tradition of ethical writing that the student would have to learn its meaning anyway if he wants to do any serious reading in the great ethical writers. He will have to keep an open mind and not look exclusively at the coercive aspect of law.

We have the following questions:
1. What is the meaning of law?
2. How did the idea of natural law develop in history?
3. What are the arguments for and against a natural law?
4. How do we come to know the natural law?
5. What is the content of natural law?
6. Is natural law invariable?
7. Is there an eternal law beyond the natural law?

MEANING OF LAW

When we say the word *law*, what comes to mind first of all is the law of the state. This is what St. Thomas seems to have in mind when he gives us his classical definition of law, though the definition is also applicable to law in a wider sense:

Law is nothing else than an ordinance of reason for the common good, promulgated by him who has care of the community.*

---

*St. Thomas, *Summa Theologica*, I-II, q. 90, a. 4

108

1. It is called an *ordinance* because it
 no mere advice, counsel, or suggestion
ut an order, a command, a mandate im-
osing the superior's will on the inferior's
nd binding with moral necessity.

2. A law is said to be of *reason* because
 must be no arbitrary whim but intelligent
irection, imposed by the superior's will
ut planned and formulated by right rea-
on. To be reasonable a law must be con-
stent with other laws and rights, just in
istributing benefits and burdens, observ-
ble as not being too harsh or difficult,
nforceable so that proper observation is
ctually secured, and useful in that the
ood it aims at is worth the price.

3. A law is for the *common good,* for
e welfare of the community as a whole,
nd not for the benefit of individuals as
ich. A command authoritatively given to
n individual about a private matter can
quire his obedience but is not a law.

4. A law must be *promulgated,* or made
nown to those whom it binds. It must be
ublished in such a manner that it can be
nown readily, though each subject need
ot be given personal notice.

5. A law must come from one who has
re of the community, from a legislator
aving authority or jurisdiction, who may
e a single individual or a body passing
ws by joint action. Not anyone who
leases may pass a law. What sets the
wgiver off from the rest and gives him
e right to command is his authority.

So a law must be mandatory, reason-
ble, community-serving, promulgated, and
athoritative. Without these characteristics
is not a genuine law and has no bind-
g force. Law in this primary and strict
nse directs *free* beings by imposing on
eir free will the restraint of obligation or
ity or oughtness, the type of necessity we
ave called *moral necessity,* which does not
nsist in physical compulsion, though the
reat of it may be used as enforcement.
ich laws can be disobeyed and often are,
it they ought not to be, and it is in this

ought not that moral necessity consists. Governance by law is the only way of regulating human acts that is consistent with the
dignity of a person.

In an extended and analogous sense the
term *law* is applied to *nonfree* beings to
express an observed uniformity or regularity in their behavior. The laws of physics,
chemistry, biology, and allied sciences may
be considered as mere formulas, and then
they are laws in a metaphorical sense only.
If it is thought that this observed uniformity does not happen accidentally but
that there is something in the very nature
of the bodies and the structure of the universe that sets their pattern of activity for
them, then this *physical necessity* constitutes
physical law.

Metaphorical uses of the term *law* go
beyond scientific formulas to express observed uniformities less closely connected
with the nature of things, such as the law
of diminishing returns in economics or
Grimm's law in philology, or to express entrenched social customs such as the laws
of etiquette and diplomatic protocol.

It was necessary to describe these various meanings of the term *law* in order
to bring out its analogous character. The
meanings are related but not wholly the
same. Nothing but untold confusion will
result if we try to talk about the *moral law*
or the *natural law* by applying to it the
modes of legislation and promulgation
proper to the civil law, or on the other
hand if we think of it in the merely figurative sense of observed regularities of behavior. It will be law in the strict sense and
not in a figurative one, but with marked
differences from the law of the state. To
make much sense of the controversy on
natural law we should first see something
about its history.

HISTORY OF NATURAL LAW

The term *natural law* has had its ups
and downs and has not been understood in

the same sense in every age. It is important to see some of these swings in meaning, for an argument or a criticism that is valid in one period will not apply to the term as understood in a different historical context.

The early Greeks contrasted *physis* (nature) and *nomos* (law), the latter being understood in the sense of human convention and contrivance, so that a union of the two words in a phrase such as *natural law* seemed contradictory. Yet they had a feeling for what is right and just beyond the laws of men. Plato is unintelligible without the Ideas of law and justice in which all human law and justice participate. Aristotle is more explicit:

> Particular law is that which each community lays down and applies to its own members: this is partly written and partly unwritten. Universal law is the law of nature. For there really is, as every one to some extent divines, a natural justice and injustice that is binding on all men, even on those who have no association or covenant with each other. It is this that Sophocles' Antigone clearly means when she says that the burial of Polyneices was a just act in spite of the prohibition: she means that it was just by nature.

> Not of today or yesterday it is,
> But lives eternal: none can date its birth.*

The Stoics were the first to make wide use of the term *natural law*. For them it is the absolutely necessary course that nature fatalistically follows, with no distinction made between physical and moral law. Reason urges us to obey it willingly rather than have it forced on us, since thus we intelligently comply with the inevitable law of our being. Cicero's remarkable passages are probably to be understood in a Stoic sense:

> There is a law, judges, not written but inborn, not learned or passed on by tradition but sucked from nature's breast. . . . †

There is truly a law, which is right reason, fitted to our nature, proclaimed to all men, constant everlasting. It calls to duty by commanding and deters from wrong by forbidding, neither commanding nor forbidding the good man in vain even when it fails to move the wicked. It can neither be evaded nor amended nor wholly abolished. No decree of Senate or people can free us from it. No explainer or interpreter of it need be sought but itself. There will not be found one law at Rome and another at Athens, one now and another later, but one law, everlasting and unchangeable, extending to all nations and all times, with one common teacher and ruler of all, God, this law's founder, promulgator, and enforcer. The man who does not obey him flees from himself and, even if he escapes other punishments normally incurred, pays the supreme penalty by the very fact that he despises the nature of man in himself.*

On the whole, the natural law as conceived by the Greeks is a rising beyond the particular and contingent to a universal and necessary ideal of conduct, describing how one must behave to be a real man, giving him a rule of life he transgresses at the peril of unhappiness in the frustration of his powers and the stultification of his being. It is not a law imposed by a legislator and enforced by his authority. With the Romans came the distinction between *jus*, or right, and *lex*, or law, between what is just *(jus)* and the command to do it *(lex)*. For the natural law the only legislator could be God, as Cicero says, but he is not yet clearly portrayed as a personal God.

The Judeo-Christian tradition introduced a new turn into this speculation by regarding nature as the product of God's creative act. God acting as lawgiver sets the law for his creation by his wisdom and enforces it by his will. His providence constitutes him governor of the universe, which he directs to its appointed end. Here we have the concept of the *eternal law* developed by St. Augustine, which is the old natural law of the Greeks but seen from the

---

*Aristotle, *Rhetoric*, bk. I, ch. 13, 1373b 4. Aristotle quotes from Sophocles' *Antigone*, lines 456-457. See also Aristotle, *Nicomachean Ethics*, bk. V, ch. 7, 1134b 18.
†Cicero, *Pro Milone*, iv, 10.

*Cicero, *De Republica*, bk. III, xxii, 33. Quoted by Lactantius, *De Institutionibus Divinis*, bk. V, ch. 8, 6-9.

side of God the creator and lawgiver. The codification of Roman law brought the civil law into contact with the natural law; the law of nations (*jus gentium*) lies in the area where the two meet and partly overlap. By the thirteenth century, studies in Roman and Canon Law, in ethics and politics, had laid the ground for an adequate philosophy of law, which first appeared in St. Thomas' *Summa Theologica* as the Treatise on Law,* with his fourfold distinction of eternal law, natural law, human law, and divine (revealed) law. But some unsolved difficulties remained. The medieval Church asserted her position as guardian of faith and morals. Are natural morals included too? Can there be an authoritative interpreter of natural law? If so, how does the law remain *natural*? These questions clouded an understanding of the natural law for some centuries and are not yet wholly dispelled.

Early Protestantism continued the medieval tradition, looking on nature as God's creation and on God as supreme lawgiver. But further difficulties arise. Any claims of the Church to be an interpreter of the natural law are rejected in favor of private individual conscience. But how shall it decide? The theory of total depravity, emphasized by Luther and still more by Calvin, seems incompatible with a natural law. Human nature, if totally depraved, offers no sure guidance for man's moral life. Nothing is left but the political state. An established religion, national rather than international, modeled on the union of nation and religion in the Old Testament, seemed to them man's best refuge. A theocracy like that of Geneva or Massachusetts, minutely regulating man's private life, was the logical outcome. In such a view the moral law is stressed, but its *natural* character seems to have disappeared.

It should be expected that the Enlightenment of the Age of Reason would carry us back to pre-Christian concepts. Natural law returns but in a new guise. God as

---

* St. Thomas, *Summa Theologica*, I-II, qq. 90-108.

lawgiver drops out. If he is acknowledged at all, he is conceived in deist fashion, unconcerned with the world and not governing it by his providence. Again we have natural law without an eternal law, without a lawgiver, without any really binding obligation. Again it is *jus* rather than *lex*, natural right or justice rather than a natural law in the strict sense. But the *natural* aspect of it, far from being abandoned, is reinforced and reinterpreted. In that rationalistic age human nature is regarded as eminently knowable by human reason. The method that reason pursues, however, is not a search for what is essential to man but for what is primitive in him, or if it seeks the essential, it endeavors to find it in the primitive. The distinction between the essential and the accidental is confused with the distinction between the natural and the artificial. The way to find human nature, it was thought, is by stripping from man the artificial accretions of civilization so that he may be seen in his native state, in the so-called *state of nature*. The natural is understood to be the native or original or primeval, and natural man is man before or without the social contract that established him in society. Human nature is not so much the abstract essence of man as the unspoiled savage. Thus the Age of Enlightenment passes into the Age of Romanticism.

In the nineteenth century, trust in rationalist procedures waned. Kant's separation of morality and legality put rights in the sphere of legality and made them a function of the civil law. He leaves no place for natural rights. He affirmed the moral law but had it known intuitively and not by reasoning from human nature; thus understood, it is a moral law, but is it a natural law? The rise of the historical school of jurisprudence and the influence of evolutionary theories in Hegel and Darwin brought in the view of human nature as something constantly developing and progressing. Laws and morals, rights and duties change with changing man; they are products of human custom, relics of traditional folkways, variable for each focus of culture and for each stage of social evolution. Legal positivism and legal pragmatism appear on the scene and relegate natural law and natural rights to the museum of discarded supersitions. The names may be kept because of the aura of veneration surrounding them, but all their substance is interpreted away. The legal profession especially is suspicious of any appeal to a higher law beyond the written law. And with good reason, if we remember the interpretations read into the "due process" clause of the Fourteenth Amendment canonizing the status quo as the only natural one and protecting vested interests. On the other hand, what guarantee have we of our rights with a judge who goes beyond the written law to decide a case by some private intuition he may have of a higher law?

The twentieth century, despite the persistence of legal positivism and pragmatism, is witnessing a tentative revival of natural law. There may have been abuses of the higher law theory, but what else do we have? The old question returns. Without natural law, what guide have our lawmakers but utility and expediency, trial and error? How can they determine what ideally ought to be the laws of states and the conduct of men? The dilemma is a serious one. Either there is no law beyond the civil law, and hence no natural rights, no court of appeal, no recourse from tyranny, and a man is subject to the arbitrary will of anyone who can control him by force; or there is beyond the civil law a higher law, but then each man is his own judge and, though it is evident to him that this higher law objectively embodies natural right and justice, his associates have no assurance that his judgment is correct. The first horn of the dilemma causes the appeal to a higher law, to which the founders of our country turned

against the arbitrary decrees of Parliament. The second horn causes the qualm of the legal positivists, who see each citizen setting aside a civil law because it disagrees with his personal interpretation of a higher law. We are back again to Antigone's problem. It is not solved by putting the matter to vote and accepting majority rule, for that would mean no rights for minorities. The tyranny of the monarch would be exchanged for the tyranny of the mob.

The problem is insoluble for any society so based on skepticism and relativism as to maintain that human nature is unknowable, that rights and duties cannot be determined, that justice is an empty abstraction, that in morals there is nothing but opinion and anybody's opinion is as good as anybody else's. Society can flourish only in some commonly breathed atmosphere of thought and principle and must rest on some public philosophy. That the natural law seems to be the only possible one is the reason for its revival in our time.

THE NATURAL LAW THEORY

That there is a natural law, at least in the sense in which the Greeks took it, without explicit reference to a divine lawgiver, is implied in much that has been said so far: the existence of values and their objective basis; the preeminence and self-justification of moral value; its irreducibility to any other value, and its absolutely imperative but noncompulsory necessity; the inner drive of each being toward the attainment of its end, which is the fulfillment of its function in the universe; the ability of man by the use of his reason reflecting on his nature to distinguish moral good from moral evil in the living of his life. What remains is to point out that all this material put together adds up to a *law*, and, since it is rooted in man's nature, to a *natural* law.

That there are laws governing the activity of beings in the universe is claimed as evident from the very existence of scientific knowledge. An utterly haphazard world could not be studied. Formulas expressing the observed regularities of natural phenomena are in many cases also rules of action carried out with remarkable constancy. Living beings, especially, direct their activity toward their self-preservation, growth, and reproduction, following the definite pattern of living prescribed for them by the kind of beings they are, by their structure and function, which is what is meant by their nature. Departure from nature's pattern does not happen spontaneously. A mild deviation imposed from the outside usually results in maladjustment and debility, an extreme one in death. To fulfill their function they *must* live according to nature's prescription, and this is the *law* of their life.

The same law of nature that applies to inanimate, vegetable, and animal nature applies likewise to human nature. As it applies to each of the other three levels with a difference, so also it applies to human nature with a difference. Man is unique in being rational and free. Though subject to physical forces like any other chemically composed body having mass and energy, to the biological drives and urges that control the world of living organisms, to the sensitive reactions and appetites characteristic of brain- and nerve-equipped animals, yet beyond all these he can intellectually *know* what is good for him and can willfully *choose* to follow it. By examining the kind of being he is, his nature, he can find the kind of conduct suitable to him and can see how this conduct alone can lead him to what is good for him. He sees that modes of conduct that are inhuman or antisocial, abusive of himself or of his fellows, while conferring a temporary advantage, must be destructive of himself and of his race in the long run. He also sees that he cannot renounce his rational nature and the responsibility bound up with it. Come what may, he must maintain his human dignity

or become intolerable to himself. He must demand that others treat him as a man, even when they refuse to, and he must deserve his own and their respect by behaving as a man.

Natural law, it is said, tests itself in the laboratory of history. Superficial observation may seem to show such differences of detail in various cultures as to eliminate any universal pattern of human living, but more careful scrutiny detects a highest common factor in all moral codes. Even the most degraded savages are recognizable as human beings, not merely by the shape of their bodies but chiefly by the way they live and act. Too great a departure from the normal mode of human behavior leads only to frustration and extinction. Individuals here and there, as well as tribes and nations here and there, may flourish though they have adopted an unnatural form of life, but they are the exceptions that prove the rule. History itself catches up with them and eventually punishes the folly of unnatural living. Living can be called unnatural only because it violates the rules set by nature, and this is what is meant by the natural law.

To sum up the argument: The only means both effective and suitable to direct man to his proper good to the fulfillment of his function in the universe, and to the attainment of his end, is the natural moral law.

1. It must be a *law*. A mere wish, counsel, hint, or suggestion would not be effective, for it would lack binding force and could be disregarded without fault or penalty. It would be an insufficient motive in the face of difficulties. It would work when it is not needed, when the path is clear and the going pleasant; but it would not work when it is needed, when we must be goaded forward over the dark and rough spots of life. Nothing less than a law will do.

2. It must be a *moral* law. Physical laws are suitable only to nonrational beings. An

internal determination or necessity of one's nature such as is found in nonrational beings would destroy man's free will and make him a living contradiction, a being made free but not able to exercise his freedom. External compulsion would mean that man must accomplish his end despite his will, and thus would do violence to human nature.

3. It must be a *natural* law. Every creature tends to its end by its activity guided by its nature, for a being's nature means nothing else but its essence considered as the principle of its activity. Man is no exception; he too has a nature, and in him it fulfills the same function. Man cannot be the only being in nature designed by his nature to go against his nature. Therefore man also can find that his nature is the means that will guide him to his end, and this is what is understood as the *natural law*.

CASE FOR AND AGAINST NATURAL LAW

Many moralists, chiefly those of the last century and the present, oppose the basing of morals on nature or on law, and especially on the combination of the two. We take up the objections first and then the replies.

1. Natural law stems from the Aristotelian concept of a fixed essence or nature in man and from the Stoic notion of universal nature. These concepts of nature have been invalidated by the experimental method of modern science, which fails to discover any such hard and fast categories among things, and the theory of evolution, which shows that there are no invariable classes of living things. Process philosophies see everything on the move, becoming something quite new, with no static patterns of behavior to be forever repeated. If there is no fixed human nature, there can be no obligation arising from it.

2. There is not as much uniformity in human behavior as natural law theorists assume. It is not the man who conforms who is the best example of the human race, but the one who has the courage to break out of the narrow circle of conformity and to initiate new ways. As the thinker and creator, he pushes beyond the dictates of nature and expresses the uniqueness of his personality. Natural law with its static ideals is actually contrary to man's rationality and a drawback to self-development.

3. What regularity we observe in human behavior does not come from any law in man. The general tendencies of mankind are simply there, urging man to certain kinds of behavior, chiefly of the physical kind, but imposing no obligation to act in a definite way. To see a law in this behavior is the fallacy of mistaking the figurative for the literal. The state governs man by law; to see man as also governed by nature is a mere figurative expression personifying nature as a lawgiver and represents no real government or real law.

4. A natural law should be easily known by those in whose nature such a law is supposed to reside. Men disagree not only on how to fulfill their obligations but also on what their obligations are and whether they have any. Even those who admit a natural law do not agree on its content, interpretation, or application. Hence, even if a natural law existed, it would be practically useless as a guide to moral living.

5. The natural law is a useless figure of speech unless it is imposed by some superior who has the power of enforcement. The most logical thinkers, therefore, are those who deduce a natural law from an eternal law in God. But not all men accept a theistic philosophy. Those who admit a direct governance of man by God need to have something by which God manifests to man the divine decrees. If there are no such decrees, no manifestation of God's will need be written in man's nature.

6. Christian revelation sees human nature infected with the evil of sin, especially

that sin inherited from the original fall of man, however interpreted. Some consider that human nature is so essentially depraved in its fallen state that it can be no trustworthy guide to human living; in fact, the important thing is to rise above nature by the help of grace, and unless one does so, one has not even begun the ethical life. Thus natural law, which is of no value to nontheists, is also of little value to a large group of theists.

7. Natural law has been used to justify any kind of act one wants to impose on mankind. All one has to do is to refer glibly to what one declares to be a natural law precept. Likewise, it has been used to excuse any kind of conduct. One merely says that the act, though perhaps not very laudatory, is not forbidden by any natural law precept. Thus natural law is a device for having and proving any kind of conduct one wants. Though abuse does not destroy the use of a thing, anything that is set down as the absolute standard of morality should not be capable of such ready and frequent abuse.

8. Natural law is the source of the legalism, casuistry, pharisaism, and bourgeois smugness that have characterized so much ethical thought. The man, the person, is made to serve some abstract formulation, as if man is for the law rather than the law for man. Instead of tightening himself up with more and more rules, adding to civil law and social custom still more hidden laws behind the obvious laws, man ought to declare his independence, exert his freedom, and express the uniqueness of his personality.

9. Law and love are so opposed that it is difficult to reconcile them. It is true that they may both coincide in such a way that the law commands what love prompts. But the motives are so different that it is psychologically disrupting to try to act from both motives at once. Love is so far superior to law that it is better to trust to love alone and to disregard the motive of

law. The fear of transgressing a law should be wholly overcome in following the inspiration of love.

These and similar arguments are of sufficient weight to require serious consideration, so much so that several succeeding chapters will be needed to explore them. Only a word on each is possible now. Natural law theorists claim that they are based on a misunderstanding of what natural law purports to mean. They answer:

1. Aristotelianism and Stoicism both logically lead to some kind of natural law, but the converse does not follow. One can accept natural law without interpreting nature either in an Aristotelian or in a Stoic sense. Modern science may have blurred the edges of hard and fast categories, but we can still tell a man from other kinds of beings. It is true that evolution of species held no place in historical Aristotelianism, but the two need not be totally irreconcilable. In Aristotle, nature itself is a principle of development, of process, of passage from potentiality to actuality; its extension from the individual to the species, from the ontogenetic to the phylogenetic, might be judged a legitimate modification of Aristotelianism to suit modern discoveries. However, there is no necessity of holding to a strictly Aristotelian interpretation of nature to have a natural law.

2. There is no need of considering the nature of a being as absolutely static. Especially, a rational being could not be static and also faithful to its own rationality. It is because man is by nature rational that he is a thinker and creator. In developing the arts and sciences, in establishing and furthering civilization, man is acting most in accord with his nature. In particular, it is by his rational nature that he develops his morals and advances to clearer formulations of the ideals of conduct to which he ought to aspire. Besides, man is by nature a personal being, and he acts most naturally when he provides for the fullest expression of his personality.

3. The extension of the term *law* beyond the civil law to analogous modes of directing human life is a perfectly legitimate usage quite consonant with our normal mode of thought and speech. Deception should occur only if we fail to separate out the connected meanings or confuse one for the other. The natural law lacks many features of the civil law and has some features that the civil law lacks, but there are fundamental resemblances as important as the differences and justifying the use of a common if analogous concept.

4. If the natural law were known intuitively by a simple inspection of human nature and no rational study of this nature were required, then there should be no disputes about natural law. But it is not according to man's nature to know difficult and complex matters in such a simple way. Man is made to think, to reason, to argue matters out for himself, and it is in this way that he arrives at the content, interpretation, and application of natural law.

5. It is no accident that the natural law will appeal more to the theist and that he will recognize its counterpart in the eternal law. But our historical sketch showed that the Greeks recognized natural law centuries before St. Augustine developed the concept of eternal law. Eternal law would not have much meaning without its promulgation in the natural law, but natural law can be recognized even by those who in their philosophy make no direct reference to God. The argument given previously made no appeal to the eternal law, though it certainly did not deny it.

6. Ethics as a philosophical discipline must be developed independently of such theological concepts as original sin. The weaknesses of human nature are plain to all, and there is no conflict between a philosophical ethics and original sin, but there is no philosophical evidence for a theory of total depravity, and, in the opinion of most, no theological evidence for it either. The natural law can still be a good

guide even if not an infallible one, especially when there is no other.

7. One purpose of a study of natural law is to purge it of the errors and abuses that have been committed in its name. Some of its friends by overworking it have been its worst enemies. One common abuse is to give it an absoluteness it cannot have. This is not to deny that the natural law has an absolute foundation, but to recognize that a natural law must be as relative as human nature. The readiness and frequency of the abuse is hardly a valid argument; civil laws are readily and frequently abused, yet we cannot on that account deny that there are any or that we need them.

8. Legalism, casuistry, hypocrisy, and externalism can be called occupational hazards of law, of any kind of law. Men tend to follow the letter rather than the spirit, especially when the letter favors them. Since the natural law is wholly unformulated, it has no letter and is all spirit. For this reason natural law is the best corrective for an overliteral interpretation of positive law, and has been so since Antigone was portrayed as appealing to a higher law against the cruelty of her uncle the king. Since anyone possessing human nature is a person, he cannot live according to his nature without expressing the uniqueness of his personality; this is perhaps the main thing the natural law demands of him.

9. An opposition between law and love is artificially contrived and vanishes with a proper understanding of both. It is the nature of man to be a loving being, and one who would suppress all love in himself would be making of himself a kind of monster that the natural law could not approve. But it would be unrealistic to say that man's love is in no need of control. When man feels the thrust of passionate desire toward an object he is not allowed to have, he has to keep his eye both on the love and on the law, whether he finds it

psychologically disrupting or not. No man can avoid all moral crisis in his life. Love is indeed the higher motive, but law is often a needed safeguard.

The summary character of both these questions and answers is readily granted, but there is an advantage in placing them in immediate confrontation. Several of them will become clearer from our next discussion.

KNOWLEDGE OF NATURAL LAW

We tend to think of a law as a written decree or spoken command, but nothing of this sort is found in the natural law. Failure to understand that the natural law of itself is not formulated has led believers in innate ideas and other intuitionists to imagine that man has moral concepts and judgments ready made in his mind at birth or that he easily forms them by the use of some infallible special faculty. Critics of such views have hastily jumped to the conclusion that, if the natural law can be known only in this way and since there is no such knowledge, there can be no such thing as a natural law. The fallacy is in the first premise: the natural law is not known in this way.

How, then, is it known? It begins with connatural knowledge. Without study or reflection, man in a prescientific and pre-philosophical condition simply follows the bent of his nature in using his powers for the purposes for which they are obviously constructed. He is following the natural law, but he knows it only as the blind man knows the hand that leads him. The individual in his growth to maturity and the race in its development toward civilization cannot remain always in this primitive condition.

Knowledge of the natural law is a slow growth. Man's nature is a rational nature, and he finds the natural law by the use of his reason in drawing conclusions about his own nature. He has no moral judgments formed at birth and ready for use but must form them for himself. He is equipped by his nature with ability for forming such judgments and has a natural tendency to use this ability, and his own nature is the object from which he draws his moral ideas and concerning which he frames his moral judgments.

Man has a natural interest in and facility for forming rules of conduct. He can reflect on himself and, finding himself interesting, is stimulated to self-observation. He can evaluate and criticize his own actions and the actions of others like him. He can understand the needs of his own nature and the suitability of his deeds to his needs. He can compare his conduct with his nature and understand the conformity or nonconformity between them. He can therefore draw up rules of conduct that will preserve and enhance this conformity. If he becomes a legislator in human society, he formulates such rules and promulgates them to his subordinates by some external sign; the law now becomes positive law. Such rules, before formulation and external promulgation, were already natural law.

All law is promulgated through reason because it is reason alone that can understand a law. This statement is true both of the natural law and of positive law. But positive law is manifested to reason by the help of some external decree or announcement intimating the mind of the lawgiver. The natural law is manifested to reason not by any external sign but by a rationally conducted examination of human nature with all its parts and relations.

The natural law exists in a *virtual* condition in every rational being even before his reason is sufficiently developed to form actual moral judgments. An infant possesses the natural law in the same way as he has intelligence, that is, as an undeveloped power. As the person advances in the use of reason and *forms* his moral principles, either with the help of moral training or by his own efforts, in him the natural moral law passes from the *virtual* to the *formal* state. A similar advance occurs in the passage of the race from a primitive to a cultured society. To aid people in this process of moral growth is the aim of ethics as a practical science.

CONTENT OF NATURAL LAW

How do we come to know the content of the natural law—what it actually prescribes? Though man by the use of his reason is able to develop the natural law into a formal and explicit code of moral conduct, how many men actually succeed in doing so? Anyone invincibly ignorant of the prescriptions of the natural law is excused from keeping them, but if most of those possessing human *nature* were in this condition, how could it be called a *natural* law? On the one hand, the natural law must be sufficiently known to the generality of mankind. On the other hand, there is much controversy and disagreement of opinion on matters of morality, betokening a widespread ignorance. Many of these disagreements can be discounted as dealing not with the principles of morality but with their application; the law itself is clear, and the argument is only about cases. Other controversies are not so readily disposed of and concern the very principles of morality. If these principles can be unknown, how is the natural law sufficiently promulgated?

The way out of this dilemma is to recognize that the natural law consists of precepts of varying degrees of importance for the welfare of humanity, that the more fundamental principles of the natural law cannot be invincibly unknown by normal mature persons, whereas reasoned conclusions derived from them can be. St. Thomas says:

There belong to the natural law, first, certain most common precepts that are known to all; and secondly, certain secondary and more particular precepts, which are, as it were, conclusions following closely from first principles. As to the common principles, the natural law, in its universal meaning, cannot in any way be blotted out from men's hearts. But it is blotted out in the case of a particular action, in so far as reason is hindered from applying the common principle to the particular action because of concupiscence or some other passion. . . . But as to the other, the secondary precepts, the natural law can be blotted out from the human heart, either by evil persuasions, just as in speculative matters errors occur in respect of necessary conclusions; or by vicious customs and corrupt habits, as, among some men, theft, and even unnatural vices . . . were not esteemed sinful.*

LEVELS IN THE KNOWLEDGE
OF NATURAL LAW

A more precise discrimination of these principles is called for. The more general the principles, the more impossible it is for them to be unknown, whereas the more particular and determinate they become, the more possibility there is for ignorance and deception. We may distinguish:
1. The first moral principle
2. Commonly known general principles
3. Reasoned conclusions
4. Particular applications

1. *There is one first principle of the natural law,* which in the practical field corresponds to the principle of contradiction in the speculative field. We have already discussed this first moral principle,† "Do good and avoid evil," and now expressly refer it to natural law. It cannot be invincibly unknown to anyone who has the use of reason at all.

2. *There are other common or general principles based on the first principle,* following from it with inference so simple and easy that no *normal, mature* person can fail to make it. These moral axioms express the natural inclinations man has in common with all substances, such as "Preserve

---

*St. Thomas, *Summa Theologica,* I-II, q. 94, a. 6.
†See pp. 95-97.

your own being," or in common with other animals, such as "Care for your offspring," or the inclinations clearly springing from man's rationality, such as "Avoid offending those among whom you must live."* One could hardly know the first principle, "Do good and avoid evil," and fail to see what is good and what is evil in such obvious cases. These common principles cannot be invincibly unknown to persons whose reason is developed, that is, to persons of normal intelligence who have arrived at mental maturity and who have received an adequate moral education. It is to be expected that the feebleminded through incapacity and children through immaturity will be deficient in this knowledge. An adequate *moral* education is a very important factor. It need not run parallel with mental education. One may have no book learning at all and yet have received an excellent moral training; on the other hand, highly educated people of brilliant talents may be victims of defective or perverted moral training. The latter cannot be considered morally normal, for their moral reason is undeveloped. One brought up in an atmosphere of cynical misanthropy, one trained from youth in crime and degeneracy, one encouraged to rebellion against all authority, has had the moral side of his nature artificially blinded and starved. This cannot be called man's normal condition.

3. *There are remote conclusions derived by a complicated process of reasoning.* There is nothing doubtful about these conclusions; the conclusion is certain and the logic perfect, but the reasoning is long and involved, as in a difficult theorem in geometry. Untrained minds cannot follow it, and trained minds can become sidetracked through confusion or prejudice. Such moral questions as suicide, mercy killing, duelling, divorce, polygamy, slavery, and racism are examples in point. These remote conclusions can be invincibly unknown

---

*St. Thomas, *Summa Theologica*, I-II, q. 94, a. 2.

even by intelligent people living in a cultivated moral atmosphere. Since even educated people can be mistaken in other fields, such as science, history, and politics, they can likewise be mistaken in moral matters when the argumentation becomes difficult and contradictory conclusions seem equally plausible.

4. *There are applications of the principles of the natural law to particular cases.* Normal, mature men may err in their application of any principles to a concrete case. The resulting misjudgment does not mean that they do not know the principles themselves or that they are ignorant of the natural law, but only that they are inexpert in applying principles to practice, like one who knows mathematics but gets bogged down in working problems.

Thus there emerge four levels in man's knowledge of the natural law. The first principle and the simplest inferences from it cannot be invincibly unknown to normal and mature persons, whereas the remote conclusions and applications can be. Ignorance of the general principles, since they ramify into all fields of conduct and are the mainstay of all law and order on earth, would make moral life and human society utterly unlivable. Ignorance of the remote conclusions, though these are important enough, is not nearly so devastating; moral life and human society can still go on, however lamely. For example, promiscuity and polygamy are not equal in their effects. Polygamous societies have functioned and flourished, though not as well as monogamous ones, but no human society has ever been totally promiscuous or could be.

Invincible ignorance of any moral duty excuses from its observance, thus taking care of the individual's conscience. But we are concerned here with objective morality. Widespread ignorance of the general principles of morality would be disastrous to the human race, and our nature itself through the natural law ensures that such widespread ignorance does not occur. However, the remote conclusions are such that invincible ignorance of them can be tolerated without wrecking mankind, and we are left to draw these conclusions for ourselves. Just as raw materials and necessities of life are scattered throughout nature and do not fail, but we are left to our own ingenuity in developing science, culture, and civilization, so we cannot fail to know the general principles of morality but must use our own reason in working out the details of a complete moral system. And just as people depend on experts in other fields of knowledge, so those who have less ability or opportunity to study difficult matters in ethics can be guided by the teaching and example of persons whose intelligence and character they respect. Even here mistakes will occur, as they do in all things human, but we are not responsible for them if we act in good faith.

The terms *normal* and *mature*, used in the foregoing discussion, may seem too inexact, but greater preciseness in this matter is not possible because of the gradual way in which human reason develops. It depends on ability, age, opportunity, effort, habit, and environment, all of which shape the moral character of the person. There will be many borderline cases, but ethical theory must start with what is clear and normal before proceeding to the indistinct and abnormal.

APPARENT EXCEPTIONS

Many difficulties can be brought up from the customs of primitive tribes and even from some civilized practices. To cover these in detail would be too long an excursion into anthropology and sociology, but a few norms can be laid down for handling them. About any alleged practice one should ask:

1. Are the facts certain?
2. Are the moral implications properly interpreted?
3. Is this a general principle or a remote conclusion?
4. Is this a moral precept itself or its application?
5. Are these people normal and mature?
6. Is their ignorance really invincible?

The first thing is to verify the facts. The accounts of early explorers are full of fanciful tales uncritically lumped with true observations, and even modern anthropologists can draw hasty conclusions. Reports of tribes with no moral notions whatever were later disproved; primitive peoples jealously guard their traditions from strangers and share them only with proved friends. The acts of savages must be interpreted, not by the conventional standards of civilization, but against their simple forest background. To enter a house and pick up anything they see may not be theft for them, for they have no privacy and no idea that a man's home is his castle. Their cruelty and revengefulness can be exaggerated manifestations of courage and justice. In general, they learn more vices from contact with civilization and from mistreatment by colonists than they ever practiced in their native condition.

Some practices are the result of inability to resolve an apparent conflict of moral principles. Human sacrifices were made on the principle that the best thing should be offered to God, and a man's dearest possession is his child. Cannibalism was done as a religious rite, to acquire a warrior's courage by eating his heart, rather than as an ordinary source of food. Suicide, too, is sometimes done as an act of religion, as was also the custom of burning a man's wives and slaves on his funeral pyre. Killing deformed children, incurable sufferers, and the aged was thought an act of mercy, as some consider euthanasia today. Prolonged social injustice may cause one to think it right to take from the rich to help the poor. Dueling was regarded as an obligation of honor and to refuse a challenge as a manifestation of cowardice. Feuding and lynching are mistaken forms of family or public justice where organized law is not in force. These practices are not defended here but only cited to show how an apparent conflict of moral principles may result in a faulty application of them or in conclusions wrongly reasoned from them.

It is possible also for people to become victims of moral depravity introduced in previous generations. Those who introduced the immoral customs may have done so with conscious knowledge of their immorality, but succeeding generations now come to take them as a matter of course, having grown up not in a normal but in a perverted moral environment. Tribes reduced to brigandage for a living may cease to see anything wrong in theft, at least from strangers. Slaves threatened with death for bringing bad news may come to feel justified in lying. The constant tolerance of concubinage by public opinion may dull the consciences of unreflecting persons. Public apathy toward political graft and unfair patronage may cause some to view them as perquisites of office. Ignorance in all such matters is not usually invincible, but it may be, especially in extreme cases.

NATURAL LAW, ABSOLUTE OR RELATIVE

Some look on natural law as a rigid and stifling box put around their lives and cramping them into an unrelieved round of prescribed duties. Others may find natural law to be so vague and fluid as to be practically useless. In answer to such exaggerations it is said that natural law is as absolute and as relative as human nature. Even in his day St. Thomas saw this:

To the natural law belong those things to which a man is inclined naturally; and among these it is proper to man to be inclined to act according to reason. Now it belongs to the reason to proceed from what is common to what is proper. . . . The practical reason is concerned with contingent matters, which is the domain of human actions; and, consequently, although there is necessity in the common principles, the more we descend toward the particular, the more frequently we encounter defects. . . . In matters of action, truth or practical recititude is not the same for all as to what is particular, but only as to the common principles; and where there is the same rectitude in relation to particulars, it is not equally known to all.[*]

Some modern legal writers speak of a "natural law with a variable content,"[†] looking toward a compromise that will give them both the needed higher law on which human law should be modeled, and an adjustibility of this law to fit human progress. But the whole content cannot be variable, since human nature is variable only within limits, outside which the being could no longer be regarded as a man. Man is essentially and invariably a rational animal, but he is adjustable to circumstances and capable of growth. His body develops by exercise, his reason by education, and his character by habits. Likewise the race, while remaining essentially the same, grows in the course of history.

A change of essence or nature is implied in fitting man into the general scheme of biological evolution. The change is too slow to make much difference for ethics, which is strictly a human study. Prehumans were not yet human, and they followed the law of their own nature. There could be morals only when the being passed the threshold into the human state, however gradual that transition might be. If man in the far future should evolve into some being so superior or so different that he is no longer human, he would no longer be guided by the laws of human nature but of the new nature into which he has evolved. Such a law could still be called natural law, inas-

---

[*]St. Thomas, *Summa Theologica*, I-II, q. 94, a. 4.
[†]Rudolf Stammler, mentioned in Rommen, *The Natural Law*, p. 229, and Haines, *Revival of Natural Law Concepts*, p. 249.

much as a being's conduct ought to correspond with the nature it has. Since it would not be human nature, its natural law would not have wholly the same content as ours. We can leave to such hypothetical posthuman beings the development of their own ethics.

Although the core of the natural law for human beings has absolute moral necessity, there are peripheral areas that have a conditional moral necessity. Man has some natural duties that are consequent on certain conditions of life, such as marriage, employment, wealth, or leadership. They flow from man's social nature and are therefore natural, provided society has taken a certain form and man has a particular position in it. Since society itself, though natural, develops its institutions gradually, some conclusions of the natural law will not have application until a certain degree of cultural sophistication has been reached. Thus the natural law may permit to savages some forms of seizure and violence that could be only brutality or revenge in a civilized man. The former has no institutions for securing justice; the latter must use those society has established. The moral law of justice remains the same; only the mode of administering it is different. Here, to use St. Thomas' language in the foregoing quotation, practical rectitude in particular actions is different because of different conditions. In other matters there is the same rectitude concerning particulars, but it is not known to all, as with the evils of predatory warfare, slavery, or race prejudice. These evils were always contrary to the nature of man, but only lately has he become conscious of his duty to eliminate them. That he has not yet fully done so is proof of his need of further moral development.

What is said here is by no means an adoption of relativistic morals. The relativist has no anchor at all and drifts anywhere on the tide of fickle human desire, giving morals no more stability than fads and fashions. On the contrary, experience shows that human nature has stability without rigidity. It is like a fixed anchor with some slack in the line, permitting a circle of swing around the center. It is the business of the moralist to pull the line taut and fix the position close to the center, but he should not try to abolish entirely the leeway nature itself gives him. By striving for absolute strictness and mathematical certainty in morals, he would not be following the law of his own nature.

THE ETERNAL LAW

Can man, who is at least the proximate basis of the moral order, be also the ultimate basis, or must we look for something beyond man? Is the natural law sufficient for itself, or must it be a derivative of a still higher law? Naturalists and humanists make man supreme and, if they admit any moral law at all, could not admit one imposed on man from above him. They could, as the ancient Greeks did, have a natural law without an eternal law. The theist, who views the universe with man in it as created by God, understands that there can be no morals and no law independently of God. He therefore accepts the natural law as "the rational creature's participation of the eternal law."[*]

What is called the *natural law*, from the standpoint of man the subject, is called the *eternal law* from the standpoint of God the lawgiver. In a sense it is the same law looked at from the two sides. It is given different names to emphasize its double aspect: as actively proceeding from God the creator, and as passively received in man the creature. The eternal law expresses the necessary relation of the creator to his creation. It is defined by St. Augustine as: "That law by which it is just that all things be most perfectly in order"[†]

---

[*] St. Thomas, *Summa Theologica*, I-II, q. 91, a. 2.
[†] St. Augustine, *De Libero Arbitrio*, bk. I, ch. 6.

and also as "The divine reason or the will of God commanding that the natural order of things be preserved and forbidding that it be disturbed."* St. Thomas, after agreeing with St. Augustine, defines the eternal law as: "The exemplar of divine wisdom, as directing all actions and movements."† The eternal law includes both the physical laws and the moral law. God directs all his creatures to their ends, nonfree beings by the physical laws inherent in their natures and free beings by the moral law to which they are expected freely to conform their conduct. Ethics emphasizes the eternal law insofar as it contains the moral law.

St. Thomas proves the existence of the eternal law as follows:

> Law is nothing else but a dictate of practical reason emanating from the ruler who governs a perfect community. Now it is evident, granted that the world is ruled by divine providence, . . . that the whole community of the universe is governed by the divine reason. Therefore the very notion of the government of things in God, the ruler of the universe, has the nature of a law. And since the divine reason's conception of things is not subject to time, but is eternal . . . therefore it is that this kind of law must be called eternal.‡

If the premises are accepted, the argument hardly needs explanation. It contains these three steps:

1. God rules the world. Being supremely intelligent, he has a plan in creating the world and cannot be indifferent whether this plan is carried out.

2. God rules the world by law. The plan of his intellect carried out by his will is truly a law. It is an *ordinance* of divine *reason,* establishing order and harmony in creation for the *common good* of all creatures, *promulgated* by being embedded in the natures of the creatures governed by it, and emanating from supreme *authority.*

3. This law is an eternal law. God is eternal, and whatever he knows and wills is as eternal as himself. But its participation in creatures, the natural law, is not eternal but as temporal as the creatures in which it exists.

Thus the eternal law is also called the ultimate norm of morality.* The ultimate reason why a human act is good is that it shares through the eternal law in the goodness of God, and the ultimate reason why a human act is evil is that by flouting the eternal law it contradicts the source of all goodness.

SUMMARY

What obliges us to conform our conduct to a norm or standard is *law.* Law in general is a rule and measure of acts directing them to the proper ends. St. Thomas gives us the classical definition: An ordinance of reason for the common good promulgated by him who has care of the community. It must be mandatory in form, reasonable in content, community-serving in purpose, knowable in manifestation, and authoritative in source.

Law directing nonfree beings to their ends by the necessitation of their nature is *physical* law. Law directing free beings toward their ends by imposing moral obligation on their free will is *moral* law. Law can also be used in a figurative sense to mean observed uniformity and regularity without the idea of necessitation.

The *natural law* theory has had a long history in ethics: as natural justice for the Greeks and Romans, as participation in the eternal law for medieval Christians, as moral law imposed on corrupt human nature in early Protestantism, as the native and primitive in the Age of Enlighten-

---

*St. Augustine, *Contra Faustum Manichaeum,* bk. XXII, ch. 27.
†St. Thomas, *Summa Theologica,* I-II, q. 93, a. 1.
‡St. Thomas, *Summa Theologica,* I-II, q. 91, a. 1.

*St. Thomas, *Summa Theologica,* I-II, q. 21, a. 1.

ment, as almost extinct in the positivistic outlook of the nineteenth century, and as staging a fairly vigorous revival at present.

General argument for the natural law theory: Man must be guided to his end by means that are effective and suited to man's nature. Such means must be a *law* with binding force, for advice is not heeded; a *moral* law, for inner necessity or outer compulsion would destroy man's free will; and a *natural* law, for man is not an exception to the general direction of every being toward its end by its nature.

Natural law is objected to as being outworn Aristotelianism and Stoicism, as repressing creativity for the sake of conformity, as being unknown by most men, as having no method of enforcement, as justifying any kind of conduct one wants, as the source of legalism and pharisaism, as opposed to the higher motive of love. Natural law theorists think that such difficulties are based on misinterpretation of the theory and merely shoot down a caricature of the natural law, leaving the real thing intact.

Natural law is said to be *promulgated* to man through his *reason*, and its *content* to be sufficiently *knowable*. Its *general principles* cannot be invincibly unknown by normal and mature persons, though its

remote conclusions can be. The first moral principle, *Do good and avoid evil,* is known to all. Simple and obvious deductions escape only the abnormal or the immature or those with defective moral training. Difficult conclusions and applications can be invincibly unknown even by the learned, just as error occurs in any field of knowledge. Hence the diversity of opinion in morals.

Natural law should be as variable and invariable as human nature. Man remains man, though his abilities develop. Natural law should be absolute only in its core but admit of relativity in details and applications. Since it is man's nature to live in history, it is natural for him to undergo moral growth.

Beyond natural law must there be a further law, an eternal law? Naturalists and humanists say no. Theists argue thus: God cannot without contradiction be indifferent to the carrying out of his plan of creation. The plan of his intellect and decree of his will that creatures attain their ends is the *eternal law*. It fulfills the definition of a *law*, and it is an *eternal* law, for whatever is in God is eternal and identified with him. Its temporal participation in creatures is the natural law.

QUESTIONS FOR DISCUSSION

1 Is the natural law so tied up with the Greek concept of nature that those who have discarded the Platonic Ideas and Aristotelian forms have no place in their philosophy for a human nature and a law founded on it? Or is natural law to be taken in a broader sense?

2 Of what value is a law that is unformulated? Then each man must formulate it for himself, and we have subjectivism, or society must formulate it, and we seem to be back among the social pressure theories. Is there a way out of this dilemma?

3 Why should the natural law be clearer in its more general principles and become more obscure as one descends to details? What

use is a law that seems to disappear when it is to be applied to concrete cases?

4   Should we say that the natural law itself develops or only that our knowledge of it develops? Is the unchangeableness of the natural law compatible with an evolutionary theory? If man has an evolving nature, will the natural law evolve with him?

5   Is it possible that some things thought to pertain to the natural law are only the cultural heritage of Western civilization? Must ethics continue to examine and evaluate the alleged content of natural law?

READINGS

As instances of the recognition of the natural law among the ancients, see Sophocles' *Antigone*, especially lines 450-460; Cicero's *Pro Milone* (For Milo), iv; *De Republica* (On the State), bk. III, xxii; *De Legibus* (On Laws), bk. I, v, to bk. II, vii. Cicero probably understood the natural law in a Stoic sense.

St. Augustine's notions on the eternal law are found in *De Libero Arbitrio* (On Free Choice) and in *Contra Faustum Manichaeum* (Reply to Faustus the Manichaean); there are several English translations.

St. Thomas, *Summa Theologica*, I-II, qq. 90-97, is known as his Treatise on Law. See also Suarez, *De Legibus* (On Laws), bk. II, ch. 1-15, translated in J. B. Scott, *The Classics of International Law: Selections from Three Works of Francisco Suarez.*

Modern philosophical treatments of the natural law include: Yves Simon, *The Tradition of the Natural Law;* Heinrich Rommen, *The Natural Law,* all-inclusive, and his *The State in Catholic Thought,* ch. 5-8, mainly political; A. P. d'Entrèves, *Natural Law,* stressing the historical and legal side; and Johannes Messner, *Social Ethics,* bk. I, pt. I. Jacques Maritain's *Rights of Man and Natural Law* is a very valuable little book, to be read with his essay "Natural Law and Moral Law," the latter found in Ruth Nanda Anshen's *Moral Principles of Action,* ch. 4. John Wild's *Plato's Modern Enemies and the Theory of Natural Law* is a modern defense of natural law. See also H. L. A. Hart, *The Concept of Law,* ch. 9.

The legal profession has recently written much on the natural law. Charles G. Haines' *Revival of Natural Law Concepts* is the chief work in this field. The *Natural Law Institute Proceedings,* published over some years at Notre Dame, contains many fine articles. Arthur L. Harding edited the results of similar conferences at Southern Methodist University in *Natural Law and Natural Rights.* There are many good articles in *Law and Philosophy,* edited by Sidney Hook, and in *Natural Law and Modern Society,* edited by the Center for the Study of Democratic Institutions. The *Natural Law Forum* is a periodical devoted wholly to the subject.

Attack against the natural law is presented in Hans Kelsen's *What is Justice?* and in the writings of Reinhold Niebuhr.

Austin Fagothey, *Right and Reason—an Anthology,* contains much of St. Thomas' "Treatise on Law" from the *Summa Theologica.*

CHAPTER 12

DUTY

PROBLEM

There are those who hold for the existence of a moral law without conceiving it in terms of a natural law. Usually they do not deny that it is a natural law, but the idea of each thing having its own nature is not emphasized in their philosophy. They may not be sure whether the natures of things can be clearly known, but they are quite sure of the existence and force of moral obligation. It speaks to them with the stern voice of duty, and it is in the concept of duty rather than in that of nature that they would locate the foundations of ethics.

The connection between law and duty is obvious. If there is a law, there is a duty to observe it. If there is a duty, it can only be because some law imposes it. But the moral law binds without the use of external physical force and without any inner determination necessitating observance. What is this duty or obligation or oughtness that the moral law imposes? How does it accomplish its effect? Where does it obtain and how does it exert its binding force?

The theory of duty for duty's sake, of obeying the law purely and simply because it is the law, has been made famous by Immanuel Kant. His aim is the laudable one of keeping morality free from the taint of self-interest, from the lure of reward and the fear of punishment, from the reduction of morality to a mere means instead of an end in itself, from the mercenary motive of living the moral life only if it pays off in some good other than the moral good. There is the further aim of safeguarding man's freedom, autonomy, and personal dignity so that he is under orders from no one, of solving the dilemma of how man can be governed by law and yet not be the slave of the lawgiver. Then, too, there is the case of the man who does good accidentally and how he differs from the morally good man. The outward effects are the same, but the former, not intending or foreseeing the good, accomplishes only a physical good by a morally indifferent act; the latter differs from him by intending the good, acting from the motive of duty and out of respect for the law, thus performing a morally good act.

We shall first outline a sketch of Kant's moral theory with some difficulties connected with it, then expose an alternative theory, and finally propose some recommendations on the place of duty in an ethical system. We have these questions:

1. Can man impose moral obligation on himself?
2. Can there be moral obligation without a lawgiver?
3. Does all moral obligation come through the moral law?
4. Is the moral law enforced by sanction?

KANT'S AUTONOMOUS MORALITY

Kant never tired of saying that two things ever filled him with admiration, "the starry sky above and the moral law within." On the moral law he based the whole structure of his philosophy, for after he had devoted his *Critique of Pure Reason* to breaking down the ability of human reason to penetrate beyond phenomena speculatively, he tried to build it all up again on a practical and moral foundation. His ethical views are found chiefly in his *Critique of Practical Reason* and in his *Fundamental Principles of the Metaphysic of Morals.*

EXPOSITION

He begins by stating that the good taken purely and simply is found only in a *good will,* and a good will is one that acts, not from natural inclination, but from *duty.* Only acts done from duty have moral worth. Even acts done in the line of duty but not from the motive of duty have no moral value. They lack the *form* of morality, that which precisely gives them their moral quality, and this can be nothing else but *respect for the law,* which is what he means by duty. Thus an act is not good because of the end to which it leads, but solely because of the motive of duty from which it is performed.

The moral worth of an action does not lie in the effect which is expected from it or in any principle of action which has to borrow its motive from this expected effect. For all these effects (agreeableness of condition, indeed even the promotion of the happiness of others) could be brought about through other causes and would not require the will of a rational being, while the highest and unconditional good can be found only in such a will. Therefore the pre-eminent good can consist only in the conception of the law itself (which can be present only in a rational being) so far as this conception and not the hoped-for effect is the determining ground of the will. This pre-eminent good, which we call moral, is already present in the person who acts according to this conception and we do not have to expect it first in the result.°

°Kant, *Fundamental Principles of the Metaphysic of Morals,* sec. I.

What is this law, respect for which must be the motive of an act to make it moral? It must be the pure concept of law as such. If any act I do is to be moral, I must ask myself: Can I make the maxim or principle on which this act rests into a universal law binding all?

The shortest but most infallible way to find the answer to the question as to whether a deceitful promise is consistent with duty is to ask myself: Would I be content that my maxim (of extricating myself from difficulty by a false promise) should hold as a universal law for myself as well as for others? And could I say to myself that everyone may make a false promise when he is in a difficulty from which he otherwise cannot escape? I immediately see that I could will the lie but not a universal law to lie. For with such a law there would be no promises at all inasmuch as it would be futile to make a pretense of my intention in regard to future actions to those who would not believe this pretense or—if they over-hastily did so—who would pay me back in my own coin. Thus my maxim would necessarily destroy itself as soon as it was made a universal law.°

Kant goes on to say that, whereas everything in nature works according to laws, only rational beings can have an idea of law and consciously conform their conduct to principles. This capacity is *will,* which is the same as *practical reason.* An objective principle of law binding the will is a command, stated as an *imperative* expressing the *ought.* An imperative may be *hypothetical* (if you want this end, you must use these means), or *categorical* (you must do this absolutely).

If the action is good only as a means to something else, the imperative is hypothetical; but if it is thought of as good in itself, and hence as necessary in a will which of itself conforms to reason as the principle of this will, the imperative is categorical. . . .

It concerns not the material of the action and its intended result but the form and principle from which it results. What is essentially good in it consists in the intention, the result being what it may. This imperative may be called the imperative of morality. . . .

°*Ibid.*

There is . . . only one categorical imperative. It is: Act only according to that maxim by which you can at the same time will that it should become a universal law.*

This statement of the categorical imperative is repeated often by Kant, sometimes with a slightly different wording and emphasis, but the underlying meaning is always the same. What in Kant's view makes an act morally wrong? It is in making an exception for myself. While asserting the universality of the law for everybody, including myself. Thus I try to make myself an exception and not an exception. No one can reasonably will such a contradiction.

When we observe ourselves in any transgression of duty, we find that we do not actually will that our maxim should become a universal law. That is impossible for us; rather, the contrary of this maxim should remain as a law generally, and we only take the liberty of making an exception to it for ourselves or for the sake of our inclination, and for this one occasion.†

The fundamental reason why such conduct is wrong is that it subjects other persons (as means) to myself (as end), perverting the whole *realm of ends,* according to which each rational being, each *person,* must be treated never merely as a means but always as an end in himself. The dignity of the rational being, the nobility of a person as such, is therefore the fundamental reason why I must be moral. But this principle involves a further and startling conclusion. If I must not subject other persons as means to myself as end, I myself am not subjected as means to another as end.

Who, then, imposes the moral law on me? I impose it on myself. This is what Kant calls the *autonomy* of the will.

Reason, therefore, relates every maxim of the will as giving universal laws to every other will and also to every action toward itself; it does not do so for the sake of any other practical motive or future advantage but rather from the idea of the dignity of a rational being, which obeys no law except that which he himself also gives. . . .

He is thus fitted to be a member in a possible realm of ends to which his own nature already destined him. For, as an end in himself, he is destined to be legislative in the realm of ends, free from all laws of nature and obedient only to those which he himself gives. Accordingly, his maxims can belong to a universal legislation to which he is at the same time also subject. . . . Autonomy is thus the basis of the dignity of both human nature and every rational nature.*

Kant goes on to derive from the moral law the three truths that he thought could not be established by speculative reason: the freedom of the will, the immortality of the soul, and the existence of God. Unless we are free, we can neither legislate the moral law for ourselves nor observe it. We can never reach but only approximate a perfect fulfillment of the moral law, but since our function in existence is always to tend to realize it more perfectly, we must be immortal. The one who does realize it perfectly, who is the absolute fulfillment of holiness and the ideal of all goodness, is God.

Granted that the pure moral law inexorably binds every man as a command (not as a rule of prudence), the righteous man may say: I will that there be a God, that my existence in this world be also an existence in a pure world of the understanding outside the system of natural connections,† and finally that my duration be endless. I stand by this and will not give up this belief.‡

Thus these truths are neither mere hypotheses nor rational convictions, but practical postulates demanded by our moral needs, which we accept on *belief,* an attitude Kant calls *pure rational faith.*

---

*Op. cit., sec. II.
†Ibid.

---

*Ibid.
†By "outside the system of natural connections," Kant means that which is *not causally predetermined, as physical nature seems to be, but possessing free will.*
‡Kant, *Critique of Practical Reason,* pt. I, bk. II, ch. II, § viii. See also § v.

CRITICISM

Kant's vigorous assertion of the moral law, his stern preachment of the claims of duty, the paramount importance he attached to the ethical issue, and the high seriousness with which he approached the fundamental problems of philosophy acted as a powerful antidote to the materialism and hedonism of a shallower age. All this was to the good, but his critics pick out certain difficulties in his theory, especially concerning three points:

1. The motive of duty
2. The categorical imperative
3. The autonomy of the will

1. To rest all morality on the motive of *duty* is unnatural and inhuman. Kant nowhere says that an act not done from duty is immoral, only that it is nonmoral; nor does he say that to be moral it must be done from pure duty alone. All he says is that unless the motive of duty is present it cannot be moral, and, if it is done from both duty and inclination, it is the motive of duty that gives it its morality. But even this statement overplays the role of duty. Is it only her sense of duty and not her love for her child that gives morality to a mother's devotion? Is it only cold obligation and not large-hearted generosity that makes relief of the poor a moral act? Certainly a sense of duty will be present in such cases, but love and generosity are always esteemed as higher motives than mere duty and give the act a greater moral worth. We fall back on duty only when other motives fail. Duty is rather the last bulwark against wrong acting than the highest motive for right acting.

How could Kant explain heroic acts, such as giving one's life for one's friend? These acts are always thought the noblest and best precisely because they go beyond the call of duty. Kant is then faced with this dilemma: either he must deny that heroic acts are moral, thus putting the best of human acts outside the pale of moral goodness; or he must make heroic acts a duty, thus putting a burden on human nature that it cannot bear and robbing these acts of the very quality that makes them heroic.

2. That the moral law commands us with a *categorical imperative* is undoubtedly true, and Kant emphasizes it well, but his formulation of it is faulty. The moral imperative is properly, "Do good and avoid evil," plus the more definite principle derived from this, rather than Kant's formula, "So act that the maxim from which you act can be made a universal law," which is only a negative rule. Evil ways of acting could never become universal laws, for they are self-destructive; but there are also good ways of acting that can never become universal laws, such as a life of celibacy. Hence the reason for the moral goodness of an act is not the fact that it can be made a universal law. Kant might answer that we can will celibacy to be a universal law for a definite type of person in definite circumstances; but this answer is no help, for if we start making exceptions of this sort, the term *universal law* loses all meaning. It finally narrows down to just one single case. To use Kant's own example of a lying promise, I might will that anyone in my peculiar predicament could get out of it by lying, and still have the law universal for that class of people.

To determine the goodness of an act wholly from the motive that governs it and not at all from the end to which it naturally leads is to adopt a purely subjective norm of morality. It is difficult to square Kant's view not only with objective morality but also with intrinsic morality, since in his view no acts are good or bad in themselves but only because of the motive of the doer.

3. Kant's recognition of the dignity of the human person is one of the most admired parts of his philosophy, but he carries it so far as to make a *created* person impossible. We must never use each other merely as means, but God may do with us

what he pleases, short of contradicting his own attibutes. To make the human will *autonomous* does violence to the rights of God the creator. Kant is forced to this position by his rejection of the traditional proofs for God's existence. In Kant's system our reason for accepting God's existence is ultimately that we will his existence, for we need him to justify morality to ourselves. As Kant says, this is a practical faith rather than a reasoned conviction. Here his critics see a dilemma. God either does or does not exist; if he does not exist, we cannot will him into existence simply because we feel a need of him; if he does exist, the human will cannot be wholly autonomous but is subject to the law God imposes on us.

Kant sees clearly that there can be no morality without free will, but in his discussion of freedom there is always a confusion between freedom of choice and freedom of independence, as if one could not retain free will and still be under the command of another's law. To save freedom he demands autonomy, but by demanding autonomy he destroys all real obligation and therefore all real law.

The obligation an autonomous will imposes on itself is an obligation only in name. A will that binds itself is no more bound than a man who locks himself in but still holds the key in his hand. Kant does not think that we may either make or not make the moral law for ourselves as we please, or that we frame its provisions arbitrarily. We cannot escape from the categorical imperative, and the maxims that we will into universal laws cannot be otherwise than they are. Why not? If this necessity is founded on the very nature of things (and Kant thinks that it is, for it is our one grasp of the *noumenon,* the thing-in-itself), then it is determined for us by something other than our own will unless we want to set ourselves up as creators of the universe. Either there is no obligation or it is imposed on us from outside our

own will. The only other alternative is an identification of the human will with the divine, the pantheistic trend taken by Kant's followers.

TELEOLOGICAL CONCEPT OF DUTY

Kant's is the most famous expression of pure deontology, or the theory of duty for duty's sake. He sought to liberalize duty by making it autonomous, or self-imposed, but had difficulty in explaining why the self should impose it and why it should be binding. Is there any other way of having duty as stringent as Kant would make it, yet without having recourse to an external legislator?

An effort in this direction had been made by the medieval followers of Aristotle—not by Aristotle himself or by any of the ancient Greeks, whose sense of duty was limited to means and hypothetical imperatives. For them the end itself was happiness, and the living of the moral life sprang from the love of wisdom; they would think it odd to call the pursuit of happiness a duty, since happiness is so eminently desirable in itself. The medieval writers wanted something more than a hypothetical imperative and found it in God, the supreme ruler of the universe and legislator of the moral law. Since few of them wished to conceive of God as an arbitrary dictator, they cast around for some reason that the moral law ought to be followed even if it were not imposed by God. Up to a point they were able to derive moral obligation from the teleological, or purposive, character of the universe, a concept that pervades the Aristotelian outlook.

St. Thomas* notes that necessity arises from the causes of a thing. The external physical necessity of compulsion comes from the efficient cause. The internal physical necessity of determination by a being's

---

*St. Thomas, *Summa Theologica*, I, q. 82, a. 1.

nature comes from the material and formal causes constituting that nature. Moral necessity, which binds a free will without destroying its freedom, must come from the final cause, for only an end or good known by the intellect can move the will. But one cannot will an end and at the same time refuse to will the means necessary to the end; otherwise he would have a mere ineffectual wish, not a decision of the will. Four possibilities occur:

1. Neither the end nor the means are necessary.
2. The end is necessary but not the means.
3. The means are necessary but not the end.
4. Both the end and the means are necessary.

1. Obviously there is no obligation when both end and means are optional.

2. If there are several alternative means to the same end, there is no necessity of willing these means rather than those. Even if the end is absolutely necessary, other means can be used and the end can still be reached.

3. If the end is not absolutely necessary, there is no necessity of using the means even when they are the only possible means. This is always the case when the end is not an absolutely last end, for every intermediate end is also a means to a further end and is not necessary unless this further end is necessary.

4. The end is one that absolutely must be obtained at all costs, and there is but one means to it, with no substitute possible. The means are necessary *if* they are the only means and *if* the end is necessary. By fulfilling both conditions, we pass beyond hypothetical necessity to categorical necessity and arrive at the absolute *ought* of moral obligation.

Applying this analysis to man's moral life, we find both requirements fulfilled:

1. A necessary end absolutely to be obtained
2. One necessary means with no substitute possible

1. Man has an absolutely last end, attainment of which is absolutely necessary for man. The human will is not free to seek or not seek the ultimate good but must of its very nature seek it. It is the sole purpose for which man exists, the only reason why he has any being at all. The intellect perceives this design impressed on man's very nature as the objective order inherent in the universe and exacted by man's being the kind of being he is.

2. Man has only one means of fulfilling his nature and reaching his last end, morally good human acts, and only one means of perverting his nature and losing his last end, morally bad human acts. The nature of man as a free being, who must earn his own moral worth and incur his own moral guilt, makes any substitute means impossible.

Can, then, genuine moral obligation arise merely from the necessary connection of necessary means with a necessary end, independently of any commanding authority? In a sense, yes. Before any authority can command there must already exist the moral obligation of obeying the command. Moral obligation is entailed in the very idea of the highest moral value. Just as the evidence of the truth imposes itself on the theoretical reason and demands assent, so the moral ideal imposes itself on the practical reason and commands consent. Moral obligation is but the clear manifestation of the intrinsic connection between an act to be done, as the necessary means, and the love of the good, as the necessary end. One cannot love the good and refuse that act.

Only the good can be of obligation, yet not every good is of obligation. Does not this show that obligation adds to the good the notion of some authority's imposing it? Not for this reason alone. Good acts are of two kinds: those that *may* be done and those that *must* be done. The kind of good that *may* be done but is not of obligation affords an option, since the end can be obtained in another way and the necessity is not absolute. The kind of good that *must* be done is the kind whose omission would render the necessary end impossible, and thus is as necessary as the end itself. Hence even without an external legislator and simply by reason of its necessary and indispensable relation to the ideal of goodness, the living of the moral life is a moral obligation.

The explanation given so far shows how it is possible for one to recognize and accept moral obligation without a clear and certain knowledge of anyone's imposing the obligation. We can see that there is no need of trying to have ourselves impose the obligation on ourselves, as Kant thought, but, that it comes from the very way things are; from the kind of being we find ourselves possessing without our choosing; from the structure of the universe about us, which we did not produce; and from the requirements of social life, which inevitably must emerge from man's contact with man by the very nature of group living.

It is because the order of knowing does not always parallel the order of being—since in the order of being cause comes before effect but in the order of knowing the effect is often perceived first and then its cause is sought—that man can have a sufficiently workable notion of moral obligation and acknowledge its binding force without arriving at a personal lawgiver. In our way of knowing, starting with connatural knowledge, we rise from the actual values we experience to the formation of purer and higher ideals of value until we come to the ideal of the good as such, the abstract notion of absolute perfection, which has to be the highest good and the moral ideal.

Is such an ideal verified in any existing reality? So far the theist and the nontheist can agree, but here they part company. The nontheist has to leave the moral ideal in this abstract condition, since he can find

no concrete reality with which to identify it. Though the ideal can never be reached, it remains an inspiring vision of what ought to be and thus engenders the moral obligation of coming as close to it as time and effort allow. Experience shows that such an abstract ideal is capable of motivating a noble and even a heroic life. The theist agrees but thinks that it can be carried a step farther. He identifies the ideal with a concrete, really existing being, a personal God who is absolute goodness in himself and the source of goodness in us. Thus moral obligation, though founded in the nature of things, comes ultimately from the founder of the nature of things, from a personal legislator with commanding authority, the one who established the end and the means and their necessary connection, and who uses his authority, not arbitrarily, but to ensure the carrying out of the objective order of the universe. Thus for the theist moral obligation is in a truncated condition until God is put at the apex.

Our purpose here has not been to establish the theistic outlook but to see how far moral obligation can stand on its own merits. We have seen it from both the deontological and the teleological standpoints. These are often regarded as opposites, though they might be better viewed as complementary parts of the one whole truth. Both agree in seeking a firm basis for moral obligation.

IMPORTANCE OF DUTY IN THE MORAL LIFE

We have arrived at the following alternatives. Either there is no such thing as moral obligation or it does exist. If it exists, it is either imposed on us by a legislator or it is not. If not, it springs out of the nature of man and his place in the universe. If it is imposed, either we impose it on ourselves or it is imposed on us from outside us. In the latter case it must come either from God or from our fellowman, for nothing beneath us can bind us. If it comes from our fellowman, it must be from him as politically organized into the state or from the customs his society has developed. These alternatives cover a broad spectrum of ethical theories. A word on each by way of summary:

1. Moral obligation cannot be denied. It is passed over in such ethical viewpoints as hedonism and opportunism, but their inability to account for moral obligation is a deficiency that renders them untenable.

2. Moral obligation does not come from oneself. Kant's valiant and ingenious attempt to make it do so will not stand up. One cannot have authority over oneself and be subject to oneself in the same respect, be one's own superior and inferior. A lawmaker can repeal his own laws. If man made the moral law for himself, he could never violate it, for he cannot will both its observance and its violation at once, and his act of violation would be an act of repeal. Such a law could impose no obligation.

3. Moral obligation cannot come from fellowman. Moral positivism and the various social pressure theories eliminate rather than explain moral obligation. As persons all men are equal. No man or body of men has original jurisdiction over another so as to bind him under moral guilt, under pain of losing his intrinsic worth as a man. What obligation have men to obey the state? Of itself the state can exert only physical compulsion or the threat of it, unless it can appeal to the authority it receives from a source beyond itself that enjoins obedience to the state as part of the moral law, unless it can appeal to the consciences of men to do their duty as citizens. Lesser groups have even less authority. Hence moral obligation cannot come from fellowman, whether taken individually or as organized into society.

4. Moral obligation does spring out of the nature of man and his place in the universe, but this source is proximate rather than ultimate. It is the kind of grounding given to moral obligation by the natural law considered in isolation from the eternal law. Many stop here and find the abstract concept of the ideal good a morally compelling force sufficient to constitute a categorical imperative absolutely commanding the moral life. Others acknowledge that this is so but ask further why it should be so.

5. Moral obligation, though stemming proximately from the nature of man and his value as a person, finds its ultimate justification in God. This gives the answer to the previous question. We need to see just what there is about the good that constitutes its overwhelming necessitating power yet at the same time leaves us freedom of choice, so that the obligation is absolute yet a moral one. We can do so only by tracing the good to a really existing source of goodness, to the one who is goodness in person, from whom goodness descends to everything else that is good, and who wills the goodness of all other things even as he wills his own goodness. The source of all being is likewise the source of all good.

The philosopher is obliged to trace the origin of moral obligation as far back as he can. Yet, whatever be our theory on the ultimate justification of the *ought*, we cannot overestimate its importance in the moral life. Duty is hardly an attractive concept in itself. It is often made more unattractive by the harsh way in which it is first encountered. A parent's arbitrary decree obliging the child to do something disagreeable with no instruction on the reasonableness of the command naturally provokes resentment in one whose intelligence is awakening. "Do it because I say so," accompanied with an appropriate threat of punishment, may get the desired outer result but at the expense of lasting inner scars. A psychological prejudice against duty can harden into a habitual feeling of rebelliousness at the confrontation with any duty, so that one will refuse to do even what he most wants to do merely because he has been told to do it. One so conditioned can become incapable of acting with mature responsibility, which is nothing else but the assumption of the duties of adult life. The union of duty and responsibility is clear. Anyone with a duty is responsible for fulfilling it, and anyone with responsibility for anything, whether it be his own conduct or some affair put under his charge, has the duty of carrying out this responsibility.

All government of men on earth finds its ethical basis in moral obligation. All human laws, which are the only instruments by which men can be governed consistently with their rational and free nature, derive their binding force from the moral law. There are only three reasons why a person obeys a law:

1. The law commands what is personally advantageous.
2. Threat of punishment makes it expedient to obey.
3. The subject feels a sense of duty or moral obligation.

The first two reasons cannot guarantee obedience to the law. It will be kept as long as it seems advantageous or the vigilance of the police cannot be eluded. Since the subjects feel no moral obligation to keep the law, they will break it as soon as it becomes more expedient to break it than to keep it. In these cases it is not the law itself that binds the human will but the attractiveness of what the law prescribes or the fear of the punishment threatened. A law, as a law, can bind the human will only by imposing moral obligation. Positive laws can impose no moral obligation on their own account but can do so only if the moral law commands that just laws enacted by legitimate authority are to be obeyed. Therefore positive laws derive what binding force they have from the moral law.

SANCTION

Obligation is moral necessity, a necessity resulting from the final cause, which is a motive urging a person to act but not destroying his free will. The only way that a lawgiver can have his law obeyed is by proposing a motive sufficiently strong to attract the subjects to free acts of obedience. Such a motive, such a means a lawgiver uses to enforce his law, is called a *sanction*. Sanction means the promise of reward for keeping the law or the threat of punishment for breaking the law, or both; it also means the rewards or punishments themselves. Its function is *antecedent*, to induce people to keep the law and to dissuade them from breaking it, and *consequent*, to restore the objective order of justice after the law has been kept or broken.

A *natural* sanction follows from the very nature of the act performed, as when sickness follows from intemperance or loss of business from dishonesty to customers. A *positive* sanction is decided by the will of the lawmaker and has no natural connection with the act, as when a fine is levied for speeding or tax evasion is punished by imprisonment. A *perfect* sanction is one that is both *strong*, in that it provides a rational will with a sufficient motive for keeping the law, and *just*, in that it sets up equality between merit and reward, demerit and punishment. An *imperfect* sanction is in some measure either weak, unjust, or both.

Is there a sanction attached to the moral law? Observance of the moral law brings about the harmony between our acts and our nature, between our animal and rational tendencies, between our creatural, social, and proprietary relations. Barring accidents, there should result peace of mind, friendship, honor, prosperity, health, and a long life, as the result of the virtues of prudence, justice, fortitude, and temperance. Frequent violation of the moral law should result in remorse of conscience, loss of friendship, dishonor, poverty, disease, and an early death, as the expected consequences of folly, dishonesty, cowardice, and debauchery.

As life is actually lived, this sanction is

imperfect. Too often the good suffer and the wicked prosper all life long. Unforeseen calamities play a large part in life, and they are not distributed according to one's moral worth. Few violate the whole moral law, and the punishments for breaking part of it are offset by the rewards for keeping the rest. Crimes are concealed and the punishments avoided. It may be true in general that "Crime does not pay," but in many particular instances it pays well. One may find a bad conscience easy to live with for a million dollars dishonestly gained. One may be put to the supreme test, to choose between gross moral evil and death.

The theist holds that God, being a wise and just lawgiver, must assign a perfect sanction to the moral law. Since the sanction in the present life is not perfect, the perfect sanction must be applied in the life to come. It must be the gain or loss of our last end and highest good. Those who deliberately refuse to use the means should be deprived of the end, and those who deliberately choose evil should be deprived of the good. If even this threat does not always prevent wrongdoing, and experience shows that it does not, surely nothing less would do so. God is unable to provide a stronger sanction without encroaching on man's free will, for he cannot offer a greater reward or threaten a greater punishment than the gain or loss of the highest good.

SUMMARY

How does moral necessity, which is the same as oughtness, obligation, or duty, accomplish its effect?

Immanuel Kant held that we impose obligation on ourselves. Nothing, he says, is simply good except a good will. A good will is one that acts from the motive of duty. Duty is the necessity of acting from respect for law. The moral law commands with a categorical imperative: So act that the maxim from which you act can by your will be made into a universal law. The basis for the categorical imperative is the human personality. A person is never to be used as a mere means, always to be regarded as an end. The human will is an end in itself, autonomously imposing the moral law on itself.

Kant is criticized for overstressing the idea of duty, incorrectly formulating the moral imperative, and making the human will supreme while emptying obligation of all meaning.

Moral obligation is inherent in the very idea of the absolute moral good and should be conceived as logically prior to any commanding authority, which presupposes an obligation to obey the command. Yet without a lawgiver it is incomplete, for there is no one to whom one is obliged. Nontheists can and do admit moral obligation but have difficulty finding a secure basis for it.

Moral obligation cannot come from *oneself,* for any lawmaker can repeal his own laws, nor from *fellowman,* for as persons all men are equal and no one has original jurisdiction over another. Theists trace moral obligation to *God,* who determines the necessary connection between the observance of the moral law and man's last end, and makes the attainment of the last end absolutely mandatory. This determination he manifests to us through the *moral law,* which is the proximate source of all obligation; from it alone *human laws* derive their binding force.

Sanction is the promise of reward or threat of punishment added to a law to secure obedience. There is an *imperfect* sanction to the moral law in the present life, but a *perfect* sanction must be looked for in the life to come. This perfect sanction, the strongest possible without destroying human free will, must consist in the gain or loss of man's last end and highest good.

QUESTIONS FOR DISCUSSION

1   The moral imperative of the natural law is: Follow your natural inclinations! Yet much of moral living seems to consist in resisting natural inclinations. Is there a solution to this paradox?

2   What is your considered judgment on Kant's categorical imperative? Can it be reworked to express the basic moral imperative? Can we get along without any moral imperative?

3   One who places the ultimate source of moral obligation in God can, apart from revelation, know of this obligation only through his own reasoning power. Does he not really impose this obligation on himself and merely refer it to God out of deference?

4   Is there something unworthy in the concept of sanction, as if we would not be good unless we were paid for it? Should a truly sincere ethics skip the whole notion of sanction?

5   Can the claims of eudaemonism, that happiness is the aim of life, and deontologism, that duty is the aim of life, be reconciled? Has one a duty to be happy? Can one be happy in doing one's duty? Or is duty necessarily restrictive of happiness, and is happiness necessarily free from all duty?

READINGS

Aristotle, *Ethics,* bk. VII, ch. 2-3; St. Thomas, *Summa Theologica,* I, q. 13, aa. 3, 6; *Summa Contra Gentiles,* bk. III, ch. 10; Suarez, *De Legibus* (On Laws), bk. II, ch. 9. These writers give background material rather than matter directly on the subject of this chapter.

Immanuel Kant's *Fundamental Principles of the Metaphysic of Morals* and his *Critique of Practical Reason* present his ethical views. His *Lectures on Ethics* are a simpler but less famous statement of the same thing. H. J. Paton's *The Categorical Imperative* is a well-known commentary. C. D. Broad's *Five Types of Ethical Theory* has a good critique of Kant. A. C. Ewing in *Ethics,* ch. 4, comments on Kant and in ch. 8 discusses deserts and responsibility, or sanctions.

H. A. Prichard's *Moral Obligation* is a classic study. See also W. D. Ross, *The Right and the Good* and *Foundations of Ethics.* F. H. Bradley, "My Station and Its Duties" in his *Ethical Studies,* interprets duty in terms of self-realization.

Austin Fagothey, *Right and Reason—an Anthology,* contains part of Kant's *Fundamental Principles of the Metaphysic of Morals,* and H. A. Prichard's essay "Does Moral Philosophy Rest on a Mistake?" from his book, *Moral Obligation,* ch. 1.

CHAPTER 13

FREEDOM

PROBLEM

The history of philosophy is a history of pendulum swings from one extreme of thought to the other. The pendulum spends twice as much time near the middle as it does near either extreme, and the amplitude of its oscillation varies, but without extremes no oscillations could occur. The overemphasis of the last few centuries on rationalism and legalism is being balanced in our time by an emphasis, some would say overemphasis, on voluntarism and anarchism. Our three chapters on reason, duty, and law presented these subjects from a fairly moderate standpoint, but there are those who think them irrelevant to a treatment of morals. What is needed is a declaration of independence against all three, and this can best be done by a proclamation of freedom.

Freedom is hardly a new idea in man's history. Any primitive hunter caught in a trap set for animals or any tribal warrior captured by his enemies longed for escape from his bonds. As life became more complex, so did the forms of freedom. Older philosophers, though recognizing the value of freedom, have not much to say about it. They seem to take it as a condition necessary for the pursuit of other goods but do not put much emphasis on it as a good in itself. The reason may be that, though freedom looks so positive, its only definite meaning is negative. Freedom enables a person to do what he wants, but it does not tell him what to want. Freedom is not a virtue. It does not make man good. Rather, it is a condition necessary for the exercise of virtue, and good acts remain mere good intentions unless one is free to do them.

The modern emphasis on human rights and the dignity of the human person has probably had much to do with the conception of freedom as one of our chief values. From the political sphere the idea entered the moral sphere. That state is thought best which best guarantees the freedom of its citizens. Thus freedom becomes thought of as a value in itself, one that a state ought to protect and that its citizens ought even to fight for, and hence a moral value concerned with the ought. In this sense freedom, far from being opposed to law, is quite consonant with it. We shall begin with some of these older views and then take up the modern ethics of freedom. We have these questions:

1. What is the relation between law and freedom?
2. What is the existentialist view of freedom?
3. What is the case for and against existentialist ethics?
4. What is the proper place of freedom in ethics?

LAW AND FREEDOM

Freedom in its broadest sense means absence of bonds, ties, or restraints. Law is said to *bind* those subject to it, and whoever is bound finds his freedom curtailed to some extent. But not all freedom is necessarily good; in its broadest meaning the word covers a vicious license as well as true liberty. The purpose of law is to eliminate the first and promote the second. How does it produce this effect? One can be bound by various kinds of bonds, and those imposed by law are of a special nature. There are three kinds of freedom corresponding to three kinds of bonds:

1. When we think of bonds there immediately come to mind such things as chains, ropes, bars, prison walls. The one bound is subjected to force, violence, coercion, applied from outside him. Such bonds impose *external physical necessity*, which compels or restrains bodily actions only and cannot touch the inner act of the will. Freedom from such external compulsion is called freedom of *spontaneity*. In this sense a man turned out of prison is set *free*, or an uncaged animal roams about *freely*.

2. Less obvious but more rigorous bonds are imposed by the inner determination of a being's own nature. A being lacking free will is utterly subject to its own natural tendencies and instincts, and must act in the way its nature prescribes for it. The nature of a being imposes on it *internal physical necessity;* this is the domain of the physical laws, which are not the kind of laws we deal with in ethics. Freedom from such inner determination of one's nature is what is meant by freedom of *choice* or *free will*, the prerogative of a rational being. It is in this sense that a human act is said to be done voluntarily and *freely.*

3. In contrast to the two kinds of physical bonds, outer and inner, just mentioned, there are also moral bonds, which are ways of restraining the free will of rational beings by the authority of a commanding will. Moral bonds are *laws* in the strictest sense, moral laws as opposed to physical laws, and the necessity they impose is *moral necessity*, which is the same as oughtness, obligation, or duty. Freedom from law, from dictation by a commanding will, is called freedom of *independence*. In this sense Americans by the War of Independence became *free* from the laws of England, a man whose wife has died is *free* to marry again, a man who has paid a bill in full is *free* from that debt.

Because the bonds are different, one kind of freedom may exist without the other. Hence a man can retain his free will and yet be bound by a law. He may be physically free to do an act, since he is able to do it, but he may not be morally free, since he ought not to do it.

Here we see the difference between the last type of freedom, freedom of independence, and the other two types. It is a perfection to be free from the compulsion of external force and from the determinism of a rigidly necessitating principle of action in one's nature, but it is no perfection in a creature to be free from *all* law. Freedom of independence has meaning only with regard to human laws, which are not passed universally for all mankind but for certain political divisions or classes of people. A man is free from the laws of other jurisdictions to which he does not belong, but as a citizen of some country he cannot have complete freedom of independence from all human law. He can have no independence at all from the moral law conceived as rooted in universal human nature.

The freedom we have been considering is *freedom from;* more important is *freedom for*. The only reason why it is good for a person to be free *from* various restrictions and hindrances is that he may be free *for* the kind of life he is meant to live, for the attainment of his end. Freedom *from* is merely negative; freedom *for* is its positive complement. Law curtails freedom *from*, because it imposes obligations a man would otherwise be free from, but it enhances freedom *for*, because it enables a man to live the kind of life that befits him.

The purpose of law, then, is not to impose undue hardship or needless restriction on people but to protect and promote true liberty. Law tends to make men good, directing them to their last end and pointing out to them the means necessary to this end. Even in the lesser sphere of man's temporal welfare, human law fulfills the same function, that of pointing out means to end and the obligatory character of both. Law makes man free to attain his goal by directing him to the right course and keeping him on it, at the same time leaving him physically free to take or refuse this direction, since it does not destroy his free will. Thus law frees man from bondage to ignorance and error without lessening man's responsibility and self-control.

A man lost in a forest is not free to reach his destination because he does not know in what direction to go or what means to take. A signpost and a pathway do not destroy his freedom but rather free him from the necessity of staying in the forest. He is still free to follow the sign and path or not, but if he refuses, the penalty is that he remains lost. In like manner laws point out how we must act to attain our goal; we retain our free will to obey or disobey them, but the penalty for disobedience is that we cannot reach our end. True liberty, therefore, is not license to do anything at all however evil it might be, the freedom of outlaws, but the ability to direct ourselves with the help of laws to the good. In this sense it is correct to say that true freedom is the right to do what we *ought,* and law shows us where the *ought* lies. But neither law nor freedom irresistibly compels us to choose as we *ought.*

EXISTENTIALISM

We might think first of the *anarchists* as the main opponents of law and advocates of unlimited freedom, but theirs is a superficial opposition, a dislike for governments and authority. Of the twin concepts, law and order, they will take the order without the law, thinking this possible because man by nature is so good in himself that all he needs is to be let alone and his reason will guide him aright. They are not necessarily op-posed to a moral law, which operates without legislators, judges, and police.

The real opponents of law are the *existentialists,* especially those who espouse the philosophy of the absurd. Their opposition is implicit, for they make no attack on governments or civil laws and strongly insist on man's responsibility for the society in which he lives. But they assert freedom in such a way as to remove all basis on which any law could rest. They deny that man has a human nature that could be either good or bad and, in their almost morbid abhorrence of rationalism, put no trust in human reason.

Existentialism is an attitude rather than a school of thought, for its proponents resist being lumped together and tagged with a label, and much less is it a system, since they have nothing but scorn for system building. Since they do not take kindly to definitions, we are never quite sure just what they mean. We gather it indirectly from their dramas, novels, journals, and autobiographies, modes of expression they find congenial. Even their strictly philosophical works proceed by way of description and digression. What we have to say will be taken mostly from Søren Kierkegaard and Jean-Paul Sartre, as representing the theistic and atheistic wings of existentialist thought.

The initial picture is a gloomy one. We find ourselves in this world, confronted with the bare fact of existence. We did not ask for it, but the fact is that we are here, trapped into existence. The world that we live in is a wasteland that makes no sense. It is often hostile to us and, worst of all, indifferent. We look around and see that most people live an animal life, some almost a vegetable life, that is barren and empty. They are faceless ciphers going through the motions of living. The few who reflect on this meaningless existence become uneasy and restless. Life fills them with a sense of futility and despair, of anguish and nausea. What should we do? What should we believe? These are agonizing questions, but there seems to be no answer. Not only are our minds too weak to work out an answer, but even if we found one, it would be absurd. Yet we must decide because we are free. Freedom is the undefined and unproved basic datum.

Kierkegaard solves the problem by faith. He sees life in three stages. The aesthetic man lives the life of the senses to the full and finds it empty. Sensations are fleeting, sterile, buried in memory, an ever-hungry filling up of a bottomless appetite. The ethical man sees the claims of abstract duty, fitting his life into the rational grooves laid for him by the system. This is the moral life in the usual sense and better than a mere aesthetic life, but it is not an authentic existence, not a creation of one's own unique self, not an expression of one's subjectivity, but a smug and presumptuous self-sufficiency. The only authentic life is the religious life lived by the man of faith. Faith is a leap in the dark, into infinity, into absurdity. Nothing can prepare one for it. It is an acceptance of something supremely unreasonable: for Abraham the command to kill his son, ethically a detestable crime; for the Christian the commitment to the Incarnation, that God becomes Man, the Infinite finite, the impossible a fact, with all the scandal of the cross. To commit oneself to an authentic Christian life is to throw away the aesthetic and the ethical for something far higher, but we know there is this higher only by faith, and faith is a commitment to what seems to our reason to be absurd. The act of faith is not a rational act. Before deciding to believe as a pure act of our freedom, we have no way of knowing that it is the right decision, whether it is better to leap or not. For our choice we bear the full responsibility, for each man's faith is his own. Our decision is made in the midst of despair, but faith is the only way of conquering despair, transcending the absurd, and finding God's will in the calm serenity of silence. For reason life is meaningless, but faith gives it meaning and hope.

Sartre and the atheistic wing of existen-

tialists can find no comfort in faith, for they have decided already that there is no God and no future life. Man is thrown back on his own resources. The world is absurd, but the brute fact is that we are here, and we cannot avoid the necessity of choice. If the absurd cannot be transcended, it must be confronted and accepted for what it is—absurd.

If existence really does precede essence, there is no explaining things away by reference to a fixed and given human nature. In other words, there is no determinism, man is free, man is freedom. On the other hand, if God does not exist, we find no values or commands to turn to which legitimize our conduct. So, in the bright realm of values, we have no excuse behind us, nor justification before us. We are alone, with no excuses.

That is the idea I shall try to convey when I say that man is condemned to be free. Condemned, because he did not create himself, yet in other respects is free; because, once thrown into the world, he is responsible for everything he does. . . .

The existentialist does not think that man is going to help himself by finding in the world some omen by which to orient himself. Because he thinks that man will interpret the omen to suit himself. Therefore he thinks that man, with no support and no aid, is condemned every moment to invent man. . . . "Man is the future of man."*

Man begins with existence but no essence. His essence, *what* he shall be, he makes for himself by every free choice. By each decision, taken in absolute freedom, we become *authentic* individuals, not meaningless stereotypes or lifeless props on the fantastic stage of life, but meaningful characters in that drama of our own composition which is our life. By each decision we create ourselves and determine what we shall become. This is why each choice is such a dreadful but inescapable responsibility, molding both oneself and one's world into the kind of thing one has chosen it to be.

*Used by permission of Philosophical Library, Inc., from *Existentialism* by Jean-Paul Sartre, copyright, 1947, by Philosophical Library, Inc., New York, pp. 22-23.

Each man is responsible not only for himself but also for all mankind, for they, too, are conditioned by his commitments. Man is not only being-for-himself but being-for-others. He must engage in the work of society and must not shirk his social responsibilities. But ultimately and finally, for what? All a man's commitments come to a head in death. No sooner has he made himself, created his essence, achieved his authenticity by the full use of his freedom, than the whole structure is swept away in death, the ultimate and tragic absurdity, the final irrationality in all this meaningless existence. Only by freely accepting his own as well as the world's absurdity can a man rise above the nausea of despair, live with his constant quest to become the God he never can be, and embrace the fact that "man is a useless passion."

CASE FOR AND AGAINST EXISTENTIALIST ETHICS

The following are some of the reasons that can be presented for existentialist ethics, especially of the Sartrean variety:

1. Freedom must be the basis of any moral theory, for only a free act can have any morality. Since one is responsible for all his free acts and only for his free acts, any other basis would be superfluous. Nor can freedom be demonstrated. One must accept freedom by an original act of commitment to it, and such a commitment must be free, thus presupposing any freedom one might be trying to demonstrate.

2. Man has no nature, no essence. The most we can say is that he exists in the human condition. Existence is simple presence and beyond explanation. Of course, a man is a man and not something else, but that is given and unimportant. It is not what man as such, any man, is or can become that is important, but what *this* man is and can become, what I am and can make of myself. Each one must live his own life, and there is no man-in-general. In this sense man has no essence and must create it by every act he does.

3. Morality is creativity, and creativity done according to rules would not truly be creativity. If what I am to make of myself must be something wholly unique, how can I have prescribed to me ahead of time what I am to make of myself? It would not be myself but something other than myself I make myself into, thus losing myself.

4. Each one chooses his own moral principles. Values have value only if we have chosen them as valuable. There are no universally valid moral absolutes. We can change our values only by our own decision, and no omens will tell us that we have decided rightly. The approval of others or of society cannot justify our actions, nor is there any transcendent self or moral ideal to which we can look. Our transcendence is a function of our present choice, which we freely make on our own responsibility.

5. A person is in "bad faith," as Sartre calls it, if he declines to accept the fact that he is what he is, namely his past actions, present decisions, and projected future. A person is "sincere," in the pejorative sense, if he refuses to admit that he is not what he is, thus denying his freedom to become what he is not yet. In both cases one tries to live some other man's life, to be a personality with a given role in society that has been imposed on him from outside himself.

6. The ethics of ambiguity is the acceptance of this division in his being, his "is" and his "is-not," his being-in-itself and his being-for-itself, his facticity and his consciousness. Man is constantly outside himself, projecting himself, losing himself outside himself, making his own existence. This is the supreme exercise of his freedom.

7. Authenticity is this realistic grasp of the ambiguous nature of human reality. It is honesty and courage, a facing of what the inauthentic individual is afraid to face: the pursuit of transcendent goals that

are of one's own choosing and for which one is responsible both for the choice of the goals and for what one does in their pursuit.

8. There is not only the subjective commitment, by which my choice becomes relevant to myself, but also the objective commitment to society, which is all-important. Our being is also a being-for-others. We live in a world of intersubjectivity. Other people are indispensable to my own existence as well as to my knowledge about myself, and I am responsibly involved in their lives. There will always be a conflict here, between my project and others' projects, and this is part of the ambiguity I must accept as implied in life's absurdity.

Much can be learned from the existentialist viewpoint. It has brought philosophy down from the clouds of abstraction and impersonality by an eloquent probing of each one's deepest and most vital concerns. Many find fault with existentialism, not for its affirmations, but for its denials. We need to stress existence, freedom, subjectivity, meaningfulness, relevance, authenticity, commitment, and involvement. But need we go at them by way of irrationalism and absurdity?

1. There is no question of the value of freedom, whether it can be demonstrated or not, and it is true that only free acts can have morality. Many free acts, however, are morally indifferent; for them the doer is responsible but not morally responsible. Also, morality is of two kinds: good and bad. The mere fact that an act is done freely does not necessarily make it morally good. Freedom is one of the requirements of a morally good act, but it should also be the kind of act one *ought* freely to perform.

2. It is misleading to say that man has no nature or essence, when all that is meant is that he has not yet completed the living of his life and fully made himself the being he is to become. Though he is a unique person, he exists as a member of the human race. Besides his uniqueness he has a commonness with the rest of the human species, and this commonness can be as important as his uniqueness. The impossibility of resigning from the human race shows that he has an essence and that it is only within the limits of a morally decent human life that he may express the uniqueness of his person.

3. The accent on creativity is one of the best fruits of existentialist thinking. No rules can be prescribed to creativity, it is true, but that does not prevent creativity from working within rules and norms. The artist does it all the time. As in much modern art, the norms may be reduced and relaxed, but they are never wholly abandoned, or one could never judge a daub or a ditty to be bad art or no art. Pure unregulated creativity in the moral life could just as well issue in criminality or futility as in a life worth living.

4. Each one does choose his own moral principles, values, and ideals, but it is the business of ethics to guide him in this choice and not to shirk this responsibility. To choose moral principles, values, and ideals one need not originate them but only make them one's own; it is not necessary to refuse help from reason and experience. One who makes such a refusal is in no condition to find any universally valid moral absolutes (except that of freedom), but whose fault is it if not the refuser's own? What if one freely chooses to have moral absolutes? Who can outlaw this free choice as invalid if freedom is the only norm.

5. A man must surely both be what he is and be free to develop himself meaningfully. If his whole life is nothing but playing a role, he deserves the contempt Sartre has for him. But this does not mean that no one can do the normal work of society without falling into "bad faith." Must everyone express his uniqueness by exhibitionism and eccentricity, which seem to be the worst kinds of role playing? Or may one play a normal role in life but do it with a

correct existentialist attitude? If so, who or what makes any attitude correct?

6. That man is an enigma and full of ambiguity is recognized in most philosophies. That the ambiguity is unresolvable is part of Sartre's irrationalism and hopelessness. If one antecedently denies anything on which a solution could be based, one will have to accept the ambiguity. But then it is an absurd world only because one has chosen to have it absurd.

7. Authenticity is a valid and valuable concept in ethics. No man can be leading the moral life unless he is an authentic person, really himself and responsible for himself and all he does. Since no one can judge his authenticity but the man himself, we have here an affirmation that the individual conscience is the subjective norm of morality. There does not seem to be any contradiction between authenticity and objective morality if the person himself is firmly convinced that his objective norms are true. Even if he did not invent them, he has adopted them and made them his own. He would not be authentic unless he lived by them.

8. Existentialists have been at pains to include society in their ethics, but critics are not convinced that they can do so successfully. That one is responsible for his own free choices is clear, but not that one is responsible for others' choices and for the social ills that surround us. Nor does one become responsible for them by refusing suicide as a way out. A moral obligation to participate in social reform would logically follow from man's social nature, but the existentialists do not admit a human nature that could be social. If man is free to choose his own values, what gives him a moral obligation to choose social values? Being-for-others seems to be only pasted on to being-for-oneself, with no reason why the paste sticks. Hence the appeal to ambiguity and absurdity. But then why spend such an enormous flow of words trying to put meaning into the meaningless?

PLACE OF FREEDOM IN ETHICS

Freedom has no less a place in a rational than in an irrational ethics, in a meaningful view of the world than in a philosophy of the absurd. The latter takes freedom as an indefinable and unprovable basic datum, which without further examination may be only a groundless assumption, but the former after investigation fits freedom into the total scheme of a rationally ordered universe, where it finds its very important but proper place.

Freedom and responsibility necessarily entail each other, as the existentialists are not alone in emphasizing. Man is indeed responsible for the free choices he makes, but not everything in the world is of man's choosing. To make him responsible for his whole environment, physical and social, over which he has no control, is carrying responsibility beyond any accepted usage of the term. One can argue that someone must be responsible and, if there is no God, responsibility for these things must be assumed by the only responsible being we know, that is, man. But the logical answer should be that no one is responsible, since man did not create the universe, did not freely put himself in it, did not even freely choose to be free. A coherent view of responsibility makes it just as extensive as freedom and no more. Since a man has not freely willed his environment, he cannot be responsible for it, but only for his attitude toward it. And this is held by any philosophy that admits freedom.

The concept of God as a supernatural stalking-horse on whom we can throw our responsibility and shed our blame is not uncommon among unbelievers. No wonder they reject such a God. Believers, too, can treat God in this fashion, for the ways of superstition are manifold and can include psychological projection. But this is not at all what the knowledgeable believer means by faith and religion. Rather than lower his responsibility by throwing it off on another, his acceptance of God increases his responsibility and makes it meaningful. With God, he is responsible to someone, he must answer to someone, he must give an account to someone. This is surely more than responsibility to oneself, which seems to be mere language for no responsibility.

There is a temptation to pass from some of life's more galling absurdities to a castigation of the whole of life as one grand absurdity. Then we have the existentialist dilemma of either accepting the absurdity and defying it, as Sartre and Camus do, or of seeking deliverance by a nonrational act of faith, as Kierkegaard and Marcel do. In both cases philosophy as a work of reason is bankrupt. In the first case is stays bankrupt and hugs its own absurdity; in the second it is bailed out by God, who plays *Deus ex machina* in a serious sense. But there is no need for philosophy to go bankrupt, if it holds on to its treasure of wisdom and manages it with the guidance of reason, judgment, and prudence. Philosophies that do so make a great deal of sense out of our harmoniously ordered and beautiful universe, taking with a sense of humor its occasional absurdities and facing with courage the challenges it offers.

Why stir up an artificial conflict between being a free person and having a rational human nature? Trying to free man from his nature is trying to free him from himself. Man is free because he has a nature of which freedom is an essential attribute. Existentialists implicitly agree by attributing freedom to man alone. Freedom is a natural consequence of intelligence. A rational being can be free because he has within him a natural guide to the use of his freedom, his reason. Existentialists say that each one of us must have a project in life, what he will make of himself. Such a project can exist nowhere but in the mind of man directing his free choice of actions to bring about the project's fulfillment. As existing in man's

mind, such a project cannot be some wild fantasy detached from life's possibilities but must be some rational aim both worthy and capable of accomplishment. How would it differ from the moral ideal we spoke of earlier? Either such an ideal is constructed and criticized by right reason, or else it has to be some blind stab in the dark. If the former, we have a rational ethics including the benefits of the existentialist outlook; if the latter, we have an absurd philosophy fit only for an absurd world it is absurd to try to live in.

Let us by all means have freedom and as much of it as we can, while recognizing that even freedom has its limits. Of itself, freedom has no judgment. As mere freedom, it is open to anything and everything, and calls for guidance. As mere freedom, it is open to good and evil, and is willing to take either. It must be steered to the good and away from the evil, and we have nothing to steer it with but the light of reason. Reason and freedom, intellect and will, knowledge and desire work together as a team, not as separate things within man, but as concurrent emphases of his one human nature, enabling him to fulfill the project he ought to accomplish, the embodiment in himself of the moral ideal.

The upshot of all this is that the most valuable part of the existentialist philosophy is quite compatible with other ways of thinking and need not be taken in an exclusively existentialist sense. We should be very grateful, however, to the existentialists for emphasizing and eloquently presenting an extremely important but hitherto neglected aspect of ethics.

SUMMARY

Freedom is one of our most cherished values. On it some wish to build the whole of ethics.

Many see no opposition between freedom and law. They say that the purpose of law is to make the exercise of freedom possible, that the function of law is not to impose needless restraint but to direct men to their ultimate goal without destroying their free will.

There are various kinds of freedom corresponding to various kinds of bonds from which one may be free: freedom of *spontaneity*, opposed to external physical necessity (compulsion); freedom of *choice* (free will), opposed to internal physical necessity (determinism); freedom of *independence*, opposed to moral necessity (law). Law, being a moral bond, is a restraint only of the last kind of freedom and, even in this case, only of the abuse of freedom. Without the guidance of law, liberty becomes license.

Existentialism is hostile to all law. It stresses the primacy of freedom as a basic datum, the unavoidability of commitment, the dreadful responsibility of each decision, the confrontation of death, the purifying value of anguish and despair, issuing in a free act either of blind faith in God (theistic) or of accepting the ultimate absurdity of nothingness (atheistic). The latter variety especially is the philosophy of the absurd.

Many think that the positive contributions of existentialism, the values of freedom, subjectivity, authenticity, creativity, relevance, commitment, and involvement, should be stressed in any ethics, but that this can be done without the negative attitudes of nausea, despair, absurdity, alienation, ambiguity, and lawlessness that pervade existentialist thinking.

QUESTIONS FOR DISCUSSION

1 What is the difference between a norm and a law, if one takes a norm not as a mere standard but as a directing guide and a law not as an arbitrary decree but as the work of reason?

2 Do we vote for the primacy of law or for the primacy of freedom? Does law exist except for the protection and guidance of freedom? Does freedom exist except to enable one to do what the law of his nature points out to him?

3 If the good is determined merely by the fact that it is the free expression of my personality, then anything I freely do is right and good, and what I really love is myself. Is this correct reasoning?

4 Before all philosophizing is it necessary to make up one's mind about whether the universe is a reasonable place or not? If it is, there is law in it; if it is not, there cannot be. How can such a question be settled without assuming what one sets out to prove?

5 In any case this is an absurd world, whether man faces the futility of nothingness at death or the judgment of a righteous God for having lived evilly in an evil world this good God is supposed to have made. Can any sense be made of it?

READINGS

On freedom in general see Mortimer Adler, *The Idea of Freedom,* with extensive reference to the whole literature of the topic.

All the existentialist writers treat moral matters at least obliquely. It might be well to begin with Kierkegaard's *Fear and Trembling* and its sequel, *Sickness unto Death,* and then his treatment of the subjective in his *Concluding Unscientific Postscript,* pt. II, ch. 1-3, pp. 115-224, 267-322.

The philosophy of the absurd is clearly expressed in Jean-Paul Sartre's essay *Existentialism.* He has a long treatment of freedom in *Being and Nothingness,* pt. IV, ch. 1, and draws ethical implications at the end of the whole work. Albert Camus' *The Myth of Sisyphus* and *The Rebel* also expound the philosophy of the absurd.

About existentialism see Kurt Reinhardt, *The Existentialist Revolt;* James Collins, *The Existentialists;* William Barrett, *Irrational Man;* Norman Greene, *Jean-Paul Sartre: the Existentialist Ethic.*

Austin Fagothey, *Right and Reason—an Anthology,* contains Kierkegaard's "Teleological Suspension of the Ethical" from *Fear and Trembling,* and Jean-Paul Sartre's essay *Existentialism.*

CHAPTER 14

SITUATION

PROBLEM

It is notorious that we cannot just *do;* we have to do *something,* which something cannot be just anything in general but must be a definite act done in a concrete situation. This is too true to need saying, but some think that not enough has been made of it. The situation, they say, is all important. In fact, they make it so overwhelmingly important that, in the opinion of many, it seems to have swallowed up whatever was supposed to be in the situation. Because of its strong roots in existentialism and its outspoken opposition to legalism, this view logically comes up next for consideration.

Situationists are distinguished not so much by the affirmation of the situation as by the negation of universals, essences, natures, norms, standards, rules, laws, and absolutes. The negation is indeed not absolute but enough to result in a fairly drastic deflation. They argue that every situation is unique. No act considered in its totality with all its context of surrounding circumstances can ever be repeated. It has some resemblance to other acts, but we cannot judge it on its resemblances only; we must also take in the differences, which may be crucial. What, then, is the value of laws and norms and rules, since they must be applied to individual acts done under concrete conditions, and the application will be different every time? Why not simply say that there are no moral rules and every act must be judged in its concrete situation?

Our procedure will be to discuss, first, the way traditional philosophies view the situation of an act, then the theory of situation ethics as populary proposed, and finally the philosophical situation of situation ethics. We have these questions:

1. What do motives and circumstances add to an act?
2. What are the reasons for and against situation ethics?
3. What is the place of the situation in ethics?

THE THREE MORAL DETERMINANTS

Those who hold to an objective norm of morality, whatever it be, have the problem of applying the norm to concrete cases. Just in what way and how far does the act agree or disagree with the norm? What must we look for in the act to see whether it is in agreement or disagreement? There is the act itself in its own very nature as an act, and there are the circumstances in which the act is performed. Among the circumstances, one, the motive or intention of the agent, may be singled out as of such importance as to be put in a class by itself. Two men may do the same thing but from different motives, or different things from the same motive, or the same thing from the same motive but in different circumstances. In each case the act can have a different morality because of a different combination of these three elements.

The accepted terminology since St. Thomas' time is to call these three sources

147

or determinants of morality the *object,* the *end,* and the *circumstances.*[*] By *object* is meant the object of the will-act, that which the will chooses to do, and this is nothing else but the act itself, which is deliberately willed. By *end* is meant the purpose for which the act is willed, and it may mean either the purpose the act is naturally fitted to achieve or the purpose the agent personally wishes to accomplish by willing that act; here the latter meaning is taken, since the former is implied in the nature of the act. By *circumstances* are meant the various accidental surroundings of the act. In the interest of clarity we shall call these three:

1. The act itself, or what a man does (the object)
2. The motive, or why he does it (the end)
3. The circumstances, or how, where, when, etc., he does it

THE ACT ITSELF

Morality resides in the will, in the will's consent to what is presented to it as morally good or evil. But we cannot just *will;* we must will *something,* to do or omit some *act,* which is therefore the *object* of the will's consent. The consent of the will derives its morality first and foremost from the kind of act to which the will consents. This is *what* the will wills; if the act willed is a bad kind of act, the willing of it must be bad; if the act willed is a good kind of act, and if there is nothing else about it to render it evil, the willing of it must be good. This point is so obvious that it hardly needs expression.

How do we know that an act is a good kind of act or a bad kind of act? The existence of verbs in any language shows that acts can be classified. No two performances of the act are exactly alike, but they are

sufficiently so to afford a basis for a universal concept. We can make a classification in the *physical* order, regarding only the muscles used and the material objects displaced, as when we speak of sitting, standing, walking, talking, grasping, hitting, throwing. Such acts are morally indifferent in their nature; whatever morality they have must come from the motive and circumstances. We can also make a classification in the *moral* order by putting certain moral characteristics in our definition. When we speak of hating, envying, murdering, stealing, lying, or slandering, moral evil enters into the very definition of the concepts indicated by the words and thus belongs to the kind or nature of the acts described. Verbs indicative of good acts, such as loving, honoring, helping, protecting, or benefiting, do not always have such a clear moral connotation, but in some contexts it is quite evident. Acts which thus have morality included in their definition are good or bad of their very kind or nature.

What may seem to be mere circumstances in the physical order can belong to the very nature of the act in the moral order. We distinguish seizure and theft, killing and murder, speaking and lying. The first of each pair indicates only the physical act, which may be right or wrong; the second means an act that is morally wrong in its nature. Theft is not mere seizure, but the seizure of another's rightfully owned property against his will; murder is not mere killing, but the direct killing of an innocent person; lying is not mere speaking, but the saying of what one knows to be untrue. At first sight these added qualifications may seem to be mere circumstances, whether what I take is mine or another's property, whether the man I kill has lost his right to life or not, whether the words I utter express my thought or contradict it. But in the moral order these points are essential. The moral order is the order of *willing,* and some features cannot be detached from the act willed. You cannot will merely to kill

---

[*]St. Thomas, *Summa Theologica,* I-II, q. 18, aa. 2-7.

but must will to kill some definite person; you cannot will merely to take but must will to take some definite thing; you cannot will merely to say but must will to say some definite words. Thus from the moral standpoint the innocence of the victim killed, the ownership of the goods taken, the truth of the words said are not accidental or circumstantial but essential. They do not merely add to a morality already present but give the act its first moral quality and go to make up the very essence of the act in the moral order.

Here one might ask whether this traditional explanation is more than a linguistic front. It may be convenient to have words indicating acts with their morality built into them by including their moral circumstances, but how valuable is an argument drawn from a way of speaking? Are these qualifications *really* part of the act itself or added circumstances?

In a sense these are not circumstances. The *moral* order, we repeat, is the order of will. What did the person *will* when he did that act? A man whips out his gun, takes aim, fires, and kills his enemy. Would it be correct to describe this act as a mere movement of his fingers? Can we say that it is a mere circumstance that his finger moved against the trigger, which exploded the powder, which drove the bullet, which entered the victim's heart, which then stopped beating and left the man dead? In the physical order it might be described in this way, but in the moral order we can hardly say that all the man *willed* was a movement of his finger and the rest was mere circumstance. What he willed was the murder of his enemy and, especially if he was an expert marksman, the movement of his finger squeezing the trigger would be habitual and almost automatic once he had made up his mind to kill.

But in another sense these *are* circumstances. It does not make a great deal of difference whether one adopts the explanation just given or whether one says that the

act itself, considered physically, is morally indifferent but surrounded by circumstances, some of which are so bound up with the act as to be the main object of the will and to give the act its first moral character.

In either of these two explanations the act receives a moral character, whether from the nature of the thing done or from some necessary circumstance known to be present and willed with the willing of the act. Thus it seems unnecessary to ask whether perjury is an essentially different act from lying or whether it is lying accompanied by additional immoral circumstances. The important thing for ethics is that perjury is morally evil and the perjurer is guilty of all the immoral parts and aspects of his act, whether they constitute the essence of the act or are its willed accompaniments.

The reason for discussing this matter at such length is to lay the ground for our inquiry into situationism, lest it become too much a dispute on words. One such dispute concerns actions said to be intrinsically good or evil.*

THE MOTIVE

The motive is that which the agent has in mind when he acts, that which he consciously sets before himself to achieve by his act. If a man has no further reason for acting than the act itself, then the act and motive coincide, but more often a man uses his act as a means to something further. This further reason distinct from the act itself is what we are considering here. It is called by many names with subtle differences between them that are not important here: end, purpose, intent, intention, aim, goal, object, objective. Perhaps the least ambiguous name in the present context is *motive*, which stresses the influence it

---

*See p. 153, point 2, and p. 154, point 2.

has on the will in moving the agent to act.

In a murder the police look for the motive of the crime, knowing that one hardly ever kills for killing's sake, but to have revenge, to remove a rival, to seize the victim's money, to be rid of a blackmailer. The proverb "No one is a liar for nothing" recognizes the need for a motive in lying, to get out of a difficulty or obtain an advantage. That this motive influences the morality of the act prompted by it is obvious.

When a man directs his act to some consciously intended purpose, he deliberately wills this purpose together with the act, and both are voluntary. When a person deliberately uses a means to an end, in the one same act he wills both the use of the means and the attainment of the end. As the act itself can be morally good, bad, or indifferent, so can the end to which it is directed by the will of the agent. Therefore, in addition to the morality which the act has by its own nature, the act also derives morality from the motive with which it is performed.

The motive may give an indifferent act its first moral quality, either good or bad. Thus one who borrows money with the firm intention of never returning it is not a borrower but a thief; one who refuses to testify in court because he wants his innocent enemy to be convicted turns his negative act of silence into one of hatred and injustice. The motive may only increase or decrease the same kind of morality the act already has; thus one may lie that he is lying so that the first lie will be believed; a clerk who pilfers a little money each day in order to build up to a predetermined sum cannot excuse himself by the smallness of each single theft. The motive may also add to a moral act quite a new kind of morality; thus one who gives money to the poor for the sole purpose of being praised turns his act of kindness into one of vanity, and one who steals money to have the means of seducing his neighbor's wife is,

as Aristotle[*] observed, more of an adulterer than a thief.

Would it be correct to say with Abelard[†] that morality is found wholly in the intention, or with Kant[‡] that morality consists solely in a good will and the motive of duty, so that the external act is quite outside the scope of morals? Such statements can be true only in the sense that without intention and will, no act can be moral or immoral, for a voluntary act requires knowledge and consent. But if there are some acts that one is never allowed to intend or will, and if there are circumstances in which we are not allowed to intend or will an otherwise good act, morality is not entirely dependent on our good intentions or good will.

THE CIRCUMSTANCES

The circumstances are the various surroundings of the act, including everything affecting the act, except the motive just discussed. The motive, as we said, is a circumstance but was separated out for special treatment; we mean here all the other circumstances. A convenient way of listing the circumstances is to ask the familiar questions: *who? where? when? how? to whom? by what means? how often?* and the like. But not *what?* or *why?* since these questions ask for the act itself and its motive.

Some circumstances have nothing to do with morality: whether one poisons with strychnine or cyanide, slanders in English or French, steals with his right or left hand. Other circumstances do affect morality: whether one robs a rich or a poor man,

---

[*]Aristotle, *Nicomachean Ethics*, bk. V, ch. 2, 1130a 24; as quoted by St. Thomas, *Summa Theologica*, I-II, q. 18, a. 6.
[†]Peter Abelard, *Ethica seu Scito Te Ipsum* (Ethics or Know Thyself). This is what he seems to say in ch. 7 and 11; but he modifies his statements in ch. 12 and 13.
[‡]Kant, *Fundamental Principles of the Metaphysic of Morals*, sec. II.

murders a stranger or a friend or a parent, has sexual relations with a married or an unmarried person, damages another's character in private or in public, charges exorbitant prices for food in normal times or when people are starving. These latter circumstances are the only kind we consider.

Like motives, circumstances can so affect the act as to make it a different *kind* of act from the moral standpoint. Dishonor to parents is not ordinary dishonor but also a breach of filial respect. Intimate relations between persons married but not to each other are sins of injustice as well as of unchastity. Perjury in a law court is not merely lying but also a violation of religion and justice. Other circumstances only change the *degree* of goodness or badness the act already has. It is still theft, whether one steals a large or a small sum of money; it is still drunkenness, whether one has had five or fifteen too many; it is still slander, whether one has partly or wholly ruined another's reputation. Such differences, though only in degree and not in kind, can be of the utmost importance.

It is evident that a human act can have its morality colored by the circumstances in which it is done. No act can be done in the abstract; every act actually performed is surrounded by a number of concrete circumstances involving persons, quantity, quality, place, time, manner, means, frequency, and relations of all sorts. These circumstances can be foreseen and willed in the willing of the act, and thus contribute to the morality of the act.

The fact that these are called circumstances should not lead us to think that they are negligible or unimportant. Sometimes they are made more of than the act itself, and to them the will is chiefly directed. There are men who will lie but not to their mother, men who will steal but not from their friends, men who will kill but not a baby. Many otherwise indifferent acts receive their whole morality from circumstances, because they are done at the right or wrong time, in the right or wrong place, by the right or wrong means, in the right or wrong manner.

PRACTICAL APPLICATION

To be morally good a human act must agree with the norm of morality on all three counts: in its kind, its motive, and its circumstances. Disconformity in any one of them makes the act morally wrong. Just as to be physically healthy one must have all one's organs functioning rightly, and if only one organ is deranged the person is unwell, so to be morally healthy no element of immorality must be present in any of one's acts.

An *evil* act cannot become good or indifferent by a good motive or good circumstances, and much less by indifferent ones. It is wrong to begin with, and no additions to it can get the evil out. No person is ever allowed voluntarily to will that kind of act in any circumstances or for any motive. That is why we must reject the principle, "the end justifies the means," in its usual acceptation. Though a good end renders good the use of indifferent means, a good end cannot justify the use of evil means. We are never allowed to do evil that good may come of it. A good motive and good circumstances may somewhat lessen the badness of the act, but it remains bad. Each bad motive or circumstance added to a bad act makes it worse.

A *good* act becomes better by each good motive and good circumstance added to it, but any seriously bad motive or circumstance is sufficient to render the act wholly and seriously bad, no matter how good it may otherwise seem. If there is only one motive and it is slightly bad, it will make the whole act slightly bad, for the whole act is directed to this one end only. When there are several motives or circumstances, a slightly bad motive or circumstance will not render the act wholly bad but only less good. Thus a man may give alms out of

151

benevolence touched with vanity, may obey legitimate superiors but discourteously, may work at his job but lazily or negligently, may tell the truth but with a little exaggeration. Such defects, commonly called *imperfections,* even though intended, cannot wholly ruin an otherwise good act, for the act retains its natural goodness in a somewhat tarnished form.

An *indifferent* act, since it has no moral quality of its own, must derive all its moral goodness or badness from the motive and circumstances. They must all be good or at least indifferent if the act is to be morally acceptable. Simply speaking, any bad motive or circumstance will make an indifferent act morally wrong. This matter can become quite complicated. How shall we judge cases in which an indifferent act is surrounded by a mixture of good and bad motives or good and bad circumstances? When the act itself is indifferent, and each motive or circumstance can be separately willed, it is easier to consider such acts as virtually multiple, that is, as compounded of a good and a bad act. Here we really have two moral acts and can judge each on its own merits. A lawyer in defending an innocent man may win his case by bribing the jury; the act of vindicating justice for his client is good, but the act of violating justice by bribery is evil. The two parts of the total act do not necessarily imply each other and can be separately willed, for the case might be won without bribery, and bribery can be used for other purposes. However, if this be considered one whole act, it must be judged evil.

SITUATION ETHICS

Situation ethics had a religious rather than a philosophical beginning. It seems to have sprung up in Germany between the two World Wars as a protest against overlegalistic interpretations of the Christian life, both Catholic and Protestant. More recently it has been popularized by Bishop John A. T. Robinson* in England and by Joseph Fletcher† in the United States. It is sometimes called "the New Morality," though the newness is recognized as relative. It can be considered apart from any religious background as a form of a larger movement known as *contextualism.*

Situation ethics is proposed as a middle ground between two extremes, *legalism* on the one side and *antinomianism* on the other.

Legalism is understood to be an abuse of law, making prefabricated rules and abstract prescriptions of the law into such absolutes that the real good of man is to be sacrificed to them. It results in a hairsplitting and logic-chopping study of the letter of the law, either to free men from its toils or to use it sadistically to hurt rather than help people. It can result in a straightlaced, sour-faced, unloving life of meticulous duties, what Mark Twain called "a good man in the worst sense of the word."

Antinomianism, on the other hand, fares no better. It supposes no principles or maxims whatever, let alone rules and laws. It is spontaneous and extempore, resulting in a kind of moral anarchy. Those who wait for the inspiration of the Holy Spirit to tell them what to do in each particular case exemplify a religious variety of this attitude. Extreme application of the existentialist ethics of ambiguity could have similar results from a philosophical point of view.

The situationist claims to be at the proper balancing point between these extremes. He approaches every decision armed with maxims and principles, but he uses them as enlighteners and guides. He obtains from them all the good they can give him, but he will not be bound by them when they will lead to harm rather than good. He considers that no law or prin-

---

*Robinson, *Honest to God* and *Christian Morals Today.*
†Fletcher, *Situation Ethics* and *Moral Responsibility.*

ciple is absolute. The situation alters rules, and it is part of moral responsibility to have the courage to discard the rule for a greater good.

Situation ethics acknowledges its affinity with pragmatism, relativism, positivism, and personalism. Fletcher tells us that for the situationist there are no rules, none at all, but then proceeds to give us six principles, as he calls them: Love only is always good, is the only norm, is the same as justice, is not the same as liking, is the end justifying the means, and decides in the situational there and then. The bulk of his work consists of case histories, vividly and dramatically told, portraying crucial moral situations. Many of them even hardbound legalists could solve as sympathetically as Fletcher, though few would be as latitudinarian in all cases.

Fletcher's popular style does not lead itself easily to the presentation of sustained argument. The following seem to be his main contentions:

1. Situationism accepts the nominalistic interpretation of universals, that is, they are mere names, conveniences of language. There is therefore nothing real about classes of things, types of actions, kinds of conduct, so that a general rule could be formed about them. Only the individual act with all its situational concreteness can have any reality. Ethics, the science of such acts, can give only concrete description, no universal prescription.

2. Morality is not intrinsic to acts, but an extrinsic addition they acquire from the situation. Goodness is not a property of actions but only a predicate of some of them. It is not in the act but happens to it. There are therefore no kinds of acts that are intrinsically or of their own nature good or evil. If they become good or evil, it must come from the circumstances in which the act is situated. Since these are different in every case, no universal judgments or rules are possible.

3. Morality is relative, not absolute. The goodness or badness of the act that is done is relative to the situation, which alone gives it its goodness or badness. No law can be formed that could take in all varieties of all possible situations, and thus no law can be absolute. All it can do is to describe what is the best course of action in most cases, but there is always room for exceptions.

4. Laws are but illuminating guides, not authoritative commands. Laws are for people, not people for laws. Laws are to be respected for the wisdom they embody and the help they give, but not to be worshiped and idolized as unbreakable and unbendable absolutes. This is no irresponsible antinomianism but a recognition of the true place and function of law.

5. If there must be an absolute, it is love. But love does not command, it invites. Love is not a law but a lure. Love makes its decisions situationally, not prescriptively. Love is not a thing, a being, a reality apart from people, not something we *have* or *are*, but something we *do*. In meaning it is not a noun but a verb. Without love even the most legalistically correct actions are immoral. With love no legalistic prescriptions are needed for a full moral life.

Nonsituationists, while not denying the partial truth contained here, think that on the whole it is an inadequate account of the moral life. In particular:

1. Nominalism is a very shaky epistemology that, when applied to ethics, results in disaster. Universals as such are not things but abstractions, it is true. The only reality about a class of objects is the objects that make up the class. But the objects do have the properties or attributes because of which they were grouped into a common class, and thus universal class concepts have a basis in the really existing objects comprehended under them. Thus the only kind of scientific knowledge we can have, conceptual knowledge, refers to things and is true of them. There is no science of the singular, and situationism, which cannot get beyond

the singular situation, makes a science of ethics impossible.

2. Extrinsicalism merely transfers goodness and badness from acts to the situations in which they occur. Then we ask: Is goodness or badness intrinsic to the situations? Are there certain common situations in which a certain act will always be good or will always be bad? If so, we can express such situations in a general rule. If not, how can we recognize whether any act is good or bad, intrinsically or extrinsically? If moral goodness or badness does not reside intrinsically in anything, but is always attributed extrinsically from something else, how can there be any objectivity in ethics? Situationism does not want to be subjectivism, but how does it escape?

3. That there is a great deal of relativity in morals should be obvious to all. That there cannot be absolute relativity is implicitly granted by the situationists when they make love into their one absolute. There is probably no law that does not admit of some exceptions, except such general formulations as "Do good, be upright, live the moral life," even "Do the loving thing." But the fact that laws have exceptions does not mean that they do not command with authority in those matters which do not come under the exceptions.

4. There is no contradiction in a law's being both a guide and a command. Certainly, laws are for people, not people for laws; but people are not only for themselves but also for other people, and the laws merely state how they should act toward other people. To worship the dead letter of the law is the kind of idolatry called legalism, but to avoid legalism there is no need of emasculating the law by denying its commanding authority and making it into something less than law. This *is* antinomianism.

5. Let us endorse all the beautiful things said in favor of love. But is it clear enough to be a reliable guide? How do I know that this is the loving thing to do,

and not that? The love the situationists mean is not romantic love, passionate love, or even the love of friendship, all of which are exclusive, but that love of good will to all men called by the Greeks *agapē*. Since it is no subjective feeling, it must be judged by its results, that is, by the good it does to others. We are back in utilitarianism, as Fletcher admits.[*] If acts are neither good nor bad, how do we know the goodness or badness of consequences? Are they good consequences because they are the loving thing, and the loving thing because they have good consequences?

PLACE OF THE SITUATION IN ETHICS

Situationism has produced strong reactions, some hailing it as the long-awaited deliverer from the narrow confines of legalism, others dismissing it as a shallow attempt to justify the doing of anything you want and calling it moral. The proponents of situationism, because of their exaggerations, must bear the blame for its ambivalent image. At the risk of some repetition we shall try to disentangle its useful aspects from its rather glaring inadequacies.

That every act is concrete and done in a situation is no news. Traditional ethics always recognized the importance of motives and circumstances, which make up the situation or context of an act. The virtue of prudence, indispensable in moral living, is simply the habit of properly applying general principles to concrete cases. There are no rules for prudence, precisely because it deals with individually situationed acts. The trouble with legalism is a failure of prudence, a stupidly wooden application of the letter of the law, rather than a failure in the law itself. But prudence has laws to apply and recognizes exceptions intelligently, whereas situation-

---

[*] Fletcher, *Situation Ethics,* pp. 95, 115.

ism wants no laws and makes every act exceptional.

Whether any acts of their very nature are good or bad depends on how they are defined. If they are taken in the physical order only, with no moral quality entering into their definition, they must receive morality from outside themselves, from the situation. Situationists regard all acts in this way, but if some act is defined so as to include morality or immorality in its concept, then such an act is already good or bad in itself. This is the view of those who hold for intrinsic morality, and they have good grounds in the common use of language, which is full of morally tinged, even morally soaked, words. Situationists may prefer their own explanation but are hardly the ones to lay down rigid laws on the use of language.

Situationism does not like any laws but is willing to admit principles, so long as they are not absolute. Natural law is out, because they think there is no discoverable human nature. One may ask, then, whether man may live any way? If not, there is something that forbids him, and this is what is meant by law. May man make for himself any kind of law he wants? If not, he must find the law already existing, and where else but in the kind of being he is with relation to all the kinds of situations he can get into? To consider the natural law as wholly nonsituational is to caricature it. To be sure, the law can consider only *types* of situations, not this concrete situation here and now; but this is the place of prudence in the application of the law, and that laws should be applied prudently is part of the natural law itself.

Condemnation of rigid legalism is situationism's best feature. Textbook morality, with its often glib statement of rigid rules, was bound to provoke a reaction. Traditional principles, some of them resting on false facts and outworn science, some not universal to mankind but only customs of Western culture, some taken for granted

without the periodic reexamination to which even the most sacred truths must be subjected, have been asserted as absolute and immutable precepts of the natural law. Situation ethics issued the necessary dramatic challenge to this complacent dogmatism, but by its reckless exaggeration it jeopardizes its own case. There is no need of throwing away law to correct law's abuses.

Even situationists cannot do without an absolute. Natural law advocates are accused of making the whole natural law absolute, but this is a misconception. It is absolute only in the center, in its most general principle: Do good and avoid evil. As one passes from the center to the periphery, from the general to the specific, the situation comes in more and more. The more specific a precept is, the more relative it is, the more it suffers exceptions, the more careful we must be in its application lest we contradict a more general principle. Thus the natural law takes in the human situation, all of it, but does not become so situational that it ceases to be human.

Situationism balances off law against person. Laws are for persons, not persons for laws. True enough when we are talking about the abuse of law, of subordinating living people to empty abstractions, but the opposition is a false one when we are talking about law itself. Situationists quote Kant with approval when he says that we must treat each human being as a person and not as a thing, as an end and not as a means; but for Kant this is one way of stating the categorical imperative, which is an expression of the moral *law*. The dignity of a person does not come from the situation he is in but from the kind of being he is, from the rational and free *nature* he exists as. Respect for the person and respect for the moral law are but phases of the same thing, not opposed and not even separable. The reason behind natural law principles is respect for man's dignity as a person.

Another questionable opposition in situationism is that between law and love. Here the two notions are quite different, and it is possible to have one without the other. But it is also possible and usual to have both together. When the situationists insist that we must always do the loving thing, they admit no exceptions and lay it down as a law as absolute as any law could be. Of course, one does not legislate love, that is, pass laws regulating emotional love, but when the love is *agapē*, good will to all men, and is not distinguished from justice and prudence or any other form of good living, then the law of love becomes merely the law to be good, to be moral, to do the right thing—the first principle of the natural law.

If the situationists want to reduce everything to one principle, they do well to choose love. Nothing is more inspiring, more ennobling—and nothing is more difficult. How does one decide on what is the loving thing to do in the situation? Some critics are unloving enough to say that situationism encourages a kind of infantilism. St. Augustine's often quoted remark, "Love and do what you will,"* has been called the worst possible slogan for youth and a safe guide only for a saint in the autumn of his life. For if you know that you do truly love, then you can do what you wish, for you will not wish to do anything unloving. But how do you know that you truly love? It is to the situationists' credit that they do not trust to any fuzzy inner feeling, to a warm glow of self-approbation, or to a complacent judgment that it must be the loving thing to do because I, the lover, choose to do it. No, love is proved in deeds. But the question remains unsettled. What deeds?

The situation has a very important place in ethics, but the situationists have no

monopoly on it. It is important not only to have the right situation in which to act but also to do the right thing in whatever situation.

SUMMARY

To apply the norm of morality to concrete cases we must find out what there is in the act that can bring it into agreement or disagreement with the norm. We find three such sources or determinants of morality: the act itself, the motive, and the circumstances.

The *act itself* is simply what the agent wills, considering it not in the physical but in the moral order. An act receives its first morality from the kind of act it is.

The *motive,* or intention, is what the agent personally wishes to achieve by the act over and above what the act naturally tends toward. The motive, being consciously willed, contributes to the morality of the act, sometimes giving it a new kind of morality.

The *circumstances* are the accidental surroundings of the act. Some have no effect on morality; others have an effect, changing the act either in kind or in degree. Circumstances can be foreseen and, if so, are willed in the willing of the act, thus contributing to its morality.

An *evil* act cannot be made good or indifferent by motives or circumstances, though the degree of badness may be somewhat modified. A *good* act is ruined by any gravely bad motive or circumstance; slightly bad ones weaken the act's goodness but do not destroy it. An *indifferent* act receives all its morality from motives and circumstances: if any one of them is bad, the rest being indifferent, the act becomes bad; if some are good and others bad, it may be possible to resolve the physical act into two moral acts.

Situation ethics holds that there is no intrinsic morality, no acts good or bad of their very nature, but every act must be

---

*St. Augustine, *In Epistolam Joannis ad Parthos,* Tractatus VII, 8.

judged in the situation. It admits laws, but they are only illuminating guides, not prescriptive commands, and none of them is absolute. It has one absolute principle (not law), that of agapeic love, and the only rule is: Always do the loving thing.

Situationism is criticized for its nominalistic epistemology, for merely transferring morality from acts to situations, for overemphasizing the relativity of morals, for actually being antinomian while protesting that it is not, and for insisting on the doing of the loving thing while reducing the loving thing to utilitarian consequences.

The good points of situationism, the importance of seeing each act in its concrete setting, the condemnation of rigid legalism, the place of the relative in morals, the preeminence of the human person, and the primacy of love in the moral life, can be separated from the exaggerations of the situationist writers and incorporated into other ethical theories.

QUESTIONS FOR DISCUSSION

1 Is the distinction between the nature of an act and its circumstances anything more than semantics? Does it matter whether an attribute of an act be included in its definition or considered as a circumstance?

2 Are circumstances good, bad, or indifferent in the same way that acts are? Are they to be judged by the same criterion or norm of morality?

3 If making the motive the sole determinant of morality is rejected as moral subjectivism, what solution is found in referring to the act itself and the circumstances, since they must be taken not as they are in reality but as they are known by the agent and are thus equally subjective?

4 What of the principle that the end justifies the means? It is usually taken in the sense that a good end justifies the use of evil means, and is therefore rejected. Fletcher says that only a good end can justify the use of any means, and thus accepts the principle.

5 Is the double-effect principle a typical example of legalism? If you can interpret a consequence of an act as indirectly voluntary, you get it under the law and make it permissible. Is this only verbal juggling?

READINGS

St. Thomas, *Summa Theologica,* I-II, qq. 18-21, treats of the goodness and badness of human actions, and of their objects, ends, and circumstances.

Eric D'Arcy, *Human Acts,* discusses the same thing from a modern point of view.

Situationism is defended by Joseph Fletcher in *Situation Ethics* and *Moral Responsibility.* A volume of reactions to the first book is published as the *Situation Ethics Debate,* in which well-known critics participate. An able criticism is found in Paul Ramsey, *Deeds and Rules in Christian Ethics,* ch. 7. Robert Cunningham edits a book of readings entitled *Situationism and the New Morality.*

Outka and Ramsey edited *Norm and Context in Christian Ethics,* a book of readings on both situation ethics and natural law, with some excellent articles.

Ignace Lepp, *The Authentic Morality,* and Louis Monden, *Sin, Liberty, and Law,* write percep-tively on the new morality with a well-balanced judgment toward situationism.

Austin Fagothey, *Right and Reason—an Anthology,* contains St. Thomas' *Summa Theologica,* I-II, q. 18, aa. 1-4; Eric D'Arcy's *Human Acts,* ch. 1; and Joseph Fletcher's *Situation Ethics,* most of ch. 1.

CHAPTER 15

LOVE

PROBLEM

The matter of the previous chapter slides into this one. The idea of love is altogether too important to be dismissed with our few remarks on the situationists' use of it. The man who has no love in his life can hardly be thought of as human. Although love may be too blind as a guide and too uncritical as a norm, so that we cannot use it to show us what is good, it is surely the noblest inspiration and the most dynamic force we can have to drive us on toward whatever good we know.

We are sometimes given the choice of having an ethics of law or an ethics of love. Situationism has made such a choice and has opted for the ethics of love. Legalism is hardly a distinct ethical theory, but strict deontologies such as Stoicism or Kantianism opt for an ethics of law without paying much attention to love. We can ask whether any such option is necessary. Are love and law so opposed that we cannot have both?

Since we have given a fairly full exposition of law, and in our study of situationism may have seemed to short-change love, the time has come for a more thorough treatment of love. An important concept in connection with love is that of person, since love can exist only between persons. We have these points:

1. What is a person?
2. Why are persons intersubjective?
3. Why is intersubjectivity shown as love?

4. How can we love all men?
5. What is the place of love in ethics?

PERSON AND PERSONALITY
HISTORY OF PERSON

The Greeks began philosophy as a study of the external world with only scanty reflections on the self. They did not even have a word for *person* but had to express the idea indirectly. It was not until the Christians speculated on the Trinity and the Incarnation that a distinction was made between nature and person, and the word *person** came into common use. The classical definition of person was given by Boethius: "A person is an individual substance of a rational nature."† This definition, repeated and commented on through the whole medieval period, is so explained as to mean that the person is not a *what?* but a *who?*, not an object but a subject, not a thing but a self, who is master of his own acts, self-owned, self-possessed, self-controlled, with a uniqueness that is incommunicable to anything or anyone else.

Study along these lines is true enough as far as it goes, but it conceptualizes *person* and universalizes it like any other concept.

---

*The Greeks used *prosopon* (face) and the Latins *persona* (mask).
†Boethius, "A Treatise against Eutyches and Nestorius," in *The Theological Tractates*, The Loeb Classical Library. Quoted by St. Thomas, *Summa Theologica*, I, q. 29, a. 1.

Every human being is a person, just as every human being is a man, but these are not stated in quite the same way. Humanity expresses what is common to us, but personality expresses what is unique in each of us. We are all persons, but no one else can be the person I am. This I cannot share with any other member of the same species. Though it is important to know what makes a person a person, and to know how this person verifies in himself the general concept of personality, what modern thinkers are more interested in is the uniqueness of this single person in his absolute unrepeatableness.

Descartes' meditations on the "I" of "I think, therefore I am" begins the modern trend toward the subjective. Unfortunately, he identifies the "I" with the mind, which is only part of the person, though he does see that a person is a center of consciousness. Kant spoke well when he said:

> Beings whose existence does not depend on our will but on nature, if they are not rational beings, have only a relative worth as means and are therefore called "things"; on the other hand, rational beings are designated "persons," because their nature indicates that they are ends in themselves, i.e., things which may not be used merely as means.[*]

This emphasis on the dignity of the person went a long way to set up the person in the center of ethics. But in both Descartes and Kant the person is still regarded as an object to be studied or dealt with, and not as the experiencing subject in its unique selfhood.

The personalist movement in philosophy began around the turn of the century. Borden Parker Bowne in the United States founded *personalism,* a philosophy centering all knowledge about the Self, both the human and the divine personality, as an antidote to naturalism and positivism, without particularly developing the ethical side

---

[*] Kant, *Fundamental Principles of the Metaphysic of Morals,* sec. II.

of personality or the aspect of love. A stronger movement of personalism came to the fore about 1930 in France under Emmanuel Mounier and in Germany under Max Scheler, both of whom relate person and love. Some incitement toward this way of thinking may be traced to Henri Bergson, whose distinction between closed and open morality, the closed morality of laws and duties as against the open morality of inspiration from the teaching and example of noble men, led to an ethics of personal response. Martin Buber's "I-Thou" relationship helped to dramatize the intersubjectivity and interpersonality of human life and to show that the connecting link between persons is one of love.

MEANING OF PERSON

The following exposition puts together the thoughts of a number of modern thinkers, trying to extract some common elements. All writing on this subject is so notoriously imprecise as to be capable of various interpretations.

Person is not to be understood as opposed to nature, even though the two are often balanced against each other. Rather, we should say that man is a being whose nature is human, and every being with human nature is necessarily a person. Nature and person are not two things in man, not two parts of him, but they are two distinct concepts representing two aspects of him. It is possible to have an ethics so centered about man's *nature* that only the general requirements of humanity are considered, with no thought taken as to how this individual man is to apply these general requirements to his own life. It is possible to have an ethics so centered on this particular *person* as to disregard all other beings in existence, and what is left is a self-centered subject immured within his own solitude. Thus neither nature nor person alone will suffice. One can, however, admit that in man there are both nature and person, and yet say that the aspect of man that is more important for ethics is not the nature but the person. Man is obliged to live morally, not because he has a nature, since everything has a nature; nor because man's nature happens to be human nature, since that merely names man's nature among all the other natures; but because man's nature comes in the form of personality, and it is this personality that makes the moral life the appropriate life for man.[*]

Person is not to be understood as opposed to *individual,* even if we distinguish between the person and the individual in the same man. Those who hold the Aristotelian theory on individuation[†] say that by his matter, his body, a man is this individual, since the form is repeatable only by being received in a different piece of quantified matter. But the form of man, his soul, is intellectual, and this it is which enables man to be a self-guiding, freely-choosing, responsible person.[‡] One can see in this explanation why there can be individual animals, plants, and inorganic particles, without their being persons. But in man the individual is the person and the person is the individual. The kind of individuality a man has is personal individuality. Hence, though the idea of person and the idea of individual partly overlap and partly coincide, in any individual human person they are the same thing. Thus we do not deny individuality of man because he is a person, and any difference between these concepts should not be overdone. But in talking of man we must choose the right word. Individuality says: "I am myself and no other." To go no farther would be to imprison oneself forever in one's own poverty. Personality says: "I am myself but open to others." The person by

intellect and will is responsive to the whole universe and especially to other persons.

What distinguishes a person is not his spirituality or mentality. This was Descartes' mistake. The person is a center of consciousness, but in man this consciousness is linked to the body and works through the body. The person is the whole man, not a part of him, even if it be the better part. Popular language speaks correctly when it says, "He laid hands on my person" for the person includes the body. The person, therefore, is not only a unified memory or a stream of consciousness, so that it would be possible to have a split personality or successive personalities in the same body. When psychology speaks in this way, it is focusing on the integration of clusters of experienced personality traits. These clusters make up only the phenomenal personality, which psychology has explored with great ingenuity and success as part of its proper field. We are treating here of the self, which underlies all such manifestations as their subject.

What does distinguish the person is its *subjectivity.* The person is a subject, not an object. All attempts to form an objective notion of the subject are bound to fail. In a sense the only things that exist in the real world are subjects. They become objects by our knowing them. The object is something of the subject transferred by the process of knowledge into the knowing mind. Since we know only the partial aspects they present to the mind, we never finish discovering them. The peculiar thing about a person is that it is a subject that cannot become an object. We try to make it one when we form the universal concept of person, but the result is that we nowise get at the person but only at an abstract concept of personality, which is not itself a person.

It seems that we can know only our own person, since we are subjects to ourselves. But how far can we know even this? Each of us is situated at the center of our world, in the observation tower of our own per-

---

[*]See pp. 103 and 104.

[†]Aristotle, *Metaphysics,* bk. VII, ch. 8, 1034a 5; bk. XII, ch. 8, 1074a 33. See also St. Thomas, *Being and Essence,* ch. 2, 4; *Summa Theologica,* I, q. 47, a. 2; I-II, q. 63, a. 1.

[‡]Maritain, *The Person and the Common Good,* ch. 3.

sonality, from which we survey the landscape of the universe. We can look only through our own eyes, be aware only through our own consciousness. For me all the landscape consists of objects, and in the midst of it I alone am the subject. My intuition of subjectivity is existential and presents no essence to be understood in a concept. Subjectivity is thus an unknowable abyss, an impenetrable night. In this sense one can agree with the existentialists* who say that we have a hole in the midst of our being, a radical nothing in the center of our consciousness, if this is taken to mean that all our knowledge is of objects, and we cannot be an object to ourselves. But we have a vague knowledge of ourselves simply by being ourselves, by existing as subjects. This knowledge is more a feeling than a knowing, like the connatural knowledge that presents our early moral inclinations, or like the creative intuition of the artist who feels that he has hit on the right color or the right word without being able to explain why. This is not scientific knowledge, which proceeds by concepts only, nor is it philosophical knowledge if philosophy is taken as a science even in the broadest meaning of the term.

I am the center of the world, subjectively. Objectively I do not count, for objectively I am only a thing among things and have lost myself. What happens to others is a mere incident to me; what happens to me is of absolute importance to me. I oscillate miserably between the subjective and objective perspective. If I slide into an object, I am false to my uniqueness. If I absorb everything into myself, I am selfish and proud. I want to know myself as I really am, and cannot do so without making an object of myself, which is the very thing I can never do. I know myself as I am to myself, which gives me only

a subjective awareness of myself, whose objective reality I cannot certify. Others know me as object, not as subject, in the same way I know them. What they know is the I-in-them, a poor substitute for the I-in-myself. Thus I am severed from myself and wounded in my identity. From such reflections the existentialists can take off into alienation and anguish. Not all of them have discovered love.

INTERSUBJECTIVITY

We have been speaking of subjectivity. Care must be taken to distinguish it from subjectivism. The former is the condition of being a subject and the distinctive mark of personality; the latter is the theory that I exist, and whatever else seems to exist is but a state of myself. The student, hearing of the ethics of the person or of personal morality, may think of it as *my* morality, that is, any morality I personally want to adopt for my own living, and thus equate personalism with subjectivism. Nothing could be farther removed from the dignity of the human person than such an egoistic subjectivism. Any morality I happen to adopt does not become true or good by the mere fact that I adopt it. It may be wholly uninterested in the good of other persons and quite content to treat other persons as things. This would be entirely contrary to personalism as an ethics of the person.

We said that we can know others, even other persons, only as objects. Such objectification, conceptualization, or universalization is not false to essences, for that is the way they are made present to the mind and the only way we can know them. But it is false to subjectivity as subjectivity and is the reason that we cannot know it. In other words, the only way to know the other precisely as other is to *be* that other, which I can never be. Knowledge is not the only kind of communication, however. There is also the communication of love. Before dis-

---

*Sartre, *Being and Nothingness,* pt. 1, ch. 1, sec. 5.

cussing love, we must see what makes love possible.

The person is not wholly a person if alone. Being includes both subject and object. Being itself is neither interior nor exterior to the knowing self. It *is*, purely and simply. I am not being itself, but I am within being and sharing in being. I do not affirm being without affirming myself, and I do not affirm myself without affirming opposite me an object, since this too is given to me in consciousness. With some of these objects I find I can communicate by means of signs, objective but meaningful symbols, a poor substitute for subjective experience but sufficient to let me know that the other is a person, a center of consciousness, like myself. Though I know him only as an object, I know objectively that he is a subject. Just as I am taking him into myself and absorbing his thoughts and feelings insofar as he can communicate them, so he at the same moment is taking me into himself in the same way. He contributes to my growth by what he shares with me, and I contribute to his. This is intercommunication, but it is not intersubjectivity, because each is still only an object to the other, and the means of communication are objective. But this intercommunication is far more fulfilling than being alone.

We have here a transition from the I-It to the I-He relation. The other is recognized as a person like myself, though this recognition is on the objective and conceptualized plane. He is not to be treated as an It, a thing; he is not to be used or consumed as a means to my end, but to be respected as an end in himself. He is the subject of rights, and toward him I have duties. Our relation is one of justice and quite sufficient to establish a working social order. Conceptually I can put myself in his place, and I can rationally argue that I must treat him as I would want him to treat me. Between us an ethical order can be established of a high type, but not of the highest type. What is wanting is love.

PERSONAL LOVE

Human love in its fullest sense is an experience of intersubjectivity. It passes beyond the I-It and the I-He relation to I-Thou relation. *It* is a thing to be used as a means. *He* is someone else standing over there about whom we are talking; we communicate about him but not with him. But to me you are *Thou,* and I am *Thou* to you. Why not say *You?* We use the archaic English form to emphasize that it has to be singular. It signifies the relationship between one center of consciousness (I) and one other center of consciousness (Thou). If love is for a person, it is focused on that one person, and if the love is returned, it is focused back on me. Three people can love each other, but if the love is reciprocal and thus truly personal, there are six acts of love.

Love is silent. Why do I love you? Because you are you. There is no reason and it is futile to search for one. If one could be found, it would show the love to be of the lesser sort, a love for various desirable qualities you may have, and this could be more a love for the advantage those qualities may bring to me than a love for you. This lesser love of desire is genuine love and by no means to be despised, but it contains more of an element of self-love and does not rise as high as love in its fullest perfection, which goes beyond all desirable qualities of the beloved directly to the beloved as a person. It bypasses his suchness to reach his selfhood, a Self subsisting in his own goodness, not as perfective of the lover but as loved for himself in his own person.

Love is communion. Lovers love themselves but do not remain wholly within themselves. Love in a sense is one, and in another sense is two. As *one,* it is a uniting, a union, based on likeness. Because the beloved is like the lover, the lover can extend his love to the other, since he sees in the other some image of himself, and in the best love an idealized image of what he would want both himself and his beloved to be. Communion in love demands community in goodness. Love is *two* in the sense that the union does not do away with the lovers. The term of love is the selfhood of the other, his unique, irreplaceable, incommunicable subsistence as a person. The other, retaining his uniqueness as a person, which is the very reason that he is loved, still somehow becomes one with the lover. Thus that I-Thou relation remains. Love makes the other a Thou, but the Thou never loses its identity to fuse with the I.

Love is presence. Lover and beloved share in a common value that must be present in both. The subject is present to himself as the secret and profound source of all the activity that constitutes his life, the consciousness of myself as I. This is no abstract concept, but a living experience. The subject is present to the other and the other to him, not as a universal concept, not as an existing nature like other natures, not even in the abstract recognition of his subjectivity and personality, not as an It and not as a He, but in that indescribable presence, so like my own presence to myself, that is designated by the Thou. To me the Thou becomes a second self as a subject, and open to me in the same sense in which I am open to myself.

Love is self-giving. Only insofar as I love another do I really love myself. I find that what I love in myself is not confined to myself but extends out to a Thou. By my love I make myself a gift to the Thou. This self-giving is essential to the completion of my personality, but it is not consciously directed to the completion of myself but of the Thou. My goal is to make the other infinitely lovable—but not by shaping or twisting him into anything else but himself. I appreciate his freedom as I appreciate my own. Far from subjecting him to myself, I help him to become himself in the full exercise of his self-directing freedom. Because this gift of myself is never total, love can increase forever.

Love is creative. It is not a dreamy feeling or a lazy repose, but a vigorous commitment toward the fulfillment of the Thou. It influences another center of consciousness and makes it grow in the presence of the lover. Love does not create the original personality of the other but finds it. The beloved exists in the world, displays his personality there, and merely by being who he is has made his being shine into my own. I will the continued existence of the other and his autonomous development, in harmony with the ideal he is striving for and I anticipate in him. Thus love is creative by cooperating with the beloved's work of creating his own fulfilled personality.

Love is reciprocal. Loving implies both the desire and the fact of being loved. It is possible to have love that is not returned, but its unsatisfactoriness is evident. This desire to be loved manifests the inevitable component of self-love in all love, a self-love that in no sense need be selfish but is a simple regard of the worth of oneself as a person even as one regards the worth of the other as a person. Thus love links persons into a community. The reciprocal journey of the I to the Thou and of the Thou to the I results in a We. The We of love is the meeting of two subjects whose being is in each's self but whose having is in the other's self, and the awareness of this communion. It is a heterogeneous identity of the I and the Thou, not absorbing the I or the Thou, but expressing their mutuality. There can be a lesser We consisting of a mere crowd or a loose class-conscious group or an organized society of cooperating members, but the We of love is the personal I-Thou relation.

Love is the supreme value. We may question this statement, but on reflection we see that love must be all or nothing—although not in its actual exercise, for we may love more or less, and never love perfectly any more than we do anything else perfectly. In its thrust and goal, however, love is limitless and can take second place to nothing else. Love does not oppose any existing realities but animates them while respecting them. Love is its own value, which is the value of the person. But is not God the supreme value? Certainly, but God is Love. All that was said here about love between two human persons is verified on an infinitely higher plane in God, in man's love for God and God's love for man, and in God's own love for himself. Even love between human persons is unfinished unless their union is seen as a participation in the love of God, who is the very acme of personality and lovableness.

LOVE FOR ALL MANKIND

The intense personal love we have been talking about cannot be extended to all humanity. One can be friendly toward all but a friend only to a few. We can will to exclude no one from our friendship, but we can include positively only those with whom we can establish an I-Thou relation. Here we are victims of the narrowness of our experience and the limitations of our powers.

When we talk about love of the neighbor, and by neighbor mean everybody, this love has to be on a secondary plane. It extends to those we have never seen or heard of, those we cannot like, even those who have done us harm. With them we can have no experienced intimacy and no sharing in their very subjectivity. Our love for them has to be a reasoned love, the result of reflection on their condition and ours. The resultant love is unemotional because it is conceptualized, nonspontaneous because it is not evoked by the presence of the other, personal only in the sense that we objectively know the other is a person and not because we respond to the attractiveness of his personality.

Yet this is true love. It is not only possible but ethically demanded. The fact that our fellowman is a person gives him a dignity worthy of our esteem beyond mere respect for his minimum rights. Our social nature makes us see in him a companion on life's journey, one with whom we share common burdens and hopes, one destined to pursue in common with us the fulfillment of his being. As we wish ourselves all good and no evil, we must wish the same to our fellowman. This is love, not of the deep and intense form that binds lovers into one heart, but of the wide and all-embracing type that takes in the whole of humanity as our brothers and sisters.

Love of this kind includes justice but goes far beyond. Love and justice are often contrasted, and yet they spring from the same root. Justice is love limited to the absolute requirements of basic human equality. Love is justice expanded to the fullest scope of the human person's dignity. Justice is minimizing and negative in emphasis: do not take or keep from another what is rightfully his. Love is maximizing and positive: go as far as you can in giving to another what will help him. Justice and love spring from different motives. Justice is connected with law, obligation, rights, and duties, and measures out its awards according to equality or merit. Love is large-hearted and generous, giving its gifts without measure or stint, rejoicing that it has something to give. Justice and love are the two great social virtues that govern men who are living together. Since there can be no love without justice, the requirements of justice must be fulfilled first. Then, when justice is established, love urges on as far as human ability can go.

A theistic philosophy can give to love of the neighbor a dimension necessarily lacking in the various secular humanisms. Though *we* cannot establish an I-Thou relation with each and every human being in existence, God does so. He is intimately present to the subjectivity of each of his creatures, and his infinity enables him to embrace them all. Thus we can love all humanity, even those who can never enter our experience, because God, whom we love, loves them. They are persons because they are likenesses of the most personal of all beings. Our openness to God, to whom they are also open, enables our love to pass through him to them. This is why it can be said that we love our neighbor in God. Our love for each other is thus a mirror of God's love for himself and for us.

PLACE OF LOVE IN ETHICS

The ethical theory presented here may be regarded as a rather eclectic form of *personalism* and, as far as the love part is concerned, could be called *agapism*, from *agapē*, the Greek word for charity, or the highest kind of love. We did not oppose *agapē* to *erōs*, as some do. All disordered love would be *erōs* without *agapē*, and the brotherly love for the neighbor could be *agapē* without *erōs*. But the two can occur combined, and ought to in the highest type of love. One's love for God can be consumingly passionate, as the history of mysticism shows. Whether or not *erōs* is present, what gives love its moral value is the element of *agapē*.

There was no mention of sex in our treatment of love, and by design. Even *erōs* is not limited to sex but is any kind of desire. There can be love without sex and sex without love; they are two different things. There can, of course, be sex with love, and that is surely the way sex ought to be, but that is a problem for sex, not a problem for love.

Missing from this chapter is a balancing off of opposing theories. One may quarrel with details presented here, but there is no systematic opposition among philosophers to love. Would anyone claim that love is not good? The ethics of love seems to be quite compatible with all and any of the philosophical viewpoints we have described, and is rather in addition than in opposition to them. There are ethical theories that neglect love, but that is a sign of their inadequacy. What theory of morals can afford to overlook the greatest of moral values?

SUMMARY

Person was defined by Boethius as "an individual substance of a rational nature." *Personalism* is any philosophy based on the central importance and outstanding dignity of the person.

Person is not opposed to *nature* in man, even if the person be thought the more important aspect for ethics; nor to *individual*, despite the reference of individual to matter and of person to form. Though chiefly regarded as a center of consciousness, the person is the whole man, not merely his mind.

The distinguishing mark of person is *subjectivity*. We can define person only by conceptualizing it and making it an object. The subject is known only by direct experience. I have direct experience only of myself as a subject, for I am the only one I can ever be. The person is a subject that cannot become an object.

Intersubjectivity is possible, not by knowledge, but by love. We pass beyond the I-It and the I-He relation to the I-Thou relation.

Love is *silent,* for it can give no reason for itself; *communion,* because it unites two with no destruction of their identity; *presence,* by which the Thou as subject becomes a second self to the I as subject; *self-giving,* not directed to the completion of myself but of the other; *creative,* by helping the other in the creative work of fulfilling his personality; *reciprocal,* in that the meeting of the I and the Thou results in a We; *supreme value,* inasmuch as love pervades all other values, and God is Love.

Love for all mankind is a less intimate love, not based on direct experience of others' personalities but on reasoned knowledge that they are persons. It includes justice but extends beyond it. It is raised to its highest plane when suffused with the love of God, who created persons in the likeness of his own personality.

The ethics of love is not opposed to other ethical theories but is compatible with what is good in all of them.

QUESTIONS FOR DISCUSSION

1 Have you a direct experience of yourself as a person? Are you able to disengage yourself, the knowing subject, from yourself, the known object? If you cannot, what is the meaning of personality for you?

2 What is so special about a person that he should never be treated as a thing? Is it anything more than a sense of my own self-centered superiority transferred to others and redounding back to myself?

3 Would not a totally selfless love, in which one is wholly for the other without a trace of self-love to mar its fullness of giving, be a higher kind of love than that described in the text?

4 Do you think that justice and love are continuous, a lesser and a greater phase of the same thing, or are they so antithetical in motive and spirit that justice is no longer needed when there is love?

5 What about the wife who accuses her husband of no longer loving her because he refuses to do for her what his conscience clearly tells him is seriously wrong? Reverse the sexes, if you wish.

READINGS

On person read Emmanuel Mounier's *Personalism,* and Jacques Maritain's *The Person and the Common Good* and *Existence and the Existent.*

Anders Nygren started a stream of writing on love with his *Agape and Eros.* Martin D'Arcy responds to Nygren in *The Mind and Heart of Love* and adds his own development. Denis de Rougement has a well-known work, *Love in the Western World.*

Read Maurice Nédoncelle, *Love and the Person,* and Robert Johann, *The Meaning of Love.* From these, together with Maritain, much of our material was taken.

Also Martin Buber, *I and Thou;* Erich Fromm, *The Art of Loving;* C. S. Lewis, *The Four Loves;* Frederick Wilhelmsen, *The Metaphysics of Love;* Robert Hazo, *The Idea of Love;* and Rollo May, *Love and Will.*

Austin Fagothey, *Right and Reason—an Anthology,* contains Maritain's *Existence and the Existent,* ch. 3.

CHAPTER 16

HABIT

PROBLEM

The good life does not consist of unrelated good acts. The acts lead into one another, reinforce one another, and form chains of good conduct. The good life would be harrowingly difficult if each good act had to be done on its own without any influence from one's past behavior.

The only way of assuring ourselves that our acts will be morally good is by turning them into a habit. Virtue and vice are only names for morally good and morally bad habits. Virtue testifies to good acts done, for there is no other way of acquiring a virtue, but it is also and chiefly the spring of further and better moral acts in the future. Virtue stands somewhere between a single good deed and a whole good life.

This chapter is mainly descriptive, but it does contain some problems. One is the paradox that good acts produce virtue, and virtue produces good acts. Another is the Socratic concept of virtue as knowledge, from which it might seem that virtue ought to be studied rather than practiced. Another is the Stoic concept of virtue as the end itself rather than a means. A last is to determine which among the almost innumerable virtues exert the chief influence on our moral life. We ask:

1. What is the moral significance of habit?
2. Does virtue consist in knowing?
3. Is virtue its own reward?
4. How does virtue stand in the middle?
5. Which virtues are basic to all the rest?

MORAL HABITS

By derivation *habit* means a *having,* and on this score anything we have is a habit. But over the centuries the word has become narrower in its meaning. Aristotle, after putting habit under the category of quality and calling it a lasting disposition,[*] gives this definition, often quoted by St. Thomas[†]:

Habit means a disposition according to which that which is disposed is either well or ill disposed, and either in itself or with reference to something else.[‡]

So vague a definition made it necessary to distinguish *entitative* habits, or habits of being, from *operative* habits, or habits of acting. The former would be such qualities as health or strength or beauty, which we hardly call habits today. Modern language recognizes only operative habits, the tendencies we *have* in us from repeated acts.

We are born with a nature endowed with certain powers of acting. We begin to exercise these powers, and each time we do a thing we find it easier to repeat the action in the same way. Habit is beginning to take shape. It is an actualization of our

---

[*] Aristotle, *Categories,* ch. 8, 8b 27.
[†] St. Thomas, *Summa Theologica,* I-II, q. 49, a. 1, ff.
[‡] Aristotle, *Metaphysics,* bk. V, ch. 20, 1022b 10.

potencies but has the peculiar position of being somewhere between bare potency and full act. Nothing, of course, can be both in potency and in act toward the same thing in the same way, but it can in different ways. Take the example of a carpenter. As a child he was only a potential carpenter, having an undeveloped natural ability. Now that he has learned the trade, got the habit, he is an actual carpenter, one actually expert in this kind of work. But he happens at the moment to be asleep. Though he actually has the habit, he is not exercising it and is in a state of potency toward that exercise. When he awakes and starts plying his trade, he not only is an actual carpenter but is actually carpentering. Thus the habit is a sort of midway stage between undeveloped ability and expert operation.

Habit does not give us the power to *do* something; this we must have from our nature. Rather, habit enables us to do something *more easily and readily*. If the habit is good, it turns our originally fitful and clumsy efforts into quick, smooth, and masterful action. If the habit is bad, it makes us fall more easily and readily into the undesirable course. Habit has therefore been called a "second nature,"* for just as nature is the principle of action itself, so habit is the source of facility in action. The habit comes from the acts, and the acts come from the habit, but in different ways: by acting repeatedly we acquire the habit, and the habit now acquired tends to manifest itself in habitual acts.

Habits are typically *human* things. God can have no habits because he has no potentiality and does all things with perfect ease. Animals cannot have habits in the proper sense because their potentialities are too narrow and their lines of action are laid out for them by their nature through their instincts; man can train ani-

mals to quasi-habits, but they are imposed from without and not developed by the animal alone. Man has a nature plastic enough to be molded in various ways. By his free choice he can do the molding himself to some extent, and his environment will do the rest. Man cannot spread his abilities over the whole field of action possible to him but must channel them along definite lines. Habits are these channels, cut deeper with each repetition for better or for worse, until the person's native temperament is carved out into the thing we call character.

Though all habits are acquired in the sense that we are not born with any fully formed, they differ greatly in the amount of effort needed for their development. The intellectual habit of first principles, the understanding and use of such truths as the principle of noncontradiction in the speculative order and the principles of synderesis, or the first moral truths in the practical order, is virtually in the mind from the start. Other habits grow only by painstaking and persistent practice, and need constant exercise to keep them at the peak of efficiency, such as the arts, skills, and sports. Bad habits may result from defective development of our abilities, so that instead of ease and smoothness we beget a wasteful and bungling style of operation. Other habits develop no ability in us but only create a tendency to repetition; the acts are not done better but only more often until we fall into them inadvertently, as with swearing. Still other habits come from building up in oneself an organic craving, whether wholly acquired or the ripening of a predisposition, as in the use of drugs and stimulants. Finally, there are those forms of routine more properly called customs than habits, which, however often repeated, normally require a voluntary act each time, such as attendance at class.

Habits are destroyed either by disuse or by contrary acts. Disuse starves out the habit, and contrary acts replace it with the

---

*Aristotle, *Nicomachean Ethics*, bk. VII, ch. 10, 1152a 30.

opposite habit. In rooting out bad habits it is important never to allow a single slip back into the habits, for one fall can undo the work of a long and painful conquest. Habits are useful servants created in us by our own acts, but they have a tendency subtly to enslave their masters; they must be kept in their place.

VIRTUE AND VICE

Some habits perfect us only physically or mentally or socially, but if they perfect our nature taken completely, they are good habits of living or conduct and are called virtues. Originally the word *virtue,* from the Latin *vir,* meant manliness, and the Greek ἀρετή had a similar sense. From excellence in battle it came to mean any kind of excellence, and that is how ancient writers use it. Only in modern times has it become restricted to an ethical sense. *Vice* likewise meant any kind of flaw, but it now means only an ethically bad habit.

Socrates taught that virtue is knowledge and vice is ignorance. This doctrine runs throughout the writings of Plato, appearing in two often recurring questions: "Is virtue one or many?" and "Can virtue be taught?" Plato explains how knowledge is the common element in all virtues, the courageous man knowing what to do in danger, the temperate man knowing how to restrain his passions, the just man knowing what rightly belongs to himself and to others. Virtue is therefore one, and since it is knowledge it can be taught, though not in the way the Sophists tried to teach it.* He says that the philosopher alone has true virtue because he alone has true wisdom, and insists on the importance of attaining that wisdom.† Because of this con-

viction Socrates and Plato took their teaching mission so seriously.

The sublimity of Plato's thought should not blind us to its defects. If virtue is knowledge and vice ignorance, no one does wrong voluntarily; at most he could be censured for neglecting to acquire the proper knowledge. Plato admits this:

> No man voluntarily pursues evil, or that which he thinks to be evil. To prefer evil to good is not in human nature; and when a man is compelled to choose one of two evils, no one will choose the greater when he may have the less.*

In his discussion of voluntariness, Aristotle directly argues against Plato's opinion:

> The end being what we wish for, the means what we deliberate about and choose, actions concerning means must be according to choice and voluntary. Now the exercise of the virtues is concerned with means. Therefore virtue also is in our power, and so too vice. . . . Now if it is in our power to do noble or base acts, and likewise in our power not to do them, and this is what being good or bad meant, then it is in our power to be virtuous or vicious.†

If our knowledge were perfect and if our appetites were under the full control of reason, Plato's theory would be correct, but in this life our knowledge is not perfect. A vicious act requires some voluntary clouding of knowledge, a willful refusal at the moment of acting to use the knowledge we have. We seek evil not for itself but for some good found with it or through it. We try to concentrate on the good and overlook the evil; yet we know the evil is there and choose it voluntarily. Also, our control over our appetites is not the same as our control over our muscles. When we command our hand or foot, it obeys, but when we command our appetites they can and often do rebel.

---

*Plato, *Protagoras,* §359-361; *Republic,* bk. IV, §441-445.
†Plato, *Phaedo,* §68-69, 107-108; *Phaedrus,* §246-256.

*Plato, *Protagoras,* §358; see also *Laws,* bk. V, §371, bk. IX, §860.
†Aristotle, *Nicomachean Ethics,* bk. III, ch. 5, 1113b 3; see also bk. VII, ch. 2-3, 1145b 22-1147b 19, regarding continence.

The soul rules the body with a despotical rule, whereas the intellect rules the appetites with a constitutional and royal rule.*

Hence the necessity of training the other parts of our being to be subject to reason. Such training results in good habits, and these are virtues. In a virtuous person the passions and appetites are habitually subject to reason like the free citizens of a well-governed state, but in the vicious man they are an unruly mob. In any single act he can keep them in line, and it is his fault if he does not, but by and large he will find the effort too great, will relax his control, be caught unawares, and act against the law of reason. Thus, though there is some knowledge in all virtue and some ignorance in all vice, knowledge alone will not suffice to make men good.

STOICISM

Though both Plato and Aristotle center their ethics on the concept of virtue, the Stoics were the ones who carried virtue to the extreme. Just when the Epicureans were promoting pleasure as the greatest good, the Stoics were opposing them with the unyielding claims of virtue. Stoicism grew out of the Cynic school of thought, which taught that virtue is no mere means to happiness but is happiness itself. Virtue is the only good, vice the only evil, and everything else is indifferent. The essence of virtue is self-sufficiency, independence from everything and everybody. The Cynics despised riches, pleasure, comfort, family, society, culture, and sometimes even common decency.

Stoicism dropped the grossness of this attitude and made it respectable by joining it to pantheism. The world, they said, is composed of the world body, consisting of coarse matter apparent to our senses, and the world soul, fine matter that blows

as a wind through the world, giving it motion and making it a huge animal. Man's body and soul are only limited portions of the world body and the world soul. The whole world itself is God or Nature, for these are the same. Nature develops itself according to inexorable law, so that the universe can be called not only Nature and God but also Fate and Destiny, Reason and Law. Hence Stoicism is a form of *materialism, pantheism,* and *fatalism.*

Our individual natures are all parts of universal nature; on which account the chief good is to live in a manner corresponding to nature, and that means corresponding to one's own nature and to universal nature.*

Nothing else, they say, could ever happen except what does happen. Everything that will befall me is decreed by Fate; I can accept these decrees graciously or rebelliously, but accept them I must. Rebellion is only an emotional reaction against Nature, a childish pouting that can change nothing and only makes me miserable. Nature stands serene though I rail against it. The reasonable thing to do is to develop *apathy,* a state of indifference to all things, of complete control over my emotions, the only thing I can control. Emotion is irrational and bad; action according to reason, which shows me the inexorable law of Nature, alone is good—and it is *virtue.* Virtue is the only good. It is not a means to an end but the end itself. "Virtue is its own reward."

Virtue is a disposition of the mind always consistent and always harmonious; one ought to seek it out for its own sake, without being influenced by fear or hope or any external influence.†

The virtuous man stands firm though the world crashes about him; realizing his identity with Nature, he is beyond good and evil. There are no degrees in virtue,

---

*Aristotle, *Politics,* bk. I, ch. 5, 1254b 3.

*Diogenes Laertius, *Lives and Opinions of Eminent Philosophers,* bk. VII, 53.
†*Ibid.*

and he who has one virtue has all, for either he lives according to Nature or he does not; the former is the wise man or philosopher, the latter a fool.

The modern philosopher Baruch Spinoza gives us a moral system that is fundamentally Stoic in tone, though based on the physical and psychological doctrines of Descartes rather than on those of the ancient Stoics. His great work, though entitled *Ethics,* is more of a metaphysical treatise embodying a complete pantheistic philosophy, culminating in the way man can reach "blessed immortality" by deliverance from bondage to his passions and by realization of his identity with Nature, which is God.

The Stoics argued vigorously in favor of their view, especially with their rivals, the Epicureans. Of course, the Stoics would have to be utterly indifferent whether they won or lost the argument, but they felt fated to make the effort. The following are a few of their arguments:

1. Stoicism sincerely faces the facts of life, that nature is hard and inexorable, neither favoring nor disfavoring us but rolling on its relentless way with utter indifference to us. It is foolish to read into nature aspects that are merely the reflection of our own emotions. If nature is indifferent to us, the only reasonable attitude on our part is indifference to it.

2. In this attitude of apathy we are really the gainers. It is a fact that we are a part of nature, and by conforming ourselves to nature we fulfill our role in the great cosmic scheme, whatever it is. To act unnaturally brings pain, and we ourselves are the only losers by this behavior. To act naturally will not necessarily bring us pleasure, but such action will be at least as painless as possible. Surely to act thus is wisdom, and failure to do so is folly.

3. There are no rewards or punishments in nature, only natural consequences of the way we act. There is something mean and despicable about refusing to do good

unless we are rewarded for it or shunning evil only for fear of punishment. Stoic ethics is as pure and disinterested as can be, for virtue is its own reward and needs no meretricious accouterments to make it attractive.

4. It is the greatest tribute to a person to love him for himself and not for the favors he may give us. Likewise, Nature, which the Stoics identify with God, is to be loved because it is what it is and not because of any favors it might give us. Otherwise we love the favors rather than Nature or God.

5. Stoicism enables us to adopt the best attitude toward the three important philosophical questions: freedom, immortality, and God. It leaves room for the rigid determinism of natural science, and yet gives man some inner freedom to control his attitudes. It encourages apathy toward a future life: if there is one, we will have it, want it or not; if there is none, we have no way of producing it. It admits the omnipotence of God as Nature, the sum total of all that is, without trying to construct some transcendent God beyond nature, for whom it sees no evidence.

Opponents find their chief objection to Stoicism in the fatalism, materialism, and pantheism implied in the system. More specifically:

1. It is indeed foolish to be upset by those aspects of nature that we cannot control. We have to take them, like them or not. There are some things we can control, however, and we are foolish if we do not better our condition. Nature does have kindly aspects that we can use, as well as harsh aspects that we have to endure.

2. We are indeed part of nature, but we should use our *rational* nature to bring the blind forces of irrational nature under our control, insofar as we can do so to our benefit. To have a rational nature and yet to stifle it by unnatural apathy does not seem to be conformity to nature at all. Man's whole being cries out for fulfillment,

not for absorption and extinction in an impersonal universe.

3. It would be wrong to do good merely for reward and to avoid evil merely for fear of punishment, but it is quite possible to do the good for its own sake and also to accept the reward that naturally comes with it. The phrase, "Virtue is its own reward," is another way of saying that virtue has no reward. But by its very notion, virtue is a means, not an end. Virtue consists of morally good habits, and these habits are called good precisely because they lead man more easily and readily to the accomplishment of some purpose in life. Virtue is a straight way, a right direction, a true aiming at the highest good, but no one takes a way to a way or directs himself to a direction or aims at aiming. Unless some goal, mark, or target is set up, virtue has no meaning.

4. Spinoza writes sublimely on the "intellectual love of God," an unemotional approval of Nature the way it is, without expecting God to love us in return. This attitude is disinterested indeed, so disinterested as to be inhuman. Love to be perfect must be reciprocal. The only God worthy of the name is a personal God who loves us infinitely more than we can love him, not impersonal nature incapable of love.

5. The three basic philosophical topics are here bargained away. The freedom is not real freedom but slavery to the omnipotent universe of matter. An immortality so problematic cannot stir up in us the slightest glimmering of hope. The God is not a God, but only Nature, for good and evil are denied all objective reality and reduced entirely to our emotional attitudes toward things. Conformity to a universe that is not good cannot make us good, and thus the Stoic ethical ideal fails. The Stoics accuse the Epicureans of frivolity, with some justice, but there can be a stern futility as well as a frivolous one. Stoic virtue leads nowhere else and in itself offers only hopeless resignation to an indifferent and basically cruel universe.

INTELLECTUAL AND MORAL VIRTUES

It will be worthwhile to spend the rest of the chapter on the Aristotelian theory of the virtues, since it is classical and little has been added to it by modern writers.

Good habits of the intellect, enabling it to be a more efficient instrument of knowledge, are virtues in the broad sense. Their effect on a man's moral life is quite remote, for they may make him a better student of ethics but not a better living man. Failure to exercise them results rather in involuntary mistakes than in wrong conduct. However, though less important for ethics, they are very valuable in themselves.

Aristotle* distinguishes three virtues of the theoretical or speculative intellect concerned with the contemplation of the true:

1. *Understanding:* the habit of first principles, the habitual knowledge of primary self-evident truths that lie at the root of all knowledge
2. *Science:* the habit of conclusions drawn by demonstrations from first principles, the habitual knowledge of the particular sciences
3. *Wisdom:* the habit of knowing things in their highest causes, an ordering of all principles and conclusions into one vast body of truth

---

*Aristotle, *Nicomachean Ethics*, bk. VI; St. Thomas, *Summa Theologica*, I-II, q. 57. Different translations of Aristotle use different names to indicate these virtues; the following list may help to avoid confusion:

νοῦς	= understanding	= intuitive reason
ἐπιστήμη	= science	= scientific knowledge
σοφία	= wisdom	= philosophic wisdom
τέχνη	= art	= craftsmanship
φρόνησις	= prudence	= practical wisdom

Then there are two virtues of the practical intellect, concerned with making and doing, the two forms of action:

4. *Art:* the habit of knowing how to make things, how to produce some external object; it includes the mechanical, the liberal, and the fine arts

5. *Prudence:* the habit of knowing how to do things, how to direct activity that does not result in tangible products, how to live a good human life

Though even the intellectual virtues have some remote reference to moral life, those which are more directly concerned with good living are called *moral* virtues. They are good habits in the appetitive part of the soul, directing the activity of the will and governing the passions of the sense-appetite. They enable us not merely to know what to do and how to do it, but they actually assist us in the doing of it. Doing a thing well is opposed to overdoing and to underdoing it, and consists in hitting the mean between excess and defect. This is Aristotle's famous doctrine of the *mean*, which he expresses thus:

> Virtue is a state of character concerned with choice, lying in a mean, i.e. the mean relative to us, this being determined by a rational principle and by that principle by which the man of practical wisdom would determine it. Now it is a mean between two vices, that which depends on excess and that which depends on defect; and again it is a mean because the vices respectively fall short of or exceed what is right in both passions and actions, while virtue both finds and chooses that which is intermediate. Hence in respect of its substance and the definition which states its essence virtue is a mean; with regard to what is best and right, an extreme.°

° Aristotle, *Nicomachean Ethics*, bk. II, ch. 6, 1106b 36. The translation uses some unusual expressions: "state of character" is *habit,* "rational principle" is *reason,* "practical wisdom" is *prudence.* The English edition of St. Thomas shortens the definition thus: "Virtue is a habit of choosing the mean appointed by reason as a prudent man would appoint it" (*Summa Theologica,* I-II, q. 59, a. 1).

In other words, virtue is a habit of choosing the mean between the extremes of excess and defect in action, and this mean is determined by reason guided by the intellectual virtue of prudence. As too much or too little food, sleep, or exercise hurts the body but just the right amount promotes its health, so excess or defect in the habits of the soul hurts its health and "virtue stands in the middle." Virtue aims us at our end and must neither overshoot nor fall short of the mark. Courage is a mean between cowardice and rashness, temperance between gluttony and abstinence, generosity between stinginess and prodigality, friendliness between surliness and flattery.

The mean is not absolute but "relative to us," for what is the right amount for one would be too much or too little for another. A brave deed for a soldier would be foolhardy for a woman, a temperate meal for a wrestler would be overindulgence for a dyspeptic, a generous gift from a poor man would be a stingy one from a rich man. Thus the intellectual virtue of prudence is the guide by which the mean of the moral virtues is to be decided.

Criticism of Aristotle's doctrine of the mean is often vitiated by a careless reading of his text, as if he meant that we should not be too good or too moral but only moderately so. Nothing could be farther from his mind. To say that you must neither overshoot nor undershoot the mark is not the same as saying that you should aim carelessly or lackadaisically. He carefully notes that, though the virtue itself is a mean between extremes, the virtue is not to be practiced moderately but fully. The judge must go all out for justice, but justice itself is a mean between lenience and severity; the witness must be exactly truthful, but truthfulness itself is a mean between exaggeration and understatement. In acts that are bad in themselves there is no virtuous mean. It is not good to be moderately murderous or adulterous; we must simply not be so at all.

CARDINAL VIRTUES

Four virtues have been traditionally picked out as the most important in the ethical order. They are called *cardinal* virtues, from the Latin *cardo,* a hinge, because they are the four hinges on which the other virtues swing. Plato, though he probably did not invent them, makes his whole theory of the human soul and of the political state dependent on them. Aristotle centers his *Ethics* on them, and they have been universally adopted by Christian writers. St. Thomas divides the cardinal virtues as follows:

The formal principle of the virtue of which we speak now is the good as defined by reason. This good can be considered in two ways. First, as existing in the consideration itself of reason, and thus we have one principal virtue called *prudence.* Secondly, according as the reason puts its order into something else, and this either into operations, and then we have *justice,* or into passions, and then we need two virtues. For the need of putting the order of reason into the passions is due to their thwarting reason; and this occurs in two ways. First, when the passions incite to something against reason, and then they need a curb, which we thus call *temperance;* secondly, when the passions withdraw us from following the dictate of reason, e.g., through fear of danger or toil, and then man needs to be strengthened for that which reason dictates, lest he turn back, and to this end there is *fortitude.*

In like manner we find the same number if we consider the subjects of virtue. For there are four subjects of the virtue of which we now speak, viz., the power which is rational in its essence, and this is perfected by *prudence;* and that which is rational by participation, and is threefold, the will, subject of *justice,* the concupiscible power, subject of *temperance,* and the irascible power, subject of *fortitude.**

PRUDENCE

Prudence is an intellectual virtue by essence, but it enters into the field of the

moral virtues by pointing out the mean and suggesting ways of attaining it. Without prudence, fortitude becomes boldness, temperance becomes moroseness, justice becomes harshness. Prudence chooses the right means toward worthy ends; the choice of good means toward bad ends is mere cleverness or shrewdness, but not true prudence. As it is impossible to have the moral virtues without prudence, so it is impossible to have prudence without the moral virtues, for the rebellion of passion and will clouds reason and prevents the formation of a prudent judgment.

The importance of prudence in the ethical life cannot be overestimated. Whenever a general rule of conduct, such as ethics devises, must be applied to a concrete case, prudence is called for. Rules cannot be given for prudence itself, because all rules must have some universality, and prudence deals with the single instance. How to break bad news gently, when to ask one's employer for a raise, whether to punish a fault or to let it pass this time, whom to pick out as the right man for the right job, how to arrange the troops for battle in a particular terrain, what legislation will best promote the common good and conciliate all interests—all such matters, great and small, are governed by prudence. The widest possible observation and experience of human behavior are the only teachers of prudence. It has little correlation with book learning. Some pick it up readily, some otherwise intelligent persons are slow to catch on, some geniuses are deficient in it. It is hard to correct imprudence, for imprudence itself largely consists in refusing to accept advice or learn from experience. Imprudent people may commit few sins, for one does not consciously will to be imprudent, but their lives are a series of blunders. The virtue of prudence does not consist in a single prudent decision but is the acquired habit of always or nearly always using the right means to good ends.

There are a number of lesser virtues im-

---

*St. Thomas, *Summa Theologica,* I-II, q. 61, a. 2.

plied in prudence, such as foresight, care, docility, caution, and circumspection. Negligence, precipitation, inconsideration, recklessness, headstrongness, and the like indicate a defect of prudence. Craftiness, deceit, timidity, and pusillanimity may result from an excess of prudence not balanced by other virtues.

TEMPERANCE

Temperance regulates the appetite in the use of sensible pleasure. It moderates our two main drives, toward self-preservation and race-preservation, and thus acts as a curb on excessive indulgence in food and drink and in the use of sex. Its opposed vices are gluttony and lust. Temperance as a virtue, perhaps better called temperateness or moderation or self-control, does not mean total abstinence. There are same persons who find that any indulgence leads to temptations they cannot overcome, and for these total abstinence is the only cure; others for higher motives and for their spiritual perfection voluntarily give up some otherwise legitimate pleasures. But no creature is bad in itself, and natural morality merely requires that creatures be used with moderation and insofar as they help to worthy ends. The habit of doing this is temperance. Since most persons are inclined to excess in pleasure, the mean is usually short of one's desire and closer to the side of restraint. People differ greatly in the strength of their sensuous cravings, and so the mean varies with different persons.

Temperance contains the subordinate virtues of abstinence and sobriety, chastity and continence. By analogy temperance also regulates cravings that are less animal in nature and puts a proper curb on our self-esteem; in which cases it is called humility, modesty, gentleness, mildness, and docility. Lack of temperance appears in gluttony, drunkenness, lust, pride, cruelty, and vanity. Too much restraint, which is intemperance in the opposite direction, may produce in-sensibility, stolidity, sullenness, moroseness, and fanatical austerity.

COURAGE

Courage, fortitude, or bravery inclines one to face danger and toil without flinching. As temperance is a bridle, so courage is a spur. Most people are inclined to quail before danger, and courage drives us into it. But not everything that looks like a brave act is a manifestation of the virtue of courage. It does not consist in one brave act but is a habit of self-mastery. To rush into peril out of anger, ignorance, or stupidity is no sign of courage; the truly courageous man acts from a rational motive, whereby he appreciates the danger while counting it the lesser evil. To our instincts death is the most dreadful of all things, but reason tells us that there are some things better than life and others worse than death. Courage enables us to overcome our abhorrence of death, and still more of lesser evils, when it is reasonable to do so. It frees us from slavery to fear, though it need not take away fear itself. The brave man may act with fear but, in spite of it, faces the danger.

Courage is the primary requisite of the soldier, who is useless without it, but in some way it enters into all fields of life. *Active* courage consists in attacking the threatening evil, fighting against it, and overcoming it. *Passive* courage is endurance of an evil that cannot be overcome, holding one's ground and not yielding, no matter what the cost. Thus courage can exist on both sides, in the victor and the vanquished. Besides these two types of *physical* courage there is also *moral* courage, which is the same two attitudes but toward evils and dangers that do not involve bodily harm. Everyone is expected to stand up to life's troubles and misfortunes, to put in the effort to overcome them when possible, and when not possible to bear them with honor. Moral courage, in the sense of refusing to do anything morally dishonorable no matter what the consequences, is essential to any moral living.

Courage implies patience, perseverance, and constancy. Aristotle adds two unusual virtues: magnificence, to dare wisely in the matter of expense, and magnanimity, to dare wisely in the matter of honor. His often quoted picture of the magnanimous man,* the high-minded or superior man, which seems to be his ideal, has been criticized as a model of priggishness and stuffiness; perhaps each one must make up his own ideal. Lack of courage is shown in cowardice, weakness, timidity, impatience, and irresoluteness. Boldness, presumption, stubbornness, quarrelsomeness, and ruthlessness are faults of the overbrave.

JUSTICE

Justice inclines us to give to each one his own. It supposes at least two persons between whom there can be some sort of equality, so that each person receives what really belongs to him. Temperance and courage regulate our control over the lower appetites, but justice regulates the will's government over itself where dealings with another person are involved.

Justice is divided by Aristotle into general and particular. *General* justice is so broad as to cover all virtue that has any social significance and is therefore not the specific cardinal virtue of justice. *Particular* justice, which is the cardinal virtue, he divides into *distributive* and *corrective*. The latter is now more commonly called *commutative*, a name derived from the commutation or exchange of goods. We shall take them in inverse order.

Commutative justice exists between equals, that is between man and man or between groups of men acting as if they were private persons negotiating on equal

---

*Aristotle, *Nicomachean Ethics*, bk. IV, ch. 3, 1122a 33; the Oxford translation calls him "proud," a term that can easily be misinterpreted.

terms. Commutative justice is the basis of contracts. In a contract, such as barter or hire, the two persons start equal; when one has fulfilled his part of the contract the equality is unbalanced; then justice demands the restoration of equality by the other's fulfillment of his part. The same holds outside the field of voluntary contracts in those situations where nature itself demands the balance of equality. One who has injured another by depriving him of something rightfully his is obliged in justice to restore it to him. Commutative justice, when violated, carries with it the obligation of restitution. Justice remains outraged until proper compensation has been made to re-establish the balance.

Distributive justice is a relation between the community and its members. As its name indicates, it requires a fair and proper distribution of public benefits and burdens among the members of the community. Though existing in some way in all organizations, distributive justice applies chiefly to the state. It is the particular obligation of public officials and is violated by favoritism and partiality. It does not exist between equals, but between a superior and his subordinates; the equality, implied in all justice, here means that each subordinate should get his proportionate share, a share equal to his just deserts. Distributive justice has its converse, the obligation of the members to contribute to the common good. In this aspect it might be called *contributive* justice.

Social justice is a modern term that has been given various meanings by various writers. The tendency now is to identify it with St. Thomas' *legal* justice, so called because it shows itself in law-abiding conduct; it is the same as Aristotle's *general* justice. Social justice refers to the organization of society in such a way that the common good, to which all are expected to contribute in proportion to their ability and opportunity, is available to all the members for their ready use and enjoyment. It shows itself more in economic, industrial, racial, and political relations but is by no means restricted to them. It involves everything connected with being a good citizen or a good member of society and reaping what ought to be the reward of upright and cooperative social conduct, one's proper share of the benefits of social living. Any arrangement of society that excludes or hinders certain classes or groups within it from their fair share of the common good is a violation of social justice. Nearly the whole of social ethics is a study of social justice.

GROWTH IN VIRTUE

Man is obliged to train his abilities to make them fit instruments for the attainment of his end. He has a general obligation to make good use of his talents, as gifts entrusted to his stewardship, though he has no particular duty to develop any one of them rather than another. But he should choose some sphere of action proportional to his gifts and educate himself in it to the point of expertness and competence. He cannot do so without a fair degree of the intellectual virtues.

Far more important in his development as a person are the moral virtues. A man must master his passions and learn self-control. Since he must avoid evil acts, he must keep himself clear of the evil habits or vices that are the sources of such acts, and acquire as much of the contrary virtues as will ensure his ability to cope with the ordinary temptations of life. No one can succeed without a good grounding in each of the four cardinal virtues.

No one is born with virtues, and they do not come to one by chance but only by long and arduous training. Parents are the ones charged with the responsibility of beginning the training of their children to give them a moral start in life. Human life is so arranged that each succeeding generation fits into the preceding one, so that the virtues of parents, by instruction but much more by example, are passed on to their children. Parents must have what they are to transmit. Moral discipline must begin long before the child is old enough to appreciate its value or even its meaning. The exercise of parental authority should gradually dwindle until it vanishes with the coming of adulthood, which is not the time to forge the weapons for life's battle but to hold them ready for use.

Exaggeration of the so-called "generation gap" does no service to either generation. The gap has always existed, but its exaggeration is a phenomenon of our time. The prevailing atmosphere is one in which respect, honor, courtesy, and loyalty are held in small esteem. Young people, being strict conformists to the pattern of their peer group, are confirmed in their adolescent attitude by their parents' own permissiveness. Youth has always had to cut the apron strings sometime, to test its newly developed strength, and to branch out on its own. One should sympathize with this feeling of expanding powers, increasing maturity, and solidifying responsibility. But to think that such growth can be accomplished with no help from one's elders, that parents have nothing to tell one, that it is impossible even to communicate with them, is to engage in an initial folly that bids fair to wreck young lives. The time will have passed in which young people can come back to repair the mistake. Some things must be done at the right time, or they cannot be done at all. The time for parental direction is before and not after the young person has left home, and when that time has passed it cannot be made up. How to discharge their parental responsibility in these days calls for the utmost in prudence as well as in love.

Our treatment of virtue may seem too cursory for so important a topic, but it is meant only as a summary and an introduction. Most of the following chapters will consist of a more detailed examination of the various virtues. Some will be treated at greater length because of the problems they raise, but the length of a discussion does not always indicate the importance of the topic.

SUMMARY

Habit is a quality difficult to change, disposing a being well or ill, either in itself or in its relation to others. Habit is a partial actualization of our natural potencies, adding to nature by giving it ease in performance, the acts intensifying the habit and the habit facilitating the acts. Habits of acting are acquired by constant repetition, lost by disuse or contrary acts.

Good moral habits are *virtues*, evil ones *vices*. The Socratic doctrine that virtue is knowledge and vice is ignorance is countered by the Aristotelian teaching that the control of reason over the passions is not despotic but political. The appetites can rebel against reason, but they ought not and must be trained not to do so.

Stoicism holds that virtue is its own reward. It controls emotion by *apathy* and cultivates resignation to inexorable fate in a pantheistic universe. The main difficulty is that virtue is a means, not an end.

Intellectual virtues make the intellect a better instrument of knowledge. They are understanding, science, and wisdom in the speculative intellect, and art and prudence in the practical intellect.

Moral virtues govern the appetites, both rational *(will)* and sensitive *(concupiscible* and *irascible)*. According to Aristotle, they consist in the habit of choosing the *mean* between extremes, directed thereto by the intellectual virtue of prudence.

The *cardinal* virtues are the hinges on which the other virtues swing. They are *prudence* in the intellect, choosing right means toward worthy ends; *temperance* in the concupiscible appetite, restraining it from overindulgence; *courage* in the irascible appetite, spurring it on to face necessary danger; and *justice* in the will, giving each one his own or his due.

Justice is particular or general. *Particular* justice is either *commutative*, from man to man, restoring the balance of equality, or *distributive*, between the community and its members. These two comprise the cardinal virtue. *General* or *legal* or *social* justice regulates the whole of social living, comprising both the acquisition and apportionment of the common good.

QUESTIONS FOR DISCUSSION

1 If virtue can be taught, how does one go about teaching it? Is it done chiefly by precept or by example? Does it consist in supplying motivation, with the actual practice being done by the one acquiring the virtue?

2 Unless virtue is its own reward, how could moral good be an intrinsic good? Can the self-control of Stoicism be reconciled with the pleasure-seeking of hedonism?

3 If moderation is a virtue and moral virtue consists in a mean between extremes, should not all virtues be practiced only moderately? Is the moral ideal an example of an only moderately good life?

4 Are not virtues mere abstractions and their classification arbitrary?

Can you think of a better classification than the traditional one? Should some other virtue be added to the cardinal virtues?

5 Does the practice of virtue mean that one is obliged always to choose the morally best among two possible courses of action? Is choosing the lesser good among two goods a morally wrong choice?

READINGS

Plato has written little that does not deal with virtue in some respect. The *Protagoras, Phaedo, Phaedrus,* and bk. IV of the *Republic* are recommended. The *Charmides* discusses temperance, and the *Laches* courage.

Aristotle's treatment of virtue in the *Nicomachean Ethics* runs from bk. I, ch. 13, to bk. VII, ch. 10. This is the original source of most of the matter in this chapter. Henry Veatch, *Rational Man,* ch. 3-4, discusses Aristotle's theory of virtue.

The classical Stoic writings are Seneca's *Letters* and *Moral Essays,* Marcus Aurelius' *Meditations,* Epictetus' *Discourses,* and the philosophical writings of Cicero. See also Diogenes Laertius' *Lives and Opinions of Eminent Philosophers,* bk. VII.

St. Thomas follows Aristotle more thoroughly, omitting some points, developing others more thoroughly, and adding the theological virtues. His discussion of habits and virtues is found in the *Summa Theologica,* I-II, qq. 49-61; qq. 63 and 64; q. 65, a. 1; q. 66, aa. 1-5; q. 71, aa. 1-4. The Second Part of the Second Part (II-II) takes up each cardinal virtue in detail. Into this framework St. Thomas puts most of his writing on morals.

Spinoza's *Ethics* is a whole philosophy in itself. Books IV and V are pertinent here.

George Klubertanz, *Habits and Virtues,* gives a full modern treatment of this subject with an extensive bibliography. Josef Pieper has three little books, one entitled *Justice,* another *Prudence,* and a third *Fortitude and Temperance,* now all put together into one, *The Four Cardinal Virtues.* Étienne Gilson, *Moral Values and Moral Life,* ch. 5, 8-11, treats the cardinal virtues in general and each one in detail. See also his *Christian Philosophy of St. Thomas Aquinas,* pp. 256-264, 271-332.

Austin Fagothey, *Right and Reason—an Anthology,* contains part of James' ch. 4 on "Habit" from his *Principles of Psychology,* vol. I, pp. 120-127; also the appendix to bk. IV of Spinoza's *Ethics,* showing something of his Stoic tone.

CHAPTER 17

HAPPINESS

PROBLEM

The conflicting claims of happiness and duty, like those of love and law, run all through the history of ethics. The *deontologists,* champions of duty, have had their say through the mouth of Immanuel Kant. Few of them would deny the claim of happiness, but they want to keep it secondary, as an added bonus for faithfulness to duty rather than an aim consciously to be pursued. This view appeals to men of sterner stuff and to the puritanical-minded, who equate happiness with enjoyment and have never learned to enjoy themselves with a comfortable conscience. The *eudaemonists,* champions of happiness, have also been vocal. We could have begun ethics with happiness, as Aristotle does, but postponed it for the sake of a more disinterested approach, wishing to show that the good is worthy of pursuit just because it is good in itself apart from its benefit to us.

It is time now to hear the case for happiness, but not to contrast it with duty. The dichotomy is a false one. To achieve happiness is our duty if happiness is our end, and the fulfillment of such a duty necessarily results in happiness. Both duty and happiness are united in the good, for the ought and the end are good only if they have intrinsic value.

That we seek happiness in the abstract is shown in all we do. The more important question is whether we can reach it. Can our pursuit of it be successful, or are we doomed to be ever chasing a will-o'-the-wisp that constantly lures us on but ever eludes our grasp? It is a choice between ethical *optimism* and *pessimism,* according as we engage in the inevitable pursuit of happiness with hope or despair. The following points sum up our study:

1. What is the meaning of happiness?
2. Do all men seek happiness?
3. Do all men think happiness attainable?
4. Is happiness really attainable somewhere?
5. Where is happiness found, if anywhere?

MEANING OF HAPPINESS

The root meaning of *happy* is that of a person favored by fortune, one to whom good things *happen.* The equivalent word in other languages usually has the same basic meaning. Hence one may wonder, as Aristotle[*] does, whether a man should be called happy until he is dead, since misfortune may befall him in his old age. We carry the word *happiness* beyond its linguistic origin and the uses of common speech. The man who is fortunate, lucky, successful, satisfied, cheerful, glad, or joyous may be comparatively happy in the sense that he has come closer to happiness than most, or has done so in some particular line, but he is not necessarily happy in the way the philosopher speaks of happiness. Thus

---

[*]Aristotle, *Nicomachean Ethics,* bk. I, ch. 10, 1100a 1 to 1100b 10.

181

happiness is an analogous term, applying to various signs of, approaches to, and contributions toward happiness. The philosopher is not interested in these diminished manifestations but in the full concept of happiness as such.

Happiness is not a passing feeling or emotion, such as joy or gladness, but is a lasting state of being. One may be generally happy though suffering a temporary grief, just as another's chronic unhappiness may be punctuated by moments of joy. Nor is happiness a permanent quality of a person's character, a sunny disposition, a cheerful outlook on life, however much this may help to happiness; some people can maintain such a disposition in the face of disappointment, whereas happiness is satisfaction. The immature and feeble-minded can have a cheerful outlook, but it is due to lack of appreciation, not to fulfillment and possession.

Animals are incapable of happiness. They tend toward ends and have appetites that can be satisfied by things good for them. Having sense-knowledge, they can *feel* satiated and are capable of a kind of contentment. The animal that has eaten all it can is content for the moment, though it will soon be hungry again. Only intellectual beings are strictly capable of happiness. They alone can reflect on their state and *consciously* appreciate the satisfaction they enjoy. Happiness is a subjective condition entailing the existence of desire in oneself, the consciousness of the existence of the desire, the actual satisfaction of the desire, and the consciousness that this desire is being or has been satisfied. Such a state can exist only in a being capable of reflection and self-consciousness, an intellectual being.

Even in man contentment is not happiness. A man can be content if he limits his desires by a judicious compromise, being willing to forego some desires in order that he may attain others. In this life such an attitude is often necessary, but no one is ever *fully satisfied* with a compromise; it

is the best we can have in the circumstances, but we wish the circumstances would allow us more. If the desires exist, they want to be satisfied, not sacrificed for the benefit of other desires.

What, then, is happiness? From our observations it follows that happiness is the conscious state of satisfaction or fulfillment accompanying the possession of the good.

Perfect happiness comes from the complete possession of the perfect good, from that which *fully* satisfies *all* our desires. Boethius defines it as "a state made perfect by the aggregate of all good things,"[*] and St. Thomas as "the perfect good which lulls the appetite altogether."[†] *Imperfect* happiness falls off from the perfect by leaving some of our desires wholly or partially unsatisfied. One who is imperfectly happy is happy insofar as his desires are fulfilled and unhappy insofar as they are not. Resignation to this state of affairs, to a partial happiness mingled with unhappiness, is what we have called contentment; thus it is evident that contentment is not happiness itself. Perfect happiness may be taken absolutely or relatively. *Absolutely* perfect happiness is happiness to an infinite degree and pertains to God alone. *Relatively* perfect happiness is all that a finite being can have; its capacity is limited, and it is perfectly happy when that limited capacity is filled.

MAN'S NEED FOR HAPPINESS

That all men seek happiness in general, in the abstract, without specifying the object supposed to produce it, is evident from the very definition of happiness. We cannot desire something without at the same time wanting our desire to be satisfied; otherwise, we both do and do not desire it.

---

[*]Boethius, *Consolation of Philosophy*, bk. III, prose 2.
[†]St. Thomas, *Summa Theologica*, I-II, q. 2, a. 8.

But happiness is only a name for our self-conscious realization that our desires have been or are being satisfied; therefore we cannot desire anything without desiring happiness. One who would not crave happiness must have no desires, and such a one could not be human. St. Thomas put this with his usual clearness:

Happiness can be considered in two ways. First, according to the general notion of happiness; and thus of necessity every man desires happiness. For the general notion of happiness consists in the perfect good. But since good is the object of the will, the perfect good of a man is that which entirely satisfies his will. Consequently to desire happiness is nothing else than to desire that one's will be satisfied. And this everyone desires. Secondly, we may speak of happiness according to its specific notion, as to that in which it consists. And thus all do not know happiness, because they know not in what thing the general notion of happiness is found. And consequently in this respect not all desire it.*

The human will is not free with regard to happiness in general. Man is so made that he must seek it. But man is free in the choice of concrete objects by whose possession he hopes to obtain happiness. All want to be happy, but not all know how to find happiness.

It is a psychological impossibility to desire misery for its own sake. Those who seem to take a morbid delight in making themselves miserable manifest a perverted condition, an exception that proves the rule by showing how unnatural such behavior is; what they really seek, subconsciously perhaps, is some form of sadistic or masochistic gratification they receive from it, as the crank probably does from his meanness. While yearning for happiness in the abstract, one may judge that happiness in the concrete has become impossible through lack of means to reach it; the man in the throes of despair wants happiness so badly that he cannot face the idea of its loss. One may feel that it is better to endure present misery than the worse misery of making an effort to escape from it; thus the lazy abide in a filth and squalor they do not enjoy, and the timid let opportunities for self-betterment pass them by. Introverted visionaries may find the dream of happiness too engrossing to be shattered by the prosaic reality of hard work; they want happiness now in the only way they can get it now. A man who deliberately chooses an evil does so because of the good he sees bound up in it. At least he thinks it the lesser of two evils; because he wants to be less unhappy, he chooses what appears to be a relative or comparative happiness; thus the suicide seeks relief from life's wretchedness. All these examples are only seeming exceptions to the universal law that all men seek happiness.

Happiness is the basic motive in everything we do. Our every act is motivated by some desire, satisfaction of which is intended as at least a partial ingredient in the sum total of our happiness. We often have to sacrifice some goods for the sake of others, we may mistakenly choose the apparent good in place of the true good, we may foolishly prefer some temporary enjoyment here and now to lasting bliss in a better world, but we do all this for happiness. It goes to show, not that we do not want happiness, but rather that we want it so much that we cannot stand the delay in waiting for it, and impatiently snatch at its partial and imperfect forms that vividly appeal to us now.

We need not be *explicitly* thinking of happiness in all that we do. We do not pause before each action and say to ourselves, "I am doing this in order to become happier." Now and then, when we reflect on the meaning of life, we may explicitly form this intention, and it remains in the back of our minds governing the rest of our deeds. Even one who never reflects on the purpose of life is acting *implicitly* for happiness; otherwise he would not be able to act at all.

---

*Op. cit., I-II, q. 5, a. 8.

ETHICAL PESSIMISM

Is happiness attainable? No one will deny the possibility of imperfect happiness, the leading of a fairly satisfactory life of partial fulfillment, at least for the more fortunate of men, but by definition this state is not wholly satisfactory. We want to know whether *perfect* happiness, perfect not absolutely but relatively to man, is attainable by us.

A negative answer represents the pervading attitude of the philosophies of India. It is not pessimistic in the sense of encouraging a gloomy or cynical outlook. Rather, it is productive of a remarkable serenity that is the admiration of other peoples. But it must be judged pessimistic in its theoretical conclusions, in its resignation to a state of irremediable negativity.

The many systems of Hindu thought have this in common: that the only thing that really exists is Brahma; that all else is illusion; that the illusion is full of pain and sorrow, that the desires of man are part of the illusion and his thirsts are unquenchable; that since the desires cannot be filled, the thing to do is not to try to satisfy them but to extinguish them so that they are no longer felt; that unless one arrives at this state, the desire itself will reincarnate us into another round of painful existence. Therefore by asceticism and contemplation rid yourself of all longings, even to be yourself, and you will escape from the wheel of birth and sink back into the undifferentiated background of Brahma, which is all there really is anyway. Buddhism accepts most of this view, without Brahma. Despite its beautiful teachings on kindness and compassion, in its extreme form it is a sort of nihilism: nothing really exists. The soul is only what it thinks, and it thinks illusion. Again the counsel is to stifle all desire, thus escaping the cycle of rebirth and sinking into the blessed state of Nirvana, the utter peace of nonbeing. Nirvana is hardly a future heaven but a state of mind, or perhaps a nonstate of nonmind, in which there are no disappointments because there are no expectations.

Interest in Oriental thought was awakened in Europe by Arthur Schopenhauer,* the prince of pessimists. He thought that life is so full of miseries that it is better not to live. The whole universe is but the manifestation of a primeval force, the *will-to-live*, which is the source of all the struggle and misery in life. The worst thing we can do is to propagate the race, because it only brings into existence more sufferers. The chief virtue is sympathy, by which we substitute the *will-to-let-live* for the *will-to-live* and thus obtain some rest from the constant struggle. This wan glimmer of relief is all the happiness we can hope for.

Western thought in general is too hardheaded to clothe what pessimism it has in mystical garments, and too activist to sit and wait in passive resignation. The atheists and materialists among us see that a denial of God and of a future life must necessarily limit man's destiny to whatever temporary happiness is possible in the present life. Some bettering of our condition in an imperfect world and some contented moments in a fleeting existence are about the best we can hope for. We must toughen ourselves to face the fact that the quest for real happiness is futile. The following passage from Bertrand Russell eloquently states this view:

> That man is the product of causes which had no prevision of the end they were achieving; that his origin, his growth, his hopes and fears, his loves and his beliefs, are but the outcome of accidental collocations of atoms; that no fire, no heroism, no intensity of thought and feeling, can preserve an individual life beyond the grave; that all the labors of the ages, all the devotion, all the inspiration, all the noonday brightness of human genius, are destined to extinction in the vast death of the solar system, and that the whole temple of Man's achievement must inevitably be buried be-

---

*Schopenhauer's main work is *The World as Will and Idea*.

neath the debris of a universe in ruins—all these things, if not quite beyond dispute, are yet so nearly certain, that no philosophy which rejects them can hope to stand. Only within the scaffolding of these truths, only on the firm foundation of unyielding despair, can the soul's habitation henceforth be safely built.°

Even if in his later days Russell dismissed this essay as youthful rhetoric, it remains a vivid picture of the naturalist's substitute for the last judgment. Even should man succeed in his constant efforts to create utopia on earth, the relentless course of entropy will overtake him and bring all his works to naught. But, they say, enjoy the brief day and live as well as you can in it. The ethical life is still possible, but it has no ultimate goal and no meaning beyond itself.

ETHICAL OPTIMISM

Optimism rather than pessimism has characterized the Western tradition. Plato† recognized that happiness in the possession of the very Idea of the Good is the goal of human living. It is to be sought in the present life but cannot be experienced here. In a former existence, before being steeped in the river of forgetfulness and imprisoned in the body, we once had it. Our purpose now is to strive through the practice of virtue in successive lives to escape from the body, from this sensible world of becoming and decay, and to return to the intelligible world of Ideas, the world of true and lasting being, in which we shall eternally contemplate the Ideas in their full perfection. To this we are led by fleeting glimpses of the Ideas awakened in our memory by their imperfect copies in this shadowy sense-world. Happiness, though the road to it be long and arduous, is ultimately attainable.

Aristotle in his masterly analysis of happiness, though never expressly denying a future life, restricts his consideration to the present world. Happiness, he says,° is the end of man. It is not inactivity but action, or else one could be happy while asleep. It must be the highest kind of action, not done for something else but desirable for its own sake. It is not amusement, which is only relaxation between work. It is not found in producing things, since such actions are for the sake of the product, and happiness is for its own sake. It is not action of the body or senses but of what is noblest and best in us, our reason. It is not activity of the practical reason, for this is full of care and trouble, but of the speculative or theoretical reason, which acts in quiet and leisure, for we work to have leisure. Hence it is not the activity of the soldier and statesman but of the sage and scholar.

Because it is the good life, it is the life of virtue, and of the highest virtue, not merely of courage and temperance, which fit a man for practical life, but of the intellectual virtues, which fit a man for contemplation, the contemplation of the highest truth and good. The contemplative life is the most pleasant, leisurely, continuous, enduring, and self-sufficing. This is the life of God, and it is the best.

Such a life is too high for man on earth. We must interrupt our contemplation of the true and the good to take care of our bodily needs, but we should devote ourselves not to what is mortal but to what is most god-like in us, and cherish the periods of contemplation to which we can attain. Happiness of a sort is possible even in the practical life. For it we need a sufficiency of health, maturity, education, friends, worldly goods, and length of days—all of which should be made subordinate aids to the truly happy life, a life most like that of God.

These two strains of thought, one from

° Russell, "A Free Man's Worship," in *Mysticism and Logic*, ch. III.
† Plato, *Phaedo Phaedrus*, §§245-257; *Republic*, bk. VII, etc.

° Aristotle, *Nicomachean Ethics*, bk. I, ch. 4-13; and bk. X, ch. 6-9.

Plato and one from Aristotle, elevated to the supernatural plane by the teaching of Christian revelation, find their full flowering in the medieval thinkers such as St. Thomas.° But St. Thomas is primarily a theologian and only secondarily a philosopher. He nowhere makes a complete study of the end of man explicitly undertaken from the standpoint of pure reason alone. He gives the groundwork for such a study, however. We can sift out the data of Christian revelation and, putting them aside as beyond the philosopher's scope, see what is left. There remains the hypothetical natural man. The whole question of man's natural destiny rests on the question of the immortality of the human soul. If immortality cannot be proved on rational or philosophical grounds, then man's natural destiny could only be to achieve such happiness as is possible in this world. If immortality can be proved on rational or philosophical grounds, then man's destiny even in the natural order lies beyond the bounds of the present life. Only on the second hypothesis is the problem of man's ultimate happiness open for further philosophical investigation.

STATE OF THE QUESTION

The preceding material leaves us with five options:

1. To abandon the quest for happiness by extinguishing the desire for it, and to make this extinction man's chief ethical aim. This is the answer of oriental pantheism and nihilism.

2. To deny the existence of God and of a future life, and therefore to settle for the imperfect happiness of this world. This is the answer of atheism and materialism.

3. To bypass the question as unanswerable and to put all consideration of it outside the scope of philosophical ethics. This is the answer of practical agnosticism.

°St. Thomas, *Summa Theologica*, I-II, qq. 3-4.

4. To hand over the whole question to theology, admitting philosophy's inadequacy to cope with it. This is the answer of supernaturalism, which some would call theologism.

5. To take the metaphysical position that there are philosophically valid arguments for God's existence and for immortality, and then to draw the logical conclusion regarding man's destiny. This is the answer of philosophical theism.

The first two views have been discussed, and the next two put themselves outside philosophical consideration. It remains to be seen what the last opinion has to say for itself.

THE ARGUMENT
FOR ETHICAL OPTIMISM

To some theists, especially those whose theism rests on nonrational grounds or whose approach to philosophy is nonmetaphysical, the following argument will have little appeal. To nontheists, of course, it can have none, but others see it as the only logical conclusion to be drawn from the existence of God and the immortality of the human soul, taken as philosophical positions established in metaphysics. Whether one finds it convincing or not, it is worth serious consideration. The argument is stated in the form of five logically connected assertions:

1. *Man seeks happiness to the fullness of his capacity.* We have already seen that man has a desire for some kind of happiness, and that this is man's basic desire penetrating all his other desires. But man is not satisfied with only some degree of happiness. The slightest suspicion that more can be obtained will start a craving for that more. His intellect reaches out to truth indefinitely and cannot rest so long as there is anything more to know. His will reaches out to good indefinitely and cannot rest so long as there is anything more to seek. In like manner all man's abilities demand complete satisfac-

tion. Thus man wants happiness as such, and all the happiness he can hold.

2. *Man's seeking for happiness is a natural tendency, one that springs from human nature itself.* Though man has no innate ideas, he has certain native drives or urges that spring into action as soon as the requisite concepts have been gathered from experience. On the sense level both man and animal have the drives popularly called instincts. On the rational level man has similar drives peculiar to himself, and the basic one is this tendency for happiness. Among all man's tendencies the one for happiness is unique. It is *universal,* for it is found in all men without exception, appearing even in morbid and abnormal persons though with some distortion; one man may refuse to seek happiness here, another there, but no one can refuse to seek it somewhere. It is *inescapable,* for it lasts throughout life and cannot be eradicated; no man can quench the desire for happiness in himself, and no matter how hard he may try not to feed it, the hunger grows in spite of him. It is *irresistible,* for it insistently demands satisfaction; man's ceaseless unrest shown in his constant activity is only an expression of this basic impulse in varying forms; he who is not happy wants to be happy, and he who is happy wants to be happier.

3. *Such a natural tendency must have been implanted in human nature by its author, God.* There must be an adequate explanation for the existence of such a basic urge. Since it is not accidental to man or casually acquired, but rooted in the very constitution of the human being, the only possible reason is that God made human nature that way. Man seeks happiness because God made him for happiness. Therefore responsibility for the existence of this natural tendency in man must be placed in God himself.

4. *A tendency implanted in human nature by God must be intended not for frustration but for fulfillment.* Here we must suppose that God has the attributes with-

out which he could not be God, especially that he is truthful, wise, and good. His *truthfulness* will not let God mislead man into thinking that happiness is possible if it is not. His *wisdom* will not permit God to place in man's very nature an inescapable urge that serves no purpose. His *goodness* will not allow God to put into man's nature a basic craving whose sole function would be to tantalize and torment him. Truthfulness, wisdom, and goodness are found in God; lying, folly, and cruelty are not. Therefore, once God has implanted in man a drive toward happiness, he must provide *some* attainable object by which this urge can be satisfied. We are not yet concerned with what that object is, but only that there must be *something.*

5. *The fulfillment of this tendency, or the attainment of happiness, is man's last end.* From the preceding analysis it follows that God has destined man for happiness and has made it possible for him to attain it. Happiness, therefore, forms at least part of man's last end. But the happiness man naturally seeks is all-inclusive, the full satisfaction of all the desires that spring from human nature itself. We have no natural capacity for anything above, beyond, or beside it. Therefore it is no mere part but the whole of man's last end, so far as human reason can discover it.

DISCUSSION FOR AND AGAINST ETHICAL OPTIMISM

Those who object to this argument by denying the metaphysical premises on which it rests are referred to metaphysics, where these premises are investigated. There can be no discussion where there is no common ground. Others have the following difficulties drawn from the structure of the argument itself:

1. The mere fact of having a desire is no guarantee of its fulfillment. The construction of fantasies and the wishing that they might come true result from the kind

of creative imagination we have. Any mature person has long ago given up the illusion that they may someday be verified, and he does not blame God that his dreams are only dreams.

2. Even granting that the desire for happiness is a natural desire does not prove that it must be fulfilled. We naturally desire health, wealth, knowledge, and other goods but cannot always obtain them. How, then, can we be sure that the natural tendency for happiness is on a different level and cannot be destined for frustration?

3. Why should man alone have natural tendencies that must be destined for fulfillment? Animals have natural wants that we often see frustrated, and we do not think that God is obliged to provide them with a future life in which to recompense them for their present disappointments. How can we be sure that God must provide special care for man to satisfy his natural tendencies?

4. The argument can hardly be taken to suppose that unrepentant, evil-living men will actually attain perfect happiness in the world to come, since they make themselves unworthy of it. Yet they must desire it as much as anyone, since this desire is rooted in human nature, which all possess. Does this not show that the tendency to happiness not only can be but also sometimes actually is frustrated?

5. If man's natural destiny consists in seeking his own happiness, how does he avoid the charge of being naturally and essentially selfish, a very unethical trait? It is a far nobler thing to spend oneself in helping one's fellowman on earth than to spend an eternity merely resting in the enjoyment of one's own happiness.

To these and similar objections the following answers are offered:

1. The argument was so stated as to avoid the charge of mere wish-fulfillment. It is not the case of mere imaginative desires that any adult can recognize as illusory, but of the most deep-seated urgings of human nature. We can give up our wistful dreams but not ourselves. Our whole nature cries out against our becoming hopeless futilities, and we cannot believe that God has made us such.

2. The word *natural* may mean anything that is not unnatural, or it may mean something positively demanded by our nature. Health, wealth, and the other lesser tendencies are natural in the first sense, happiness in the second. The lesser goods perfect us in a partial way but must sometimes be sacrificed for the all-inclusive tendency, which is for the highest good.

3. Animals have desires, but not for happiness, of which they cannot even form an idea. Not being persons, they are subordinate to the utility of each other and of man. Nature is so arranged that one of the purposes animals are naturally destined to serve is to be food for one another. Thus they always fulfill one of the alternative purposes for which they exist: either to grow to full maturity or to be consumed in assisting others to do so. Man, being a person, is not a mere means to another's end.

4. The argument does not say that all men *will* attain happiness but only that all men *can* attain it. It must be possible for all to reach it. If man lose it, the loss must be man's own fault. God must offer it, but man is free to take or refuse the offer. Man is destined to happiness conditionally, and the condition is that he voluntarily do his part to earn it.

5. Self-seeking is selfishness only when one seeks self inordinately, in the wrong way or measure, to others' loss. Happiness does not come in limited quantities, so that if I have more, you must have less. Every man can attain all the happiness he can hold without depriving anyone else of the least. Ethics requires of man the proper kind and amount of self-love. He is responsible for seeking his own self-development and for bringing his life to its appointed goal. It makes sense to help other

if they, too, have some meaning to their lives and are not destined to futility. The greatest love one can show one's fellowmen is to help them to their ultimate happiness.

PURSUIT OF HAPPINESS

Those who accept the foregoing argument, that there must be *something* in which man can find his ultimate happiness, are faced with the next question: Where can man find this happiness? Since men are not born perfectly happy, with all their desires fully satisfied, they must achieve happiness by coming into possession of some object they previously lacked. What is this object?

Those who have followed the argument so far will have little difficulty in suspecting the answer. For the sake of method and as a kind of summary, it will be helpful to look at the various candidates suggested for this position. A process of elimination will ensure that we have examined all claims, and then we can verify the credentials of the successful claimant.

PROCESS OF ELIMINATION

The object that can make man happy must be either man himself or something that is not man but either below man or equal to man or above man. It cannot be a being that is not man but equal to man, for we know of no such being and cannot seek something we do not know. Three alternatives remain:

1. Something below man
2. Man himself
3. Something above man

1. *The first main point is that things below man cannot make man happy.* The good things of this world, such as wealth, family, honor, fame, position, power, and influence, not only can be possessed with unhappiness, but also can cause unhappiness by the care and burden they impose.

We have desires they cannot satisfy, such as the craving for knowledge and love. Some chance on them without forethought or labor, whereas others cannot secure them even with the greatest effort, and they often come to the most unworthy. When obtained they have an uncertain existence, and they must all be left at death. These goods of fortune are means, not ends. They are for man, not man for them.

2. *The second main point is that man cannot make himself happy.* He cannot find his last end either in the possession of himself or in the possession of certain qualities of himself. There are three possibilities:

a. *Goods of body.* Health, strength, beauty, physical skills, and other bodily endowments are all subject to the imperfections of the goods of fortune. Without gifts of fortune that afford them scope for their proper exercise, they are often useless. They are not lasting; the art of growing old gracefully consists in intelligently adapting oneself to their loss.

b. *Goods of soul.* Though happiness, as a subjective state experienced within the consciousness, is a good of the soul, it must be produced in the soul by the acquisition of something else, since no one is born happy. By goods of the soul are meant such things as knowledge, the good of the intellect, and virtue, the good of the will. These are both highly estimable, and a life dedicated to their pursuit is truly noble. No one could be really happy without them. But knowledge as such and virtue as such can give only partial happiness at most, since they are means to the end and not the end itself.

i. *Knowledge.* The man who devotes himself to the life of learning has chosen wisely among the good things of this world, and he will probably be happier than most men, but he is chasing a phantom if he expects from it perfect happiness. The knowledge we can obtain in the present life is acquired by hard and toilsome study, is never fully clear, cannot be completed in the longest lifetime, and disappoints by confronting the undiscovered and inaccessible. That learning can be devoted to the service of evil shows that it is only a means that can be abused, and that of itself it is not *the* good.

ii. *Virtue.* Through accompanied by peace of conscience and spiritual exaltation, the practice of virtue demands self-control, self-sacrifice, and at times even heroism. However admirable this may be, nothing painful or difficult is compatible with complete happiness, since one would be happier who could attain the same good without the pain and difficulty. Virtue is an indispensable means to happiness, as making us worthy of it, but it is not that happiness itself.

c. *Goods of body and soul together.* If the goods of neither body nor soul taken separately can make man happy, perhaps happiness should be sought in the satisfaction of the whole man, of both body and soul taken together. Here again two possibilities arise, according as one seeks this satisfaction in enjoying a good already attained or in the very process of striving to attain it. Pleasure is the enjoyment of a good attained, and progress is the process of attainment.

i. *Pleasure.* The possession of the goods discussed so far results in pleasure of some kind, either sensuous or intellectual. Most hedonists, when they propose pleasure as the aim of life, mean both sensuous and intellectual pleasure combined into one object and seek happiness in a wise blend of physical and mental delights. Pleasure must be admitted as an ingredient in happiness, for it is actually desired and we could not be satisfied without it. But those who propose pleasure as the highest good are referring to the pleasures of this life only, to be derived with our present abilities from the objects surrounding us. We have already examined the hedonist theory and seen its limitations.

ii. *Progress.* By progress is meant the actualization of all man's potentialities, either of the individual or of the race. There is indeed a moral obligation to actualize the potentialities nature has endowed us with but it will not make us completely happy. It is *one* of the ends of human life but not the last end.

Self-development results in the fully developed man, but man cannot be satisfied with himself. He is not satisfied with the mediocre abilities he has to begin with and much less with the imperfect development he can give them. The self-development possible in this life would consist in a combination of goods of soul, body and fortune. Few men can succeed in acquiring them in sufficient proportion, and no one can keep them forever.

Social progress, development of the whole human race, is a favorite view of evolutionary humanism. The end of the individual is to contribute toward the future good of humanity, and man, who is now capable of little happiness, must evolve into a higher race capable of more. But this answer is no solution. The future happiness of the race cannot benefit the individual now living, and he wants to be happy himself as well as to make others happy. This happiness could only be greater material prosperity and a higher level of culture, an increase in the goods of body, soul, and fortune, which, however increased, can never be fully satisfying. If individual men are for the whole race, then what is the whole race for? To devote oneself to the advancement of civilization is a worthy and high-minded enterprise, but it is not enough. Man cannot be satisfied even with his civilized self.

3. *The third main point is that man's happiness must be sought in something above man.* From our whole discussion so far it follows that neither things below man nor man himself can make man perfectly happy. None of these things taken

separately can satisfy, nor can the combination of them all taken together, because no one can secure all these goods in one lifetime; some of them are mutually exclusive, and any choice among them will leave other desires unsatisfied. They are all fleeting and insecure, and over the whole of them is flung the shadow of death. The fact of death alone is sufficient argument to show that none of these transitory things could be the purpose for which we live.

Above man we have *God*. No one ever suggested that man exists for the sake of some superhuman creatures to be used or consumed for their well-being in the same way as animals are for the sake of man; the fact that man is a person makes this impossible. It follows, then, by the process of elimination that the only object that can make man perfectly happy, and thus is man's absolutely last end, is God.

The validity of a process of elimination depends on the completeness of the disjunction, that is, on the assurance that no possible alternative has been overlooked. Though ethical systems have an infinite possibility of variation in detail, and as the history of philosophy progresses, future theories will be proposed to supplant their predecessors, it can be safely said that no theory is conceivable that cannot be classified under some one of the headings just given. Any such system that does not make God man's last end must, if it is to be taken seriously, fall into the category of those which make *man* his own last end. But man is inherently incapable of satisfying himself or of being his own happiness.

POSITIVE ARGUMENT

The following argument is independent of the process of elimination just given, but the two arguments reinforce each other. For our happiness God is required and sufficient. If he is required, we cannot be happy without him. If he is sufficient, nothing else is necessary.

God is *required,* for no lesser being will do. Man is by nature rational, and rationality shows itself in two main tendencies: the tendency of the intellect to know all truth, and the tendency of the will to possess all good. But God is perfect truth and goodness. Without him man's intellect and will cannot be satisfied.

God is *sufficient* for one who possesses God, though he may also enjoy creatures, has no strict need of them. There can be no desire in man that God cannot satisfy to the full. There can be no truth that is not found in truth itself, no good that is not found in goodness itself.

The upshot of all this argumentation is that, even on the purely natural plane, man must be destined to a last end which is also his highest good, that this last end subjectively is happiness and objectively is God. Does this mean the beatific vision that theology speaks of? No. Philosophy knows nothing about that. All that pure reason can discuss and try to establish is a knowledge and love of God fully proportioned to man's natural powers and capacities, so that they are not left frustrated but given thorough satisfaction. This is all that man can *naturally* aspire to.

Would such a happiness be a static condition incapable of growth or progress? Only in the sense that God does not change and there is nothing beyond God to attain to. But there is no reason for happiness to be static on the part of the creature. There is no inherent impossibility in the supposition that the knowledge and love of God would be a continuously expanding knowledge and a continuously deepening love, at each moment perfectly corresponding to the proximate capacity of the soul at that particular stage, and thus satisfying it, but with a remote capacity of indefinite growth because God is the inexhaustible source of everlasting new manifestations of his infinite perfections.

SUMMARY

Happiness is desire satisfied by the conscious possession of the good. It is a lasting subjective state that can exist only in an intellectual being. It is neither mere contentment nor a passing emotion nor a sunny disposition.

All men seek happiness in general, since all want their desires satisfied, but they differ in what they judge will make them happy. Those who appear to desire misery or choose evils are only seeming exceptions. Happiness is the basic motive in all we do, though we may seek it only implicitly.

Perfect happiness fully satisfies all our desires; *imperfect* happiness has flaws in it. Because of man's finite capacities, his happiness cannot be *absolutely* but at most *relatively* perfect.

Is such relatively perfect happiness attainable? Pessimism says no. Oriental pessimists seek relief from suffering in the extinction of individual consciousness. Atheists and materialists counsel contentment with this life and the acceptance of death as the end of all. The optimistic Western tradition holds that happiness is man's last end and is attainable. The argument, presupposing God's existence and the soul's immortality, includes these steps:

1. Man seeks all the happiness he is capable of.
2. This is a natural tendency springing from human nature.
3. Such a tendency is implanted in human nature by God.
4. God cannot intend a natural tendency for frustration.

5. He intends it for fulfillment as man's last end.

It is objected that this is mere wish-fulfillment, that animals' natural desires are left unfulfilled, that evil-living men do not deserve happiness, and that seeking one's own happiness is selfish.

It is answered that our natural desire for happiness is our basic tendency and unique, that animals have no idea of happiness, that attainment of happiness requires our cooperation, and that legitimate self-seeking is not selfishness but the very purpose of our being.

Where can man find the happiness to which he is destined? What is man's objective last end? The argument is twofold:

1. *Process of elimination.* Nothing below man can make man happy, nor can man make himself happy; therefore, only something above man can do so, and this is God. Goods of fortune and goods of body are given to few, held with anxiety, and lost in the end. Knowledge is toilsome, incomplete, and unsatisfying. Virtue, besides being hard to practice, is but a means to the end and not the end itself. Pleasure cannot be constantly enjoyed. Service of others supposes that these others have some last end. Personal progress results only in a fully developed man who cannot be satisfied with himself. Progress of the human race does no good to the individual now and leaves unanswered what the race is for.

2. *Positive argument.* God is *required* to satisfy all man's desires, because the intellect tends to all Truth and the will to all Good. God is *sufficient*, because all perfection is found in the Infinite.

QUESTIONS FOR DISCUSSION

1 Is the definition of happiness a verbal or a real definition? Is happiness really definable or an indefinable experience or the con-

cept of an indefinable possible experience? Or is it something else?

2 Does moral pessimism lead to two alternative conclusions: Live the good life anyway, even if you cannot be happy, for the good is worthy in itself; don't bother to be good, for it will not surely bring you anything? Which, if either, is more pessimistic?

3 Is there a sense in which self-realization is the end of man? Is the possession of God the most perfect self-realization? Is this the meaning of love: self-realization through possession of another and self-donation through being possessed by another?

4 Is man's natural tendency toward happiness an unconscious drive spontaneously arising in man's nature or is it a conscious desire aroused only by intellectual reflection on the purpose of human life? Could it be both?

5 Man's last end is sometimes expressed as everlasting happiness and at other times as the glory of God. Is there opposition between them? How can they be reconciled?

READINGS

In the Oriental vein: The *Bhagavadgita* is a sublime poetic expression of Hindu thought. It would be well to read some of the Buddhist *Sutras*. Of both, there are many translations and editions. Schopenhauer's attitude can be seen in his essays, edited from *Parerga and Paralipomena*, especially bk. V.

Plato's writings are full of reflections on man's purpose in life and on happiness. The *Phaedo, Phaedrus, Symposium,* and bk. X of the *Republic* give Plato's idea of man's destiny.

Aristotle's *Nicomachean Ethics*, bk. I, ch. 4-13, and bk. X, ch. 6-9, provide the basic reading material here.

St. Augustine, *De Vita Beata* (The Happy Life), *De Moribus Ecclesiae Catholicae* (Of the Morals of the Catholic Church), and *De Doctrina Christiana* (On Christian Doctrine), does not separate philosophy and religion.

St. Thomas' *Summa Theologica*, I-II, qq. 2-5, presents the views of a theologian. Hence he treats of supernatural rather than natural happiness. This is why he says that man cannot attain ultimate happiness, by which he means the supernatural beatific vision, by his natural powers. What he says is useful for philosophy with the proper reservations. The same holds true of his treatment of happiness in the *Summa Contra Gentiles*, bk. III, ch. 25-63.

Leibniz' *Principles of Nature and Grace* treats of what most modern philosophers prefer to overlook.

Étienne Gilson's *Moral Values and Moral Life*, pp. 26-51, and his *Christian Philosophy of St. Thomas Aquinas*, pp. 351-356; Leo Ward's *Values and Reality*, ch. 5-6; Mortimer Adler's *Dialectic of Morals*; and William R. O'Connor's *The Eternal Quest* have good material.

Austin Fagothey, *Right and Reason—an Anthology*, contains Aristotle's two treatments of happiness in his *Nicomachean Ethics*, bk. I, ch. 7-10, and bk. X, ch. 6-8. The selection from Maritain's *Existence and the Existent*, ch. 3, has some pertinence here.

CHAPTER 18

RIGHTS

PROBLEM

Having considered happiness as the end of the moral life, we come back to a further consideration of the means to that end. The idea of law and the virtue of justice imply the existence of such things as rights and duties. They logically form the next topic in our study, especially since the remaining part of ethics consists chiefly in determining what man's rights and duties are.

There are those who are not interested in a natural law but still claim what they call natural rights. They may not even use the term natural rights but speak of human rights, rights that belong to any and every human being simply because he is human. We shall have to examine the logic of this attitude. From where do such rights come, and what obliges anybody to respect them? There are also those who are clamorous for their own rights but are unwilling to acknowledge that they have duties, or perhaps they will admit some duties but only those they voluntarily accept. Can any sense be made of such an attitude? What happens when I assert my right and others refuse to recognize it, or when others impose on me a duty I refuse to accept? We can distribute the matter under the following questions:

1. What are rights?
2. What are the components of a right?
3. Are there natural rights?
4. How is right related to might?
5. What are duties?
6. What if rights and duties conflict?
7. What excuses one from duty?

MEANING OF A RIGHT

The English word *right* has two main meanings, as illustrated in the following sentence: "It is right (morally good) for us to demand our rights (things owed us)." The two meanings stem out of the same root idea, the ethical concept of *oughtness:* how I ought to act, and how others ought to act toward me. Hence we have:

1. Right as opposed to wrong
2. Right as correlative to duty

Right originally means something that is straight, not crooked, in opposition to *wrong*, which is wrung or twisted from the straight. Right is something that squares with a rule or norm, such as a right line or a right angle. In ethics *right* means that which squares with the norm of morality and thus is morally good. Up to now we have dealt only with this meaning of the word *right,* and we have by no means finished with it.

Right is also used to mean that which is just: a just law, just deed, just debt, just claim, that which is owed. This is *right* as correlative to *duty,* and it is this sense of *right* that we must now study.

We cannot be obliged to keep the moral law and at the same time be deprived of the means necessary to this end. This obligation requires that we have the *power* both to do the things necessary for keeping the moral law ourselves and to restrain others from interfering with our observance of the moral law. No one can be obliged to do the impossible; hence, if it is a fact that we are obliged, we must be *empowered* to fulfill our obligation. Power is of two kinds:

1. Physical power, or might
2. Moral power, or right

Might, or physical power, is the bodily strength needed to secure an end. It comprises not only our own skeleton and muscles, together with all the tools, weapons, and machinery we can use, but also the bodily strength of all other persons under our command and the force of all the instruments they can use to help us accomplish our end. Thus a whole army can be at the disposal of a single man's will and is an enormous extension of his personal might. Though applied by a will or even by many wills cooperating, physical power accomplishes its purpose by mere force, which is indifferent to the claims of justice and can be used to help or hinder the observance of the moral law. Hence might in itself is neither good nor evil, and becomes either by the will that directs it.

Right, or moral power, on the other hand, works by appeal to another's will through his intellect. It points out to him that I claim something as mine, and that respect for my claim is necessary for him if he is to attain his own purpose in life. In urging a right I equivalently say, "This is mine, a means given me to help me fulfill my moral function as a human being; if you try to interfere, you can do so only by doing wrong, incurring moral guilt, violating the moral *ought,* thus destroying your own moral worth as a man." Thus a right puts a moral bond on the free will of another so that, even if he can infringe my right physically, he cannot do so without committing an evil deed and incurring moral guilt, with its corresponding sanctions. Hence a right is said to be morally inviolable even when it is physically violable.

1. Right is defined as moral power over what is one's own, or more expressly, *moral power to do, omit, hold, or exact something.* Right as thus defined exists in the person possessing the right, and, it is right in the primary sense.

2. By a figure of speech we transfer the word *right* from the person who has the right and apply it to the thing over which he has the right. We say, "I will get my rights," meaning some object rightfully mine, and "This man is deprived of his rights," meaning some object rightfully his. *Object* here is not necessarily a physical substance but may be actions, services, or omissions. If a man were deprived of his right in the sense of moral power, he would have no right to the thing at all and could not legitimately claim it; what we mean is that he is deprived of some object to which he retains a right.

3. Rights are founded on law, and law supposes rights. They imply each other. For this reason *law* itself is sometimes called *right,* a usage common in other languages but infrequent in English. Since all right comes from law, rights are called natural or positive, divine or human, ecclesiastical or civil, according to the kind of law that confers the right.

These three meanings of right are illustrated in the following sentence: A man is unjustly deprived of his rights (an object due him); recourse is made to the code of civil rights (the law); the man is given a fair trial to which he has a right (moral power to do, omit, hold, or exact something; in this case, to exact).

COMPONENTS OF A RIGHT

A right involves a system of relations in which there are three terms and a basis or foundation on which the relations are grounded. In the example of a workman having a right to his wages, we may separate four elements, or components: the workman who has earned the wages, the employer who is bound to pay the wages, the wages the workman has earned, and the work done whereby the workman has earned the wages. In general, in every right we distinguish the following:

1. Subject: the one possessing a right
2. Term: those bound to respect or fulfill a right
3. Matter: that to which one has a right
4. Title: the reason why this subject has a right to this matter

1. The *subject* of a right can only be a *person*. Rights exist because we are obliged to guard the moral value of our being and fulfill our function by voluntary observance of the moral law, and thus to reach our last end. To this kind of action rights are essential, because if we must guide ourselves by use of our free will, we must be guaranteed immunity from hindrance in our choice of the necessary means. Since only persons have free choice and are obliged by the moral law, only persons can have rights. Other creatures, acting spontaneously and without freedom or responsibility, need no such guarantee.

The subject of a right may be not only a *physical,* or *natural,* person, an individual rational being, but also a *moral,* or *juridical,* person (sometimes called a corporate, conventional, fictitious, or artificial person), such as a society, firm, corporation, or government. People may act singly or in groups, by themselves or through representatives, and group action is in accordance with man's social nature. Man attains his end by social as well as by individual activity, but a society would be useless if it could not command the means necessary to achieve its purpose; therefore societies as well as individuals can have rights.

2. The *term* of a right must also be a *person*. This proposition is evident from the definition. The term is the one or ones morally obliged to respect or fulfill the rights of another, and only a person can have moral obligations.

3. The *matter* of a right can *never* be

a *person*. As we saw previously, a person cannot be subordinated to the interests of another to be used and consumed as a mere means for another's benefit. Since in the exercise of any right the subject always subordinates the matter to himself and uses it as a means to his own end, it follows that the matter of a right can never be a person. This conclusion does not mean that one person can never do a service for another. Social life is a constant interchange of services, and men were made by nature to be helpful to one another. When we hire people to work for us, we buy their labor, not their persons, and labor can be the matter of a right.

4. The *title* of a right is the reason this particular concrete right exists. Its purpose is to establish a connection between the subject and the matter of a right. For example, a man has a right to own property in general, but this right is abstract, not specifying any particular piece of property. Something is necessary to give this particular man rather than someone else the right to this particular piece of property, to change the abstract into a concrete right. The contract of sale does so, and this fact is his title.

According to title, rights are congenital or acquired. *Congenital,* or native, rights come with birth or even before birth; the title to these rights is the bare fact of existence as a human being. *Acquired* rights have as their title some contingent historical fact, such as purchase, inheritance, or arriving at the age of majority. In either case, the title is always some fact connecting this subject with this matter, this person with this thing.

There are three important questions connected with the subject, the matter, and the title of a right:

1. Is the *subject* of a right always and only a person, or do animals and other nonpersonal beings also have rights?
2. May a person ever be the *matter* of a

right by reason of voluntary servitude or slavery?

3. Do humans have truly inalienable rights, or may a person's *title* to a right be either given up or taken away?

ANIMAL RIGHTS

From the above explanations it follows that animals, not being persons, have no rights. Man may be as gentle and kindly toward animals as he thinks he ought to be, without at the same time trying to give them rights. If one wants to give animals rights, he must take the consequences: he must give them the basic right, the right to life, and must refrain from all slaughter of animals and from all participation in their slaughter, so that he could neither raise animals for food nor eat meat. If he gives them rights, he must also give them the corresponding duties and hold them responsible for the exercise of rights and the fulfillment of duties they can never understand. The case is different with children, who are persons even if immature ones. There must be some cutoff point between beings that do and beings that do not have rights, and the only reasonable place for it is between persons and nonpersons.

Is there, then, no wrong in cruelty to animals? Cruelty to animals is indeed wrong, but not as a violation of the animals' rights. Rather, it is a perversion of the natural relation that should exist between man and animals, and violates the duty man owes to himself. Man must use animals in a way befitting man's own rational nature, and to inflict needless pain is unreasonable conduct. It is also an offense against the Creator, who has provided man with these creatures to be used for any reasonable and good purpose they can serve, but not merely to pander to man's sadistic craving for cruelty.

Vivisection is not wrong in itself, because animals are for man and may be used to help in the curing of man's diseases just as

they may be used for other human purposes. But vivisection can easily become wrong through circumstances, by being performed in an unnecessarily inhumane or cruel manner. On this subject much sentimental nonsense is written. Why draw a line between pets and pests? Even the staunchest defenders of so-called animal rights think it proper to get rid of vermin, and it is irrational to acknowledge rights only in those animals that happen to please us. If dogs have rights, so must fleas.

The zeal of some environmentalists leads them to give rights even to trees. They say, "In these circumstances this tree has a right not to be cut down." Now, no one objects to the use of metaphorical language, but it would make no sense to take this statement literally. It would make the chopping down of a tree murder in the same way that the killing of a man is murder. The quoted expression can only mean that man has a duty not to squander the goods of this world and not to cut down trees wantonly and wastefully. The existence of right and duties in man sufficiently takes care of the case without giving fictitious rights to trees.

SLAVERY

Slavery is wrong because it comes so close to treating a person as a thing. It is impossible to own a person, if we understand the word *person* in a philosophical sense. To own a slave's person would be to own not merely his body but also his intellect and will. These, however, always remain under the slave's control, and he is responsible for his voluntary acts like any other human being. It is precisely because a person is an intellectual being capable of voluntary and free acts that he cannot be owned. Though the slaveholder does not deprive a man of his internal freedom in the sense of free will, he does deprive the slave of his external freedom, which is one of the most precious attributes of a person and one of his most fundamental rights.

Slavery might be imposed as punishment for crime. If the state can put criminals to death, it should be able to impose lesser punishments. Imprisonment for crime is used in all societies, and the distinction between it and slavery is rather nominal. When a man hires out his labor, he can always quit and thus save his personal dignity; the slave and the prisoner cannot. Under desperate conditions a man might sell himself into slavery. If he can hire out his services for pay, why not for mere maintenance; if he can do it for a time, why not for life? One would hardly condemn a desperate man for saving himself in this way, but one would condemn a society for allowing such intolerable conditions to exist. For the public good the state should forbid such a contract. These two forms of servitude, the penal and the voluntary, are the only ones for which even a semblance of moral justification can be found.

Slavery as a historical institution looked on slaves as property, as animated tools, to be bought and sold. There can hardly be anything more degrading to human dignity or more destructive of human rights than this revolting practice. There can be no possible moral defense for slave-hunting, nor for letting children be born into slavery, and what begins unjustly and in bad faith cannot be righted by the mere passage of time. That the civilized world accepted this institution for so long illustrates the slow growth of moral social consciousness and the difficulty of seeing remote conclusions of the natural law.

INALIENABLE RIGHTS

The terms *alienable* and *inalienable* rights cause so much confusion as to be practically unusable in ethics. To alienate is to give away or to take away. No right, if it is a genuine right, can be taken away except by the one who has granted it. Positive rights can be taken away by the grantor and given up by the possessor. Natural rights, since they are granted by God through the natural law, cannot be taken away by man's authority and are in this sense inalienable. Can they be given up, waived, or renounced by the possessor? Some of them can, for though granted by nature, they are not strictly necessary in all possible conditions of life. Thus a man may bind himself not to own property or not to marry, but other rights are so indispensable that their exercise is also a duty. These rights may not be arbitrarily taken away nor voluntarily renounced and are in this sense inalienable, but they may be lost as punishment for misuse. Thus parents have the natural right to rear their children but may lose it because of incompetence or cruelty. Even so basic a right as that to life may be lost for serious crime. Some try to explain the loss of rights by saying that the man keeps the right itself while losing the right to its exercise, but this seems a meaningless subtlety. Moral power that *cannot* or *must not* be exercised is not moral power. It is better to say that the right itself is lost but can be restored under changed conditions. The only rights that would be absolutely inalienable in all senses would be such highly abstract formulations as the right to lead a moral life or the right to be treated justly. In much of the literature the term *inalienable right* simply stands for *natural right*.

NATURAL RIGHTS

We need not prove that there are such things as rights, for no one denies it. To deny all rights, one would have to deny all law, and even the most extreme anarchists would admit some form of customary law. All law supposes rights, and all rights suppose law. The concepts are inseparable. There cannot be a right unless all others are bound to respect that right, and that which binds them is law. There cannot be a law unless someone is charged with moral power to exact obedience to the law, that is, with the right to enforce it, and law exists for the purpose of protecting someone's rights. Hence the saying, "No law, no rights," and vice versa.

Unanimity ceases when we ask: Which law is the origin of rights? Since no one denies that there are positive laws, no one denies that there are positive rights. The problem, then, centers on the existence of the natural law. If there is a natural law, there should be natural rights; if not, there can be none. So the main cleavage of thought is as follows:

1. Are there no rights but positive rights?
2. Besides positive rights are there also natural rights?

POSITIVIST VIEW OF RIGHTS

Moral and *legal positivists* are logically compelled to adopt the first position. If there is no natural law, there can be no natural rights, because there would be nothing to oblige people to respect such rights. Some moral positivists use the term *natural rights*, but by it Hobbes* means only that in the state of nature a man had a right to do whatever he was able to do, and Spinoza,† consistently with his pantheistic determinism, cannot distinguish between natural moral law and natural physical law, so that a man's natural rights are on the same plane as that of a rose to bloom or of a cat to purr. Such uses of the word *right* make it but an empty name, as Rousseau‡ correctly observes. Moral positivists must either deny that the commonly accepted natural rights of man are really rights or reduce them somehow to positive rights.

There is also a group of compromisers who will not go so far as to deny a natural moral law but think that civil law should be studied independently of it. They make a complete separation between the juridical order of rights founded on the civil law and the ethical order of morals founded on the natural law. Hence they are not strictly *moral* positivists (no natural morality) nor *legal* positivists (no natural law), but *juridical* positivists (no natural rights). All moral and legal positivists must also be juridical positivists, but not vice versa. Of course, if one defines the word *right* in such a way that it can apply to positive rights only, then there would be merely a dispute on words, but these writers do not admit natural rights under any other name and thus are denying not the word but the thing. Because of these differences and the importance of the matter, it is worth risking some repetition to outline these views briefly. The chief sources suggested by moral, legal, and juridical positivists for all the rights they admit are:

1. The state, by its constitution and statutes
2. A contract, expressed or implied
3. The concept of freedom, universal for all men
4. Custom, manifesting the spirit of the people

1. *The state.* The notion that no one has any rights except those given him by the state has always been widespread in practice, if not in philosophical theory, throughout all ages from the ancient oriental despotisms to their modern counterparts. Tyrants have acted as if their groveling subjects' right to live and breathe were their own graciously granted favor. Even today some otherwise enlightened states declare in their constitution that the citizens have no rights except those expressly granted them by the state. Hobbes* gave this doctrine, that all true rights come from the state, its first clear philosophical expression; in it he is followed by others,

---

*Hobbes, *Leviathan*, ch. 14.

†Spinoza, *Theologico-Political Treatise*, ch. 16; *Political Treatise*, ch. 2.

‡Rousseau, *Social Contract*, bk. I, ch. 3-4.

*Hobbes, *loc. cit.*

such as Spinoza,* whose total system is of quite a different cast. Among American jurists Justice Oliver Wendell Holmes† said that a right is only a prophecy that the state will use its courts and its might to sustain a man's claim.

Criticism of this view may be summed up as follows. The state cannot be the source of its own right to existence, for it would have already to exist before it could confer this right on itself. Either the state has no right to exist, or there is some source of rights prior to the state. Apart from force and fear, the state can bind its citizens to respect the positive rights it confers only by appeal to its own natural right to exist and function as a state. If the state were the source of all rights, it could give itself and withhold from its subjects any right it wished, it could do no wrong, tyranny would be impossible, individuals could have no rights against the state, one state could have no rights against another state, and since a state can rule only its own subjects, there would be an end to all international rights.

2. *Contract.* Hobbes and Rousseau, holding that the state originated by the social contract, trace the origin of rights both to the state and to a contract. But they differ in emphasis, Hobbes stressing the state more than the contract, and Rousseau the contract more than the state.

Critics of this theory say that though many rights originate in contracts, not all rights can result from contracts, and no right can be wholly grounded on contract alone. Before making a contract the contracting parties must first have the right to enter into such a contract, which might come from a previous contract, but the series cannot be infinite. Contracts receive their binding force from something existing prior to all contracts, the moral law, which requires the observance of just pledges and agreements. The right to life and other non-renounceable rights cannot result from a contract freely made, since such a contract would be voidable at will, and such rights cannot be contracted away. One cannot by contract acquire a right to commit a wrong, as another's murder, for the man to be murdered already has his right to life and did not obtain it by contract.

3. *Concept of freedom.* Kant separates legality from morality, the juridical order from the ethical order, saying that right, or legality, has to do with external action and comes from the state; ethics, or morality, has to do with the inner motive of duty and comes from the moral law. Both are derived from the absolute freedom of man, which is twofold: freedom from inner compulsion, the basis of morals, and freedom from outer compulsion, the basis of rights. Kant says:

> There is only one innate right. Freedom (independence from the constraint of another's will), insofar as it is compatible with the freedom of everyone else in accordance with a universal law, is the one and sole original right that belongs to every human being by virtue of his humanity.*

All men have equal shares in the external goods of the world and the right to use as much of them as is consonant with the equal right of every other man. Right pertains only to this external use; the motive from which he acts, whether the moral motive of duty or any other, pertains to the private sphere of ethics. This system of equal shares of free external action is the system of rights.

This view is criticized for the following reasons. Both the internal act and the external act, the inner motive and the outward deed, form one voluntary human act. The legal order is part of the moral order, and hence there can be no complete sepa-

---

*Spinoza, *loc. cit.*
†Holmes, *Collected Legal Papers,* "The Path of the Law," "Natural Law."

*Kant, *The Metaphysics of Morals,* pt. I, The Metaphysical Elements of Justice, Division of the Theory of Justice, B. [LLA ed., p. 43].

ration of legality from morality. Apart from morals the word *right* has no real meaning, for all rights suppose obligation somewhere, and obligation belongs to morality. Not all rights are deducible from the concept of freedom limited only by the equal freedom of all others. A child's right to support from its parents is due to its natural needs rather than to any freedom it cannot yet exercise. If all rights are based on freedom, we should have the right freely to give up any right, even those we are not morally allowed to surrender. To say that we have a *right* to do anything we wish, so long as it hurts no one else, would give us a right to practice private vices, provided we allow others to do likewise. No amount of equally shared freedom among men can create a right to do what there is a moral duty not to do.

4. *Custom.* The historical school of jurisprudence, a reaction against Kant, grew out of the philosophy of Hegel and found its juristic expression in the writings of Friedrich Karl von Savigny. It holds that every people unconsciously develops its own speech, manners, art, and culture, much as an individual develops his mannerisms and personality. Rights are part of this development and are grounded in immemorial customs, which are the outward expression and unconscious product of the spirit of a people. The state is not the origin of rights but can and should assist in their development, since the people show their spirit in their political institutions as well as in every other features of their national life.

Critics grant that some rights do originate in custom, for some laws originate in custom and rights come from law, but deny that this can be true of all rights or be the basic source of any right. The people must already have a right to originate and follow such a custom. With this theory how could one obtain a right to do anything new? There would be no rights until a custom has been sufficiently established; by what right, then, were the first acts performed? Customs, even national customs,

can be evil as well as good. By doing bad acts often enough a people could secure a right to do them. Rights customarily violated could not be vindicated, since it would then become the custom, and therefore a right, to violate them. Man is not so wholly absorbed in his tribe, race, or state that he has no rights but those they are accustomed to give him.

ARGUMENT FOR NATURAL RIGHTS

The foregoing criticism of the various forms of juridical positivism can be taken as a negative argument for natural rights. Having seen something of the historical background of this controversy, we are now ready to see how the natural law theorists view the problem. On the premises they accept, their positive argument is very simple:

There exists a natural law, which imposes obligations on man to achieve the purpose of which he exists as a human person and to conform his conduct to the norm of morality as the only means to this end. But man cannot have such obligations unless he has a right to fulfill them and a consequent right to prevent others from interfering with his fulfillment of them. Therefore there are rights that stem from the natural law, and they by definition are natural rights.

RIGHT AND MIGHT

The separation of the legal and juridical order from the ethical order, that is, the separation of rights from morals, is practically equivalent to identifying right with might, for if rights do not rest on moral obligation, they rest on physical force or the threat of it. Right was defined as moral power and might as physical power, but now it is necessary to examine more thoroughly the relation between these two.

1. *Right and might are not the same.* An interesting discussion of the claims of

right and might occurs in Plato's *Republic*,* where Thrasymachus defends the proposition that right is might, or justice is the interest of the stronger, claiming that all laws and rights are framed by men in power for their own advantage and to keep the rest in subjection. In the *Gorgias*† Callicles maintains the contrary proposition, that justice is the interest of the weaker, who by sheer force of numbers are able to extort concessions from the few strong, and these concessions become the people's rights bulwarked by laws and conventions; such is conventional justice only, for by natural justice the stronger ought to prevail simply because they are stronger. Plato agrees with neither of these views on justice but has Socrates define it as "the having and doing what is a man's own"‡ whether he be strong or weak.

Right and might are two different things because there can be right without might and might without right. By natural right each one is entitled to the means necessary for living the moral life, but each one is not granted the physical force necessary for securing and defending these means. The child depends on its parents, the wife on her husband, the sick and the aged on those who care for them. In fact, no man, however strong he be physically, is wholly independent of others. Since all men are equal in their ultimate destiny and in their common moral obligations, but unequal in physical strength and also in wealth and authority by which they can command the physical strength of others, some safeguard must be provided against the encroachments of physical force. This safeguard is provided in the form of rights, natural rights from the natural law and positive rights from positive law. Therefore, since right and might do not always correspond, they cannot be the same thing.

2. *Some rights, but not all, imply the right to use might*. Though right and might are not the same thing, there is evidently some connection between them, because violated rights can be redressed only by the use of force. What is this connection? Hegel holds that not all might is right, but all right is might or at least implies might. He says:

> Abstract right is a right to coerce, because the wrong which transgresses it is an exercise of force against the existence of my freedom in an external thing. The maintenance of this existent against the exercise of force therefore itself takes the form of an external act and an exercise of force annulling the force originally brought against it.*

Since the first use of force against a free being is a crime, not all might is right; right implies a second use of force, repelling the first, unjustified use of it.

Two objections can be brought against this view: it restricts rights to external physical objects and acts only, and it confuses the essence of a right with a property of some rights.

a. One could limit the word *right* to external matters, but both English usage and the concept of a right as *moral* power counsel otherwise. We speak of a mother's right to her children's love, of a benefactor's right to gratitude, of a man's right to his friends' loyalty. The subject imposes a duty on the term, even though there is no way of physically compelling fulfillment of the duty; violation of the duty produces moral guilt, which is the proper effect of the exercise of moral power. Here there seems to be everything needed to constitute a genuine right.

b. Other rights can be enforced by the use of might. Physical actions can be exerted or restrained, and physical objects can be defended or recovered by the use of physical force. Rights to such matters would be useless unless we were morally allowed to use physical force in protecting and se-

---

*See bk. I, from §336 on.
†From §481 on.
‡Plato, *Republic,* bk. IV, §433.

*Hegel, *Philosophy of Right,* §94.

curing them. Even here the ability to resort to force is not the essence of the right. The right must already be a right before it can be vindicated by might. There is really a double right: the original right, such as the right to life or property, and a secondary right annexed to it, the right to use might in defense of life or property.

Rights that may thus be upheld by recourse to might, force, or coercion are *coercive* rights; they are also *juridical* rights, because they can be sued for in a law court which enforces its verdict by appeal to the executive arm or might of the state. In contrast to rights founded on loyalty, gratitude, friendship, benevolence, and similar virtues, all coercive or juridical rights are founded on *justice*. Their enforcement should normally be entrusted to the civil government, since the maintenance of justice, the adjudication of disputes, and the protection of its citizens' rights is the chief function of the state.

DUTIES

Limitation is a property of rights. Limitation is that point beyond which a right cannot be exercised without violating the right of another. Moral laws make up one organic system much like the physical organism. The functions of one organ are limited by the other organs of the body, each being apportioned its share of nutriment and having its sphere of exercise, but not to the detriment of other organs. No one organ is the whole organism, which is the complexus of all organs working harmoniously. If any organ encroaches on another, it works harm to the whole body. Thus each man has an end to fulfill and is endowed with rights for this purpose, but the whole of creation also has an end to fulfill, and no man may seek his own end in such a way as to frustrate the end of the whole.

Right is limited by duty. I may exercise my right up to the point where my duty

to others supersedes my right. A right ceases to be a right when it injures others' rights. I have a right to build a bonfire on my own property, but not when it endangers the property of my neighbors. Parents have a right to their children's obedience, but not in choosing their state of life.

Duty is *the moral necessity to do or omit something.* Though compulsion may be used to enforce a duty, the duty exists and obliges independently of enforcement. This *moral* necessity laid on a person is duty in the primary sense. In a transferred sense duty also means the thing that must be done or omitted.

Rights and duties, as we have defined them, are correlative and complementary. That they are so follows from the moral inviolability of a right. If I have a right, everyone else has the duty to respect my right; thus the term of a right becomes the subject of a duty. If I have a duty, someone else has a right to the thing I must do or omit; if no other man appears to have such a right, then at least God has it, as in my duty to preserve my life. If I have a duty, I have also the right to fulfill that duty and do all the things necessary for its fulfillment; otherwise it could not be a genuine duty. But if I have a right, I have not necessarily a duty to exercise that right; in fact, no man can exercise all his rights but must choose among them, for some of them are simultaneously incompatible, such as the right to stand and the right to sit.

All duties, like all rights, come from law. Duties are divided in the same way as the corresponding rights and thus are natural or positive, divine or human, ecclesiastical or civil. In addition, there is another classification of importance here: into affirmative and negative duties.

Affirmative duties follow from affirmative laws (commands) and require the performance of an act. *Negative* duties follow from negative laws (prohibitions) and require the omission or avoidance of an act. Care should be taken not to call affirmative laws and duties *positive,* for the word *positive* is already used in another sense, as the opposite of *natural.* Affirmative duties may connote negative duties, as "Honor your parents" connotes "Do not dishonor your parents." The importance of the distinction between affirmative and negative duties is that they impose a different type of obligation. Negative laws and duties require constant fulfillment every moment; one must never be doing the thing forbidden. Affirmative laws and duties impose a lasting obligation, in the sense that one is never exempt from it, but the obligation does not require constant fulfillment every moment: a property owner is *always obliged* to pay taxes by reason of his permanent status of taxpayer; yet he is not obliged to be *always paying* taxes but only when they are due.

CONFLICT OF RIGHTS AND DUTIES

The conflict between rights and duties is a very practical problem, for it sometimes happens that one person has moral power to do a thing and another has moral power to prevent his doing it, or two persons have moral power to do or hold or exact the same individual thing each for himself, or the same person has two incompatible duties to discharge for two different people at the same time, or the same individual has a duty to one person to do a thing and also a duty to another person to refrain from doing it. What is to be done when a right conflicts with a right, a duty with a duty, or a right with a duty?

This question is easy enough to answer in theory. There can be no real conflict of rights and duties, either with one another or among themselves. All rights and duties are derived from law, and all law is a reasonable ordinance that cannot both command and forbid the same thing. Therefore the conflict is only apparent. The stronger right or duty prevails; the weaker simply ceases to be a right or duty at all. In other circumstances it would be an existing right or duty, but in these circumstances it vanishes in the face of a higher claim. The stronger right or duty does not conflict with lesser ones but extinguishes them.

How can we determine which is the stronger right or duty? In practice such determinations can become exceedingly intricate and beyond the competence of the ordinary person. One of the chief functions of positive law, drawn up by professional legislators and applied through the courts of justice, is to settle disputed claims. Both reason and experience prescribe that we shall set up such means for determining just which right or duty prevails, and in most of the matters that come under this jurisdiction the decisions of the courts, unless manifestly unjust, are binding in conscience. But not all matters are subject to the civil law and its courts; often the decision must be made on the basis of natural ethics. We can lay down only a few general norms. Other things being equal, the stronger right or duty can be determined from the following scheme:

The subject
1. *The higher-ranking person:* God before man
2. *The closer relationship:* relatives and friends before strangers

The term
3. *The more common good:* world peace before personal comfort
4. *The wider social order:* the country before the family

The matter
5. *The graver matter:* life before property
6. *The greater urgency:* fighting a fire before reading a book

The title
7. *The higher law:* natural law before positive law
8. *The clearer title:* a certain claim before a doubtful one

What makes these norms hard to apply is that in concrete cases other things are not equal. One right or duty may appear stronger according to one of the headings just listed, and the opposite right or duty according to another heading. The main use of the scheme is to show us what to look for, not to give us automatic rules.

1. A doctor is about to attend divine worship on Sunday when an emergency call comes for an urgent case; God comes before man, but the case cannot be postponed, and the man may die.

2. A young man wants to take a college education but has no funds; the mind comes before the body, but if he does not eat, he cannot study.

3. A son has been disinherited in a civilly valid will but for dubiously just reasons; the natural law prevails over the positive, but the positive title is clear and the natural one doubtful.

4. In time of war a man is torn between duty to his country and to his family; the common good prevails over a private good, but his family is related to him more closely than the bulk of the citizens.

For a solution to these and similar apparent conflicts of rights and duties, no hard-and-fast rules can be drawn up. Each case must be taken in its concrete setting and every circumstance carefully weighed. In these matters there is no substitute for common sense, which is another name for the cardinal virtue of prudence. Most cases are settled by working out some proportion or compromise between the various factors and claims, except that the negative duty of never doing anything inherently evil prevails over everything else. In the foregoing cases:

1. It would be wrong for a doctor to be so engrossed in his profession as to have no time at all for the worship of God, but in this instance God can be served later and the sick man cannot; the doctor should tend to the patient.

2. A man must live before he can live well; the student must first provide for himself the minimum requirements of life, and thereafter he does well to devote himself to the things of the mind rather than to the things of the body.

3. The disinherited son may contest the will, but if the will is upheld in the civil courts, he has no choice but to accept this decision; the parent may have done a private wrong in disinheriting him, but the son would commit a public crime if he attempted to seize the property by force.

4. A country at war can require its citizens to come to its defense, yet defer or exempt those who can least easily be spared by their dependents; this policy balances the claims of private and public good, and brings in the element of urgency.

It may happen that after the most careful investigation two rights or two duties or a right and a duty seem equally valid and equally certain. In this case one may do either, or, if the matter is divisible, do part of both. The bankruptcy laws are an instance of the latter, where no creditor can be satisfied in full, but as equitable a distribution is made as the matter allows.

EXCUSES FROM DUTY

Duty is imposed by law, which by definition is reasonable and for the common good. The purpose is not to crush man with unreasonable burdens out of proportion to the good aimed at. According to the principle of double effect, the physical evils (burdens, losses, restrictions, inconveniences, dangers) sometimes unavoidable in the fulfillment of duty are to be incidental to the accomplishment of good and not disproportionate to it. Hence there are causes that can excuse from duty, because in these cases the duty really invades our right.

No one can do the impossible, and all excuses from duty can be reduced to impossibility of fulfillment taken in a broad and relative sense; we shall call it *hard-*

ship. Some norms can be established by putting together four elements:

1. The kind of hardship, inherent or incidental
2. The amount of hardship, normal or excessive
3. The kind of duty, affirmative or negative
4. The kind of law, natural or positive

1. Only incidental and excessive hardship excuses from a duty. *Incidental* hardship arises from the particular circumstances of the person concerned, such as being sick, disabled, captive, or destitute. If hardship essential to or inherent in the duty itself could excuse, there would be no duties; thus workmen are not excused from their work because it makes them sweat nor soldiers from battle because it endangers their lives. Hardship may run from practical impossibility through extreme, grave, and moderate difficulty to slight inconvenience. To be an excuse it must be *excessive,* out of proportion to the importance of the duty. A duty can be so necessary as not to admit of excuse, even in the face of death.

2. A *negative* duty arising from the *natural* law admits of no excuse whatever. Such a duty concerns matters so evil in themselves or in their situation that nothing could justify them. We are obliged to choose death rather than commit them. There is question here of the worst possible evil, moral evil, to which no other evil can be proportioned. Even here subjective excuses can arise from the modifiers of responsibility, such as ignorance or passion, but we are speaking now of objective morality and fully responsible agents.

3. An *affirmative* duty arising from the *natural* law admits of excuse because of impossibility or excessive hardship. There must, however, be no violation of negative natural duty involved; for instance, the omission of an act of honor toward someone must not give the impression of contempt. Since affirmative duties do not require constant fulfillment every moment, the acts can often be postponed for more favorable circumstances when the hardship will not be present, and then they must be done; if they cannot be postponed, the obligation ceases entirely.

4. A duty arising from *human positive* law, whether *affirmative* or *negative,* admits of excuse because of impossibility or excessive hardship. Here also no violation of negative natural duty must be involved. Merely human duties, even the negative ones, concern matter that is morally indifferent in itself, and the human laws that impose them are meant to be a help rather than a hindrance to human living.

SUMMARY

We have seen *right* as opposed to *wrong;* now we take up *right* as correlative to *duty.* In the latter sense *right* is moral power, appealing to another's will through his intellect, as opposed to *might,* which is physical power or force. Right is defined as moral power to do, omit, hold, or exact something. Things to which we have a right are often called our *rights.*

A right has four components: *subject,* the one possessing the right; *term,* the one bound to respect the right; *matter,* that to which one has a right; and *title,* the reason why this person has a right to this thing. The subject and term must always be persons; hence animals have no rights. The matter can never be a person; even slavery, one of the world's most flagrant violations of human rights, supposed a right only to the slave's services, not to his person.

All rights come from law, *natural* rights from natural law, *positive* rights from positive law. All admit positive rights, but are there natural rights? Moral and legal positivists deny the natural law; they can have no natural rights. Juridical positivists deny natural rights, though they may admit a natural law. Both these groups derive all rights from one or several of the following sources:

1. *The state.* If so, the state itself has no right to exist, has no basis for the positive rights it grants, can withhold from its subjects any right it wishes, and can have no rights against another state.

2. *Contract.* If so, the first contract was made without any right to do so, contracts have no binding power but force, nonrenounceable rights are subjected to contract, and one can by contract obtain a right to anything, however evil.

3. *Equal freedom for all.* If so, rights are limited to external acts, legality is separated from morality which alone gives it meaning, all rights can be freely surrendered, and we can have a right to immoral acts provided they hurt no one else.

4. *Custom.* If so, mere repetition of acts begets a right to them, there were no rights until the custom was established, evil customs can create rights, and man becomes the victim of the customs his race unconsciously develops.

Natural rights are deduced from the natural law. The natural law imposes obligations on man, who must therefore have moral power to fulfill them and prevent others from interfering with this fulfillment; such rights coming from the natural law are natural rights.

Right and *might* are different because they can exist separately. All men have equal moral obligations but differ greatly in physical strength. Rights are our moral safeguard against the encroachment of superior might. Rights concerning external matters due in justice imply the right to use might in their defense or recovery. This right of coercion is not the essence of any right, but a property of some rights.

Right is limited by *duty*, which is the moral necessity to do or omit something. Every right supposes a duty, and vice versa. *Negative* duties require constant fulfillment, *affirmative* do not.

There can be no real conflict of rights and duties; the stronger extinguishes the weaker. In practice it can be very difficult to determine which is the stronger right. The subject, term, matter, and title must be considered together with the factor of urgency.

Impossibility and excessive hardship are excuses from duty. Hardship inherent in the duty never excuses from it. Disproportionate hardship, depending on the importance of the matter, excuses from *affirmative* duty under *natural* law, and from both *affirmative* and *negative* duty under *human positive* law. *Negative* duty under *natural* law admits of no excuse whatever.

QUESTIONS FOR DISCUSSION

1 Which concept is primary, law or right? Do laws exist for the sake of guaranteeing rights, or do rights exist for the purpose of fulfilling law? Or are the two concepts coordinate and reciprocal?

2 It has been said that duty is primary to right. Is this so? Do we have rights in order to be able to fulfill our duty, or are there duties only because there is a previous right in someone?

3 Is it possible to have rights in existentialist and situation ethics? What can be the meaning of right where there is no essence, nature, principle, or law? Can it be: I cannot be authentic to myself

unless I grant others the right to their authenticity? Is this meaningful?

4 Are rights founded on human nature or on the human person? Is personal dignity the ultimate reason why we have rights? In speaking of human nature in this context, is the stress more on "human" than on "nature"? Is "human rights" a better expression than "natural rights"?

5 Go through the Bill of Rights, the first ten Amendments to the United States Constitution, and separate the natural from the civil rights. You may also find some civil rights with a natural basis.

READINGS

Read Plato's *Republic*, bk. I, §336, to bk. II, §368, on the relative merits of justice and injustice, right and might. Read Aristotle's defense of natural slavery in his *Politics*, bk. I, ch. 4-7, to see how disappointing a great man can sometimes be. One might hope for a correction in St. Thomas' *Commentary*, but he merely expounds Aristotle. Cicero's *De Officiis* (On Duties) is rather a treatise on morals in general and runs through man's chief duties as connected with the cardinal virtues and one's state in life.

The little that St. Thomas has to say on rights is found in the *Summa Theologica*, II-II, q. 57. A discussion of the term *jus* (right) as related to *lex* (law) in the usage of Roman law is found in Suarez, *De Legibus* (On Laws), bk. I, ch. 2, translated in J. B. Scott, *Classics of International Law: Suarez.*

Immanuel Kant, *The Metaphysics of Morals,* is published in two small volumes by The Library of Liberal Arts, part I as *The Metaphysical Elements of Justice,* and part II as *The Metaphysical Principles of Virtue.* The whole is a different work from Kant's *Fundamental Principles of the Metaphysic of Morals.*

W. D. Ross, *The Right and the Good,* pp. 48-56, has some objections against correlativity of rights and duties, partly because of his admitting that we have duties to animals, though animals have no rights.

There have been numerous attempts to codify fundamental human rights. That of UNESCO, published in its own symposium entitled *Human Rights,* is worth considering and that suggested by Jacques Maritain in *The Rights of Man and Natural Law.* Le Buffe and Hayes, *The American Philosophy of Law,* ch. 5, lists various codifications; it also contains an appendix by John C. Ford, criticizing Justice Holmes' legal philosophy. Holmes' views are found in his *Collected Legal Papers,* especially "The Path of the Law" and "Natural Law," and in the *Holmes Pollock Letters.*

David Ritchie's *Natural Rights* and Leo Strauss' *Natural Rights and History* are well-known studies. See also Heinrich Rommen's *Natural Law,* ch. 12; and Arthur Harding's *Natural Law and Natural Rights.*

Austin Fagothey, *Right and Reason—an Anthology* contains some selections indirectly involving rights, those from St. Thomas, Hobbes, Locke, Rousseau, Kant, Thoreau, Murray, King, and Stevick.

CHAPTER 19

LIFE

PROBLEM

Since ethics is not only a normative but also a practical science, it cannot be satisfied to give only the general norms of morally good conduct but must try to apply these norms to the chief types of human conduct. Though human acts taken individually are indefinitely variable so that no two are ever exactly alike, they can be classified under certain headings, and the general norms can be made more specific so as to bring out more clearly the goodness or badness of each class of acts.

Older writers, such as St. Thomas, built their whole treatment of applied ethics around the classification of the virtues and opposed vices. Some modern writers prefer to make a specific investigation of the rights conferred and the duties imposed by the moral law. The first method, unless used skillfully, tends to become a sterile process of naming and cataloging. The second method gives the impression that ethics is restricted to the minimum of goodness imposed by law. Our method will consist of mapping out certain *areas of concern* in man's moral life, involving rights and duties, habits and virtues, aspirations and ideals, that pertain to each of these areas.

First in dignity come man's relations to God. Man's whole moral life is the fulfillment of his duty and the expression of his love toward God. On this problem the findings of philosophical ethics appear so thin, compared with the rich offerings of religion and theology, that we will hand over this whole topic to these studies.

Among man's rights the right to life is fundamental, for there can be no further rights or duties unless there is someone there to have them. That this is a natural right is evident. The only way he can fulfill his function as a man, reach the goal of his existence, and achieve his highest good, is by performing morally good acts. To perform such acts he must live. The very nature of man, therefore, demands that he have the right to life.

Is this right a nonrenounceable one, so that not only may no one lawfully take it away from him but also even the person himself may not give it up? Is it a right that is also a duty? Is it always wrong to deprive another of his life, even incurable sufferers, even unborn babies? What about self-defense, when a man can save his own life only at the expense of another's? Here we deal only with deliberate destruction of human life, saving marginal questions for the next chapter. Our questions are:

1. May one kill oneself?
2. May one kill another man?
3. May one kill the incurable?
4. May one kill the unborn?
5. May one kill in self-defense?

SUICIDE

Suicide is here taken in the strict sense as *the direct killing of oneself on one's own authority.*

Direct killing is an act of killing that is

directly voluntary; that is, death is intended either as an end or as a means to an end. Either the action is capable of only one effect and that effect is death, or the action is capable of several effects, including death, and among these death is the effect intended, either for its own sake or as a means to something else.

Indirect killing is an act of killing that is indirectly voluntary; death is not intended, either as an end or as a means to an end, but is only permitted as an unavoidable consequence. The action is capable of at least two effects, one of which is death, and the agent intends, not death, but the other effect. To avoid misunderstanding it is better not to speak of the indirect killing of oneself as killing at all, but as the deliberate exposure of one's life to serious danger. Such exposure is not what is meant by suicide.

The killing is not suicide unless it is done *on one's own authority.* Two others might be thought of as having authority in the matter: God and the state. God, having a supreme dominion over human life, could order a man to kill himself, but to know God's will in such a case, a special revelation would be needed, for which there is no provision in philosophical ethics. The state, supposing that it has the right of capital punishment, might appoint a man condemned to death to be his own executioner. Whatever be the morality of such an uncommon and questionable practice, it is not suicide according to the accepted definition.

Suicide can be committed positively, by the performance of some death-dealing act against oneself; or negatively, by omitting to use the ordinary means of preserving one's life. It is suicide to starve oneself to death, to refuse to step out of the way of an oncoming train, to neglect to use the ordinary remedies against an otherwise fatal disease.

Among the arguments proposed in favor of the moral permissibility of suicide are the following:

1. It is understood that no one should commit suicide for whom life holds out some hope or promise, and that people suffering from temporary despondency should be prevented from harming themselves, but there are always some for whom life has become an intolerable and irremediable burden. They are useless to society and to themselves. It is better for all concerned that they retire from the scene of life through the ever open door.

2. It is an act of supreme personal self-determination to summon death when life's value has been spent. Man is expected to manage his life intelligently and not to be merely passive in the face of inexorable nature. When reason shows that life has no more to offer, it is folly to drag out life to its last bitter breath. Man preserves his dignity and self-mastery by ending his life at the moment when all its worth and meaning for him are exhausted.

3. It is allowed to choose a lesser evil to avoid a greater. Since there are worse evils than death, why cannot death be chosen as the lesser evil? There is nothing unnatural about it. If it is not wrong to interfere with nature to prolong life, as medical science does, why should it be wrong to interfere with nature to shorten life? In both cases it is done for the benefit of the person concerned and by his own consenting will.

4. Even admitting that God has given us our life, yet it is truly a gift. A gift belongs to the receiver, who may now do whatever he wills with it. No gift is expected to be retained indefinitely at the expense and to the harm of the receiver. When its possession becomes more injurious than its surrender, it should be in accordance with the will of a good God and a wise use of his gift to relinquish it.

5. To suppose that suicide in any way defrauds God of his supreme right is to have a very naive idea of God. No crea-

ture could possibly defraud God of anything. In giving us the gift of life, God knew how we would use it and expected us to use our intelligence and freedom in managing it. He allows us to destroy animals and plants, other life, for our purposes. Why should our own life be withdrawn from our control?

6. In the case of self-defense we have the right to destroy other human lives for our own safety. The state claims the same right in war and capital punishment. It seems, then, that God can and sometimes does give us direct ownership over human life. Why must it be only over others' lives? The reasons for suicide are often stronger than for self-defense, either personal or national. Why not kill ourselves when we have become our own greatest enemy?

These rather persuasive arguments are countered by opposing arguments:

1. Suicide is often regarded as an act of cowardice and a refusal to face life like a man. It is the easy way out for one who thrusts the burdens he cannot bear onto the shoulders of his dependents. But not all are in this case; rather, they themselves are a burden on others. Yet they must not forget the worth of their own person. Who can be called useless? Suffering has no earthly value and might be called the worst of earthly disvalues, but its moral and spiritual value can be tremendous. Courage and patience cannot be discounted in any moral appraisal of human life.

2. It is a natural prompting of well-ordered self-love to keep one's person in being against all destructive forces. There are times when one must face death without flinching, but there is something inordinate in willfully acting as that destructive force oneself. Everything naturally seeks its own being and tends to keep itself in being as long as possible. Our intelligence is meant to promote and not to counteract that natural urge.

3. The lesser of two physical evils may be chosen when there is no moral evil involved, but moral evil may never be chosen to avoid a physical evil. Medical science is an intelligent use and development of the remedies nature provides to preserve life. To use them to destroy life is not wise management but a wrecking of what has been entrusted to our care. Man would be free to wreck himself if he were responsible only to himself, but this is not so if there is a God to whom he is ultimately responsible.

4. Life is a gift from God, but some gifts are given outright and others have strings attached. All God's gifts are restricted, not because of any lack in his generosity, but because he has to make us responsible for their use when he entrusts them to our free will. Free will itself is perhaps his greatest gift, but we are not allowed, though we are able, to misuse it. Life has been given, and its allotted span goes with the gift. It is not ours to decide when we have had enough of it and to tell God that we are quitting his service.

5. Man can never actually defraud God, but he is not allowed even to *try* or to be willing to do what would defraud God were he not infinitely beyond all possible harm. God allows us to destroy animals and plants because they are not persons and are provided for our use and consumption. Human life is not on the same level as other life; personality makes the difference.

6. In self-defense the defender kills the attacker not on his own authority but on God's authority implicit in the defender's own natural right to life. The defender has no ownership over the attacker's life but only repels force by force, a situation the attacker brought on himself by his crime. The state also acts on authority given to it by God as a natural society, authority not to be used in any way the state pleases but only in defense against the nation's internal and external destroyers. The suicide is both attacker and attacked, and there is no defense. Crime and punishment are here

simultaneous and extreme. He is his own executioner at the moment of committing his own murder.

It can be readily seen that from a non-theistic viewpoint there is no argument against suicide. One who acknowledges no higher being than himself assumes supreme mastership over his life and can do with it as he pleases. The fact that a theistic philosophy sees life as a gift from God does not of itself make suicide wrong, for an outright gift may be used or abandoned in any way the recipient wishes. The case against suicide, then, requires proof that God's gift of life to us is not an outright but a restricted gift, that he has not given us full ownership and control over our person with the right to consume and destroy it at our discretion, but he has given us only the use of ourselves, the right of stewardship and management, for which he will demand an account. Since philosophy cannot ask God what he willed to do, its only recourse is to show that God not only did not but *could not* give man full ownership over his person.

The reason that God must reserve to himself full mastership over human life is the peculiar nature of a rational and free being, such as man is. Man can attain the end for which he has been created only by freely choosing to do morally good acts. These acts take time, and the length of each man's life is the opportunity allotted to him for doing them. It is for God and not for man to say when man has done enough well enough to deserve the end. The suicide equivalently tells God that he will have to take the deeds performed and virtues developed so far, and that he will simply get no more. The creature thus tries to dictate what God will have to be satisfied with, in contradiction to what God in creating him has a right to demand from him. God cannot give such authority to a creature without making the creature supreme over him. The suicide, by making further works of his own impossible, in-

vades God's exclusive right, is a rebel against his creator, and commits moral wrong.

MURDER

In ethics we find the civil law's distinction between murder and manslaughter of little help. Murder supposes malice aforethought and thus full voluntariness, but the civil law can judge only by external criteria. Morality, which resides chiefly in the inner act of the will preceded by knowledge, does not always correspond with the amount and kind of evidence presentable in court. So long as the act of killing another man is both directly voluntary and unjust, we shall call it *murder,* following the usage of common language rather than the technical terms of the civil law.

Murder is defined as *the direct killing of an innocent person.* It is *direct* killing, directly voluntary, so that death is intended as end or as means. Indirect killing, or the exposure of life to serious danger, is discussed later; it does not come under the heading of murder.

An *innocent* person is one who has not forfeited his right to life. Murder is *unjust* killing, done without legitimate authority. This excludes killing another on the authority of God or the state, as mentioned before under suicide. The soldier killing the enemy in war and the executioner putting criminals to death are acting on the state's authority. The state, however, can commit murder by acting outside the scope of its legitimate authority. Killing in self-defense is not murder because the defender acts by authority of his natural right to life, as will be discussed later. The word *innocent* must be understood as objectively innocent, for it is not murder to kill a maniac in self-defense.

That murder is morally wrong hardly needs a separate proof if the argument against suicide is already admitted, for if a man is not allowed to take even his own life, much less would he be allowed to take the life of another. Murder is morally wrong because it violates the right of God, who has exclusive full ownership over human life, the right of use ownership that each man has over his own life, and the right of the state to administer justice and preserve public order.

Murder can be treated briefly because no one in his right mind, not even a philosopher, has ventured to defend it. It has always been recognized as one of the worst of crimes and as the most glaring example of a morally evil act. But some are not convinced of the injustice contained in certain types of direct killing, and these must be examined further.

MERCY KILLING

Mercy killing, or *euthanasia,* is the giving of an easy, painless death to one suffering from an incurable or agonizing ailment. Its advocates argue that the person will die anyway, that the purpose is not to invade the person's right to his life but only to substitute a painless for a painful death, that the shortening of the person's life merely deprives him of a bit of existence that is not only useless but unbearable, that for all the good he can do to himself or others his life has reached its term anyway. Some would leave the decision to a qualified physician; most would require the subject's consent.

Although one can sympathize with the sentiments of pity and mercy inspiring this proposal, moral judgment on it falls into the two categories of action just described. If administered by oneself, euthanasia is suicide. If administered by another without the victim's consent, it is murder. If administered by another with the victim's consent or cooperation, it is suicide and murder combined. Nontheistic ethics has no solid argument against it, unless it were done without the victim's consent. Theistic ethics has to condemn it, and say that, even

if it should be made permissible by civil law, for which there is strong propaganda in some quarters, it still remains an immoral act.

Until recently, *euthanasia* had only this meaning. It is still the only meaning appropriate to the term *mercy killing,* where *killing* has an active sense. However, *euthanasia* is now being used in an extended sense, and a distinction is being made between *active* euthanasia, which is killing the person, and *passive* euthanasia, which is letting the person die. Passive euthanasia is an indirectly voluntary act, and among other risks to life will be considered on pp. 228 and 229.

ABORTION

Abortion is a hotly controverted moral issue of our day. Both the proabortion and the antiabortion forces seem to engage in immoral and dishonest tactics to carry their point. We shall strive for a dispassionate and philosophical discussion of the topic. We must distinguish carefully between the morality of abortion itself and the morality of its legalization, which we will remark on later.

MORALITY OF ABORTION

Abortion is the expulsion of a fetus from the womb before it is viable, that is, before it can live outside the mother. It is not the premature delivery of a viable fetus. To hasten birth is not wrong if the child can be kept alive, but it presents such a serious risk that grave reasons are required to make it permissible. It can be justified by the principle of double effect, the proportionate reasons being the danger to the health of the mother, child, or both, if the gestation be allowed to reach its natural term.

A spontaneous *miscarriage* is nobody's fault. Our discussion is about *induced* abortion, which is voluntarily brought about.

If the death of the child is intended as end or as means, it is a *direct killing,* and no mere exposure of the child to danger, for by this act it is taken from the only place where it can live and is put in a place where it cannot live; there is no more efficient way of killing a person. No one can seriously say that the child dies from natural causes after it has been born; it has not been allowed to be born properly. All killing consists in interfering with nature in such a way that a person dies of it.

The principle of double effect is of no value in cases of direct abortion. The act itself is directly destructive of the fetus, and the bad effect, death to the fetus, is no merely permitted side effect but is the means used for the accomplishment of whatever good effect may accrue to the mother. Since the first two conditions of the double-effect principle are not verified, it makes no difference whether there is a good intention and a sufficient proportion. Thus it is futile to attempt any moral justification for direct abortion on the basis of the double-effect principle. Any justification, if possible, would have to be based on other principles.

It is a different situation if the death of an unborn child is only indirect, so that it is merely permitted and not willed as a means or an end. This situation of *indirect abortion* arises when the mother has some serious illness (pregnancy itself is not an illness but a natural condition), and the only workable treatment, whether medical or surgical, will have two effects: the cure of the mother's disease and the death of the child. This is the type of case to which the principle of double effect readily applies. The child is not directly attacked, and its death, even if certain to follow, is an incidental and unavoidable by-product in the performance of a legitimate act. The mother herself needs the treatment no matter what effect it may have on the child, and the death of the child is not the means by which she is

cured. She has a right to take such treatment and is morally allowed to do so. The doctor has the responsibility of deciding whether the mother's condition is truly pathological and whether the treatment contemplated is the only effective remedy.

To sum up the distinctions necessary for an understanding of the arguments: Abortion can be *spontaneous,* a miscarriage that is no one's fault, or *induced,* voluntarily brought about. Induced abortion can be *indirect,* the foreseen but unwanted consequence of doing something else, or *direct,* the expulsion of the fetus intended as end or means. Direct abortion is called *therapeutic* if the purpose is the saving of the mother's life or health, or *criminal* if the purpose is anything else not accepted by the laws. The first two distinctions are important for the moralist as dividing the involuntary from the voluntary and the indirectly voluntary from the directly voluntary. The last distinction from the civil law is of little value to the moralist.

Not all the following arguments favoring abortion look on it in the same light, since some favor abortion on demand and others would allow it only under stringent conditions.

1. To talk about abortion as being murder is nonsense, because the human fetus is not a human being. Either it is part of the mother, to be treated as any other appendage, or it is a separate living thing within the mother but not yet arrived at human status. In the first case it may be removed from the mother's body as an undesirable excrescence. In the second case it may be put out of the way for a good reason just as we kill animals and other forms of subhuman life.

2. Whether the fetus is human or not is a question no one can settle, since no experimental evidence is possible on the moment when it receives a human soul. Many moderns say the moment of conception, but an honorable ancient and medieval theory said several weeks later. Since

certainty is not possible on this question, we must have recourse to probabilities. We can therefore act on the probability that the fetus is not human and for good reason terminate the pregnancy.

3. Even if the fetus, because of biological continuity and chromosomal inheritance, be regarded not merely as a potential but as an actual human being, it has not yet become a human person. Only a person has rights, including the right to life. Since the fetus does not yet possess the right to life, its life may be terminated for a good reason without any breach of good morals.

4. Even if the fetus be granted a right to life, in any collision of rights the fetus' right yields to that of the mother. On all possible counts the mother's right takes preference. She is an adult person, exercising her intelligence and freely controlling her life, with already assumed responsibilities toward her family and others. For the fetus all this is future. It barely lives, is not conscious, and is wholly dependent. The mother can live without it, but it cannot live without the mother.

5. In some cases the child can be considered an unjust aggressor against the physical or mental health of the mother. The danger to the mother's physical health in certain pregnancies is the reason that most states allow therapeutic abortion. But mental health is every bit as important as physical health. To make the rest of the mother's life an intolerable torture of psychic derangement is too much of a price to ask. The mother is morally allowed an adequate defense against such a prospect, and the only defense is the elimination of the cause.

6. At least in those cases, now fortunately rare, in which both mother and child will certainly die unless the child is aborted, only a benighted legalism could oblige the obstetrician to let both die rather than to save one. No fine distinctions between direct and indirect actions, principal and incidental effects, wanted and permitted consequences, and similar rules should be adored as fetishes while a life is at stake. Necessity knows no law.

7. No unwanted child should exist. A child demands love and cannot live a normal life without it. The unwanted child is an unloved child. Some parents can learn to love it later, but even the child can detect the strained feeling behind the show of love. In many instances there is not even the show of love, and the child grows up rejected and resentful, to take out his spite later on against his own society or all humanity. Such misfits should not be brought into the world.

8. Why should a woman be obliged to pay for an indiscretion with many years of sacrifice in bringing up an unwanted child, especially when the father can disappear without a trace? Why should a married woman be stigmatized and her life ruined, when her husband could do the same thing she has done without detection? The prejudice against abortion has been made by men and should be removed by women.

9. The population must be controlled. So urgent is this need that some individual rights will probably have to be submerged for the greater good, the very survival of the human race. Contraception and sterilization would be better methods than abortion, but human beings are too unpredictable and uncontrollable to eliminate the need for abortion entirely. Rather than forbid abortions we should promote them, and should be gratified that they are being done voluntarily, thus putting off the time when we may have to make them compulsory. We have come to the point of global ethics, in which lesser issues are transcended.

Opponents of abortion find these arguments unconvincing, especially as not providing for the interests of the child. They answer:

1. All biological evidence confirms the

fact that the human fetus is nothing else but human. The fertilized ovum has the human chromosome pattern containing all the inheritable factors, and it can never grow into anything but a human being. Also, biologists are unanimous in testifying that fetal life is distinct from the mother's life, even though the two are connected during the period of gestation. Therefore any analogy with the surgical removal of tumors or with the killing of animals is inapplicable to the case of abortion.

2. Aristotle* thought that the embryo does not become human until some time after conception, and this may be why he saw no wrong in early abortion. St. Thomas† accepted Aristotle's opinion as a probable physical theory but drew no such ethical conclusion. We do not know and probably never will know the exact moment when the human soul comes to the body to make it a human being, and thus for all practical purposes we must consider it human from the moment of conception. We cannot use probabilism here, for there is no doubt about law or obligation, only about a matter of fact. Just as we may not bury a man if he is only probably dead, so we may not kill a fetus if it is only probably nonhuman. In such matters the morally safer course must be followed, which is to treat the embryo as a living human being.

3. If we could prove that the fetus, even if human in some sense, is not yet a person, it would have no right to life and could be killed like an animal. But what criterion will we take for personality? If we take the actual use of intelligence and freedom, we could kill children for some years after birth. Whether the child is inside or outside the mother is a physical and local difference that can hardly constitute the essence of personality. The only way to deal with this matter is to consider the human embryo or fetus as a human person with all the rights, including the right to life, that go with personality. In this consideration the child is not a potential person but an actual person, though full use of his personality will have to wait on his gradual attainment of maturity.

4. All human beings are equal in their right to life, and age gives no priority. If there is question only of indirectly permitting the death of one or the other, that one should be chosen who has the better chance of survival. But a collision of rights cannot be settled by a direct killing of an innocent person who has done nothing to lose his right to life. In this case each one's right yields to each one's duty, and neither may be killed. The mother may not kill any of her born children to be free of her various responsibilities; why the unborn?

5. It seems absurd to consider an unborn child as an aggressor against its parents, who by their own voluntary act caused its presence in the mother's womb. Aggression does not consist in merely being present but in *doing* something; there must be an actual attack. If the pregnancy is not developing normally, this is one of those accidents that are no one's fault, surely no more the child's than the parents'. The mental health angle is different. Here the mother is the one who needs therapy, and the killing of the child is no moral solution, any more than the remedy for paranoia is the slaughter of all the imagined persecutors.

6. No moralist wants doctors to be remiss in their professional duty of saving human life. They must use all legitimate means, but they must not use means that are morally evil. Doctors have no more right than anyone else to put innocent persons to death. The fact that the unborn child cannot protect itself does not mean

---

*Aristotle, *On the Generation of Animals*, bk. II, ch. 3, 736a 24-737a 17. See also *Politics*, bk. VII, ch. 16, 1335b 24.

†St. Thomas, *Summa Theologica*, I, q. 118, a. 2, reply to obj. 2; *Summa Contra Gentiles*, bk. II, ch. 89.

that its right can be invaded at anyone's discretion. Protection of the child's right to life is not legalism but the correct use of law. That necessity knows no law may be a popular proverb, but it has little standing as a moral guide. Some kind of necessity could be thought up for anything.

7. All recognize the importance of love in the child's life. But shall we say that if the child is not loved, the thing to do is to kill it? Let us put the blame for the unwanted child on the right parties, on those who conceived it. When they did what they did, they took the chance of conception and are responsible for the result. Whether or not they can learn to feel emotional love toward it, they have the obligation of caring for it and showing it as much love as possible. Even unloved children would rather live than be put to death. Who has the right to make this decision for them before they are born?

8. Indiscretion is a euphemism to cover up a moral fault committed, except in the case of rape, voluntarily on both sides. That women are responsible for what they do is not a masculine invention any more than the biological structure that has the female bear the child. That a man can be coward enough to abandon a woman he has mistreated is the man's moral crime. Abortion is a woman's more difficult way of seeking equality in iniquity. A second wrong is not the way of righting the first one.

9. We are all conscious of the population problem and know that something must be done about it. Whatever solution we arrive at, if there is one, will have to accord with morality. Widespread abortion is not the answer. Compulsory abortion would be so flagrant a violation of human rights that any people would have the right to resist it violently. We do need global ethics, but if it consists of global immorality, there is no ethics left.

The conclusion that follows from this debate is that there is no moral justifica-tion for direct abortion, even of the thera-peutic variety. Man has no right to engage in a direct killing of the innocent, and if anyone is innocent, it is the unborn child. The only line of investigation open to those who still wish to make a moral case for abortion is to establish somehow that the fetus is not a human person and thus has no right to life, or to demonstrate that the fetus is actually an unwitting aggressor against the mother and thus forfeits its right to life. So far this has not been done successfully, but there is no reason why scholars should not work at it.

LEGALIZATION OF ABORTION

A further question arises on the control of abortion by the civil law. It is one thing to hold an action immoral and another thing to forbid and punish it by civil legis-lation. It is not the business of the state to regulate the whole private life of its citi-zens, and many immoral practices must be tolerated by the civil law as being outside its scope.* Can we say that abortion be-longs wholly to the moral sphere and that civil law should not attempt to deal with it?

Most such cases deal with victimless crimes and consenting adults, such as pros-titution, homosexuality, and such matters. Though many proabortionists try to reduce abortion to this category, it will not fit. Abortion invades the child's right to life, and the protection of its people's rights is the chief business of the state. No state can overlook murder as not its business; abor-tion, whether called murder or not, in-volves the same right to life. Even when the state does not define the unborn as a citizen, the question remains whether the state can get rid of an obligation merely by defining it away. Abortion concerns not only the consenting adults, mother, doctor,

---

*See St. Thomas, *Summa Theologica*, I-II, q. 96, a. 2.

and father (who is even occasionally consulted), but also the nonconsenting nonadult, the child, whose stake in the matter is crucial but whose interest is often wholly overlooked. Is not the state obliged to come to the defense of the otherwise defenseless victim? This is a strong argument for severe, even rigorous, abortion laws.

On the other side there is the nature of the political state itself and what can be accomplished by its laws. A state, especially the pluralistic state of today, must operate within a framework of popular consensus. The argument for the immorality of abortion, the theory of rights on which it rests, and the philosophy of the person underlying the ethics of rights are not admitted by a large part of the population. There is popular consensus on the wrongness of murder, theft, and similar crimes; the defense is never that the act was not wrong but that the accused did not do it. Abortions, however, are readily admitted, and the defense is that it is not a wrong act but one within the rights of the mother. Does one group of citizens, whether majority or minority does not matter so long as the group is considerable, have the right to impose its opinions and the philosophical backing for those opinions on another group that disagrees? A democratic and pluralistic state will say no.

Hence there are many who think that there should be no laws on abortion. Some do not want abortion to be legalized, since that may be interpreted as approving of it, but rather decriminalized. Without approval, the state simply does not punish such acts and turns them over to the individual consciences of its citizens. Would not the state, then, fail in its duty to protect the rights of the innocent? Every antiabortionist will say yes. But such failure is inherent in the limited function and power of the state. The state cannot force all its citizens to adopt the same philosophy of rights, the same respect for human rights, and the same judgment on the personality of the human fetus. To attempt it would involve a grave violation of the freedom of its citizens. On the other hand, no doctor should be obliged to perform an abortion, no nurse to assist at one, and no hospital board to allow one to be done with the hospital facilities. These persons also should not be pressured to act against their conscience.

As can be seen from balancing both sides of this debate, there is a conflict between two very basic moral principles: that of the right to life and that of the right to freedom. Is the right to life so great that we can force our fellow citizens to accept our view of it against their conviction, or is the freedom of the citizen to think and act according to his convictions strong enough that to defend it 'we are allowed to entrust unborn children to the tender mercy of their mothers? Many think that the best solution would be to spend less effort on legislation and more effort on moral persuasion of the mothers.

SELF-DEFENSE

Man's right to life implies a right to the means necessary to preserve his life. The right to life is a coercive or juridical right, one that may be protected by the use of physical force. It is often impossible, when one's life is attacked, to appeal to the civil government, the normal custodian of our rights. After the attack is over, punishment of the offender belongs to the civil government alone, because the factor of urgency is not present, but at the moment of the attack the victim must often use *self*-defense or there will be no defense. On what principles is self-defense morally justified, and how far may one go in defending one's own right to life?

The act of violating or attempting to violate another's right is *aggression*. As we use the term, it always means an *unjust* attack. Mere intention to attack without any external attempt is not aggression, but there may be aggression without deliberate intention, as in an assault by a maniac. The distinction between an intentional and an unintentional aggressor describes the guilt or innocence of the person attacking, but we are interested here in what the man who is attacked may do. He needs to repel the threat to his life, whether the assailant means it or not.

CONDITIONS OF A BLAMELESS SELF-DEFENSE

Man has a right of self-defense, but only under certain conditions. There are four of them, and they stem from the very notion of defense:

1. *The motive must be self-defense alone.* If self-defense is only a mask for hatred or revenge, the act becomes evil because of evil intent.

2. *Force may be used only at the time of the attack.* The danger to one's life must be actual, not merely prospective. The mere fact that a man sends me a threatening letter does not allow me to go out and kill him, for many threats are never followed up. There would be an end to public order if anyone could use force to repel merely imagined attacks.

3. *Force may be used only when there is no other way of repelling the attack.* Recourse must be made to the police and public authority when possible. One need not run away from every fight but should try not to provoke one. Persuasion or other nonforceful methods should be used if there is any reasonable hope of success.

4. *No more injury may be inflicted than is necessary to avert actual danger.* If I can save my life by injury less than death, I must not proceed further. If the assailant is knocked unconscious, there is no need to kill him. More harm than necessary may not be inflicted for the sole purpose of defense.

The second of these conditions has the most difficult application. In concrete cases it is often hard to determine just when preparation for attack turns into actual aggression. Mere purchase of a gun by my enemy with declaration that he intends to shoot me is not aggression, but I do not have to wait until he has actually shot at me, for then no further defense may be possible. Defense may begin as soon as the aggressor lifts his gun or even approaches the oncoming fray, depending on the circumstances. Here the common estimate of men must be taken into consideration. In a matter so crucial, when the action to be efficient must be swift, it is impossible to draw fine lines and make delicate discriminations, and it is better to favor the defender of life than the attacker. Individual conscience will decide subjective guilt or innocence in concrete cases; we are trying to discover objective principles for any act of self-defense.

MORALITY OF SELF-DEFENSE

Self-defense seems to be merely an application of the principle of double effect, and so St. Thomas considers it. He says:

Nothing hinders one act from having two effects, only one of which is intended, while the other is beside the intention. Now moral acts take their species according to what is intended, and not according to what is beside the intention, since this is accidental. . . . Accordingly the act of self-defense may have two effects, one is the saving of one's own life, the other is the slaying of the aggressor. Therefore this act, since one's intention is to save one's own life, is not unlawful, seeing that it is natural to everything to keep itself in *being*, as far as possible. And yet, though proceeding from a good intention, an act may be rendered unlawful, if it be out of proportion to the end. Wherefore if a man, in self-defense, uses more than necessary violence, it will be unlawful: whereas if he repel force with moderation his defense will be lawful, because according to the jurists, *it is lawful to repel force by force, provided one does not exceed the limits of a blameless defense.* . . . It is not lawful for a man to intend killing a man in self-defense, except for such as have public authority, who while intending to kill a man in self-defense, refer this to the public good, as in the case of a soldier fighting against the foe, and in the minister of the judge struggling with robbers, although even these sin if they be moved by private animosity.*

It should be easy to recognize in this passage the source from which the principle of double effect was derived, by broadening it to suit other questions besides that of self-defense. However, in applying the principle of double effect to self-defense a crucial problem about the first two conditions arises: Is not the killing of an assailant a *direct* killing, so that in defending my life I am using an evil as means to a good? On this matter there are two opinions:

One opinion holds that legitimate self-defense is always only an *indirect* killing. Though more fully expressed by his commentator Cajetan,† this opinion seems to be that of St. Thomas. Only one in public authority may *intend* killing another, even in self-defense. According to this opinion, all that I as a private person may do in defending myself is to produce a state of quiet or nonactivity in the assailant so that he cannot continue his attack. If my attempts to produce this nonactivity, a thing that is morally indifferent, result in death, that is incidental and regrettable. But I must not *intend* anything more than the quieting of the adversary, not his death.

The other opinion holds that in self-defense the killing may be *direct*. John de Lugo puts it as follows:

We may intend whatever is necessary for the defense of our life. Sometimes the striking of blows alone is insufficient for this purpose, but the death of the adversary is necessary. His stubbornness is such that he will not cease from attacking you, either by himself or others, unless he dies. Therefore you can intend his death, not merely as the striking of a blow [from which death may follow] but as death, because it is

useful to your safety not otherwise than as death. . . . The death of the aggressor is not merely connected with another means that is intended, but it itself, and as death, is useful and judged necessary to your defense.*

This latter opinion falls back on a *collision of rights*. By the very fact that the assailant's attack is unjust, his right to life yields to that of the person attacked. The right to life of the two parties is no longer equal, but the aggressor temporarily loses his right to life by his unjust act of aggression. Killing in itself is not wrong, but what makes it wrong is its *injustice*, the invasion of another man's right. If that right is extinguished, there is no injustice present to make the act of killing wrong. This second opinion has the double advantage of eliminating the subtle distinction between killing and quieting, and of permitting both direct and indirect killing in self-defense.

Whichever of these explanations be preferred, there is no doubt about the existence of the right of self-defense. The use of force is not in itself wrong. It is so only when one has no right to use it. Man must have a natural right to self-defense for the following reasons:

1. The assailant who breaks the moral law cannot thereby acquire a better right to life than the innocent person who keeps the moral law, so that on being unjustly attacked a man finds that his right to life becomes a duty to die.

2. The good and upright members of the population cannot have the duty to let the criminal element, by their indiscriminate and unchecked use of force, seize control of human society and thus pervert it into an instrument of evil.

Therefore man's natural right to life would defeat itself unless, under proper conditions, it carried with it authorization to use force even to killing in self-defense.

*St. Thomas, *Summa Theologica*, II-II, q. 64, a. 7.
†Cajetan, *Commentaria* (Commentaries on the Works of St. Thomas), on the above passage. This is found in the Leonine Edition of St. Thomas, vol. IX.

*De Lugo, *De Justitia et Jure* (On Justice and Right), Disputation X, sec. VI, §149.

The argument proves that man has a *right* to self-defense. Is it also a *duty?* No. As we shall see, man has the duty to use ordinary means to preserve his life, but the killing of a human being, even if he is an aggressor, is surely an extraordinary means. Therefore nothing prevents a man from choosing the heroic course of giving up his own life rather than taking another's. Only in unusual circumstances could self-defense become a duty, for example, in the case of a public personage indispensable to the community's welfare.

One may come to the assistance of another whose life is unjustly attacked. Such assistance becomes a duty for custodians of public order because of their office, and for husbands, fathers, and others who have a natural duty to protect their charges. The casual bystander has a general duty in common humanity to come to another's assistance in distress; if this action goes so far as to require the killing of an assailant, it usually entails serious risk to his own life, a risk he is allowed but not obliged to take.

UNINTENTIONAL AGGRESSION

The preceding argument is expressly directed at *intentional* aggression but applies with proper reservations to *unintentional* aggression. A man who has lost the use of his reason, either permanently or temporarily, cannot perform a voluntary act and cannot incur moral guilt, but he can be just as serious a threat to other people's lives. The same is true of a man who has the use of reason but does not realize that the act he is doing at the moment will kill someone; for him the act is voluntary only as far as he sees it, and its unforeseen consequences, though involuntary, can be fatal to others, who have a right to protect themselves against them.

Such acts are unjust aggression from the standpoint of the person attacked, because his right is actually, though unintentionally, violated. He may protect himself even to the killing of the assailant under the four conditions of a blameless self-defense. The unintentional aggressor's right yields to the defender's, not because of the former's fault, but because of his misfortune. Human lives cannot be placed at the mercy of madmen, however blameless they may be, nor are we obliged to give up our lives in deference to another man's ignorance. Most assailants are malicious, but it is not necessary that they be so in order that we may exercise our right of self-defense against them.

GOODS EQUIVALENT TO LIFE

Man has a right not only to life itself but to a human life, a normal and decent life fit for a rational being. Man's right to defend his life would be of small value if he could not also defend his right to live that life in a manner befitting a man. This right entails the possession of certain goods that make life worth living, goods that some writers call equivalent to life. Force may be used to defend such goods—even to the killing of the unjust aggressor, under the same conditions that apply to the defense of life itself. Personal goods considered equivalent to life are liberty, sanity, chastity, and bodily completeness. Many would rather die than submit to such evils as rape, insanity, blindness, or enslavement, and, whether they would or not, why should anyone have to yield to a fiend who tries to inflict them?

Material goods, even of great value, may seem so disproportionate to human life that we may never kill to defend them. On the other hand, the social as well as the personal aspect must be considered, and the good of society requires that people be secure in their possessions, especially those on which their whole livelihood depends. Acts of violence, whether against one's person or against one's property, cannot be allowed to go unchecked in society, and in the last resort they can be checked only by opposed violence. The attacker can easily save his life simply by desisting from his aggression.

Honor and *reputation* have been deliberately omitted here. They are as important as any of the goods just listed, for their loss can mean utter ruin, but they are not the kind of thing that can be defended by force. Self-defense is the repelling of force by force. Lies and slander are words and cannot be beaten back by fists or swords or pistols. The only weapon against them is the truth. The use of physical force against a liar would only prove me physically stronger than he but would not restore my reputation; if I use strength to force from him a recantation, it would not be generally believed under the circumstances. However, force short of killing may be the only way of closing the mouth of a reviler or slanderer who refuses to stop. Here physical force can be effective.

The former practice of *dueling,* which was supposed to deal with matters of honor, cannot be morally justified. Dueling with intent to kill on both sides is a combination of murder and suicide. The intent to kill the adversary makes it murder, and the exposure of one's own life to an unnecessary risk makes it suicide. The imputation of cowardice against one who refuses a challenge is unjust and at best the result of an erroneous conscience. The civilized world is well rid of this immoral custom.

SUMMARY

Man's right to life is based on the fact that he must achieve his goal and fulfillment by morally good acts, and to do so he must live.

Suicide is the direct killing of oneself on one's own authority. Arguments favoring suicide are that life can become intolerable and a worse evil than death, that God's gift of life is to be used intelligently and surrendered when useless, that God gives us rights over others' lives and why not over our own?

Arguments against suicide are that God gives man only *indirect* dominion over himself, the stewardship of his person, but no *direct* dominion, no right to destroy his person, for this is so exclusively God's that He cannot give it away; it is for God to decide that man has had sufficient opportunity for a good life; by suicide man arrogates this privilege to himself and invades God's exclusive right.

Murder, the direct killing of an innocent person, is morally wrong because it violates the right of God over all human life, of an innocent man to his life, and of the state to public order and safety.

Mercy killing, or active euthanasia, is suicide if done by oneself, murder if done by another with or without the victim's consent.

Abortion is the expulsion of the fetus from the mother before it is viable. If the mother has a serious illness, she may be given necessary treatment even though the death of the child *indirectly* results. But the double-effect principle cannot be applied to *direct* abortion.

Arguments favoring direct abortion are that the fetus is only a part of the mother, or not yet a human being, or at least not yet a human person, and hence not a possessor of rights. The fetus can be an unjust aggressor against the mother. The woman is unfairly penalized for sex faults. No unwanted child should exist. Population control may even require compulsory abortion.

Arguments against direct abortion deny both the alleged facts and the conclusions. Though we do not know just when the human soul enters the embryo or when it becomes a human person, we cannot use probabilities here but must follow the morally safer course. From the moment of conception the child is biologically determined and can never be anything else than human; it must be treated as a human being with full right to life. No convenience, not even that of the mother, justifies putting an innocent child to death.

How far the civil law should go in protecting the child involves almost insoluble difficulties in a pluralistic society. There are good reasons for strong abortion laws and also for no laws on abortion.

Self-defense, the repelling of force by force, should ordinarily be entrusted to the civil government but sometimes must be done personally. There are four conditions of a blameless self-defense:

1. The motive must be self-defense alone.
2. Force must be used only at the time of attack.
3. There must be no other way of repelling the attack.
4. No more injury may be inflicted than necessary.

Some say that self-defense must aim only at the quieting of the assailant, and death must be indirect. Others think that even a direct killing is allowable because of a collision of rights.

The natural right to life implies the right to protect that life, even by the killing of the assailant if necessary. Otherwise, criminals have a better right to life than the innocent, and the criminal element get a free hand in the control of society.

Self-defense is a right but normally not a duty. We may defend others who are attacked, but we are not obliged to risk our lives for those not under our charge.

We may defend ourselves against *unintentional* aggressors, because they are actually though guiltlessly invading our right.

We may also defend goods equivalent to life: limbs and faculties, sanity, liberty, chastity, material goods of great value. But honor cannot be defended by force; hence dueling is wrong.

QUESTIONS FOR DISCUSSION

1. Has a nontheistic philosophy any valid argument to prove that in no case is suicide morally allowable? If a man owes nothing to a power higher than himself, has he the final say in the disposal of himself?

2. Is there any way a man can acquire a moral right to destroy himself if it is necessary for the common good, say, if he were going to be tortured to reveal a secret that would cost the lives of thousands of his countrymen and he foresees that he could not hold out?

3. Nature intends that man shall use his intelligence in discovering means to overcome the evil of useless pain. Since death itself is natural, why cannot it be used when no other means is possible?

4. Can therapeutic abortion be allowed on the grounds of a collision of rights: that the mother is certainly a human person but the child only probably so, and that the mother already has duties to an existing family but the child has no such obligations?

5. When does the human offspring become a human person with a right to life? Can we argue that if a child may be aborted therapeutically, it may for the same reason be killed after birth if it is defective? Does the process of birth itself make it a human person?

READINGS

Read Plato's *Phaedo*, §61-62, which shows that Socrates, whatever we may think of his drinking the hemlock, certainly did not intend to commit suicide; the famous death scene is at the end of the *Phaedo*. Plato in the *Laws*, bk. IX, proposed what he thinks are the best laws on homicide and assault.

St. Augustine, *City of God*, bk. I, ch. 17-27, treats of suicide. David Hume and Arthur Schopenhauer each have short essays on suicide; they can be read in Abelson, *Ethics and Metaethics*, pp. 108-121. Émile Durkheim's work, *Suicide*, is a classic. Albert Camus' *The Myth of Sisyphus* and *The Rebel* contain an existentialist's views, the first on suicide and the second on murder, with many other reflections.

St. Thomas treats of all kinds of killing in the *Summa Theologica*, II-II, q. 64. There is no English translation of Cajetan or de Lugo to make accessible their views on self-defense. Michael Cronin, *The Science of Ethics*, vol. II, pp. 93-110, and Joseph Rickaby, *Moral Philosophy*, pp. 202-224, argue for Cajetan's position.

The legal as well as the moral angle is developed by Norman St. John-Stevas in *The Right to Life; Life, Death, and the Law;* and *Law and Morals.*

On abortion: Robert E. Cooke and others edit a symposium entitled *The Terrible Choice: the Abortion Dilemma.* See also David Granfield, *The Abortion Decision;* Daniel Callahan, *Abortion: Law, Choice, and Morality;* Germain Grisez, *Abortion, the Myths, the Realities, and the Arguments;* John T. Noonan, *The Morality of Abortion: Legal and Historical Perspectives.*

Austin Fagothey, *Right and Reason—an Anthology,* reprints a number of passages from Dietrich Bonhoeffer's *Ethics,* containing his reflections on most of these problems.

CHAPTER 20

HEALTH

PROBLEM

Life can be lost not only by deliberate killing but also by lack of proper positive maintenance. Health and safety are means toward the preservation of life and thus pertain to man's stewardship over himself. To what extent must one go to preserve life and health? May a man expose himself to serious danger or even to certain death in a good cause? Must he keep himself whole as well as alive, and what if he cannot do both? We must discuss:

1. When may a man risk his life?
2. How much care must be given to health?
3. What morality is involved in the drug problem?
4. Are mutilation and sterilization justified?

RISK TO LIFE

Suicide, or the direct killing of oneself on one's own authority, meets with rather general moral disapproval, but the indirect killing of oneself or the deliberate endangering of one's life, even when the danger may be so great that death is certain, can be a praiseworthy act. When we say that life is a nonrenounceable right and its preservation a duty, we do not mean that a person may never sacrifice it under any conditions, but only that he may not give it up at pleasure. When a person may rightfully risk his life is determined by the four conditions of the principle of double effect:

1. The act involving the risk must be allowable in itself apart from its consequences.
2. Death must be an incidental by-product and not the means by which the good is attained.
3. Death, even though foreseen, must be merely permitted and not intended for itself.
4. There must be some proportionate good that makes the risk worth taking.

Cases frequently arise in which all the conditions are fulfilled. In this event, provided any other evil circumstances arising from other possible sources are excluded, the deliberate exposure of oneself to the risk of death is not morally wrong.

This we all know through ordinary experience in the hazards of life. If we could never risk our lives, no one could nurse the plague-stricken or undergo a serious operation or mine coal or build a skyscraper or fly an airplane or even drive on the highways. Human life as we know it would come to a standstill.

The fourth condition, the proportion, requires some additional remarks. How is it to be estimated? Except in cases in which death is certain, we must not balance the good we seek against death itself but against the *risk* of death. Is the good proportioned to the danger?

The danger may be:

1. *Ordinary* or *extraordinary*
2. *Proximate* or *remote*
3. *Certain*, *probable*, or barely *possible*

The greater the risk, the greater must be the desired good that can justify such a risk. There is an ordinary, remote, and possible hazard in driving a car or flying a plane, and yet one may do so for mere pleasure. To drive on sleety streets or fly in bad weather is much more dangerous and requires a better reason. Conditions can become so bad that no driving or flying is allowable, except perhaps to save a life, and then we must see how much that life is endangered.

To save another from certain death, we may expose ourselves to certain death. Such an act is usually allowable but becomes obligatory only under special conditions. Those who, either by nature or by contract, have charge over the lives of others may and sometimes must take greater risks to protect their charges. Husbands will sacrifice themselves for their wives and parents for their children. Soldiers, sailors, policemen, firemen, doctors, nurses, and others are obliged by the contract implicit in their occupation to fulfill their duties even in the most serious danger.

The greater benefit an action or occupation is to society, the more dangerous it may be without overbalancing the proportion. Columbus could take chances not otherwise permitted because of the enormous boon to mankind a successful voyage would bring, and so may astronauts of the present and space travelers of the future. Dangerous work with radiation is justified when truly directed to the advancement of science or to national defense, under proper precautions both for the investigators and the public. A man may do right in facing the ordinary risks of a hazardous occupation such as coal mining or dynamite manufacturing, and at the same time do wrong by creating extraordinary dangers for himself and others in his way of working, especially by despising the usual safety precautions.

Is mere entertainment sufficient reason for risking one's life or health? It can be, if the proportion is kept. Acrobats and daredevils are morally allowed to ply their trade because their skill renders the danger remote; when age blunts their skill, they must lower their pitch and finally bow out. Auto racing, because of increased speeds over courses not made to take them, may in some contests have already passed the morally tolerable point. Injuries in football and other body-contact sports are accidents outside the game's structure and presumably outside the players' intention, and thus come under the indirect voluntary and the double-effect principles. The same cannot be said for prizefighting, which lacks its climax unless it ends in a knockout; the knockout is the direct intention of each contestant and shouted for by the spectators. We now know more about the effect of the knockout blow on the human brain than we formerly did; each one produces some irreparable lesion, adding up to a progressive brain deterioration known as the "punch-drunk" condition. Promoters and backers of the sport, perhaps more than the participants, therefore have a serious moral problem on their hands. Some moralists would ban the sport entirely, most would require at least firmer regulation, and only few would see no moral problem at all in it.

The infinite variety of possibilities in this whole question of risk to life and health rules out the setting of any hard-and-fast norms. Positive law and custom, crystallizing man's age-old experience with danger, are helpful guides but are not infallible. We must ultimately fall back on the intellectual virtue of prudence; this we call common sense, and for it there is no substitute.

CARE OF HEALTH

Health is a good that requires reasonable care. This does not mean becoming a health crank but using the ordinary means of keeping healthy Not to do so would be needless exposure of one's life to danger, for life itself is dependent on health. By ordinary means we refer to proper food, clothing, and shelter, due moderation in work and exercise, the avoidance of foolish risks and dangers, taking the usual remedies in sickness, and seeking and following medical advice when necessary; all such care supposes rather normal conditions and does not contradict what was just said about exposing one's life to danger.

Man is not obliged to preserve life and health by extraordinary means, for no one is obliged to do what is practically impossible or disproportionately difficult. A man in moderate circumstances is not obliged to undergo a serious and costly operation, to break up his home and move to another climate, or to adopt some regimen that would prevent him from earning a living and make him a burden on others. Health must be preserved, but not at all costs. Whether a means is extraordinary or not must be judged, not absolutely, but relatively to the person. A form of life tolerable to one man would be unbearable to another. Hence a person's subjective attitude must be considered here as well as his social and financial condition.

One is certainly bound to avoid excesses ruinous to health, but the chief wrong in dissipation and debauchery comes not so much from the ruination of one's health as of one's character. The evil of drunkenness consists partly in the physical deterioration it gradually induces, but far more in the unseating of reason from its ruling position, making the man a temporary beast, and in the disastrous social consequences involved in becoming unfit for any responsible work, such as holding a job and supporting a family. The evil of indiscriminate sex indulgence often meets a natural punishment in the form of venereal disease, which one is obliged to avoid, but the real malice of unchastity is quite independent of such accidental physical effects. Acts of overindulgence are wrong as violations of the virtue of temperance, but an added evil accrues to them from the effect they can have on one's health.

DRUGS

The use of narcotic and psychedelic drugs poses a problem that is becoming ever more acute. These drugs are not evil in themselves and are to be judged from their effects. Under a doctor's supervision they are merciful means for the alleviation of pain. The doctor must balance their desirable and undesirable effects and judge by the principle of double effect that the good they will do outweighs the harm that must be tolerated. The chief danger is that of addiction, but even this danger may sometimes be chanced for a proportionately great good.

People who voluntarily take to addictive drugs for the thrill of it know quite well what they are letting themselves in for. No one is morally allowed to bring on himself the physical deterioration and personality collapse that results from addiction to opium derivatives such as morphine and heroin. From an individual evil it branches out into a social evil, since addicts easily resort to crime to sustain the increasing expense of greater supplies of the dwindlingly effective drug. No individual is allowed, apart from accomplishing his personal ruin, to make himself the burden on society that nearly all addicts are.

The allegedly nonaddictive psychedelic drugs pose a lesser but still very important problem. They have not yet been sufficiently explored to warrant a firm categorical judgment about them. Their liberating and mind-clarifying effects on some are paralleled by suicidal and dangerous tendencies in others, and in the same person at different times. Since the effects are so uncertain and since no one can predict how he will react at a particular time, one who takes these drugs is chancing what may happen and is responsible in cause for any untoward consequences. To take such risks in any other area of human life would be branded as criminal folly, so why not here? No one is allowed to play fast and loose with his body, mind, and character for no better justifying reason than the thrill of a "trip." The pity of it is that adolescents are the least qualified to experiment intelligently with these mind-blowing chemicals, and yet they are the ones who find them most appealing. Further knowledge may lead to a revised opinion, and we may find that under proper supervision man's heightened powers may lead to marvelously beneficial results, but that is problematic, and we can make moral decisions only in the light of what we know now. The accomplishments of the drug subculture to date are hardly reassuring.

THE RIGHT TO DIE

Much is being written and discussed these days about a person's right to die, especially to die in peace and dignity. This issue has always been more in the domain of the medical profession than of the moralists. Most doctors take seriously the Hippocratic oath and feel a strong obligation to keep the patient alive to the last possible breath with the use of all the means that medical science can provide. This attitude is much to be praised, and we could have no trust in the medical profession if it adopted the opposite. However, even the best of attitudes can become exaggerated, and with the advance of medical technology, the more human aspects of the science have sometimes been lost. The present interest in passive euthanasia is a proper corrective of this exaggeration, though it can be subject to an exaggeration of its own.

Moralists have been able to preserve a balanced attitude on this question precisely because of their distinction between ordinary and extraordinary means. They see that means and techniques have value not in themselves but in the end to which they lead, that mere biological life is not human life in any valuable sense, and that the death of the person is to be determined by the presence of consciousness and self-control rather than by the mechanically stimulated functioning of certain organs. Hence the distinction between ordinary and extraordinary means is to be measured *humanly* rather than scientifically. A treatment may be common medical practice or involve standard hospital equipment; yet for a particular person the cure may be worse than the disease. The patient, if he or his family speaking for him want it, should be given all the treatment medical science can offer, but there is no moral obligation to ask for it. The doctor should not urge it but clearly explain the alternatives. Especially in terminal cases, there is no point in prolonging life, regardless of trouble and expense, for a few more days, weeks, or even years of torment or coma. It is often better to let nature take its course so that the patient can die in peace. This is what is meant by passive euthanasia, and from the moral standpoint, supposing the proper conditions present, it seems justified.

Physicians, of course, have their legal and professional responsibilities to consider and must protect themselves against malpractice suits. They should secure written permission from the patient or his representative. Some doctors have no trouble about not using extraordinary techniques in the beginning but cannot bring themselves to turn off a machine that has already been functioning, to "pull the plug." The first is letting nature take its course, but the second looks like direct intervention. Most moralists think that they may be spared such scruples. The initial decision to use or not use the machine is not significantly different from the decision to continue or not continue using the machine now that the case has turned hopeless, and there is no moral obligation to continue doing something useless. The main thrust of the doctor's will here is toward helping the patient, not toward running a machine.

More is being written nowadays on preparing the patient for death. As a rule the medical profession has been unsympathetic in this regard, perhaps because the aim of the whole profession is the preservation of life, and the loss of a patient is regarded as somehow a medical failure. The profession itself is now seeing more clearly that death is part of life and that the time comes when a particular human life just cannot be saved any longer. Not to save a patient who can be saved for further profitable living is medical failure, though often no one's fault, but the aim of the profession cannot be to make all men live forever. It should be part of the purpose of the medical profession to assist people to die well when it has exhausted its resources to help them to live well, and physicians should cooperate with nurses, family, friends, social workers, and others to help the patient perform with peace and dignity his last act.

MUTILATION

Mutilation is an action by which some part or function of the body is injured or destroyed. To paralyze a part of the body by cutting the nerves is mutilation, but a mere wounding or incision that will heal and leave no disability is not.

The same argument which proves that suicide is wrong also proves that unnecessary mutilation is wrong, whether we inflict it on ourselves or allow others to do it to us. If we have only stewardship or use-ownership over our person, we are obliged to keep intact what has been entrusted to our care. We may therefore not part with our members or carve up our bodies on our own authority.

SURGERY

We are also obliged to preserve life and health, which is sometimes impossible without surgery. Must we undergo it? If the operation involves great pain or risk, or reduces one to a condition in which life would not be worth living, it would be an extraordinary means of preserving life, and one would not be morally obliged to submit to it. But this is not always the case.

What makes mutilation allowable? It is not a mere permitting of an evil, such as can be justified by the principle of double effect, but a direct attack on the wholeness of the body, an action directly voluntary, and therefore the accomplishment of a good by means of an evil. It is true that it is only a physical evil, but it is morally wrong to inflict physical evil unless one has a right to do so. We do have this right. The principle involved here is the *principle of totality: The part is for the sake of the whole.* By the natural order of things a part of the human body is subordinated to the good of the whole, the various organs and members and functions existing not for their own sakes but for the purpose of maintaining life in the whole organism. The part is the means and the whole is the end. Hence it is a legitimate act of care for one's life and health to sacrifice, when necessary, the part for the sake of the whole.

Well-founded hope of notable improvement in health, efficiency, or appearance can be proportionate reason for lesser operations.

ORGAN TRANSPLANTS

Organ transplantation is a highly technical matter, on which we can make only a few remarks. Blood transfusions, skin and bone grafts, and transplants from animals and from human cadavers are legitimate. The moral difficulty about transplants from other living humans is the unavoidable disability left in the one from whom the organ is taken. If the disability is not disproportionate to the good accomplished, some allow the operation, not on the principle of totality, which does not apply, but on the grounds of love for the neighbor, of which it is a most noble and generous instance.

Heart transplants offer no particular moral difficulty except that it must be certain that the donor is already dead and not killed for the purpose. In this case death cannot be determined by the ceasing of the heartbeat, for a man can be kept alive with an artificial heart, and a heart can be kept going outside the man. It seems safe in practice to conclude that a man is dead when the brain has so deteriorated that no restoration of consciousness will ever be possible. Medical science, whose business it is to make such judgments, follows the criteria of a flat encephalogram over sufficient time and the absence of all reflexes or other indications of life. Until further research discovers more, we do well to follow the best information available.

STERILIZATION

Sterilization is a form of mutilation, for, though it can be done simply by ligature without depriving the body of a physical part, it renders impossible one of the body's natural functions, the power of reproduction. Because this power is for the race rather than the individual, it involves a special problem.

1. *Indirect* sterilization, when sterility is but the foreseen effect of something else that is done, is allowable by the double-effect principle. *Direct* sterilization is the production of sterility itself as an end or a means. It follows the principles set down for mutilation: it is allowable if required for the life or health of the whole body. Mere sterilization is not at present the remedy for any disease, but should it be-

come so it may be done. This form might be called *therapeutic* sterilization.

2. May the state impose sterilization as a punishment for crime, especially for sex crimes? On the one hand, if the state can put criminals to death, it can decree lesser punishments, and for sex offenders it is a punishment that fits the crime. On the other hand, sterilization is useless because it destroys neither the desire nor the possibility of sex satisfaction, but only renders it unfruitful, a situation sex criminals would not resent. Hence *punitive* sterilization, despite a theoretical justifiability, is practically ineffective.

3. Some people wish to undergo sterilization to avoid parenthood, and some doctors wish to produce it when they foresee danger in future pregnancy. It is being advocated as a means of controlling overpopulation, especially in underdeveloped countries. Such *contraceptive* sterilization has the same morality as that of contraception, with the added effect of making it a permanent condition. Contraception is discussed later.

4. Sterilization is proposed also as a *eugenic* measure. The study of eugenics deals with the development of a better breed of human beings by methods commonly used in the breeding of animals. Eugenists are alarmed by the low birth rate among the more successful classes of society, and by the high birth rate among the less gifted groups, especially the mentally deficient. They see the best families dying off, while the diseased, feeble-minded, shiftless, and criminal elements are multiplying apace, thus bringing about a gradual deterioration in the general level of human excellence. Therefore they argue that defective strains must be eliminated from the race.

The factual case for eugenics is very shaky. Most scientists agree that there is no real evidence that the human race is deteriorating and that, even if it were, sterilization is not the remedy. Even if sterilization were effective, is it a means that is morally permissible? Though surgically only a minor operation, sterilization is a major mutilation because is deprives one of a very important natural function. No one is allowed to submit to a major mutilation unless it is necessary to save his life or health. Eugenic sterilization is not done for the sake of the individual's life or health but solely for some problematic effect it may have on the future of the race. Therefore in eugenic sterilization the reasons that alone can justify mutilation are not present, and this act is morally wrong.

If *voluntary* sterilization is thus morally wrong, the state has no right to order *compulsory* sterilization. Eugenic sterilization is not inflicted in punishment of crime, since it deals with disabilities that are presumably only hereditary. The state has the obligation to protect the individual in his rights and not to maim him for something not his fault. The good of society may require the segregation of harmful defectives, which adequately prevents any damage they can cause. The main reason that the state favors sterilization is that it can then turn defectives loose on society without fear that they will burden the state with families they cannot care for. This financial argument has no moral value whatever.

It may be objected that just as the members of the individual body exist for the sake of the whole and may be sacrificed for the good of the whole, so may the members of the social body; defectives may be called on to sacrifice the possibility of offspring for the benefit of society. Only in a totalitarian state could such an argument be admitted. The citizen is not wholly for the state and has natural rights the state must protect, among which is the right to bodily completeness. According to this argument the state could kill them just as readily. No matter how much it would help the public welfare, the state has no right to kill or mutilate its citizens except

in punishment for proved crimes, and not all admit that it has such a right even then.

CONCLUSION

This and the preceding chapter deal with the dignity of the human person as a living being. The exercise of the right to life can be looked down on as "mere survival" and rated low on the scale of values as something brutish rather than ennobling. So it may appear if we overdo the contrast between it and the heroic sacrifice of one's life in a great cause. But man is not always faced with such sharp alternatives, and it is in the calm flow of his everyday life that the pattern of right living appears. Man has to respect his own person and the person of others. He may not tamper irresponsibly with his own body or neglect its proper care. He may not subject other persons to himself by treating them as things to be destroyed for his own advantage. He may assert his right when attacked and defend himself manfully against aggression, since he is not made to be misused by others. Life itself is beset with many risks, and man cannot shrink from all of them without losing his manhood, but if he must live dangerously, the danger must be such as to be worthy of him. Life is entrusted to man to be used responsibly as befits one endowed with the dignity of being a person.

SUMMARY

Deliberate exposure of life to risk is allowable when the four conditions of the *principle of double effect* are satisfied. To estimate the proportion, note that danger may be ordinary or extraordinary, proximate or remote, certain or probable or barely possible. Even when we are allowed to risk our lives, we are not obliged to do so, except under special conditions.

Man must take reasonable care of his

health but is not obliged to use extraordinary means.

The use of addictive drugs is immoral because of their disastrous personal and social consequences. The use of nonaddictive psychedelic drugs, because of their effects, is the taking of a morally unwarranted risk.

Man has a right to die in peace and dignity. In terminal cases there is no need to prolong life uselessly by extraordinary means. This is passive euthanasia.

Mutilation is the destruction of some member or function of the body. Since we have only use-ownership over ourselves, mutilation is not allowable at will. Mutilation, since it is a direct attack on the wholeness of the body, is justified on the principle that *the part is for the sake of the whole,* and is allowable only to save life or, in lesser mutilations, to obtain a proportionate improvement in well-being. Organ transplants can be justified within limits.

Sterilization is depriving a person of the reproductive function. Like other mutilations it is lawful when necessary for life or health. As a punishment for sex crimes, it would be lawful if it were effective, but it is not. As a contraceptive measure, its morality must be judged the same as that of contraception. As a eugenic measure, it can neither be justified if done voluntarily, because it is not required to save the life or health of the individual, nor if done compulsorily by the state, because the victim is guilty of no crime by which he would forfeit his natural rights.

QUESTIONS FOR DISCUSSION

1 How do we reconcile the efforts to limit the population with the efforts to preserve existing life as long as possible, even when a person is deformed or diseased?

2 Could sterilization be set by law as a penalty for mothers or fathers notoriously neglecting their children and incapable of reform? Why let them have more children they will continue to neglect?

3 St. Thomas uses the "part for the whole" principle as a defense of capital punishment, applying it to the social body as well as to the physical body. Why not extend it to eugenic sterilization, which is also for the benefit of the social body?

4 Marijuana is thought by many to be no more harmful than alcohol, perhaps even less, and our laws about it to be benighted and overly severe. Should it be exempted from the class of harmful drugs?

5 What judgment should be made on the so-called drug subculture? Is it moral for a person to make drugs so much a part of his life that he retires from society and lives chiefly in a dreamworld?

232

READINGS

The matter of this chapter is hardly touched on by the older writers. St. Thomas has one article in the *Summa Theologica,* II-II, q. 65, a. 1.

Most of the problems in this chapter are discussed at length in books on medical ethics. See Edwin Healy, *Medical Ethics;* Charles McFadden, *Medical Ethics;* Thomas O'Donnell, *Morals in Medicine;* Gerald Kelly, *Medico-Moral Problems;* John Kenny, *Principles of Medical Ethics;* Bernard Ficarra, *Newer Ethical Problems in Medicine and Surgery;* and Peter Flood (ed.), *New Problems in Medical Ethics, Medical Experimentation on Man,* and *The Ethics of Brain Surgery.* The last three works are symposia of French doctors, too technical for the general reader but valuable to the medical student, with good ethical summaries.

Interest in consciousness-expanding drugs was accelerated by some of Aldous Huxley's works, especially *The Doors of Perception* and *Island.* Numerous periodical articles have appeared, enthusiastic, condemnatory, and neutral. See Sidney Cohen, *The Beyond Within,* and Richard Blum, *Utopiates.* For a dramatic presentation there is Eugene O'Neill's *Long Day's Journey into Night.*

Austin Fagothey, *Right and Reason—an Anthology,* has selections from Dietrich Bonhoeffer's *Ethics,* which have some pertinence here.

CHAPTER 21

TRUTHFULNESS

PROBLEM

Man has not only a right to be but a right to know, not only a right to life but a right to truth. He demands respect for his own intellect and must show similar respect for his neighbor's intellect by putting right order in the communications between his own mind and the minds of others. He who speaks is obliged to speak the truth.

The problem arises from the fact that a man may also have a right or a duty to conceal the truth. He has a right to privacy. He may be entrusted with a secret that he must not divulge. There might be little trouble on this point if people did not have the habit of asking questions, but the privilege of inquiring goes with the gift of speech. What can a man do when he is questioned point blank on a matter he must keep secret? How can we veil our speech to guard the truth as well as to communicate it? We need to explain:
1. What is a lie?
2. Are all deceptions lies?
3. Why and how far is lying wrong?
4. Why must secrets be kept?
5. How can secrets be kept without lying?

MEANING OF A LIE

What is a lie? The literal-minded person may define a lie as any statement not in strict literal accord with actual facts. But no one with the faintest spark of imag-ination or the most primitive inkling of courtesy could confine his speech within such narrow bounds. Speech not only exchanges information but also contributes to the amenities of life. Candor has its place, but the outspoken telling of the unvarnished truth on every occasion would lose us all our friends and make us unfit for society. Speech need not always be used thus, and this literal-minded definition would require a distinction between lies that are allowable and those that are not, between so-called white lies and black lies. A better procedure is to reserve the word *lie* for the misuse of speech that is morally wrong and to define it accordingly. To distinguish it from the looser usages of everyday speech we may call it a *strict* or *formal* lie. We are concerned with it alone.

Commenting on St. Augustine's[*] definition of a lie as "a false statement uttered with intent to deceive," St. Thomas[†] says that it contains three things:

1. The falsity of the statement. This provides the material for a lie, for it is not a lie to say what is actually false while thinking it true, though it is a lie to say what is actually true while thinking it false.

2. The will to tell the falsity. The essential element of a lie as a human act

---

[*]St. Augustine, *De Mendacio* (On Lying), ch. 4; *Contra Mendacium* (Against Lying), ch. 12.
[†]St. Thomas, *Summa Theologica*, II-II, q. 110, a. 1.

is the willful disconformity between one's thought and one's speech, so that it is "speech contrary to one's mind."*

3. The intention to deceive. This is the usual motive for lying and indicates its normal effect on the one lied to. The intent need not be efficacious, as when a liar knows that he will not be believed.

Some add a fourth element, that a lie must be:

4. Told to one who has a right to the truth. If this addition is properly understood, it will make the explanation of lying much simpler and clearer. It should not mean that we can say anything and everything we want to a person merely because he has no strict right to demand the truth of us. It must be presumed that anyone to whom we speak has the right to be spoken to truthfully if we speak to him seriously on any matter at all. Respect for him as a person requires that we treat him so. He loses this right only when we have the greater right to withhold the truth from him and cannot do so by silence. In this case speech must be used to conceal rather than reveal the truth, and what we are really communicating to him is the fact that we are not communicating. He should be able to take the hint that he is not being lied to but is being put off.

The problem comes down to the nature of speech as a medium of communication and its function in human society. For a strict lie there must be indication, at least in the circumstances, that:

1. Serious communication is going on.
2. It is meant to be taken as the truth.
3. It is being accepted by the hearer as truth.
4. Yet is it known by the speaker to be false.

---

*A commonly accepted definition of lying, but embodying only the first two elements.

CONVENTIONALITY OF SPEECH

It is natural for man to speak, but apart from a few obvious gestures and imitative sounds, there is no natural language. The so-called natural languages are merely those which were never consciously invented but grew up historically. Language is *conventional,* the symbols used being developed by human artifice and dictated by custom. Hardly any word has a single univocal meaning whenever used, like the symbols of mathematics. Language is a peculiar mixture of logic and tradition, in which the conventions are undergoing subtle but continual change. By convention we distinguish fact and fiction, literal and figurative expressions, jokes and serious statements, emotional outbursts and sober information, ironical allusions and scientific data, polite compliments and solemn testimony. Often nothing but circumstances indicates the difference.

1. Communication is not limited to words but is *any sign used to convey thought.* Looks, gestures, nods, winks, shrugs, facial expressions, tones of voice, and even the circumstances in which something is said are all signs capable of telling another what we think and, if used for this purpose, are communication. Lying is possible by any of these means.

2. The sign must be *intended* by the speaker *to convey a meaning.* Involuntary looks and gestures are not communication. It is not lying to conceal our emotions under outward calm nor to appear cheerful when we are sad, for we are not then intentionally using our appearance to express our real feelings.

3. The sign must be made *to another person,* for communication is between minds. It is impossible to lie to oneself, nor would it be lying to confide untruths to one's dog. Talk in other people's presence, when it is clearly not directed to them, is not communication to them. Eavesdroppers listen at their own peril.

4. The sign must be such as to *express the speaker's own judgment*, what he believes to be true. To lie, therefore, the speaker must express as true something he thinks to be untrue, or as certain something he does not know for certain. If he mistakenly thinks that what he says is true, though in fact it is not, he does not lie; his speech is untrue but not untruthful.

5. *Fiction* is not lying, for the story is used as an expression of one's creative imagination and entertaining ability, not of one's factual judgment. Jokes and exagerations are not lies if there is any circumstance to indicate that they are not to be taken seriously.

6. *Figures of speech* are not lies. When a word has several meanings, its sense in this particular statement must be judged by the context and the meaning of the whole statement by the total situation. Sometimes we speak literally, sometimes figuratively, and the figurative meaning can be just as genuine as the literal.

7. Many *polite expressions* and *stereotyped formulas* have lost old meanings and acquired new ones through convention. "Not guilty" in a law court is a legal plea by which the accused does not confess but demands that the case be proved against him. "Good morning," "goodbye," "how do you do," "see you later" once meant something but are now mere forms of greeting and parting. There are times when compliments must be paid: "very becoming hat," "most enjoyable evening," "such a beautiful baby." Only the most naive would accept these remarks at their face value. How far one can go in the use of polite excuses depends on convention. "Not at home," "in conference," "occupied," "too busy," "previous engagement" are recognized as urbane ways of putting one off, depending on the circumstances. Once these probably were lies, but use has softened their import.

8. *Circumstances* can be such that, though words are used, there is no formal speech because no communication is intended nor should it be expected. A captured soldier, for instance, may regale his captors with tall stories about the disposition of his own troops. Even if they are foolish enough to believe him, he is not lying because circumstances show that he is entertaining and not communicating. The case is different if a prisoner is put on parole and seriously accepts the conditions.

LYING AND DECEPTION

Deception is the usual motive for lying, but we must not confuse these two concepts. Feints, disguises, impersonations, fictitious names, and other such pretenses are deceptions but not lies. The difference is in the lack of communication in the sense just explained. Deception is not wrong in itself but can become wrong from motives and circumstances if intended or foreseen as a cause of harm. The wrong comes not from the act done, which is indifferent, but from the harm that follows.

Most games are built on harmless deception. Even harmful deception may be permitted in the protection or vindication of one's rights, according to the principle of double effect. Thus stratagems and military maneuvers in war may be designed deliberately to mislead the enemy. Such deceptions are not lies because nothing is *said*, no judgment is expressed, no statement is made by the usual symbols of communication. Actions are done, it is true, but if the enemy takes a meaning out of them, he does so at his own peril. The intent to deceive may be justified on the grounds that one is defending one's own rights and merely permitting the enemy to harm himself. Some even classify the presentation of forged passports and other documents to elude an unjust government as deceptions but not lies, because circumstances show that they are not communications but only an external compliance with demands the officials have no right to make.

Hugo Grotius* correctly distinguishes between lies and stratagems, but his application is poor; he classes among stratagems some actions that really are lies: to tell a falsehood in order to do someone a service, to use false intelligence to encourage troops, and his approbation of Plato's "noble lie"† told for the public welfare. These are not stratagems, actions capable of a deceptive interpretation, but lies. A free hand cannot be given to one of the worst forms of lying yet invented, mass propaganda of militant nationalism.

ARGUMENTS ON LYING

We have shaved down a lie to the minimum because people use speech loosely and give it other social functions besides that of communicating thought. There remains an irreducible residue: speech meant and taken in all seriousness as communication from mind to mind. The hearer trusts the speaker and has a right to be told the truth if he is told anything. Hence lying in the sense defined and explained, which we have called a *strict* or *formal* lie, is a morally evil act. St. Thomas' argument cites Aristotle and St. Augustine:

As words are naturally signs of intellectual acts, it is unnatural and undue for anyone to signify by words something that is not in his mind. Hence the Philosopher‡ says that lying is in itself evil and to be shunned, while truthfulness is good and worthy of praise. Therefore every lie is a sin, as also Augustine§ declares.‖

---

*Grotius, *Rights of War and Peace,* bk. III, ch. 1.
†Plato, *Republic,* bk. III, §389-414.
‡Aristotle, *Nicomachean Ethics,* bk. IV, ch. 7, 1127a 28.
§St. Augustine, *Contra Mendacium* (Against Lying), ch. 1.
‖St. Thomas, *Summa Theologica,* II-II, q. 110, a. 3.

The first of the following arguments is an expansion of St. Thomas' argument, and the other two are additions to it.

1. *Argument from the abuse of a natural ability.* It is natural to intelligent beings to have some means of communicating their thoughts so as to win assent from others. To communicate as thought what is not thought, to convey seriously to another as true what one knows to be untrue, is to abuse this means of communication and to render it unfit for its purpose. Hence lying is an act against man's nature and a violation of the natural law.

2. *Argument from the social nature of man.* Human society is built on mutual trust and faith among men. If lying were morally allowed, we could never tell when a person is lying and when he is not, whether his next statement will be a lie or the truth; we could not even accept his assurance that the statement he is now making is the truth. His speech would cease to have any meaning for us, and if this practice became widespread, there would be an end to human communication and thus to human society.

3. *Argument from the dignity of the human person.* No man's intelligence ought to be insulted by being fed falsehood instead of truth under the assurance that it is truth. This is precisely what the liar does. By subjecting another's noblest attribute, his intellect, to himself as a means to his own advantage, he degrades the person of his fellowman and in so doing degrades his own person.

No moralist advocates lying as a normal practice or thinks that we may play fast and loose with the truth as we please, but some, and not only relativists, object to the rigidity and absoluteness of the arguments just given. There are occasions, they think, when lying is allowed and perhaps even required.

1. Words are a means to an end and have no sacredness in themselves. They may be used for communicating or for

withholding the truth. There is no reason why one should be a natural use and the other an unnatural abuse. We use other abilities for purposes not directly intended by nature, as when an acrobat walks on his hands, without considering it an abuse. Why should speech be treated differently?

2. Everyone recognizes the social value of speech and the need for trust among men. But the good of society may sometimes be promoted more by a lie than by the truth, for instance, to save an innocent man's life or to avert war. Kant thought that if I were hiding a friend from a pursuing murderer, I could not save him by telling the lie that he is not here.* Such idolatry of principle would be more antisocial than social. It would destroy the fugitive's trust in me, and even the pursuer, while accepting my betrayal, would despise me for it.

3. A person should be morally allowed to lie, not arbitrarily, but only in limited social situations. The person would be using the lie to protect himself, and the greater the lie, the more extreme would have to be his peril to justify it. The rest of us can usually recognize when a man is cornered and can make due allowances for the truth value of his speech. We actually do so anyway; yet the social value of communication is not thereby destroyed.

4. If self-defense allows us to go so far as to kill an attacker, why may we not save ourselves at much less cost by telling a lie when lying would get us out of the situation? Why should physical force be an allowable means of self-defense and the spoken word an immoral one? To let a man be deceived is a far less evil to him than to kill him.

5. In self-defense the means of defense are to be proportioned to the means of attack. If we may repel force by force, why should we not repel a lie with a lie? Force cannot defend against speech, it is true, but speech can defend against speech. One who slanders my good name can be deterred by knowing that he will receive the same treatment from me.

6. The difference between a lie and other kinds of deception is that a lie uses the common symbols of communication called speech, whereas other forms of deception use actions capable of misinterpretation. Why make so much of this difference? Why not consider a lie as any other feint or stratagem, and treat it on the same terms?

There is value to some of these objections. Others have already been considered in determining the factors necessary for a lie to be a lie in the strict sense.

1. Many prefer not to use the argument from the abuse of a natural ability, not as denying that such abilities can be abused, but as questioning how we decide what uses are unnatural abuses, since many things in nature have several alternative uses. Walking on one's hands does not unfit them for their normal use, but to drive nails by punching them in with one's bare fist would soon do so. The boy in the fable who cried "Wolf!" so ruined his speech that he could no longer communicate when it became necessary. Does such a result come from a lie or two, or from the reputation of being a habitual liar?

2. The telling of a lie seems a small price to pay for saving life or averting war. But where does one stop? Murder or any other crime could be done for similar reasons. Not the size of the evil but the kind is what counts. Moral evil may not be done to avert even the greatest of physical evils. All this makes sense only if the lie is really a lie in the full meaning of the term. Murderers have no right to know where their intended victim is, and nothing said to them has the character of communication. This is not an example of a real lie, and there is

---

*Kant, "On a Supposed Right to Tell Lies from Benevolent Motives," in Abbott, *Kant's Theory of Ethics,* Appendix I, pp. 361-365.

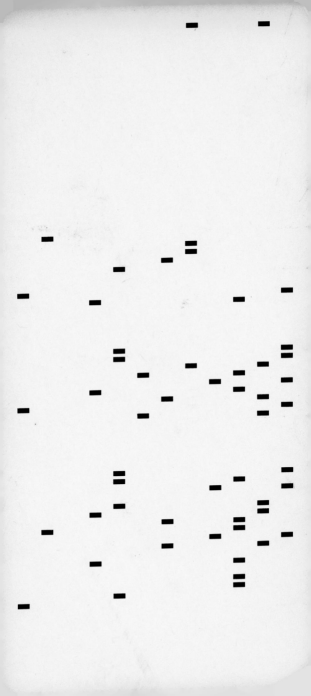

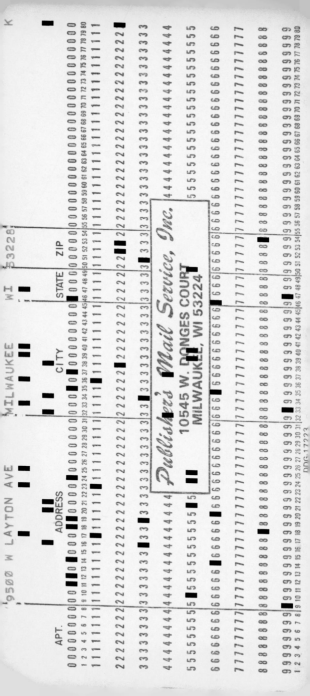

no need of following Kant's rigid interpretation of duty.

3. The same answer is applicable to a man in extreme difficulty. We do not expect literal truth from him because we know that he is not communicating. The case is different when he is put under oath in court, for then what he says is taken seriously by those who have a right to know, unless the court itself is corrupt and a vehicle of injustice, a fact to be proved and not presumed.

4. One may summon all one's powers to aid in defense against an unjust attack, but one must not misuse these powers so that they become evil means to a good end. We should certainly defend ourselves by speech rather than by killing, if the speech can be morally justified in any legitimate way, but not if it is a real lie in the strict and formal sense previously discussed. Physical force can be a moral or immoral means of self-defense, depending on how it is used, and so can speech. A strict lie is an immoral means by definition. If in most such cases the adversary would not have a right to the truth, what is said to him would not be a strict lie.

5. We have here a different case from the preceding. It is not a case of warding off physical attack by speech rather than by force, but of trading off lie for lie. To answer a lie by telling another lie is returning evil for evil and not a repelling of the first evil. A lie against me is a wrong use of speech and is properly repelled by my own right use of speech, which is telling the truth.

6. The value of our examination into the factors that make up a lie in the strict sense here becomes apparent. Speech may often be used as a means of deception, as we have seen partly and will see more clearly. Feints, stratagems, and other forms of deception may not be used indiscriminately, and neither may speech. A lie in the strict sense is always an immoral use of speech and not just any form of deception.

SECRETS

If our speech is such that it is serious communication, what we say must be true, but there are times when we may and times when we must refuse to speak. We must reveal the truth when the other party has a right to it. Such would be a lawful superior, a judge in court, or a party to a contract. We must not reveal the truth when it is a strict secret. A secret is knowledge that the possessor has the right or the duty to conceal. For want of a better term we shall call a truth that one has a *duty* to conceal a *strict* secret. A person may be obliged to keep a secret because:

1. The knowledge of its very nature is private
2. He has promised not to reveal it

The first is a *natural* secret, because the matter it deals with is private in nature. What belongs to a person's private life, to the closed circle of the family, to the status of business firms and corporations, to military and diplomatic affairs of governments, cannot be aired in public without injury to the parties concerned. Those who share in such matters are bound to keep them secret. Others who happen to find out about them are also bound to keep them secret, but not to the jeopardy of their own rightful interests.

The second comprises secrets of *promise,* when one already has the knowledge and then promises not to divulge it; and secrets of *trust,* when the knowledge is confided to him only under the condition, expressed or implied, that the matter is confidential and not to be revealed. Both of these may also be natural secrets or not, depending on the nature of the matter. Professional secrets are typical examples of secrets of trust and are usually natural secrets also. A secret of trust is the strictest kind of secret and binds in justice, because it is based on a contract expressed or implied.

That man is at times *permitted* to conceal the truth should be evident from the nature of man. Besides being a member of society, a man is also an individual. He has not only social and public relations but also private and personal affairs of his own. Man has a right to his own personal dignity and independence, to freedom from meddling and prying into his private affairs.

Furthermore, man is at times *obliged* to conceal the truth. One of the purposes of speech and of human society itself is that man can get help from his fellowman, that he can get advice from his friends and consult experts without danger of making private affairs public, that when he organizes with other men for the pursuit of a common goal, they can exchange information without fear of betrayal to a hostile group. One of the main purposes of speech would be lost unless we can also control how far the knowledge we communicate will spread.

How far does the duty of keeping a secret extend? This question concerns a conflict of rights, when the right of one party to have a certain matter kept secret conflicts with the difficulties the other party experiences in trying to keep it secret. In general, one is no longer bound to secrecy:

1. If the matter has otherwise been divulged
2. If the other party's consent can rightly be supposed

The first of these conditions is evident, since the secret no longer exists, but the second needs some explanation. One may be expressly released from the obligation of secrecy and then is no longer bound. Even if this release is not expressly given, conditions may be such that it can reasonably be presumed, for no one has the right to expect a man to keep a rather ordinary secret at the expense of his life. The laws on excuses from duty, as previously explained, apply to natural secrets and secrets of promise; one is no longer held to keep the secret when doing so would cause disproportionate hardship.

However, one who has expressly promised to keep the secret even under grave or extreme hardship must keep his promise, unless it were morally wrong for him to have made such a promise. Greater reasons are required to release one from a secret of trust, but even such a strict secret may cease to bind if the holding of the secret would cause serious damage, not merely hardship, to the parties concerned, to a third party, or to the community. Sometimes, however, the revealing of a secret, such as a military secret, would cause such damage to the community that it must be guarded even at the expense of one's life.

What means can one use to keep a secret when directly questioned about it? The following four are customarily noted:

1. *Silence.* The normal way to treat an impertinent question is to refuse to answer it. A courteous statement that one is not free to talk of such matters usually ends the subject. Persistent pryers are not put off, however, and silence is often interpreted as consent.

2. *Evasion.* The use of evasion distracts the questioner without giving him the information he wants, by changing the conversation, answering a question with a question, passing it off as a joke, or assuming an injured air. Evasion requires more ready wit than some people can command.

3. *Equivocation.* By the use of double-meaning expressions the speaker says what is true, though his words are capable of another meaning that is false; if the incautious hearer takes the wrong meaning, he is deceiving himself. Thus a person may speak of his child without saying whether it is his child by birth or adoption; the hearer who assumes one rather than the other is making a hasty judgment. For equivocation to be legitimate, both meanings must be discoverable by the hearer, even though one meaning is much more obvious.

4. *Mental reservation.* Mental reservation is the limiting of the obvious sense of

words to some particular meaning intended by the speaker. It is the truth but not the whole truth. Part of the truth is reserved in the speaker's mind, lending a possibly deceptive coloring to the part that is expressed. For mental reservation to be legitimate, some outward clue to the limited meaning must be objectively present, though the speaker hopes that it will not be noticed by the listener. The clue may be nothing else but the circumstances in which the words are said. A doctor is asked whether his patient has a certain disease and answers, "I don't know," meaning, "I don't know, secrets apart and in my nonprofessional capacity." He may even answer, "No," meaning, "No, not insofar as I can tell you." The very fact of his profession is sufficient clue to his meaning, for the questioner ought to know that the doctor cannot speak in his professional capacity. Thus this example can be taken as a mental reservation but is better interpreted as an instance of noncommunication.

May a person use evasions, equivocations, and mental reservations at any time and for any reason? No. They are not lies and not wrong in themselves, but an act can become wrong by its motive or its circumstances. An unrestricted use of these means of concealment would have ruinous social effects and would break down mutual trust among men. It is not the normal mode of speech, and we cannot be constantly combing over every sentence uttered to us to find possible hidden meanings. We expect our neighbor to speak to us with candor and sincerity, and we take his words in their obvious sense in the ordinary transactions of life. These combinations of speech and nonspeech are to be used only as a refuge to guard a secret from prying questioners who have no right to the information they seek. With this motive and in these circumstances they are morally allowable.

Legitimate as these subterfuges may be, they should not be overstressed. Most cases of allowable verbal deception can be explained simply by the fact that speech is not being used in its function of serious communication.

CONCLUSION

By nature man is a social being, and the gift of speech is perhaps the chief means by which man's social life is carried on. Like all other gifts, speech may be used or abused. Thus truthfulness is good and lying is wrong.

Speech can be abused in two ways: by seriously communicating as truth what one knows to be untrue or by revealing truths one has no right to reveal. One is never allowed to do the former, since the hearer has a right to the truth. One would have no difficulty about the latter were it not for other people's prying minds and impertinent questions; against them a man has a right to protect himself, a right that often becomes a duty when other people are involved. One in such a difficult situation is allowed, sometimes obliged, to summon all his ingenuity to extricate himself from the difficulty and to guard the trust others have placed in him. Apart from such situations, sincerity and candor should rule man's speech.

SUMMARY

A lie in the strict sense is speech contrary to one's mind with intent to deceive someone who has a right to the truth. Speech is any sign used to communicate thought, including language, gestures, tones of voice, and even circumstances. To lie a speaker must outwardly show that he seriously intends to express to another person as his true judgment a judgment that he knows is untrue. Deception is the normal motive for lying, but not all deceptions are lies. Fiction, jokes, figures of speech, and expressions of politeness are not lies, since speech must be interpreted according to convention. The important thing about a strict lie is that it has all the appearance of serious communication of truth when the speaker knows it is not.

Lying is *morally wrong* because it is an abuse of the natural ability of communication, because it is contrary to man's social nature, which requires mutual trust among men, and because it debases the dignity of the human person, whose mind is made for truth.

It is argued that a lie is not always wrong, because it is merely a use of words to conceal rather than reveal, it can sometimes help society more than the truth, it can be less harmful than force as self-defense, and should be classed among the legitimate stratagems.

It is answered that lying is not mere use of speech for a secondary end, leaving the primary end intact. It may promote a particular good, but by evil means and at the expense of a greater good, mutual trust. There is no parallel between killing in self-defense and lying in self-defense, for one is a right use of force, the other a wrong use of speech.

A *secret* is knowledge the possessor has a right or a duty to conceal. A *natural* secret deals with matter private in nature, a secret of *promise* with matter one has promised to conceal after finding it out, and a secret of *trust* with matter confided after exacting a promise of secrecy.

Concealment of the truth is often permitted, sometimes required. Man has a right to personal dignity, freedom from meddlers, and the right to seek advice without betrayal of his private affairs.

We are excused from secrecy if the matter has otherwise been divulged, or with the other party's expressed or presumed consent. Even a secret of trust ceases to bind if serious damage would result from keeping it.

The ways of keeping a secret are *silence, evasion, equivocation,* and *mental reservation.* The last two require that there be some outward clue to the speaker's meaning, though the hearer may fail to take it.

QUESTIONS FOR DISCUSSION

1 If lying is wrong because its purpose is to deceive, yet not all deception is wrong, why is deception by lying wrong? In what does the specific malice of lying consist?

2 A lie is wrong because it is harmful to society, since misuse of the gift of speech is misuse of a social ability. If a man is sure that his lie will not harm but will benefit society, why should he not tell it?

3 The shaving down of the definition of a lie to such a narrow meaning shows that lying is not wrong in itself but only in certain circumstances. Would it not be better to acknowledge this fact rather than to lie about lying, as we seem to have been doing?

4 A person against whom a mental reservation has been used, however technically correct it might be, would feel just as deceived as if he had been lied to. Do not both equally destroy mutual trust among men?

5 When a man tells his troubles to another, he ought to forfeit all right to secrecy. If he does not want something known, let him keep it to himself. Would not this obviate all the refinements of definition and casuistry found in this chapter?

READINGS

Despite the fact that he allowed the "noble lie" in the *Republic*, bk. II, §382, and bk. III, §414, Plato really has not much use for lying. Read the *Republic*, bk. II, §381-383, and bk. V, §484-490. See Aristotle's *Nicomachean Ethics*, bk. IV, ch. 7.

St. Augustine in *De Mendacio* (On Lying) and *Contra Mendacium* (Against Lying), both translated into English, is treating a special aspect of the subject and later expressed dissatisfaction with his work.

St. Thomas deals with lying in the *Summa Theologica*, II-II, qq. 109-110. In the following three questions he continues with a discussion of hypocrisy, boasting, and irony, which are subjects kindred to truthfulness and lying.

Hugo Grotius explains his view in *The Rights of War and Peace*, bk. III, ch. 1.

Kant's views on lying are found in the *Fundamental Principles of the Metaphysic of Morals* and in the monograph "On a Supposed Right to Tell Lies from Benevolent Motives," both in Abbott, *Kant's Theory of Ethics*.

Cardinal Newman's *Apologia pro Vita Sua*, note G, contains his reflections on equivocation. See Joseph Rickaby's *Moral Philosophy*, pp. 224-237.

J. A. Dorszynski, *Catholic Teaching About the Morality of Falsehood*, accepts the broader view.

Joseph Fletcher's *Morals and Medicine*, ch. 2, treats of the right of the sick to know their condition.

Austin Fagothey, *Right and Reason—an Anthology*, contains a selection from Kant's *Fundamental Principles of the Metaphysic of Morals*, in which he uses lying and promise breaking as examples.

CHAPTER 22

SOCIETY

PROBLEM

We start with the easily observed fact that a man is not alone in the world but lives in company with others like himself. Many living beings thrive in groups, clusters, colonies, or herds, in which there may be some degree of cooperation and even a primitive form of leadership. Society is considered to be uniquely human and therefore must consist in something more than mere togetherness, be it of place or of activity. Given the fact that man does live in society, we ask why he does so and what there is about human society that makes it different from other ways of living together. We may formulate our questions as follows:

1. Why do men live in society?
2. What is society?
3. What is the common good?
4. Must there be authority in society?
5. What are the main kinds of society?

NATURALNESS OF SOCIETY

The moralist's problem about society is different from the sociologist's. The moralist wants to know whether man lives in society by his own choice, so that society itself is but a product of human invention, or whether man is so fitted by his very being for social living that any other form of living would be unnatural for him. Since society imposes serious obligations on man, are they only such as man has created for himself, so that he may extricate himself

from them at will, or do they stem out of man's very nature, so that they become unavoidable moral obligations? This question is basic to any treatment of the moral aspects of man's social life.

Throughout ancient and medieval times, except for a flurry of dissent among the Greek Sophists, it was taken for granted that man is a social being by nature. This view is implicit in Plato and expressly formulated by Aristotle in the beginning of his *Politics,* where he declares: "Man is by nature a political animal."[*]

In the seventeenth and eighteenth centuries this view was challenged by Hobbes and Rousseau. Both envision a primitive condition called the *state of nature,* of man without society. Hobbes, who makes man antisocial, pictures the state of nature as one of constant predatory warfare. Rousseau, who thinks man only extrasocial, describes it as an era of blithe and carefree innocence. According to both, man's gift of intellect enabled him to see the advantages of cooperative action, to frame the social contract, and thus to pass from the state of nature to that of society. Having given up his liberties by the social contract he need never have made, man is now the slave of the monster he has created. Society is not natural to man but only conventional; its undoubted advantages are counterbalanced by its unnatural restrictions. Now, it is impossible to return to

---

[*]Aristotle, *Politics,* bk. I, ch. 2, 1253a 2.

the state of nature, and man must make the best of the situation. Hobbes counsels complete submission to the all-powerful *Leviathan;* Rousseau, a fight for a recovery of at least some of our lost liberties. The "back to nature" movement with its hatred for the artificialities and conventionalities of civilization found its inspiration in Rousseau, the great Romanticist.

The nineteenth century gave a new turn to the philosophy of *evolutionism.* The theory of biological evolution, which is almost universally accepted today, was eagerly seized on by materialists of the last century as a way in which mind can be reduced to matter and man's specifically human characteristics leveled to mere continuations of ancestral animal traits. Since man evolved from animal ancestors of the herding type, man is naturally social, but his sociality is only a more developed form of his instinctual gregariousness rather than a product of his intelligent and free conformity to his moral requirements. The tendency today is to recognize the evolutionary aspect of this view without necessarily interpreting it in a materialistic sense.

The view that man is not naturally social has some plausibility to it:

1. There is much truth in Hobbes' oversimplified description. Think away the products of human convention, and what is left is man's natural condition. Each man competes for food, protects himself against wild beasts, and hoards against all comers what he can wrest from niggardly nature. Man's greatest enemy is man, the only one with intelligence like himself to outwit him. To stop the wasteful war of all against all, his natural condition, he fashions the social contract by agreement with other men and thus creates society by his own intellect and will. Society is thus a conventional and artificial product of man's own ingenuity.

2. One can discount Rousseau's romantic picture of man's natural condition, but even in those regions in which struggle for survival was less acute, men would see the advantages of cooperation, with cooperation would come quarrels, and again the need of a social contract as a means of living peacefully and safely with others. Here also society is something to which nature is indifferent, something that man has introduced, something conventional and artificial which man pays for by the loss of much that was natural.

3. Society would not have arisen until man was sufficiently evolved to reflect on himself, to set his own purposes and choose the means to them. If we distinguish the social tendency from the herding instinct, we see that man is naturally gregarious and has lifted this instinct to the social level by his own intelligence. Society is thus something that man himself has added to his nature, a human contrivance that he must constantly modify to suit his continuing cultural development.

4. The growth of man's social consciousness over the ages shows the artificiality of human society. It took man ages to emerge from the tribal condition to political organization. Only recently has he become conscious of such global troubles as war, racism, poverty, and ecology. They are problems he has artificially created, to which he has not yet found the solution. Since the problems are not natural, neither is the society from which they spring.

Opponents admit most of the facts here cited but say that they have to do only with the form society took in particular instances and do not show that man is not meant by his nature to live in some kind of society. Their arguments:

1. Man abhors solitude and craves companionship. Some solitude is good for man, perhaps more than most men have, but excessive solitude can go so far as to unhinge reason. Men spontaneously seek others and enjoy their company, whereas loneliness sets up a veritable hunger in the soul. Hobbes' picture fits some miserable

outcast from the tribe, not the normal situation. Even primitive man had relatives and friends, without whom survival must have been nearly impossible. The more primitive the society, the more immediately dependent a man is on it.

2. Man cannot take care of himself alone. The child must be reared by its parents for many years. Even in adult life a solitary man cannot supply himself with the bare means of subsistence, not to speak of the goods required for living a decent life befitting a human being. Without the family no children grow up, and living in the family implies cooperation right from the beginning of each one's life. The mode of cooperation may be by convention or agreement, but the fact of cooperation is a requirement of man's nature for any kind of life at all.

3. The gift of language fits man to communicate with his fellows, to discuss projects of common interest, to agree on means and ends for cooperative effort. Thus the ability of speech indicates that man was meant to live a social life. Speech itself is natural to man, though each particular language is a construction of human art. Likewise man's social tendencies are the form gregariousness naturally takes in an intelligent being, though capable of development by human ingenuity. Any particular culture is a work of human art and to this extent artificial, but to tend toward the development of some culture, although not natural to unintelligent animals, is natural to intelligent man. Only man has human nature, not his prehuman forebears, and only man's nature is claimed to be social.

4. Intellectual and moral development require constant communication of ideas among men, an exchange possible only in society. If small, isolated communities stagnate because they are out of touch with new ideas, how much more would this condition be true of single individuals? That man's social consciousness has grown

over the ages hardly shows that society is not natural. What is more natural than growth? That man is now becoming more conscious of global social problems is a hopeful sign that he is gradually edging closer to social maturity.

What emerges from this discussion is the conclusion that man is social by nature and that society is natural to man. But socialization is no automatically operating instinct. Rather, it is a demand on his mind and will to set up for himself a mode of living with his fellowmen that will satisfy his needs as a human being for safety and fulfillment, and that will extend these benefits to the rest of mankind. The methods are largely left to his own ingenuity, and the actual societies that he forms, this particular family and this particular state, are human products. The imperfections of society come from the fact that man is only partially successful in this effort, just as he is only partially successful in his private life. As he has the moral obligation to seek constantly his own personal improvement, so he has the moral obligation to work with others for the social betterment of all mankind.

It is not enough for society that men live together and haphazardly give one another occasional assistance when the mood strikes them. Mere communal living is not necessarily society. For society some organization is required, whereby men at least implicitly bind themselves to cooperate for common ends by the use of common means, each guaranteeing his help to the rest so that all can depend on it. When men bind themselves together in this fashion, they have formed a society in the strict sense. Since they so act by the prompting of nature, society is natural to man. Insofar as the means to be used and the mode of organization are not determined by nature but chosen by man, society can be regarded as a work of human artifice and contrivance.

Society is essential to man in general

Not every individual must live in society, nor is a hermit's life wrong in itself. Society can get along without the few who count themselves out by renouncing both its burdens and benefits, so long as they do nothing to impede its functioning. A solitary life can be good or bad depending on its motive, but it cannot be the life of most men. Aristotle is right in saying that the life of solitude is fit only for a beast or a god.*

DEFINITION OF SOCIETY

What sort of thing is society as it emerges from the foregoing discussion? We notice that several elements are necessary:

1. There can be no actually existing society without *members*. Only rational beings can form a society, since it is a union based on agreement of wills. The number of persons is not specified, but there must be at least two; otherwise there can be no togetherness or commonness of interests and activity.

2. The members must be united in a *stable*, or *enduring*, way. A single act of working together may be only a haphazard occurrence. The union need not last forever or for life but must last for some considerable time.

3. The members must *cooperate*, or work together for the attainment of some *end*. This end will be some *common good* that all the members will share in and that no member could accomplish singly. The end differs for each kind of society and determines the nature of the society more than any other factor.

4. Society is held together by bonds, *moral bonds* of means and end. Either the members bind themselves by contract, pledge, or agreement, or else the bonds are imposed on them by some law, natural or positive. It is this moral bond that dis-

tinguishes a society from a crowd, makes the individuals committed members, and obliges them to their commitment.

5. To guide the cooperative effort to the common good, society must be equipped with that moral power called *authority*. Authority is the right to determine the means and direct the members in their use.

Hence society may be defined as an *enduring union of a number of persons morally bound under authority to cooperate for a common good.*

Some clarity may be found by putting it in terms of the Aristotelian four causes: The *material* cause is the members. The *formal* cause is the moral bond uniting the members. The *efficient* cause is the founder of the society for its origin, and later leaders for its continuance. The *final* cause is the common good sought by the members.

It is easily seen that society is not a physical thing. The only thing physical about it is the members and their actions. But it would be a mistake to say that society is not real. Of course, it is not a substance, for it has no existence of its own separate from the individuals who compose it; it is not a kind of superperson built out of people, as the living body is made up of cells. Metaphysically, society falls under the category of *relation*. A society is not a single relation but a number of relations unified and systematized into an *order*. These relations link men together in a definite way. An order is not a substantial entity distinct from the things that are ordered, but this does not mean that the order and the relations constituting it are not real. The order is real if there are real beings ordered in that way.

If society is not a physical being, what kind of being is it? It has more than ideal or mental being, for that would only make it an idea or thought in the mind of some thinker. Perhaps it is best called a *moral being*. Not every relation, but only a uni-

---

*Aristotle, *Politics*, bk. I, ch. 2, 1253a 29.

fied system of relations, is an order. Not every order, but only an order resulting from a human act, a decision of the will relating means to end, is a moral being. Not every moral being, but only a moral being resulting from the simultaneous decisions of many human wills to cooperate toward a common end and achieve a common good, is a society.

THE COMMON GOOD

The common good is the end for which society exists. The common good is an intermediate end, an end that is also a means toward man's ultimate end. To say that the common good is *the* end of society means that it is the end that is distinctive of society as such. Society is a temporal thing, and it exists for a good realizable in this world.

The common good is the temporal welfare of the community, taken both collectively and distributively. The collectivist stresses the first element only, making the common good an entity over and above the individual good, the former absorbing the latter. The individualist sees only the second element, making the common good a mere sum of individual goods. An adequate view of society and the common good must find a place between these extremes. The common good is realized only in the individuals who make up society, but it is a good that they could achieve only by the interaction of many cooperators.

To have a common good that can be the end of society, it is not enough that it concern several persons. That might give us two interdependent private goods, such as we find in contracts of exchange. If an employer is interested only in profits from business and an employee only in wages from his labor, each benefits the other, but they have not a common good in the strict sense. To have a common good as the end of their joint effort, the employer must be genuinely interested in the welfare of his employee, the employee must have at heart the success of the business he works for, and these two interests must be merged into one common enterprise. They must help each other not only accidentally, because their private goods are entangled, but essentially, because they share in the one same good. For lack of this common good, the employer-employee relation normally found today is not a society.

Negatively, the common good consists in the establishment and maintenance of *order*. Each knows his place, his relations to others, his rights and duties as compared with others' rights and duties toward him. Each can rely on the other not to interfere; each is guaranteed a wide enough scope for private action and the development of his own personality. There result peace, harmony, security, opportunity, and freedom. Cooperation for the maintenance of order must be done by all for the benefit of all and is thus a truly common good. But alone it is not enough.

Positively, the common good consists in giving to others and receiving from them powers and resources that as individuals none would possess. It is both active and passive, both supplementation and participation; a single word for it is *union,* or better, *communion.* Scattered raindrops over a wide enough area may, if added together, equal the force of a waterfall, but they cannot do the work of a waterfall harnessed to a turbine. The common good is not an arithmetical sum of each individual's contribution but something new resulting from the channeling of human energy and the mobilization of nature's resources. The economic products of an advanced civilization depend on the genius and labor of thousands of men who invented the machines, developed the processes, and continue to work them. The literature and art of a culture must be built up over the centuries and stored in books, monuments, libraries, and museums that we may now enjoy them and absorb the great minds of the past into our own. A family depends on the two sexes and the love between them; mutual protection and support exemplify the negative common good of order, but the begetting and rearing of children is the best illustration of the positive common good of communion.

The means society uses to develop and share the common good are often called *institutions,* such as schools, libraries, laboratories, hospitals, police, military forces, public utilities, corporations, banks, stock exchanges, law courts, and countless others. Some of them are also societies in their own right, but as institutions they are regarded as instrumental agencies used by society for storing and distributing the common good.

The common good is to be shared in by all. The negative aspect of the common good should be shared in *equally,* for it consists in the absence of interference and the affording of opportunity. Even if nature does not give equal opportunity to all, there should be no artificial human restrictions on such opportunities as nature does offer. The positive aspect of the common good should be shared in not equally but *proportionately.* The proportion is a blend of equal and unequal elements. There should be equality between one's contribution to society and one's share in the distribution of society's benefits, but since not all contribute equally, neither should all receive equally. This establishment of social justice, the foremost task of society, is so difficult that in this imperfect world we can hope for no more than an approximation.

The dynamic character of the common good becomes apparent here. It is the end of society, but, since it is never perfectly attained, society is never static. Temporal welfare is a thing that can be constantly bettered. Even if a society should once achieve a condition of perfect social justice, new conditions would arise with new difficulties to be met, and the problem of adjustment would have to be faced anew. The common good is thus the driving force in social progress.

If the common good is constantly changing, how can men agree on it so as to will it together? The common good taken formally, or abstractly (the general welfare as such, without specifying anything definite), always remains the same abstract ideal and must be willed by all the members of society. Thus society always has an end and the same end. But the common good taken materially, or concretely (the specific good to be achieved here and now and the means to it), varies with circumstances and need not be willed or even known by each and every member; it is sufficient that each accomplish his part. Each soldier wills victory, the abstract common good, but only the high command plans the precise steps by which the battle is won, the concrete common good. Each nation in the world wills or ought to will peace, the abstract common good, but how to achieve it, the concrete common good, has so far eluded us. How the parts the members play fit together is determined and willed by the leaders of society in their exercise of authority.

AUTHORITY IN SOCIETY

Authority is the right of a society to direct and control the members so that they cooperate toward the attainment of the end of that society. It should be evident that no society can function without authority, but this proposition is denied by the *anarchists.* They argue that social life and the absence of all restraint are compatible, that authority is necessary now only because of the imperfect condition of society. They say that society has evolved from despotic to monarchic, from monarchic to aristocratic, from aristocratic to democratic, and that the next step should be from democratic to anarchic. There is a gradual lessening of authority as man rises to a higher degree of development. Communists, despite their differences with the anarchists, have the same idea of the fully developed communist society, when "the state will have withered away." The difference is rather about the means of accomplishing this end than about the character of the goal itself.

Anarchism is understandable as a reaction against the abuse of authority in an overly regimented society, but it takes an exaggeratedly optimistic view of human nature. We must take human nature as it is, untinted with any rosy colors supplied by our imagination. A realistic appraisal shows that no society could endure without authority. Authority is needed:

1. *To remedy ignorance.* Only the more general principles of good living are evident to all; the remote conclusions are not easily grasped and must be enforced by one having the moral power or authority to do so for the common good and public order.

2. *To enforce justice.* Men are eager to claim benefits but prone to shirk duties; someone must see to it that both are distributed fairly, and that the greedy are restrained and the slothful stimulated. Besides direction, enforcement with the right to use penalties is necessary.

3. *To provide leadership.* Though all may agree on the end of human society, there may be many disputes on the means to be used in attaining the end; someone must be empowered to choose the means and to insist on the cooperative use of the means chosen. Cooperation is impossible without direction and control.

Authority is therefore essential to every society, since without it the society cannot exist or fulfill its function. The first two points mentioned stress the *substitutional* function of authority, by which it remedies human deficiencies either of intellect or of will. This kind of authority tends to diminish and become unnecessary the more it fulfills its function; thus paternal authority disappears when the child reaches adulthood, and corrective authority ceases when the delinquent has been reformed. A chief difficulty of the anarchists is that they consider this function of authority alone. The third point mentioned brings out the *essential* function of authority, which would exist even in a society of perfect human beings. Because there could be several sets of equally effective means to the end, yet only one set can be used cooperatively, someone would have to choose between them and prescribe the one to use.

NATURAL AND CONVENTIONAL SOCIETIES

When it is said that man is naturally social, that he lives in society and that society is natural to him, no reference is made to any specific grouping. Society in this sense is the abstract concept of men living together in interdependence and interaction for the sake of some unspecified common good. This is *society* but not *a society*. It is society-at-large, so to speak, the whole community of mankind, but not a definite social entity. In concrete fact men break up into numerous overlapping divisions, each of which is a society in the definite sense.

Some of these societies are informal and unorganized *groups*: ethnic, linguistic, geographical, neighborhood, class, and cultural. They are united by the fact of their common location or interest rather than by any deliberate act of the will. They find themselves together rather than get together. Opposed to these are *associations* or *organizations*, which are deliberately instituted with a determinate structure for specified ends under a definite authority. These groups are societies in the strictest sense. There are many kinds, but for our urpose we classify them under two main eadings: conventional and natural.

Conventional societies are artificial products of human contrivance, founded by ne free agreement of men who set the nd and choose the means. Clubs, fraernities, athletic leagues, business firms, bor unions—all such organizations are onventional. They may be established or bolished without affecting human nature s such. If some of them are necessary to fe as we know it, their necessity is not bsolute but dependent on historical conngencies that are not universal, and for hem other arrangements could be subtituted.

Natural societies, on the other hand, are hose conceived of as required by nature nd having their end set by nature. The ature referred to here is human nature, nasmuch as man, reasoning on his own ature and its needs, perceives that he is norally obliged to form such societies, ince without them he would be unable o live in a way consonant with his human lignity. Are there any such natural soieties? The mere fact that it is natural o man to live in society does not lead to he conclusion that nature specifies any lefinite societies to which he must belong. This question must therefore be settled ndependently for each society for which his claim is made. For the time being we an note that the commonly held specific natural societies are two: the family and he state.

Before taking up each of these societies n turn, it will be helpful to see the different ways in which authority manifests tself in conventional and in natural soieties, and thus bring out the ethical importance of this social topic.

In a *conventional* society authority comes from the members contracting to organize themselves, who vest the authority in a head or leader of their choosing, either a single person or some type of governing board. With no authority there would be no society; but since the authority is wholly conferred by the members, they can withdraw it, limit it, or extend it as they please. In such a society the right of direction and control is hypothetical, for it affects a person only so long as he is a member; the extreme penalty for disobedience is expulsion from the society. Any member is free to repudiate the authority by resigning from the organization. Hence, if the family and the state were only conventional societies, they could have no more authority than the contracting parties in marriage or the founding fathers of the state possessed as individual persons, and association with these societies would be terminable at pleasure. Man would have no more obligation to them than is contained in the voluntary contract of membership.

In a *natural* society, supposing for the time being that the family and the state are such, a very different situation prevails. Men enter into natural societies by the prompting of their human nature and remain members by the continuing demand of their nature. Fulfillment of their duty as members of a natural society is enjoined on them by the very requirements of human living and cannot be extinguished by expulsion or resignation from the society. A natural society supposes a scope of authority, an extent of direction and control, a right to inject itself into the lives of its members and demand of them the utmost in loyalty and dedication, which the members as individuals never had or can have. Hence authority in a natural society cannot come from the individuals composing the society, since they do not have it to give, but has to come from some higher source.

What could such a higher source be? The natural law theorists find it in natural law. For them a natural society is one that is required by natural law and has its authority conferred on it by natural law. But just as there are some who find

251

natural law objectionable but accept natural rights, which they may prefer to name human rights, so there are those, mostly the same ones, who disapprove of natural law but see the necessity of natural societies or, as they may prefer to call them, natural institutions. If they do not wish to appeal to natural law, they may find a satisfactory basis in the dignity of the human person. What is important here is that such societies or institutions are required by the kind of being a human person is; because of the dignity of the human person which no one can renounce, they are equipped with authority to confer moral rights and impose moral duties of a type more stringent than can result from mere human agreement.

Here the theist is in a better position than the nontheist. On the theist's premises, a natural society is ultimately traced to the author of man's nature. Authority in a natural society is conferred by God, who created man with a social nature and is thus the ultimate founder of natural societies, which he equips with all they need for their proper functioning. Not that he dictates the exact structure of the society or picks out the persons to lead it, but through the natural law he gives authority to the society and its leaders as soon as man, by the prompting of the natural law, brings the society into being.

SUMMARY

Is society natural to man?

That man is not naturally social, but that all society results from convention, is claimed: man is a natural predator and wars against all, man passed from a natural to a social state by a man-made social contract, man had to evolve intellectually before he could become social, and man's work of socializing himself is not yet finished.

That man is naturally social is argued from these properties of human nature:

man abhors solitude and craves companionship, man cannot supply even his basic needs alone, language fits man for communication and cooperation, and progress in culture is impossible outside society.

The conclusion that emerges is that man is obliged by his nature to form society and live in it, but the detailed shape society takes is the work of man's own art.

Society may be *defined* as an enduring union of a number of persons morally bound under authority to cooperate for a common good. The four causes of society are *material,* the members; *formal,* the moral bond; *efficient,* the founder; and *final,* the end or common good. Society is not a physical thing distinct from the members but a moral being consisting of a system of real relations coordinating the members' activities among themselves and toward a common end.

The *common good* consists negatively in *order,* a maintenance of peace and affording of opportunity, and positively in *communion,* an increase of powers by their mutual supplementation. Institutions are means established for the storing and distribution of the common good. Social justice is the equal or proportionate sharing by the members in the common good.

Anarchists think that society can get along without authority. This opinion is too optimistic, for what is socially good for man is not known equally by all, benefits and burdens must be distributed fairly to all, and someone must choose among various means the ones to be cooperatively used.

Besides society-at-large, there are particular societies existing as unorganized *groups* or organized *associations.* Societies are *natural* or *conventional,* according as they are requirements of human nature itself or have no other basis than the free agreement of men. Two natural societies are recognized: the family and the state.

Authority in a conventional society

comes from the members, and one may quit at will. Authority in a natural society must come from a higher source, since it binds individual members more strongly than they can bind themselves. Even apart from natural law, it can be deduced from the dignity and requirements of the human person. Most logically it is derived from the natural law proximately and from God ultimately.

QUESTIONS FOR DISCUSSION

1 If man is naturally a social being, how do we explain his antisocial tendencies, the constant wars, fights, and quarrels that mar his every attempt to organize himself socially?

2 Society exists for the common good, but the common good seems to mean nothing more than the social good. That society should exist for the social good is an empty truism. Can this statement be made more definite?

3 How is the common good determined? What society puts the determination of this common good up for vote among the members? Does each society have a different common good? If it is different, what is common about it?

4 If man is naturally social, why should society need authority? Authority is needed only to repress the antisocial element in society. Is not authority only accidental to society, and should it not disappear as society progresses?

5 To say that all authority comes from God is to say that man has no authority in himself, that there can be no such thing as sovereignty of the people, and that man has to go to God or his representatives for every social decision. How is this common objection answered?

READINGS

The ancients did not treat of society apart from its specific forms, such as the family and the state.

The following modern authors have matter pertinent to this chapter: Johannes Messner, *Social Ethics*, bk. I, pt. II, but the whole is a monumental work on all phases of society; Heinrich Rommen, *The State in Catholic Thought*, ch. 1 on social being and ch. 13 on the common good; Yves Simon, *The Nature and Functions of Authority*, a lecture expanded and developed in *The Philosophy of Democratic Government*, ch. 1; and Frank Sheed, *Society and Sanity*.

All books on sociology necessarily treat of society, but not all from a philosophical or ethical standpoint. The following have interesting chapters on most of the forms of society and social disorders to be discussed later: Walter Lippmann, *The Good Society*; Pitrim Sorokin, *The Crisis of Our Age*, and other works; Gabriel Marcel, *Man Against Mass Society*; David Riesman, *The Lonely Crowd*; Harvey Cox, *The Secular City*; and many other popular works.

Austin Fagothey, *Right and Reason—an Anthology*, contains Aristotle's *Politics*, bk. I, ch. 1-2; Hobbes', *Leviathan*, ch. 13-15, 17; Rousseau's *Social Contract*, bk. I, ch. 1-6, 8; St. Augustine's *City of God*, bk. XIX, ch. 12-14, 17; St. Thomas' *Treatise on Law*.

CHAPTER 23

FAMILY

PROBLEM

If any group of human beings has the right to be called a society, that group is the family. Furthermore, if any society can call itself a natural society, there can be no better claim than that of the family. In every group of human beings, from the most primitive to the most cultivated, we find the family immemorially entrenched. Human sexuality naturally dictates a union of man and woman, and nature provides the children, whose care further cements the union of husband and wife. It is no wonder that marriage has been considered a natural institution.

But the philosopher cannot take anything for granted. He has to ask whether it is so and why it is so. Ever since the beginning of ethics and the Greeks' first probing into human customs, the question was raised whether marriage is a natural institution necessary for the human race or only the prevailing convention we have grown to accept as a matter of course. If the former, it would seem that marriage is the only morally allowable arrangement between the sexes; if the latter, marriage may still be the most desirable arrangement but not the only possible one even from the ethical standpoint. If marriage is a natural institution, the family is a natural society; otherwise it is not. The importance of this question for ethics is obvious.

Other questions immediately follow. Who can marry, why do they marry, how do they marry, how many wives or husbands may one have, how long does the marriage last, what happens when a marriage goes bad? We have space in this survey for only the most basic questions. We ask:

1. What is marriage?
2. Is marriage a natural institution?
3. What are the conditions of the marriage contract?
4. Must all marriage be monogamous?
5. What about divorce?

MARRIAGE AND THE FAMILY

We begin with a description of the family as existing today and through most of history. In former times the word *family* was extended in two different ways: it included all blood relatives, whether they lived together or not; on the other hand, it also meant all who lived together in the same household, including servants, retainers, and other nonrelated persons. We take the more restricted meaning of the word: the family is a society consisting of husband or father, wife or mother, and their children.

The family, or domestic society, consists of two components, or subsocieties: a horizontal component, the union of husband and wife, called *conjugal* society; and a vertical component, the union of parents and children, called *parental* society. There are not really two distinct societies, but two aspects or directors within the family. Accidentally a family may have one component only, but this is not the normal case.

The *material* cause of the family, as of all societies, consists of the members or persons constituting it: a man, a woman, and their children. The *formal* cause is the moral bond between them, consisting of a definite group of rights and duties, guaranteed by contract in conjugal society and imposed by the nature of things in parental society. The *final* cause of the family is the good of all parties concerned, achieved by their living together in mutual love. The *efficient* cause of the family is the contract of marriage, or more properly the contracting parties, for by marriage the family is brought into existence and maintained.

Marriage may be considered as the act of getting married (wedding) or as the state of being married (wedlock). The first is the marriage contract, by which a man and a woman give and receive rights and duties toward each other concerning cohabitation and intercourse. As a state, marriage is a society or lasting union of a man and a woman resulting from such a contract. We shall consider the state of marriage first, for people get married in order to live in the married state; hence the nature and conditions of the contract are determined from the state that the contract aims to produce.

The state of marriage implies four chief conditions:

1. There must be a union of *opposite sexes*. Since marriage has to do with the reproduction of the human race, this requirement is obvious. Thus marriage differs from homosexuality and autoeroticism. Marriage is not necessarily between only one man and only one woman, though monogamy is considered the ideal.

2. Marriage is a *permanent* union. It must last at least as long as is necessary for the fulfillment of its purpose and the discharge of its obligations, and hence until the last child is capable of living an independent life. Thus marriage differs from promiscuity. Marriage, at least when con-

tracted, is intended to involve lifelong permanence.

3. It is an *exclusive* union. The partners agree to share relations only with each other, so that extramarital acts are a violation of justice. Thus adultery is a crime against marriage.

4. Its permanence and exclusiveness are guaranteed by *contract*. Mere living together without being bound to do so does not constitute marriage, even though the partners actually remain together for life, because they do not form a society. This contract makes the difference between marriage and concubinage.

MARRIAGE AS NATURAL OR CONVENTIONAL

There are those who favor the view that man gradually developed from primitive promiscuity through various forms of polygamy to the monogamous marriage, the stage corresponding to his present development; future evolution will probably lead on to some more advanced arrangement; hence, though man may be naturally social in a broad sense, marriage is a purely human institution that may be abandoned for something better. Those moral positivists who hold that man is not naturally social should logically deny that the family is a natural society, but they seem to be thinking rather of the political state than of the family in this connection; at any rate Rousseau° says that the family is the only natural society. Those who hold that marriage is merely conventional may advocate the abolition of the convention in favor of freer relations between the sexes, or they may think that on utilitarian grounds it is an excellent convention by all means to be maintained.

On the other hand, the prevailing and traditional belief is that marriage is no

---

°Rousseau, *Social Contract*, bk. I, ch. 2.

mere convention but a natural institution. Aristotle's sagacious words deserve quoting because they contain the germ of the argument as well as a penetrating insight into human nature:

Between man and wife friendship seems to exist by nature; for man is naturally inclined to form couples—even more than to form cities, inasmuch as the household is earlier and more necessary than the city, and reproduction is more common to man with the animals.° With the other animals the union extends only to this point, but human beings live together not only for the sake of reproduction but also for the various purposes of life; from the start the functions are divided, and those of man and woman are different; so they help each other by throwing their peculiar gifts into the common stock. It is for these reasons that both utility and pleasure seem to be found in this kind of friendship. But this friendship may be based also on virtue, if the parties are good; for each has its own virtue and they will delight in the fact. And children seem to be a bond of union (which is the reason why childless people part more easily); for children are a common good to both and what is common holds them together.†

The Thomistic statement is built on this passage but casts the idea into a more formal type of argument:

That is said to be natural to which nature inclines, although it comes to pass through the intervention of the free will; thus acts of virtue and the virtues themselves are called natural; and in this way matrimony is natural, because natural reason inclines thereto in two ways. First, in relation to the principal end of matrimony, namely the good of the offspring. For nature intends not only the begetting of offspring, but also its education and development until it reach the perfect state of man as man, and that is the state of virtue. Hence, according to the Philosopher‡ we derive three things from our parents, namely existence, nourishment, and education. Now a child cannot

be brought up and instructed unless it have certain and definite parents, and this would not be the case unless there were a tie between the man and a definite woman, and it is in this way that matrimony consists. Secondly, in relation to the secondary end of matrimony, which is the mutual services which married persons render one another in household matters. For just as natural reason dictates that men should live together, since one is not self-sufficient in all things concerning life, for which reason man is described as being naturally inclined to political society, so too among those works that are necessary for human life some are becoming to men, others to women. Wherefore nature inculcated that society of man and woman which consists in matrimony.°

The argument may be restated in the following fashion, carrying it along by steps and bringing out each point expressly:

1. Nature intends the continuance of the human race, because nature has given human beings the faculty and instinct for reproduction. Nature intends that this occur by a union of man and woman, because human beings are made to reproduce in the sexual manner. People may marry for a variety of motives, for love, for companionship, for money, for position. The idea of begetting children may be very subordinate, perhaps only tolerated rather than desired, in the minds of many marrying couples; it need not be psychologically uppermost in their minds. There is no doubt, however, that it is uppermost in nature's design. Men eat mostly for the pleasure of it and rarely think of its necessity for sustaining life; yet they recognize on reflection that the latter is the objective purpose of eating. The same is true regarding the sexual relation; it may be done for a number of subjective reasons, such as pleasure or attraction or love, but its objective, natural purpose is to sustain the race. In race preservation, nature has not trusted to logic, by which man might reason to his duty in this

---

°"Reproduction is more common to man with the animals" than forming cities is common to man with the animals. Reproduction is common to man and *all* animals, but political or quasi-political organization is common to man and *some* animals only, such as bees and ants.
†Aristotle, *Nicomachean Ethics*, bk. VIII, ch. 12, 1162a 16-28.
‡*Ibid.*, ch. 11, 1161a 17.

°St. Thomas, *Summa Theologica*, III, Supplement, q. 41, a. 1.

regard, but has implanted an instinct so strong that most human beings follow it. Thus the whole economy of nature in establishing the sexes leads to the child.

2. The duty of caring for the child naturally devolves on the parents. The parents are the cause of the child's existence and therefore are charged with caring for its welfare. There is nothing so helpless as the human infant. Some animals can fend for themselves shortly after birth, and none require a long period of care. Natural instinct prompts the parent animals, when both are necessary, to remain together until the offspring are sufficiently reared to care for themselves. In no case does this last until the next mating season, and therefore promiscuous mating does no harm to the offspring of animals and allows well for the fulfillment of nature's purpose. The same cannot be said of human beings. The human child cannot live at all without intense care for several years, and on the whole needs from fifteen to twenty years of rearing before it is really able to live a fully independent human life. The ones equipped by nature with the means for rearing the child and normally impelled to it by natural instinct and love are the parents. Other agencies are poor makeshifts in this regard. Therefore the parents are designated by nature as the child's proper guardians.

3. The duty of rearing the child belongs to both parents, and not to one alone. That this duty belongs to the mother is clear from the fact that she must bear the child and nurse it; otherwise it cannot survive even the first few days of life. But the father is equally the cause of the child's existence and therefore is equally charged by nature with the child's welfare. Together they gave the child life and together they must care for it, not in lives apart and independent, but in that joint life which makes up the society of the family. Ordinarily neither mother nor child can procure the means of subsistence, and who

else in nature's plan has this duty except the father, the one responsible for the condition of mother and child? The possibility that the mother may have wealth of her own is accidental and outside of nature's provision. The help of the father is necessary, not only in the first years of the child's life but throughout the whole period of the child's rearing. In fact, it is rather toward the latter part of the training period that the father's influence is most necessary, when he must fit his children, especially the boys, to take their place in human life. Nature has given father and mother different capacities that are psychologically as well as physically complementary, and the influence of the father's sternness as well as of the mother's sweetness is necessary for the adequate training of the child.

From these three points it follows that nature demands a permanent and exclusive union between the sexes, and one guaranteed by contract, in other words, that marriage is a natural institution.

Those who hold that marriage is not a natural but only a conventional institution do not usually deny the facts cited in the argument given but deny that they warrant the conclusion drawn from them. In particular:

1. We must give some explanation why marriage is so widespread a phenomenon, but the fact that it has been universal up to now does not prove that it is necessary for all time. Children must be taken care of and provided with a home, but communal care in state nurseries might accomplish the same end as well or better. Parents had to care for them when no one else could, but we have now arrived at a condition of social organization when parents can be relieved of this obligation and can pursue their independent careers free of this all-absorbing hindrance.

2. When a man and a woman remain together, either for the sake of the child or for the sake of each other, why should they have to bind themselves by contract?

Their actual love for each other or their duty to the child should be enough to hold them together; when it is not, no mere ceremonial contract will make much difference. The marriage contract should be optional for those who want it, but it should not be necessary for all who intend to live together.

3. If the argument for marriage as a natural institution is drawn from the parents' obligation to the child, it would seem that childless marriages are not really marriages but only attempts at marriage. When it becomes evident that no children will be forthcoming, the parties should be free to separate and seek fruitful unions elsewhere.

4. The argument supposes that the help of both mother and father working together is necessary for the upbringing of the child, but nature sometimes allows the child to be deprived of father or mother or both. Why should human beings be obliged by nature to accomplish an end set by nature, when nature itself often fails to keep its own law? If marriage is regarded as a mere human convention, not so much is expected of it.

5. If marriage is a natural institution, then it should be contrary to nature not to marry. What is natural to man pertains to all who have human nature. Those who uphold marriage as a natural institution should agree with those who condemn voluntary celibacy as a failure to fulfill a natural duty. Yet some want illogically to approve both states as natural.

6. A natural institution should not be capable of so much mismanagement and unhappiness. Marriage cannot be regarded as particularly successful among human endeavors. That there have been happy marriages goes without saying, but one of the greatest sources of human misery is a brace of mismatched partners whose home is a den of spite and strife. How can one say that it is natural for them to remain together? If marriage is conventional, a bad marriage is but a human mistake which the partners can rectify by agreeing to disband.

7. Marriage contains too much in it of human contrivance to be called natural. Nature does not tell whether one should marry, does not select the partners, does not teach married couples how to get along with each other, does not prescribe just how to raise the children, does not automatically supply the family with its needs. All these things must be discovered by human ingenuity. Why not say that the whole institution is only a human device and one that man seems to be rapidly outgrowing?

Those who hold that marriage is a natural institution find these objections unconvincing.

1. Modern psychology reinforces what has always been known: the child's need for love. If state-operated institutions can take care of some children, as they do, enough of them could take care of all, but this institutional upbringing is a poor makeshift for the home. We have to resort to it when necessary but recognize that it is far from the ideal. There is no substitute for the child's experience of its parents' personal love. Events over which they have no control excuse parents from their obligation, but they are not allowed to shed it voluntarily.

2. Parental society requires no contract, since the infant cannot make a contract, and later on it finds itself already a member of parental society by disposition of nature itself. The same is not true of conjugal society, which is entered into freely by adults. Each must be assured of the other partner's faithfulness before assuming the heavy burdens that marriage entails. An implicit understanding might do for the partners themselves, but marriage is a public and social affair, not solely a private and personal one. Public order requires that it be publicly known who is married to whom and where responsibility for the family lies. Thus society has a right to in-

sist on the registration of marriages and other formalities.

3. There is no marriage unless the partners transfer rights and assume duties toward one another, which in the normal course of nature should issue in the existence of children. Nature sets the end but does not guarantee that it will be attained in every case. Childless couples form a family in its conjugal relation, even though the parental relation never becomes actualized. They have the same duties toward one another as any other married couple, but their duties as parents are in abeyance so long as they have no child.

4. The design of nature must be judged from the normal instance. Loss of a parent, and much more of both, is a great misfortune in a child's life. Nothing in nature ensures against misfortune, and a parent's early death is one. Those who are alive and able to fulfill their obligations are not excused because of other people's death or inability. Adoption into another family is the best way of caring for orphans, but this supposes that there should be families. If the family is natural, nature here supplies its own remedy.

5. Marriage is a duty for the race but not for the individual. The individual's good can be obtained only by the individual's effort; thus no man can live by getting others to eat for him, but the good of the race can be obtained if a sufficient number tend toward it. Marriage would be a duty for each individual only if the human race would be in danger of dying out, but there is little need to fear on this score.

6. Man can mismanage anything. The blame is not to be put on nature but on the mismanagers. Man can ruin his health, stultify his mind, pervert his will, squander nature's bounty, pollute the earth's surface, and even blow himself off the map. Abuse of these natural things does not render them not natural. That man reserves some of his most exquisite folly for the mismanagement of marriage does not make marriage any less natural.

7. What is natural to man does not preclude the use of human ingenuity but requires it. Since man's nature is rational and free, he is expected to use his rationality and freedom even in the exercise of those things which are most natural to him. Thus man follows the prompting of nature in entering into marriage and approving the existence of marriage in his society, but most of the details of marriage and family life are left to his ingenuity.

THE MARRIAGE CONTRACT

The married state of individuals begins by a contract entered into by the mutual free consent of the man and the woman. People are not born married and may remain unmarried throughout their lives. Nature does not select the partners for marriage. There must be something that determines *whether* one shall marry and *whom* one shall marry. Since nature does not determine it, the partners themselves do, and they do it by the marriage contract.

The marriage contract pertains to marriage in its institutional aspect. Some dislike the word *contract* as too businesslike and prefer *covenant* or *agreement*, but the word does not change the reality. *Contract* is a general word for any voluntary meeting of minds concerning the transfer of rights. Marriage is a contract in the full sense of the word. It must fulfill all the conditions requisite for a contract in general, as well as some peculiar to itself.* By it the parties transfer to each other strict rights and thereby incur toward each other strict duties, which they henceforth owe to each other in justice. The essential right transferred is the right to the use of the other person's body for the performance of the generative act. Cohabitation, support,

*See pp. 336-339 on contracts in general.

sharing of goods, and the like are consequent rights. The transference of the essential right is permanent and exclusive; failure to make it so invalidates the contract.

By its very nature as a contract, marriage requires mutual free consent and the absence of error and fear. Freedom of consent is particularly important in marriage, because marriage supposes love, and love cannot be extorted, besides the fact that marriage imposes heavy burdens that no one is obliged to assume, much less to assume in company with a particular person.

An impediment to marriage is some inability in the contracting party that makes the marriage contract either invalid or illicit. The first kind renders the contract null and void from the beginning, so that the parties never were actually married. The second kind simply makes it wrong for a person to marry under such conditions, but if he does so, the marriage contract holds. The chief invalidating impediments from nature itself are impotence, too close kinship, and being already married. The church, because of the religious and sacramental aspect of marriage, and the state, for the sake of the common good, can establish additional impediments of either grade.

The ban of kinship may need a few remarks. The crime of incest has always been regarded with particular horror. Any marriage between parent and child is absolutely outlawed by nature as utterly opposed to the parental relation already existing. Marriage between brother and sister is not absolutely contrary to nature, but the only condition under which it could be considered allowable would be that otherwise the race could not propagate. The reason for banning marriage between brother and sister is the fact that they grow up in the same home and develop during their immaturity a kind of love free from all passion; anything else

would mean the utter ruin of the family and make the home an unlivable place.

MONOGAMY OR POLYGAMY

That marriage must be between man and woman follows from its nature and purpose. Between how many men or women? The marriage of only one man with only one woman at the same time is *monogamy;* marriage to two at the same time is *bigamy;* marriage to more than one at the same time without specifying the number is *polygamy.* Polygamy is said of either sex; it is:

1. Polygyny, when one husband has more than one wife
2. Polyandry, when one wife has more than one husband

Polygyny does not wholly subvert the purpose of marriage. It places no hindrance to the birth of children and allows at least the essentials of the child's rearing. Each mother can devote herself to the rearing of her own children while supported by the father. Unless the number of wives is extremely large, the father also should be able to assist somewhat in the training of the children.

But polygyny falls far short of realizing the ideal of marriage. The father cannot give the same attention to the training of the children of several wives that he could give to those of one wife. The mutual love and help that should exist between husband and wife are weakened by being single in one direction and divided in the other. There can be no equality between husband and wife when she is only one among several, and there is little wonder that in polygamous countries the position of woman is not far above that of a slave. Jealousy among the wives is to be expected when each vies for the husband's favor and each is ambitious for her own children. Almost superhuman ingenuity is required of the husband to be perfectly fair to the wives and the children, and this kind of society seems possible only when the woman's condition is so degraded that her will does not count. Though such evils may occur in a monogamous family, they occur there only accidentally, through the fault of the parties concerned and not through the nature of the institution; but in a polygynous family these evils spring from the system and can be avoided only accidentally. Hence polygyny should not be approved as a morally acceptable form of marriage.

Polyandry wholly subverts the purpose of marriage. The only alleviating factor is that the several husbands would all be pledged to the support of one wife and all the children she would have. But material support is not the main element in marriage. The excuse of polygyny, quicker propagation of the race, is absent in polyandry, for a woman cannot bear more children to many husbands than to one. The rearing of the children as nature intends becomes impossible, because the father cannot be determined with certainty and is thus unable to perform his function of giving help and guidance to his children. The children would naturally quarrel over which husband is the father of which child. All the fathers might try to fulfill these duties to all the children or divide them arbitrarily, but the resulting relation cannot be truly parental.

STABILITY OR DIVORCE

We said before that marriage must be lasting, but we did not say for how long. Can it be dissolved, or must it last until the death of one of the partners? Married persons may break up their home in either of two ways:

1. By separation from bed and board
2. By attempted dissolution of the marriage bond

A *separation* means that the two parties cease to live together and to discharge marital functions but remain married; the marriage bond remains intact so that neither party is free to contract a new marriage. It is easy to see that such a separation is sometimes necessary, but it should be undertaken only for the gravest of reasons. People who intend only a separation may sometimes have to obtain a civil divorce to protect themselves from the other party, to gain support for and custody of the children, or to effect a civilly valid distribution of property. Divorce in such cases touches only the civil effects of marriage and need not be intended to dissolve the marriage bond.

The term *divorce* is usually understood to mean an attempt to dissolve the marriage bond itself, so that the parties are free to contract new marriages with other persons. Divorce, like the marriage contract that it tries to dissolve, is regulated by ecclesiastical and civil law. We are obliged to consider the matter from the standpoint of natural morality alone, a limitation that necessarily makes our treatment incomplete.

Parents' duties to their children require that the marriage endure until the family is fully reared. Marriage, as we saw, has as its aim not only the begetting but also the rearing of children. Nature itself requires that marriage last until this end is accomplished, until the child is fully reared and able to live an independent life of its own. To rear one child normally takes from fifteen to twenty years, but if the parents must live together for that time, other children are ordinarily to be expected. Hence marriage must last for at least fifteen years after the birth of the youngest child. The woman is capable of bearing children up to the age of about 45 years. Normally, therefore, marriage must last until husband and wife are 60 years old.

Love between the married couple requires that the marriage last until the death of one of the partners. When married people have reached advanced age, hardly any reason could justify a separation. Life together could not have been too intolerable. Most separations occur in the early years of marriage, in the difficult period of mutual adjustment, when the romantic mist has blown away to reveal each to the other in the hard light of reality. It would be absurd to think that this has not already happened to an elderly couple who have shared all the joys and sorrows of life together for so long. The man is the natural support of the woman, and he who has enjoyed her whole period of youth, beauty, and fertility owes her love and protection in her old age. Likewise the woman who has taken her husband's support and protection in the years of his strength cannot leave him to loneliness at the end. And what kind of rearing would parents give to their children if they ruined it all by the bad example of breaking up their own home in their old age?

The chief reason against divorce is the havoc it works in the life of the child. The child is the one who pays for the parents' failure. Parents who break up the home deprive the child of the environment in which by the intention of nature it should grow up. Cases happen in which the child profits by being removed from a bad home, but nature considers what is normal, not what is accidental. The new husband or wife of a divorced person can often do quite well in rearing the children but in too many cases is bitterly resented. The children may love both their real parents and become confused as to which side to take or why they should have to take sides. The situation is anything but ideal.

Even the strongest proponents of divorce recognize it as a serious social evil and a breakdown in social morality. Those who consider marriage a mere human convention should logically allow divorce for the asking. In their view there should be nothing binding in the contract but the parties' continued will, even if they orig-inally meant it for life. If marriage is a natural institution, the case is different. Then marriage is a free contract in the sense that one may either marry or not, but the conditions of marriage are laid down by nature itself and not by the contracting parties, and the term for marriage is until the death of one of the partners.

How inexorable is nature? Take the case of a marriage that for some reason, whether it involves moral fault in either or both of the parties concerned or whether it is one of those situations that is nobody's fault, has gone so bad that there is no chance whatever of rehabilitating it. Must the parties, since they cannot live together, spend the rest of their lives in continent singleness until one of them dies? What is the reasonableness of demanding any such thing?

From the standpoint of pure reason it is hard to see any reasonableness in it. The marriage does not fulfill any of the purposes of marriage. Love is dead, the home is broken up, the children are not being reared by both parents together, and there will be no more children. Much stress has been placed on the wedge argument: that the granting of divorce for the gravest reasons gradually leads to a letting down of the bars until trifling excuses are accepted. History shows that there is a great deal of truth to this argument. However, we do not apply it with such absolute stringency to other affairs in life, and why should we do so here? It seems unjust to punish people who have genuinely valid reasons because others make the same demands under flimsy pretenses. Also, one can sermonize on how important a step marriage is, and how those who enter it hastily or with little sense of its serious obligations must pay the price of their folly. But not all divorced persons entered marriage hastily or foolishly, and those who did are now paying the price. In all the other affairs of life one can get out of an irredeemably bad bargain and start over. Against this it is argued that laws are made for the common good, and since divorce is ruinous to society generally, individuals will have to uphold the common good of marital stability at personal sacrifice. Any law, however, admits exceptions, especially where failure to do so would circumvent the purpose of the law itself. We have such a case here.

Thus the voice of reason seems to speak. But marriage has its religious as well as its natural aspect. Proof that no valid marriage can ever be dissolved will have to be sought from theological sources, and even here most religious bodies admit at least a few specified exceptions.

Nothing said here was meant to impugn the stability of marriage or to advocate divorce as a general remedy for marital unhappiness. There was question only of certain hopeless cases. Looking at the divorce record in most countries of the world today, one is forced to the conclusion that most divorces are morally unjustified. What is particularly noxious is the bad example of many prominent people who never intended their marriage to be stable and are willing to shuck husband or wife whenever a more desirable person comes in view. This form of successive polygamy has perhaps done most to make a mockery of marriage as a social institution. The antidote is to point to the many happy homes in which a healthy family life is actually flourishing.

SUMMARY

The family, the most primitive society, consists of two subsocieties: *conjugal*, the husband-wife relation, and *parental*, the parent-child relation. Marriage, which creates and maintains the family, means both the contract and the resulting state. The married state supposes a man and a woman united by contract in a permanent and exclusive union of shared life and love.

Is marriage merely a human convention or a natural institution? That it is a natural institution is argued thus:
1. Nature's design in establishing sex is the propagation of the race.
2. The parents' duty of caring for the child lasts over many years.
3. The rearing of the child belongs to both parents jointly.

Therefore nature demands a permanent and exclusive union guaranteed by contract—that is, marriage.

Objections: Children can be brought up in state-operated nurseries, a ceremonial contract is but an empty rite, sterile unions would not be marriages, nature often leaves orphans, all would have a natural duty to marry, a natural institution should not be open to so much abuse, and married life has to be run by human ingenuity.

Replies: Institutions cannot supply parental love, public order requires external formalities, childless couples have the conjugal relation, orphanhood is an unfortunate exception, marriage is a duty for the race but not for the individual, possibility of abuse does not make a thing not natural, and man is expected to use his rationality in natural matters.

By the marriage *contract* each transfers to the other the right to intercourse and cohabitation. It must fulfill all the requisites for contracts in general and be free of error and fear. Any fault in the essentials of the contract renders it invalid. Impotence, too close kinship, and being already married are natural impediments. Church and state may add others, rendering the contract either invalid or illicit.

Polygamy has two forms. *Polygyny*, one husband with several wives, makes the rearing of the children difficult, degrades the status of woman, fosters jealousy, and is divisive of the huband's love. *Polyandry*, one wife with several husbands, wholly subverts the purpose of marriage.

Divorce means not a mere separation

but an attempted dissolution of the marriage bond, so as to leave the partners free to remarry. Marriage requires the partners to remain together until the last child is reared; since they are then 60 years old, no justifying reason can be found for breaking the marriage. Accidentally divorce may not be harmful in individual cases, but its widespread practice is a serious social and moral evil.

QUESTIONS FOR DISCUSSION

1 Does it not seem anthropologically and sociologically established that religious taboos have turned man's natural promiscuity into the institution called marriage and that marriage is not natural to man but the result of convention?

2 Why should not marriage be optional, so that those who wish to proclaim their enduring union may celebrate it publicly, and those who prefer to keep such matters private may be free to do so?

3 Marriage is for love, and if love grows cold, it should be dissolved in favor of another marriage that will afford the parties greater love. Is marriage for man, or is man for the sake of some abstract entity called marriage?

4 Monogamy happens to be the prevailing convention here, polygamy elsewhere. To assert that monogamy is better is only a manifestation of our personal bias. How could so widespread an institution as polygamy be called unnatural?

5 A contract seems to make marriage into a sort of business affair, most glaringly in dynastic marriages and those planned by parents for family prestige. Are these really marriages or only economic and political arrangements?

READINGS

Plato's dissolution of the family for the guardians in his ideal state, *Republic*, bk. V, is well known. Aristotle's refutation is in the *Politics*, bk. II, ch. 1-4; otherwise he has only passing remarks on the family in the *Nicomachean Ethics*, bk. VIII, ch. 10-12, and in the *Politics*, bk. I, ch. 2.

The treatise on marriage in the *Summa Theologica*, pt. III, Supplement, qq. 41-68, added by St. Thomas' followers from his other writings, is mainly theological but discusses some philosophical aspects in qq. 41, 44-48, 51, 54, 65, 67.

The *Pastoral Constitution on the Church in the Modern World* of the Second Vatican Council is an important document that should be read; the theological viewpoint rests on a philosophical basis. John Ford and Gerald Kelly's *Contemporary Moral Theology*, vol. II, treats the whole of marriage and is one of the best expressions of the conservative attitude. Bertrand Russell, *Marriage and Morals*, represents the radical view.

Cardinal Suenens' *Love and Control* is excellent. See also: T. G. Wayne, *Morals and Marriage*, a little book for those contemplating marriage; Dietrich von Hildebrand's two short books, *Marriage* and *In Defense of Purity*; Jacques Leclercq, *Marriage and the Family*; Wingfield Hope, *Life Together*; and Gustave Thibon, *What God Has Joined Together*.

Austin Fagothey, *Right and Reason—an Anthology*, contains "The Virtue of Chastity" from John Macmurray's *Reason and Emotion*, which is remotely pertinent to this chapter.

CHAPTER 24

SEX

PROBLEM

The difficult but unavoidable problem of sex is thrust at us from every side. Since the dam of Victorian inhibitions has burst, the flood of sex has risen to overwhelm us in art, literature, psychology, advertising, journalism, and even conversation, until one begins to suffocate in it. Our treatment of it will be restrained, not that it is unimportant, but because there is no use adding another voice to the overpowering chorus. What was said about marriage and the family in the last chapter sufficiently indicates the meaning and function of sex in the world and disposes of a number of opinions that could be adopted only by those who see no essential value in marriage. If marriage is the institution dictated by nature for the proper use of sex in human beings, no use of sex unrelated to marriage can find any moral justification. We shall limit ourselves to a few questions in which it seems possible to say something on both sides. We ask:

1. What is the place of love and sex in marriage?
2. May married people have sex without children?
3. What ought to be said about premarital sex?

LOVE AND SEX IN MARRIAGE

In treating marriage as an institution, stress is placed on its objective, external, legal, and juridical aspect. This is unavoidable, for marriage is a social fact. Every government in the world finds it necessary to regulate marriage and to include domestic relations in its civil law; primitive tribes enforce with social sanctions their traditional marriage customs, and nearly every religion makes the wedding ceremony a religious rite. It is the business of the moralist to evaluate these practices, and thus he too must consider the institutional side of marriage.

Marriage is not only an institution; it is also a personal experience, one of the most profound a human being can undergo. Marriage cannot mean to the detached outsider what it means to the married couple, an intersubjective union unique to the two who share it and incommunicable to anyone else. Any discussion of marriage that omits the love of husband and wife is like an interpretation of a poem limited to the grammar of the sentences.

The traditional distinction between the primary and the secondary ends of marriage is out of favor today. It looked on marriage wholly from its institutional aspect. The primary end was seen as the perpetuation of the human race through the begetting and rearing of children. Begetting implies the moral obligation of rearing or education, which is to be understood in the broadest sense as full physical, mental, and moral development, fitting the children to face life, to pursue their ultimate goal, and to work with their fellows for the common good. This is the public task married people take on themselves, for which they are responsible, and for which they bind themselves into the permanent contractual union called marriage rather than meet in a temporary, indiscriminate union that would not be marriage.

In this older view the secondary ends of marriage were summed up in the mutual love and help exchanged between husband and wife. Chief among these would undoubtedly be the fulfillment of true human love, directed to the other as a person with qualities of mind, heart, and soul, and the intertwining of their lives in the mutual gift of each to the other. Included also were the goods of cohabitation: the companionship resulting from the fact that the two sexes are ideally suited to each other, since the qualities of man and woman are naturally supplementary; the legitimation of sexual desire, which most people are unable to forego but cannot satisfy in a moral way outside marriage; and the urge toward self-perpetuation, by which one leaves behind an image of onself and sets one's mark on the universe by carrying on the family strain. It should be noted that these ends, though called secondary, were never meant to be incidental or unimportant. They were called secondary because they take second place in a legal or juridical consideration of marriage as an institution, which could continue to exist without them.

The tendency today is to play down the distinction between primary and secondary ends of marriage because of misplaced emphasis. It is thought that marriage should not be looked at from the outside only, but more from the standpoint of the married couple. For them the legal and juridical aspect takes second place to the interpersonal love and intimacy that has changed their whole way of life. Hence it is suggested that there is but one overriding end of marriage, and that is *love*. Love is here to be taken in its widest possible scope and on all possible levels.

1. On the highest level love is between persons who are attracted to each other as persons. It is simultaneously self-fulfillment and fulfillment of the beloved. Each gives himself or herself to the other, so that in a sense the two lives are merged into one greater life. Together they share life's joys and bear up one another in life's sorrows. Love does not always require the intensity of romantic passion but shows itself more enduringly in quiet devotion. Marriage at its least, as an institution, can exist without love, but at its best, as an ideal, it cannot. It should be a seeking of a life situation or environment in which love can flourish and grow, for love is a developing thing that the lovers themselves must foster.

2. Human love involves not only the spirit but also the body, and hence married love includes sex. Married people are not supposed to use each other merely as means of sexual satisfaction, which would be love of self rather than of the other, but sexual union is a normal expression of married love and a means toward growth in personal love. Since it is naturally fruitful, it should result in the creation of new life, in that permanent mingling of the qualities of the two wedded lovers in a new person who mirrors both. Actual fruitfulness cannot be guaranteed in any marriage, but the right to do that which normally produces children is the basic right transferred in the marriage contract.

3. Living together results in constant companionship, which is mutually beneficial in a practical way apart from personal love and sexual passion. The wife needs support and protection, whereas the husband needs someone to manage the home. The psychological temperament of each sex needs its complement. There results a love of friendship on a more prosaic level that acquires greater significance in old age. Some marriages have been successful almost on this level alone, though it hardly represents the ideal.

If love is taken as the one essential end of marriage, it must be taken in all three of the aspects just mentioned: personal, sexual, and companionate. The first is undoubtedly the noblest and most important, but it is the least subject to external regulation. Love in its highest sense is attracted, not commanded, and cannot be reduced to a contract. Rights and duties based on justice belong to the contractual aspect of marriage, but love alone can inspire the ideal of marriage and make it what it ought to be. In this sense love is the essential end of marriage.

It is essential also in this sense, that no marriage could be successful that was consciously limited by the married couple to its legal and juridical aspects, to the insisting on rights and the fulfilling of duties. Love is generous, and love in marriage is subject to the paradox of generosity—that it requires one to do more than one is strictly required to do. There is no better illustration of the continuity of justice and love and of the fact that the mere fulfillment of duty is not enough for the good life.

BIRTH CONTROL

Can there be immoral uses of sex within as well as outside marriage? Any use of sex between husband and wife is right and good, unless it is perverted by being done in some unnatural way. The main point of interest here is the hotly controverted issue of birth control. Is it unnatural?

Birth control ought to mean any way of controlling births, including abstinence from intercourse and its limitation to sterile periods. But it is usually taken to mean *artificial contraception*, the use of mechanical, physical, or chemical means to make the sexual act possible without a resulting conception. This is the sense in which the term is taken in the present discussion.

Some such methods have been used from the earliest times, but they were crude and ineffective and overlaid with superstition. The advance in medical knowledge and the widespread marketing of perfected devices have brought contraception within the reach of most and have made it a social as well as a moral problem. It is propagandized as a method of counteracting overpopulation, of reducing the breeding of subnormals, of relieving economic distress in overlarge families, and of obtaining the optimum number and spacing of children in normal families. Few would oppose these ends, but the use of contraception as a means to these ends has met constant moral opposition. The moral condemnation of contraception is traditional; its widespread acceptance is new. Today the immorality of contraception continues to be maintained by large sections of society, especially by those who hold a natural law ethic, for the reasons alleged reduce to the *unnaturalness* of the practice. The chief reasons seem to be the following:

1. The primary end of marriage is the begetting and rearing of children. Even those who no longer speak of primary and secondary ends admit that procreation is an essential end. Marriage is a natural institution, and to take advantage of this natural institution contrary to its primary or essential purpose is to subvert the order of nature and thus to act immorally. Contraception is such a subversion of nature and therefore against the natural law.

2. The sex faculty, as everyone knows and biologists know scientifically, is obviously meant for reproduction. There is nothing wrong in abstaining from its use, but if it is used, it must not be deliberately frustrated of its natural issue. To frustrate a natural faculty of its primary and essential purpose is to go against nature, to act in a manner directly contrary to the norm of morality, and to do something intrinsically wrong. There is a natural teleology in the reproductive process by which the whole of it is directed

to the child. Man's personal teleology must accord with nature's, not contradict it.

3. Artificial contraception is wrong for the reason that it is an unnatural vice of the same sort as homosexuality and auto-eroticism. It has been described as mutual masturbation, a using of each other for mere animal indulgence rather than for the expression of true human love, which is creative of new life. To turn nature's instruments away from their natural purpose, the good of the race, to a mere means of individual satisfaction is what is meant by perversion. This is precisely what artificial contraception does.

4. Contraception is seeking the pleasure while at the same time avoiding the responsibility. The strong desire that animals, including the human animal, feel for sex gratification is nature's way of alluring them to breed. Since nature attaches the pleasure as an inducement to accept the responsibility, the acceptance of the pleasure together with a deliberate repudiation of the responsibility is acting against nature. It has been likened to deliberately vomiting after eating, so as to have the pleasure of additional eating while preventing the natural consequence of nourishment. If we want the pleasure, we must take the consequence nature has attached to it.

5. Contraception is a contamination of one's bodily temple. Married couples are privileged to cooperate with the Creator in the noble work of creation, and it is for this reason that they are fruitful. Thus there is something sacred about the reproductive ability. It is not one's own in the same sense as other abilities but is consecrated to the good of the race. Hence it may not be withdrawn from the fulfillment of nature's purpose and devoted to some secondary purpose of one's own.

6. Contraception cannot be engaged in without necessarily having an evil intention. One who performs the sex act is seeking the procreative good, for it is not pos-sible to use the procreative powers otherwise. By contraceptive intent the person is intending the hindrance of the procreative good at the same moment and in the same act in which he is intending the seeking of the procreative good. Since both intentions are unavoidable in contraception and contradictory in purpose, contraception is necessarily evil in intent and therefore immoral.

7. Contraceptive intercourse is psychologically unsatisfactory. The barrier put between husband and wife to prevent conception means that neither can derive full sexual satisfaction. But nature obviously intends this satisfaction by attaching it to the normal and unimpeded use of sex, thus teaching us how this ability is to be used. An unsatisfactory sex life leads not only to psychological disturbances but also to loss of love, and hence it attacks the nature of marriage itself.

8. The marriage act should be the perfect expression of conjugal love. There should be no reserve in the surrender of each to the other. Mature sexuality is a complete self-fulfilling and other-fulfilling interpersonal relationship. The use of contraception is a reserve in the surrender, a withholding of what ought to be given, a defrauding of what is due to the other, an acceptance of the other's affection but a refusal of the other's substance. Hence contraception prevents marriage from being the perfect expression of conjugal love that nature intends it to be.

These arguments overlap greatly, but each lights up a different side of the question. They are a strong presentation of the traditional view, but the publicity given to contraception, its ready acceptance by so many well-meaning people, the medical and economic problems families face, the unsatisfactoriness of continence and rhythm, the hopelessness in underprivileged areas, and especially the zooming population explosion, all these force on us a rethinking of the whole question. Even some adherents of the natural law ethic challenge the foregoing arguments, and on two main counts:

1. Biological knowledge requires that we revise some of our opinions on the exact natural character of the reproductive process.
2. Ethical sincerity requires that we reconsider some of our assumptions concerning the proper interpretation of the natural law.

Specifically, the following sort of counterarguments have been proposed:

1. The begetting and rearing of children certainly constitute an essential end of marriage (call it primary or not), which no marriage can wholly exclude. But must it be sought every time the sex act is used? Man's other abilities have no such restriction. Also, the rearing of children is a part of the primary end as much as the begetting of children. One of the chief reasons given by people for practicing contraception is that any more children would render difficult or impossible the proper rearing of the children they already have. Hence the primary end of marriage may require family limitation as well as family expansion.

2. There is a natural teleology in the reproductive process, but that does not mean that man may never interfere with it. In a way many applications of human science or art are frustrations of nature, making nature accomplish human ends rather than the ends their own nature drives them to. The design of God must be respected, but just what is that design? It includes the fact that man is to use his intelligence and modify nature to suit his legitimate aims. Should not man also intellectually govern his sexuality and moderate his fertility by responsible parenthood? That contraception is an evil way to doing so is assumed but not proved in the argument.

3. Analogies drawn from homosexuality and autoeroticism are beside the point. These acts are not between married people,

who have to live together and express a proper love for each other, who have done their duty to the race by generating a large enough family but happen to be overfertile. Married people can use each other for selfish indulgence, which is wrong, but they can also love each other too strongly for abstinence, even periodic, and yet cannot afford to have more children.

4. One must take a responsibility that necessarily comes, but it is necessary to create that responsibility? One must care for the child one has, but must one conceive it? Why must the responsibility for procreation prevail over the responsibility for education? The old notion that sex pleasure is somehow wrong unless justified by an excuse, and the only excuse is children, is challenged today as having Manichaean overtones. Sex is good in itself as the expression of love between husband and wife, and it needs no excuse. It can be overused, just as eating can be overdone, and in both cases the virtue of temperance must be exercised.

5. That there is something more sacred about the reproductive ability than about other abilities does not seem to have any standing in philosophical ethics. Parents cooperate with the Creator in the starting of new life and also in its continuance, so that every act parents do for their child later on should also be sacred, together with the abilities they use in doing it. Is not the love aspect of sexuality as much the Creator's purpose as its fertility aspect? We must avoid an unnatural preoccupation with the biological side of sex to the exclusion of its human significance.

6. Married couples must seek the procreative good, but must they seek it in every single act of intercourse? Mutual love and parenthood, sexuality and fertility, seem to be two separable moral intentions. Nature itself separates them most of the time, since the sterile part of the woman's period is longer than the fertile

part, and in periodic continence one is deliberately sought without the other. Why cannot they separate these intentions also in a contraceptive act? Because contraception is forbidden? But this is the point to be proved, not assumed.

7. Whether or not contraceptive intercourse is psychologically unsatisfactory, psychological satisfaction is not a matter of obligation so that it must be obtained in every act. There is far more psychological dissatisfaction, even neurotic anxiety, in the prospect of an overabundant family with all the worries of providing for it. For many the rhythm method is psychologically most unsatisfactory, forbidding intercourse when it is desired and allowing it when it is not wanted. The "pill" puts no barrier in the performance of the sex act and solves at least this aspect of the question.

8. A contraceptive act is certainly not the perfect expression of conjugal love and is by no means the ideal. This is readily granted. But the ideal cannot always be realized. More children might make ideal family life impossible. Continence and rhythm can play havoc with the proper expression of love and can divert conjugal love even farther from the ideal. Though we should always strive for the ideal, we must often adjust to situations in which the ideal is recognized as unattainable.

This balancing off of arguments represents the state of the question as it is today. Many find the traditional arguments thoroughly convincing, others find them unsatisfactory, and still others hold to the traditional conclusion but seek new arguments or a reformulation of the old ones. The question is complicated by some other factors: traditional views are not lightly to be thrown aside, since they are our heritage, yet serious and difficult obligations are not to be imposed unless they are certain; such intimate matters should be entirely a family matter and withdrawn from public discussion, yet the size of families has social effects that are the concern of all; many will decide the question for themselves on religious grounds, yet religion has little to offer besides ethical and natural law arguments.

The idea of *responsible parenthood* is commonly admitted today by both sides. Parents are not obliged to have as many children as possible and should determine their number and spacing for the good of the whole family. The only controversy is on the morality of the means. Opponents of contraception have two means: continence and rhythm.

Marital *continence* is refraining from relations with mutual consent. Marriage transfers rights, and it is a violation of the marriage contract to refuse them to the spouse who reasonably demands them, but there is no obligation to demand them. Both must agree to abstain and must be able to do so without proximate danger of yielding to temptation. Marital continence is not easy, but it is not as impossible as some seem to think.

Rhythm, or periodic continence, is the limitation of relations to the sterile period that nature itself provides. Since there is no obligation to demand marriage rights at all, there is no obligation to demand them at one time rather than another. It is known that the act will be unfruitful, but nature itself has made it so. There is no question here of using unnatural means, and thus rhythm is not a form of artificial contraception. The intention may be the same, but unless it is an intention of never having any children at all, it is a legitimate exercise of responsible parenthood. That it be responsible, some justifying reason, medical, eugenic, economic, or social, should be present.

The contraceptive *pill* remains a problem. It is still under experimentation, and it is too soon to observe all its effects. This uncertain state of science leaves us without the facts on which to make a solid judgment. However, the undesirable side-effects belong under the question of risk to health and are irrelevant to the contraception issue. Even if all the side-effects were eliminated, that would not of itself legitimize the use of the pill, if contraception itself is regarded as morally wrong.

There should be no objection to a pill that would merely regularize a woman's cycle so as to make the use of rhythm surer. It is hard to interpret any existing pills as working in precisely this way. Some consider the existing pills as destructive of a possibly fertilized ovum and thus as abortive. Others consider them as delaying ovulation, which may be direct temporary sterilization and wrong on that count (if anything so temporary really should be called sterilization at all). Others think of the pill as merely prolonging nature's sterile period and thus as assisting nature rather than opposing it; they find nothing wrong in it. The pill has the advantage over mechanical and physical contraceptives in that it does not interfere with the ordinary performance of the sex act and commends itself to those who distinguish between sexuality and fertility as two possibly separable intentions. At all events, future developments of the pill seem to offer the best hope of finding some sure means of family limitation that can be accepted by people of all moral persuasions.

At best, contraception is a makeshift and far from the ideal. There should be no opposition between the natural teleology of a human process and the personal choice of human beings. An intensive study of the laws of nature is called for, so that nature can be tamed, regulated, and developed by reason in such a way that nature's reproductive finality need not be shut off in the interest of family planning or personal fulfillment. Increased knowledge of fertility should be combined with a more human use of sexuality, but behind both there will always remain the ethical need of responsible self-govern-ment. In the exercise of this self-government most people will settle their consciences not by philosophical reason alone but by the tenets of their religious faith, not by natural law alone but by natural law as interpreted in the official pronouncements of the church to which they have given their adherence. And rightly so, especially on such a complex question, where the deliverances of mere ethical reasoning are so equivocal and the need of surer guidance is so acutely felt.

PREMARITAL SEX

The great crime against marriage is *adultery*. Its wrongness is evident from the exclusive nature of the marriage contract, whether marriage be regarded as a natural institution or only as a conventional arrangement. So long as there is marriage at all, the parties pledge fidelity to each other, which means that they are for each other exclusively. To try to have marriage without this exclusiveness would render marriage futile, for a person could do the same thing with one to whom he is not married as with one to whom he is married.

It was formerly thought that the establishment of marriage as a natural institution automatically disposed of any allowability of *fornication*. Its wrongness was clearly visible in that it made no provision for a home for the child whose existence the parties chanced when they had sexual relations. It was thus a gross violation of nature's provision for the human child and an attack on the institution of marriage, which exists to make nature's provision real. The argument was sound for those unable to control the possibility of offspring, and is still sound for those now in such a condition. But with the advent of effective and available contraceptives a different picture emerges. Now it is possible to have sexual relations with the possibility of offspring almost entirely precluded.

It does not immediately follow that there is no moral wrong in fornication provided contraceptives are used. The old argument never said that the *only* wrong in it is the harm to a possible child, but this reason was seen as so glaring that no other need be sought. Now the question has to be reopened. Is there anything right or wrong in sexual relations between unmarried persons when no harm can come to a third party?

The following reasons have been put forth in favor of the moral allowability of premarital sex, understanding by this term that the parties probably will be married sometime, though not necessarily to each other.

1. Aside from cases of prostitution and seduction, where sex is bought and sold like a commodity or where undue advantage is taken of another's innocence, it is hard to see any wrong in a sex act guarded against possible pregnancy. The sex act itself is purely natural, neither right nor wrong. The idea that it is bad in itself or that it needs some excuse, such as procreation, for its performance is an old, irrational tabu, from which we are now emancipated.

2. It is false that sex is cheapened and degraded unless severe restrictions are put on it. Married persons might want to protect and rationalize their situation by interdicting sex to the unmarried, but they should have no right to impose their prejudices on the unmarried. A casual affair may not have the depth of married love, but that does not make it wrong.

3. Premarital relations do not in any way harm the marriage possibilities of the two involved, neither if they marry one another nor if they marry someone else. Virginity in one's spouse can still be honored as a desirable trait for those who esteem it, but because some prefer it is no reason for making it a universal law. Premarital sex neither attacks the institution of marriage as such nor renders difficult any of its aims.

4. Premarital relations should, in fact, be the best preparation for marriage. In no other important business of life is one expected to go into it wholly unprepared and inexperienced. Premarital relations will teach the two the difficult art of sexual performance, will enable them to decide whether what they feel is mere sexual attraction or true love, will preclude many a disastrous marriage made only because the parties could not wait.

5. Our society requires great maturity in partners binding themselves together by a lifelong contract and setting themselves up in an independent home, but human sexuality manifests itself much earlier and is very insistent. It is unnatural that youth should be obliged to curb sexuality when they feel it most strongly, and postpone marriage to a time when they will be emotionally mature and economically secure. Since marriage requires these conditions, the young should have some earlier way of satisfying their natural urge.

6. What is so important about a ceremony and a certificate? How can a few words and a piece of paper change an act from immoral to moral? Those who seriously love each other should be able to satisfy their love without asking anyone's permission or going through an empty ritual. At least those whose intimacy is not casual but serious have from nature itself the right to sexual relations. If society insists on it, they can go through the formalities later.

Those who maintain the immorality of premarital sex, even with the precautions mentioned, consider these arguments irrelevant and focus their attention on the persons of the two involved rather than on any harmful effects.

1. The sex act in itself is natural and morally neutral, but motives and circumstances must be considered in any act. If the two parties are merely using each other

as means of gratification with no real love between them, they are guilty of serious crime against each other's person, of degrading a person to the level of a thing. No one is morally allowed to do this to another or let it be done to oneself. The casual type of premarital sex differs little from prostitution except for the commercial aspect.

2. Premarital sex is not wrong because of any supposed monopoly of sex by the married. Precisely what is wrong with casual affairs is that they cannot have that depth of love without which sex is cheapened and degraded because those engaging in it cheapen and degrade themselves. Only if they commit themselves unreservedly to one another for a lifelong union of shared love can they preserve their dignity as persons and respect the person of the other. This is what married people do and what the unmarried, as long as they are unmarried, fail to do.

3. Premarital relations seem to have no effect on subsequent marriage, and those who indulge in them can make just as good husbands or wives as those who come to marriage with their virginity intact. Thus the prevalence of premarital sex is not a danger to the institution of marriage, which continues to flourish anyway. No argument against premarital sex should be drawn from these sources. Its wrongness does not stem from its effects but from itself, from a failure of a complete and wholehearted giving of each self to the other, in which love consists.

4. The same difficulty exists in trial marriages. You can try on a suit of clothes because it is a thing. You cannot try on a person without reducing him to the level of a thing. If you test to see is someone is fit for a certain job, you are testing his work, not the person himself. But the sex act is not the rendering of a service, as prostitution makes it, but the full surrendering of oneself in the completest union possible between two persons. It is reasonable to try out things; it is a supreme

insult to experiment with persons as if they were things. That the insult is accepted is no excuse.

5. Early marriage is no answer to the problem of youthful continence, since early marriages are by far the most precarious. If evil will not be avoided, premarital sex is a lesser evil than a binding but intolerable marriage. However, it is not at all impossible for young people to contain themselves, especially if they have been brought up in an environment neither too permissive nor too repressive. The fact that so many do so proves its possibility. Self-control has to be learned sometime. Why not in youth?

6. If a man and woman really do love each other with total commitment and seriously intend to share their lives together, then as far as nature, philosophy, and sure reason are concerned, they are married. If they seal their commitment by intercourse, their use of sex is not so much premarital as preceremonial. It is true that the state and the church have the right to regulate the public and social condition of marriage with certain formalities, even to the making of a marriage invalid unless they are complied with. No one who belongs to either or both of these societies should engage in a common-law marriage, and surely not as an act of defiance against them. However, it is not a certificate or a ceremony that marries them but their declaration of total commitment to each other. It is this which the marriage ceremony solemnizes and celebrates.

It follows that the only case of premarital sex which is morally allowable, a total, lifelong, exclusive commitment of love, turns out to be not premarital at all. If the two persons have felt this way about each other for sufficient time to know that they are serious, there seems to be no reason why they should refuse to go through a marriage ceremony before engaging in sex relations. There seems to be no excuse but ignorance, negligence, or defiance for a common-law marriage. Thus the conclusion to be drawn is that there is no moral justification for premarital sex.

SELF-CONTROL AND SEX

There is nothing in human life more capable of abuse and mismanagement than sex. What is governed so easily and naturally in animals by means of their instinct must be regulated in man by his free will guided by his reason. Success or failure in life depends to a very great extent on the individual's ability to control this strongest of all passions. Marriage is the institution demanded by nature for securing this control. Any number of otherwise successful people have wrecked their lives by failing to succeed in their relations with the opposite sex. The selecting of the right partner in life and the preservation of fidelity to the marriage vow are not matters of accident but of wise human conduct. Marriage also requires traits of character that are not accidentally achieved but must be sedulously developed. Success in the married state is possible only by the practice of the cardinal virtues of prudence, justice, fortitude, and temperance in a high degree. Marriage therefore calls for a virtuous life and entails heavy responsibilities, but it also brings with it one of the best of earthly rewards, the founding and maintenance of a happy home.

SUMMARY

This chapter continues the previous one.

Marriage regarded legally as an institution was said to have as its *primary end* the begetting and rearing of children and as its *secondary end* the mutual love and help between the spouses. But marriage regarded as an ideal and as a personal experience can be said to have only one end, and that is *love* in its widest scope and on all levels, personal, sexual, and companionate.

Birth control, in the sense of artificial *contraception,* has been traditionally regarded as an unnatural use of sex within marriage and hence immoral. Its unnaturalness is now being challenged.

Arguments against contraception: Contraception frustrates the primary end of marriage, interferes with nature's design, is a form of unnatural perversion, seeks the pleasure while avoiding the responsibility, contaminates the temple of one's body, seeks and simultaneously hinders the procreative good, is psychologically unsatisfying, and impugns the totality of the surrender in marriage.

Replies: The rearing of children is as primary as their begetting, all human art and science interfere with nature, not fertility itself but overfertility is controlled, responsibilities need not be created, reproduction is not more sacred than other acts, the procreative good need not be sought in every act, an overlarge family is psychologically frustrating, and the ideal cannot always be realized.

Continence and *rhythm,* not being forms of *artificial* contraception, are morally acceptable means of family limitation.

Adultery is the chief crime against marriage, since it violates its exclusiveness. *Fornication* is traditionally condemned as failure to provide for the possible child.

Premarital sex, a euphemism for fornication under certain circumstances, is being defended today, for if contraceptives are used, it causes harm to no one. But it is necessary to look not only for harmful effects but also at the persons involved. If the sex act is only a casual encounter, it degrades the person to the level of a thing, an end to a mere means. If it is meant as a serious and permanent commitment of love with all its responsibilties, it amounts to a common-law marriage and is not really premarital. Common-law marriages have an antisocial aspect about them and do not deserve moral approval.

QUESTIONS FOR DISCUSSION

1 Each one's sex life seems to be so private that it should hardly be discussed in ethics. Here, if anywhere, personal conscience should reign supreme. So long as no one is hurt, what a person does is his own business. What of this argument?

2 No laws can be laid down to love and its sexual manifestation. Attempts by busybodies throughout history to regulate it have all been unsuccessful. Why continue this futile interference?

3 Do you agree that contraception has been one of the greatest steps in the emancipation of women, freeing them from the slavery of childbearing and rearing? Whatever increases human freedom is morally good.

4 What is wrong with adultery when approved by one's spouse? Should not the frigid approve of it? What is wrong with spouse-swapping or marital communes composed of congenial people who want more variety in life?

5 Perhaps we had better adjust to the fact that, with contraception, premarital sex is here to stay. Why look for new arguments to prove it immoral? Why not accept it as moral because man's ingenuity has circumvented the evils formerly present in it? Is it wrong to circumvent evil?

READINGS

On love and sex in general see Ignace Lepp, *The Psychology of Loving;* Marc Oraison, *The Human Mystery of Sexuality;* Erich Fromm, *The Art of Loving;* C. S. Lewis, *The Four Loves;* Peter Bertocci, *Sex, Love, and the Person;* John Wilson, *Logic and Sexual Morality;* and many others.

Helmut Thielecke, *The Ethics of Sex,* is a well-known work from the standpoint of Protestant theology.

On birth control: John T. Noonan's *Contraception* is a thorough scholarly study; Louis Dupré, *Contraception and Catholics,* questions traditional views, whereas Germain Grisez, *Contraception and the Natural Law,* upholds them in a new way; John L. Thomas, *Marriage and Rhythm,* explores that particular subject; John Rock, *The Time Has Come,* argues for the "pill" he helped to discover. Dorothy Bromley, *Catholics and Birth Control,* offers a well-balanced short study by a non-Catholic. Archbishop T. D. Roberts, *Contraception and Holiness;* William Birmingham, *What Modern Catholics Think about Birth Control;* and Michael Novak, *The Experience of Marriage,* are collections of essays airing both sides of the question.

Read Pius XI's encyclical *Casti Connubii* (Christian Marriage) and Paul VI's *Humanae Vitae* (Of Human Life).

On premarital sex: Evelyn Duvall, *Why Wait Till Marriage?* Lester Kirkendall, *Premarital Intercourse and Interpersonal Relations.* Burgess and Wallen, *Engagement and Marriage,* ch. 12, is a factual study without a moral judgment.

Austin Fagothey, *Right and Reason—an Anthology,* contains John Macmurray's "The Virtue of Chastity" from *Reason and Emotion,* and Evelyn Duvall's *Why Wait Till Marriage?* ch. 12.

275

CHAPTER 25

STATE

PROBLEM

After studying the family as the more primitive and fundamental institution, we now take up the more elaborate type of universally acknowledged society known as the state. This part of ethics is sometimes called political philosophy, as midway between political science on the one hand and pure ethical theory on the other. In this chapter we shall deal with the state itself, its origin, properties, purpose, and structure. In the following chapter we shall discuss the functioning of the state, or government. The matter for the present chapter can be arranged under the following headings:

1. Is the state a natural outgrowth of the family?
2. How far does the state depend on contract?
3. How far is the state sovereign?
4. Is the state for man or man for the state?
5. How is the state built up out of its elements?

Our first problem deals with the origin of the state itself as a political entity, the transition of a people from a nonorganized to a politically organized condition. On this point there are two main opinions:

1. The state is a natural society because it arose as a natural outgrowth of the family.
2. The state is a merely conventional society because it arose from a social contract freely entered into.

NATURAL ORIGIN THEORY

The Greeks took it for granted that the state is a natural society, although they do not call it that, perhaps because they have no word for *society* in general but use the word *polis*, city, to stand for both state and society.

Plato derives the state from man's economic needs, which of course are natural needs. He says:

A state, I said, arises, as I conceive, out of the needs of mankind; no one is self-sufficing, but all of us have many wants. Can any other origin of a State be imagined?

There can be no other.

Then, as we have many wants, and many persons are needed to supply them, one takes a helper for one purpose and another for another; and when these partners and helpers are gathered together in one habitation the body of inhabitants is termed a State.

True, he said.

And they exchange with one another, and one gives, and another receives, under the idea that the exchange will be for their good.

Very true.

Then, I said, let us begin and create in idea a State; and yet the true creator is necessity, who is the mother of our invention.*

Aristotle derives the state from the family, but not without due consideration for man's economic needs. Plato could hardly have stressed the family when he was going to abolish it among the rulers and guardians, but Aristotle is strong for the family. Here are his words:

---

*Plato, *Republic,* bk. II, §369.

He who thus considers things in their first growth and origin, whether a state or anything else, will obtain the clearest view of them. . . .

Out of these two relationships between man and woman, master and slave, the first thing to arise is the family. . . . The family is an association established by nature for the supply of men's everyday wants. . . . But when several families are united, and the association aims at something more than the supply of daily needs, the first society to be formed is the village. And the most natural form of the village appears to be that of a colony from the family, composed of children and grandchildren. . . .

When several villages are united in a single complete community, large enough to be nearly or quite self-sufficing, the state comes into existence, originating in the bare needs of life, and continuing in existence for the sake of a good life. And therefore, if the earlier forms of society are natural, so is the state, for it is the end of them, and the nature of a thing is its end. For what each thing is when fully developed, we call its nature, whether we are speaking of a man, a horse, or a family. Besides, the final cause and end of a thing is the best, and to be self-sufficing is the end and the best.

Hence it is evident that the state is a creature of nature, and that man is by nature a political animal. . . . And it is characteristic of man that he alone has any sense of good and evil, of just and unjust, and the like, and the association of living beings who have this sense makes a family and a state.*

The foregoing passage from Aristotle was quoted at such length because of its fundamental importance. Before examining his argument, we have three preliminary remarks to make:

First, we have to speculate on the origin of the state by observing the forms of primitive society in existence today and by examining the traditions handed down among people now civilized. Of particular value are the Greeks, whose literature developed so early as to reflect both tribal and political life.

Second, we are interested in the passage of mankind from nonpolitical to political existence, the formation of the state

as such, not of this or that particular state. The states in existence today have risen by colonization, conquest, revolution, or similar causes, in which we see only the patterning of new states on the ready-made framework of old ones, not the original formation of political society.

Third, the first formation of the state must have been gradual. As a rule men do not consciously aim at things of which they have had no experience. As various needs arose and better solutions to them were devised, men were unconsciously forming the self-sufficient state. It was spontaneous but also guided by reason as a product of many converging acts of human thought. The first states were not vast empires but, rather, slight though real improvements on tribal organization.

In the light of these remarks Aristotle's theory can be expressed under the following points:

1. *The most elementary form of society is the family.* The family is here taken in the extended sense to mean all blood relatives living together and any servants or others adopted into the household. It can provide for its own welfare in mere daily wants, but it cannot provide for a broader human life. The arts and appliances of civilization could never be developed within one family; for these there is needed the cooperation of many minds and many hands through accumulated generations.

2. *As the family grows, the end it can attain also grows.* The children reach maturity and found new families, usually nearby. In several generations a group of families all interrelated live close to one another. Division of labor comes in; people begin to specialize in different kinds of work and to exchange their products.

3. *The interrelated group has become a clan or tribe.* A clan is a smaller group with a tradition of descent from a common ancestor. A tribe is a larger group and may be an amalgamation of several

*Aristotle, *Politics*, bk. I, ch. 2, 1252a 24 to 1253a 18.

clans; at least the blood relationship is not so clear. Some tribes never get beyond the tribal condition, either because of nomadic habits, because they are wholly occupied in war, or because they show no ingenuity in developing the earth's resources. In forming a state a peaceful, industrious settlement—a central village where the people trade—is necessary.

4. *The village community can supply more of its wants than a single family, but it is not yet self-sufficient.* Military organization against enemies from without, economic organization against famine and want, and legal organization for settling internal disputes are still wanting. These things are handled rather arbitrarily by the tribal chief with his council of elders. This chief may be the patriarch or founder of the whole family, or his eldest son, or one of his descendants appointed by him, or one elected by the tribe to be their leader, or one who simply assumes leadership and keeps it by his ability.

5. *From the village community or an aggregate of such villages the state is formed.* One village composed of people all descended from a common ancestor may expand to such a size in such a favorable location that it is now able to take care of all its needs and has become self-sufficient. More probably several such villages would aggregate and organize for common defense, mutual trade, and a common legal system. As soon as these things have been determined and an authority has been established to enforce them, the state has come into existence.

The argument can be summarized as follows: The family is demanded by nature and is a natural society, but the state is a natural outgrowth of the family and becomes necessary for human living when a number of families realize the need of cooperation for their common good under authoritative leadership. Therefore in these circumstances the state is demanded by nature and is a natural society.

SOCIAL CONTRACT THEORY

The theory opposed to the natural origin of the state is the contractual theory. Since it is the only theory consistent with moral, legal, and juridical positivism, we must expect the names familiar to us from those movements to recur.

To what we said previously about *Thomas Hobbes'* description of the state of nature we may add his description of the formation of political society:

> The only way to erect such a common power, as may be able to defend them from the invasion of foreigners and the injuries of one another, and thereby to secure them in such sort as that, by their own industry, and by the fruits of the earth, they may nourish themselves and live contentedly, is, to confer all their power and strength upon one man, or upon one assembly of men, that may reduce all their wills, by plurality of voices, unto one will; which is as much as to say, to appoint one man, or assembly of men, to bear their person, and everyone to own and acknowledge himself to be the author of whatsoever he, that so beareth their person, shall act or cause to be acted in those things which concern the common peace and safety, and therein to submit their wills, everyone to his will, and their judgments to his judgment. This is more than consent, or concord; it is a real unity of them all, in one and the same person, made by covenant of every man with every man, in such manner as if every man should say to every man, *"I authorize and give up my right of governing myself to this man, or to this assembly of men, on this condition, that thou give up thy right to him, and authorize all his actions in like manner."* This done, the multitude so united in one person, is called a *commonwealth,* in Latin *civitas.* This is the generation of that great *Leviathan,* or rather, to speak more reverently, of that *mortal god,* to whom we owe under the *immortal God,* our peace and defense.*

Since Hobbes' view cannot be gathered from one paragraph, however long, we append the following summary. Man by nature is not social but antisocial. In the state of nature, before the founding of the commonwealth, "man was a wolf to man," there was a "war of all against all," there

---

*Hobbes, *Leviathan,* ch. 17.

was not right or wrong, no justice and injustice, for there was no law. Force and fraud governed men's actions. This condition was intolerable, and one powerful impulse, self-preservation, drove men to seek a remedy for constant warfare. The remedy was the *social contract*, by which men agreed to hand over all their liberties to some one man or body of men, provided every other man did likewise. Thus they created authority, to which all are now subject and which directs the destinies of all. The power of the ruler is the aggregate of the powers of the individuals. The social contract, once effected, is irrevocable. The sovereignty of the ruler is absolute within the terms of the contract, and rebellion can never be lawful; only if he can no longer protect his subjects does obligation to him cease. We have no rights except those granted back to us by the sovereign of the all-powerful state.

Jean Jacques Rousseau is as strong a proponent of the contractual theory as Hobbes, though the two differ in their interpretation of the social contract. Rousseau says:

To find a form of association which may defend and protect with the whole force of the community the person and property of every associate, and by means of which, coalescing with all, each may nevertheless obey only himself, and remain as free as before. Such is the fundamental problem of which the social contract furnishes the solution. . . .

In short, each giving himself to all, gives himself to nobody; and as there is not one associate over whom we do not acquire the same rights which we concede to him over ourselves, we gain the equivalent of all that we lose, and more power to preserve what we have.

If, then, we set aside what is not of the essence of the social contract, we shall find that it is reducible to the following terms: "Each of us puts in common his person and his whole power under the supreme direction of the general will; and in return we receive every member as an indivisible part of the whole."

Forthwith, instead of the individual personalities of all the contracting parties, this act of association produces a moral and collective body, which is composed of as many members as the assembly has voices, and which receives from this same act its unity, its common self, its life, and its will. This public person, which is thus formed by the union of all the individual members, formerly took the name of *City*, and now takes that of *Republic* or *Body Politic*, which is called by its members *State* when it is passive, *sovereign* when it is active, *power* when it is compared to similar bodies.[*]

The following supplies the background for the passages quoted. Man is not naturally antisocial but only extrasocial. In the state of nature man lived a carefree life in the forests, sufficient for himself, bound by no obligations, subordinate to no one. Man is naturally good, and there was no war of all against all, but the establishment of private property, due to man's natural inventiveness, brought with it frauds, disputes, and conflict. Then the state had to be established as a necessary evil to keep the peace. The state was set up by the *social contract*, by which each man handed over all his power of self-rule to a sort of universal person, the *general will*, provided all the rest did the same. Thus the individual will becomes part of the general will, the individual person part of this general personality, the right of the state the accumulation of all individual rights. In obeying the general will a man really obeys himself as part of the general will, because in the social contract itself he has willed that the general will shall be his will, and shall prevail over any particular decision he makes. The general will is always sovereign and, even if it appoints representatives, cannot transfer sovereignty to them. Especially in this last point Rousseau parts company with Hobbes.

A combination of the natural and contractual origin of the state is found in *John Locke*. He believes that man is naturally social, that there is a natural law conferring natural rights, but he thinks that po-

---

[*]Rousseau, *Social Contract*, bk. I, ch. 6.

litical society could begin only by the social contract, which, however, men are impelled to make by the demands of their nature. He says:

Men being, as has been said, by nature all free, equal, and independent, no one can be put out of this estate and subjected to the political power of another without his own consent. The only way whereby any one divests himself of his natural liberty, and puts on the bonds of civil society, is by agreeing with other men to join and unite into a community for their comfortable, safe, and peaceable living one amongst another. . . .

And thus that which begins and actually constitutes any political society is nothing but the consent of any number of freemen capable of a majority to unite and incorporate into such a society. And this is that, and that only, which did or could give beginning to any lawful government in the world.*

There seems to be no warranted objection to placing an implicit contract as the actual instrument by which many particular states were founded. Locke's critics point to his making such a contract a universal requirement for the origin of all states, to his basing every state on majority rule, to his requiring implicit renewal of the contract by each citizen on reaching adulthood, and to his making the chief function of the state the protection of property. But these important details are not our present concern, which is not to prove or disprove a contract but to ask whether the state is a natural society or an arbitrary creation of merely human deciding, and whether, if there was a contract, men were impelled to make it by the requirements of human nature and the dictate of the moral law.

The *case for* the social contract theory of the state has just been presented in the authors' own words. The *case against* consists mainly of criticisms of Hobbes and Rousseau, who deny that the state is a

natural society, rather than against Locke, who does not:

1. Man is naturally social, not antisocial or extrasocial. He is neither utterly depraved nor thoroughly upright in nature, but inclined both to good and evil. There is no evidence that man ever lived in this state of nature, and it is probably not intended to be historical, but it does not give a correct view of human nature.

2. There never was a state of nonmorality, without rights, duties, justice, or law. There was always the natural law, and from it rights and duties immediately flow. The first child would set up a whole system of rights and duties. There never was an utter absence of private property, for anything occupied becomes such, and ownership immediately involves justice and injustice.

3. The function of the family in preparing for the state cannot be overlooked. Human beings had to live at least temporarily in some society to be able to survive as a race. A mere animal life, whether predatory or carefree, is impossible for man, for no man can supply his needs unaided. Family life naturally develops into the clan or tribe, and from there into the state.

4. There are certain rights of the individual and of the family that it is immoral to transfer to another, for they belong to the dignity of the human person and to the very nature of the family. A social contract that requires the transference of all rights is contrary to the nature of man.

5. A social contract that is not a requirement of human nature as such but a mere convention could not bind posterity. The unborn were not parties to the contract and might refuse to enter into it. No one would become a citizen of the state by birth, and anyone could resign from the state at will.

6. The social contract cannot have greater authority than the contracting parties give it. There are rights of the state

---

*Locke, *Second Treatise of Civil Government*, ch. 8, §95, 99.

that no individual can possess, because they concern the common good. In the contract theory there is no way in which the state can legitimately obtain them.

SELF-SUFFICIENCY AND SOVEREIGNTY

The state is said to be a natural society, which the family is also, and a self-sufficient society, which the family is not. A *self-sufficient* society is one that is independent, autonomous, and sovereign. As a society, whether it function well or ill, the state is not tributary to, or dependent on, another society for the attainment of its end. It is because the family is not self-sufficient, is unable to protect itself and to provide its members with all they need for the good life, that the state is necessary. If the state itself were not self-sufficient, it would require a higher society on which it could depend. Such a series could not be infinite, and by the name *state* we mean precisely that society which is self-sufficient and independent.

Self-sufficiency here does not mean *autarky,* or economic isolation. The state need not grow all its own food or produce all its own manufactures if it can obtain them by trade from other countries. It need not have an army that can stand off any other army in the world if it can secure its own protection by treaties and alliances. It must be independent in the sense that it acknowledges no dictation from other nations in its internal affairs and negotiates with them as an equal in external affairs. Such a state is self-governing, a law to itself, autonomous. Considered as a quality in the will of a people and their rulers, this autonomy is called *sovereignty,* the independent power of self-rule by which a state controls its citizens and its territory in such a way that there is no higher appeal in the political order. Sovereignty in the state corresponds somewhat to personality in the individual man.

Such qualities cannot be absolute or unlimited. As there are restrictions on the freedom and independence of the individual person, so also are there on the state. Its right to do what it pleases is limited by the natural rights of mankind, by the existence of other states with equal sovereignty. All nations form the world community to which they belong, like it or not, by the fact that they all exist on this same earth and cannot avoid each other. A League of Nations or United Nations does not form a superstate or destroy the sovereignty of individual states. Nor would a tighter federation of states destroy sovereignty, though it might limit it still further. A union of all mankind into a single world state would so absorb the sovereignty of individual states as practically to reduce them to mere provinces. Whether this would be desirable is a debatable question. What we are saying here is that it would not mean the end of political society but the substitution of one political state for many. And this one state would have to be self-sufficient, independent, autonomous, and sovereign.

THE STATE AND THE PERSON

The fact that the state is sovereign and in a sense supreme brings up the question of its relation to its members. How can the autonomy of the individual person be reconciled with the supremacy of the state? Aristotle touches this question in a passage immediately following the one quoted earlier:

Further, the state is by nature clearly prior to the family and to the individual, since the whole is of necessity prior to the part. . . . The proof that the state is a creation of nature and prior to the individual is that the individual, when isolated, is not self-sufficient; and therefore he is like a part in relation to the whole. But he who is unable to live in society, or who has no need because he is sufficient for himself, must be either a beast or a god; he is no part of the state. A social instinct is implanted in all men by nature, and yet he who first founded the state was the greatest of benefactors. For man, when perfected, is the best of animals, but, when separated from law and justice, he is the worst of all.*

Contrast this quotation with the one cited in the chapter on the family:

Man is naturally inclined to form couples—even more so than to form cities, inasmuch as the household is earlier and more necessary than the city.†

The individual and the family are prior to the state in *time,* as being earlier, but the state is prior to the individual and the family in *nature,* as being their end and purpose. Does this mean that the individual and the family exist for the sake of the state? So it would seem, but it would be an anachronism to make Aristotle a totalitarian. He is only mirroring his own Greek society, where ethical life was inconceivable apart from the civic life of the *polis,* and all citizens took a more active part in civic affairs than is customary in modern life. Besides, no Greek developed the theory of the human person, which is one of Christianity's historical contributions to philosophy; thus Aristotle failed to see that the dignity of the human person prevents him from being subordinated as a means to an end, even if that end be his collective good manifested in the state.

Whatever Aristotle himself may have thought, we are interested in his problem:

1. Is the state for man?
2. Is man for the state?

If we must choose one or the other of these alternatives without qualification, we ought unhesitatingly to choose the first: The state is for man, not man for the state. But an unqualified answer is too superficial. Individuals and families are often obliged to subordinate their private good to the common good, as is evident from the very idea of the state. Nor is it sufficient answer to say that the common good redounds to the benefit of all the individuals making up the community. An individual is sometimes obliged to sacrifice his life for the state, as in war, and receives no personal good from it at all. If the state is for him, why must he die for it? There is, then, a qualified sense in which the individual is subordinate to the state. We must still say that the state is for man, but not for any single member of the state to the detriment of all.

A solution that gets at the metaphysical roots of this problem is developed by Jacques Maritain.* He argues from two apparently opposed passages in St. Thomas: "Every individual person is compared to the whole community, as part to whole"† and: "Man is not ordained to the body politic according to all that he is and has."‡ The whole man is a part of the state, but he is not a part of the state by reason of all that is in him. When a man runs, the whole man runs, but by reason of his muscles and not by reason of his knowledge of astronomy. Thus the whole man is an individual person, a member of the family, and a citizen of the state, but there is something different in him that sets him up in each of these relations.

The human being is a person but not the highest type of person. As a person he is for himself and cannot be subordinated to a greater whole, but because his self-sufficiency is so limited he must band with his fellows to supply his needs.

Because he is a *person,* man transcends all temporal societies, for he has a destiny beyond this life and in his immortality will outlast all the empires of this world. There

---

*Aristotle, *Politics,* bk. I, ch. 2, 1253a 19 to 1253a 39. See p. 277.
†Aristotle, *Nicomachean Ethics,* bk. VIII, ch. 12, 1162a 17, quoted on p. 256.

*Maritain, *Scholasticism and Politics,* ch. 3; *The Rights of Man and the Natural Law,* ch. 1; *The Person and the Common Good.*
†St. Thomas, *Summa Theologica,* II-II, q. 64, a. 2.
‡*Op. cit.,* I-II, q. 21, a. 4, obj. 3.

is nothing above human personality but God, and herein lies its high dignity. In this sense human society exists for each person and is subordinate to him. The state must not compromise man's natural rights, because they are given by a higher law than the state's. The state itself is only one of the means granted to man by the natural law to help him in achieving his last end, and he casts it aside as an outworn instrument when he passes out of earthly society into the kingdom of heaven.

However, because man is such a *lowly type* of person, subject indeed to no being but God above himself, but utterly dependent on his equals for every kind of service and abounding in needs and wants, both physical and intellectual, that only his fellowmen can supply, man during his earthly life becomes a part of a larger whole whose common temporal good is greater than the individual temporal good of each member taken separately. In this sense the common welfare takes precedence over private comfort and security. Since the state exists to protect the life, liberty, and property of all, the individual may be called on to play his part in the common defense even at the expense of his own life, liberty, and property.

The theory continues with an exploration of the concepts of personality and individuality as verified in the selfsame individual person. The whole man is a person, and the whole man is an individual; personality and individuality are only mentally distinguished aspects. According to the Aristotelian theory that quantified matter is the principle of individuation, man is an individual by reason of his body. But man is a person by reason of his soul, since a person is an intellectual being, and man is intellectual by reason of his form, or soul. Thus by reason of his individuality founded on his temporal needs man is a member of the political community and subordinate to it, but by reason of his personality based on his eternal destiny man

transcends the political community and subordinates it to himself.

STRUCTURE OF THE STATE

The building blocks of the state are the members, the individual human beings of whom the state is composed. How is the state built up out of these materials? Is it composed directly of individuals with no structures or subgroups in between, or is it made up of families, which in turn are made up of individuals? Should we include other groupings larger than the family but smaller than the state? Are such groups essential to the state or only incidentally found in some states? There are three main views:

1. The *atomistic* concept of the state holds that the state is made up directly and proximately of individuals. Each citizen is like an atom in a homogeneous mass. He counts for one and no more than one, not representing others under him. No intermediate groups such as the family, the business firm, or the labor union are recognized as structural units in the state. They exist, of course, and the state must deal with them extensively, but they are not regarded as part of the state's essential makeup. In the state each individual is expected to act for himself alone, banding with others only for mutual self-interest in a contractual relation. The atomistic view is characteristic of laissez-faire individualism.

2. The *biological* concept of the state gives the state not merely a moral union but a physical entity over and above the members that compose it. It overdoes the analogy between a society and a living organism. Just as the organs and members of the living body have no life of their own but live with the life of the whole, so also the individual person and the family are thought to be as completely submerged in the state as a cell or organ in the living body. There are various interpretations of this view, but the most extreme as well as

the most logical is the *totalitarian* concept, in which the individual counts for nothing. There is just a global mass of social humanity in which the individual has not even the independence of an atom.

3. The *hierarchical* concept of the state stands between these extremes. The state is seen as a complex structure of individuals and families, so that the family is an essential ingredient in the state's composition. Some individuals live singly outside families, and members of families have some relations to the state independently of their family status, but the very existence of the state depends on a healthy flourishing of family life among its people. Within modern states there are also a number of voluntary associations with semipolitical functions, carrying on work for the common good that the state would otherwise have to do by itself. These voluntary associations are not essential to the state in the same way as the family but are sort of properties pertaining to a well-developed state. This structure of individuals, families, voluntary associations, and the state forms a hierarchical arrangement. Some writers call this the *organic* theory and contrast it with the biological theory, which they call *organismic,* but the similarity of names is confusing, especially since other writers call organic any theory opposed to the atomistic. Care must be taken to stress that the state is not a physical organism but a moral organization in which individuals and families retain their identity, rights, functions, and relative autonomy.

Of these three views the hierarchical one alone contains a proper balance of the individual and the social. It insists on the *principle of subsidiarity:* that no higher organization should take over work that a lower organization can do satisfactorily. The higher does not exist to absorb or extinguish the lower but to supplement and extend it. Otherwise the rights given by nature to the individual and to the family, and man's freedom to organize for lesser

pursuits within the state, are rendered meaningless. On the other hand, the state should provide a favorable environment in which individuals, families, and voluntary associations can fulfill their functions properly. It has the right and duty to intervene when they fail to function as they ought or cannot harmonize their activities for the common good.

SUMMARY

The state is held to be a *natural* society and not merely a conventional society, because the family naturally broadens out into the tribe with a central village and becomes a state when it achieves self-sufficiency under a common authority. Any group arriving at this condition is bound by the demands of nature to organize itself into political society.

Opposed to this theory is the *contractual theory* of Hobbes and Rousseau, according to which the state is an artificial product of human agreement. The *social contract* supposes a nonsocial and nonmoral state of nature, overlooks the natural expansion of the family, requires the alienation of inalienable rights, cannot logically bind posterity, and does not account for all the rights the state claims.

The state is a *self-sufficient* society, independent, autonomous, and sovereign. It has all it needs to fulfill its end and depends on no higher society. But its sovereignty is not absolute, for it is limited by the moral law and the equal rights of other states.

The state is for man, not man for the state. This cannot be said without qualification, because man must sometimes sacrifice himself for the state. Maritain explains it thus: The whole man is part of the state, but not by reason of all that is in him. Because he is a *person,* man transcends all temporal societies and is subordinate only to God. Because he is a *lowly type* of person, poor in self-sufficiency, the individual man is dependent on his fellows for his temporal welfare and must sacrifice his personal good for the common good. The state itself, however, is not for itself as a state but for all its people.

The *structure* of the state is the arrangement of its components. The *atomistic* view has the state built up proximately of individuals, like atoms in a homogeneous mass.

The *biological* view submerges the individual in the whole, like a cell in the living body. The *hierarchical* view sees the state as a structure of individuals, families, and voluntary associations that retain their identity, rights, and functions while directed to the common good by the state, according to the *principle of subsidiarity*.

QUESTIONS FOR DISCUSSION

1 How can the state be a natural society? Since there was a time when political society did not exist, how can man live without something natural to him? Are all primitive peoples immoral because they are not politically organized?

2 Could not the state still be a natural society even if formed by a voluntary agreement among those who are to be its members? What is wrong about an origin by contract?

3 The political state has been the greatest exploiter of man. History is a bloody record of tyranny, oppression, wars, and injustices within the nation and against other nations. If the state is a natural society, it seems to be an immoral one. Can man be morally obliged to belong to an immoral society?

4 If the state is for man, and man as a person transcends the state, why should man have to give up his life, the most personal thing about him, for the benefit of an abstraction such as the state?

5 How can the principle of subsidiarity be proved? Is it a moral requirement or only a way of indicating that we prefer to have our societies limited?

READINGS

The great classics of political philosophy include such works as Plato's *Republic,* Aristotle's *Politics,* Cicero's *De Republica* and *De Legibus,* St. Thomas' *De Regimine Principum,* Niccolò Machiavelli's *The Prince* and *Discourses,* Jean Bodin's *De la République,* Robert Bellarmine's *De Laicis,* Francis Suarez' *De Legibus,* Thomas Hobbes' *Leviathan,* John Locke's *Two Treatises on Government,* Montesquieu's *Spirit of the Laws,* Jean Jacques Rousseau's *Social Contract,* Hamilton, Madison, and Jay's *Federalist Papers,* and John Stuart Mill's *Representative Govern-*

ment. From this formidable array the student should find something to interest him.

On the matter of this chapter read Plato's *Republic,* bk. II, §369-374, and *Laws,* bk. III, §676-682; Aristotle's *Politics,* bk. I, ch. 1-2; Hobbes' *Leviathan,* pt. I and II; Locke's *Second Treatise on Government,* ch. 1-4, 7-10; and Rousseau's *Social Contract,* bk. I-III.

Read Jacques Maritain's *Man and the State,* which sums up the results of his important work in political philosophy. Two earlier booklets of his are recommended: *The Person and* the Common Good and *The Rights of Man and Natural Law.* Yves Simon's *Philosophy of Democratic Government* is a unique and rewarding work; see ch. 1. Read Heinrich Rommen's *The State in Catholic Thought,* ch. 4, 9-12, 17-18; Johannes Messner's *Social Ethics,* bk. III, pt. I and II; and George Catlin's *Story of Political Philosophers,* ch. 3, 5-9, 14. See

Reinhold Niebuhr's *Moral Man and Immoral Society* for a different approach.

Austin Fagothey, *Right and Reason—an Anthology,* contains Aristotle's *Politics,* bk. I, ch. 1-2; selections from Hobbes' *Leviathan,* ch. 13-15, 17; Rousseau's *Social Contract,* bk. I, ch. 1-6, 8; and Locke's *Second Treatise on Government,* ch. 5, which gives his views on property.

CHAPTER 26

GOVERNMENT

PROBLEM

A state is said to rule, or govern. Government primarily means the actual exercise of the state's function, its direction of its citizens to their common good. To accomplish this purpose a state can be organized in various ways. The particular organization used in a certain state is called its constitution. It determines the number of officers, how they are chosen, their coordination and subordination, their powers and duties, and the apportionment of authority among them. Government often means the constitution, especially when we speak of the form of government. Men tend to concretize abstractions and refer to the body of legislative and administrative officers, the group of persons officially exercising government, as *the government* of that particular state. Thus government means the act of governing, the constitution, and the persons holding political power.

There can be no society without authority. It is evident that if authority exists anywhere in a state, it must exist in the government. How do the government officials obtain it? How should they use it? We shall discuss the following topics:

1. How is the recipient of authority designated?
2. Is there any best form of government?
3. How much should the state interfere in private life?
4. Why must the moral law be supplemented by positive law?
5. Is there a law between natural law and positive law?
6. Are we morally obliged to keep the civil law?
7. Why and to what extent does the state have the right to punish?

RECIPIENT OF AUTHORITY

In a conventional society the same convention or agreement that establishes the society determines the mode of selecting its officials. In the natural society of the family the qualities of aggressiveness and leadership normally preponderant in the male designate the husband as the responsible head of the family, at least as traditionally viewed. How authority in *political* society begins to reside in one person or group of persons is a controverted matter. Among those who accept the state as a natural society, rather than as a merely conventional one, three main explanations have been devised:

1. The theory of the divine right of kings
2. The theory of popular consent
3. The patriarchal theory

1. The theory of the *divine right of kings*, defended by King James I of England and by Sir Robert Filmer, held that the actual rulers have their authority by an immediate personal grant from God, who not only gives authority to the state but even selects the rulers, either by positive intervention as in the case of King Saul in the Jewish theocracy, or by tacit

approval of the ruler selected by appointment, election, hereditary succession, or some other traditionally recognized manner. Most is made of the title of hereditary succession. The kings were not loath to have their thrones bolstered by this theory, which would make it immoral to unseat them no matter how badly they governed.

2. The endeavor of kings to bend philosophy to their service provoked an immediate reaction. The formerly prevailing view, that of popular consent, also called the *translation* or *transmission* theory, implicit and undeveloped in medieval writers, was more expressly formulated by St. Robert Bellarmine in his *De Laicis* (On the Laity) and by Francis Suarez in his *De Legibus* (On Laws) and *Defensio Fidei Catholicae* (Defense of the Catholic Faith). John Locke wrote his *Two Treatises of Government* against Filmer's *Patriarcha*.

Bellarmine and Suarez, whose opinions are substantially the same on this point, hold that the state is a natural society, that men are not free to form the state or not as they please but are obliged to do so by their natural needs and inclinations, and that all authority comes from God and is no mere product of human convention. Nevertheless, though the people themselves do not give authority to the state, they are the ones who select the ruler who is to bear that authority. God immediately confers authority on the whole people civilly united; the people then determine the form of government and transfer the authority to an individual or a group for its actual use.

That families are descended from a common ancestor, live near one another, have common needs and interests, and have organized themselves into a tribe with a central village are all causes disposing groups of men toward statehood and making the formation of a state naturally imperative. But the formation of an actual concrete state with a definite ruler and a definite type of organization requires the consent of the people, which is the proximate efficient cause of this particular state. The consent of the people may be either express or tacit, either direct or indirect, but in all cases it is the original title a ruler has for his authority. Though neither Bellarmine nor Suarez uses the exact words of Jefferson's phrase, "Governments derive their just powers from the consent of the governed," it aptly summarizes their opinion.

The difference between this theory and the contractualism of Hobbes and Rousseau should be apparent at a glance (see top of p. 289).

3. Some antiliberals of the nineteenth century, alarmed by the excesses of the French Revolution, tried to steer between the divine right of kings and the basically democratic theory of Bellarmine and Suarez. The *patriarchal*, or *designation*, theory, stemming from the work of Joseph de Maistre,* Donoso-Cortés,† Karl von Haller,‡ and Aloysius Taparelli,§ holds that when civil society is first formed, some man or group of men may be so outstanding in fitness and leadership as to receive an immediate grant of authority through the natural law independently of the consent of the people. Some natural fact indicates this person or group. He may be the patriarch himself, or the eldest son of the eldest branch of the family, or the tribal chieftain, or a victorious military leader, or a man who by gifts of intellect and will has done most to weld the people into a body politic. Such a man receives his grant of authority immediately from God, inde-

---

*de Maistre, *Du Pape* (On the Pope).
†Donoso-Cortés, Ensayo sobre el Catholicismo, el *Liberalismo y el Socialismo* (Essay on Catholicism, Liberalism, and Socialism).
‡von Haller, *Restauration der Staatswissenschaften* (Restoration of Political Sciences).
§Taparelli, *Saggio teoretico di diritto naturale* (Theoretical Essay on Natural Right).

Hobbes-Rousseau	Bellarmine-Suarez
Man is not naturally social and forms the state only out of expediency.	Man is naturally social and is obliged by the natural law to form the state.
The state is an artificial institution and a pure invention of man.	The state is a natural society based on man's natural needs and instincts.
The social contract establishes political society itself as an institution.	The contract determines only the form of government and the ruler.
Authority is but an aggregate of individual human wills.	Authority comes from God to the people, who transfer it to the ruler.
The ruler somehow acquires rights the people have no power to give him.	The state receives its superior powers from God through the natural law.
The contracting parties bind posterity but with no valid authority to do so.	The natural law binds posterity to honor the state's just commitments.

pendently of the consent of the people, for they are obliged by the natural law not to refuse his leadership. Even when no such man appears and the people choose their leader, he receives his authority so directly from God that it does not pass through the people.

The theory of the *divine right of kings* is easily disposed of. Except in the Jewish theocracy, no act of divine intervention designating the form of government and the person of the ruler has occurred in history.

The *patriarchal theory* argues against the popular consent theory thus:

1. The patriarch or chieftain already had some sort of authority in the tribe before it passed into statehood, and it is natural that he should keep it.

2. Authority is essentially an attribute of a ruler, whether an individual or a group, and cannot dwell in the community as such. The whole people are too unwieldy to exercise authority.

3. Popular consent, though one of the titles, is not the only title to political power. It cannot be proved historically that all original rulers were elected by the people.

The *popular consent theory* answers these arguments as follows:

1. The patriarch or chieftain probably would become the ruler of a newly formed state, but not without the people's consent, at least tacit, if the state is not to start as a tyranny instead of a just government. There is no need of express consent in the form of a vote.

2. Formal authority ready for immediate use resides in the ruler, but basic authority resides in the whole community. Because they are too unwieldy a body, the people transfer the exercise of authority to an individual or group charged with the task of governing.

3. There are many titles to political power, but they are all derivative except the one basic title of popular consent. No other title is valid by itself but becomes so only when confirmed by at least tacit consent of the people. Rule against the people's will, maintained chiefly by force, is the perversion of government.

Besides, during an interregnum there is no person in the state holding supreme authority; if authority vanishes, the state itself vanishes. The patriarchal theory cannot solve this difficulty, but the popular consent theory simply has the authority revert to the people. Also, natural law must provide some remedy for tyranny. Tyrants can be removed only by revolution, but no one can authorize a revolution except the people themselves, and to do so some form of authority must already dwell in them. By its very nature all government must be *for* the people, since its purpose is the common good. The popular consent theory says that it should also be *of* the people, arising from their consent and with their authorization; whether it should be *by* the people, so that they do the governing themselves, depends on the adoption of a democratic form. The popular consent theory does not require this last element but finds it congenial.

FORMS OF GOVERNMENT

From the earliest times political writers have tried to classify the forms of government. Plato* has a fivefold division based on a gradual falling-off from the ideal (aristocracy, timocracy, oligarchy, democracy, tyranny). Aristotle† has a sixfold division based on a double principle, the number of rulers and the quality of their rule; he lists three good forms (monarchy, aristocracy, polity) and three perversions (tyranny, oligarchy, democracy). These ancient divisions have yielded in the popular mind to the threefold classification into monarchy, which may be absolute or limited; aristocracy, which may be of birth or wealth; and democracy, which may be pure or representative. These forms may be combined in so many ways that no two governments are exactly alike.

There is nothing ethically wrong with any of these forms or their combinations. Moralists think that the way a government functions is more important than the way it is constituted. Government is a means to the end of the state, the common good, the temporal welfare of the people. Any

---

*Plato, *Republic,* bk. VIII.
†Aristotle, *Politics,* bk. III, ch. 7, 1279a 22 to 1279b 10. For the ancients democracy meant mob rule; hence it is listed among the perversions.

government that actually fulfills this end to the satisfaction of human expectation is good; any that does not, but governs for the benefit of the few at the expense of the many, is not good.

There have been efforts to prove that representative democracy is the best form of government. A distinction must be made between the relatively best, the best for this people in these circumstances with these traditions and in this stage of its historical development, and the absolutely best, the best for an enlightened and mature people in almost ideal conditions. In the first case one type of government will be best for one people, another for another; which to adopt or maintain is a matter of political prudence. In the second case one can make out a good argument for democracy, since, other things being equal, it is more fitting for a free people not only to be ruled but also to share in the act of ruling. In actual fact, however, other things hardly ever are equal, and for democracy to work a people must have had a long apprenticeship in self-government.

In structure, all forms of government are ethically acceptable. In function, only those forms can be approved which actually succeed in realizing the end of the state. It is wrong to force on a people a type of government they do not want. Tyranny, the misuse of government, is perhaps the worst moral crime that can be committed, because it hurts so many. Leaders of the state, and to some extent the people, have a serious moral obligation in justice to do what they can toward correcting the defects in their government.

GOVERNMENT CONTROL

Having seen how authority comes to reside in the governing body of a state, and the chief forms it takes, we now ask how far the government should go in the exercise of its authority, in controlling the lives of its citizens. Including untenable extremes, we can list five possible views, grading them from the least to the most interference. Government should:

1. Be abolished as unnecessary
2. Be mostly negative and limited to mere policing
3. Positively assist private initiative for the common good
4. Assume direction and control of all public affairs
5. Absorb the whole of human life

We shall discuss these opinions, beginning with the extremes and working toward the center. Nothing further need be said about the first opinion, *anarchism*, and the fifth opinion, *totalitarianism*. Both are clearly contrary to the nature of man, since the first denies the rights of society and the other the rights of the person.

The second opinion is *individualism*. The nineteenth century called it *liberalism*; today it would be regarded as reactionary conservatism. It is a theory of economics as well as of politics. It was advocated by the Physiocrats in France,* who coined the phrase "laissez faire," and by the Economic Liberals and the Manchester School in England.† It is resentful of all government interference in business and wants no more government interference elsewhere than is strictly necessary. The activity of the state should be limited to keeping public order, protecting property, punishing criminals, and defending against foreign attack. Because its functions would be mainly negative, it is sometimes called the *watchman state*. It is also known as the *minimizing* theory, since it can be summed up in the statement: "The best government is the least government."

The fourth opinion, so far as it falls short of totalitarianism, is called *statism* and *paternalism*. Its corresponding economic theory is socialism, but it can exist without

socialism, as in the mercantilist monarchies before the French Revolution. If not socialistic, it allows private property but leaves little scope for private enterprise in its use. It imposes the minutest regulations on all business and makes the undertaking of nearly all public works a state monopoly. Though free from theoretical convictions that the individual and the family are mere cogs in the state machine, in practice it interferes unduly in the personal and family lives of its people and infringes on their natural rights. As the name *paternalism* indicates, it looks on its subjects as incapable children rather than responsible citizens.

The third opinion seems to gravitate to the center and to maintain the proper balance between the claims of the individual and the state. It does not want any more government interference than necessary but is willing to admit it when necessary. It leaves the way open for private initiative but is ready to come to its assistance when private initiative fails. It not only protects but positively promotes all enterprises undertaken for the common good. It carefully respects the rights of the individual and of the family, does not try to usurp their duties, and helps them rather by offering opportunities than by regimenting their behavior. On the other hand, it does not hesitate to correct abuses, by legislation if necessary, when it becomes apparent that private influences cannot cope with them. No government has ever put this theory into practice perfectly, but it represents the ideal of many governments, including our own. No term unequivocally designates this ideal, and we shall simply call it the *middle way*. It can still be the middle way even if it has leanings to one side or the other, as in the conservative and liberal elements of our own country.

Individualism may work successfully for a while, especially in a land of unlimited opportunity, such as in the early days of our own country, but sooner or later proves inadequate to cope with the social stresses

---

*François Quesnay, Anne Robert Turgot.
†Adam Smith, David Ricardo, Richard Cobden, John Bright.

and strains of an advanced society. Paternalism may be necessary in colonial administration and among backward peoples not yet fit for self-rule, but even here should assume the role of a temporary educator rather than that of a permanent dictator. Whatever be the form of government or type of constitution in a state, the middle way represents the only way in which a government can exercise its powers consistently with the dignity of a mature and free people.

NEED FOR POSITIVE LAW

If man is already governed by the moral law, whether conceived precisely as natural law or generally as whatever source of moral obligation there is, it may seem that other laws are superfluous. However, we have seen that the natural law is clear to all only in its most general principles; it is unequally known because knowledge of it must be gradually developed, and in any case it lacks statement in an expressed formula. This formulation human legislators supply by enacting positive laws.

Human positive laws may assume two forms. *Declarative* positive laws simply declare in so many words what the moral law prescribes or draw conclusions deducible from it. Such would be laws forbidding murder, theft, perjury, and the like. These laws differ from the moral law only in the mode of promulgation. *Determinative* positive laws determine or fix ways of acting in accordance with the moral law but not deducible from it. Such would be traffic laws, ways of collecting taxes, times and methods of electing magistrates, the conditions for contracts, and the like.

The moral law needs to be supplemented by positive law, both declarative and determinative, for these main reasons:

1. *The dictates of right reason may be obscured in some persons.* In every community there are some with defective or perverted moral education. Against such individuals society must be protected by a code of laws drawn up by the more responsible members of society, expressly stating what right reason demands and setting up some mode of enforcement.

2. There is no definite natural penalty for wrongdoing. Many are willing to live with a reproachful conscience, if only they can satisfy their selfish will, but these people cannot be allowed to destroy society. Hence society has the duty to compile a code of criminal law, specifying definite and just punishments for definite crimes.

3. *There is often a choice of means to the end.* In merely individual action each one may pursue his own method, but sometimes the end must be achieved by concerted social action. Where teamwork is necessary, individual preferences must be sacrificed. Hence some social authority must decide among all these legitimate means and possible methods just which one is to be used in a given case.

4. *Complex social life continually changes.* To these changed conditions human society must be harmoniously adjusted, and new applications must be made to fit the new situation. Thus the industrial revolution brought up problems undreamed of before, and, though the principles of justice remain the same, they must now be applied to this new form of social organization. To prevent untold confusion positive laws providing a social and cooperative solution of these problems must be passed.

THE LAW OF NATIONS

The great lawgivers of antiquity were the Romans, whose legal system is the basis of nearly all modern law in the European tradition. The Romans developed their law in the early days of their Republic, but when they began to expand and incorporate other nations into their empire, they left a good deal of autonomy to their subject nations, allowing them to run most of their internal affairs according to their own laws. Difficulties arose when cases were to be decided between a Roman citizen and an individual of a subject nation or between individuals of different subject nations. They solved the problem by extracting the common elements from the laws and customs of all their subject peoples. This highest common factor they developed into the *jus gentium,* or *law of nations.* It was a gradual growth, but at the height of the Roman Empire it had become an impressive body of customary law. The new nations that resulted from the breakup of the Roman Empire continued to use this law of nations with which they were familiar, and on it they built the structure of this own laws.

The other source of European law is the customs of the Germanic tribes, but on the Continent these customs were grafted onto Roman law. The only comparable rival to the Roman law of nations is the English *common law,* which is the basis of English and American law. The common law consists of unwritten precedents and decisions of the common courts handed down through the centuries, as distinguished from statute law, or acts of Parliament. The English common law is independent of the Roman law of nations but has been greatly influenced by it.

The *jus gentium* is not the same as natural law. The *jus gentium* is positive law, for it is a sifting out of the common elements in the legal codes and customs of various peoples. However, since it abstracts from the peculiarities of different peoples, it is in great part an embodiment of natural law. The first clear distinction between natural law and the law of nations is found in St. Isidore of Seville.

Natural law is common to all peoples in that it is had by an instinct of nature, not by any human agreement, as the marriage of man and woman, the begetting and rearing of children, the common possession of all, the one freedom of all, the acquisition of those things that are taken

in the air or sea or on land; likewise the restoring of property entrusted or lent, the repelling of violence by force. For this or whatever is like this could never constitute an injustice but must be considered in accord with natural equity.[*]

The law of nations is the occupation of territory, the building and fortification of cities and castles, wars, captivities, enslavements, the recovery of rights of postliminy, treaties of peace and others, the scruple which protects ambassadors from violence, and prohibitions of marriage between persons of different nationality. This is therefore called the law of nations because nearly all nations have made such things their custom.[†]

The law of nations in the sense of the *jus gentium* is not the same as international law. International law aims to regulate the mutual relations of states as states. The *jus gentium* was a general law within all nations, not between nations, and dealt with activities of individuals without considering their nationality; it was supranational rather than international. The term *law of nations* is used by most modern writers to mean international law, thus causing much unfortunate ambiguity.

From this brief survey it can be seen that the *jus gentium* holds somewhat of a middle place between natural law and civil law. The *jus gentium* is limited both in space and time. It is derived only from Western peoples and at a particular era of their history. It does not represent the whole natural law, and it contains some things not required by natural law. Despite these limitations, it is of great help to the moralist.

MORAL OBLIGATION OF CIVIL LAW

Besides the law of nations, there are also the civil laws of particular states. What sort of obligation do they impose—a mere

---

[*]St. Isidore of Seville (570-636), *Etymologiae,* bk. V, ch. 4.
[†]*Ibid.,* ch. 6. (Translation of both passages taken from Le Buffe and Hayes, *Jurisprudence,* pp. 64-65.)

civil obligation of outward conformity or also a moral obligation binding on the moral conscience? The answer is implicit in what we have seen. If the state is a natural society required by the moral law for directing man's social life, is endowed by nature with authority for this purpose, and is the institution entrusted with the task of enacting and enforcing the positive laws needed to supplement the moral law, then the moral law itself imposes obedience to the civil law.

The argument, put this way, is general. Man is morally obliged to be a law-abiding citizen. Some points come up regarding the extent and seriousness of this moral obligation:

1. *Is the individual obliged or only the group?* One might argue that the state will not be destroyed by occasional disobedience of individual citizens, and therefore only the citizenry taken collectively and not the individual is morally obliged to obey the civil law. We see that the state continues despite individual acts of disobedience, but general disobedience would overthrow the state and make it futile. No one citizen has a better right to disobey than another; it is a case of all or none. To allow all to disobey would be to allow general disobedience. Therefore no one is allowed to disobey. We must not overlook the fact that the citizens as citizens are united into one body demanding cooperative action; each must contribute to the common good, and he does so by keeping the laws.

2. *Must the lawmaker intend to bind in conscience?* Some argue that many modern lawmakers no longer believe in genuine moral obligation and hence cannot intend civil laws to be morally binding. A formal and explicit intention of making the law binding in conscience is not necessary. Whatever be the theoretical beliefs of these lawmakers, they often have the practical intention of giving to their laws full authority, of making them bind as thoroughly as

laws can bind. This is an implicit intention and is sufficient to constitute a real law. Even when the legislator's authority does not demand their observance, the common good may.

3. *Is popular acceptance necessary for civil laws?* Not unless the nature of the state or of the law requires it. In a pure democracy, and in laws requiring a popular referendum, the people themselves are the lawmakers, and the law becomes valid only by their consent. Ordinarily legislative authority is handed over to one person or a group, who have authority while in office to pass laws without referring them back to the direct vote of the people. Such laws should be changed by petitioning the lawmakers or electing new ones, not by disobedience. The refusal of the people to accept a law or general disobedience to it does not of itself nullify a law. At most it may arouse suspicion of some radical defect in the law, that it may be unreasonable or unjust or against the common good, and therefore not really a law; investigation can then verify or dissipate such a suspicion. Sometimes a legislator does not expressly repeal a law but tacitly lets it become a dead letter; this may be equivalent to repeal by the legislator, and if so, the law ceases to bind. A true law cannot be got rid of except by repeal, express or tacit, by the authoratative legislator, and until he does so it continues to bind morally.

4. *How are laws to be interpreted?* Interpretation of a law is its genuine explanation according to the mind of the lawgiver. Laws may be interpreted by the lawgiver himself, or by lawyers and jurists of standing, or by custom that has the tacit approval of the lawgiver. Custom has been called the best interpreter of law. The custom must not be reprobated by the lawgiver but must receive at least his tolerance and silent approval. It is this attitude of the lawgiver toward the custom that gives it authority as an interpreter of

law and prevents it from being an illegitimate assumption of authority by those subject to the law. With the tacit approval of the lawgiver, custom may not only interpret but also establish or abolish laws. A too rigid interpretation of the letter of the law may go contrary to its spirit and do more harm than good. Hence most governments admit the principle of *equity*, a tempering of the rigor of the law in the interest of reasonableness and natural justice.

PURELY PENAL LAWS

There are certain civil laws that many good people feel no qualm in violating. They know their conduct is illegal, but they do not consider it immoral. A man who breaks traffic laws when there is no danger, or gets something through the customs office without paying duty, or operates a business without a license, does not feel that he has committed a morally evil act. A penal law is any law provided with a penalty, and a *purely penal law* means one that imposes no obligation in conscience but has a penalty attached for violation.

Purely penal laws pose a problem. They are commonly regarded by the people as genuine laws; yet a law that would impose no obligation whatever does not seem to have what the idea of a law demands. We seem to be faced with the dilemma that either these so-called laws are not really laws or that they do bind in conscience. In either case we go against the widespread opinion of well-meaning and conscientious persons.

Many writers of the intellectualist tradition, that law is mainly an act of reason guiding man to the good, will not admit the concept of purely penal law. They argue that a law is a work of reason and meant for the common good; if, therefore, a lawmaker intends a law at all, he must intend its full observance. Some say that

all civil laws, unless manifestly unjust, bind in conscience, and their violation is a moral fault measured by the seriousness of the matter. Others require that a true law be really *necessary* for the common good, and admit that certain so-called laws are only rules and regulations for civil decorum and public good order, whose violation does not imply a breach of morals unless accompanied by contempt for authority. This group, then, either will not hear of purely penal laws at all or, if they use the term, mean so-called laws that are not really laws.

Those of the voluntarist tradition, that law is mainly an imposition of another's will, generally accept purely penal laws. Since for them law is essentially an act of the lawmaker's free will, he may choose not to invoke his power of binding in conscience. A common explanation of this theory is that a purely penal law imposes a disjunctive obligation: either obey the law literally or be willing to pay the penalty if caught breaking it. Thus the law is really a law because it does impose moral obligation, though a disjunctive one. The legislator, it is said, can intend to make the obligation disjunctive, with an option for fulfilling it in one way or the other, even though he indicates his preference for literal observance. By assessing heavy penalties out of all proportion to the crime, the legislator seems to show that he is not averse to allowing the act if one will pay the price. Some laws, especially those designed to raise revenue, may attain their end in this way, for the fines collected for breaking the law may exceed what the law would have brought in had it been kept by all. The fact that modern states rely so heavily on police machinery to enforce such laws, rather than on an appeal to duty, is considered an indication of the lawmaker's mind.

In summary, there are three possible views on the moral obligation of the civil law: all bind in conscience, or none do, or some do and some do not. The first view, though it has its defenders, is too severe and contrary to common opinion and practice. The second view is too lax and plainly false, for some civil laws are evidently necessary for the common good. The third view seems the only reasonable solution, but it brings up the problem of distinguishing which laws bind in conscience and which do not. Those which do not can be called purely penal laws with a disjunctive obligation, according to the voluntarist theory; or it can be said that they are mere directives and not really laws, according to the intellectualist theory. In either case civil laws which are thought not to bind in conscience can be recognized if their main purpose is raising revenue, if the penalty is much too severe for the offense, if police methods are exclusively resorted to, or if they involve mere technicalities of procedure.

TAXATION

The state's right to exist and to pursue its end implies the right to the necessary means. Since no state can get along without revenue, the state has a right to tax its citizens. Since no right is unlimited, legislators are morally obliged in justice to keep taxes within reasonable limits, to account for the use of public funds, and to distribute the tax load as equitably as possible. How taxes ought to be arranged to preserve distributive justice is the business of political and economic experts. Ethics can only point out to them their obligation.

If the state has the right to impose taxes, the citizen has the duty to pay taxes. One who is not too poor to pay some taxes yet pays none whatever is plainly failing in an important duty concerning the common good. Indirect taxes now make this condition almost impossible. Is one morally obliged to pay all the taxes imposed? If the tax is clearly unjust, there can be no moral obligation. The judgment that taxes are unjust must not be made hastily; people are always complaining about taxes even when there is no doubt of their necessity. Yet is there an obligation to support the waste, graft, and inefficiency rampant in almost all governments? Some distinguish between the duty of paying taxes in general, a clear moral obligation, and the duty of paying this or that particular tax, a controverted issue. Can the latter, that is, certain particular tax laws, be regarded as purely penal law? For those who admit that there are purely penal laws, there is some probability to this opinion, especially when one considers the previously mentioned four criteria for discerning which laws might be purely penal. In financial matters even idealists tend to cut corners and find it hard to break away from a narrowly legalistic interpretation of moral duty.

PUNISHMENT

Laws are useless without enforcement, and enforcement supposes the right to punish. Punishment is applied by the executive power of the state, but the judgment that punishment is deserved is rendered by the judicial power. Punitive justice involves distributive and legal justice (sometimes also commutative) in the function of restoring the balance of equality upset by crime.

The following discussion has no reference to the punishment of animals, children, maniacs, or others who cannot be guilty of moral evil. This is not punishment in the strict sense but a figurative extension of the term. There is a resemblance in the means used, but the purpose is quite different: not to repay for crime committed but only to train or restrain irresponsible beings.

Punishment in the strict sense has three functions, one looking to the past and two to the future. As looking to the past, punishment is *retributive*, because it pays back the criminal for his crime, gives him his just deserts, reestablishes the equal balance of justice which has been outraged, and reasserts the authority of the lawgiver which the criminal has flouted. As looking to the future, punishment may take two forms. If directed to the improvement of the offender and his rehabilitation as a member of society, it is *corrective*. If directed to preventing similar crimes by others, showing by example what happens to offenders, it is *deterrent*. An ideal punishment should fulfill all three functions and thus serve all parties concerned. It should be:

1. Retributive, vindicating the rights of the offended
2. Corrective, rehabilitating the offender
3. Deterrent, forewarning the community at large

In most acts of wrongdoing punishable by society three things are usually involved: an injury against the individual, a crime against the state, and a sin against God. For the *injury* done to the individual the offender is obliged to make restitution or compensation for the loss inflicted. This is only part of what is demanded by justice, for it merely restores things the way they were before the offense. It involves no payment for the crime as a crime and therefore is not punishment. The offender simply did not get away with it this time and may try again later. The individual offended, as an individual, is not entitled to more than compensation and has no right to wreak private vengeance, but the offense is a *crime* against the state as well as an injury to the individual. Hence, besides receiving compensation, the offended party can turn the criminal over to the state for punishment. The state has the right to exact retribution for the breach of public order and the assault on the majesty of the law, as well as the duty of trying to reform its wayward citizen and deter others from like crimes. A theistic ethics will also look on the evil act as a *sin* against God. Neither the individual offended nor the state can do anything about this. Forgiveness and punishment must be left to God, who is both merciful and just.

BASIS OF PUNISHMENT

There is no difficulty about the corrective and deterrent aspects of punishment. Everyone sees that without them human society is impossible. But much has been written on retributive punishment in modern times, and some have thrown it out as a relic of benighted barbarism. They argue that it is mere revenge and is therefore immoral in itself, that it only adds one evil to another and does not overcome evil by good. This is not a new idea—it is found in Plato:

> No one punishes the evil-doer under the notion, or for the reason, that he has done wrong; only the unreasonable fury of the beast acts in that manner. But he who desires to inflict rational punishment does not retaliate for a past wrong which cannot be undone; he has regard to the future, and is desirous that the man who is punished, and he who sees him punished, may be deterred from doing wrong again. He punishes for the sake of prevention.°

Plato, as logic requires, connects his theory of punishment with his view that no one does wrong voluntarily. He also expresses the very modern notion that crime is a disease and should be treated as such. Many modern writers adopt Plato's theory on other grounds; they are determinists in psychology and utilitarians in ethics; no one can be guilty of crime if there is no free will, and there is nothing useful to the public welfare about merely retributive punishment.

It is well to pay tribute to the humanity of these well-meaning people, but we must not so emphasize mercy as to destroy jus-

---

°Plato, *Protagoras*, §324. See also *Laws*, bk. XI, §934; Gorgias, §525.

tice. They are right in condemning revenge, but revenge and retributive punishment are not the same. Revenge aims at the emotional pleasure one receives from hurting an enemy, retributive punishment at securing justice simply. This is one reason that justice is best administered by a neutral party. Retribution is not merely adding one evil to another, unless one were to hold that justice itself is not a good. Many of the punishments used in former times were unjust and cruel, but that is an abuse and no argument against punishment itself. Some criminals are mentally ill, and they should be restrained, not punished; but to call *all* criminals mentally ill is to adopt an a priori theory that contradicts the evidence.

The reason we cannot abolish the retributive function of punishment, and limit ourselves to the corrective and deterrent functions, is that all punishment to be justified must be based on retribution. Retribution may not be uppermost in mind, but it must be present; otherwise the infliction of any punishment is morally wrong.

1. Punishment may not be inflicted unless a crime has been committed. If punishment were merely corrective and deterrent, we could inflict pain on any person to improve him or deter others from wrongdoing, whether he were guilty or not. But in these cases we can only threaten punishment, not inflict it. Guilt calls for retribution and gives us the right to inflict punishment so that it is not the use of an evil means to a good end. We may then also make the punishment corrective and deterrent as additional functions.

2. Punishment should be proportioned to the crime, but if the corrective and deterrent functions of punishment were the only ones, punishment should be proportioned to them. Not the guilt of the offender but what is necessary to correct him or to protect society should measure the penalty. If the criminal could be frightened from ever committing this crime

again, or be made such an example of as to deter many others from attempting it, we should be justified in punishing him far beyond his deserts, but such punishment would reduce a person to a mere tool for his own or others' improvement. All admit that for good reasons punishment may be mitigated but never increased beyond what the guilt of the offender demands, no matter how much good it may do. Why? Because it is not deserved; just retribution does not call for it. Hence retribution is an essential element in punishment.

To sum up: It is immoral to punish unless the accused is guilty, no matter how much good the infliction of pain may do him or society. It is moral to punish the guilty even if there is no hope of correcting him or deterring others from crime. Therefore neither correction nor deterrence but retribution is the basis on which punishment is justified. However, the corrective and deterrent functions of punishment are very important, and human rulers should devise their punishments with these functions uppermost in mind, leaving full retribution to God, but they cannot overlook retribution entirely, for this alone makes punishment allowable.

CAPITAL PUNISHMENT

From the beginning of recorded history the state has used capital punishment rather freely, often excessively. If the death penalty is out of all proportion to the crime, the state does wrong in using it. We are speaking of it here only as applied to very serious crimes, such as murder and treason, which all who approve of capital punishment acknowledge as its proper sphere.

The state exists to maintain justice, and one of its chief purposes is the prevention and punishment of crime. The contractualist theory has no way of explaining how the citizens who have no private right of taking others' lives can give this right to the state. The natural law theory has no such difficulty. In receiving its authority from God through the natural law, the state also receives from him the right to use the necessary means for attainment of its end. The death penalty is used as such a means. It fulfills the retributive function of punishment by reestablishing as far as possible the balance of outraged justice and is thought to be the only effectual deterrent against the most serious crimes.

By its very nature capital punishment cannot be corrective. But correction, desirable though it be in a punishment, is not absolutely necessary; in the most serious crimes the claims of retribution and deterrence are so imperative that the corrective aspect must be waived, if necessary. What other penalty could be used against criminals already under life sentence? If capital punishment often fails as a deterrent, the fault may lie rather in the way it is administered than in the nature of the punishment itself. The law's long delays can empty the lesson of all its meaning. To be an effective deterrent, punishment should be swift, summary, and sure. Enough time must be allowed to gather evidence and to give the accused a fair trial, but in their effort to protect the criminal our judges, lawyers, and juries can lose the proper sense of civic responsibility. On the other hand, many argue that the death penalty, no matter how well applied, has almost no deterrent effect.

Even if the state has the right of capital punishment, it need not exercise the right if it can protect itself from criminals in another way. In former ages life imprisonment for all major criminals was impossible because the jails did not exist. If the state is convinced that it can effectively handle crime without the death penalty, it may be argued that it not only need not but should not use it. Factual confirmation is supplied by the many states that have abolished the death penalty with no increase in crime. The conclusion seems to be that capital punishment has outlived its usefulness and those states are to be praised which have abolished it.

PRISON REFORM

The prison, which is supposed to reform the prisoner, is itself in need of reform. Everyone knows that there are some classes of criminals that have to be locked up for the protection of the public, and therefore there is no question of abolishing all places of detention. However, we seem to have reduced all punishment down to fine, imprisonment, or both, and have not had the imagination to devise other suitable punishments that could be called neither cruel nor unusual. Years ago we abolished the debtors' prison, which made it impossible for one ever to pay off the debt. Now it seems time to divert from imprisonment to other forms of punishment those who have committed a crime but are no menace to the public safety.

The effect of prison life on one who is not yet a habitual criminal is often to make him one. He is perverted by the criminals he has to associate with and embittered against society, which forced this condition on him, and he often comes out of prison far worse than when he entered. This effect is not the intention of the penal system, but it seems to happen too often for it to be dismissed as merely incidental. Hence arises the moral problem: Can we continue to use a method of punishment whose bad effects in so many instances outweigh its good effects? Not, surely, if we can find something better, and we are obliged to search for something better.

Just how to reform the penal system is a matter for penologists, criminologists, and other experts. The excellent work some of them have done so far only points to how much there is yet to be done. It is not the business of the ethician to try to do their job for them but only to point out the many moral inadequacies in the present system.

In discussing this matter, it is not well to put too much stress on the prisoner's rights. He retains, of course, his natural rights as a human being, which no amount of waywardness can cause a man to forfeit, such as the right to justice, decency, and respect for his person, and not to be brutalized, degraded, or treated cruelly. But the prisoner does not necessarily retain his right to property, to liberty, or even to his life (where capital punishment prevails), since the punishment consists precisely in the privation of these things. What civil rights the prisoner retains is decided by the civil state, which is the grantor of such rights. The prisoner by his crime forfeits them, and the state can do as it pleases in applying the forfeit.

Any mode of prison reform will be enormously costly, but our present system is enormously costly without producing enough of the desired results. Any additional cost that would produce better results is worth the price.

SUMMARY

Government means the act of governing, the constitution of the state, or the persons holding political power. Government supposes authority. How does that authority become lodged in a particular ruler or ruling group?

1. The *divine right of kings* theory, holding that the ruler is directly appointed by God, is deservedly obsolete.

2. The *popular* consent theory of Bellarmine and Suarez holds that God gives authority to the whole people civilly united, who then transfer its exercise to an individual or group. The implied contract does not establish political society as such, but only the form of government and the ruler; all government exists by the consent, at least tacit, of the governed.

3. The *patriarchal* theory holds that a man or group can be so outstanding in qualities of leadership as to receive a grant of authority from God without the people's consent; authority dwells only in the ruler, not even basically in the people.

Of the last two theories the popular consent theory seems preferable. It alone can explain an interregnum and a justified revolution. Any government in which there is not at least tacit consent of the people must be a tyranny.

The functioning of government is more important than its structure. Monarchy, aristocracy, and democracy are all ethically acceptable in principle. Some think that democracy is absolutely best, but in practice we must consider the relatively best: which form is best *for a people* depends on their traditions and circumstances.

How far should government interfere with private life? Theories run from *anarchism,* no interference at all, to *totalitarianism,* total absorption of everything into the state. *Individualism* and *paternalism* are more moderate but still exaggerate the function either of the individual or of the state. The ideal is the middle position, one of giving positive assistance to private initiative, correcting its abuses while scrupulously respecting its rights.

Positive law, both *declarative* and *determinative,* is needed to supplement the natural law because:

1. The ignorant need instruction and control by the wise.
2. Definite penalties are required for the safety of society.
3. Concerted action demands teamwork and leadership.
4. Society must meet changed conditions harmoniously.

The *jus gentium,* or Roman *law of nations,* the source of most modern legal codes, was both a highest common factor among the positive laws of ancient civilized peoples and an approach to natural equity. The English *common law* is analogous to it in the latter function. They are both positive law embodying much of natural law.

There is a moral obligation to maintain the state and obey the civil law, because the state is demanded by man's social nature and accomplishes its end by the civil law. Laws are binding on each individual citizen, whatever be the theoretical beliefs of the lawmaker. General disobedience does not nullify a law, and contrary customs require at least tacit approval of the authorities.

Are there *purely penal laws,* laws that do not oblige in conscience but have a penalty attached for violation? Some say that they are real laws imposing a disjunctive obligation, either to keep the law or to pay the penalty if caught. Others think that they are not real laws but merely directives for public order. Others discard the concept entirely.

The state has the right to *tax,* since it needs revenue, but not to overtax. It must distribute the tax load fairly. The citizens must pay taxes, but *some* particular tax laws seem to be either purely penal laws or mere directives.

Punishment has three functions: retributive, corrective, and deterrent. It reestablishes the balance of outraged justice, rehabilitates the criminal, and prevents others from similar crimes. If we abolish the retributive function, we make all punishment unjust. It is immoral to punish unless the accused is guilty, no matter how much good the punishment may do him or society. It is moral to punish the guilty even if there is no hope of correcting him or deterring others from crime.

The state has the right of *capital punishment,* which it exercises by the authority God gives it to attain its end. If it can curb criminals in another way, it need not and probably should not use this right.

The penal system is in need of thorough overhaul. The obligation is moral, but only experts can devise and carry out proper reforms.

QUESTIONS FOR DISCUSSION

1 Is it not enough that civil laws should bind us civilly without adding a moral obligation? Does the appeal to a moral obligation mean that the government is trying to get ethics and religion to do its job for it?

2 What do you think of calling capital punishment legalized murder? Why should the state have power over life and death when individuals cannot? Is the state usurping God's power?

3 If taxes are just, people must pay them; if taxes are unjust, people should not pay them. Why try to take a middle ground and reduce some taxes to purely penal laws? Is not the whole notion of purely penal law a subterfuge, a law that is not a law?

4 It seems that popular consent government is only a modern phenomenon. How, then, can it enter into the structure of a state, which is a natural society and independent of the accidents of time and history?

5 Is all endeavor to work out a philosophy of government futile, because all government is a historical growth that takes place without consultation of philosophy or philosophers?

READINGS

On the philosophy of government in general see A. P. d'Entrèves' *Aquinas, Selected Political Writings,* containing a translation of *De Regimine Principum* and of other political passages in St. Thomas' works, together with d'Entrèves' introduction; Jacques Maritain's *Freedom in the Modern World,* pt. I and III, *True Humanism,* ch. 4-7, *Scholasticism and Politics,* ch. 1, 3-4; Yves Simon's *Philosophy of Democratic Government,* ch. 2-5; Heinrich Rommen's *The State in Catholic Thought,* ch. 13-14, 19-21; and Frank Sheed's *Society and Sanity,* ch. 11-16.

On the recipient of authority, *The Political Works of James I,* edited by Charles McIlwain, and Sir Robert Filmer's *Patriarcha* are balanced by Robert Bellarmine's *De Laicis* (On the Laity); Francis Suarez' *De Legibus* (On Laws), bk. III, ch. 2-4, and John Locke's *Two Treatises of Government,* of which the first is a refutation of Filmer and the second (the important one) is an exposition of Locke's own views. John Figgis' *The Divine Right of Kings* is a standard work.

On forms of government, Plato's classification is found in his *Republic,* bk. VIII-IX; Aristotle's classification in his *Politics,* bk. III, ch. 6-9, 15-17, and bk. IV; and Cicero's observations in his *De Republica,* bk. I, ch. 22-47.

On state control and interference see Johannes Messner, *Social Ethics,* bk. III, pt. III; George Catlin, *The Story of Political Philosophers,* ch. 13, 20-22; as well as the works of Maritain, Simon, and Rommen mentioned previously. Walter Lippmann's *The Public Philosophy* is an interesting study of the natural law philosophy he considers inherent in the American form of government.

On human law read St. Thomas, *Summa Theologica,* I-II, qq. 95-97; q. 100, a. 2. Also read II-II, q. 57, a. 3, on *jus gentium;* q. 64, aa. 2-3, and q. 69, a. 4, on capital punishment; and q. 108, on vengeance, which he considers a virtue (retributive justice). Francis de Vitoria's *De Jure Gentium et Naturali* (On the Law of Nations and the Natural Law) is translated in J. B. Scott, *The Spanish Origin of International Law: Francisco de Vitoria and his Law of Nations,* appendix E. Francis Suarez' *De Legibus* (On Laws) is translated in part in J. B. Scott, *Classics of International Law: Suarez;* read bk. II, ch. 16-20; bk. III, ch. 1; bk. IV, ch. 9; and bk. VII, which is all on custom.

On punishment see Plato, *Protagoras,* §324, *Gorgias,* §525, and *Laws,* bk. XI, §934. Aristotle's *Nicomachean Ethics,* bk. V, on justice, contains much pertinent matter. Cesare Beccaria's *On Crimes and Punishments* did much to reduce the cruelty of punishments. J. D. Mabbott in his article "Punishment" in *Mind,* XLVIII (1939), and in his *Introduction to Ethics,* ch. 11, defends retributive punishment; this and opposing articles are printed in Joel Feinberg (ed.), *Reason and Responsibility.*

John Courtney Murray's *We Hold These Truths* interprets the ethics of America's pluralistic society. Paul Douglas' *Ethics in Government* and George A. Graham's *Morality in American Politics* discuss the practical aspects of ethics in political life.

Austin Fagothey, *Right and Reason—an Anthology,* contains selections from the writings of Aristotle, St. Thomas, Hobbes, Locke, and Rousseau, all of which have some relevance to this chapter.

CHAPTER 27

PROTEST

PROBLEM

No government is ever perfect. Change from within is part of its life, and necessary lest it suffer political death by stagnation. Change rarely comes from the top, where the ruling class is satisfied with its position and power. Growth in a state most often comes from groups within the body of citizens, who must have some way of redressing the grievances under which they labor and of initiating the improvements they feel desirable. Growth is a development from out of the past, not a putting to death of the past and a wholly new creation. Since not all see this lesson of history, in every state that is politically alive there will be tension between two extremes, the unbudging defenders of the status quo and the starry-eyed visionaries of a new dream. How and where to find a reasonably progressive midpoint is the problem. Some observations on it from the ethical angle are now in order:

1. May the state limit freedom of speech?
2. Must the state respect the individual conscience?
3. What of the relations between church and state?
4. What about the rights of races and minorities?
5. Is there a right of civil disobedience?
6. Are rebellion and revolution ever morally justified?

CITIZENS' FREEDOMS

One of the ironies of history is the need for a Bill of Rights. The state, which exists to safeguard its citizens in the free exercise of their natural rights, has been a notorious violator of them. The history of the last few centuries portrays the victory of the people in their long struggle to get back from the state fundamental rights the state had usurped and liberties it had suppressed. Hardly had the victory been achieved when totalitarianism arose as the most ruthless destroyer of freedom yet to appear. The ferment of today is a further continuation of the people's self-assertion. We can discuss only three of these rights, perhaps the last to be won and the first to be lost in a people's fight to be free.

FREEDOM OF SPEECH

The fact that speech is a natural ability means that man has a right to use it. Speech is not merely repeating what one has been told to say but is the manifestation of one's own thoughts. Therefore a man has a natural right to say what he thinks. But no right is wholly unlimited. A man can have no moral right to say things that are untrue or injurious to another person or harmful to the public welfare.

The state has the right to limit freedom of speech and of the press (which is only an extension of the right of speech) insofar as is necessary for the welfare of the

303

community. Libel, obscenity, and the active fomenting of rebellion are rightly suppressed, since a man has a right to his good name, the public has a right not to be assaulted by the foul mouthings of dirty minds, and the state has a right to continued peaceful existence.

It is one thing to admit that the state has a *right* to limit freedom of speech, and quite a different thing to ask how far the state should go in the *prudent exercise* of its right. Obscenity and pornography pose well-nigh insoluble problems. The civil law has not even devised a workable definition, and the courts' judgments are arbitrarily discordant. Attempts of local communities to guard their public morals are made futile by nationwide communication. Filth will proliferate wherever it makes money, and it makes plenty. Its purveyors claim the right of free speech, but what they are asserting is a right to the abuse of speech. If the law acts leniently toward them, it is not because they have any right but because it is so difficult to control this kind of thing by law. There are two schools of thought. Zealots would move in and create what would amount to a police state governed by their own narrow prejudices. Permissivists would drop almost all legislation as ineffective and hope that, with the forbidden-fruit aspect gone, the evil would subside to a tolerable level. Neither side convinces the other.

In political matters, history has shown that an overactive censorship is an unwise policy, and that it is better to tolerate some abuses for the sake of liberty than to correct all abuses by suppressing liberty. A government afraid of criticism confesses its own weakness, and a government that stifles all criticism is tyrannical. Constructive criticism and free expression of opinion are the best way in which the government itself can find out how it stands with its people, what their needs are, and what reforms should be instituted for the common good.

A practically unrestricted right of free speech supposes an enlightened and responsible citizenry. If the government is not to restrict them, they must restrict themselves. A paradox occurs when a citizen abuses the right of free speech to advocate the overthrow of the government that guarantees free speech and the substitution of one that would abolish it. This behavior can be taken indulgently only as long as such persons are an uninfluential minority. Any government allowing it on a large scale is committing political suicide.

A sort of inverse of the right of speech is the right to listen. No government has the right to spy on what is said within the family, nor has it the right to censor its citizens' mail except during wartime, and then only within certain limits. The use of modern listening devices poses a very difficult problem. The right to privacy is too important to be trifled with, and yet a government must have some way of gathering information about criminals and protecting the people from them. If used at all, listening devices should be under the strictest supervision, and the public should know when and where they can find guaranteed privacy with sufficient opportunity to enjoy it. The right of the government does not take away the rights of the individual and the family.

FREEDOM OF CONSCIENCE

Freedom of conscience is a natural and inalienable right. Just as a citizen has a right to say what he thinks, so he has a right to do what he sincerely believes is required of him. No state has the right to force a citizen to perform acts that he considers immoral or to forbid him to carry out duties that he judges to be morally binding on him. The citizen's conscience concerning war will be considered when we come to that topic.

Each one's conscience is his own. In a sense, conscience has an inside but no outside. What goes on in a person's conscience can be known only from his own report, but actions dictated by conscience can have a social as well as an individual impact, and thus we can have a difficult situation. Every large society contains its quota of peculiar people, running all the way from mild cranks to wild lunatics, some of whom may feel driven by conscience to highly antisocial and destructive behavior. Society is obliged for its own protection to restrain them. Because antisocial speech can be tolerated more easily than antisocial action, there is a limit to freedom of conscience in its external expression. Where to draw the line between the normal and the abnormal, between the tolerable and the dangerous, takes a great deal of political prudence. The legal rule of "clear and present danger" is not always easy to apply.

Even within the compass of the normal there can be difficulties. Should genuine believers in polygamy be denied a right to follow their belief in a prevailingly monogamous country? Should those who would let their child die for want of a blood transfusion, because they consider transfusions immoral, be allowed to have their way, or should the state intervene for the sake of the child? Some help may be found in the principle that a negative duty of never doing anything wrong is stronger than an affirmative duty whose fulfillment may be excused or postponed; thus the people will more easily tolerate the forbidding of actions they think right than the command to do positive actions they think wrong. But this guideline does not cover all cases.

FREEDOM OF WORSHIP

The only way in which a man can accept religious teaching is by being intellectually convinced of its truth. If he is convinced of its truth, he is morally bound to accept it; if he is convinced of its falsity, he is morally bound to reject it; if he is

doubtful, he has the right to reserve judgment until further investigation convinces him one way or another. The state has no means at its command to enforce its will but the use or threat of physical coercion, which might produce a hypocritical conformity but cannot beget conviction.

Religious persecution must be condemned as an immoral violation of a natural right. Religious tolerance came late in history, though it was advocated in theory long before it could be put into practice. What retarded its advent was the failure to distinguish between the belief and the believer, between error and the erring. Any religion that considers itself as the only true religion will consider contradictory religions to be false. This attitude is not confined to religion but includes any body of knowledge of which one is firmly convinced. But intolerance toward the belief does not justify intolerance toward the believer. As a person he has to find truth for himself; he has the right to make the search and to accept the results he sincerely arrives at. It is said that error has no rights. In a sense this is so, for only persons have rights, and error is not a person. In this sense neither has truth any rights. But the *person's* right must be respected. To grant it implies no approval of the beliefs he holds. There is nothing to prevent people of different faiths from living harmoniously side by side and aggreeing to differ in religious belief, each respecting the other's political right to follow his conscience. In reading the history of religious conflicts it is well to mark the distinction between the official teachings of a religious body and the behavior of some of its overzealous but misguided members.

Church and state are independent but related societies. The church is supreme in purely religious matters, the state in purely temporal matters. The church must not interfere in matters of a merely civic character, nor the state in the teaching and practice of religon. However, there will always be some relation between church and state because the same persons who are members of one society are also members of the other. The two societies should harmoniously cooperate where their interests touch and should arrive at a working agreement.

The *separation of church and state* is a difficult problem because of the ambiguity in the word *separation.* How far does it go? If all citizens belonged to the same church, church and state would coincide in membership but differ in purpose and function, and be at least *distinct,* if not separate. Even here provision would be necessary for the freedom of possible dissenters and minority groups to follow their own conscience openly and peaceably. In a pluralistic society such as ours, where the people profess many different religions and are split into any number of sects, a practical separation of church and state seems to be the only workable arrangement. As the facts of history show, it has succeeded admirably.

It is well to note that the term *separation of church and state* is used in different senses in different parts of the world. In countries where anticlericalism is strong it often is only a euphemism for subordination of church to state and suppression of religious freedom. This is the same thing as persecution.

WOMEN'S LIBERATION

That half the human race would accept a subordinate position, with denial of some of the most basic of human rights, and let this situation continue for many centuries, is one of the curious facts of history. There were ancient matriarchies, and women were always able to exert a great deal of influence, especially in the indirect way in which they are so expert, but for the most part men arrogated the work of government to themselves, gave women no place in it, and seriously curtailed women's

rights. Plato* was one great exception, but even he, though he grants women full equality of opportunity, does not think that women in general are quite as capable as men.

The emancipation of women, as it was called then, began in earnest in the last part of the nineteenth century with the campaign for the vote. It was the logical place to begin, for only by vote could they make their voice effective. Then, having achieved the vote, they went back to several decades of apathy. Only recently has a rearoused women's liberation movement made itself felt. What women want now is not only political but also economic, social, psychological, and cultural parity with men.

The moral philosopher should applaud the general thrust of the women's liberation movement. Women are human beings with all the natural rights that belong to human beings. How could any moral justification be made for denying these rights to fully human persons? Civil rights depend on the will of the citizens; yet only the most artificial arrangements of society could make women incapable of discharging the main functions of a citizen. If in earlier days citizenship was connected with military duty and political office with military leadership, there is no excuse in these times for perpetuating so obsolete a social structure. No woman should be excluded by reason of her sex from any of the rights and privileges that go with citizenship in the state. She should be eligible for the highest office in the land and should be able to compete with men on the sole basis of her ability.

A chief complaint is in the economic sphere. Women are not paid equally with men for the same kind and amount of work. Since women are relatively new to the working force, this inequality arose be-

---

*Plato, *Republic,* especially bk. V, §§ 451-458.

cause many women took jobs temporarily, never intending to be permanent members of the business but only waiting to acquire a husband. It was thought equitable that men, who were to make their whole career in that business, should be encouraged by greater pay. But this situation is no longer the prevalent one, and there are nearly as many women as men making a permanent career in a particular business. From the standpoint of justice, which is that of morals, women should have equal pay with men for equal work.

Another matter is that of careers for women. Some still maintain that woman's place is in the home, that she is supposed to find her fulfillment in bearing children to her husband, in taking care of his house, and in general acting as his unpaid servant. Many women find this a satisfactory life and defend it as woman's proper sphere. It surely can be for many, but there is increasing revolt among women against the stultifying life of a household drudge. Educated women need something better to occupy their minds and cannot always find it in the trivia of suburban life. Woman has a right to a career, to a form of life that is intellectually and emotionally satisfying. Why should she have a lesser right to it than her husband? It is especially in the latter part of her life, when the children are grown and she has much time on her hands, that women, especially those fitted for it by education, should have something worthwhile to which to devote their energies.

There are other, less agreeable features of the women's liberation movement. Despite the fundamental equality of the two sexes, each sex has its own peculiar characteristics that cannot be denied unless we want to deny that there are two sexes. If the human race is to be propagated, women will still have to spend nine months bearing the child and several more years intensely caring for it. If the woman is to go in for motherhood at all, she will have to discharge the responsibilities that go with it. Nature has not been equal to the sexes in the amount of time and care that must be spent on the child that is the common fruit of their union. That this cuts into a woman's career more than a man's is obvious. Common state nurseries are not the answer. It is futile for women to rebel against nature's provision and to try to emancipate themselves from the obligation of caring for and raising their own offspring. How to fit this in with a career is a matter for women's own ingenuity. If they cannot find the solution, who can?

The women's liberation movement has been hampered by some of its more hysterical supporters. It has unfortunately given its backing to causes, such as abortion, that would not liberate them *as* women but would liberate them from being women in any admirable sense. But when it is kept within proper bounds and restricts itself to rights women should possess, it is a moral claim for justice and the righting of a great historical wrong.

RACES AND MINORITIES

The world in general and our country in particular have become more acutely conscious of the huge wrongs done to minorities. The horrors of the slave trade and the injustice of slavery as an institution came at last to be recognized for what they always were, the most enormous of social crimes. But the freeing of the slaves was only the first step in rectifying a gross evil. The hundred years' failure to integrate the freed slaves and their descendants into the nation's society on equal terms, as human beings with full human rights, was a culpable prolongation of the crime of the past. Now the minority racial groups have dramatized their plight by voice and deed, and made it the burning issue of the day.

The correction of these injustices is a moral problem of the first magnitude, involving a vast social, economic, political, educational, and cultural task. However, the philosophical part of the problem is simple and clear, which may explain why philosophical ethicians have said so little about it. No philosopher of note has ever attempted to defend racial discrimination. Philosophers prefer arguable questions. This one has all the reasons on one side and none on the other.

All human beings have the rights that go with human nature. To differentiate men by their color, race, caste, or class, and not by their dignity and value as human persons, is to succumb to one of the grossest of irrational prejudices. To deprive others of equal rights because of racial or other accidental characteristics is to commit serious injustice. There is a moral obligation on all, where such discrimination prevails, to cooperate in working for its removal. How to do it, especially where the prejudices are long ingrained, may tax the virtue of prudence to the limit, but the duty is there and must not be indefinitely postponed.

There are a number of rights involved in racial discrimination: the right to vote, to a fair trial, to equal application of the laws, to fair employment practices, to admission to labor unions, to desegregated schools, to nondiscrimination in housing, to the unhindered use of public facilities. One's private right to choose one's friends and company does not extend to denying others the public goods of the community. The supplying of *separate but equal* facilities is a fiction and an insulting one, since on the whole the facilities are not equal and the separateness is meant to be a stigma of inferiority.

What means may racial minorities use to obtain their rights? In any established society legal means must first be used and exhausted. What happens when courts are prejudiced, juries are loaded, state laws conflict with federal laws, and justice is constantly denied? Then the means of se-

curing justice become the means of perpetuating and enforcing injustice. The right to vote can be denied by making registration impossible. The right of peaceful assembly and petition can be curtailed by the requiring of licenses for the use of meeting halls, public streets, and other places of assembly. The perpetual refusal of license renders nugatory the right the government itself is bound to protect. If such a situation were only temporary, the greater good might require that it be endured for a time, but when no legal remedy is in sight, there is no recourse except to extralegal methods.

The use of petition, assembly, and demonstration to obtain their constitutional and civil rights will not wholly relieve the plight of the black people in America. The law is conservative and does not usually initiate social change. All that the law could do, even if it were perfectly administered, would be to integrate the black into the mainstream of white culture. The whites are mostly under the illusion that since this is what they have unjustly denied to the blacks in the past, the granting of it will rectify the evil and give them what they are protesting for. What the whites fail to see is that their own unjust use of the law has in the eyes of the blacks ruined the law as a means of justice. The law itself has been the means by which the whites have hitherto kept the black in subjection, reinforcing the negative self-image of inferiority, which the blacks have been taught by a predominantly white society, and producing a profound alienation and resentment against the whole notion of law and order, which to the blacks means only white law and order. Since they have received nothing from law and order but segregation, repression, and degradation, it is little wonder that they have no respect for it. Homogenization into the standard middle class may be an acceptable goal for some black people, but it is not at all what a great many of them want. They have seen this culture from the outside and have learned to despise it. The revulsion can be emotional and in its exaggerated form unjust, but the fact is there.

What, then, do they want? That they want self-respect, pride in their origin, recognition of their own culture, besides equality and nondiscrimination, goes without saying. How to reduce these abstractions to some concrete form is the problem. The answer will have to come from the black people themselves. Even the right answer would not be accepted from any other source. So far the voices of the black community are in conflict. Unless some outstanding leader can bring them into harmony, their efforts may remain a protest *against* rather than a program *for*. Even so, the negative part of the work is not yet finished. The removal of discrimination remains a worthwhile, if interim, goal.

The black people have learned by painful experience that nothing but blatant and persistent militancy will produce results. The white man immediately forgets about the black man's plight unless it is constantly and dramatically thrust before him, and the black man slides back into apathy and resignation unless he is keyed up by ceaseless harping on the theme. The word *militancy* should not shock us. It need not be violent. It is organized and aggressive, of course, but it can be kept within legal limits. It can also step beyond legal limits to the extralegal or, as some prefer to call it, the supralegal.

Our concentration on the problems of the blacks in America has not been meant as neglect of other minorities, of the Mexican-American Chicanos or of the American Indians. Though neither have suffered the degradation of slavery, the Chicanos have a language difference to cope with, and the Indians are slowly reviving from virtual extinction. We took the blacks because of their effectiveness in dramatizing

their plight. The fact that race riots have quieted down does not mean that a moral investigation of the question is no longer pertinent.

America has no monopoly on problems arising from differences in race, language, religion, and culture. Glance at the world map and try to find a place wholly free from oppression by a dominant group. The same principles, arguments, and conclusions are applicable, with allowance for varied circumstances, to all oppressed and underprivileged peoples.

Since discrimination and its remedies, including appeal to the extralegal, are not restricted to the race question, this is the place to take up the topic of protests in general and the militant means that may be used to obtain justified ends. They run from civil demonstrations through civil disobedience and rebellion to a complete political revolution.

CIVIL DISOBEDIENCE

Civil disobedience as *disobedience* is a deliberate breaking of a government law one is bound to obey, not a strike or boycott or some other form of private harassment. As *civil* disobedience, it must be nonviolent, nonrevolutionary, aimed not at overturning the state itself but at rectifying an evil or attaining a good within the existing poltical framework. It is used as a means of protest and therefore must be *public;* a mere breaking of the law for personal advantage, such as robbing a bank, is disobedience but not civil disobedience. It may be a refusal to obey the very law against which protest is directed, as when such a law is thought unjust or otherwise immoral; or it may be a violation of other laws, just in themselves, such as trespassing, blocking streets, disturbing the peace, acting without a license, and similar troublesome but not permanently harmful acts, as a means of dramatizing the demands. This indirect method is the only way when a law is needed but does not exist, or when the breaking of the unjust law would cause too much disturbance.

It has been claimed that civil disobedience can never be moral:

1. Society requires order for its existence. The means that it uses to preserve order is law. To disobey the laws of society is to revolt against society itself. Whatever be the good intentions of the civilly disobedient, they are engaged in actual rebellion.

2. Any advanced society has means within it for the interpretation of its laws and for their just implementation. Since these means are within the legal structure itself, it is never necessary to resort to extralegal means. A higher authority can always be appealed to against an adverse decision of a lower authority.

3. There are as many consciences as there are people. Who is to decide that a certain law is unjust or that redress cannot be obtained by legal means? To set the private conscience up against the public conscience and let each one decide for himself what laws he will or will not obey is to substitute anarchy for government.

4. The social consequences of disobedience are always worse than those of obedience. It is impossible to engage in civil disobedience without violating somebody's rights, at least those of the public to peace and order. Even if some immediate advantage is gained, the long-range result is always a lessening of respect for law and an increase of contempt for authority.

5. Experience shows that peaceful civil demonstrations easily degenerate into riots. The mob is notoriously a dangerous thing, gets out of hand, is swayed by demagogues, draws to itself irresponsible agitators, ceases to be representative of the cause, and becomes demonstration for demonstration's sake. Riots, with the accompanying looting and destruction, are an inexcusable descent into barbarism and are morally indefensible.

6. Those who thus pass from extralegal to extramoral methods begin actually to defend their destructive behavior in principle. Nonviolent means of peaceful protests, they say, are too slow and ineffectual, whereas a few summers of rioting, looting, and burning made both the people and the government take notice and start acting. Some even defend looting and burning as involving mere property rights, which are not to be compared with the more important human rights.

Others claim that such arguments, drawn from theory, fail to face the actual facts of the situation:

1. Civil disobedience by its very nature is not an attack on society itself. No society is so perfect that it never needs reform. What is wanted is not an abolition of society but the correction of particular defects and injustices for society's own benefit. Not all protesters have such morally pure motives, but a good cause is not ruined by some immoral hangers-on.

2. Civil disobedience is to be used only when legal means have been tried and exhausted. It is not true that legal means are always available or that appeals will always be heard. What one has to look for here is the very purpose of law in general. Law does not exist for its own sake but for the sake of guaranteeing to the people their rights as human beings. Laws do not exist singly and independently but form a system of means for the common good. When observance of a single law produces the opposite effect, then it must yield, for it is irrational to insist on a means that makes the attainment of the end impossible.

3. Legality and morality do not always coincide, and there can be unjust laws. Except for the cumbrous process of judicial review, the law itself will not admit that it is unjust. Only the individual conscience can make that judgment. It should not do

so lightly but only after a thorough investigation or a prolonged experience of frustration. It can be confirmed in its judgment by the agreeing judgment of many other people, sometimes almost the whole people except the entrenched ruling clique.

4. The principle of proportion must be maintained. The cause agitated for must be worth the disturbance, and the means used must be kept within reasonable bounds. But it is absurd to think that some must continue forever to suffer gross injustices because the effort to remove them will cause others some inconvenience. The best way to lessen respect and produce contempt for the whole system of law and authority is to keep unjust laws on the books or to administer even just laws in an unjust manner.

5. No civil demonstration can be morally allowable unless it is under competent and responsible leadership, whose business it is to keep it within bounds and prevent it from turning into a riot. Otherwise the proportion of good to evil is violated and the rights of people in general are outraged. Experience shows that protests involving civil disobedience are quite possible without riot or violence, especially those in which the protesters willingly accept the penalty.

6. Extramoral methods can only mean immoral methods. Even justice cannot be obtained at the price of wreaking deliberate injustice on others. That property rights yield to human rights is a slogan with some truth to it, but it can be misapplied. It is not a question of comparing a man to a thing. Property rights are human rights in the sense that they are rights of human beings over their property. To destroy the property of innocent people, the ones usually hurt in a riot, is to attack the freedom of human beings to enjoy the fruits of their labor, and freedom is surely a human right. Destruction in a riot cannot be laughed off as if no one were responsible for it. They are responsible who did it or incited others to do it. It has no place in *civil* disobedience.

Civil disobedience strives to correct injustices and to seek redress within the existing structure of the state. It can also happen that the very structure of the state is the source of injustice, or the ruling power has become committed to exploitation. Then the stage is set for revolution.

REBELLION AND REVOLUTION

Rebellion is open, organized, and armed resistance to constituted authority. Revolt, insurrection, and sedition are more localized forms of the same thing. There will always be malcontents and disaffected groups even in the best of human societies. For the common good a government must try to keep them contented, which it can best do by scrupulous regard for minority rights, but no authority can allow itself to be openly defied. Since the state has the right to exist, it also has the right to put down rebellion by all efficient and legitimate means.

What if rebellion is provoked by abuse of power on the part of the ruler? Abuse of power does not by itself take away the right to power. A father unjustly punishing his son does not lose his paternal right, nor does a man putting his money to unjust use lose the ownership of it. Small abuses of power are occurring constantly and serious ones occasionally in every state, because rulers are only human and fallible. Such causes cannot justify rebellion, though they call for protest and redress.

What may a private citizen do when he is unjustly oppressed? Unjust laws have only the appearance of laws and can impose no moral obligation. Injustice in a law must not lightly be presumed but clearly established.

1. Passive resistance or nonobedience is required if the citizen is ordered to do something evil in itself, for no human law

can cancel the already existing obligation of the moral law. A so-called law that is unjust but does not order the doing of something evil in itself may be resisted or obeyed, as the subject thinks expedient. It is wrong to do injustice, but it is not wrong to suffer injustice. To prevent greater evils one may have an incidental obligation to obey, but there are some things one must refuse to do, no matter what the penalty.

2. Active resistance without physical force, by petitions, speeches, protests, books, pamphlets, editorials, and propaganda of all sorts, is always morally allowed against unjust laws and tyrannical rulers. But it is characteristic of tyrants to deny any opportunity for such peaceful methods.

3. Active resistance with physical force is allowed against a tyrant attempting to inflict grave personal injury, for the ruler in this case becomes an unjust aggressor. The rules of a blameless self-defense must be observed. If some citizens are unjustly attacked by a tyrannical ruler, others may come to their assistance against him.

Despite occasional injustice, it is wrong to stir up and wage civil war against a *rightful* ruler, that is, one who retains his right to rule. The right referred to here is not so much legal right as moral right. He may observe all legal and technical formalities and yet be a tyrant. Moral right means that he has not acted in such a way as to forfeit the office that still belongs to him in justice. If he is the rightful ruler, no one may rightfully depose him.

How can a ruler lose his right to rule? There are two ways. First, abuse of power may destroy the title on which the right is held. If the ruler took office bound by certain conditions and breaks his side of the contract, the people are not bound to theirs; in feudal times subjects were released from their oath of allegiance, and modern republics have the machinery of impeachment. Second, no matter how ab-

solute a ruler may be or how legitimate his title to office, he always loses his moral right to rule by certain, continued, and excessive tyranny. In this case rebellion against him becomes a justified revolution.

Revolution is a fundamental change in political organization or in a government or constitution: the overthrow or renunciation of one government or ruler and the substitution of another by the governed. Rebellion cannot be allowed unless it is the means for accomplishing a justified revolution. In a revolution a new kind of government may be established, or the same type may be retained with new personnel. The theory behind a justified revolution is that the ruler lost his right to rule by his tyrannical behavior, and that sovereignty reverts to the people in whom it always dwells basically anyway (according to the theory of Bellarmine and Suarez). Consequently, it is not directed against a rightful ruler, since he has lost his right, nor is it by private authority, but by the public authority of the whole people civilly united.

The following conditions for a justified revolution are set down not as absolute requirements, for historical contingencies are too diverse, but as useful norms:

1. The government has become habitually tyrannical and works for its own selfish aims to the harm of the people, with no prospect of a change for the better within a reasonable time.

2. All legal and peaceful means available to the citizens have been exhausted to recall the ruler to a sense of duty.

3. There is reasonable probability that resistance will be successful, or at least that it will secure a betterment proportional to the effort and suffering involved in a civil war.

4. The judgment that the government is tyrannical should be truly representative of the people as a whole. It should not be a movement of a single faction or party,

of one geographical district, or of one social class or economic interest.

Nothing said here is intended to weaken the authority of legitimately established and functioning governments, whose laws the citizens are morally bound to obey. But the moral law, which condemns tyranny as one of the worst of crimes because it wreaks injustice on so many, cannot oblige men meekly to submit to being ground into the dust with no hope of relief. The power of a ruler is too sacred a trust to be used irresponsibly yet kept indefinitely.

SUMMARY

The state must be responsive to the people's need for change and development.

The state must acknowledge the citizens' right of *free speech* and not limit it more than the common good demands. It is better to allow more than less freedom of speech, but libel, obscenity, and incitement to rebellion need some curb.

The state must respect *freedom of conscience,* but it should protect the people against external antisocial behavior.

The state must allow *freedom of worship.* Religious persecution is morally wrong. We should distinguish the belief and the believer, condemning false beliefs while respecting the right of persons to profess what they sincerely believe. Separation of church and state is often the best working arrangement.

Women have equal human rights with men, especially to equal pay for equal work and to a career of their own.

The state is obliged in social justice to correct *racial prejudice* and any disabilities resulting from merely accidental differences of birth, race, color, or class. Minorities may seek their rights first by legal means and, these failing, even by extralegal but moral means.

It is argued that *civil disobedience* can never be moral, because it flouts law and order, it bypasses the means within the legal structure, it opposes private to public conscience, it breeds contempt for law and authority, it degenerates into riots, and it results generally in more evil than good.

In answer it is said that civil disobedience wishes to correct injustice in society, may be used only when legal means have been exhausted, has to rely on individual judgment, must observe the principle of proportion, should be under responsible leadership, and can be kept from descending into anarchy.

The state's right to *suppress rebellion* is implied in its right to existence. Occasional injustice does not destroy a ruler's right to rule. A citizen may resist tyrannical acts by protest but may use violence only in self-defense against personal injury.

Citizens have the right of *revolution* only when the ruler has lost his right to rule. The conditions are habitual tyranny, no hope of improvement, the last resort, fair chance of success, and the backing of the people as a whole.

QUESTIONS FOR DISCUSSION

1 As a man has a right to think what he wants, so he has a right to say what he thinks. Why should the state have the right to muzzle the free expression of any opinion whatever? Wrong opinions should be counteracted by right opinions, not by suppression.

2   How can a state's right to put down rebellion be compatible with the people's right to stage a justified revolution? Will not the state always consider it an unjustified rebellion and the insurgents think it a justified revolution?

3   Have the black people in America the right to large sums of money in recompense for their many generations of servitude? Do all oppressed people have a right to remuneration for their years under tyranny?

4   What is the obligation of insurance companies regarding property destroyed in a civil protest that degenerated into a riot? Must the government make good? If it does, will it be subsidizing riots?

5   Are those arrested while engaged in civil disobedience criminal offenders or political prisoners? Those engaged in nonviolent breaking of the law? Those engaged in violent destruction? Is destruction of property without hurting people basically nonviolent?

READINGS

Plato's *Republic,* bk. VIII and IX, describes the degeneration of the state into tyranny. Aristotle's treatment of revolutions in the *Politics,* bk. V, is more factual than ethical. St. Thomas, *Summa Theologica,* II-II, q. 42, deals with sedition.

Famous works in defense of liberty are John Milton's *Areopagitica,* John Locke's *Letter Concerning Toleration,* and John Stuart Mill's essay *On Liberty.*

Locke's *Second Treatise on Government,* ch. 18-19, contains his idea of an appeal to heaven against tyranny.

Some well-known works on women's liberation are Simone de Beauvoir, *The Second Sex,* Betty Friedan, *The Feminine Mystique,* and Germaine Greer, *The Female Eunuch.*

Henry David Thoreau's article *Civil Disobedience* is dated but a classic. Martin Luther King's "Letter from Birmingham Jail" is on the way to becoming a classic statement. The *Autobiography of Malcolm X* is a vivid presentation of the black man's case.

Daniel Stevick in *Civil Disobedience and the Christian* gives a well-balanced and constructive analysis of the problem. See also Robert Drinan, *Democracy, Dissent, and Disorder,* and Hugo Bedeau, *Civil Disobedience: Theory and Practice.*

Bierman and Gould, *Philosophy for a New Generation,* is an unusual collection of articles, many of them most pertinent to the matter of this chapter.

Austin Fagothey, *Right and Reason—an Anthology,* contains Thoreau's *Civil Disobedience,* Martin Luther King's "Letter from Birmingham Jail," and selections from Stevick's *Civil Disobedience and the Christian.*

CHAPTER 28

EDUCATION

PROBLEM

That both the family and the state have an interest in education is admitted by all. The child is born and grows up as a member of the family so that he may take his place later as a citizen of the state. Having seen these two societies, we now ask how education fits into both of them.

However educators may define education, we take it to mean any process of training the physical, mental, and moral powers of a human being to render him fit for the duties of life. Our question deals only with education during the formative period of a child's life and with education for the common duties of a human life. It does not deal with adult education, which is subsequent to the formative period, nor with vocational training, which is a requirement only for those pursuing that vocation. We are discussing the kind of education a child has a right to have and someone the duty to provide, a situation that sets up a special relation between teacher and pupil. Anyone who knows something has the right to teach it if he can get people to listen to him, but he cannot impose his teaching with authority. We are dealing here with education which the teacher has authority to impart and which the pupil has the duty to submit to respectfully, though his intellectual acceptance of what he is taught depends on his being convinced of its truth.

We have one main problem, which branches out into several others. We shall treat them as follows:

1. Who has the primary right to educate?
2. Have state and church any rights in education?
3. Who is to conduct schools?
4. What of academic freedom?
5. How should we judge the student revolt?

PARENTS' PRIMARY RIGHT

The right to educate their children belongs to the parents as a natural right. Nature itself imposes on the parents the *duty* to educate their children. The very reason that marriage exists as a natural institution is that both parents must provide for the long period of training necessary to raise a child. But one cannot have a duty without the right to fulfill that duty. Therefore parents have the natural *right* to educate their children.

Since the parents are responsible for the child's existence, they are also responsible for all the child will need to live a decent and useful human life. They do not fulfill their duty simply by feeding, clothing, and sheltering the child; they must also see to it that the child, when grown, can take his place as a useful member of society, since society is natural to man. Therefore they must teach him the means of acquiring an independent livelihood, the means of communication with his fellowman, and the social virtues needed for life in common with others. More important still, the child is dependent on his parents for the formation of those good moral habits which the child will need for his own personal morality and for attaining his purpose in life. The parents can do this job, and they can do it best. Hence they are chosen by nature for this work.

How much education is the child entitled to? At least the minimum essentials just described. Whether the child can expect more education depends on the child's ability, the circumstances of the family, the educational facilities available, and the prevalent level of culture. Parents should try to do the best they can for their children but are not obliged to make extraordinary sacrifices. In this country one can hardly get along without knowing how to read and write, but this is not the case everywhere. The amount of education therefore depends on a combination of individual, family, and community requirements.

RIGHTS OF STATE AND CHURCH

The state has no right to interfere in what strictly belongs to the family. Education cannot belong to both family and state in the same way and on the same plane, for there would be a conflict of rights and duties. The family is prior to the state and had the obligation of educating the children before there was any state. The state is founded to supplement the family, not to destroy it, and hence cannot take away from the family its already existing right.

However, the state has secondary rights in education, which by no means contravene the parents' primary right. The state has a right to all the means necessary for the fulfillment of its ends, and education comes within the scope of these means. The state has the right and the duty to compel parents to fulfill their duty in educating their children. This is called a sec-

ondary right and duty, because it is valid only when the parents themselves fail in their duty. The state can compel parents to feed their children if they neglect to do so, but it has no right to interfere when the parents discharge their obligation satisfactorily. The same is true in the matter of education. The state's right is not so much to *do* the work of education as to see that it is done. In this function it is protecting the child.

Has not the state, especially a democratic state, a particular interest in the education of its future citizens, so that this right transcends that of parents? The state has a right to a sufficiently educated citizenry, especially a democratic state that depends on an intelligent vote; hence, if the parents do not fulfill their duty, the state may force them to do so, not only for the child's sake but also for the state's sake. But this right is always secondary. The state has the right to see that parents educate their children into competent citizens but no direct right to take over this duty itself. Otherwise the state is encroaching on an essential right of the family, crowding the family out of its rights, and thus verging on totalitarianism.

In its own sphere the church also has secondary rights in education. It has the right and the duty to oblige parents who are its own members to give their children the proper religious education, but the church has authority only over its own members and uses no temporal sanctions to obtain its ends. Since the members belong to the church voluntarily, they are rightly expected to cooperate with their own church's educational program.

SCHOOLS

Our discussion has been about education and not about schools, for schooling is only a means, and not always an absolutely necessary one, toward education. Parents had the duty of educating their children long before there were any schools, and the duty would remain were all schools abolished. Even today, if the parents have the ability and the leisure to give adequate instruction to their children at home, they have no moral obligation to send them to school at all. Few parents are qualified for this task today. If they can afford it, they can employ a private tutor; if the tutor is properly qualified, it is hard to see how the state would have any right to object. But the home-educated child is handicapped by lacking the socializing influence of contact with those of his own age.

Ordinarily parents hand over the work of formal instruction and mental training to schools, but not entirely; the parents themselves must do the work of preschool education or hire someone to do it for them. This is the most important part of education and is best done by the parents themselves. Even when the child goes to school, the parents must continue their training out of school hours and must constantly watch the child's progress at school. The mere handing over of the child to others to educate does not absolve the the parents of their responsibility. Parents must inform themselves on the character of the schools to which they send their children, and should remove them if the influence threatens to prove harmful.

What are the rights of the state regarding schools? The state has the right to open and conduct schools when private initiative is insufficient for this work. The state must look after the common welfare and promote all works that are socially necessary. If private schools are too few and small, they must be supplemented by state schools, and where there are no private schools, the state must furnish all the facilities. If this work is already being done adequately by private schools, the state has no right to put them out of business by unfair tax-supported competition.

The state has not the right to monopolize education. Education is a legitimate form of private enterprise, subject indeed to a certain amount of government regulation, but there is nothing in its nature that makes it a public or state monopoly. In undertaking the work of education the state is simply supplying the parents with facilities to fulfill their duty. If the parents have other facilities at their command, they have no obligation to use those the state provides.

The state's right in education is entirely secondary and supplementary. The state may not make attendance at state schools compulsory, either by law or by undue favoritism. It may not force parents to send their children to one definite school, public or private, rather than another, though it may refuse to accept children from other tax-supported districts. It may not close private schools already operating, unless they have proved to be public menaces or frauds, nor may it refuse to allow the opening of new private schools. Even in its own public schools the state is acting under the authority delegated to it by the parents, who have the primary right; the state is only their agent and trustee. Therefore the state must conduct these schools with a regard for the parents' wishes and not force on the children a type of education the parents disapprove. This does not put on the state the impossible task of listening to every parent's whim, but it must give the general type of education the parents as a group demand. This is not true of private schools, for they provide another option to parents who do not want their children to attend a public school operated by the state or local municipality. It would be true of them, however, if they carried the whole educational burden, for then they would be in a position like that of a privately owned public utility, which is obliged to put the common good before private interests.

The state has the right to regulate education within certain limits. As a measure of public protection, it may set reasonable standards to which schools, both public and private, must conform. It may set standards of qualification for teachers. It may protect the young against injurious policies and attitudes, just as it can forbid the sale of tainted food. It may prescribe courses in citizenship and encourage a patriotic spirit in the schools, but it has no right to dominate the whole curriculum. The proper integration of courses in a school and the methods of teaching to be adopted are the business of educators, not of politicians.

What are the rights of the church regarding schools? The church has the right to teach its own members their religion and for this purpose may open schools of religious instruction. Secular education does not directly belong to the church's sphere of work, but if it is either not being given at all or is being given in a way hostile to religious faith, there is no reason why the church should not add a secular curriculum to the religious studies and thus develop its schools (while preserving the denominational aspect) into ordinary private schools. The church got into the work of secular education by historical accident, opening schools in the early Middle Ages, when there were no schools and no one else fit to start any. Various denominations have adjusted to the modern educational scene differently in different countries as circumstances seemed to warrant, either fitting their religious program into the state school system or continuing to conduct their own independent schools. At least, denominational schools are legitimate private schools, and a church has the right to continue those in existence and to establish others if doing so seems expedient for promoting the faith of its members.

ACADEMIC FREEDOM

Academic freedom is the name given to a teacher's privilege of teaching the doc-

trines and opinions he holds, without undue censorship by the state or even by the school that employs him. It is understood that academic freedom is expected chiefly at the college and university level, but it is extended somewhat to secondary and primary education.

The reasons for academic freedom are obvious. Advancement in science and culture is possible only when investigators are free to pursue truth wherever it leads. The teacher is supposed to be an expert in his field, and it is illogical to put him under the dictation of those who know less about the subject than he. He cannot be morally obliged to play the hypocrite and teach what he thinks false. He earns his living by teaching and should not be in constant fear of dismissal because his superiors adopt a change of view or policy, so that he would have to teach one year the contradictory of what he had taught the previous year. This last remark shows the connection between academic freedom and tenure.

It cannot be maintained, however, that academic freedom is absolute. First of all, it is subject to the same limitations as the right of free speech, and may not be defamatory, obscene, subversive, or otherwise malicious, since no one can acquire a right to immoral conduct. Academic freedom is subject to further restrictions because of the teacher's relation:

1. To his pupils
2. To their parents
3. To the school employing him

1. *To pupils.* The elementary and high school teacher, and even the college professor on the undergraduate level, is dealing with immature minds, unable to compete with him on the same level, as yet untrained to give an exact appraisal of all he says or to argue with him from a rich background of experience. Speaking to these impressionable minds with the authority of his position, he must consider not only his own convictions and theories

but also what effect they will have on the minds of the young. He is supposed to be forming and developing youth, not merely using them as a sounding board for any sort of idea he may have. If he feels that loyalty to his own convictions requires him to preach doctrines commonly regarded as inflammatory and subversive, let him give up teaching and enter the public arena to cross swords with his equals. It is one thing to present the students with an intellectual challenge, another to make it a policy to unsettle all the ideals and convictions the students have received at home and then leave them in this state of vacuity and disorientation. Such abusers of academic freedom are among the greatest enemies of youth.

2. *To parents.* The teacher, especially on the primary and secondary levels, is the agent and trustee of the parents. He has no independent authority over the child but must work in harmony with the parents, supplement the training of the home, and in general give the type of education the parents contract for. On the other hand, parents send their children to him because he is supposed to be an expert in his field, and he cannot adjust his teaching or the school's curriculum to meet every ignorant or meddelsome parent's demand. Here arises a conflict of rights and duties in which the application of the ordinary principles may become difficult. The best solution seems to be the establishment of many schools with a wide variety of curricula and policies among which parents may choose. Thus the parents can obtain the kind of education they want for their children, and the teachers can teach what they believe.

3. *To the school.* The teacher has definite responsibilities to his employers and must fulfill the contract he makes with them. Before accepting the position he must inform himself on the ideals and policies of the school, for he has no right to take the position if he disagrees with

them or intends to be disloyal to them. Academic freedom cannot be stretched to the point of allowing him publicly to oppose the policy of the school where he teaches; if he feels that he must, because of some change in his own views, he should seek other employment. The right of tenure may be invoked against arbitrary dismissal, but there can be no ethical ground for making it a reason that a school must tolerate treason in its own house. The school has a moral obligation to pupils and parents, and must be able to get rid of undesirable teachers as well as uncooperative pupils.

On the whole, we can consider the teacher in a threefold capacity: as a private individual expressing his personal opinions, as a scholar presenting the fruit of his research to the learned world, and precisely as a teacher in contact with his students. So far we have been discussing him in the last function. As a private individual, he may act as any other private person, so long as he makes clear that he is speaking for himself alone. As a scholar, he is somewhat in between; he is speaking to his equals and is open to their criticism on the same level, but he is under obligation to his school, from which he derives his academic standing and on which his views may reflect; he cannot exempt himself entirely from their approval. This relation to his school puts some limitation on his academic freedom.*

Let it be understood, however, that academic freedom certainly has its place, and a policy of overactive censorship, especially on the part of the state, would be unwise. Any restriction of teaching

---

*See "Academic Freedom and Tenure, Statement of Principles, 1940" in *Bulletin of the American Association of University Professors*, vol. 27, no. 1 (Spring, 1941), p. 40. Also "Statement on Procedural Standards in Renewal or Nonrenewal of Faculty Appointments," *ibid.*, vol. 57, no. 2 (Summer, 1971), p. 206.

should be done by the schools, which are capable of handling such matters, rather than by the state, which is capable of supplying the facilities for education but not of deciding what ought or ought not to be taught.

In speaking of academic freedom in the teacher, we have implied that there is also an academic freedom in the school to be the kind of school it wants to be, so that it can require its teachers' cooperation in its policies. Is there also academic freedom for the student? Certainly no student should be forced to accept what he does not believe. He should not be penalized for the expression of any opinion, within the limits of free speech, no matter how much it may differ from that of his teacher or of anyone else. But besides matters of opinion, there is also an undebatable content in learning. Refusal to do the work of learning or to perform assigned academic tasks, though it be a freedom, is not an academic freedom and properly results in academic penalty.

STUDENT UNREST

The student unrest of a few years ago has all but disappeared, and it may seem futile to discuss it now. It is said that there is nothing so dead as last year's demonstration, but there were some real moral issues involved, at which we should cast at least a cursory glance.

What did youth want? Youth makes just about every protest its own. It is concerned with nuclear war, conscientious objection, the race problem, poverty, ecology, inner cities, the third world, the military-industrial complex, technology, the drug culture, free sex, and anything else. It was also concerned with the stuffy traditionality of the education offered it and was disillusioned with the society it was being prepared to enter. There are wrongs and injustices about us that are glaringly inexcusible, and there are remedies for them

that are logically evident. Why cannot people be persuaded to use the remedies and cure the evil? If the older generation will not remedy the mess it has made, the only thing to do is to take the power from them and create a future not like the past.

When it came to a positive program, however, youth was inarticulate. Its only answer was a vigorous assertion of what it did not want. Negative criticism is easy even for the immature; positive construction, to be effective, needs maturity and experience. Then, too, it is not possible to neglect established channels, such as existing political parties. They are too entrenched and politically wise to be easily displaced; independent political action is ineffective. Another thing that youth forgot is that the hardest thing in the world to move is the mass of the people; it is easier to send rockets to the moon. Thus anything like instant utopia is impossible in this world. It may take generations to get people to do what everybody knows ought to be done.

Most of the ideals and aspirations of youth are highly commendable. The moral question was about the means. May students use confrontations, sit-ins, and boycotts, and even shut down the university in order to achieve them? A university campus is in an unusual situation, being only semipublic even in state institutions, so that there is always a tension between such forces of public order as the police and the private means the university employs to keep order on the campus. The police adopt a hands-off policy unless they are summoned and expect the university to handle the disciplining of its refractory members. The lines of demarcation are not clear, and uprisings can occur more easily on a campus than they can on the city streets. When they overflow into the neighborhood, the situation becomes more complicated.

The view that disturbances are less justified on campus than off is based on the nature of a university as a place of learning, where intelligence and reasonableness should prevail. The pursuit of learning cannot go on under disturbed conditions, and the rights of students who want peace and quiet for their studies can be seriously interfered with.

An opposite view would hold that the campus is the logical place for students to air their grievances, since that is where the students are and where their grievances occur. What is the use of peace and quiet for the pursuit of studies which the protesters object to, and for the training of new inductees into a kind of society the protesters do not approve?

There seems to be validity to both these claims. At first sight they seem irreconcilable. To keep the campus in a state of perpetual turmoil while disruptive campaigns are being conducted against every conceivable social ill would mean the end of the university as an educational institution. On the other hand, to deny the students any forum for expressing their aspirations and for seeking what they conceive as long overdue reforms is to interfere with their rights as persons and to fasten on education a dictatorial regime. Who is to yield?

Some answer may be found in the principles laid down previously for civil disobedience. Student demonstrations are not precisely civil disobedience, though they may involve it incidentally, but the relation of student to university has sufficient similarity to the relation of citizen to government for both of them to fall under similar moral requirements. In both there must be a proportion between the good sought and the evil permitted, there must be competent leadership and control, riot and violence and destruction are morally inexcusable, and the aim must be the betterment of the educational system and not its overthrow. The moral principles here are not too difficult, but the problem seems to have disappeared of its own inertia rather than to have been solved on moral principles.

SUMMARY

By *education* we mean any process of training the physical, mental, and moral powers of a human being to render him fit for the duties of life. We deal with general and formative education only.

The *parents have the primary right* to educate their children, for education belongs to the essential purpose of marriage, and where there is a duty there is a right to exercise that duty. The amount of education depends on the child's capacity, the family's resources, and the cultural level of the community.

State and church have *secondary or supplementary rights* in education, each within its proper sphere. They are not to interfere when parents do the work adequately, but they have the right to see that it is done.

Schools are the ordinary means of education, but they do not take the whole burden from the parents. The *state* should respect the rights of private schools, supply facilities when private initiative is inadequate, give the general type of education the parents approve, set minimum standards, and make inspections if necessary. The state must *not* monopolize education or dominate the whole curriculum. The *church* has the right to establish religious schools and to add to religious teaching a secular curriculum.

Academic freedom, the teacher's privilege to teach what he believes without undue censorship, is a necessary part of the educator's life, but it has its limits. The teacher has special obligations to his *pupils* because of their youth and inexperience, to the *parents*, whose agent and trustee he is, and to the *school*, whose ideals and policies he is not allowed to subvert. As a private individual he may say what he wishes, as a scholar he has some obligation to the school employing him, but precisely as a teacher he must form the minds of the young by continuing the child's home training according to the program of his school.

The *student unrest* pits the students' demands for a more relevant education against the slow-moving traditionalism of educational institutions. Students' use of demonstrations and other disruptive techniques are subject to the same moral requirements as those for civil disobedience. They must be nonviolent and respectful of the rights of others, especially of their fellow students' right to finish their education in a satisfactory manner.

QUESTIONS FOR DISCUSSION

1 May a boy with good intellectual talent quit school at the legal age but against his parents' wishes and go to work at a menial job? May he stay at this job permanently? Do his parents have any moral obligation here?

2 In the interest of justice and equity, how do you reconcile the exempting of private school property from taxation with the taxing of citizens for the support of public schools when they send their children to private schools?

3 Is democracy in education a viable concept considering the differences in intellectual potential of the human being? Is an intellectual elite unavoidable even in the most democratic society?

4 In grading students, in disciplining them, and in recommending them for higher studies or for jobs, the teacher must balance the good of the individual student against the good of the class, of the school, of other schools, and of the community, as well as of his own reputation. Have you any guiding norms to suggest?

5 Is cheating in schoolwork a moral fault, a violation of educational etiquette, or something quite all right if you get away with it? Can there be acts that are dishonorable but have no moral quality?

READINGS

Education is constantly referred to throughout Plato's works, but especially in the *Republic*, bk. II, III, IV, and VII, and in the *Laws*, bk. VII. Aristotle's views are found in his *Politics*, bk. VII, ch. 13, to the end of bk. VIII, where he does not get beyond elementary education. St. Augustine and St. Thomas both have tracts entitled *De Magistro* (On the Teacher), both translated into English. These have little reference to the matter of this chapter, which deals only with ethical problems raised by education. John Henry Cardinal Newman, *The Idea of a University*, is one of the great classics on higher education but does not emphasize the moral aspect.

The following discuss the right of the family, church, and state in education: Heinrich Rommen, *The State in Catholic Thought*, ch. 15; and Leo Ward, *Christian Ethics*, ch. 14.

Russell Kirk's *Academic Freedom* and Robert MacIver's *Academic Freedom in Our Time* treat this knotty subject.

John Dewey's *Democracy and Education* is one of the great classics of modern education theory. John Brubacher's *Eclectic Philosophy of Edu-*

cation is a book of readings from authors holding widely diverse positions.

On the revolt of youth and student unrest there is already a bulk of literature. For a quick look see Robert Drinan, *Democracy, Dissent, and Disorder,* ch. 3. Kenneth Keniston, *The Uncommitted* and *Young Radicals,* is one of the more perceptive observers of the modern scene. Bierman and Gould, *Philosophy for a New Generation,* contains several representative articles.

Austin Fagothey, *Right and Reason—an Anthology,* has no article directly on education, but the selections from Thoreau, King, and Stevick on civil disobedience are pertinent at least obliquely to campus disturbances.

Chapter 29

PROPERTY

PROBLEM

Man cannot live his life on earth without using the material goods with which the earth abounds. In doing so he makes them *his own,* his *property.* The more recent challenges to the right of property we shall leave to a later chapter. Here we limit ourselves to an investigation of the institution of private property as it has been accepted throughout most of the world's history and try to find what moral basis it has. We can distribute the matter under the following headings:

1. What is ownership?
2. Why may we use material goods for sustenance?
3. What is theft and why is it wrong?
4. What are the chief economic systems?
5. How is the system of private property justified?
6. What are the main titles to property?

OWNERSHIP

The words *mine* and *thine* represent notions too elementary to be made simpler. The expression *one's own* universalizes the idea and makes it applicable to any person. A thing is said to be *one's own* when it is reserved to a certain person and all others are excluded from it. The one who holds a thing as *his own* is said to *own* it, to be its *owner,* to have the right of own-

ership over it. Things owned are said to *belong* to the owner and are called his *belongings.* So much any child knows. The English language feels more scientific when it dresses ideas in Latin derivatives; thus *one's own* is *proper* (in its old meaning as contrasted with *common*), an *owner* is a *proprietor, ownership* is *proprietorship,* and *belongings* are *property.*

Since we all know what ownership is, a definition may seem superfluous, but the following will help to clarify our ideas.

Ownership is the *right of exclusive control and disposal over a thing at will.* It is:

1. A *right.* Thus we distinguish between ownership and the mere holding of a thing in one's possession. A thief has possession of stolen goods, but he does not own them, because he cannot acquire a right to them.

2. *Exclusive.* This term pertains to keeping others from the use of the thing owned. A thing over which everybody has equal rights is not owned at all. Several or many persons may own a thing together, either in joint ownership or as a corporation, but anyone outside the group is excluded from the property.

3. *Control and disposal.* This means doing anything possible with it: keeping, changing, giving away, selling, using, consuming, destroying. Of itself ownership is unlimited, though limitation may come from another source: from rights of a

higher order, from love of the neighbor, or from the civil law.

4. *Over a thing.* The matter of the right cannot be further detailed except to say that whatever can be controlled or disposed of can be owned. We think of it first as a material object, but it can be actions, services, goodwill, or credit.

5. *At will.* The owner acts for himself, in his own name, and need consult no one else as far as mere ownership is concerned. An agent or trustee may be given the right to control a thing or dispose of it, but only on behalf of the owner and in his name.

Property may be defined as *that which is owned* or that over which one has the exclusive right of control and disposal at will. Not everything can become property. The air, the sunlight, the ocean cannot be owned and can never be property; they must remain *common.* Wild beasts, fish in the sea, land in an unexplored wilderness are not actually owned but can be; they are potentially property but actually nobody's; they are *common* now but need not remain so.

There are various *kinds* of ownership, a few of which we can define briefly. Since a group can be an owner, and there is no limit to the size of this group, the whole community as such can own property: the federal government, the state, the county, the city. This is *public* as opposed to *private* ownership. In all ownership we must consider the substance of the thing owned as distinct from its use and fruits. *Full* ownership supposes right of control over all three; *limited* ownership denotes right of control over any one or two of these, but not over all three together. Lending, borrowing, renting, leasing, and the like render ownership limited. Only the one who retains control over the substance is properly called the *owner,* but it is obvious that the other has partial property rights in the matter and hence some sort of limited ownership. Ownership over the substance is called *direct* ownership; ownership over the use or fruits or both is referred to as *indirect.*

PROPERTY AS SUSTENANCE

The right of ownership or the right to property in its simplest and most primitive form enables man to take and use for his sustenance, comfort, and development the goods that nature's bounty provides. That man has a right to act in this way is evident from his natural right to life. The material goods of this world are naturally fitted to become man's property. In nature some beings are for the sake of others, for nature has so constructed them. Living things cannot maintain their lives except by the use and consumption of other beings, both living and inanimate. Since man is a person, he is for nothing else, and all other things are for him to take and use. Nature does not portion out her goods to definite individuals. If no other man has already taken them, they are there for anyone to take. One who does so *appropriates* them, or makes them into his property. Man has intellect and will, by which he can indicate his intention of keeping material goods for his own use and of excluding others from them. His intellect and will naturally equip him to become a self-provider, with ingenuity to control nature and make it supply his wants. Animals can only take what they find, as their instinct prompts them, but man, because of the control he can exert over nature, is naturally fitted for ownership.

The argument may be put as follows: Man has a natural right to life, and not only to mere survival but also to the kind of life befitting a human being: a decent life with opportunity for physical, mental, and moral self-development. But the use of material goods is absolutely necessary for the maintenance of life and for proper self-development. Therefore man has a natural right to use the material goods of this world.

THEFT

The violation of the right of property is called *theft* or *stealing*. Hence the proof that man has a right to property is proof that theft is wrong. Theft can be defined as the *unjust taking of another's property,* and the taking is unjust when it goes against the owner's reasonable will. The word *reasonable* is put here because, though the owner may be unwilling to give me what I need, there are cases, as we shall see, in which his refusal is unreasonable, and I may take it against his will.

If nature were uniformly bountiful and no effort were needed to take and develop her products, there would be little motive for stealing. Its peculiar malice consists in the fact that one seizes the products another has gathered, labored on, and stored for his own use. No one reasonably wills to have the product of his labor taken from him without his consent. Thus the thief virtually reduces another person to the status of a slave working for the thief without recompense and, by disturbing the fundamental equality of all human persons, commits an act of injustice. Even an owner who has not worked to acquire the goods that the thief steals owns them by some other legitimate title, which does not cease without his consent. The wrong of theft is rectified first by restitution, the restoring of the stolen goods or their equivalent, and then by punishment, for theft is a crime upsetting the social order as well as an injury to the owner.

What happens when the right to life and the right to property come into apparent conflict? The general principle solving such conflicts is that the stronger right prevails. Obviously, property is for life, not life for property. Life is identified with the man himself; property is but a means to support life and minister to its needs. Life is indivisible, property divisible. A dead man has no use for property, but a live man who has lost his property can acquire new property and in the meantime be sustained by borrowing another's excess property. Natural rights, however, cannot be contradictory. It cannot be that every man has a natural right to life and to the means necessary for supporting life while at the same time some men have such rights over property as to nullify other men's right to life. Therefore man's right to use material goods for the maintenance of his life prevails, as the stronger right, over any acquired right to property.

The argument as given refers to extreme need but is valid, with due proportion, for serious but less drastic emergencies. If I am attacked and have no weapon of my own, I may use another's weapon even against his will in order to defend myself, unless he has equal need of it. If I am pursued by bandits, I may commandeer another's car or horse or any other means of escape. If the only way I can get out of a place in which my life is endangered lies through another's property, I need not worry about trespassing. In all such cases I must ask permission if time and circumstances permit, but if this is impossible or the permission is refused, I may do these things anyway. I have no obligation to die or suffer very serious loss because some people are selfish. Of course, I must restore goods so taken as soon as the emergency is over. The owner is entitled to reimbursement for loss or damage done, to be paid eventually by the party at fault, if any. Civil law will have to decide disputes on indemnification.

If a man is starving, he should first try to obtain food by every legitimate means. He must seek honest work, and if he finds it, he must take it, even if it be of a menial character. He must contact public agencies of relief and not be too proud to accept their help. But if his every effort has met with rebuff and he sees that it is practically impossible for him to respect other people's property and at the same time to keep alive, then he has the right to seize what he needs even though it is the property of another. This is not theft or stealing. Others have the duty to come to his relief, and if they do not, their lesser right to their property yields to his greater right to his life.

We may sum up the points made so far. Man has a right to use the goods of this world. He has a right not only to the goods absolutely necessary for subsistence but also to goods needed for a decent human life befitting his rational nature. Theft, or the unjust seizure of rightfully owned property, is morally wrong, but the right to property must yield to the right to life. It is not theft to seize goods needed for life or safety, even if they are someone else's property, unless he is in equal need. Rather, there is an obligation to share goods with those in extreme need, since supplying human needs is the primary function of property.

DISTRIBUTION OF WEALTH

We come now to a more intricate question, that of the *economic system* that ought to prevail in society. Here we no longer deal with the basic form of property stemming out of basic human needs but with that more advanced form of property called *wealth*. Should nature's resources be left unowned for each to take what he needs, or be divided up among private owners, or be publicly owned and operated by the state? We can distinguish three primary systems for dividing the community's wealth:

1. Each one takes from nature's supply the goods that he needs for his use at present or in the near future, without hoarding up goods for the far future. Land, especially, is left common as the hunting ground of the tribe. Property does not extend much beyond personal movable implements. This is the system of *primitive collectivism* as found among savages and barbarians.

2. Nearly all the resources of nature and goods of the community are divided up among particular owners. The land is marked off and distributed, with trespassing forbidden or restricted. Only that is left common which everybody judges worthless. What individuals do not own, the state owns, but the bulk of the property is in private hands. This is the system of *private ownership*.

3. The community or the state owns nearly everything, especially all the means of production, the farms and factories. The produce is distributed to the people in return for their work. Private property is allowed for use and consumption only. Here again hardly anything is left common as found in nature, though it may be called common in the sense of community-owned. This is the system of *socialism* and *communism*.

No enlightened person advocates a return to primitive collectivism. The system of private ownership has prevailed historically in almost all civilized countries up to the present century. Now some countries have substituted either socialism or communism for the system of private ownership. Because of its historical priority and former worldwide acceptance, the system of private ownership will be examined first, and then in a later chapter its possible replacement by socialism or communism.

PRIVATE OWNERSHIP OF WEALTH

What ethical justification has been offered for private ownership as the economic system of a community? There are three main opinions:

1. Private ownership of wealth rests on *convention*. It may be thought a good convention to be preserved or a bad convention causing most of our social woes. It is not a natural right.
2. Private ownership of wealth rests on the *jus gentium*, or law of nations. It agrees with natural law but is not de-

manded by it as a natural right. It is
a morally acceptable system.

3. Private ownership of wealth rests on
natural law as a natural right. It not
only agrees with natural law but is
demanded by it. It is the *only* morally acceptable system.

THE CONVENTIONAL BASIS
FOR PRIVATE OWNERSHIP

Those who hold that man is antisocial
or extrasocial by nature and that society
itself results from convention make the
various appurtenances of society also conventional. Hobbes and Rousseau (but not
Locke) make the right to property part of
the social contract. Man transferred all
his liberties to the state and received some
of them back in the form of rights, among
which is the right to property. Logically,
the state could take back from individual
owners the property right it has allocated
to them, could abolish all private property
and institute some other system for the distribution of wealth. Hobbes and Rousseau,
having no prevision of modern socialism or
communism, accepted the private property
system, but they had no reason for thinking it necessary or fixed for all time. It is
not a natural but only a civil right.

This view of the moral and legal positivists should likewise be adopted by utilitarians, pragmatists, and relativists, even
though they may repudiate a contractual
origin for human society, for they do not
admit a natural law or any rights and duties
stemming from human nature. The institution of private property is relative to the
state of culture to which we have arrived,
and is to be judged by its practical effectiveness in promoting human welfare. It
should be preserved in default of something better, but it is a human device, not
a natural right.

The Marxists, because they put such
stress on man's economic needs as the
basic factor in every culture, are less se-

vere on the institution of private property
than one might think. For them it was an
essential step in man's historical progress,
and no civilization would have been possible without it. As the dialectic of history
unfolds, however, it must give way to the
superior system of socialism or communism. The private property system, therefore, is to be approved as an inevitable
transitory arrangement. It becomes evil
when, in its decadent capitalistic form,
it is perpetuated into the future, now that
the time is ripe for the great economic
and social revolution. Far from being natural or necessary to man, the system of
private property must necessarily disappear. This view will be discussed at length
later.

THE JUS GENTIUM BASIS
FOR PRIVATE OWNERSHIP

It might be thought that St. Thomas and
other medieval defenders of natural law
would make the system of private ownership a requirement of natural law. But such
is not the case. St. Thomas, while approving the system of private ownership, bases
it on the law of nations, or *jus gentium*. It
may be well first to see his very cautious
and enlightened treatment of this subject:

Two things are competent to man in respect
of exterior things. One is the power to procure
and dispense them, and in this regard it is lawful
for man to possess property. Moreover this is
necessary to human life for three reasons. First,
because every man is more careful to procure
what is for himself alone than that which is common to many or to all: since each one would shirk
the labor and leave to another that which concerns the community, as happens where there is
a great number of servants. Secondly, because
human affairs are conducted in more orderly
fashion if each man is charged with taking care
of some particular thing himself, whereas there
would be confusion if everyone had to look after
any one thing indeterminately. Thirdly, because
a more peaceful state is ensured to man if each
one is contented with his own. Hence it is to be
observed that quarrels arise more frequently where
there is no division of the things possessed.

The second thing that is competent to man with regard to external things is their use. In this respect man ought to possess external things, not as his own, but as common, so that, to wit, he is ready to communicate them to others in their need. . . .

Community of goods is ascribed to the natural law, not that the natural law dictates that all things should be possessed in common, and that nothing should be possessed as one's own: but because the division of possessions is not according to the natural law, but rather arose from human agreement which belongs to positive law, as stated above (q. 57, aa. 2, 3). Hence the ownership of possessions is not contrary to the natural law, but an addition thereto devised by human reason.°

Several things are to be noted in this remarkable passage:

1. The first is that St. Thomas defends the institution of private property as a good thing, and by the usual arguments, suggested by Aristotle's† criticism of Plato's communistic ideas.

2. The second is St. Thomas' approval of Aristotle's theory that property should be privately owned but its use should be common. This arrangement was especially applicable to the ancient and medieval system of large landed estates, privately held but with definitely understood public obligations. The modern counterpart is the social function of private capital invested in industries and corporations serving public needs and supplying livelihood to thousands of employees.

3. The third point is that St. Thomas bases the division of goods into private hands on the law of nations, the *jus gentium*, which he discusses in question 57, to which he refers.

This third point is our present question. By his words St. Thomas seems to be making private ownership of wealth something allowed but not required by natural law, something coming from human agreement

sanctioned by positive law and permitted by natural law, with an option for another arrangement equally in accord with natural law. This interpretation may be reading into St. Thomas more than is actually there, for he is not thinking of other possible economic systems as substitutes. He maintains that the institution of private property is a morally justified system, but he neither affirms nor denies that it is the only morally justified system. It is remarkable, however, that a man of his time should be so careful not to step beyond the bounds of his evidence and to leave room for future speculation. Many today agree with his view that the system of "ownership of possessions is not contrary to the natural law, but an addition thereto devised by human reason."

THE NATURAL LAW BASIS FOR PRIVATE OWNERSHIP

Many think that we can go beyond St. Thomas' arguments and prove that the system of private ownership is the only method of managing the world's wealth consistent with natural law, that private ownership is demanded by the requirements and aspirations of human nature, and that it admits of no possible substitute and is therefore a natural right. Being of the cumulative type, the argument is rather cumbersome in statement:

1. In the working up of nature's gifts, man impresses the *stamp of his personality* on his products. Natural objects are changed by man's labor and bear the impress of his thought and energy. These objects which man has shaped after the design of his own mind should naturally belong to him. Who else can have an equal right to them? Nature in leaving things common supplies only potential wealth, which becomes actual wealth only when man has developed it. To develop it man must possess it, for otherwise he cannot work on it; after development man can

---

°St. Thomas, *Summa Theologica*, II-II, q. 66, a. 2.
†Aristotle, *Politics*, bk. II, ch. 1-6, especially ch. 5, 1263a-1264b.

keep and use it, because it was for this purpose that he worked on it.

2. Nature does not provide continuously but *only in season*. A man must put away enough goods to last him through the winter; to do so he must own these goods and exclude others from them, thus acquiring the right to store and own this produce at least for a year. But there is no reason for ownership to stop then. A man pioneering in a new country clears the ground and sows the seed; that field is his at least until harvest. There is no reason that he should have to hand this field to others and clear a new field for next year's crop; thus the field remains his permanently. Here he builds his house and settles with his family; these is no reason that he should have to vacate it, for he was there first, or to share it with others, for he has a right to privacy.

3. Man has the right and duty to *provide for his family*. He must rear his children and give them a start in life. He should then amass more goods than are necessary for his family's immediate use. He appropriates more land than he can now use with a view to the future needs of his growing children. At any time he may die or be disabled, and should leave his family well secured against the time when he can no longer work. If he has the right to provide for them, they have the right to receive these goods in the form of inheritance.

4. Inability to be expert in everything brought about a *division of labor*. Men specialize in certain kinds of work and exchange their products. Livelihood on this basis implies a right to store the products, to keep enough on hand to trade for present and future necessities. But storage is impossible without ownership. Besides, a storage of excess goods is the only way in which a man can provide for himself in sickness and old age, when he can no longer work. There is no reason that a man should have to be dependent on others during these times, for he fulfills his duty to society better and lightens its burden if he can take care of his own keep.

5. The *profit motive*, rooted in human nature, is the strongest motive in getting men to work. Men take pride in the work they have accomplished. If they cannot enjoy the fruits of their toil, they lose interest and turn to something else they think more profitable. They take care of the things they own, whereas it is notorious how common possessions are neglected and squandered. "What is everybody's business is nobody's business." Men also want to be independent, to choose their place of residence and their kind of work. They will not undertake projects for the taming of nature unless they can share in owning the results. Thus human progress and the advancement of civilization depend on private ownership.

6. The state is founded on a *solid middle class*, as Aristotle observed,* on families of fairly prosperous citizens who own a moderate amount of property. Their property is sufficient to give them the pride of ownership, yet not so abundant as to let them live in idleness. They have some resources for new undertakings and also the incentive to put their wealth to work. They are the equalizing influence between tyranny and anarchy, thus opposing the extreme tendencies of the rulers and the mob. Their continued prosperity depends on the maintenance of peace and order, without which business cannot function, and they exert pressure on the rulers to see that it is kept.

The foregoing argument should be a telling answer to the theory of the moral and legal positivists, that private ownership has no basis in natural law, that it is the mere result of a free compact entered

---

*Aristotle, *Politics*, bk. IV, ch. 11, 1295b 25; ch. 12, 1296b 35.

into by men or of a grant by the state, and therefore entirely conventional. The system of private ownership is certainly in agreement with natural law and approved by it. It is the system men naturally take to in the absence of any other, because it corresponds so well with the needs of human nature. It gives a good account of what must have been the historical development of the private property system. Since private ownership was the universal custom of civilized peoples applying the natural law to their social life, it was properly included within the *jus gentium.* Does the argument prove all that its backers ask of it? Does it prove that private ownership of wealth is so demanded by the natural law that there can be no substitute for it? Not without an examination of possible substitutes. This thesis must therefore remain incomplete until such substitutes as socialism and communism have been examined.

PROPERTY TITLES

The foregoing discussion was theoretical, asking whether there should be such a right as ownership and such a thing as property and on what moral grounds. Taking property as an existing fact, we now ask: How does this man come to own this or that piece of property? A man by the fact that he is a man has the right of ownership in general, and yet he may never exercise this right, may never actually own anything. Something must make this man acquire this piece of property, that man that piece, a function fulfilled by the title. A *title* to property is a historical fact that changes the abstract right of ownership in general into the concrete right of ownership over this particular piece of property. There are seven chief titles to property:

1. *Occupancy* is the original way of changing into property the objects that nature leaves common. It is defined as the taking of a thing that belongs to no one with manifest intent of holding it as one's own. It does not require dwelling or inhabiting, as the word *occupy* might suggest. There are three requirements: the thing taken must not actually be owned by anyone though capable of being owned, it must be effectively possessed with intent to hold it, and this intent must be made known to others by some suitable sign. The sign depends on custom: putting up a notice, fencing a field, staking a claim, recording the deed, keeping the thing on one's own person or in one's house. Some labor may be involved in securing possession, but the object itself is not the product of one's toil.

2. *Labor* cannot be the original title of ownership, because the raw materials must first be owned before one has the right to work on them. Labor, transforming raw materials into useful objects, creates new values that belong to the worker as products of his energy. Mental no less than physical labor is a natural title to its fruits. When the material belongs to one owner and the labor to another, the ownership of the finished product has already been determined by a contract of hire; the owner of the material keeps the product, and the worker is paid for his labor. Some think that labor is the only title to property; they can do so only by taking so broad a definition of labor as to include the act of occupancy, as John Locke[*] seems to do, or, like Karl Marx,[†] by restricting property to consumable goods distributed by the community to individuals in return for their labor.

3. *Gift* is a gratuitous transfer of ownership to another and is implied in the owner's right of disposing of his property at will. In the making of a gift the property is alienated only on condition that it be accepted by the person to whom it is

[*]Locke, *Second Treatise on Government,* ch. 5.
[†]Marx, *Capital,* vol. I, pt. I, ch. I, sec. 1.

offered. Hence the title of gift is a variety of contract, though the benefit is all one way.

4. *Trade* is any form of exchange, running all the way from *barter,* through *buying and selling,* up to and including the intricate enterprises of world *commerce.* In fact, trade, whether money is used or not, is only mutual gift, but it is better to class it as a separate title because of the different attitude we have toward gifts and purchases. Trade is the logical consequence of the division of labor and necessary for the good of mankind, resting on the mutual help demanded by man's social nature, for each does help the other though personal gain be the motive.

5. *Inheritance* indicates that property on the death of the owner does not become common, to be occupied by the first comer, but passes to designated persons. If there is no will, the property goes to the natural heirs, the wife or husband and the children. Property is for the good not only of the individual but of the family, and after death it should continue to fulfill the function of supporting them. Civil law determines inheritance; it should be based on natural justice and protect the natural heirs. The goods of a man dying intestate without relatives or dependents would naturally become common if the state did not usually settle the matter by taking possession itself. *Bequest,* the disposing of property by a will, is a valid title, for a gift can be made to take effect at any time including the moment of death. In bequeathing his goods the owner is in duty bound to provide for his natural heirs, but beyond this he may make any disposal of his property he would be allowed to make when alive.

6. *Accession* is the title by which one gains ownership of the increment accruing to one's property. New trees in timberland, new births in a herd, new soil washed down on one's fields are examples of natural accession. The addition belongs to the owner of the property added to. Artificial accession, the inseparable mixing of two people's property without a previous agreement, such as painting a picture on another's canvas or building a house on another's land, can be settled by agreement or by the civil law. The property should go to the one who contributed the greater value, with compensation to the other.

7. *Prescription,* also called *adverse possession,* is the extinction of a previous owner's title and its transference to the present possessor through lapse of time. It concerns not only property itself but also such easements as passing across others' land and fishing or mining in certain areas. For occupancy the goods must have no actual owner; for prescription the goods must, unknown to the present holder, be actually owned by someone else. Prescription is a civil title with a basis in natural law. To be valid it must fulfill these conditions: the matter must not be protected against prescription by civil law; the possessor must have intended ownership, been in constant peaceful possession, and in good faith; the time determined by the civil law must have elapsed. Without prescription much modern ownership would be uncertain. Most property is obtained from former owners, who must transmit it with a clear title. Memories fail, witnesses die, documents perish. New claimants could constantly arise, basing their pretensions on forgotten transactions centuries old. Present owners would be in jeopardy of having to prove and re-prove their right against all comers. The only remedy is the extinction of all titles and claims that go back beyond the time set by law. In all this the civil law is using the authority given to it by the natural law; it is an exercise of eminent domain.

Several of the seven titles to property (gift, trade, inheritance, and labor except labor for oneself) can be reduced to the general heading of *contract.* Not all contracts are about property, and not all property is acquired by contract, but all deliberate transfer of property from one owner to another implies offer and acceptance resulting in a mutual agreement, and hence a contract. Contracts in general and property contracts in particular form our next topic.

SUMMARY

Ownership is the right of exclusive control and disposal over a thing at will. What is owned is *property*. Ownership is *public* if the property belongs to the community as such; otherwise it is *private*. *Full* ownersip is control over the substance, use, and fruits, all three; otherwise it is *limited*. Ownership over the substance is *direct;* over the other two, *indirect*.

Every man has a natural right to use the material goods of this world. Nature leaves things common; man is naturally a self-provider with ingenuity to make nature supply his wants.

Theft, as the unjust seizure of rightfully owned property, is wrong, but life comes before property. Nature cannot allow men to acquire such a right to property as to extinguish the right to life that nature has already given to all at birth. In grave need a man can commandeer another's property without the guilt of theft.

There are three main *economic systems:* primitive collectivism, private ownership of wealth, and socialism or communism.

Many derive the system of private ownership of wealth wholly from human *convention*. Others, including St. Thomas, base it on the *jus gentium*. Some modern writers wish to base it more directly on *natural law*, for man should own the products on which he has put the stamp of his personality, nature is seasonal and a man must provide for the future of himself and family, division of labor requires storage of products for future trade, the profit motive is the most effective in getting men to work industriously, and the state functions best with a solid middle class of the moderately prosperous. To be conclusive such arguments would have to show that there is no possible substitute.

A title to property is a historical fact that changes the abstract right of ownership in general into the concrete right to this particular piece of property. There are seven titles:

1. *Occupancy:* appropriating what belongs to no one
2. *Labor:* adding new values to raw materials
3. *Gift:* gratuitous transfer of ownership to another
4. *Trade:* any kind of exchange including purchase
5. *Inheritance:* gift to take effect at one's death
6. *Accession:* increment accruing to one's property
7. *Prescription:* possession in good faith over a long time

QUESTIONS FOR DISCUSSION

1   Since nature leaves things common and does not portion them out to individual owners, how can the private property system, which counteracts nature in this matter, be considered natural and moral?

2   Private property has spawned the twin evils of greed and poverty. If man has a moral duty to get rid of these evils, how can he do so except by getting rid of the cause, private property?

3 Private property rests only on the custom of civilized peoples, and it is a bad custom. It may be natural because it involves the profit motive and man wants to hog as much as he can get, but does that make it moral?

4 Is there a natural limit to the amount of wealth one is morally allowed to amass? If so, does this limit come from something intrinsic to the notion of wealth itself or from the needs of other people?

5 Is not property in a way more sacred than life, because life is only the original gift in which man has no say, but property is the result of his labor and ingenuity, bearing the stamp of his personality and giving his life its meaning?

READINGS

Plato describes the origin of property together with the origin of the state in the *Republic*, bk. II. Read Aristotle's *Politics*, bk. II, especially ch. 5-6, where he defends private ownership against Plato's theories. St. Thomas' *Summa Theologica*, II-II, q. 66, is based on Aristotle, and both are primary sources for the matter found here.

Read John Locke's *Second Treatise on Government*, especially ch. 5. Locke is a firm and even excessive defender of private property.

Pope Leo XIII's *Rerum Novarum* (Condition of the Workingman), Pius XI's *Quadragesimo Anno* (Reconstruction of the Social Order), and John XXIII's *Mater et Magistra* (Christianity and Social Progress) can be found in many editions, some with excellent commentaries. They treat of many matters not pertinent to this chapter, but what they have to say on private ownership is much to the point.

John A. Ryan's *Distributive Justice*, ch. 4 and 18, though old, is still valuable. See Gottfried Dietz, *In Defense of Property*. Johannes Messner's *Social Ethics*, bk. IV, pt. II, has supplied a good deal of material for this chapter, especially on the natural law basis for private ownership.

Pierre Prudhon's *What is property?* is an old and fiery attack; his answer to his question is "Theft!"

Austin Fagothey, *Right and Reason—an Anthology*, contains Locke's *Second Treatise on Government*, ch. 5, and selections from Karl Marx's *Communist Manifesto*. They make a good contrast.

CHAPTER 30

CONTRACTS

PROBLEM

Why should there be justice among men? The question hardly needs to be asked. The notion of justice is too primitive to need proof. It is not innate but arises very early in our experience. Children and savages can tell fair from foul play. Even if they cannot define or explain justice, they know when they have been cheated. But reflective knowledge must go beyond inarticulate feelings and attempt a philosophical justification of justice.

Justice is derived from *equality*. Though unequal in many respects, all men have a certain basic equality. We all have the same human nature. We all live under the same norm of morality and have the same moral obligations. To fulfill them we all have natural rights, which are the same for all and entitle all to what they need to achieve the purpose of life. To live as befits a man one needs not only life but food, clothing, shelter, liberty, education, property, recreation, companionship, and all that goes to make life tolerable as well as possible. To interfere with a man's use of these in such a way as to make his life a hardship and a burden, especially when we refuse to take the same ourselves, is to destroy his fundamental equality with us, to invade his rights, to be unjust.

Moral law and natural rights are thus the source from which justice flows. To protect himself in these rights man has instituted human law, the paramount expression of which is the civil law. The primary aim of the state and of civil law is to secure for its citizens the greatest benefits that can be derived from communal living and to distribute these benefits justly.

There are many transactions that are too personal in scope to be determined by the civil law. In these matters the parties concerned determine what they shall do by free agreement. Such mutual agreements, which concern the transfer of a right, are called *contracts*. In a typical contract two men agree to exchange goods, services, or whatever can be transferred. As far as this transaction is concerned, they start equal; then one carries out his side of the bargain and upsets the original equality, whereupon the other is now obliged to do his part and restore the equality. Until the second party does his part, he is said to *owe* it, and it is said to be *due* the first party. What obliges each to do his part in view of the other's doing his part is commutative justice.

Thus we see three main sources of human rights, the preservation of which is justice and the violation injustice. To violate a *natural right* is to take from another man something that God has given him, an act of injustice against both God and man. To violate a *civil right* is to take from another man something the state owes him in distributive justice, and our interference with the state's duty to him is a crime against social justice. To violate a *contractual right* (if we may use the term, for a contract does not originate rights but transfers them) is not only a breaking of one's plighted word but a violation of commutative justice. No one is obliged to make a contract, but if he makes it, he is bound in commutative justice to keep it. Both moral law and civil law protect the sanctity of contracts, each in its own sphere. The civil law can enforce only those contracts that fall within its jurisdiction, but the moral law is the guardian of all justice.

About these exchanges of goods and services, which are the embodiment of commutative justice and expressed in contracts, we ask:

1. What is meant by a contract?
2. When is a contract binding and when void?
3. What are the obligations of buyers and sellers?
4. Is there such a thing as a just price?
5. Is monopoly necessarily evil?
6. What are the duties of partners and stockholders?
7. Why is interest-taking allowable today?
8. Are gambling and speculation wrong?

NATURE OF A CONTRACT

Many moralists define a contract as a *mutual agreement concerning the transfer of a right.* The commonly accepted legal definition is that of Blackstone: "An agreement upon sufficient consideration to do or not to do a particular thing."* These definitions are not opposed but help to explain one another.

1. A contract is an *agreement,* for there must be consent of at least two wills to the same object; an offer that is made but not accepted cannot be a contract, for only one party consents.

2. It is a *mutual* agreement, for the consent on one side must be given in view of the consent on the other side; two people

who accidentally happened to will the same thing without doing so in view of each other's consent would not form a contract.

3. The parties transfer a *right* and therefore bind themselves in *commutative justice;* pacts, promises, and engagements based on truthfulness, loyalty, friendship, or benevolence can impose serious obligations but are not strictly contracts. The transfer of a right produces a corresponding duty of doing or omitting something.

4. Apart from civil law a valuable *consideration* or recompense is not necessary in all contracts, and thus there can be gratuitous contracts such as gift or promise. Even here some intangible consideration in the form of affection, gratitude, or goodwill is normally to be expected.

5. Since the obligation in justice may be on both sides or only on one side, contracts may be bilateral or unilateral, onerous or gratuitous, but the *consent* must always be on both sides.

That there is a moral obligation to keep contracts hardly needs proof. One who makes a contract transfers a right to another. Then by breaking the contract he violates the right of another, the very right he has just transferred, and thus acts unjustly.

To be binding a contract must be valid, and to be morally allowable it should also be licit. Any alleged contract may be valid or licit, or both or neither. A *valid* contract is one that really is a contract, one that holds good and binds the parties to it. An *invalid* contract is null and void and therefore not a contract, though it may look like one. A *licit* contract is one that the contracting parties were morally or civilly allowed to make. An *illicit* contract is one that is morally or civilly forbidden. Thus buying an article from its owner with my own money is valid and licit; buying extravagant articles with hardship to my dependents is valid but morally illicit; buying stolen articles without knowing that

---

*Blackstone, *Commentaries,* bk. II, ch. 30, p. 442.

they are stolen is invalid but licit; buying an article that I know to be stolen is invalid and illicit. In the example given, the buyer of extravagant articles must pay for them if he cannot return them, and thus the contract is valid, but he did wrong in making the contract, and thus it is illicit. Because it is always illicit to attempt a contract one knows to be invalid, it is only through invincible ignorance that a contract can be invalid but licit.

VALIDITY OF CONTRACTS

In every contract we can distinguish the contracting parties, the matter of the contract, and the mutual consent. These contribute the three main conditions for a valid contract:

1. The contracting parties must be competent persons.
2. The matter must be suitable for a contract.
3. The consent must be mutual, free, and in proper form.

CONTRACTING PARTIES

That the contracting parties must be competent persons means that they must be able to understand the terms of the contract so that they can give voluntary consent to them. Because the making of a contract is a human act, one incapable of a human act is incapable of making a contract. The parties must have sufficient use of reason at least when agreeing to the contract. Infants and the insane are excluded, as are intoxicated, drugged, and hypnotized persons while in that condition.

The state, its purpose being to promote the common good, has as a natural society the authority to regulate contracts within the sphere of its jurisdiction. This authority it often exercises by decreeing that certain classes of persons are incompetent subjects with regard to certain contracts, or by setting down conditions for their competence, thus invalidating contracts they may attempt to make to their own or others' harm.

MATTER OF A CONTRACT

In a contract the matter is that which the contracting parties agree to do or not to do. A contract can concern goods, services, actions, or omissions. For a contract to be valid the matter must be something *possible* under the terms specified and not unduly difficult, something *definite* so that both parties know what they are agreeing to, something morally *permissible* and not contravening prior obligations; if the matter is a physical object, it must be *existing* either in fact or in prospect, and must *belong to* the contracting party so that he has the right to dispose of it. These conditions merely express the fact that a contract involves the transfer of a right and the assumption of an obligation. One must have a right in order to transfer it and must be capable of an obligation before assuming it.

A contract *to do evil* is invalid, that is, null and void, for a contract imposes obligation, and an obligation to do evil is canceled by a prior obligation not to do it. One who has agreed to do evil is not allowed to carry out the supposed contract. He did wrong to begin with in entering into such an engagement and would do further wrong by attempting to fulfill it. If he has been paid in advance, he must return the price, which he cannot claim by any title. The whole is a bad bargain, and both must withdraw from it.

What if the evil is already done? It must be undone, if possible. If the act is irreversible, opinion is divided. The first opinion says that if the conditions for a valid contract are not met, the whole transaction is void; both agents ought to have known that neither is bound to anything. The second opinion makes a distinction, arguing that the promise to do evil was indeed invalid, but the act by which it was carried out was a real expenditure of physical effort or mental ingenuity worth a price—that here was a valid subsidiary contract attached to the main invalid contract. Each of the parties may follow the probable opinion that is to his advantage, the one demanding and the other refusing payment. The doer of the evil deed may certainly ask for and accept the price, for even if he has no right to it by contract, he may always ask for and take a gift.

Bribery is the offering of money for evildoing, especially for the shrinking of duty. If the money is offered or promised on condition that one do the evil act and this condition is accepted, there is an attempt to make a contract about illegitimate matter, and the principles just stated apply: the evil act must be avoided and the money returned, or if the act has been done, the money either must be returned, if one adopts the opinion that the whole transaction is void, or the money may be kept, if one follows the opinion that the payment of the price for service rendered is a valid contract attached to the invalid evil contract. But if the money is offered merely to persuade or allure someone to do wrong, there is no contract because there is no promise in return. Though it is understood why the money is given, the absence of mutual agreement makes it no more than a gift; if we regard only the purely contractual aspect of commutative justice, one could take the money and still refuse to do the evil act. But morality is not limited to strict justice. No self-respecting person will soil his hands with a bribe, and public officials particularly must not jeopardize their freedom to act impartially for the common good.

MUTUAL CONSENT

That which gives the contract its essence is the mutual consent of the parties.

Consent implies offer and acceptance. The *offer* remains open as long as the offerer wishes. It may cease by withdrawal on the part of the offerer, by refusal on the part of the one to whom it was offered, or by lapse of time. *Acceptance* may not be revoked, for it seals the contract. Conditions attached to the offer or to the acceptance must be made known to and accepted by both parties. Regulation of contracts is a typical matter for human law and custom. In the absence of an agreement to the contrary the prevailing conventions should be followed.

Mutual consent must be an external manifestation of a free internal act of the will. It must be externally manifested, because a contract is between two persons and supposes communication between them. It must be internally given by a free act, because a contract is a *human act*, requiring an act of the will consequent on knowledge. Freedom of consent may be nullified by error or by fear.

Error voids a contract only insofar as it excludes consent. Any *substantial* error, whether involving deceit or not, invalidates the contract, for then the person consents to something quite different from the actual matter proposed, as when a person buys what he thinks is a live horse and gets a hobbyhorse. Errors about unimportant qualities do not affect the contract, as when a person finds that the horse he bought is not the color he thought it was. However, if such qualities were expressly stipulated so that the contract would not have been made except for them, the contract is invalid if the stipulations are not adhered to. Hence what is substantial to a contract may be determined not only by the nature of the matter concerned but also by the will of the contracting parties when they make a certain condition essential to the contract.

Fear voids a contract only if it destroys the use of reason, making voluntary consent impossible. This would be the strongly emotional, not the intellectual, type of fear. Since even grave fear does not normally destroy voluntariness, contracts made from the motive of fear are naturally valid. Fear may be artificially aroused in a person by the use of threats to extort his consent. Such unjust intimidation, though it leaves the contract valid, makes it voidable, that is, capable of being canceled without the intimidator's consent. It is valid because it is a human act but voidable because it is the result of injury which the intimidator is bound to repair. Positive law, for the sake of the common good, also has the authority to render invalid from the beginning contracts extorted under intimidation and duress. Whether it does so and under what conditions, the positive law itself would have to declare.

So much about contracts in general. They all deal with the transfer of rights and the consequent assumption of duties, to the observance of which each party binds himself in justice. Implicit understandings may be sufficient among friends, but the public solemnity of the formal contract acts as a guarantee to each party concerned that the other party will respect the right transferred, fulfill the duty assumed, and thus maintain justice.

The remaining sections deal with various business and property contracts.

BUYING AND SELLING

The contract of *buying* and *selling*, or *purchase* and *sale*, is a contract whereby two persons agree to exchange a commodity for a certain price. If differs from *barter* by using money as the medium of exchange. The two are essentially the same sort of contract, but the idea of price brings up some special problems. The expression of consent to each other is normally enough to seal the contract, but the civil law may add certain formalities necessary for validity, as in the transfer of real estate, where it is important for the common good that

the state know who owns the property.

The *seller* must own the object he sells, manifest its hidden defects, and deliver the actual article bought. Articles belonging to another, whether stolen or held by mistake, cannot be validly sold, and anyone who possesses them must return them to the real owner as soon as his ownership becomes evident; a seller in bad faith must stand the loss, both refunding the price and seeing that the true owner receives his property, but no one need be disturbed about purchases made in good faith on the open market. The seller must manifest hidden substantial defects even without inquiry, for they touch the essence of the contract, but he need not manifest hidden accidental defects except on inquiry, when he must tell the truth; in any case he must lower the price proportionately.

The *buyer* must accept on delivery the goods contracted for and pay in full within a reasonable time, either specified in the contract or dictated by custom. Precious objects should not be bought for a song from children or simpletons, and the law protects them by making consent of their guardians necessary. The buyer need not inform the seller of the use he will make of the property or the profit he expects from it, but to have a meeting of minds, both should know the *nature* of the goods even if they differ about their value.

Both buyer and seller, though neither need assist the other to make a good bargain, since each is out for his own advantage, must see to it that the contract is valid according to the norms set down for contracts in general. They are also bound to see that justice is done and therefore must agree on a just price.

THE JUST PRICE

In some economic circles the *just price* is regarded as a medieval notion inapplicable to the competitive methods of modern business. Since economics is not ethics, economists are privileged to ignore the idea of justice as being outside their field and to pursue their study in an ethical vacuum. In theory the two sciences must be kept distinct, but in practice no man can divide his life in that way. One does not cease to be a man by becoming a businessman. A business transaction has both a commercial and a moral aspect: commercial insofar as it involves a *price*, and moral insofar as it involves what is *just*. As it can be good or poor business, so it can be moral or immoral conduct, and these two spheres do not always coincide. To be viewed adequately as a piece of human endeavor, the act must be seen from both standpoints.

It solves nothing to say that the just price is that which gives the seller a fair profit after deducting his own expenses. This is only a rule of thumb, supposing an already existing price structure, prices for materials, machines, labor, and upkeep, besides prices for the commodities needed for a man's support and purchased with his profit. We want to know how this price structure itself arises and what can make it just.

Our discussion will begin with *staple* commodities bought and sold in the market by people *in business*, not with rare articles or occasional private transactions outside the haunts of commerce. The former alone can give us a standard of value according to which prices can be scaled; the latter must also conform to the just price, but here it can be arrived at only by analogy and derivation from the former source.

The *price* of a thing is its value in terms of money. *Value* is the capacity of goods to satisfy human wants, and *money* is the accepted medium of exchange. The *just price*, then, is the true money value of the commodity, a price that can purchase other commodities having equal capacity for satisfying human wants as the commodity sold. The whole concept of commutative justice is based on the idea

of equality, and trade itself with all its modern complexities is only a development of the same idea: that a man receives the equal of what he gives. The purpose of trade is social, to allow men to supply themselves with the commodities they need in exchange for those they have in surplus. Nor is this concept of equality contradictory to the idea of profit, for a man is entitled to the fruit of his superior industry and ingenuity, and he may make as good a bargain as possible without violating justice. There are limits set by justice, and human commerce is not allowed to have the antisocial purpose of prospering on the calamities and misfortune of others.

The problem is: How can the equal capacity of commodities for satisfying human wants be calculated? Two extreme views can be considered:

1. Each commodity has an exactly fixed money value.
2. Any price the buyer is willing to pay is just.

The first extreme is impossible. There is no way of determining what any individual man will want, for human needs and desires differ too widely from person to person, vary too much from time to time in the same person, and depend on too many purely psychological factors such as taste and fashion. One will pay a king's ransom for an article that another would not take as a gift. Hence it is foolish to look for a just price as an absolutely fixed sum. It could only be a range within which prices fluctuate, and the whole range varies with the times.

The second extreme is immoral. A starving man would be willing to pay all he possesses for a bit of food, for he cannot eat his money, but no one would be allowed to take such an advantage of his plight. Were prices determined by what an individual is willing to pay, we should have the absurd situation that, as a man's needs increase, the purchasing power of his money decreases, until in desperate straits it is practically worthless. The example given here is an extreme case, it is true, but it only goes to show how false the principle is. It would thwart the whole idea of money as a medium of exchange, of trade as a function of society, and of commutative justice as a moral virtue.

The just price, then, must be determined by the usefulness of the commodity not to this or that individual but to men generally. The price must represent the judgment of the buying public on the value of the article, eliminating the subjective conditions peculiar to the individual. This judgment is expressed in the open market, where buyers and sellers freely compete with one another and thus establish a true equation between the capacities of different commodities for satisfying human wants. The competitive price is the *natural* price that will drive out all other prices, and this is also the just price where there is pure competition.

There is not much pure competition remaining. Wants are artificially created by our huge advertising programs, and prices are monopolistically determined, but even an artificially induced want is a want and competes with other wants. Monopolistic prices can be judged outrageous or exorbitant, and the thing so priced will not sell, thus showing that the just price concept still obtains. Because there are conspiracies to boost or lower prices artificially, the government may step in and regulate prices; a price thus set by law is the *legal* price, and it is the just price if properly calculated to offset the distortion artificially induced. The government may also set legal prices to protect certain occupations, such as agriculture, that are essential to the public welfare.

The just price is elastic, a range between a *highest just price* and a *lowest just price*. Outside these limits justice is violated, but between them any price is just. The reason for this elasticity is that the wants of the buying and selling public continually alter and take some time to make themselves felt, so that the market lags a bit behind these changes. To sell above the highest just price is to take an antisocial advantage of the buyer's needs and to make a profit out of human misery; to buy below the lowest just price is to take the opposite advantage of the seller's need to get rid of his goods in exchange for what he needs more. To act thus is to be guilty of injustice, and one who does so is morally bound to make restitution even without a legal decision.

Since possibility of loss or of long-deferred payment may excuse from the market price, there is nothing wrong with the practice of a periodic "bargain sale" at reduced rates for the purpose of clearing out old stock or attracting new customers. The seller may raise the price if the article has personal or sentimental value for himself, because he deserves compensation for this loss, but not if it has such value for the buyer only, because the seller does not possess this extra value and loses nothing on account of it.

The prices of rare articles, such as curios, museum pieces, collector's items, and objects of art and luxury, are determined by the narrow community that deals in such things. There is still a just price, but it is much more elastic. If the object is unique, the community may be narrowed down to one buyer and seller, and almost any price agreed on is just.

Auction is a sale in which the highest bidder becomes the purchaser. The highest bid determines the just price. Since no one is bound to buy in this manner, auctions work no injustice if the conventions are followed and free bidding is not interfered with.

MONOPOLY

Monopoly is exclusive control over a market. Monopolies may be state controlled or privately controlled; they may owe their existence to the nature of the marketable commodity or be granted by law.

Monopoly is *just* when it uses its control for the common welfare. Thus copyright and patent rights secure to men the fruits of their ingenuity and industry, large outlays of capital for railroads and toll bridges need protection, the state may establish a monopoly over a luxury as a source of revenue. The putting of so much economic power into the hands of one or a few is not wrong in itself. The whole question is how that power is used, for or against the common good. Once a monopoly over important commodities and services has been secured, it ceases to have a purely private interest and becomes a matter of public and social interest.

Monopoly is *unjust* when it uses its control against the common welfare. It is not unjust to undersell competitors, even though this act puts others out of business and tends to create a monopoly, provided one does not sell under the lowest just price. This is how competitive business works, though there are other obligations besides those of mere justice. The classic abuse of monopoly is to cut prices below the lowest just price for the purpose of driving out competitors and cornering the market, and then, when the monopolist has gained control, to raise the price above the highest just price. In such a process the monopolist has as his ultimate aim the charging of unjust prices and the using of economic dictatorship for his personal profit contrary to the common good.

PARTNERSHIP

Partnership is a contract by which several persons put together their money or labor or skill into a business and share the profit and loss proportionately. We limit ourselves to a few remarks on its ethical aspects.

In the *firm* or company each partner is bound by a personal obligation and, in case of default, must make good out of his personal belongings for the total liability of the firm unless it is a "limited" firm. A *corporation* is a legal person having corporate rights and duties, each member being bound in proportion to the amount of capital he has subscribed. Besides limiting the members' liability, the corporation is endowed with a sort of immortality, continuing in existence indefinitely though all the members have changed.

The ethical disadvantage of the corporation is the diminished sense of responsibility on the part of the stockholders who leave the whole management of the corporation to the directors. Many never reflect that their money may be put to the perpetration of the grossest injustices by unscrupulous directors. Securely shielded behind the impersonal front of the corporation, they may feel that they have sloughed off all personal responsibility onto the directors' shoulders. But it is impossible to avoid moral responsibility in this way, and the principles concerning *cooperation in evil* apply. As a rule people who have invested their money in reputable enterprises need not be disturbed, but if anything occurs to raise serious doubts, they must investigate.

There is nothing wrong in principle with the more complex forms of business association such as trusts, cartels, syndicates, holding companies, and conglomerates, but they are open to abuse and unjust monopolistic practices. They require supervision and control.

INTEREST AND USURY

Loan of money generally carries with it a contract of interest. Formerly all interest was called *usury*, from the Latin *usura*, the price for the use of a thing; but now usury means only excessive interest. It is well to note this point in reading Aristotle's and St. Thomas' condemnation of *usury;* they do not mean excessive interest only, but any interest. Since they were only reflecting the common view of their day, we ask: Why was interest-taking formerly thought wrong and now is the accepted thing? According to Aristotle:

> The most hated sort [of wealth-getting], and with the greatest reason, is usury, which makes a gain out of money itself, and not from the natural object of it. For money was intended to be used in exchange, but not to increase at interest. And this term interest, which means the birth of money from money, is applied to the breeding of money because the offspring resembles the parent. Wherefore of all modes of getting wealth this is the most unnatural.°

St. Thomas accepts Aristotle's theory and works out the argument in greater detail. He says:

> To take usury for money lent is unjust in itself, because this is to sell what does not exist, and this evidently leads to inequality which is contrary to justice.
>
> In order to make this evident, we must observe that there are certain things the use of which consists in their consumption: thus we consume wine when we use it for drink, and we consume wheat when we use it for food. . . . He commits injustice who lends wine or wheat, and asks for double payment, viz., one, the return of the thing in equal measure, the other, the price of the use, which is called usury. . . .
>
> Now money, according to the philosopher, was invented chiefly for the purpose of exchange: and consequently the proper and principal use of money is its consumption or alienation whereby it is sunk in exchange. Hence it is by its very nature unlawful to take payment for the use of money lent, which payment is known as usury: and just as a man is bound to restore other ill-gotten goods, so is he bound to restore the money which he has taken in usury.†

These views are no longer held, not because of any change in the moral principles of justice involved, but because of a change in the function of money. Interest was condemned as an attempt to get gain by no labor, expense, or risk from something which does not fructify (money) and hence can afford no just title for the gain.

In former ages Aristotle's statement that money is merely a medium of exchange was literally true. It could not be easily turned into capital. There were only handicrafts, no large factories. The only capital worth the name was land, and land, since it was owned by the nobility and was the title to their rank, was not generally on the market for sale. All that a man could do with his surplus money was to keep it locked in a chest or spend it on furnishings and luxuries.

The change in the function of money was brought about by the introduction of the capitalistic system, appearing first in the merchantile and later in the industrial form. When feudalism was breaking up and the new class of wealthy burghers was coming into prominence, the latter formed *joint stock companies* to finance projects greater than the wealth of any single man, the profit to be distributed in proportion to the amount contributed. Since the development of these enterprises and more so after the industrial revolution, money can always find profitable investments and can be readily turned into capital. By such investments money brings profit, breeds more money, and so does fructify.

Nowadays the person who lends money to another deprives himself of the opportunity of investing his money in profitable enterprises and is deserving of compensation for this loss. This is the modern function of interest. Now that anyone can readily invest his money and turn it into capital, there is no reason why he should ever lend money to another unless he can receive profit in the form of interest. To charge an excessive rate is unjust and has now become the crime of usury.

That this modern idea of interest does not rest on a change of moral principles,

---

°Aristotle, *Politics*, bk. I, ch. 10, 1258b 2-8.
†St. Thomas, *Summa Theologica*, II-II, q. 78, a. 1.

but only on a new interpretation of money, is confirmed by the fact that even the ancients admitted the right to compensation for the expenses of the transaction, the loss of the opportunity to seize good bargains, and the risk of not recovering the principal. In ancient times these were not always present or were negligible; now the reverse is true.

The foregoing refers to private loans only, in which the just rate of interest would be calculated to offset the loss of potential gain incurred in each case. How may we explain the uniform rates of interest prevailing in the money markets? And how is a man justified in taking interest on money loaned to the capitalistic enterprises themselves, in supporting those very institutions that make interest-taking on private loans almost an economic necessity? An investor in stocks is entitled to dividends, which are his share in the profits, but why is the holder of bonds, who owns no share in the company, entitled to interest on his money?

The answer must be based on the function of credit in the modern financial world. The granting of credit is the placing of economic power at somebody's disposal. It is an economic service and as such is worth its price like any other service. He who makes his property available for another's use charges rent for it. He who makes his money or credit available for another's use can likewise charge for this use in the form of interest. Interest in this sense has changed radically from interest on private loans. It ceases to be the old contract of interest and becomes much like one of hire or lease. It is rendering a service to the enterprise and thereby to the whole community, whose economic prosperity consists in the total complex of these enterprises. It sets up a market in money as in any other commodity, and the just price is determined in the same way as the price for any other service. The natural rate of interest is what people in general are willing to pay on the open market, and the legal rate is fixed by law.

CONTRACTS OF CHANCE

Contracts of chance have to do with some uncertain event whose outcome results from luck, skill, or a combination of the two. Since a person may dispose of his property as he pleases, gambling is not wrong in itself. However, contracts of chance, besides conforming to the requirements of contracts in general, must observe some special conditions of their own if they are to be conducted on a moral plane:

1. One must wager only what belongs to oneself and is not needed for satisfying other obligations, such as paying creditors or supporting one's family.

2. The matter of the contract must be something lawful in itself and understood in the same sense by all parties. Equality is not necessary, but inequalities should be made known. Odds and handicaps should be offered by the favored side but may be waived by the other side.

3. The outcome should be objectively uncertain and not a sure thing, if it is to be truly a contract of chance. Each may feel subjectively certain that he will win but must not have so manipulated the matter beforehand as to cut down the other's chance. If one insists on betting against another's protestation of certainty, he is making a gift, not placing a bet.

4. There must be no cheating, either by fixing the outcome beforehand or by engaging in an illegitimate style of play. What constitutes cheating depends on the conventions accepted in that kind of bet or game. Winnings through cheating are fraudulently acquired and must be refunded.

5. The loser must pay. This is evident from the whole supposition of the contract. One would have no right to take the winnings unless he is prepared to stand the losses, since he imposes this obligation

on the other party, and the obligation is mutual.

What if gambling is outlawed? If a civil law forbids gambling, it is either a purely penal law, leaving the contract valid and the obligation standing, or it is a law that binds morally, voiding the contract from the start, so that the principles on evil contracts apply. In the former case one does no moral wrong in gambling but must pay. In the latter case one probably need not pay but commits a wrong in the act of gambling.

Gambling, though not in itself morally wrong, is open to serious abuse. Some people get gambling in their blood and cannot stop until they have brought about their own and their family's ruin. For them gambling becomes a vice leading to many others. Just as some must practice total abstinence regarding drink, others must stay completely away from all forms of gambling, not because it is objectively wrong, but because of the subjective danger of excess in certain persons. Besides, professional gambling is conducted in such an atmosphere of general moral laxity as to provide many temptations beyond those of gambling itself. The civil law, instead of trying to forbid gambling, would spend its energies better in inspecting gambling facilities and seeing that they are run honestly.

Insurance has a purpose different from that of other contracts of chance, for it is not to make money quickly but to guard against loss. Gambling creates a risk where none existed before; insurance covers a risk that was already present. Insurance fills a definite need in modern society. Its contract, whose written form is called a policy, must follow the laws of contracts in general. Any fraudulent concealment or failure to live up to the terms of the contract is an act of injustice demanding restitution. Deliberately to cause damage in order to collect insurance money is the obvious crime here, removing the element of

chance essential to the contract. Insurance companies must have the funds to pay indemnities for losses occurring at the normal rate, but not to cover all at once. Insurance has become so common and has assumed such social significance that the civil law has the right and duty to regulate it strictly.

Operations on the stock exchange and similar markets are in the first instance only buying and selling, though on a grand scale. The size of the transaction does not change its nature or the moral principles on which it rests. It becomes a contract of chance when it assumes the form of *speculation,* which consists in betting on future changes of price, and is thus a kind of gambling. In itself speculation is not morally wrong, and it follows the laws of betting. Those who engage in it, however, must consider not only themselves and their competitors, those willing to play the game, but also the producers of commodities and the vast horde of small investors whose interests are bound up with their own. Unscrupulous speculation on the market and its resulting artificial manipulation of prices can work serious harm to thousands of people and can wreck the economy of nations. To ruin others for one's own profit cannot be condoned by any law of justice or charity, and those who cause these evils bear a staggering load of moral responsibility.

SUMMARY

Justice is derived from the fundamental *equality* of all men, based on their common human nature. To maintain this equality man is endowed with natural rights, defines for himself civil rights, and transfers alienable rights by contract. Justice demands respect for all three kinds of rights; interference with any is injustice. Commutative justice guarantees the sanctity of contracts and obliges to their observance.

A *contract* is a mutual agreement by

which two or more persons bind themselves to do or omit something. A *valid* contract holds good and really binds, and a *licit* contract is one lawfully entered into; a contract can be valid without being licit, and vice versa.

The *contracting parties* must be competent persons, with sufficient use of reason for a human act. Positive law may add further conditions.

The *matter* must be possible, existing, definite, transferable, and lawful. A contract to do evil is invalid, and one is forbidden to fulfill it; one who has done so may ask and accept the price, though the other probably need not pay it.

The *mutual consent* means that each freely consents in view of the other's consent. Substantial error voids a contract, but not accidental error, unless it is about something expressly stipulated. Fear that destroys consent voids a contract; positive law may void naturally valid contracts made under duress.

The title to property is transferred by *contract*. The *seller* must own the object he sells, manifest its hidden defects, and deliver the article bought; the *buyer* must accept the goods on delivery and pay within a reasonable time.

The *just price* is one that can purchase other commodities having equal capacity for satisfying human wants. It is neither an absolutely fixed money value nor any sum the buyer is willing to pay, but represents the judgment of the buying public in general, found by free competition on the open market. It is the *natural* price; if fixed by law, it is the *legal* price. The just price is elastic, a range between a *highest* and a *lowest* just price. To buy or sell outside these limits is unjust and demands restitution. Rare articles, bargain sales, and auctions are exceptions.

Monopoly, exclusive control over a market, is just when used for the common welfare, unjust when exploited for selfish ends.

Partnership is good in itself, though monopolistic forms need regulation. In a *firm* each partner has total liability. In a *corporation* liability is limited by the proportion of shares held. Stockholders cannot slough off onto the directors responsibility for immoral use of their capital.

Interest was formerly condemned as an attempt to get gain from what does not fructify. Capitalism, with unlimited opportunities for investment, changed the function of money so that it can fructify. Interest compensates the lender for the gain he might otherwise have made and for the service he renders. Now only excessive interest, *usury*, is wrong.

Contracts of chance deal with an uncertain event. Gambling, though not wrong in itself under proper conditions, is a great moral danger to certain people. Cheating demands restitution, and gambling debts must be paid. Insurance is a legitimate social necessity. Market speculation, a complex form of betting, is capable of wreaking great harm unless kept within responsible control.

QUESTIONS FOR DISCUSSION

1 If people really trusted one another, there would be no need of binding another with a formal contract. Do contracts spring out of man's immorality, and would they have no place if ethics were fully observed?

2 Why should not buying and selling be a free contract, in which any

price the seller asks is just, and if the buyer does not want it at that price, he need not take it? Should not the only moral restriction be that each really owns what he exchanges?

3 Economists insist that the exact determination of the true worth of a commodity is practically impossible. How can there be a just price for something that is continually fluctuating?

4 Is the morality of charging interest so connected with capitalism that a change to a different economic system would again make the charging of interest immoral? Or is the fruitfulness of money here to stay in any kind of economy?

5 States vary greatly in their gambling laws. Is it better for the state to be restrictive or permissive on the gambling issue? Since people will gamble, no matter what, why try to regulate it at all?

READINGS

On justice: Plato's treatise on justice takes up bk. I and the first part of bk. II of the *Republic.* Aristotle's *Nicomachean Ethics,* bk. V, is all on justice. St. Thomas writes on justice in the *Summa Theologica,* II-II, qq. 58-62. Of modern writers read Étienne Gilson's *Moral Values and Moral Life,* ch. 9, and his *Christian Philosophy of St. Thomas Aquinas,* pt. III, ch. 4; Heinrich Rommen's *The State in Catholic Thought,* pp. 184-192, 319-326; and Josef Pieper's little book *Justice* or the section on justice in his *The Four Cardinal Virtues.*

On economics: Aristotle, as the founder of economics as well as of so many other sciences, writes on household management and on wealth in his *Politics,* bk. I, ch. 8-11. St. Thomas discusses cheating and usury in the *Summa Theologica,* II-II, qq. 77-78. On usury, John T. Noonan's

Scholastic Analysis of Usury is a thorough scholarly study. On the moral aspects of economics see John A. Ryan, *Distributive Justice,* ch. 7, 10-11, 16; and Johannes Messner, *Social Ethics,* bk. IV, pt. I.

On the ethics of various particular business practices see Herbert Johnston's *Business Ethics,* Henry Wirtenberger's *Morality and Business,* Thomas M. Garrett's *Ethics in Business,* Marquis Childs and Douglas Cater's *Ethics in a Business Society,* and Luther Hodges' *The Business Conscience.* The *Harvard Business Review* has an ethically oriented article in nearly every issue.

Austin Fagothey, *Right and Reason—an Anthology,* contains background material in the selections from Locke, Marx, and Pieper.

CHAPTER 31

WORK

PROBLEM

Most men get the property they need by working for it. By the wage contract a man hires out his labor to another for a definite sum of money known as a wage or salary. We single out the wage contract for special treatment because it brings up the whole question of industrial relations, the problem of management and labor. We must discuss the following:

1. Is the wage system just?
2. How is the minimum just wage determined?
3. Has a man a right to work?
4. Are labor unions justified?
5. Why and when have workmen a right to strike?
6. Are lockouts and boycotts justified?

THE WAGE SYSTEM

A man who finds his business becoming too large to be run by himself alone must either curtail its volume or engage the help of others. In the latter event, he may choose to take others into partnership and share with them the control of the business, or he may wish to keep the control in his own hands and merely hire others to do part of the work. Partnership usually supposes an investment of capital in the business and is rewarded by a share in the profits. Employment does not suppose an investment in the business, and it is rewarded by the definite monetary return contracted for. The wage system seems to

be as old as history and is accepted everywhere. Though perhaps not the only possible arrangement between employer and employee, it is in itself a valid and just form of contract.

Under the wage system the workman receives a fixed wage but has no share in the profits and losses, whereas the owner receives the profits and also sustains the losses. Thus the workman has income security, which he needs most because of his lack of capital; the owner takes the risks and losses, which his reserve capital enables him to absorb, and he also has the profits as his compensation for the risks and losses. It is a fair bargain. Neither side can have it both ways. The *owner* may not take all the profits and then put off the losses on the laborer when profits fail. The paying of a fixed wage is his first obligation, taking precedence over all others. The *workman* is assured of a steady income from his labor, which is all he has to sell and on which he depends for his immediate support.

A fixed wage means that it is fixed over a certain period specified by contract, not that it is wholly static. The workman has no right to share in the immediate profits resulting from temporary fluctuations, but he has a right to share in the increasing wealth and prosperity of the community of which he forms a part, whether this community be the industry, the nation, or the whole world. Though the workman who is already being paid a just wage has no right to demand more merely because his company happens at the moment to be making a temporary increase in profit, which a prudent owner will hold as a cushion against possible reverses, any really lasting increase in efficiency of productivity should be reflected in a higher wage scale.

The foregoing is an extremely simple view of the matter, but it is necessary to get down to fundamentals, or the problem cannot be seen at all. Our highly organized industrial society brings in a number of other factors, but the basic ones we have mentioned still remain. Many suggest a combination of the wage and partnership systems: that the worker be paid a fixed wage sufficient for his own and his family's support, and that over and above this wage he be given some shares in the business; and that these shares be not in the form of an occasional bonus but part of the employment contract. We have some discussion of such schemes later. Note here that they do not eliminate the wage contract, which remains the basic source of the worker's income.

MINIMUM JUST WAGE

The minimum just wage means the least amount any regular workman ought to be paid for his work. By *regular workman* is meant here an adult, competent, full-time employee who makes his living by giving his whole working day to his employer—not children, the physically or mentally handicapped, or those engaged part time or temporarily. These persons also must be paid justly, but they cannot furnish a standard; their pay will be a fair proportion of the regular workman's wage. The *minimum* just wage is not the minimum for a particular kind of work but for *any* work; it will apply chiefly to the unskilled worker, since skilled work will be worth so much more. We shall make no attempt to calculate the actual minimum wage in dollars and cents, for it will vary with the times, but only to find the *principle* that ought to govern any such calculation. How can it be determined?

1. Not by the length of time spent in work, for time itself has no definitely fixed and constant value; no man today could live on the wage given fifty years ago; the value of labor-time fluctuates, and time itself can form no standard.

2. Not by the value of the products of labor, for labor costs are included in the sale price of the product, thus supposing that the price of labor has already been set by some other standard.

3. Not by the usefulness of a certain laborer to his employer, for this is rewarded by wages above the minimum but cannot set a standard for the minimum itself; the minimum wage means the least wage any regular workman should be paid if he is employed at all.

4. Not by the law of supply and demand, for labor is no ordinary commodity on a par with the rest, since it involves the dignity of the human person; there is a point below which it cannot go without degrading the human person to a subhuman condition.

5. The only way in which the minimum just wage can be determined is from the function of human labor itself. *Why do men work?* Why are they willing to put in a day's labor for a sum of money? A man works to make a living, to support himself and his dependents. This is why a man will spend his life working for himself, as an independent farmer, artisan, or shopkeeper. If a man, instead of working for himself, sells his labor to another, he does it for the same reason. If he cannot make a living by his work, there is no reason why he should work. The minimum just wage, therefore, is a wage capable of supplying the essentials of a human life.

What are these essentials? More than bare subsistence, for a man is not a beast of burden, and more than would satisfy the simple wants of a savage, for a man has a right to share in the civilization of which he forms a part and in the general progress of humanity. Man has a right to the essentials of a human life precisely as *human,* a decent life befitting the rational kind of being man is by nature. A minimum standard of living implies at least adequate housing, sufficient and wholesome food, time for sleep and relaxation, some inexpensive recreation, and a small surplus for emergency.

Is the minimum just wage a *personal* wage or a *family* wage, that is, must it be only enough for the worker alone or also enable him to support his dependents? It must be a family wage. The just price of labor, as of anything else, is determined in the open market by the common estimate of men, and the ordinary reason given by men for judging that a wage is too low is: "A man cannot support a family on such a wage." A wage sufficient only for the worker's personal support is not really sufficient even for this purpose, for since he is bound to share it with his family, not enough of it would be left even to support him personally. The moral obligation is clear: an employer who monopolizes all the earning power of the father of a family is morally obliged to pay him a wage that will enable him to fulfill his natural duties to his family.

Should this family wage be *relative* or *absolute,* that is, should it be scaled to the size of the particular workman's family or be adjusted to the average family? The foregoing argument might seem to prove that it should be relative, for the workman must support the actual family he has, not some mathematical medium that may not be verified in his case. However, a relative wage would lead to untold confusion and conflict. The employer would be faced with an almost hopeless task of clerical work, would be unable to estimate his labor cost for the coming year, and would have too strong a temptation to employ men of smaller families. There would be dissatis-

faction among the employees paid differently for the same work, and those with the largest families, who most need work, would have the most difficulty finding and keeping it. Therefore the wage should be adjusted to the average family. Some sort of public subsidy might be necessary for very large families, but this is not strictly the employer's business; it devolves on society as a whole or on the state.

Have only married men a right to a family wage? No, this wage must be paid to all. Unmarried men have a right to marry or to save money for future marriage, and only a family wage will enable them to do so. It is one of the main motives driving young men to work industriously. Even an elderly single man has the right to marry, though he may never exercise it, and he should not be penalized for not doing what he does not have to do. Besides, distinction in wages on this score would lead to trouble, for grasping employers would find pretexts to dismiss men when they marry and to hire unmarried men in their places.

A word of caution may be useful here. While stressing the obligation of the employer, we must not forget the other side of the picture. Our American standard of living is so high that we have come to confuse necessities with luxuries, and our habits of spending are eliminating all regard for thrift, a quality needed for survival in most parts of the world. If a man wants luxuries, he should earn them by developing himself into a skilled worker who will receive a wage far above the minimum.

The changed condition of the modern family adds its problems. Formerly the husband walked to work and had to live nearby; now he needs a car. Formerly the wife contributed more to the family's sustenance by her personal services; she churned the butter, baked the bread, spun the wool, and made the clothes besides cooking the meals and sweeping the house. Now there are prepared foods, manufactured clothes, washing machines, vacuum cleaners, automatic kitchens, and countless other appliances. These cost money to buy and operate, and unless the wife is gainfully employed, must be paid for out of the husband's earnings. How many of these things are minimum requirements for a decent human life in our society, so that any employer must pay enough to provide them? Any answer given now would soon be obsolete.

EMPLOYMENT

Has a man a right to work, that is, to a steady job? The argument may be put very simply: If a man has a right to live, and can live only by work, then he has a right to work. The logic of the argument is perfect, but the second part of the hypothesis, that a man can live only by work, is normally and generally, but not universally and necessarily, true. The very rich are only an apparent exception because their capital works for them, but even outside this class there are always many who live by their wits and have no steady income. Some men turn green at the very mention of work, and yet manage to stay alive. But work is the normal way of obtaining a living, and the economic structure of modern society is geared to it.

If the jobs do not exist, how can workmen rightly demand them? In time of general calamity, such as widespread financial depression, workmen will suffer as well as everyone else. Employers are obliged to tide over short periods of depression and not to lay men off too quickly, for to take the losses as well as the profits is part of their risk, but it is absurd to think that they can run private businesses indefinitely at a loss. By trying to employ too many men, they would soon be able to employ none. In such conditions the only one that can come to the workman's assistance is society itself and, as a last resort, the state. How to do it best is a matter of prac-

tical expediency and human ingenuity, but the duty itself is moral and binds in justice.

Under modern economic conditions society must see to it that there are enough jobs to go around for all who need them. Does this mean a planned economy? The phrase "planned economy" is often used to mean that the state should take over the work of private business, prescribing how much is to be produced and how many jobs are to be provided. Nothing of the kind is advocated here, but no enterprise can succeed without some planning. The state need not do the planning, but someone must; if private business cannot or will not, the state must either do it or see that it is done. Harmonious cooperation between them is the ideal.

The following groups are sore spots in the employment problem:

1. The first group is *temporarily unemployed* because of some financial crisis or industrial disturbance. The real cure is to remedy the financial or industrial situation and to take measures to prevent a recurrence. Until we find a way of reducing these troubles, a partial remedy can be found in employment bureaus, in a combination of periodic occupations, in social insurance, in temporary subsidy to private companies, and in the undertaking of public works.

2. The *unemployable* are a perennial problem. Since competitive business cannot afford to employ them, their care must be the duty of society in general. Institutions must be established for those who cannot be cared for privately. Those who are physically or mentally handicapped but not institutional cases may be given part-time employment, with the rest of their support made up by the state or by private foundations. The quarrelsome, the drunkard, and the drug addict are the worst problems, but society cannot let them starve.

3. *Vagrants* deliberately put themselves outside the pale of human society and thus

cut themselves off from any real right to social assistance. Begging is not in itself morally wrong, for anyone may ask another for help. We are speaking here of those professional beggars who could support themselves otherwise but refuse to do so. Since these persons often take to crime and are a menace to society, vagrancy laws are necessary. Compulsory labor is probably useless as a remedy. On the other hand, there seems to be no ethical reason why a man may not adopt a wandering life, especially if he has no dependents and is willing to do temporary work for his daily needs.

RETIREMENT

The idea of unemployment brings up that of retirement. We are much concerned today with our senior citizens, and the concern is most laudable. There is not much that can be said on the subject from the ethical standpoint, except that each community should do its best for its older people. What it can do depends on its social structure and the means at its disposal, as well as what its people are willing to support.

We cannot expect business companies to keep employing those who have passed their time of usefulness. Since we grow old at varying rates, it is better not to have a fixed mandatory retirement age but to adjust retirement to the individual. In this way the talents of older persons are not sacrificed to a mathematical number but can be used for the benefit of both the individual and society. But some older people will not recognize that they are beyond their time, and the company must have some way of easing them out. Perhaps the largest industries can manage the problem only by having mandatory retirement at a fixed age.

How are these retired persons to spend the rest of their days? Not long ago the large patriarchal family supported its aged in honor and dignity in the ancestral home. Nothing seems to have taken the place of this tradition in our urbanized society. For the most part senior citizens live in apartments separated from their children, and prefer it so. If ill or feeble, they are shunted off to rest homes, which in many instances are the only places equipped to care for them. The older person often has either a lonely or a semihospitalized existence, neither of which he finds satisfactory. He is supposed to have provided for his own old age by savings, pension, or insurance, or at least by social security. On the whole his life is depersonalized and institutionalized at the very time when he has leisure for more friendly personal relations. More efforts are now being made to bring senior citizens together and to provide them with meaningful activities.

Social justice requires that senior citizens partake in the benefits of social living in due proportion to their place in society and in regard for their contributions to society in their heyday. Just how to arrange the means to accomplish this end is a matter of social and political prudence. Ethics points out this obligation of society and counsels the community to be as generous as it can afford.

LABOR UNIONS

The individual workman is at a distinct disadvantage in bargaining with his employer for a suitable wage. The workman is without capital or power or influence, is usually of lower educational attainments, is trained for only one kind of work, cannot travel but must take present opportunities, and needs a job immediately in order to live. The employer needs workmen, but not any particular man, and thus can employ the man who will work for the lowest wage. The workman would have to take any terms the employer wanted to give him unless he could band with his fellow workers for the purpose of *collective bargaining*. A large group of workmen banded together can bargain with the employer on equal terms, since he is as dependent on them as they are on him.

That the labor union is ethically justified is hardly any longer in dispute. The labor union is the *only means* the workman has of obtaining the fair wages and fair treatment to which he as a person has a strict right. Unless the relation of management and labor is to be regimented by the state, the individual worker is at the mercy of the employer. The labor union is also a *legitimate means*. There is nothing contrary to justice or to good morals in an association of workers or in collective bargaining. What it is lawful to do separately, it is lawful to do together. If employers and producers can organize themselves into associations, so can the workers. If employers can agree among themselves on what wages they will pay, so can the workers on what wages they will take.

Like everything else, labor unions are open to abuse. They can make exorbitant demands, call unjustified strikes, ruin fair-dealing employers, operate in restraint of trade, become hotbeds of radicalism, and be betrayed by unscrupulous leaders. The remedy is not to destroy the unions but to correct the abuses. Capital also has been seriously abused by unjust management, as history from the beginning of the industrial revolution to today amply testifies; yet the remedy lies not necessarily in the abolition of capitalism, supposing it a legitimate system, but in the correction of its abuses. When management failed to correct its own abuses, legislation became necessary; if labor will not be clear-sighted enough to put its own house in order, it must submit to the same remedy. In neither case does abuse destroy the use.

There is nothing wrong in principle with the *closed shop* or the *union shop*, but in practice both are open to abuse. No one should be forced to join a union, it is true, but if the situation is such that the union cannot achieve its end unless all the workers are organized, or if some are taking the benefits gained by union activity while evading the burdens of membership, it seems right that those who will not join should be denied jobs. No one has a right to this particular job, and he who wants it should take the conditions attached to it. But if a large part of the workers do not want unionization, it would be unjust to force it on them. The so-called "right-to-work laws," outlawing both the closed shop and the union shop, do not seem justified unless the abuses cannot be handled by less drastic measures, a controverted issue dependent on local conditions.

Likewise the *closed union* is not wrong in principle. Unions have a right to limit membership and form a closed union if otherwise their trade will be glutted with too many new men seeking to displace tried and reliable members who have given the union its strength. If limited membership is used, as sometimes happens, to create unduly high wages through artificial scarcity of workers, an unjust monopoly of labor is created against the public good.

STRIKES

The strike is the chief weapon in the hands of labor for enforcing its demands. Since the purpose of organized labor is to equalize the bargaining power between employer and employee, the only way to counteract refusal to pay fairly is by a concerted refusal to work.

A strike is an organized cessation of work by a number of workers to obtain their employer's assent to certain demands. In the strict sense a strike is of employees only, not of students or prisoners or other unpaid groups. A strike is a walkout of a large enough number to cripple the business. It is an organized movement; even a large, simultaneous quitting without organization is not a strike, unless the lack of organization is only pretended. The purpose of a strike is not to seek employment elsewhere but to regain the old jobs on better terms; therefore a mass movement from one employer to another who pays better is not a strike against the first.

Are strikes morally justifiable? To answer this question we must first distinguish three main kinds of strike:

1. The *direct* strike, by workers actually laboring under the same industrial grievance
2. The *sympathetic* strike, by those who have no grievance of their own but act in support of others who have
3. The *general* strike, by all the workers of the community to support some political demand

THE DIRECT STRIKE

The basic and original form of strike is the direct strike. Any workman has the right to quit his job provided he has fulfilled his contract, just as any employer who has fulfilled his contract need not rehire him. An *organized* cessation of work, especially in a large and essential industry, ceases to be a private affair and assumes a social significance. It brings about serious evils to:

1. The employer, through loss of profits
2. The worker, through loss of wages needed for support
3. The consumer, through lack of goods and services
4. The public, through general economic dislocation

Because it brings about these foreseen evils, which affect not only the persons concerned in the strike but the community at large, a direct strike involves among other principles that of double effect. It is quite possible and often happens that the four conditions are satisfied:

1. The direct strike is not wrong in itself. It contains four elements, none of which is essentially wrong. *Cessation of work* is not wrong in itself; otherwise, one could never quit work. *Organization* is not essentially wrong; if each may quit work separately, all may do it together and for their common benefit. *Just demands,* presented and refused, are the cause of the strike; no strike can be lawful unless these demands are just, but they can be and often are, such as insufficient pay or intolerable working conditions; the contract may have run its term, or been violated by the employers, or become null through an unforeseen change in the economic situation. *Circumstances* connected with a strike are not always and necessarily evil; violence and bloodshed have occurred in strikes, but there is nothing in the very idea of a strike that requires them.

2. The good effect is not obtained by means of the bad effect. The evils to the worker, to the consumer, and to the public are not means of rectifying the workers' condition, and they only accidentally put added pressure on the employer. But is not the good effect obtained through the evil to the employer? This is the crucial point. The strike is so designed as to hit the employer where it hurts, in his pocketbook; this financial loss is the strikers' means of moving the employer to yield at last to their demands. True, but the fact that a strike works in this way does not make it morally wrong. The principle of the *conflict of rights* comes in here to validate the double-effect principle. Financial loss is a physical evil that one can have a right to inflict; a judge does so when he imposes a fine as punishment. The strikers do no injustice to their unjust employer when they stop work for the purpose of stopping his profits and thereby forcing him to stop his injustice toward them. To end the evil of loss to himself, all the employer need do is to behave justly toward his men. Hence the evil is one the employer brings on himself.

3. The strikers must not intend the evil

in itself, but only the just wages and proper working conditions to which they have a right. The strike must not be aimed at fomenting hatred and class war, but only at getting back the old jobs on better terms. Personal hatred is morally wrong for individuals indulging in it, but it does not of itself invalidate an otherwise just cause.

4. There must be sufficient proportion between the good and the evil effect. The more painful and widespread the evil, the greater must be the cause required to balance it. A strike among the military is unthinkable, and among policemen and firemen almost never justifiable. A strike in a nationwide industry that would paralyze the country needs an overwhelmingly strong cause. This requirement does not put all the burden on the workingman but emphasizes the duty of employers to anticipate trouble and to see that a really just cause for striking never arises. It would be out of proportion to call or continue a strike that had no hope of even partial success. The proportion depends on many factors that must be separately determined for each concrete case.

The fourth point can be determined more in detail by considering the following four conditions of a justified strike:

1. *There must be a just cause.* Too little pay, too long hours, brutal treatment, and unsafe or unsanitary working conditions are certainly genuine grievances, whereas personal feuds, petty rivalries, and the ambitions of individual leaders are not. The workers may strike for the minimum just wage, and skilled workers for the wage prevalent for the kind of work they do. When negotiating a new contract, they may refuse to work for the minimum just wage, even though it is a just wage, and may demand more. No law obliges men to take the least they have a right to, and the very idea of bargaining supposes the hope of getting more. But the proportion is upset if the workers strike for the very

last cent of the highest just wage, though they may ask it, or if the owners stage a lockout because the workers refuse to accept the bare minimum. To stick adamantly to either extreme, unless some important principle is at stake, is really a refusal to bargain, and neither side has the right to be stubborn at the expense of the public.

2. *There should be proper authorization.* The decision to strike should come from the men themselves by a free and unintimidated vote. Organized workers must have their strike backed by their union. If the employer can bargain with his workers only through the union, the workers must also use the same channel. Hence "wildcat" strikes are outlawed unless the circumstances are so unusual that the unions have ceased really to represent the workers and are repudiated by them.

3. *The strike must be the last resort.* Every other less painful means must have been exhausted. There is no need of trying plainly futile measures, but each side is morally bound to explore all avenues that offer any reasonable hope. This requirement is all the more important in strike threats that would paralyze the community, in which case the state as protector of the common good may have a duty to intervene. Arbitration, mediation, cooling-off periods, and fact-finding boards may be disagreeable to either side, but they must be used if they have a reasonable chance of success.

4. *Only rightful means may be used.* These means are two: work stoppage and persuasion of other workers to keep the work stopped until the demands are met. Strikers have no right to injure the employer in his person or property. There is no excuse for sabotage or violence. Peaceful picketing is a lawful means of persuasion, but strikers are not entitled to use physical force against those who try to cross the picket line, whether they be customers, nonstriking co-workers, or new

workers genuinely seeking employment. Employers may hire peaceful workers to take the place of the strikers, but not professional strikebreakers, who, it is foreseen, will inevitably provoke violence. In a justified strike the strikers have a right to be returned to their jobs, for it was merely in defense of their rights that they struck in the first place. Whoever begins the use of violence in a strike does wrong; once it has begun, each one has the right of self-defense. But violence is not a legitimate means of either winning or breaking a strike as such.

THE SYMPATHETIC STRIKE

There is great difference of opinion regarding the sympathetic strike. Some see red at the very mention of it, whereas others think it only a natural extension of the direct strike. The moderate view distinguishes two possible cases.

1. The first case involves several groups of workmen belonging to different unions but hired by the same employer. One group strikes for a just demand, but because the members are too few to enforce it, they appeal to the other groups employed by the same company. This kind of sympathetic strike seems justified, provided all the other conditions for a just strike are fulfilled, because it is directed against the same unjust employer. Such a strike may even be directed against several employers when they bind themselves into an employers' or producers' association to adopt a common policy toward their employees and this policy is unjust, or when one employer comes to the aid of another for the purpose of breaking a justified strike. Concerted effort on the part of management is met by concerted effort on the part of labor. A real grievance is spread among all strikers, who direct their efforts against actually unjust employers.

2. The second case involves groups of workmen hired by different and unassociated employers. One group strikes because of a grievance, and to support them the other group goes out on strike against their own wholly blameless employer. The idea seems to be that solidarity among the forces of labor must be achieved at all costs. This second type of sympathetic strike seems unlawful for several reasons: *It is a violation of the wage contract.* These workers have no grievance against their own employer, and yet refuse to do for him what they contracted to do, a breach of commutative justice. *The evil caused is out of proportion to the original demands.* If such a sympathetic strike spreads far enough, the public at large rather than the unjust employer of the original strikers is the chief one to suffer from it. *There is no logical place where such a sympathetic strike should stop.* All businesses are more or less connected. All use public utilities and, if these go out in sympathy, the whole city or country comes to a standstill.

THE GENERAL STRIKE

The general strike is a political rather than an economic weapon and has the characteristics of rebellion or revolution. As a *mere strike,* it is out of all proportion. It aims not to remedy an evil but to inflict injury—not to bring pressure on unjust persons to make them fulfill the demands of justice, but to destroy their property and overthrow the order of society. A grave moral crime is thus perpetrated. As a *method of revolution,* its morality depends on the justifiability of the revolution, toward which it could be a legitimate means. We are talking here of a serious strike. In some countries a general strike of a few hours or even of a whole day is used for political demonstration. This type of strike does not seem wrong if the people are willing to tolerate this sort of inconvenience and if no violence is used or permanent harm done.

LOCKOUTS AND BOYCOTTS

The *lockout* is the inverse of the strike. The employer, unwilling to grant the demands of his striking employees, shuts down the whole plant, thus putting out of work even those who are not striking. The lockout is the employer's weapon against the strike. As the workers are not obliged to submit to unjust treatment, neither is the employer. He cannot keep his plant running when key workers have quit and production is stalled, nor can he continue to pay wages without income. If the strike is justified, the lockout is not; but if the strike is unjustified, a lockout can be permissible so long as it conforms to the same conditions and restrictions that apply to the strike. The *sympathetic lockout,* the closing down of all the factories of the region to break a strike in one of them, causes a disproportionate amount of suffering. The employer has wealth and credit to tide him over, but the workers have not.

A *boycott* is a concerted refusal to patronize a certain business establishment and a persuading of others to join in this refusal. A boycott is justifiable for the same reasons and on the same conditions as a strike. No one is obliged to trade in one place rather than another, and a person may refuse to trade with unjust persons; there is no reason why he may not persuade others to do likewise, so long as he limits his efforts to persuasion and does not resort to violence. The *secondary boycott* is directed against other firms that do business with the boycotted firm; if they do not join in the boycott, they will be boycotted themselves. The secondary boycott is much like the sympathetic strike and follows the same principles. These other firms are not unjust and should not be made to suffer for something they cannot help. Often they cannot obtain materials or services elsewhere to keep themselves going, or they have contracts with the boycotted firm that they are bound in justice to fulfill. If they cooperate with or connive at injustice, economic pressure can legitimately be brought against them.

INDUSTRIAL RESPONSIBILITY

The establishment and maintenance of good industrial relations is one of the most important problems of our age. Ethics is not called on to solve it but merely to point out some moral issues involved. It is not difficult to see in the abstract what ought to be done; the hard part is to get men to do what they know they ought. The ethical concept running through this whole discussion is that of justice. Justice itself never changes, but it must be applied to the new economic facts of the present day.

When our sense of social justice is outraged by the industrial unrest of today, we must not forget the enormous advances that social justice actually has made in the last hundred years. Capital, which formerly wielded its power with imperious recklessness, has been gradually though grudgingly brought to a better sense of public welfare; it still has a long enough way to go in eliminating greed and selfishness. Labor, once so powerless, has by dogged persistence won for itself a position of impregnable strength; it is time for it to assume a larger share of social responsibility.

Union leaders have a delicate and difficult task. They must be upright and just men, true leaders of their unions and jealous of their rights, but also men with a broad social vision embracing the welfare of the whole nation and not merely of the economic class they represent. The rank and file of labor have the obligation to attend meetings and vote, so as to make sure that the union will not fall prey to irresponsible leadership or adopt unjust policies. If a strike is to be called, workers have the duty to inform themselves on the justice of the strike, either by a direct study of the situation or, if they are incapable of this, by assuring themselves of the character and uprightness of their leaders.

Because it sets the pattern of industry, management's responsibility is inescapable. Despite its reforms hitherto, perhaps more of the vast wealth and energy devoted to expanding plants, developing new products, advertising its wares, opening up new markets, and attracting capital investment could be diverted to that extremely important but often forgotten cog in the whole machinery: the contented employee.

SUMMARY

By the *wage contract* a man hires out his labor to another for a definite sum of money. Thus the workman has income security, which his lack of capital demands, whereas the employer takes the profits and losses, against which his capital acts as a cushion.

The *minimum just wage* is the least amount any regular unskilled workman should be paid. It is not determined like other commodities, because the dignity of the human person places a point below which it must not fall. It is determined by the reason a man works: to earn a livelihood. It must be a *family wage*, one sufficient to supply the essentials of a decent human life for an average-size family, whether the worker is married or not.

In our economy a man has a *right to work*, and society the duty to provide jobs. If no one else will, the state must. Means must be taken to cure unemployment, care for the unemployable, and regulate vagrancy. Senior citizens must be provided for in any society.

Labor unions are morally justified as the only practical means of obtaining fair wages and fair treatment for the worker. By banding together for *collective bargaining*, workmen can overcome their disadvantage and make the employer as dependent on them as they are on him.

The *strike*, an organized cessation of work to obtain certain demands, is labor's chief weapon. The *direct* strike can be justified by the two principles of double effect and conflict of rights; the strikers have the right to demand justice by inflicting on the employer a loss of profits he seeks to gain unjustly. There is sufficient proportion if the strike is for a just grievance, is backed by a recognized union, is the last resort, and limits itself to peacefully persuasive means. The *sympathetic* strike is justified if directed against unjust employers only; otherwise it is an injustice against innocent people. The *general* strike, if more than a demonstration, is out of proportion as a strike; it may be the means of a justified revolution. Lockouts and boycotts follow the same principles as the strike.

Great strides have been made toward *social justice*, but both management and labor need a still higher sense of social responsibility.

QUESTIONS FOR DISCUSSION

1 What government could set a minimum wage so high as to give a decent livelihood to a family? Must not a minimum wage necessarily be unjust by the fact that the legal minimum must fall below the moral minimum?

2 Some states have "right-to-work" laws. What is their purpose? Do they guarantee a man a job, make employment easier, free the

worker from being dominated by the unions, or make it easier for union workers to obtain their rights?

3 Is there any substitute for the strike, or is the right to strike essential to unionism? Is there any substitute for unionism, or is unionism essential to a free-enterprise economy? If not, are we doomed to intermittent industrial disturbance forever without remedy?

4 Since a strike to be just must have a just grievance, why can workers strike for a wage above the minimum just wage for their kind of work? Where is the injustice?

5 What do you think of unions for agricultural workers, teachers, doctors, lawyers, and other professions? How otherwise can they obtain what is rightfully theirs?

READINGS

Pope Leo XIII's *Rerum Novarum* (Condition of the Workingman), Pius XI's *Quadragesimo Anno* (Reconstruction of the Social Order), and John XXIII's *Mater et Magistra* (Christianity and Social Progress) are among the most important documents on the moral aspects of industrial relations. Their treatment of the subject is not primarily philosophical, but the ethical background is clearly brought out. There are numerous commentaries; outstanding among them is Oswald von Nell-Breuning's *Reorganization of Social Economy*.

See Johannes Messner's *Social Ethics*, bk. II, pt.

II, and John F. Cronin's *Catholic Social Principles*, ch. 9-11, the latter with an annotated bibliography.

On particular problems: William J. Smith, *Spotlight on Labor Unions;* Jerome Toner, *The Closed Shop;* Benjamin Selekman, *A Moral Philosophy for Management;* Frank Tannenbaum, *A Philosophy of Labor;* and Harwood Merrill, *Responsibilities of Business Leadership.*

Austin Fagothey, *Right and Reason—an Anthology,* contains Josef Pieper's *Leisure, the Basis of Culture* and Marx's *Communist Manifesto.*

CHAPTER 32

CAPITALISM

PROBLEM

Earning a living is not the highest activity of man in point of dignity, but it consumes most of the ordinary person's time and effort. The economic side of man's nature, unlike the domestic and political, is not taken care of by a corresponding natural society. There already is an economic aspect both to the family and to the state, the one extending up and the other down into the middle region between these two societies. Families and states are alike in having their essential functions prescribed for them by the natural law, but nature does not assign any definite association man must enter into for his economic support. That man must organize in some way for this purpose is evident, but *how* to do it is left to human ingenuity. As in most things human, man's efforts over the centuries in building up a socioeconomic order have been only partially successful. Its remarkable complexity is balanced by haphazard performance, its astonishing fertility in production by its glaring injustice in distribution.

Must we give wholehearted approval to capitalism? No, neither in its present form nor in any form. The world existed for many centuries with private property, yet without that specific form of it called capitalism. We shall not enter into a dispute about the proper definition of modern capitalism but can take it loosely as the economic system characterized by four things: private ownership, free enterprise,

the profit motive, and invested funds. The last element is important in distinguishing it from earlier forms of the private property system. Capitalism, both the system itself and the present form it has assumed, is a contingent historical occurrence. There are many details, adjuncts, and conditions not essential to the system of capitalism itself. Its development is constantly continuing, and there seems to be no final pattern into which it must necessarily congeal. When, if ever, it shall have changed so much as no longer to deserve the name of capitalism is a semantic question. However, though capitalism in its practical working is far from ideal, we are hard put to find another system of private property and free enterprise that could be substituted for it in an advanced society today.

We cannot turn back the clock of history and induce people to give up the comforts of modern living for the simple life. Nor was this life wholly desirable. One can romanticize the past by overlooking its disagreeable features, which for the mass of mankind were far worse than anything we have today. The slave economy of ancient times made civilization possible by developing a leisured class, but only by the most hateful form of social injustice. The medieval knight could pursue his noble adventures only by the support of a horde of peasants and serfs who were excluded by birth from his privileges. Laissez-faire individualism, with its disregard for the dignity of the human person, proved its insufficiency within recent memory; the modern worker would embrace communism rather than return to it.

On the other hand, no one has proposed a totally new economic system that can be taken with any seriousness. The working out of an ideal economy poses a challenging task for human ingenuity, but the finished blueprint would have to be highly practical as well as intellectually satisfying. The slightest knowledge of history shows that human institutions develop gradually and that men will not adopt a system that has no strong link with the past. To be practical any such scheme would have to compromise with existing facts and thus could be no radical break with historical continuity.

One attitude toward capitalism is *conservative* and pessimistic. In itself conservatism is indifferent; it all depends on what one wants to conserve, whether it be good or bad. The conservatism that cherishes all that is valuable in the culture of the past is the very life of civilization. The conservatism that perpetuates the diseases of society is a force that makes for death. It is the latter form that is up for criticism, the attitude of wanting to maintain the economic status quo unchanged despite its acknowledged defects. We have arrived, they say, at an uneasy balance of individualism and statism. To stop the state's constant encroachment on private rights we must fight hard for the retention of as much individualism as we can hold on to. Every suggestion for reform is branded as creeping socialism. If the present situation is bad, any other can only be worse. The best we can hope for in the losing battle is a stalemate. How should such an attitude be judged? It is natural that those whose economic situation is satisfactory should be loath to give up their advantages or compromise their position, but selfishness cannot be approved. The desire to preserve modes of conduct that are unjust is morally wrong. We are allowed to tolerate evils when they cannot be remedied, but the refusal even to seek a remedy for existing evils is not an ethically defensible position.

The other attitude is *progressive* and optimistic, recognizing the deficiencies of our present economic system and social order but seeking to remedy them gradually and peacefully. Utopia is impossible, and therefore optimism should be restrained; but though a perfect economy can never be achieved among fallible human beings, a better one is possible. The present arrangement manifests certain obvious defects that are not beyond improvement by human ingenuity. There has been constant progress in social and economic relations in the past, and there is no reason that the trend cannot be continued toward improvement. Violent agitation will accomplish nothing, but gradual pressure and persuasion can bring about more valuable if less spectacular results.

What are the areas in which improvement seems both desirable and possible, and what are the corrective measures most often proposed? This field is very controversial, and our remarks should be taken as tentative and suggestive. We ask:

1. Can competition be mitigated by cooperation?
2. Is strife between management and labor inevitable?
3. Can business learn to regulate itself?
4. What, if anything, is wrong with bigness and centralization?
5. Is man being overmastered by his own technology?

COMPETITION AND COOPERATION

Up to now a distinguishing mark of the capitalistic system has been the principle of competition. At the close of the feudal period, aristocracy of birth gave way to aristocracy of wealth. Business ability is no greater guarantee of morality than noble birth was. Ability is determined by success, and success by competition, which crowns the winner and eliminates the loser, for whom it makes no provision. Many have succeeded in economic competition without descent into the unethical, but it takes an extra measure of ability to win from those who do not play the game clean. In pure competition there are no rules to the game, and the most ruthless has the best chance of winning. Thus the principle of pure competition puts a premium on selfishness and injustice, as well as on intelligence and energy.

There is no way to eliminate all competition and maintain free enterprise. Only if the state were to set prices, fix wages, assign markets, allot quotas, and practically run all business would it be possible to do away with competition. The result would be full socialism, not free enterprise. Competition keeps the economy flexible, dynamic, progressive, resourceful, and efficient, but we learned from our own experience the need of putting a brake on unlimited individualism to protect the common good.

There is no question of abolishing competition, but it must be supplemented by another principle, that of voluntary cooperation. Enterprise can remain free private enterprise while devoted to a common end as well as to an individual end. Citizens do not lose their freedom while voluntarily cooperating, and neither should business associations. Much cooperation actually goes on: against price slashing, against depletion of natural resources, against useless duplication of services, against false advertising, against a mad scramble for markets. Initiative for this cooperation had to come from legislation, but companies now recognize the value of most of this legislation and accept its protection. Now that the lesson has been learned, there is no reason that more cooperation cannot be initiated voluntarily without pressure from the law.

The population of the world is increasing so rapidly that it cannot be supported without a careful husbanding of the earth's resources. The earth can sustain a far larger population, but not by any haphazard methods of production and distribution. The answer of communism is to abolish private enterprise and establish a state-dominated economy. In a sparsely settled country such as America we can afford to brush this answer aside, but we cannot overlook the appeal it has to the teeming populations of Asia and the new nations of Africa, struggling to rise above their substandard living conditions. The capitalist economy must meet this problem and can do so only by a union of free enterprise with voluntary cooperation, the whole organized to work efficiently. Unless it sets up the machinery soon enough, the capitalistic system may not survive.

CLASS ANTAGONISM AND SOLIDARITY

At present, capital and management are lined up on one side and labor with its unions on the other. Because of the unfortunate history of long-standing hostility, it is assumed that these two groups are necessarily opposed. There is organization among employers, including the tightly knit organization of the company itself and the looser grouping of various companies into employers' associations. Workers are organized into unions and local unions into industrywide unions and nationwide federations. Between the two there is collective bargaining, each trying to obtain as much as possible for itself, often with little consideration for the long-term benefit of both or for the nation and society as a whole. Even when relations are amicable, the atmosphere is that of each side protecting and furthering its own interests against the other's encroachments.

There has been too much class conflict, but Marxists are wrong in thinking it essential to capitalism. Collective bargaining cannot be eliminated in a free economy, but such negotiations need not be conducted in an antagonistic spirit of class against class. Two sides can vie with each other where their interests differ, and yet unite where their interests agree. In the realm of sports we have each team striving its utmost to win the game, though both belong to the same league that scheduled the game and made common arrangements for the public's enjoyment. Economic rivalry is far more serious, but the analogy holds. Cooperation and competition are not mutually exclusive, but there can be cooperation for the sake of legitimate competition. Just as more cooperation is needed between companies competing for the market, so more cooperation is needed between management and labor engaged in the same field of production.

The proposal to unite both the management group and the labor group concerned in the same industry into a larger organization for the benefit of the whole industry seems eminently reasonable. There have been overtures toward labor-management cooperation, some of which have been successful, and this movement should be sedulously encouraged. But the effort has been partial and sporadic; it needs definite organization into recognized bodies for fact finding, policy making, standard setting, problem solving, and mediation service, in no way extinguishing or absorbing existing groups but setting the climate for individual enterprise. Man's organizing genius is surely capable of filling this gaping hole in the social structure.

STATISM AND SUBSIDIARITY

Like it or not, business is now regulated to a great extent by the government. The economic order teeters precariously between the extremes of freedom and control. Conservatives stress the evils of statism and its bureaucracy and ask for a return to more individualism. Liberals note the

failure of disorganized individualism and call for increased state intervention in economic life. Neither alternative is acceptable, and neither is necessary.

Government intervention came when and as it did because there was no mechanism in the business world for self-regulation. So huge and important a thing as man's economic life cannot simply be let go undirected and uncontrolled. Individualism was mistaken in thinking that there are natural economic laws which, if left alone, will automatically bring about the best results for all concerned. Individualism failed, not only because it put a premium on waste, greed, and selfishness, but chiefly because it could not deal with the human person, who demanded respect for his dignity and enough security to make his freedom worth having. In the absence of any other power to help him, the state gradually became conscious of its duty to protect its citizens' welfare, stepped into the vacuum, and now finds itself burdened with functions that many think do not properly belong to it.

There is no question of eliminating all government influence from economic affairs. That would be neither desirable nor possible. The state is responsible for the welfare of its people and cannot be left out of any consideration of man's economic life. There are fundamental laws regarding economic matters that any modern state must enact and enforce, but not everything should be the business of government. By the *principle of subsidiarity* a higher organization should not take over work that can be handled adequately by a lower organization.

In the dilemma between no control offered by individualism and state control offered by complete socialism, there is a possible third alternative, that of self-control. With a proper degree of self-government of the industry by the industry, there could be a foreseeable limit to state regulation. Perhaps more governmental intervention than we now have may be necessary in our increasingly complex society. If we are to stop somewhere short of complete socialism, a definite mechanism has to be set up to handle those problems that ought to be kept on a lower than governmental level.

BIGNESS AND DECENTRALIZATION

Concentration of wealth in the hands of a few is one of the main criticisms of capitalist economy. The economy is dominated by a few huge corporations, in each of which the directorship is lodged in a few persons. This centralization of economic power is not wrong in itself and often makes for greater efficiency, but it has its attendant evils: the crowding out of small businesses, with the extinction of pride of ownership and sense of achievement; the danger of monopoly, which can be used for selfish as opposed to social purposes; and the pressure on government that can be exerted when the whole nation's economic life is dependent on a few powerful men. Some see in bigness a chief threat to our socioeconomic order and advocate a program of decentralization.

An older movement in this direction was *distributism*—a greater distribution of property, return to the land from the cities, benefits to rural areas, the making of farm life more attractive, tax favoritism to small farmers and businesses, more stringent antitrust laws, prohibition of large mergers and combines, and other modes of encouraging the "little man." Many think that any such regression to the past has long since ceased to be feasible without repressive governmental control.

The *cooperative movement* is a more promising scheme for decentralization. Its purpose is chiefly to eliminate the middleman by bringing producer in direct contact with consumer, thus saving money for both. There are thus both producers' cooperatives and consumers' cooperatives,

and the two can form one larger cooperative. There is no giant corporation with directors and hired personnel; policies are determined in meetings of the members, in which each person has only one vote no matter how large his share. Thus there is diffused ownership and democratic control. The profit motive is played down, to be supplanted by the ideal of community service. The cooperative movement has met with considerable success, especially in agriculture, but not everywhere. A factory cannot be run on democratic principles; a cooperative factory would have to hire managers and foremen with an unquestioned right to give orders; conditions of work would not differ much from the present factory owned by capital investors. Governing boards of cooperatives would differ little from those of our present corporations. Cooperatives deserve encouragement, but they are not a universal remedy.

A more modest approach is that of *profit sharing*. It is proposed as a supplement to the wage contract, not as a substitute for it. The worker would have his pay determined by collective bargaining and over and above this some share in the profits or even in the ownership of the business. Such schemes have been used successfully but by and large meet with resistance both from business and from labor. The purpose is to allay industrial unrest, to increase the worker's loyalty by making him feel a part of the enterprise, and to make sustained production his advantage. But workers are suspicious that it is only a means of speeding up production, of tying them to the job, of giving them a poor substitute for increased wages, and of hamstringing their unions' efforts at collective bargaining. Profit sharing might work better when this attitude of suspicion fostered by class antagonism has been outgrown.

A still more controverted issue is that of *management sharing*. Most employers will not hear of it, and labor has been rather indifferent to it. To give ordinary laborers a place on the board of directors would be unrealistic, but recent efforts toward labor-management cooperation may finally break down much existing prejudice. Intelligent workers often have good suggestions, if not about handling the company's finances, at least about efficient ways of running the factory. Contrariwise, management may obtain better results by explaining the reasons for their decisions instead of simply handing out flat orders. Companies have become acutely conscious of "human relations," and these efforts may work out into better labor-management teamwork, if not into actual management sharing. Since management and labor do have different functions, perhaps they had best be kept distinct, with emphasis put on increasing communication, cooperation, and integration between them.

Perhaps bigness is a feature of the modern world we must learn to live with. The negative approach of trust-busting legislation has met with indifferent success. More can be accomplished by the positive approach of dispersing industries into outlying areas, giving the worker a chance to own at least his own home, and demonstrating that everybody's prosperity depends most on increased production. After all, the goal is not an equal distribution of wealth but a standard of living that affords all a decent life befitting human dignity.

TECHNOLOGY AND LEISURE

The mention of human dignity leads to a consideration of the evils of technology and mass production, which would be a problem for socialism as well as for capitalism. It is said that the gain in productiveness, making available to nearly all a vast variety of comforts and luxuries formerly beyond the dreams of the most wealthy, is matched by the degradation of the worker, chained to the machine, condemned to a stultifying routine of ac-

tions in which he has not the slightest interest. The assembly line reduces the worker to a robot, stunts his personality, and starves his artistic spirit, leaving him with no pride of ownership, no joy in creativeness, no satisfaction except his pay.

What can be done about this state of affairs? No one, least of all the worker himself, will return to handicraft methods of manufacture. It takes too much effort to produce too little. Comparing the two economies, we see that in the handicraft system it was possible to work at what one liked with a sense of pride and creativeness, but one worked long hours for a pittance, whereas now one may work at a routine, noncreative task, it is true, but for shorter hours with good wages, making possible a style of living unthinkable for such workers a generation ago. Whenever was work free from drudgery? If the tedium of the factory were so much worse than the tedium of the farm, how explain the ceaseless movement from farm to factory? The creativeness of the worker was always limited by his ability to sell his product; not what he wants but what the buyer will want must be his guide if he expects to make a living by his work.

Nevertheless, the problem is there. Many leading industries recognize it and take some steps to alleviate it by fitting workers into jobs for which they are best suited, rotating them from one job to another, determining optimum length of work and rest periods, and providing psychological counseling and social service facilities. However, there is no way of turning all work into play, so that the man on the job can do only what he finds personally interesting.

Automation is looked at fearfully by some as the final step in the degradation of man to the level of the machines he has created, but machines can do only what they have been constructed and programmed to do. They are the best servants man has yet found, and their judicious use can be the most liberalizing influence history has afforded. Automation, far from being feared, should be welcomed as a marvelous blessing. It will take over more and more of the disagreeable side of mass production, freeing men from repetitious drudgery, presenting them with the challenge of intellectual effort in the use of the machines, and giving them vastly increased leisure. The final effect will be to make work shorter, easier, safer, and pleasanter. The problem will be one of adjustment to a new society in which fewer workers will be needed out of a greatly increased population. There will be many initial dislocations, whose severity can be eased by the cooperative planning of management and labor with the assistance of the government. Men will have to be retrained to run the new machines, fitted for different jobs, or retired to pass an honorable old age at public expense. A moral obligation rests on management, labor, and government to initiate farsighted measures cooperatively and to begin doing so soon enough.

We should get rid of the concept of work as being something sacred. It is a mere means, not an end in itself. Leisure is the end, and leisure is not idleness but the freedom to do what one wants to do. We shall have to educate the worker so that he can make the best use of the many free hours technology will enable him to enjoy. The worker will still be economically bound to his job, but he will be bound to it for less and less of his time. If he has any creativeness in his makeup, he will at least have some opportunity to exercise it, if not on the job, then in his off time, whereas formerly most workers had no opportunity at all.

It is as foolish to paint too rosy a picture of the technological age as it is to overromanticize the preindustrial period. Socialism and communism have nothing to offer here, except greater regimentation of the worker than need be feared under private enterprise. If this vexation cannot be eliminated from the capitalist economy, neither can it be eliminated from any workable economy in our modern age.

CONCLUSION

The preceding investigation has been unsatisfactory because it involves too much prophecy. The moral philosopher is not called on to solve the economic ills of mankind but merely to point out the moral obligation of society to seek a solution for those ills. By detailing a few of the suggested remedies, we have shown at least that not all men are standing by idly in smug complacency at the present or wringing their hands in futile fear of the future. Many things can be done, and those mentioned here may not be the only ones or the best.

The obligation bears on society, not on single companies or single unions, much less on single individuals, except that they must show a willingness to cooperate with others in working out a solution and in adopting measures to implement the solution. The larger the industry or union, the greater the obligation of the leaders to point the way and to take the first steps along it. The advance toward social justice is a serious moral obligation that stands squarely on the leaders of society who have the power and influence to do something about it. It will not happen automatically but requires the cooperative effort of all under the leadership of the most able.

SUMMARY

Capitalism is not an immoral economic system, but it should be revised to eliminate some of its worst defects:

1. For the exclusive use of *competition,* substitute a spirit of *cooperation.* Competition is necessary to free enterprise, but unlimited competition was so greedy and wasteful that it had to be limited by law.

Only greater cooperation can care for the increased population of the future.

2. For *strife* between management and labor, substitute *associations* or *councils* embracing both, representing the whole industry or field of occupational endeavor.

3. For too much *state control* and bureaucracy, substitute *self-control* by the industry itself on all levels of management and labor, and observe the principle of subsidiarity.

4. For *concentration* of economic control in the hands of too few, substitute a wider *distribution* of control. *Distributism* would prohibit mergers, break up combines, help small business, and promote rural life, all by means of state benefits and taxation. The *cooperative movement* eliminates the middleman, putting control in the owners rather than in boards of directors. *Profit sharing* would take the workers into the business as small owners, and *management sharing* would give them some control in its operation. These schemes all have some advantages and some drawbacks.

5. For the stultifying effects of *mass production*, substitute training in the proper use of *leisure*. Since technology and automation are here to stay and will increase, it would be better to adapt ourselves to them than to try to stop them. Education is faced with the great task of teaching the worker how to use profitably his vastly increased leisure.

To remedy our economic ills and establish social justice is a serious moral obligation on society. No one can do it alone, but all are obliged to seek remedies and to cooperate in the use of those agreed on.

QUESTIONS FOR DISCUSSION

1 Is the antagonism of classes necessary to keep any one class from dominating our society? Management, labor, and agriculture, each pursuing its own ends, keep the others in their places and give us a balanced society.

2 Would it be true to say that profit sharing and management sharing are viewed with suspicion only because they have not really been tried on a wide enough scale? How could their benefits be obtained without their defects?

3 What do you think of voluntary associations uniting management and labor in a single industry? Would they solve the problem of industrial conflict or create more and worse problems? Is any such arrangement workable?

4 What steps can be taken to integrate automation into our industrial pattern? Is this merely an economic and social problem, or has it an ethical import? Has an individual displaced worker a right to be taken care of?

5 Does technology really dehumanize man? Is our urbanized civilization better or worse than the mainly rural life of our ancestors? Is more liberal education the answer to our greatly increased leisure?

READINGS

Thorstein, Veblen, *The Theory of the Leisure Class;* Max Weber, *The Protestant Ethic and the Spirit of Capitalism;* and Richard Tawney, *Religion and the Rise of Capitalism* are well-known works on capitalism.

The following discuss the issues raised or lay the background for them: William Feree, *The Act of Social Justice;* William Drummond, *Social Justice;* Richard Mulcahy, *The Economics of Heinrich Pesch,* ch. 7; John F. Cronin, *Catholic Social Principles,* ch. 1, 7, 8, 13, 16; and Johannes Messner, *Social Ethics,* bk. I, pt. IV; bk. II, pt. II; bk. IV, pt. III.

On the evils of technology read Gabriel Marcel, *Man Against Mass Society,* and his shorter statement of the same theme, *The Decline of Wisdom.* Friedrich Jünger, *The Failure of Technology,* and Jacques Ellul, *The Technological Society,* are strongly critical. Leon Bagrit, *The Age of Automation;* John Diebold, *Beyond Automation;* John Dunlop, *Automation and Technical Change;* and Walter Buckingham, *Automation: its Impact on Business and People,* express a more hopeful view.

Francis X. Quinn edits a symposium, *The Ethical Aftermath of Automation,* now somewhat dated.

Austin Fagothey, *Right and Reason—an Anthology,* contains Josef Pieper's *Leisure, the Basis of Culture.*

CHAPTER 33

COMMUNISM

PROBLEM

The desire for a more equitable distribution of the world's goods is very ancient. The system of private ownership goes back farther than our earliest historical records. So, too, do the abuses of private property, enormous wealth and dire poverty. As soon as any region became so settled that there was no longer any free land, all economic advancement had to be accomplished by the wealth already in one's possession. Because some men are more clever in trading than others, wealth tends to concentrate in the hands of a few. Classes of society based on wealth are established and the inequality is perpetuated. Thinkers began to speculate on the inequality of wealth, its causes and remedies.

Communism and socialism are proposed as remedies for this evil. Though in their present form these are modern theories, products of the industrial revolution, some of the basic ideas behind communism and socialism have an ancient lineage.

HISTORY OF UTOPIAN SCHEMES

The Institutions of Lycurgus* at Sparta embodied many features of communism: equal distribution of land, abolition of luxury, use of iron money valueless outside the state, common meals and dormitories, a rigid system of state education, prohibition of travel, and exclusion of strangers.

Plato's *Republic** proposes a drastic communism, but it is quite unlike any modern form. His motive was political, not economic. The state will be good only when ruled by the best men, the most qualified statesmen, the philosopher kings. To develop such persons a system of state education must be set up. All, men and women alike, will be given equal opportunity. From them the state will select its rulers by rigid examinations in which only the truly able will succeed. Thus the state will secure competent rulers. To eliminate fraud and graft, to secure public-spirited rulers who will administer the state for the common good and not for their private benefit, communism must be established for the guardians, the two upper classes of rulers and soldiers, but not for the third class of producers. The guardians would be allowed no property, and the state would supply their needs. Lest they have any temptation to amass wealth or gain privileges for their wives and children, wives and children should be held in common as wards of the state. A strict system of eugenics will ensure the purity of the race and the development of the best talent.

St. Thomas More's *Utopia* is a satire on contemporary conditions but contains communistic notions. In Utopia money is abolished and gold is held in dishonor, all per-

---

*Life of Lycurgus in Plutarch's *Lives*.

*See bk. III-V, especially the end of bk. III.

sons must work, six hours a day are given to labor and the rest to learned leisure, property is held in common, there are common meals and apartments but the family is preserved, tolerance is accorded to all religions and opinions, and government is by an absolute monarch elected by the people.

The nineteenth century saw the rise of a number of socialist and communist movements. Claude de Saint-Simon advocated abolition of inheritance, socialization of the means of production, distribution based on merit, and a state ruled by economists and industrialists. Charles Fourier would organize the world into phalansteries, or self-contained communal units, consisting of land, shops, and dwellings, where each would contribute his labor and receive his share of the produce. Brook Farm in Massachusetts was the best known of his thirty-four establishments. Robert Owen, after successfully setting up a model textile factory, turned to the running of communal villages and cooperative communities. His foundation at New Harmony, Indiana, ended in discord. Pierre Proudhon insisted that property is theft, labor is the only measure of value, and man's ethical progress will make property unnecessary. He partly inspired the Paris Commune of 1871.

With the coming of Karl Marx the utopian era of socialism and communism ended. Marx made of socialism and communism a scientific theory and a practical movement. His *Communist Manifesto,* a brief call to the workmen of the world to unite, and his great work *Capital,* the bible of modern socialism and communism, are works of a far different spirit from anything that had preceded them.

Karl Marx, born in 1818 of Jewish parents at Trier in the Rhineland, attended the universities of Bonn and Berlin, where he absorbed the then popular philosophy of Hegel, and took his doctorate at Jena with a thesis on the materialistic philosophy of Epicurus. As editor of a radical newspaper, he came in contact with the working classes and was deeply affected by their plight. He went to Paris, then the center of socialistic movements, where he was influenced by, though he disagreed with, Proudhon. On reading the materialistic works of Ludwig Feuerbach, he conceived his own distinctive philosophy, an application of Hegel's method to Feuerbach's content. In 1848 he published the *Communist Manifesto* with Friedrich Engels, his constant collaborator. Expelled successively from Paris and Brussels, he moved to London, where he spent the rest of his life in poverty. He helped in the organization of the First International. He kept working on his great book, *Capital,* until his death in 1883.

EXPLANATION OF MARXISM

Interest has been aroused today in Marx's earlier writings as being less doctrinaire and philosophically more interesting, especially for his development of the concept of alienation. But it was Marx's later writings that had the impact on history. We shall first give a rapid bird's-eye view of the main points of the Marxist system and then take up each point for evaluation and criticism. We can arrange the points as follows:

1. In *philosophy:* dialectical materialism
2. In *history:* economic determinism, class struggle
3. In *economics:* surplus-value, concentration of wealth
4. In *sociology:* progressive pauperization, financial crises
5. In *politics:* the revolution, dictatorship of the proletariat

PHILOSOPHY: DIALECTICAL MATERIALISM

Marx's unique philosophy was a union of the dialectical method of Hegel with the historical materialism of Feuerbach. Marx thought that Hegel had the correct method of development but made the wrong thing evolve—thought instead of matter; Feuerbach, on the other hand made reality consist of the right thing, matter, but left its development to chance, which explains nothing. Marx insists that his is not a vulgar mechanistic materialism.

The *Hegelian dialectic,* to give only the barest outline of it, is the process of development that pervades everything. For Hegel there is only one reality, which he calls the Idea. Only the rational is real, and the Idea is Thought itself thinking itself out. The process of thinking itself out is the *dialectic.* Thinking consists in contrasting each thought with its opposite, whereupon there arises a higher thought that is the union of the two. Thus the thought of *being* leads to the thought of its opposite, which is *nothing;* the union is *becoming,* or the passage from nothing to being. In every case the first stage is simply given or posited, the second stage is its negation, and the third stage, or the negation of the negation, is the union of the first two. What underlies this process is that reality itself is basically contradictory; thought first takes up one side of the contradiction (thesis), and then the other (antithesis), and finally succeeds in fusing the two (synthesis). Any thought contains only part of the truth; there is some truth also in the opposite, and only when both are reconciled in a higher union does the whole truth appear. The process continues because each synthesis now becomes a thesis for further development.

In thinking itself out, thought arrives at the main antithesis to itself, which is inert matter. At this point the Idea objectifies itself in matter, turns into its opposite, contradicts its unity and totality, fractions itself into this manifold world of experience, and spreads itself out to become Nature. This, for Hegel, is the creation of the world. World evolution continues along dialectical lines. The first inkling of synthesis is life, in which thought reappears in matter, organizing plants, manifesting conscious instinct in animals, and arriving at self-consciousness in man, the spearhead of the process. In man the dialectic continues through human history, in which man has passed to higher and higher forms of social organization, culminating at present in the political state. Thus thought and matter, spirit and nature, are united in man. The final synthesis will be a combination of the thesis (the Idea thinking itself out) with the antithesis (the Idea spread out into Nature) into the synthesis (Nature gathered back into the Idea in full self-consciousness as Absolute Spirit). The whole process can be looked on as the life of God, whose evolution is the universe, of which human history forms a leading part.

Marx kept the dialectic but substituted matter in place of thought. The Hegelian dialectic is an *idealism;* matter is only a transient appearance of the Idea in the stage of otherness. Marx does not admit the existence of anything but matter. He nowhere defines exactly what he means by matter, but he certainly refers to the sensed world of bodies. He makes the dialectic a dialectical *materialism* instead of an idealism by having *matter* the evolving reality. He puts into matter itself the principle of its own evolution, which proceeds according to the three Hegelian stages and forms itself into our present universe. Marx is particularly interested in that part of the dialectic which refers to human history, which he says is conditioned by man's primitive material economic needs.

HISTORY: ECONOMIC DETERMINISM

What Marx calls the *materialistic conception of history* is usually known as the *economic interpretation of history* or *eco-*

nomic determinism. He thinks that the main motive explaining the whole of human behavior and therefore of history is economic. The way we produce goods and exchange products determines our life. Society gradually evolved from primitive collectivism, through savagery and barbarism, to civilization. At first men lived by hunting and fishing, then by domestication of animals and a nomad life, then by agriculture on settled farms, then by handicraft industry in the towns, and finally by power machinery and the factory system in huge industrial centers. The degree of civilization depends on the economic system. Religious, ethical, philosophical, artistic, social, and political ideas have their value in shaping history, but they are ultimately conditioned by economic motives. Any society will develop that type of religious belief, moral customs, philosophical outlook, artistic expression, social strata, and form of government which corresponds with the prevailing economy in that society's particular degree of cultural development.*

From this follows the theory of *class struggle.* Marx says: "The history of all hitherto existing society is the history of class struggle."† Classes arise out of the economic life of society: those who have and those who have not. In ancient times there were the masters and slaves, those who had and those who did not have freedom; in medieval times there were lords and serfs, those who owned and those who did not own the land; in modern times there are employers and employees, those who own the means of production and those who have nothing to sell but their labor. In history the lower class has always emancipated itself. This age can be no exception. The proletariat will rise against its oppressors, but this time it will destroy all class rule and thus emancipate all society from the evil of class struggle. Marx thinks that not only is the *thesis* of primitive collectivism long past but the *antithesis* of private property is now coming to an end, and the *synthesis* of communism is in sight.

ECONOMICS: SURPLUS-VALUE

Marx adopts from the liberal economists, Adam Smith, David Ricardo, and others, the *labor theory of value,* that labor is the sole source of economic value. The unit of wealth is a commodity, which, as Aristotle* had pointed out centuries before, has a twofold value: *use-value,* its capacity to satisfy a human want, depending on its physical and chemical properties, such as bread used for food; and *exchange-value,* the ratio according to which different use-values may be bartered for one another depending on the object's social desirability, such as bread to be sold in the market. Marx goes on to argue that exchange-value is wholly independent of use-value:

As use-values, commodities are, above all, of different qualities but as exchange-values they are merely different quantities, and consequently do not contain an atom of use-value. If then we leave out of consideration the use-value of commodities, they have only one common property left, that of being products of labor. . . .

A use-value, or useful article, therefore, has value only because human labor in the abstract has been embodied or materialized in it. How, then, is the magnitude of this value to be measured? Plainly, by the quantity of the value-creating substance, the labor, contained in the article. The quantity of labor, however, is measured by its duration, and labor-time in its turn finds its standard in weeks, days, and hours.†

Hence the value of an object consists solely in the amount of abstract homogeneous human labor socially necessary for its pro-

---

*Marx, *A Contribution to the Critique of Political Economy* (1859), preface.
†Marx, Beginning of the *Communist Manifesto.*

*Aristotle, *Politics*, bk. I, ch. 9, 1257a 7.
†Marx, *Capital*, bk. I, pt. I, ch. I, sec. 1.

duction. Since this labor cannot be accurately calculated, the actual price of a commodity fluctuates about its true value.

Marx's chief innovation is the concept of *surplus-value*. The modern workman, not owning machines and unable to compete by handicraft with those who do own them, must sell his labor-power to the capitalist, for labor-power is all he has. This labor-power has use-value and exchange-value like any other commodity. The use-value of labor-power is the improvement of the raw materials into the finished product. The exchange-value of labor-power is wages, what the workman gets in exchange for his work. The capitalist pays only the price of the exchange-value of the labor (wages); yet he takes the whole of the use-value of that labor (the finished product). The exchange-value of labor is a daily wage sufficient to buy the amount of goods necessary to sustain a man for a day, but in a day's work the workman produces goods of much higher value than that, so that the use-value of his labor far exceeds its exchange-value. This excess goes wholly to the capitalist, and for it no recompense is made to the workman. The workman may be able in the first few hours to create value equal to his wages; yet he is obliged to work several hours more. The value he creates in this second part of the day is what Marx calls *surplus-value.** It may be defined as the use-value of the workman's labor-power minus its exchange-value.

The ratio of surplus-value is the measure of *exploitation of the worker*. Since the value of the finished product sold by the employer is measured wholly by the labor put into it, and the employer pays the workman only for part of that labor, the employer is robbing the workman to

the extent of the surplus-value. The surplus-value is put back by the employer into his business and used to facilitate production; it thus produces more surplus-value, and so becomes *capital*.

The lower the wages, the greater is the surplus-value. The total capital may be divided into two parts: constant and variable. Constant capital is used for raw materials, machines, buildings, and upkeep, and is not productive of more capital, for these expenses cannot be diminished without ruining the business. Variable capital is used for wages and also creates surplus-value; the more wages are lowered, the more surplus-value there is for the employer in the form of profit. Marx's solution to this problem is to eliminate the capitalist and have the workers own the factory or farm. Then the total value of his labor, its full use-value, goes back to the worker.

SOCIOLOGY: PROGRESSIVE PAUPERIZATION

If surplus-value leads to an *accumulation of capital* by the employer, the unbridled competition which is the life of trade in the capitalistic system leads to its *concentration in monopolies*. As in the mercantile age, when capital was invested in raw materials, nations scrambled for colonies, so in the industrial age, when capital is invested in machinery, there is a scramble for markets. Since the cheapest product gets the market, competition means lower and lower wages. But competition is self-destructive, for logically there is no place where the forcing out of competitors should stop until everything is in the hands of one. Competition inevitably breeds monopoly, which, now that the zest of competition is eliminated, acts as a shackle on production and tends to bring about industrial stagnation. Industry becomes concentrated more and more in a few gigantic trusts, and capital

---

*Marx, *Wage Labor and Capital;* see Engels' very lucid introduction to this pamphlet. In *Karl Marx's Selected Works,* vol. I, p. 242 ff.

becomes concentrated more and more in the hands of a few.

The effect of the factory system on the working masses is their gradual degradation. With the concentration of capital in the hands of the few, the rich grow richer and the poor, poorer. The large companies squeeze out or absorb the smaller. Small manufacturers yield their plants to the big monopolies, and the former owners, once independent capitalists, now become proletarians working for the larger company. The middle class of society is gradually eliminated and swells the ranks of the proletariat.

The proletariat concentrate more and more around the centers of production, leaving the countryside and gathering in the industrial cities, where they form the bulk of the slum population. This concentration is good for the capitalists because it provides them with a vast reserve of cheap labor. When the demand for work exceeds the supply of available jobs, wages go down, surplus-value goes up, and there is more profit to the capitalist. The invention of labor-saving devices decreases the number of workers needed and turns them out of the factories to swell the *industrial reserve army,* Marx's name for the unemployed.

The occurrence of *cyclical financial crises* accentuates the process. Every ten years or so a financial crisis occurs, a major one every twenty years, and these crises become progressively worse. They are necessarily bound up with the capitalistic system. When wages are low, industry makes use of the cheap labor to increase production. Now the markets become flooded, demand slackens, the factory shuts down, and the workers are thrown out on the streets. These oscillations are unavoidable in an economy of unregulated competition, and the greater the concentration of industry, the greater they must become. The time must come when a crisis of such magnitude will occur as to eventuate in the utter collapse of the capitalistic system.

Along with the constantly diminishing number of the magnates of capital, who usurp and monopolise all advantages of this process of transformation, grows the mass of misery, oppression, slavery, degradation, exploitation; but with this too grows the revolt of the working-class, a class always increasing in numbers, and disciplined, united, organised by the very mechanism of the process of capitalist production itself. The monopoly of capital becomes a fetter upon the mode of production, which has sprung up and flourished along with, and under it. Centralisation of the means of production and socialisation of labour at last reach a point where they become incompatible with their capitalist integument. This integument is burst asunder. The knell of capitalist private property sounds. The expropriators are expropriated.[*]

POLITICS: THE REVOLUTION

The dialectic of history shows the *inevitability of the revolution.* People can stand only so much. When the situation of the proletariat becomes absolutely unbearable, they will revolt. The Communists must be ready to take charge of this revolt and guide it the right way. Since it is inevitable, we may as well promote it and have done with it. As Marx and Engels put it:

In short the Communists everywhere support every revolutionary movement against the existing social and political order of things.

In all these movements they bring to the front, as the leading question in each, the property question, no matter what its degree of development at the time.

Finally, they labor everywhere for the union and agreement of the democratic parties of all countries.

The Communists disdain to conceal their views and aims. They openly declare that their ends can be attained only by the forcible overthrow of all existing social conditions. Let the ruling classes tremble at a Communistic revolution. The prole-

---

[*]Marx, *Capital,* vol. I, ch. 32, toward the end.

tarians have nothing to lose but their chains. They have a world to win.

Workingmen of all countries, unite!*

Though they join them for tactical purposes of infiltration, Marxists have little sympathy with trade unionism or with attempts to alleviate the condition of the working class. These attempts, they say, are only palliatives, which can cause only temporary relief. The people must be taught to see that the capitalistic system itself is hopelessly rotten, that it cannot be patched up but must be entirely scrapped in favor of a new economy. Let capitalism collapse, as it must. Then the revolution will come, when the exploiters will be driven out, the expropriators will be expropriated, and the workers of the world will seize the means of production and set up the socialist or communist state.

This change can hardly be made without a wrench. The bourgeoisie will fight back, and to cope with them a transitory period of the *dictatorship of the proletariat* will be necessary, during which the Communist Party will be the spearhead of the revolutionary movement. The dictatorship of the proletariat, perhaps lasting some generations, will be followed by the period of *state socialism*, but the state will gradually wither away and give place to the long-desired era of pure communism. The end result will be the *classless society*, which will put a finish to the class struggle because there will be only one class. The era of exploitation will be over because the means of production will belong collectively to all. Then the communist utopia will be realized, for all men will share justly in the goods of the earth and the produce of their labor. Society, having passed dialectically from the thesis of the savage tribe's primitive collectivism,

through the antithesis of private property by which civilization was developed, will at last be gathered into the synthesis of a new collectivism in which the evils of property will have been eliminated and the benefits of civilization retained for further progress.

EVALUATION OF MARXISM

This summary, inadequate as it must be in the space allotted, sketches the general outline of Marxist teachings. We must now turn to a critical appraisal of the points raised.

CRITICISM OF DIALECTICAL MATERIALISM

Hegel's dialectic is criticized as going counter to two self-evident principles that are the foundation of all thinking, the principle of noncontradiction and the principle of causality. To take contradiction itself as the inner essence of all reality is to make both reality and knowledge impossible, for that which is self-contradictory can neither be nor be thought. Nor does it help to make the contradictory stages successive rather than simultaneous, for then the Idea is made to evolve out of itself what is not contained in itself or derived from any other source. The whole system rests on this assumption, but there is no reason for making this assumption, and the contradictory assumption should be equally true.

Materialism, the theory that nothing exists but matter, is criticized for denying the existence of God and of the human soul, and for its inability to explain the universe and man without them. Marx's materialism is rather halfhearted. He wants to emphasize the exclusion of God and the hereafter from his system and to contrast his materialism with Hegel's idealism.

Though the materialism is halfhearted, it does not combine coherently with the

---

*Marx and Engels, *Communist Manifesto,* at the end.

dialectic. It invests matter with the qualities of spirit, and spirit with the properties of matter. The human mind is reduced to a mere function of matter, whereby any explanation of reflective intelligence in man is rendered impossible, while at the same time matter is made a self-moving principle of development and orderly progress, a function impossible without a guiding intelligence.

CRITICISM OF ECONOMIC DETERMINISM

No one would deny that economic factors have largely influenced history. Before everything man must live, must find food, clothing, and shelter. But man does not live on bread alone. Marxists assert that they do not make economic motives the *sole* factors of history, but then they equivalently deny their assertion by making ethical, religious, philosophical, artistic, social, and political ideas the result of economic conditions.

Economic determinism is a distorted view of history. True, ancient civilization rested on a slave economy, but that form of economy was common to the whole ancient world. There was nothing distinctive in their economics that developed the Greeks' intellectual genius and the Romans' power in conquest. Even the peculiar position of the Jews is explained more by their religion than by their economics. The origin and spread of Christianity were not the result of methods of production and exchange. The Renaissance and the Reformation contained strong economic factors, but humanistic and religious causes were even more fundamental. Alexander, Caesar, Charlemagne, Napoleon, and other conquerors changed the course of history, but not so much for economic motives as for the love of glory and the pride of conquest. In all these movements an economic aspect can be discerned, and there were other events in which the economic motive was primary, but to make the economic motive primary in *all* events is to oversimplify the really complex character of history.

The class struggle theory is a gross exaggeration. Ancient history is full of wars of conquest between nations and despots, but relatively few class struggles are recorded. The masses were oppressed but usually bore their yoke with mute resignation. Slave uprisings were quickly and ruthlessly suppressed. The castes of India and the masses of China remained in subjection for 3,000 years; movements to liberate them have come rather from the outside than from their own class-conscious efforts. Only in the late Middle Ages in Europe with the rise of the bourgeoisie did class struggle come to the fore, and only in the industrial revolution did it become a major force in history. Marx is cunningly selective in picking his events.

Even if class struggles have always occurred, they do not explain all the main events of history. The civilization of Greece was developed by free citizens, not by an uprising of slaves. The empire of Rome was a conquest of Roman arms, not a revolt of downtrodden masses. Christianity spread by the appeal of a religious idea to all classes, high and low. The Renaissance was a movement of educated people, not a rising of the lower classes against their masters. The Reformation was imposed from above by the kings and princes of northern Europe, and succeeded only in those countries where it was supported by the ruler. The voyages of discovery, which all admit had an undoubted economic motive, were financed and promoted by the ruling classes; they were no spontaneous revolt of the downtrodden seeking an outlet against oppression. Only after its discovery was America used as a refuge by the oppressed, whose oppression was as much religious as economic. Even the industrial revolution itself, though resulting in class struggles, was not produced by a class struggle but by inventive genius in the creation of new machines, and this genius was not restricted by class lines. The point of these examples is not to deny that class struggles have existed but to show that they do not explain the whole of history.

CRITICISM OF SURPLUS-VALUE

The theory of surplus-value as explained by Marx is rejected by all but Marxian economists. It is untrue that exchange-value is wholly independent of use-value, and that the so-called surplus-value is necessarily exploitation.

The exchange-value of a commodity is not determined by labor alone. People will not buy articles merely because somebody has labored on them but because they are somehow useful to the buyer. Hence the common element in all commodities is not labor but the ability of a thing to satisfy some human need, its desirability or goodness, for which reason we call these things *goods*. If a thing is already plentiful and everybody's need for it is satisfied, it will not command a price no matter how much labor was spent on it. If a thing can satisfy a need better, it will sell at a higher price even though less labor went into it. Hence labor is only one of the factors determining the price of a desirable object; utility and scarcity are equally important. Marx admits this fact when he says that the only labor that counts is socially useful labor and that if a thing is useless, so also is the labor contained in it; but this admission contradicts all that he had said, for then utility, and not labor, would be the standard of value.

The theory of surplus-value depends on the labor theory of value, and stands or falls with it. The contract between employer and employee is simply one of hire. Marx supposes that the exchange-value, or hire-value, of labor is determined as the minimum amount required to support a man and his family; a man cannot work for less, and the employer will not pay more. This statement, however, merely expresses the norm for a minimum wage, and wages are not held down to the minimum. One man is more experienced, talented, skillful, and reliable than another. The first man will be hired sooner and receive more pay because he has more utility to the employer. The second man may have a larger family and therefore need more support, but he receives less because he is a less desirable worker; he is certainly entitled to a minimum just wage but can earn more if he makes his work more useful to his employer. Hence the exchange-value of labor is not measured solely by the number of hours spent at it. Nor is it correct to say that the value of skilled labor can always be expressed in terms of so much more unskilled labor, for few useful products can be made with unskilled labor alone. The quality of the labor is as important as its quantity.

It is not true that the capitalist necessarily exploits the worker. That capitalists have done so in the past and that some still do so, by paying too low wages and taking too much profit, is readily granted, but exploitation is an abuse of the system and by no means essential to it. Marx says that the capitalist appropriates all the surplus-value, which belongs properly to the laborer, and thus exploits him. If the capitalist manages his own plant, he certainly works in a way requiring more effort, skill, and training than the common laborer; Marx acknowledges this fact and would grant him the equivalent of a wage proportionate to his work; he, too, must live, and such a return would not be regarded as profit. What Marx objects to is the kind of profit that is put back into the business, so that capital produces more capital. But how otherwise could any sort of economic development be possible? The idea of capital cannot be avoided. Even if the state takes over all the means of production, it will need some resources to begin new enterprises and must have built up these resources from previous enterprises, and these resources are capital. The individual workman could have no more say in the use of these resources or this capital whether it were state owned or privately owned, whether his employer were a private entrepreneur or a state functionary.

CRITICISM OF PROGRESSIVE PAUPERIZATION

Marx's views on the accumulation of capital and the concentration of industry have a fair amount of plausibility. The formation of huge trusts and monopolies, with the squeezing out of small firms, has certainly occurred. Legislation has been necessary to correct this abuse, and it has not been wholly successful, but not all the evils that Marx expected from this concentration have come to pass. Trusts and monopolies have become vast stock companies, so that the capital, rather than being concentrated in the hands of a few, is scattered among many. However, it is all too true that the control of these huge companies rests in the hands of a powerful few, and decentralization of this control seems desirable. The elimination of the middle class was a groundless fear. Those who gave up their small businesses to work for larger companies are paid good salaries and are not pauperized. Many workers today invest part of their wages in capitalistic enterprises and thus become both workmen and small capitalists.

When Marx wrote, there was real fear of progressive pauperization, but his preoccupation with economics in history made him a poor prophet. He failed to consider political and humanitarian influences. The rich have indeed grown richer, but the poor have not grown poorer. Wages and living standards have continually improved. The workers have not sunk into growing insecurity, misery, oppression, slavery, degradation, and exploitation, as Marx gloomily predicted. Not everywhere in the world has the position of labor grown as strong as it has in this country, but that labor has prospered especially in the world's most industrialized nation gives the lie to Marx's whole theory. Most of the demands for bettering the condition of labor have been put into effect by collective bargaining between labor unions and employers. It is true that the workers will stand only so much, but they will not stand as much as Marx thought they might, and they took means into their own hands to improve their condition. This improvement has occurred within the framework of capitalistic economy. Here we are not trying to prove that capitalism is the best economic system, but only to show that socialism and communism are not necessary to remedy the workingman's plight.

The industrial reserve army in the Marxist sense is a myth. There always has been unemployment, but it is not desired by the capitalists, nor do they make a profit on it. Good times are beneficial to both capitalist and proletarian, and hard times hit proletarian and capitalist alike. The unemployed worker loses his wages, and the capitalist loses his market and his profits. New inventions put men out of work temporarily but often result in the opening up of new industries with increased opportunities for employment. The invention of the automobile ruined the carriage and harness trade, but today the automotive, and allied industries provide millions of jobs more than the corresponding occupations in the horse-and-buggy days.

Business cycles and financial crises are still with us. How they can be avoided or controlled is a prime economic problem, but there is no proof that they will necessitate a collapse of the capitalistic system. Panics caused by huge frauds and swindles in the stock market, such as have occurred in the past, should be preventable by a vigilant government exercising the moderate control over business we have all come

378

to recognize as necessary. The periodic shutdown of factories has been largely corrected, either because management voluntarily geared itself to a steady rather than a fitful output or because it was forced to do so by collective bargaining with the unions. Privately owned enterprises can be regulated by law as effectively as socialistically operated factories. How far governmental regulation of business should go is a disputed point, but the state need not own industries in order to regulate them.

CRITICISM OF THE REVOLUTION

The inevitable collapse of capitalism through its own inherent rottenness shows no sign of imminence. The capitalistic system survived the world crisis of the 1930's and proved its efficiency in the stress of the world's greatest war. Communism owes what strength it has to militant agitators, not to any spontaneous rebellion by the workers. Marx thought that communism would appear in highly industrialized countries such as Germany or England, but the first country to adopt the communistic system was Russia, one of the least fit because it was one of the least industrialized. Communism was imposed on Russia by a small minority when the nation was leaderless and demoralized, and it was maintained only by the most ruthless oppression and terrorism. The Russian Revolution was no inevitable rising of the proletariat but was deliberately engineered by trained revolutionaries who forcefully imposed their will on the helpless masses.

The classless society, the goal of communism, is as far off as ever. Certainly it has shown not the slightest sign of appearing in the communist governments so far established. Marxists answer that the process is still in the stage of dictatorship of the proletariat, but there is no indication that this period will ever come to an end. It is not even a dictatorship of the whole proletariat but of a few dominant men. Will men who have so entrenched themselves in absolute power ever freely consent to let it "wither away"?

SOCIALISM

The previous discussion has been a criticism of Marx, whose orthodox followers today, accepting the development of Marx's doctrine by Lenin, are known as *communists*. Those who adopt milder views of the same general tendency and limit them more to the economic sphere are called *socialists*. The terms *communist* and *socialist* have been variously used at different times in the history of the Marxist movement. One point of distinction is that the communists believe in achieving their ends by violent revolution, the socialists by peaceful evolution in cooperation with existing governments and by legal procedures. Many find a more significant distinction in the fact that the socialists have dropped almost all Marxian theory from their program.

Stripped of any doctrinaire significance, the word *socialism* may mean only the opposite pole to *individualism*. One emphasizes the rights of society and the common welfare, the other the rights of the individual and personal liberty. Since both have rights, the only acceptable position is somewhere in between. Unless one wants to be a rugged individualist, one must admit some degree of *socialization*. We already have public education and social security, public power plants and utilities, socialized medicine and compulsory insurance; we see other nations with nationalized railroads and subsidized merchant marine, and we can conceive of nationalized banks and stock exchanges. There is nothing morally wrong with these things, and each nation may decide for itself how far it wishes to go along the road of government-operated social service to its people. Even the welfare state, which some look on as being one step short of socialism, should not be criticized on ethical grounds but on those of expediency. Though the cost is heavy in taxes, it leaves most property in private hands and plenty of scope for private enterprise.

The case is different with organized, doctrinaire socialism, which has as its goal the fully socialized state, in which *all* the means of production are taken from private hands and turned over to the state. Even when purged of the Marxian atheistic and materialistic ideology and limited to the economic and politicoeconomic sphere, this kind of full-blown socialism has its ethical difficulties. Short of a complete submersion of individual human rights and the institution of an absolutely totalitarian regime, how could the full socialistic program be inaugurated and maintained?

Advocates of full socialism and communism, even as merely economic and politicoeconomic systems, must find a way of implementing their program without destroying the rights of the individual before they can offer a morally acceptable alternative to the private enterprise system. And they must prove that their system is not only as good but better—better enough to justify the dislocation inseparable from so vast a reorganization.

CONCLUSION

Both communism and full-blown socialism go counter to too many things fundamental in human nature. Their view of human nature is too high, too optimistic, when they think that men will spontaneously cooperate in harmony without the profit motive, and that such an enormous bureaucracy could function without a vast amount of corruption. Their view of human nature is too low, too degraded, when they think that men will not rebel against a stultifying regimentation unless it is enforced by tyranny and terror, and that the whole purpose of human life is con-

fined to the temporal, mundane, economic sphere.

The only solution can be a compromise between the two goods, individual liberty and economic security. Economic liberalism, rugged individualism, laissez faire, is one exaggeration; communism and full socialism exaggerate the other side. Man must have both liberty and security, but each limits the other. Just where to draw the line in this delicate balance is the crux of the whole economic problem, but neither extreme accords with right reason and human nature, which is the standard of moral action.

SUMMARY

Communism and socialism are proposed remedies for the inequality of wealth. Many utopian schemes were put forth both in ancient and modern times, but none of them can compare with that of Karl Marx, who made communism a scientific theory and a practical movement. Marx's system includes the following points:

1. *Dialectical materialism.* Marx combined the dialectical method of Hegel with the materialism of Feuerbach. Nothing exists but matter, which contains within itself the principle of its own development from thesis through antithesis to synthesis; man is the spearhead of this necessary evolution. *Criticism:* Hegel's dialectic is an idealism that runs counter to the principles of noncontradiction and of causality; materialism cannot explain the intellectual life of man; the combination of the two philosophies is incoherent.

2. *Economic determinism.* The underlying motive in all human history is economic; as the economy, so the civilization. Economic life establishes classes, the *haves* and the *have-nots,* and all history is the history of class struggles; the lower class always succeeds in emancipating itself. *Criticism:* This is a gross exaggeration of the role of economics and of the class

struggle in history; it achieves plausibility only by selecting a few movements and neglecting whole areas of history.

3. *Surplus-value.* Exchange-value is entirely separate from use-value; the capitalist takes the whole use-value of a man's labor while paying only for the exchange-value; the workman creates more value than he is paid for, and this surplus-value goes to the employer, who exploits the workman to that extent. The employer puts this surplus-value back into his business, and this constitutes capital. The lower the wages, the more capital to the capitalist. *Criticism:* Labor is not the only source of value; labor-value differs qualitatively as well as quantitatively; capital is needed to begin new enterprises, and if it is not privately owned, it is state owned.

4. *Progressive pauperization.* Competition breeds monopoly; the rich grow richer and the poor, poorer; the middle class is eliminated and swells the ranks of the proletariat, which concentrate in industrial centers and form a vast supply of cheap labor, the industrial reserve army. Financial crises, inseparable from the capitalistic system, accentuate the degrading process. *Criticism:* Wealth and industry do tend to concentrate, but the poor have not grown poorer; legislation and labor unions have largely remedied the workman's plight. Capitalists do not want unemployment because it hurts their markets; financial crises are not wholly beyond control.

5. *The Revolution.* The collapse of capitalism is inevitable; the masses will revolt, seize the means of production, establish the dictatorship of the proletariat, which after a phase of state socialism will emerge as the classless society, the communist utopia. *Criticism:* Capitalism survived war and depression; communism was imposed on Russia by a few and is maintained by force; the classless society shows no signs of appearing.

Socialism relies on evolution rather than revolution. People may choose how much socialization they want, even as far as the welfare state, but full doctrinaire socialism, even if limited to the economic and political sphere, cannot be morally justified unless it can solve its practical difficulties without destroying man's inherent rights.

Man must have both individual liberty and economic security. As rugged individualism exaggerates liberty, so communism and full socialism exaggerate security. Neither corresponds with right reason.

QUESTIONS FOR DISCUSSION

1 Why do we insert a discussion of communism in the study of ethics? Is it correct to say that the communists have no ethics and to expect it of them is unrealistic?

2 Is Marx's criticism of nineteenth century capitalism valid for that age? If so, what has happened to change the picture? If not, what is invalid about it?

3 Do present-day communists care anything about Hegel and Feuerbach and the dialectical materialism that Marx put together from their philosophies? Is it not wholly a practical movement, whose purpose is, as Marx said, not to know the world but to change it?

4 Is it not logical, if a future life is denied, to seek one's happiness in

this world? And can there be any happiness in this world so long as most of mankind is in dire poverty? Is it not true that man's basic needs are economic?

5 Do you think that communism will grant more and more scope to free enterprise and that free enterprise will admit more and more socialistic control, until the two systems grow together into one? Or is a final showdown between the two inevitable?

READINGS

G. W. F. Hegel's dialectical process is described in his *Phenomenology of Mind, Science of Logic,* and *Encyclopedia of the Philosophical Sciences in Outline,* all difficult writings. There is a very simple but critical exposition in Frank Sheed, *Communism and Man;* and an indispensable one in Sidney Hook, *From Hegel to Marx.* Ludwig Feuerbach, *Essence of Christianity,* is readily available, though only remotely related to this chapter.

Read Karl Marx and Friedrich Engels, *Communist Manifesto,* a historical document of utmost significance. Marx's great work, *Capital,* should be looked at and the first few chapters read. Adoratsky (ed.), *Selected Works of Marx and Engels,* and Emile Burns (ed.), *Handbook of Marxism,* contain what Marxists consider the most important works and documents. V. I. Lenin, *Materialism and Empirio-Criticism,* is his most theoretical work. Josef Stalin, *Dialectical and Historical Materialism,* is a short and readable exposition that was once authoritative. Mao Tse-tung's works have now achieved importance.

Herbert Marcuse wrote a scholarly study, *Reason and Revolution: Hegel and the Rise of Social Theory,* before becoming the philosophical prophet of the New Left in *One Dimensional Man* and *An Essay on Liberation.*

Robert C. Tucker, *Philosophy and Myth in Karl Marx,* is an excellent study. Louis Dupré, *Philosophical Foundations of Marxism,* follows Marx's development. J. Sommerville, *Soviet Philosophy,* and G. D. H. Cole, *Meaning of Marxism,* represent the Marxist view. Charles McFadden, *Philosophy of Communism;* R. N. Carew Hunt, *Theory and Practice of Communism;* H. B. Mayo, *Democracy and Marxism;* and G. Wetter, *Dialectical Materialism,* are critical.

On particular points there are Benedetto Croce, *Historical Materialism and the Economics of Karl Marx;* and Nicholas Berdyaev, *Origin of Russian Communism.*

On socialism Paul Sweezy, *Socialism,* and Howard Selsam, *Socialism and Ethics,* are favorable; Ludwig von Mises, *Socialism,* is critical; and Joseph Schumpeter, *Capitalism, Socialism, and Democracy,* is an important general work.

Edmund Wilson's *To the Finland Station* is a fascinating description of the development of Marxism.

Austin Fagothey, *Right and Reason—an Anthology,* contains Marx and Engels' *Communist Manifesto.*

CHAPTER 34

EARTH

PROBLEM

Both capitalistic and communistic economics, and indeed any other economic system one might imagine, suppose that there will be goods of the earth that can be managed, developed, and distributed. The resources and productivity of the earth have been taken for granted and used as if they were inexhaustible. Now we are shocked to find that some resources are nearly depleted and that nature's capacity for renewal is inadequate to cope with man's capacity to pollute. We were used to the picture of little man against the vast forces of nature. Now we see the possibility of too many men swarming over a globe that can support only a limited number. Ecology has come to the fore as the science of the relation of living organisms to their environment. The place of man in the general ecology of nature is being increasingly recognized. Not only can man upset the natural interdependence of animals and plants in a region by his interference, but he is an animal as thoroughly dependent for survival on his environment as any other living being. Man is beginning to see that unless a halt is called soon to his improvident exploitation of nature, he will destroy himself by the excess of his own cleverness.

In such a wide-ranging subject, we shall have to restrict ourselves to the ethical issues involved. There is one ethical issue that we find running through most of the writings on this subject, that of intellectual honesty. The writers tend to become carried away by their emotional commitment to either one or the other side of the question, and to write in a strong vein of propaganda, so that it is difficult to derive from their statements a cool, objective, balanced, and honest appraisal of the question.

One school is that of the prophets of gloom, very vocal and strident, proclaiming that man has already destroyed himself, that he has carried the pollution of nature beyond the point of no return, that he has nothing to face but disease and starvation because of his foolish wasting of nature's goods, that the world is already much overpopulated, and that doomsday awaits us in the near future unless we curtail our numbers. The opposite school cavalierly dismisses the problem, as if the resources of the earth were inexhaustible, as if the solution to the world's poverty were just around the corner, as if the cleaning up of our pollution were an easy and inexpensive task, and as if the earth could support an almost indefinite number of people. In gathering the facts we shall have to go on the assumption that the truth probably lies somewhere between these extremes, and on that basis try to form a moral judgment. Here the chief enemies are apathy and hysteria.

There are several important ethical issues:

1. Exploitation: is man naturally and inevitably an exploiter?
2. Resources: has man a moral obligation toward future generations?

3. Pollution: how much pollution of the environment is ethically tolerable?
4. Poverty: have rich nations a duty to help poor nations in their basic economic needs?
5. Population: are there ethical ways of controlling population growth?

EXPLOITATION

Some ecologists distinguish two attitudes toward nature. One is living in harmony with nature, adapting our lives to nature's cycle, integrating our activities into nature's rhythm, finding our equal place with all other natural objects, and subordinating ourselves as parts in the whole of nature's plan. The other attitude is to concentrate on our uniqueness, to celebrate our rationality as the only thinking beings in the world, to consider the other things in nature as objects to be used as means toward our own ends, and to exploit and dominate nature. Some connect the first attitude with primitive man, with a general pantheistic outlook, and with the contemplative character of Eastern thought, whereas they connect the second attitude with sophisticated society, with the activism of the West, and with the Judeo-Christian theism of a personal God. In particular they refer to the biblical command, "Be fertile and multiply; fill the earth and subdue it. Have dominion over the fish of the sea, the birds of the air, and all the living things that move on the earth."* Thus, they say, man has found divine approval for his reckless exploitation of the earth. Others answer that the passage must be taken in context, that the first man was put into the Garden of Eden to till it and keep it, and that man's function is one of stewardship, of responsible management of things entrusted to him, for which he will have to give an account to his Creator.

*Gen. 1:28.

Scripture is quoted here by both sides, not as an argument, but as representing the attitudes of two cultures, the one supposed to be gentle and natural, the other hostile and domineering.

It does not seem that we can draw a hard-and-fast line between these two attitudes: of submitting oneself to nature or of submitting nature to oneself. We do a bit of both, which is not contradictory, for we do it in different ways. Every living thing uses the environment for its own support, consuming other beings for food and thus subordinating them to itself. Man does so more than any other being and is more ingenious in manipulating nature to serve him, but there are limits beyond which nature cannot be bent, and in observing those limits man submits himself to nature's scheme. The practical result of ecology as a science is to define those limits and to keep man's manipulation of nature within its proper bounds.

Rather than blame man's exploitation of nature on the Judeo-Christian outlook, let us rather carry it back to man's first major interferences with nature: his domestication of animals and his development of agriculture. Here man freed himself from the food supply nature haphazardly offered by developing new strains of animals and plants whose whole purpose is to serve man. This legitimate use of man's ingenuity is in accordance with his intelligent nature, which is capable of foresight, planning, and creativity. It is true that nature can get along without man, as it did for millions of years, but it is a mistake to think of man as an intruder into nature, as if he were not continuous with his evolutionary forebears and as if there were something unnatural about a being that thinks for himself. Man also has a tendency toward greed, toward overdoing his adaptation of nature, toward exhausting nature's fertility by stimulating it to overproduction. The remedy for his own greed man can find in his reason, when he sees that he has upset nature's balance too far and must pull back to more reasonable limits the demands he makes on nature. Here is where the voice of ethics speaks. It must condemn greed, avarice, or cupidity as the excessive and unreasonable indulgence of one's desires. Just where the desires become excessive must be judged by other criteria: by the quantity of nature's available stock, by the fairness of the distribution methods, and by the ease with which the goods can be replenished. Here ethics comes to ecology and allied sciences for a factual judgment. Thus ecology and ethics work hand in hand. The one determines when man's use of nature is fair and proper, as well as when it is exploitative and destructive; the other insists on man's obligation to use nature fairly and properly, with an eye to both present and future generations.

RESOURCES

Only the ethics of selfishness could say that man has no responsibility for future generations. If justice requires a fair distribution of nature's goods among people now living, and love for one's fellowman requires a concern for his welfare, there is no reason that this justice and love should include all those living in various parts of space but exclude those living at different ages of time. It is true that only those who are existing are able to receive our benefit, but we should not make life intolerable for those whom we intend to bring into existence on this earth. A future generation does not yet exist to be the subject of a right, but the present generation does exist as the subject of a duty. When we exercise the right of procreation, we undertake the accompanying duty of supplying our offspring with the conditions for a proper human life. As parents have such an obligation toward their future children, so in a wider sense the present generation of all humanity has such an obligation to future generations.

How far into the future? We have no notion of what life will be like a thousand years from now and are incapable of providing for it. With such problems we tend to use the phrase "foreseeable future." It is vague enough to fit almost anyone's interpretation and useless for providing any precise calculations; yet we may ask whether greater precision is possible or desirable. We can calculate, for example, the oil reserves in the earth, with their present rate of depletion, and can thus come to some fair idea of how much will be left for the next generation or two, and of when man can no longer depend on this source of energy. It was thus that we calculated timber sources and, after the reckless deforestation of the previous century, have come to some measures of conservation and reforestation. In this matter of looking into the future, there seems to be a moderate position between saying that we cannot predict the future and therefore can do nothing about it, and trying to lay down a detailed blueprint for the future that the future is not going to follow. The future will have surprises and will solve some of our present problems in ways we cannot now imagine, besides bringing up new problems beyond our wildest suspicions. Some things are certain, and some conjectures have too much validity to be easily dismissed. We cannot continue to abuse certain aspects of nature in the way we are doing and command nature to come up with a remedy for our own folly.

Should we not let future generations solve their own problems? We had to solve ours. Why not let the next generation do as we had to do? But this is what is in question: was it moral of the last generation to have handed its unsolved problems on to us? No one can require that they solve insoluble problems, nor can that be expected of us. But was it moral for them to have refused to solve what they could have solved? Will it be moral for us to let the future generation do our job for us?

Where we clearly see a trend in our behavior now that will almost surely lead to disaster for future generations, are not we the ones who must desist from that behavior? Would it be according to the virture of prudence to continue as we are doing and expect some unforseen discovery to come to our assistance? Occasionally a stroke of good fortune rescues us from our stupidity, but to bank on such a rescue is stupidity squared.

It seems, then, that we do have the moral obligation of providing for future generations, of so using the resources of the earth as not to deprive our descendants of their use, and of acting as stewards or good managers of what has been put in our keeping. If we have not yet worked out the details of what we ought to do, we have the moral obligation of putting our effort into that work, of using the best scientific information available, and of alerting humanity in general to the problems that face us.

POLLUTION

How much pollution can nature tolerate? In a sense nature pollutes itself. Volcanoes spew ash and gases into the atmosphere, dust and sand storms blow over the world's deserts, lakes have a lifetime and then gradually silt up, the seas are the dumping ground for all nature's refuse. Nature maintains an equilibrum for a very long while, but that pattern of equilibrium breaks up and is succeeded by another pattern. Without any interference from man, the fauna and flora of many an age passed away because nature itself made conditions of life impossible for them. Because such changes occurred so slowly, we do not call them pollution, and yet the essence of it is there: the environment is rendered unsuitable for the survival of some formerly thriving species of living things. Nature dirties itself and does not have to wait for man to do the job, but we reserve the words *dirt* and *pollution* for what man does to nature,

because he can change nature so quickly and drastically, and because he is capable of controlling and avoiding his own action.

Man cannot prevent the natural pollution that occurs within nature's own scheme, nor can he stop the minimum pollution that follows from the very fact of keeping himself alive. There is no moral issue here. What does involve the moral issue is the voluntary indulgence in excess, the production of refuse that nature cannot recycle and that results in constantly growing piles of useless and indestructible material.

The pollution of the air by smog resulting chiefly from the automobile; the pollution of the rivers by the dumping of raw sewage and industrial wastes; the death of lakes such as Lake Erie, which has lost its oxygen and its stock of fish by a man-created imbalance; the poisoning of the land by an overuse of fertilizers, which are then washed off into the streams instead of forming part of nature's cycle; the overuse of DDT and other pesticides and herbicides that leave an indestructible residue; and even the fouling of nature's last repository, the ocean, which is even now giving notice that its power of recuperation is being taxed to the breaking point—all these facts testify that man is in fact a polluter of his environment, that his advancing technology is enabling him to pollute it still more, that it is not enough even to hold to the present level, but that he is obliged to reverse his mode of behavior and repair as much as possible the damage he has done.

One thing about the pollution aspect is that there is much that can be done about it. Unlike the depletion of natural resources, which when consumed cannot be restored, pollution is a constant process going on by man's activity, and he can simply cease or be forced to cease from his polluting activity. The difficulty is not physical but political. How do you persuade people to do what is necessary for their welfare?

Pollution is not leading to such swift and dire consequences as the prophets of gloom predict. All is not lost yet. Something, but not nearly enough, is being done about it. The moral obligation is to intensify the efforts toward pollution control up to but not beyond the point where the remedy would be worse than the disease. There may be need of more political control of the economy to make pollution control economically feasible. The cost of pollution control is considerable; it must either be absorbed by the government and paid for by increased taxes, or be imposed by the government and paid for by increased prices. Either way is a moral way, but neither way is palatable. Since the end is socially mandatory and since neither producer nor consumer is willing to contribute voluntarily to pollution control, there seems to be no other remedy than enforcement by the government.

Then there is the problem of making this control international. It seems to be almost beyond human ingenuity to persuade the nations of the world to agree on a matter that concerns them all if they can squeeze the slightest advantage out of independent action. Yet no individual country is excused from its moral duty because its neighbors fail to fulfill theirs. If a sufficient number of countries succeed in agreeing, they can exert pressure on the rest.

POVERTY

One of the ironies about food production is the claim that the earth cannot feed even its present population, for one third of the human race goes to bed hungry each night. However, we see that some governments pay their farmers to keep land out of production so as to keep up the price, thus making inevitable the prevalence of hunger. The problem is not one of production, since production is deliberately curtailed, but of distribution, and the distribution in-

volves economics and politics. We cannot motivate people to work hard at growing food for those who cannot pay for it, and therefore the richer countries must subsidize the growing of food and give it away to countries in need. Food is actually given away, though the process is disguised in various fashions. Very few people die of starvation, as they would do if the poorest countries were left entirely in their own plight, but many die of the effects of malnutrition or semistarvation, which shows that the help given to needy countries is insufficient.

What moral obligation do the rich countries of the world have to come to the assistance of poor countries? If each country is independent and supposedly self-sufficient, it should be able to take care of the basic needs of its people, either by growing its own food or by trading for it. If political boundaries were drawn with an eye to a proper allocation of resources, this argument might have something to it, but such is not the case. Some countries have political independence, which they will not give up even though they are economically inviable, and they will have to be supported by the other nations of the world. Every family has children, the elderly, and other unproductive members to support. Nations may not think of themselves as having such family obligations, but how otherwise are the indigent members of the family of nations to be supported? What is the alternative? Letting other human beings starve to death or suffer serious want because they are not your concern? Is such an attitude compatible with any ethics?

Social justice is not confined by the boundaries of political states, so that one has obligations to one's compatriots only, and to no one else. Our common humanity transcends any artificial grouping we may make, no matter how deeply these groupings are rooted in history and tradition. Other things being equal, our first obligation is to our own, but when we discuss the relation between rich and poor countries, other things are not equal. One country's basic requirements for survival are pitted against another country's luxuries and superfluities.

Just as the wealthy as a class of people have the moral obligation of contributing to the support of the needy, both for relieving immediate distress and for working toward a long-range solution of the poverty problem, so wealthy countries have the obligation of contributing toward the relief of needy countries, both in times of crisis from disaster and famine, and in the long-range plan of assisting such countries toward economic adequacy. Very few nations are willing publicly to repudiate such an obligation, but fulfillment of it is spotty. In too many instances hungry countries are fed rhetoric instead of food, and each nation is quite willing to let other nations take the initiative. This modest behavior is in marked contrast to the seizing of any advantage that might contribute to the nation's selfish benefit. The moral weaknesses of individuals become intensified in the behavior of nations. Here is an area where the United Nations should be able to contribute its services. It has tried to do so, but though it has accomplished something, its efforts have been impaired by the selfish attitude of the nations of which it is composed. In all this matter the moral obligation seems clear. The difficulty here, as it is in so many areas of ethics, is in getting men to do what they know they ought to do.

POPULATION

Many persons think that the only remedy for our ecological ills lies in a restriction on the growth of the population. The trouble always comes down to "too many people." There is no doubt of the zooming population. It is doubling itself in increasingly shorter periods. The thesis of Malthus* may not be fulfilled in exactly the way Malthus proposed it, but in general lines his prophecy is coming true. Our efforts to stave off starvation and malnutrition are brought to nought by the fact that every increased food supply is met by an even more greatly increased number of mouths to feed. Thus we are constantly falling behind in our attempt to feed humanity. It is true that the earth can produce much more food than it actually does, and therefore a short-term remedy may be possible. However, such a remedy is no answer to the fact that the population is exploding at an exponential rate, and the time must eventually come when there is no room on the earth for another human being. Before any such time arrives, the population explosion will have been contained by starvation and other disasters. The ethical problem is: Can we allow the population to increase at this alarming rate so as to make conditions of life impossible for a great part of the human race, or must we stop our rate of increase and contain it within reasonable limits? The problem is a new one. We had hitherto assumed that "the more the merrier" was a valid principle and that there was plenty of room for all. It is our own efficiency in controlling death that now requires us to control birth. Formerly nature eliminated the unfit; we have succeeded in enabling almost all to live.

There is an ethical obligation on the human race as a whole to limit its increase. Just as there was the ethical obligation to increase and multiply when there was a population shortage, so now there is the ethical obligation to keep reproduction within the bounds of the earth's finite capacity. If man is fitted by his nature to live on this earth, his numbers must also be geared to what the earth can support. Though the earth can support, with human

---

*Malthus, *Essay on the Principle of Population,* 1798.

ingenuity, perhaps many times the number of people existing now, it cannot support the indefinite number toward which our exponential increase is rapidly leading. The time is growing short, and plans must be made now for setting a limit to our numbers.

How can this general obligation be applied to individual persons and families? Just as there is the general obligation on the human race to reproduce and continue itself, but no particular individual is obliged to marry and raise a family because enough will do so anyway, so a general obligation on the human race to limit its numbers would not fall on a particular individual or family, so long as enough were limiting their reproductive capacity to keep the size of the human race within proper bounds.

The best way to accomplish this limitation of births is by persuading people to limit their families voluntarily. A variety of methods has been suggested, some of them acceptable from a moral standpoint and others not. Infanticide would be the most objectionable, so much so that most people would simply refuse to do it or let it happen. Abortion is an acceptable method to those who see no moral wrong in abortion, but it is quite unacceptable to those who regard the fetus as a human being with a right to life; even those who do not condemn abortion think of it rather as a last resort for those for whom contraception has failed. Voluntary sterilization, of either the male or female, is another method advocated by those who see no moral obligation to preserve one's physical wholeness and who regard sterilization as a condition of permanent contraception, against which they have no moral scruples. Contraception is the favored method for those who do not consider contraception an unnatural or immoral act. Abstinence and the rhythm method are means that should be morally acceptable to all, but not all find them feasible. Late marriage is an efficient method of keeping down the birth rate in some parts of the world, but not all peoples would accept it, and it becomes useless if people indulge in premarital sex without contraceptives. In fact, the whole population problem would be greatly eased, though not entirely solved, by eliminating two human vices, adultery and fornication, by which illegitimate children are brought into the world. Planning for the future, however, cannot bank on any marked reduction in extramarital sex, and one can only urge that if it is indulged in, it be with the use of efficient contraceptives.

Thus it is seen that the question of population control is bound up with most of the moral problems that concern the right to life and the use of sex. Most agree that the end, population control, is good and is morally required in these times of actually existing or rapidly approaching overpopulation. The dispute is on the means, since a good end does not justify the use of immoral means.

Some advocate compulsory limitation of population. Not all the advocates of zero population growth (ZPG) favor compulsory methods, but some do. Their argument is that voluntary methods are insufficient, that people will practice them only halfheartedly, and that not enough people will practice them to make them effective. The governments of all the nations of the world will have to step in, to order the destruction of all children beyond the two who will replace their parents (to be more exact, 2.2 children on an average to each married couple) and to sterilize those parents who exceed this number. Their reasoning is that otherwise the human race will not survive, and the obligation on the race toward survival is stronger than the right of any individual to survive and stronger than the right of parents to have as many children as they please. There is something very strange about this argument, as if the normal but undesirable controlling factors such as famine, war, and disease would become inoperative, that they would not serve to thin the population, but that the whole human race would arrive at the point of extinction at once. Thus, rather than let these factors thin the population for us, we should step in and kill those who would otherwise die. What is the purport of such an argument? Does it not come down to saying that since there is not enough to go around, we will make sure that we are the ones who will survive? How moral is this attitude? Hitherto it would have been called selfishness. Does it become different when done on global scale?

Most moralists would hold that only persuasive and voluntary methods can be used. Not only do those methods alone show the proper respect for individuals' rights, but they are the only ones that have a chance of succeeding. The surest way of producing worldwide revolution, and hence the destruction of humanity that the ZPG advocates want to avoid, would be the autocratic and forceful interference with the family necessary to implement compulsory population control.

But voluntary methods will reduce the population only slightly, not enough to save humanity! It seems, then, that we will have to live with continued population growth. Most of the developed countries have a fairly stable population. Runaway population growth is occurring chiefly in the developing countries. The aim today of both the developed and the developing countries is to turn the developing countries into developed countries. If this trend is followed, then when all the countries of the world are economically developed and have arrived at cultural and political maturity, all the countries of the world will also have arrived close to zero population growth. This will be a slower process and will allow for a larger world population than the more fanatical ZPG advocates desire, but it seems to be the only way in which the absolute long-run evils of unlimited population growth can be avoided in a man-

ner consistent with sound morals and a respect for the rights of the individual person.

The growth of urbanization, which is itself a kind of blight on the landscape, will help in lowering the population. Children are an asset on the farm but a liability in the city. More two- and three-children families will become the rule as the cities spread and set the fashion for the rural regions. Thus, although voluntary family limitation lacks that definite mathematical precision which a compulsory limitation would achieve, voluntary limitation seems to be the only way that is morally allowable, as well as being the only way that is politically and socially feasible. Whether it is enough to solve the problem, time alone will tell.

CONCLUSION

The moral questions involved in this chapter are fairly simple in principle but extremely difficult in practical application. No one has the right to use the gifts of nature in such a way as to produce widespread and intolerable harm to others. Few are going to do much about this social crime against humanity unless curbed by law, and lawmakers need more courage than they have so far shown to resist the pressure of vested interests. Legislation on the local level is usually not enough, nor even on the national level, and international cooperation is the most difficult thing in the world to come by. What laws to enact and how to enforce them is the business of environmental experts and political agencies. The ordinary citizen can cooperate by disposing of his own refuse in a way that does not add to the general litter and by reinforcing the pressure of public opinion on his political representatives. That the public has become conscious of the problems is a great step forward but will mean little unless followed by continual resistance against greed and apathy.

SUMMARY

Ecology, the science of the relation of living organisms to their environment, has assumed increasing importance since man has come to experience the effects of his reckless exploitation of nature. We must guard against the exaggerations of the more hysterical environmentalists and the apathy counseled by the defenders of the status quo and vested interests. There are several ethical issues involved.

Exploitation. It is claimed that man is by nature an exploiter, that his natural greed is furthered by the Judeo-Christian ethic of dominating nature, and that the only remedy is to adopt the Eastern attitude of submission to nature, fostered by the pantheistic outlook of man's continuity with all things. Many think that these attitudes are not incompatible and that man as a steward is meant to use and adapt nature to his purposes but always within the limits imposed by nature itself.

Resources. Nature has many nonrenewable resources that we are using up more and more swiftly as our technology develops. Does man have a moral obligation to future generations to save for them a proper share in nature's bounty? It would be difficult to deny such an obligation, though it is also difficult to give it exact limits. At least there can be no moral defense for sheer wastefulness. Now that we recognize our wastefulness, we have a moral obligation to correct it.

Pollution. Man adds to nature's own pollution of the environment. Nature's pollution cannot be corrected; man's can. The environment is not so hopelessly spoiled as some prophets of doom proclaim, but the trend toward man-made pollution must be reversed. Man's selfishness is such that this reversal will not be accomplished without strict government control, both on the national and international level. The cost will be great, but it must be faced because the alternative is not tolerable.

Poverty. Rich nations have the same moral obligation to come to the aid of poor nations that individual rich men have to come to the aid of individual poor people in their society. One basic lack in poor nations is food. Though there is little actual starvation, there is malnutrition and its attendant diseases. The obligation is twofold: to relieve immediate needs from famine and drought, and to establish a far-reaching program of helping economically disadvantaged nations to attain economic self-sufficiency.

Population. The population explosion has been blamed for all these ecological ills. This is a gross exaggeration, for some of these ills are not tied to population, but the rapid multiplication of the population is itself a problem that will not go away by ignoring it. Population growth must be curtailed, and moral methods must be used. Infanticide, abortion, sterilization, contraception, rhythm, abstinence, and late marriages are the most commonly suggested methods. The first three are morally disapproved by many, and the last three are morally acceptable to most but ineffectual in practice. Family limitation by contraception seems to be an effective method that most people would probably approve. To practice it morally, one should be convinced of the moral rightness of contraception. *Compulsory* population limitation goes against the fundamental rights of mankind and would be an immoral solution of a moral problem. Only persuasive and *voluntary* methods may be used. They already work in developed countries. When all developing countries have become developed, perhaps world population will be fairly well stabilized.

QUESTIONS FOR DISCUSSION

1 The phrase "spaceship earth" is commonly used. Is it a legitimate expression? In what respects is the earth like a spaceship and in what respects is it quite different? Does any moral issue follow from this metaphor?

2 Colonization has always been a way of relieving population pressure. Now that there are no more empty lands to colonize on earth, is it not a logical extension of man's colonizing tendency to look for new homes among the stars and planets? Even when space travel becomes possible, will it relieve excess population on earth?

3 Getting the nations of the world to cooperate on food, poverty, and pollution is as difficult as getting the United Nations to prevent a war. Is not the only realistic answer an acceptance of certain evils as inevitable?

4 Some blame all our ecological ills on the advancing state of human technology. Everything has become so artificial that we have lost our sense of continuity with nature. The only thing to do is to declare a moratorium on technology, to halt our scientific advance until our human values have had a chance to catch up.

5 What would you do if ordered by the state to limit your children to two, the penalty for failure being the destruction of the third child and your and your wife's or husband's sterilization?

READINGS

Interest in ecology and a warning on what we are doing to our environment was sparked by Rachel Carson's *Silent Spring.* She greatly overstates her case but is well worth reading.

Barry Commoner's *The Closing Circle* is one of the most influential books from the environmentalist standpoint. See also his *Science and Survival,* and his many articles. Ian McHarg's *Design With Nature* is an expensively produced work on nature and environment, with actual studies of Washington, Philadelphia, etc., and with reflections on man the exploiter. John Black puts out a small book, *The Dominion of Man: the Search for Ecological Responsibility;* he concentrates on the ethical and religious aspects: exploitation vs. stewardship. Ian Barbour edits a series of essays entitled *Earth Might be Fair.* Bruce Allsopp has a little book, *The Garden Earth: the Case for Ecological Morality,* that is rather far out.

On the other side there is John Maddox, *The Doomsday Syndrome,* an interesting protest against such gloomy prophets as Carson, Commoner, and Ehrlich. Though antienvironmentalist, it seems to be fairly well balanced.

Who Speaks for Earth? is a small volume edited by Maurice F. Strong, containing speeches delivered at the International Institute for Environmental Affairs and the Population Institute, United Nations Conference on the Human Environment, Stockholm, June, 1972. The speakers are Barbara Ward, René Dubos, Thor Heyerdahl, Gunnar Myrdal, Carmen Miró, Lord Zuckerman, and Aurelio Peccei, an array certainly worth listening to.

Barbara Ward's *The Rich Nations and the Poor Nations,* though a bit old, is still a vital work from one of the world's best-known economists. Her later pamphlet, *A New Creation? Reflections on the Environmental Issue,* is very well done, environmentalist but restrained.

The great beginner of population studies and demography is Thomas Malthus. The first edition (1798) of his *Essay on the Principle of Population* is worth reading. Here he announces his principle that population increases geometrically, whereas food production increases only arithmetically. He sees war, famine, and pestilence as the only ways of regulating the population.

Paul Ehrlich's *The Population Bomb* exploded on the scene in 1968, together with the author's frequent speeches and the foundation of the Zero Population Growth movement. With his wife, Anne, he published *Population, Resources, Environment,* a more restrained version of the former. They are necessary reading on this subject, but beware of the strong propagandist presentation and test carefully every conclusion.

Austin Fagothey, *Right and Reason—an Anthology,* does not contain any article directly related to this chapter, though our technological society is criticized in Josef Pieper's *Leisure, the Basis of Culture.*

CHAPTER 35

NATIONS

PROBLEM

International relations are complicated by the fact that individual sovereign states have no superior to whom they can appeal and whose authority they respect. The state itself is a society of individuals and families, and one of its chief functions is to judge disputes between them, but when states themselves conflict they have nothing ultimately to appeal to but force, and that is war. There is no more inefficient way of settling disputes than war. To avoid its horrors, if possible, or at least to reduce them as far as can be, states have developed the instrument known as international law. We will discuss the following questions:

1. What is international law and how did it arise?
2. Is international law really law?
3. Are states bound by the natural law?
4. What duties in justice do states have to one another?
5. What duties in amity do states have to one another?

RISE OF INTERNATIONAL LAW

The ancients seem to have looked on foreign nations as enemies and their property as booty. Homer pictures the Greeks as supporting themselves by forays on other villages about Troy, and the custom was to kill or enslave the conquered. There was some unwritten code of honor among warriors, for they held sacred the person of heralds and had truces for burying the dead and exchanging prisoners. The Amphictyonic League was an attempt to bring harmony among the Greek city-states and to establish among them some common rules of action, but it met with little success.

The Romans, as we have seen, developed the *jus gentium,* which is not international law but what they found to be the common element in the internal laws of all their subjugated peoples. The *jus gentium,* because it was common to all peoples with whom the Romans came into contact, closely approached the natural law and became one of the sources from which international law was later to be drawn, but the Romans felt no need for international law in the modern sense. Their final solution to the differences between nations was to absorb them all into their own vast Empire. Rome took on herself the task of keeping order in the civilized world, and her great achievement was the *Pax Romana.*

When the world emerged from the wreckage of the Roman Empire, there was one great international institution to which all Christian nations could turn for an adjudication of disputes, the Church. A common faith and a common code of morality did much to standardize the behavior of kings and princes into a common Christian pattern and to outlaw certain practices as unworthy of a Christian anywhere. The ideals of chivalry and knighthood, with their high sense of honor, exerted an enormous humanizing influence. Definite rules and customs, founded on the natural law, the *jus gentium,* and even the Church's Canon Law to some extent, governed the relations between states. Diplomatic negotiations, as we understand them now, seem to have originated among the medieval Italian city-states. Though without any force to impose her decisions and relying solely on her moral position, the Church arbitrated countless quarrels and did much to mitigate the horrors of war and conquest. Even so, the feudal period was all too barbarous, but at least between Christian peoples there was nothing like the wholesale enslavement of ancient times or the almost total war of today.

The breakdown of united Christendom in the sixteenth century and the ensuing lack of any common court of appeal acceptable to all Christian nations led to the formation of the concept of *international law* in the modern sense. Though it was prepared for by the work of Francis de Vitoria and Francis Suarez, who tried to codify existing customs and apply them to the rising nationalism of their day, the founding of international law is commonly attributed to Hugo Grotius, author of *The Rights of War and Peace.* He saw that henceforth, in the absence of a higher tribunal, relations between nations must be governed both by the natural law, which as the law of reason is common to all men, and by voluntary agreement among states, based on their enlightened self-interest. His codification of existing customs, tested by these criteria, passed into the texture of modern international law.

International law is the result not of any definite enactment but of long custom and usage. Its rules can be found in recognized writers commenting on these customs, in treaties between civilized nations, in state papers and diplomatic correspondence, in decisions of international tribunals, and in court decisions of partic-

ular countries regarding citizenship, alien property, admiralty cases, and similar matters.

International law comprises the rules determining the conduct of political states in their dealings with each other. Which political organizations are *states?* In practice, a *state* is one so recognized by the nations of the world generally, and admitted to their circle. The theory on which this practice seems to be based is that a *state* is here taken in the strictest sense to mean one having the fullest degree of independent sovereignty.

This concept of the state supposes enough development and organization to make the state self-sufficient and capable of self-rule; it also supposes the actual possession of self-rule, full jurisdiction over the whole people in all departments of life, internal and external. Primitive and uncivilized tribes, though they have their natural rights, are not states because they lack the first requirement; the individual states of the United States, under the theory of divided sovereignty, have handed over control of foreign affairs to the federal government and thus fail in the second requirement.

The position of *client states,* whether they be called provinces, colonies, tributaries, dependencies, protectorates, 'or mandates, is a knotty question. Some of them retain a technical sovereignty and basic jurisdiction over all affairs, yet in practice have handed over to another state some of their affairs and especially their foreign relations. Those which are technically sovereign come under international law in theory, but foreign nations disregard this theoretical position in practice, since they cannot treat with them directly but only through the state that manages their foreign relations. Their position is somewhat like that of a minor, who has inherent personal rights equal to those of anyone else but is under his guardian's tutelage for the transaction of business. Some, especially colonies, gradually grow to a condition of full independence, but others show little initiative toward responsible self-rule.

MORAL ASPECTS OF INTERNATIONAL LAW

It may be argued that international law is not truly law because there is no one who has care of the community of nations, no common authoritative ruler over all states. In fact, the requirement that the states be fully sovereign makes it impossible for any real law to exist between states.

Natural law theorists answer this difficulty by distinguishing two parts of international law. Some parts of international law arise out of the very nature of the state and are merely reaffirmations of, or deductions from, the natural law, such as the right of a nation to defend itself when unjustly attacked, or its duty to fulfill just contracts freely made. Such rights and duties constitute *natural* international law. Other parts of international law are the result of express or tacit agreements made between nations and not directly deducible from the natural law, such as the diplomatic immunity accorded ambassadors, or the internment of warships by neutrals in war time. These areas of law constitute *conventional* or *contractual* international law.

Ethics is concerned with natural international law only, and this is truly law in the sense in which natural, or moral, law is said to be law, as embodying natural rights, natural justice, and natural morality. But contractual international law depends only on compact and agreement, and relies for its enforcement only on the good faith of the contracting parties. There is nothing in the nature of things that demands the making of such contracts, and they are freely entered into for mutual benefit like contracts between private persons. Hence they are not laws in the strict sense.

We cannot conclude that such laws have no binding force. Contracts between individuals, though not themselves laws, impose obligation from the moral law, which prescribes that *just contracts must be kept*. The same is true of international agreements. Though they are entered into voluntarily and are not guaranteed by any higher authority on earth than the contracting parties, once made they bind nations and their rulers in conscience. Hence the distinction between natural and contractual international law, necessary for studying and formulating this law, is of less importance when there is the mere practical question of keeping its obligations. In both cases the obligation comes from the moral law, but in different ways: in natural international law, without any medium; and in contractual international law, though the intermediacy of a voluntary contract. In the first case the obligation cannot be avoided; in the second, it can be avoided by refusing to be a party to the contract.

The solution just given is based on the supposition that states are bound by morality and the moral law. It is a deplorable fact that many states have behaved as if they were not bound by any consideration of morality, but this observation does not mean that they approved this kind of action in theory. Nations most ruthless in violating the rights of others often shout loudest when their own rights are attacked, thus offering lip service, when it suits them, to the idea of international morality. But some philosophers and jurists insist that even in theory international law is outside the scope of morality.

Moral positivists, holding that all morality comes from the state, must logically accept this conclusion, but one need not be a moral positivist to do so. One may attempt a compromise, admitting individual morality but denying international morality on the grounds that the individual has a destiny beyond this world, where-

396

as the state is merely a temporal affair; that morality deals with eternal ideals of conduct, whereas states are concerned with worldly needs and material wants; and that an individual can afford to be idealistic, but a state must be hardheadedly realistic.

History should be a sufficient lesson to mankind about the horrendous results of conducting international affairs on the principle that might makes right. That states are bound by the moral law hardly needs any separate proof, but the following remarks will serve as a review:

1. The state is a natural institution, with a natural right to exist, based on the social nature of man. It cannot be exempt from the law that created it, maintains it, and gives it all its rights and authority.

2. The state is composed of human beings and is carried on by their activity. No human being can be exempt from the moral law, which governs every possible form of human conduct. It is absurd to think that a man can rid himself of obligations merely by associating with others, or that anything is allowable as long as men do it together.

3. International law cannot be based entirely on agreement, for what would oblige the states to keep their agreements except some previous agreement? An infinite series of agreements is impossible. The source of all obligation is the moral law, which holds for states as well as for individuals.

4. That rights and duties exist between persons is as true of corporate persons (societies) as of physical persons (individual men). The state is a corporate person, and as a natural society has a sort of natural incorporation. Business firms have obligations in natural justice; so likewise has the state.

5. The individual citizens of one state have natural rights and duties toward the citizens of other states. Justice does not end at the boundaries of states. Conflict of these rights and duties often cannot be settled except through the intermediacy of the states concerned, and they will be governed by international law based on natural justice.

INTERNATIONAL JUSTICE

Men as men have equal rights because they all have the same human nature, the same origin and goal. On this foundation the virtue of justice rests. They can be subordinated to one another only because of some other reason, when they are organized to achieve some lesser end, as when children are subordinated to parents, pupils to teachers, employees to employers, citizens to ruler. The family, the school, the business, and the state are organized each for a definite social function as well as for helping individual persons. Within these societies there is subordination, but between societies of the same kind there is equality of rights. Each is a corporate person and must be treated as an equal by its equals, not merely as a means for another's convenience.

Thus each state exercising full sovereignty has equal rights with every other state. They all have the same end, to promote the temporal welfare of their peoples, and derive their authority from nature and nature's God, not from any other state. No such state is subordinate to any other and may not be treated as subordinate. The rights of a sovereign state are not scaled to its political size or strength, any more than the individual's rights are dependent on his physical size or strength. Whether or not states should curtail their sovereignty by becoming members of a world organization is a topic to be treated later, but even then the various states would be equal among themselves and not subordinate to one another, though they would come under the whole organization.

We must now discuss from the standpoint of morals some of the rights and duties states have in justice:

1. Independence
2. Entirety
3. Property
4. Colonization
5. Free action
6. Treaties

INDEPENDENCE

No state has the right wantonly to destroy the independent existence of another state. Independence is to a state what life is to an individual. As an individual has the right of self-defense against an unjust aggressor, so has a state. An individual may kill in self-defense under the proper conditions; so also a state may deprive another of independence if its own independent existence is so seriously threatened as to leave no other remedy, but this is the only reason. These questions will be treated under war.

A state may be destroyed not only by attack from without but also by the fomentation of sedition and the stirring up of civil war. No state has the right to interfere in this way against its neighbor; a state has the right not only to bare existence but also to a peaceful and orderly existence.

We should note one difference between the life of an individual and of a state. An individual may not take his own life, since he is a physical person whose life is indivisible and incommunicable. A society, being a corporate person, does not have these attributes. Societies can merge or divide, and even revive after extinction. A state can agree to unite with another or others in the formation of a larger state, as the thirteen American states formed the United States. What was formerly one state may split up into several, as in the dissolution of the Austro-Hungarian Empire after the first World War.

ENTIRETY

Each sovereign state has a right to the whole of its territory and of its population. No state need submit to mutilation by its neighbors. Diseases of the kind that attack states are not cured by surgery; the principle that *the part is for the sake of the whole*, which justifies individual mutilation, cannot be applied to states, since the state exists for the benefit of the members. A state's right to expand is limited by its neighbor's right to all its land and all its people. We are not speaking here of border regions to which there are conflicting claims, but of the seizure of neighboring territory that certainly belongs to another state.

The *nationalist ideal*, that the state and the nation, the political unit and the ethnic unit, should be coterminous, would be a legitimate ambition if it could be accomplished without trampling on the rights of other states equally sovereign, but this ideal is rarely attainable. There is nothing in the nature of things that demands that all people of the same racial stock, language, and culture should be assimilated into the same political unit. Other things being equal, a homogeneous totality of population has certain advantages, but other things are hardly ever equal. The Swiss, for example, do not want to be divided among the neighboring states to which they have linguistic and cultural affinities. On the other hand, there is no reason why a number of small principalities should not voluntarily unite along nationalist lines, if they find it expedient and can do so without violating any rights.

Nor is it necessary, as the theory of *autarky*, or economic self-sufficiency, supposes, that the political unit be an economic unit. The self-sufficiency required for sovereignty does not mean that the country must produce all it consumes, but only that it be able to support itself adequately, either by produce, by trade, or by any other means. A state need not be both agricultural and industrial but can engage in a sort of economic symbiosis with another state. Remedy for surplus population, formerly found in emigration and colonization, must be sought in some other way and not in seizing the neighboring state's territory.

PROPERTY

The state, being a corporate person, can own property. The state's titles to property are about the same as those of individual ownership; the main difference is that the state has the additional title of legitimate conquest but lacks the title of inheritance as a natural heir, though it can accept bequests.

Property can come under the jurisdiction of the state in three ways. There is exclusively state-owned property, such as warships, forts, highways, and public buildings. Then there is the private property of its citizens both at home and abroad, for which the state has a responsibility, since to protect its people's property is one of the reasons for the state's existence. Lastly, the very territory of the state, though most of it is divided up among private owners, comes under the state's administration as far as foreign relations are concerned. Seizure of any of this territory by a foreign power is international theft, and culpable damage to it calls for indemnification.

COLONIZATION

Colonization is obsolete, and we can now only judge the past actions of colonizing nations. Of itself there is nothing morally wrong in colonization, though it was subject to the most flagrant abuses. A state could take possession of territory not belonging to any other state and own it by title of occupancy. Mere discovery did not suffice, but annexation and settlement were necessary.

Land that was recognized as the territory of an existing state was not open to colonization, nor land that was adequately occupied by a people capable of statehood but with only incipient political organization. The territory could not be seized without violating the rights of those already in possession. These people either had a state of their own or were on the verge of forming one, and could not rightfully be deprived of their independence. Instead of trying to annex this emergent state, more advanced nations had the obligation of recognizing it and assisting it in its transition to full political stature.

The only land that was legitimately open to colonization was land periodically overrun by nomadic hordes or very sparsely settled by primitive tribes. Nomads had no real possession of the soil, and could not reserve for their exclusive use a whole wilderness that they only occasionally visited and did nothing to develop. Many settled tribes effectively occupied only their own villages and the immediate environs; over their vast hunting grounds they had no more definite control than nomads over the desert steppes. The world's teeming population could not be kept out of these regions forever. Any state might send in a colony, being careful meanwhile to respect the natives' genuine rights. The land was incorporated into the state's political territory and put under its government, but the natives retained the personal ownership of their private property and became citizens or at least wards of the state, which was now bound not only to respect but to defend their rights. These people were not deprived of political independence, for they have never had any political society. Great injustices have occurred in this type of colonization, not the least of them in our own country, but they are not essential to colonization as such.

Now that the colonial era is over, we are faced with a host of problems it left as its aftermath. Praise is due to those nations that prepared their colonies for future independence and responsible self-government, blame to those that were forced to turn them loose unprepared or still try to keep them in tutelage. The hates generated by colonialism did not just happen through nobody's fault, and we have to thank immoral colonizers for the moral problems they left us. These problems will not be solved by recriminations for the past but by cooperative effort toward the future.

FREE ACTION

A state has the right to develop itself in any way it sees fit that does not conflict with the strict right of another state. It may adopt the form of government it wishes, change its constitution to suit itself, enter into commercial relations with others, trade with whom it likes, impose what tariffs it thinks just, and make treaties and carry on other negotiations. Some of these functions may be incidentally detrimental to other nations but are not unjust unless they violate others' rights. States may not prevent the development of other states on the mere plea that they are threatened with rivalry, any more than individuals are allowed forcibly to extinguish legitimate competitors. Free competition is not aggression and does not justify counteraggression.

Nations should have free access to the raw materials that nature provides, and should be able to obtain them by trade. These goods are intended by nature for all mankind, and no nation is allowed to monopolize them in such a way that the rest of the world must suffer. Here the rules of monopoly apply; a country has a right to a legitimate profit on its natural monopolies but should not raise the price beyond the reach of other nations in genuine need of these products.

What nations can do to one another in this respect has been dramatized for us recently by the action of the oil-producing states. Oil is a natural monopoly, and nations that have it, especially if they have little else, are entitled to profit by their one main resource. They enter into relationships with the customer nations, and inconsiderate unilateral action on either side goes counter to the dependence that has been established between them. The oil-buying nations may have kept the price too long at an artificially low level by an abuse of their monopoly of capital, which they invested in the oil-producing country by developing the wells. The oil-producing nations should have been gradually brought more and more into the possession of their own natural resource, so that a proper balance of profit would accrue to both the owner and the developer. However, the answer to this abuse is not to engage in one or the other side. The way to adjust the grievance is by economic and political discussion and agreement, not by a sudden, world-upsetting use of monopolistic power. These remarks are not meant to suggest a simple solution to a complex problem but to reflect on the fact that almost everybody in the world has had his life seriously interfered with by this action, on how enormous economic power can be, and on how important it is to use it responsibly.

TREATIES

A treaty is a contract between sovereign states as states. It differs from a contract between a state and a private individual or corporation, and also from a contract between states not acting in a strictly political capacity, as when one government purchases food or munitions from another. To be binding a treaty must be an act of the sovereign authority in this state, which must ratify the result of previous diplomatic negotiations. The conditions for a valid treaty are the same as those for any valid contract. Treaties, because they are contracts, bind in commutative justice and derive their binding force from the moral law.

Do unjust treaties bind? If the terms of the treaty are clearly and certainly unjust, there can be no contract, for no one can be bound in justice to do or suffer injustice. A state forcing such a treaty on another is morally bound to withdraw it and repair any damage caused. The injustice of a treaty is not to be lightly presumed, but proved with objectively certain reasons. Any nation can trump up dishonest reasons for repudiating perfectly valid treaties when they prove burdensome. The unilateral denunciation of a treaty as unjust before its fulfillment or expiration is very much to be suspected.

Do treaties made under duress bind? Ordinarily a contract made under duress is rendered null and void by positive law, but there is no positive law above states to regulate their actions or to set down conditions for the validity of their contracts. Hence treaties cannot become invalid for this reason. Moreover, the reason that positive law invalidates contracts made under duress is to protect the common good and discourage violence, but the invalidation of *treaties* made under duress would have the opposite effect. The typical treaty made under duress is the peace treaty at the end of a war. If an unjust aggressor is victorious, the treaty he imposes is unjust and therefore invalid. We are speaking here only of just treaties; at the end of a war even they are imposed under duress. The defeated nation is driven by force of arms to accept unfavorable conditions, but it was for the very purpose of imposing such conditions that the war was fought. If such treaties were invalid, wars could never end. It is surely wrong for a nation to accept a treaty to secure cessation of hostilities and then to repudiate the treaty in order to avoid paying just reparations. The only case in which just

treaties made under duress do not bind is when the signer of the treaty is subjected to *personal* threats or violence, for then the presumption is that he is acting solely from motives of personal safety and is not truly the representative of his government.

When do treaties cease to bind? A treaty becomes extinct in the same way as any other contract: when its object is completely fulfilled, by mutual consent of the parties, when one of the parties ceases to exist, when it becomes impossible of fulfillment, when an essential condition no longer holds good, or if it conflicts with a higher or more universal law. If a treaty is valid at the time when it is made, there are as a rule only two reasons that can justify its repudiation: failure of the other party to fulfill an essential part of his obligation, or extinction of the state resulting from fulfillment of the treaty unless that were part of the treaty itself. But the mere fact that a treaty becomes more burdensome to a state than was expected does not at all absolve a state from its obligation. It took this risk when it made the treaty, and such risks are involved in all contracts, private as well as international.

INTERNATIONAL AMITY

The term *amity* means friendly relations, especially between states. Call it benevolence, helpfulness, humanity, cooperation, friendliness, goodwill, or any other name you prefer. The duties of amity or friendship between states are about the same as the duties of love or charity between individuals. One state should come to the aid of another in distress, provided it can do so without serious hardship to itself, in the same way that an individual should help another in trouble. But there is one main difference between the state and the individual. An individual is allowed, though not obliged, to risk certain death in order to protect another; a state would not be allowed to do so because its first obligation is to its own people, whose rights it is not allowed to sacrifice. An individual is for himself, but a state is for its people.

NATIONALISM

Patriotism, or love of country, is a virtue akin to piety or love of parents and must be developed by every citizen. It can go so far as to demand the supreme sacrifice of life itself, as in national defense. True *patriotism,* however, must be distinguished from its caricature, *nationalism,* just as proper self-love differs from selfishness. To love self we need not hate others.

The state, even though self-sufficient and sovereign, is not superior to the common humanity that binds all men into the great family of mankind. Political differences do not take away human likenesses, and the general welfare of the whole human race takes precedence over the welfare of any particular group. Each single state is organized for mutual helpfulness among its members, and this same principle that prevails within each state should also prevail between states. States exist for the sake of promoting a full human life, and the full development of man's social nature is not limited by any artificial political boundaries. Hence an exaggerated *nationalism,* which shows itself in hatred of all foreigners, is to some extent inhuman and therefore immoral, as contradicting man's essentially social nature. It is also poor service to one's own nation to seek its interests so exclusively as to make it a bad member among the family of nations. Selfishness can exist on a national as well as on an individual scale.

INTERVENTION

The *principle of nonintervention,* defended especially by nineteenth century liberalism, is that no state may interfere in the internal affairs of another state for any reason, except where its own interests are involved. To do so is considered an infringement of sovereignty.

This opinion takes too narrow a view of sovereignty and violates the amity or helpfulness spoken of earlier. It is true that no state may meddle with another except for the most serious of reasons, but such reasons can and do sometimes exist. A state can come to the aid of a weaker state unjustly attacked by a stronger, can help a state put down unjustified insurrection, can establish order in a state hopelessly harassed by continual anarchy, can help a people throw off the yoke of unbearable tyranny, and can enforce some policy absolutely necessary for the peace of the world. When one country appeals to another for assistance in such matters, there is no reason why the appeal must be rejected because of the fictitious principle of nonintervention. We may as well say that we have no right to interfere in a family when the man is killing his wife or torturing his children. On the other hand, it would be wrong to try to run their family for them or to interfere when there is no call for it. Hence the principle of nonintervention is invalid as a sweeping generalization, but it has its validity within limits.

CONCLUSION

It is impossible for us to go deeper into the problem of international relations. Contractual international law is quite outside our scope, except insofar as it may conflict with morality. The complexity of international relations in the modern world raises many difficult questions, answers to which have not yet been thoroughly worked out. Students of ethics, law, and politics have here a promisingly fertile field for their efforts. However, it is one thing to devise a solution in theory and quite another to induce the nations of the world to adopt it.

The point that remains of prime importance to the moralist is that the political state is as thoroughly subject to the norms and demands of morality as the individual person. The acts of states are all the more important because they affect the lives of millions of people, and in our days even of the whole world. The rulers of states bear a responsibility proportionate to their power, and in a democracy this responsibility is partially shared by the people. In the course of history the world has paid a terrible price for international immorality, for injustice on a grand and global scale. Immoral conduct is inhuman conduct, and unless nations come to a better sense of justice and honor in their dealings, we must be prepared to see more of man's inhumanity to man.

SUMMARY

International law, a gradual growth of custom and usage, comprises the rules determining the conduct of political states in their dealings with one another. A *state* here means one with full independent sovereignty, not client states whose foreign affairs are managed by others.

Since sovereign states have no superior, *is international law really law?* Natural international law, embodying natural right, justice, and morality, is law. *Contractual* international law, comprising free contracts between states, is not really law, though the contracts bind like any others.

States are bound by the moral law, for they derive their rights and authority from it, are composed of men subject to it in all their conduct, rely on it to give binding force to their contracts, are corporate persons with rights and duties based on it, and must see that natural justice is done between their own citizens and foreigners.

States have rights and duties to one another in *justice.* Every state has a right to:

1. *Independence.* This is a state's life; a state may defend itself against unjust attack and against undue interference by other states in its affairs.

2. *Entirety.* All its territory and population belong to it and must be free from encroachment by other states seeking to satisfy nationalistic or economic ambitions.

3. *Property.* The state, like any society, can own and administer property; it must also protect its citizens' property and maintain its territory, even the part of it that is privately owned.

4. *Colonization.* The state may annex and settle unclaimed and politically unorganized regions, with proper respect for the rights of nomads and aborigines, but the days of colonization are over.

5. *Free action.* Each state may develop itself in its own way, with access to the earth's raw materials, which other states may not withhold from it by unjust monopoly.

6. *Treaties.* These contracts between sovereign states as states bind in justice like any other contract. Unjust treaties cannot bind, but the injustice must be certain. Treaties made under duress, such as peace treaties, bind unless the negotiator signs under threat of personal violence. A valid treaty may be repudiated only if the other party fails to fulfill it or if it would mean the extinction of the state.

States also have duties in *amity* or friendship to one another, but their duty to their own people comes first. Exaggerated *nationalism* is immoral, against man's duty to his fellowman of whatever nation. *Intervention* in another nation's internal affairs is normally wrong, but there can be sufficient reasons to justify it.

QUESTIONS FOR DISCUSSION

1 How can there be morality between nations, since nations have no last end to attain by the use of morally good means? Their end is their temporal welfare, and what right have we to expect more of them?

2 Is not the division of men into political states merely an accident of history, so that it is unrealistic to think of states as having rights or duties? Rights and duties belong to men, but not to mere groupings of men. How can such groups have a right to independence, freedom, and similar abstract qualities?

3 How can one try to justify colonialism, which has been nothing but the exploitation of a weaker people by a stronger? Here abuse seems to have destroyed any legitimate use.

4 Can we say that any state that so guards its borders as to prevent the emigration of its people to other parts of the world is making slaves of its citizens and denying them a basic human right?

5 Must a state tolerate the existence of hostile states around it, so long as they do not engage in any overt belligerent act? How can such a state protect itself from having these neighbors used as preparation places for future attack?

READINGS

Francis de Vitoria faced the new moral problem of the Spanish conquest of the Americas. The translation of the text of his *De Indis* (On the Indians) and *De Jure Belli* (On the Right of War) is given in J. B. Scott, *Francisco de Vitoria and His Law of Nations*, together with Scott's comments. Francis Suarez' ideas on international law are gathered from his great work *De Legibus* (On Laws); the translation of bk. II, ch. 17-20, in J. B. Scott, *Classics of International Law: Suarez*, vol. II, shows how his thinking prepared the way for modern international law. See also J. B. Scott, *Catholic Conception of International Law*, treating of Vitoria, Suarez, and others.

Hugo Grotius, *Rights of War and Peace*, is a classic of international law.

From among modern writers see: John Eppstein, *The Catholic Tradition of the Law of Nations* and *Code of International Ethics*, with many quotations and documents; Don Luigi Sturzo, *Nationalism and Internationalism;* Alfred de Soras, *International Morality;* Robert Delavignette, *Christianity and Colonialism;* Heinrich Rommen, *The State in Catholic Thought,* ch. 28; and Johannes Messner, *Social Ethics*, bk II, pt. IV.

Austin Fagothey, *Right and Reason—an Anthology*, contains Kant's *Perpetual Peace* and John Courtney Murray's *We Hold These Truths*, ch. 11, which are indirectly relevant to this chapter.

CHAPTER 36

WAR

PROBLEM

War is the ultimate in human social failure. Unlike natural disasters, war is a wholly man-made affair, the result of man's greed, envy, hate, ambition, and passion, something utterly useless and unnecessary. No war taken as a whole can ever be justified, for it must start from some original injustice. Granted that the original injustice has been done, must it simply be suffered by the aggrieved nation, or is there a right to resistance and redress? The behavior of mankind throughout history evidences a choice of the second alternative, but the mere fact that nations have acted in this way does not make it moral. Can any moral justification be made out, not for war itself as a whole, but for a nation fighting for its rights in a war not of its own making?

We shall first give the traditional teaching on war and then discuss the more terrible forms of modern warfare. We cannot judge whether or not the old views still prevail until we know what they are. We ask the following questions:

1. Is there a medium between militarism and pacifism?
2. Is there a moral justification for war?
3. What is the just war theory and its conditions?
4. How do we distinguish aggression from defense?
5. What can be said of modern nuclear warfare?
6. What is the ultimate limit to which war could morally go?
7. How far is disarmament mandatory?

MILITARISM AND PACIFISM

There are two extreme attitudes on war between which most people try to find some intermediate position. *Militarists* look on war as inevitable, as a natural expression of man's aggressive instincts, as a necessary element in a nation's growth, and as the normal means by which it plays its role in history. *Pacifists* think that violence and bloodshed, whatever tendencies man may have toward indulging his fighting instincts, are so wrong in themselves that to use them even for defense is to use an evil means for a good end.

Militarism was tacitly assumed in practice by most of the world's empires, but it had almost no philosophical defenders until the nineteenth century, when Fichte identified morality with struggle, Hegel made war a necessary stage in the passage from peace to victory, and Nietzsche extolled master morality as the ethics of the will-to-power. Hitler's Nazism was doubtless inspired by these views. Revolutionary communism, inheriting Hegel's dialectic without his idealism, had its militaristic phase in the absorption of numerous satellite nations and in its behavior toward them at any stirring of independence. Militarism is dismissed by all right-thinking people as an untenable position from any moral standpoint.

Pacifism is not a simple movement and exists on several levels. *Absolute pacifists* condemn all war. A man, they say, is not allowed to raise his hand against his neighbor even for personal defense; neither may a nation go to war to preserve its freedom. This attitude is usually adopted on religious grounds, on the statements and example of Christ in the New Testament,° without attempt at philosophical justification. Gandhi[†] in India made of pacifism a practical movement. War will be impossible, he argues, if people refuse to fight. Violence must be met by nonviolence, by the active nonviolent resistance of noncooperation. It is as wrong to run away as it is to fight. There must be no hatred toward the enemy and no show of cowardice, but simply a peaceful refusal to obey. If enough people can be persuaded to act thus, the enemy can achieve only a hollow victory, and force will cease to be a factor in history. The cost may be severe to the present generation, but nonviolence will ultimately triumph. Gandhi's critics think his views noble but impractical. They were not tested in a real war between sovereign states but only against an Empire that was already on the verge of dissolution.

Relative pacifists are less extreme, objecting only to certain kinds of wars or certain uses of force. In particular there are the *nuclear* pacifists, who admit that in principle there can be such a thing as a just war but that modern and especially thermonuclear war has grown so destructive as to be utterly unjustifiable. We shall see more about them later.

MORAL JUSTIFICATION FOR WAR

Most people see that the truth must lie somewhere between the extremes of militarism and pacifism, that war is to be regretted and avoided as far as possible but that occasions can arise in which it is in-

evitable. A nation may have war thrust upon it against its will by an enemy's aggression and find no solution in pacifism. When a nation that refuses to fight for itself has been reduced to vassalage or slavery, it may then be forced to fight *for* its masters in their further conquests rather than against them. In such a world there will be no peace.

Why is the political state such a thing that men should defend it with their lives? The reason is that man by nature is a political animal, not made to live alone but in society, and not only in the basic society of the family but in the larger organization of the political state. Since one of the main motives for political organization is mutual defense against enemies from without, there is no sense or purpose to political society unless it can defend itself and its people.

As an individual is allowed to use force in self-defense and also for the recovery of what is rightly his when recourse to higher authority is impossible, so may the state, and for the same reasons. War in itself is a physical evil; it becomes a moral evil only when there is injustice on the part of the one using the force. A nation against which injustice is being committed justly defends itself, according to the principle of the unjust aggressor. It may likewise seek the recovery of goods it has been unjustly deprived of, since there is no higher authority to which it can appeal. Though no war can be just on both sides (except subjectively, through mistaken judgment) and a war can be unjust on both sides (each nation violating the other's rights), it is possible for a war to be just on one side and unjust on the other.

The argument for the possibility of a just war can be stated thus: The state, since it is a natural society, has a natural right to use the means necessary for its preservation and proper functioning. However, conditions may be such that the only means by which a state can preserve itself in

---

°Matthew 5, 39-40; 26, 52.
†Gandhi, *Non-Violence in Peace and War*, throughout.

being, and can protect or recover its lawful rights, is by war. Therefore under such conditions the state has a natural right to wage war.

A state that would not wage war under any circumstances, however serious, would condemn itself to political death, to loss of independence, which is the very life of a state, and to servitude under the feet of its aggressive neighbors. If morality demanded this sacrifice, it would be giving only to immoral states a moral right to existence. It would impose on man the moral obligation to organize himself politically, and at the same time deny him the means necessary for attaining that end. If a state cannot protect the lives and liberties of its citizens, it is failing in its chief function. If it cannot do so except through force, it must have the right to use force.

THE JUST WAR THEORY

The endeavor to steer between the extremes of militarism and pacifism led to the development of the *just war theory.* Little help could be found in the ancient writers. Plato and Aristotle condemned militarism but saw that war was a possibility that even an ideal state would have to provide for. The early Christians deplored the existence of war, as anyone should, but only in general terms. The Fathers of the Church have some very pacifistic statements, but the context shows that they are talking about resistance to persecution, gladiatorial combats, or imperialistic aggression. The first noted writer to treat expressly of the morality of war was St. Augustine. He derived, seemingly from Cicero, certain conditions for a just war and is thus regarded as the founder of the just war theory. These conditions, scattered among St. Augustine's works, are gathered together and systematized by St. Thomas:

In order for a war to be just, three things are necessary. First, the authority of the sovereign by whose command the war is to be waged. For it is not the business of a private individual to declare war, because he can seek for redress of his rights from the tribunal of his superior. Moreover, it is not the business of a private individual to summon together the people, which has to be done in war time. And as the care of the common weal is committed to those who are in authority, it is their business to watch over the common weal of the city, kingdom or province subject to them. And just as it is lawful for them to have recourse to the sword in defending that common weal against internal disturbances, when they punish evil-doers, . . . so too it is their business to have recourse to the sword of war in defending the common weal against external enemies. . . . And for this reason Augustine says:° The natural order conducive to peace among mortals demands that the power to declare and counsel war should be in the hands of those who hold supreme authority.

Secondly, a just cause is required, namely that those who are attacked should be attacked because they deserve it on account of some fault. Wherefore Augustine says:† A just war is wont to be described as one that avenges wrongs, when a nation or state has to be punished, for refusing to make amends for the wrongs inflicted by its subjects, or to restore what it has seized unjustly.

Thirdly, it is necessary that the belligerents should have a rightful intention, so that they intend the advancement of the good, or the avoidance of evil. Hence Augustine says:‡ True religion looks upon as peaceful those wars that are waged not for motives of aggrandizement or cruelty, but with the object of securing peace, of punishing evil-doers, and of uplifting the good. For it may happen that the war is declared by the legitimate authority, and for a just cause, and yet be rendered unlawful through a wicked intention. Hence Augustine says:§ The passion for inflicting harm, the cruel thirst for vengence, an unpacific and relentless spirit, the

---

°St. Augustine, *Contra Faustum Manichaeum,* bk. XXII, ch. 75.

†St. Augustine, *Quaestiones in Heptateuchum,* bk. VI, q. 10, on Josue viii.

‡Not found in St. Augustine but in the *Decretum Gratiani* (Decree of Gratian, a medieval compilation of Canon Law), pt. II, causa 23, q. 1, canon 6.

§St. Augustine, *Contra Faustum Manichaeum,* bk. XXII, ch. 74.

fever of revolt, the lust for power, and suchlike things, all these are rightly condemned in war.*

In the remaining articles of question 40, St. Thomas takes up the question of ecclesiastics engaging in warfare, of laying ambushes, and of fighting on holy days. Except the second, these are obsolete medieval matters; they are mentioned here only to show that St. Thomas recognized that a war could be just in its cause yet become immoral because of the way it is fought. Hence, for a war to be morally allowable, besides the three conditions of lawful authority, just cause, and right intention, there is also to be considered the right use of means.

St. Thomas' opinions, stated so generally, needed further development. Among his many commentators, Vitoria, Suarez, and Bellarmine are outstanding in interpreting these conditions and applying them to the new nationalistic warfare of their day. Since these are the principles on which all prenuclear warfare was based, we must see them in greater detail.

LAWFUL AUTHORITY

War is an act of the political state as such. Hence only the person or body designated in the constitution of the state as having the authority to declare war can do so legitimately. Killing is wrong only when unjust, but it is always unjust when done by private authority outside the case of blameless self-defense. The soldier receives his right to kill by being legally and publicly designated as an agent of his country in the prosecution of a just war. This formality, however, is not necessary in a purely defensive war, and the authority is rightly presumed. If the country is actually being overrun by the enemy, there is no need to wait for formal induction into the armed services.

---

*St. Thomas, *Summa Theologica*, II-II, q. 40, a. 1.

Guerrilla warfare in the sense of raids unauthorized by any lawful government cannot be justified, but guerrilla tactics may be employed in a war declared by legitimate authority, especially in regions occupied by the enemy. Even the fact that a government has surrendered to an unjust invader does not mean that all underground resistance movements must cease for lack of proper authorization, for they began legitimately and may continue with hope of foreign assistance. When the government abdicated, sovereignty reverted to the people, who now tacitly acknowledge the leaders of the resistance as their temporary leaders. But after all possibility of success has been lost and the people have withdrawn their backing, guerrilla fighters would become outlaws.

JUST CAUSE

In every case just cause must be the violation, attempted or accomplished, of the nation's strict right. Such might be the carrying off of part of its population, the seizing of its territory or resources or property, or such a serious blow to the nation's honor as to weaken its authority and jeopardize its control. Territorial aggrandizement, glory and renown, envy of a neighbor's possessions, apprehension of a growing rival, personal spites and jealousies between monarchs—these and the like are invalid reasons. The just cause implies several subordinate conditions:

1. There must be a *sufficient proportion* between the good to be accomplished and the accompanying evil. War is so horrible an evil that only the most serious reasons can make it permissible. Nations must tolerate minor evils until changed times make their peaceful redress feasible. On the other hand, a nation need not be victimized by the Hitlerian technique of a series of small injuries and unjust demands, no one of which is worth fighting over, but adding up to a gradual loss of independence. Re-

sistance is allowable as soon as the aggressive intent becomes morally certain.

2. War must be *the last resort.* Before a nation takes to war it must have exhausted every peaceful means consistent with its dignity: negotiation, mediation, arbitration, diplomatic pressure, economic sanctions, ultimatums, and every other means known to enlightened statesmanship. Otherwise there is no proof that war is unavoidable and hence no sufficient proportion.

3. There must also be *fair hope of success.* This hope need not amount to moral certainty, for the fortunes of war involve too many unpredictable elements, and moral certainty could occur only when the strongest nations are fighting the weakest. There is a fair hope when it is proportionate to the evils expected. To fight when there is not even possibility of advantage is to impose evils on the nation to no purpose. However, a small nation may resist invasion as a protest against injustice and as a refusal to submit to conquest, with the hope that other nations may come to its aid.

RIGHT INTENTION

A state may have objectively good grounds for war, or be subjectively convinced that it has, and yet fight it for other reasons. It may use a just cause as an excuse to seek wrong ends, and thus spoil a good act by a bad intention. This intention may exist only in the minds of the rulers, whereas the people do no wrong in fighting because they have no such evil motives. Or an individual soldier fighting for his country in a just war kills for a motive of hatred and cruelty; his country's cause is good, but his own personal conduct is bad.

Note that a wrong intention will make the war subjectively immoral but not necessarily unjust. It is not morally allowed to continue an unjust war, and reparation must be made for the damage done; but in the prosecution of a just war an evil intention, if present at the beginning, can be corrected and the war continued for a worthy purpose.

That the war be fought with a right intention, the nation's cause must not only be just but *known to be just.* This can be presumed in a purely defensive war, but international relations have become so complex and affairs of state are kept so secret that the ordinary citizen is not always able to judge the justice of a war. Even the most bellicose nations refuse to admit that they are aggressors and put out reams of propaganda to deceive their own citizens as well as the rest of the world. After the war has been fought and all the documents are open to inspection, historians cannot always agree on war guilt.

This quandary can be handled in a practical way only by the rules for forming one's conscience. When the objective truth cannot be known, yet immediate action is imperative, there is no other recourse but to use reflex principles and arrive at a prudentially certain subjective judgment of conscience. Not only private citizens but even statesmen themselves may be obliged to rely on their consciences when objective truth cannot be determined. Thus, though no war can be objectively just on both sides, the people and their leaders on both sides may be in a state of invincible ignorance, subjectively convinced of the justice of their cause, and acting with the right intention of saving their country. Bellarmine puts this clearly, as far as soldiers are concerned:

> The cause of war should be neither trivial nor doubtful, but weighty and certain, lest perchance the war bring about more harm than the hoped-for good; hence if there is any doubt a distinction must be made between the ruler and the soldiers, for the ruler himself sins, without doubt; for war is an act of retributive justice, but it is unjust to punish any one for a cause not yet proved; but the soldiers do not sin unless it is plainly evident that the war is unlawful, for subjects ought to obey

their superior, nor should they criticize his commands, but they should rather suppose that their ruler has a good reason, unless they clearly know the contrary; just as when the offense of some particular individual is doubtful, the judge who condemns him sins, but not the executioner who carries out the sentence of death imposed on the condemned; for the executioner is not bound to criticize the sentence of the judge.[*]

Bellarmine hastens to add that he is speaking of the regular army (to which he would add conscripts and draftees, if he had heard of them), but not of volunteers and mercenaries. Since these latter are not obliged to fight but offer themselves for it, they must make certain that the cause is just.

Conscientious objection is a painful problem in which the conscience of the individual clashes with that of the nation's leaders. The ethical principles involved are fairly simple and were explained in our chapter on conscience. No country has the right to force a citizen to do what he is firmly convinced is morally wrong. One drafted by his country to fight in what seems to him a certainly unjust war, whether he has this attitude toward all war or only toward this particular war, is morally obliged to refuse to fight. Whether his judgment is objectively right or wrong is not the question here, for we are considering one who has done his best to settle his conscience and finds himself convinced that his participation in the war would be morally wrong. As we have seen, one is obliged to follow a certain conscience even when it is invincibly erroneous. Nations should have provisions for conscientious objection, and anyone whose conscience forbids him to fight is morally obliged to avail himself of them. It seems reasonable to expect that he would be required to substitute for military engagement some equivalent peaceful service to his country. One whose sincerely made plea for exemption is not granted must make his coopera-

tion in the war as remote as possible, depending on how far his conscience will let him participate in it at all.

The attitude that, to qualify as a conscientious objector, one must be a pacifist opposed to all war is logically indefensible. It supposes only two alternatives, both impossible for most: either all wars whatever are wrong, or all wars that my country fights are right merely because my country fights them. The whole idea behind the just war theory is that any country can fight a just war or an unjust war, and the judgment must be made about the particular war in question. Many judge that our response to Hitler's aggression was justified but our continued involvement in Vietnam was not. Selective conscientious objection is the only kind that makes sense. True, it may be difficult to administer so as to detect cowards and liars, and also the individual is opposing his own judgment to that of the leaders of the country, but both these difficulties are inherent in any kind of conscientious objection, and draft boards are faced with a particular war anyway. Morally acceptable legislation on this subject is a crying need not obviated by the fact that a particular crisis is over.

RIGHT USE OF MEANS

It is morally wrong to seek a good end through evil means. Hence a war might be justified in every other respect, and yet become morally wrong because of the way in which it is fought. War is an ugly thing no matter how we look on it or for what noble purposes we may undertake it. The essential means is force, and the use of force is a brutal matter admitting of no finely drawn distinctions and delicate niceties. The soldier in the heat of battle can hardly be expected to fight with a gun in one hand and a textbook of ethics in the other. Much must be excused on the grounds of invincible ignorance, the cloud-

---

[*]Bellarmine, *De Laicis,* ch. 15.

ing of reason by passion and fear, and the general background of war hysteria and propaganda. But none of this excuses us, as students of ethics, from a peacetime discussion of objective right and wrong in the fighting of a war.

It is very difficult to determine from pure reason and natural morality the means that are allowed and those that are forbidden in the fighting of a just war. Older writers tend to allow almost anything except the direct killing of the innocent. Suarez, for example, says:

> After war has been begun, and during the whole period thereof up to the attainment of victory, it is just to visit upon the enemy all losses which may seem necessary either for obtaining satisfaction or for securing victory, provided these losses do not involve intrinsic injury to innocent persons, which would be in itself an evil.°

The following points are generally agreed on in the just war theory:

1. The purpose of a just war is to put the enemy's war machine out of commission so that he can no longer use violence to wreak injustice. If this end could be attained without bloodshed, so much the better, but so far there is no method of stopping an attacking enemy without killing. In war an effective agent of an unjust government is an unjust aggressor, and he may be killed so long as he is in that condition, that is, until he is disarmed. He need not be personally guilty of his nation's unjust war, nor need he be at the moment engaged in battle. It suffices that he is an active member of an armed force seeking to inflict or maintain injustice. His opposite number, the soldier of a just government fighting a just war, is commissioned by his country's public authority to eliminate this constant menace to its safety and its rights. The soldier acts not as a private individual but as an agent of his state and with its authority. War is not

between person and person but between state and state, not a matter of individual but of national defense. The attack on the nation continues as long as the war lasts, not merely as long as this particular soldier is in danger.

2. The guilty may thus be killed, but not those who are clearly innocent. The term *guilty* here means objectively guilty, the effective agent of a nation waging an unjust war, for no one in battle could examine each enemy soldier's conscience to determine his subjective guilt. Hence in actual fighting *guilty* and *innocent* amount to the same as *combatants* and *noncombatants*, supposing them on the unjust side. In the simpler days of hand-to-hand fighting the distinction was easy to apply. There was no excuse for deliberately chopping up defenseless women and children with the sword or shooting them down with muskets. In the more complex conditions of today combatants are held to be all those who belong to the armed forces of belligerent nations and all who actively and proximately cooperate in the military effort. Since cooperation shades imperceptibly from proximate to remote, this norm may be difficult to apply. Those who perform auxiliary military services, such as workers on arms, munitions, transport, communications, and the like, despite their technical civilian status, are actually combatants; their work is directly military in nature and can have no other purpose. The same is not true of farmers, shopkeepers, and taxpayers, even though the military may need them; their cooperation is too remote. In between there will be many borderline cases.

3. On the treatment of prisoners and spies, the use of siege and blockade, the question of reprisals and hostages, the commandeering and disposal of enemy property, the rights of neutral nations, and the reparations to be exacted, natural morality can suggest only the vaguest generalities. The details have to be worked out

---

°Suarez, *The Three Theological Virtues: On Charity,* disp. XIII, sec. VII, no. 6.

by international agreement, with a view to reducing war's barbarism as far as possible. No civilized nation today could be morally justified in refusing to subscribe to such international agreements when the other nations of the world are willing to do so. States that are parties to such agreements are bound by the moral law to keep them, unless they have been substantially broken by the enemy, and even here the fact that one side does something inherently immoral gives no permission to the other side to do so. Cruelty and atrocity, barbarism and treachery are outlawed not merely by agreement but by the moral law itself.

AGGRESSION AND DEFENSE

Those who developed the just war theory seem to have had in mind chiefly offensive war and even punitive war. Defensive war appeared to them so eminently a just cause that it was either unnecessary to stipulate any conditions for it, or they were automatically fulfilled.[*] For the sake of clarity we need to lay down a few definitions.

All know what war is, some by bitter experience, so that the word itself is clearer than any definition. If we must have one, we can take that of Karl von Clausewitz: "War is an act of violence intended to compel our opponent to fulfill our will."[†] The merit of this definition is the utterly stark way in which it lays bare the essence of war: the end is to impose our will on another, and the means is violence. This definition very properly leaves out any consideration of right or justice as not belonging to war as such.

War, in the strict sense in which it is taken here, is between one whole state, sovereign and independent, and another whole state, sovereign and independent; it is not between a state and some individuals, nor between a government and its people. Sedition, insurrection, rebellion, and revolution are often called civil war but are not war in the strict sense. People in a condition of revolution are virtually in a condition of war, and it becomes formal war if the insurgents succeed in establishing a working *de facto* government in the territory they control. War is *armed* hostility; commercial rivalry and diplomatic tilts are not strictly war, nor is the so-called "cold war." War is *active* hostility; mere preparation for future aggression or defense is not war, but there must be actual fighting, though it may be intermittent.

The older writers divided war into *defensive* and *aggressive* war. There seems to be a fairly common opinion that the nation which declares war or makes the first attack is waging aggressive war, whereas the nation against which war is declared or which is attacked first is waging defensive war. But this view is too superficial and formalistic. Hear Suarez on the subject:

> It remains for us to explain what constitutes an aggressive war, and what, on the other hand, constitutes a defensive war; for sometimes that which is merely an act of defence may present the appearance of an aggressive act. . . . We have to consider whether the injustice is, practically speaking, simply about to take place; or whether it has already done so, and redress is sought through war. In this second case, the war is aggressive. In the former case, war has the character of self-defence, provided that it is waged with a moderation which is blameless.[*]

Hence a nation is fighting a defensive war if its sole purpose is to protect itself against actual or imminent aggression, even if its defense assumes the appearance of attack. Just as a man need not wait until he has been shot at before defending

---

[*]Vitoria, *De Jure Belli* (On the Right of War), no. 1, 3, and 13. Vanderpol, A., *Le droit de guerre d' après les théologiens et les canonistes du moyen âge*, pp. 42-43.

[†]Clausewitz, *On War*, vol. I, beginning.

---

[*]Suarez, *The Three Theological Virtues: On Charity*, disp. XIII, sec. I, no. 6.

himself, so a nation need not wait until it is actually invaded before using means of defense. Moral certainty of the enemy's intention seems sufficient. The formality of declaring war has been discarded by some states, and modern nations must be prepared to meet a sneak attack. The advantage of striking the first blow is so great in modern warfare that no nation, not even one merely defending itself, can afford to give this edge to the enemy. This seems to be what some modern writers call *preemptive* as opposed to *preventive* war.

Since the word *aggression* is now taken almost always in a bad sense, it is more consonant with modern usage to divide war into *offensive* and *defensive,* according to the nation responsible for provoking (not necessarily beginning) hostilities, and into *just* and *unjust,* according to the nation having moral right on its side. Aggression can then be reserved for unjust offensive war.

Punitive war, a war undertaken to punish a guilty nation, would come under the heading of a just offensive war. This is not understood to mean a war to force an unjust aggressor to give up his ill-gotten gains, which is mere restitution, but to go farther and punish him for his crime. And even if the war was not undertaken for the purpose of punishment as its chief aim, still the question of punishing those responsible for unjust aggression and barbarous conduct arises at the end of the war. The older writers, St. Augustine, St. Thomas, Vitoria, Bellarmine, and Suarez, for example, think that a punitive war can be justified. Suarez is explicit:

> Just as within a state some lawful power to punish crime is necessary to the preservation of domestic peace; so in the world as a whole, there must exist, in order that the various states may dwell in concord, some power for the punishment of injuries inflicted by one state upon another; and this power is not to be found in any superior, for we assume that these states have no commonly acknowledged superior; therefore, the power in question must reside in the sovereign prince of the injured state, to whom, by reason of that injury, the opposing prince is made subject; and consequently, war of the kind in question has been instituted in place of a tribunal administering just punishment.[°]

This opinion is opposed by those who argue that punishment is an act of jurisdiction and must be inflicted by a superior on his inferior; since no state has jurisdiction over another, punishment of a guilty nation cannot be justified. This view seems too legalistic, as if there could be no law but positive law. Where there is a superior with jurisdiction, he and not the interested party is the one to pass sentence and administer punishment, but the mere fact that there happens to be no superior distinct from the parties concerned should not make the attainment of justice impossible. Here natural law, natural right, and natural justice take over.

The same reasoning applies to the trial of *war criminals,* even though the whole war was not fought as a punitive war. It seems absurd to string a man on the gallows for a single peacetime murder and then to let those who have engaged in a set program of mass murder go scot-free, simply because nations have failed to enact a law providing for their punishment. It is hard to see how anyone who admits a morality independent of politics can call the punishment of war criminals unjust. Whether it is expedient or not is a different question. It does set a dangerous precedent that future unjust aggressors who happen to be victorious can use with deadly ferocity against their blameless victims.

So much for the traditional theory of the just war. What war in history, we may well ask, ever observed all these rules? Probably none. They are not meant to be rules or laws that are authoritatively prescribed. Who has such authority and who

---

[°]Suarez, *The Three Theological Virtues: On Charity,* disp. XIII, sec. IV, no. 5.

could possibly enforce them? Rather, they are criteria for judging war. Some wars come closer to fulfilling more of them than others and can thus be said to be more just than others: to be more legitimately authorized, to have a better objective cause, to pursue it with nobler intent, and to be more humane in its fighting conduct. We call a man good though he has some faults; we say that he is a just man though he has committed some unjust acts. So we can call a war just if it approximates justice close enough and rates high on most of the points detailed in the just war theory. War is too complex an affair to achieve a hundred percent score on all points.

NUCLEAR WAR

It is customary today to distinguish between *conventional* warfare, which includes all the wars fought hitherto, and *nuclear* warfare, which threatens to be the war of the future. The dropping of atomic bombs on Hiroshima and Nagasaki is regarded as the transition from one to the other. We need pass no moral judgment on this particular incident to discuss the principles of war in general. Past immoral use, if such it was, does not preclude a weapon's future legitimate use.

The reason for making such a sharp distinction between conventional and nuclear warfare is that some see here a difference not merely of degree but of kind. The new weapons are so utterly destructive as to introduce a new element in warfare, absent from the wars of the past, so that the old principles no longer apply. Nuclear war, it is said, essentially violates the principles of the just war. In particular nuclear pacifists argue thus:

1. *The right use of means.* Modern weapons are immoral in themselves. They cannot be directed at military targets only. Their sphere of destruction is so widespread that they must by their very nature cause more damage to civilian life and property than to military personnel and installations. They cannot be used in such a way that civilian damage is merely a regrettable by-product. The wiping out of whole cities involves the destruction of the guilty and the innocent indiscriminately. This is but mass murder on a grand scale.

2. *Reasonable hope of success.* It is impossible to win a modern-style war. Both sides lose. The losses sustained even by the technically victorious side would nullify any benefit received. Modern war is mass suicide as well as mass murder.

3. *Just cause.* The violation of a nation's strict rights is just cause for seeking redress, but not necessarily by means of war. No injured rights could be so precious as to justify the wiping out of a nation's population and the rendering of a large part of its territory uninhabitable for years to come.

4. *The proportion of good to evil.* Modern war spreads to the whole world. Even if a single nation could achieve all its war aims, the good would be canceled by the evils inflicted on all humanity through the poisoning of the atmosphere, producing diseases and mutations that would be passed on to future generations. Some go so far as to say that it would be better to accept slavery under tyranny and try to oppose it from within by nonviolent methods, hoping to infiltrate into it and eventually control it, than to engage in mass suicide by fighting it. "Better red than dead" is the slogan of this group.

5. *Legitimate authority.* No one on earth has the authority to order a nation into modern war. The complications of modern diplomacy and the efficiency of modern propaganda make it practically impossible for the ordinary citizen to determine the justice of his country's cause. How otherwise explain the millions who fought for Hitler? No longer can we blindly trust our leaders when the weight of evidence points to their probably being more wrong than right.

These and similar arguments cannot be

taken lightly. They certainly call for a re-examination of the traditional ethics of war.

1. Can the arguments be answered and nuclear war justified on the old principles?
2. Can new principles be found on which nuclear war ought to be based?
3. Can the old principles be retained but modified and reinterpreted to suit modern conditions?
4. Or is nuclear war flatly immoral, so that it must not be used even defensively?

The first question denies that there is any problem, and the last question admits that the problem is basically insoluble. The best hope of an answer is found in either of the two central questions, and perhaps in a combination of them. By modifying the traditional principles of the just war and adding one or two new restrictions, a plausible case can be made for the theory of limited nuclear war.

LIMITED NUCLEAR WAR

Bombing in itself is not intrinsically wrong. A bomb is simply a larger military weapon and, like any other, may be used against military targets; the killing of civilians, if any occurs, is incidental. Indiscriminate bombing of a city or area, with no attempt to distinguish military from non-military objectives, has been rightly considered in conventional war as mass murder. The phrase *military necessity*, which has its proper use, can be misused and twisted to cover any act, however immoral. Nor is it excused by the desire to destroy the enemy's morale and terrorize him into submission, for terror can also be produced by the grossest and most bestial atrocities without in any way making these acts moral. Thus conventional bombing can be moral or immoral, depending on how it is used.

Since a nuclear bomb is merely a bigger and more destructive bomb, its use is gov-erned by the same principles. A military target may be extensive enough to warrant the use of a nuclear bomb without disproportionate civilian damage; for example, a fleet at sea or an isolated munitions plant. The enemy cannot claim sanctuary by putting such a plant in a civilian sector and has the responsibility of evacuating the civilian population from the danger spot. If a nation is allowed to destroy a military target with a hundred ordinary bombs, why not with one nuclear bomb? Nor can it be said that the atom bomb may have legitimate use but not the hydrogen bomb. Though one works by fission and the other by fusion, it is not the method but the extent and control of the destructiveness that have moral significance. These two types of bomb overlap, the largest fission bomb being considerably more destructive and emitting more fallout than the smallest fusion bomb.

Nuclear bombs pose the problem of radioactive contamination that is absent in conventional bombs. The point of strike and its environs are not only destroyed but rendered uninhabitable for some time. The radioactive cloud is blown to civilian sectors and even to neutral countries. However, the amount reduces so rapidly as to come well within the limits of human tolerance, except near the center of the blast. Since there is natural radioactivity in the earth's crust and in cosmic rays, a nuclear explosion does not produce something entirely new but increases what is already there. Can a slightly added susceptibility to bone cancer, leukemia, and mutational defects in the germ plasm be considered a by-product of the war that can be permitted to occur in the civilian population by the principle of double effect? How much worse would this be than our peacetime pollution of the atmosphere by automobile exhausts and factory chimneys? In any war the civilians suffer greatly anyway, and in a world war even neutral nations are seriously affected, at least economically, with the possibility of malnutrition and other repercussions on the rest of their life. To impose these effects on others is not out of proportion to a nation's right to its freedom. The hazard, however, must be reduced as far as possible, and the endeavor to develop cleaner bombs is a recognized moral requirement.

Guided missiles, whether intercontinental or of shorter range, cannot be considered wrong in themselves. What is important is the charge they carry and how accurately they are directed. If a nuclear bomb is justified, so also is this means of delivering it. It must be launched at military objectives only, and its accuracy must be such that civilian casualties caused by it are only incidental.

As bombs are legitimate weapons if used properly, so also are chemical and bacteriological weapons. The difficulty in these two types of warfare is one of control. Any means of waging war that is by its very nature uncontrollable cannot be condoned on any moral principle.

It was thought necessary to make these remarks here lest anyone argue from the very nature of the weapons used. Nuclear weapons are not of their very nature immoral. They can be controlled, they can be directed against military installations and personnel, and they can be used in accordance with the principle of double effect, which allows direct attack against the guilty but permits only incidental harm to the innocent.

Despite what has been said, the terrible and extensive nature of the weapons used in a nuclear war even of a limited character imposes some restrictions not present in former wars. Some* think that we must make the following additions to the theory

of the just war. They can be formulated in two propositions:

1. *Any war of aggression, even a just offensive war, is morally forbidden.* This statement goes counter to the traditional teaching on the just war, according to which war was a legitimate means of recovering violated rights. One reason is that the character of modern war requires much more serious reasons to justify it. Any nation that initiates war, even for the best of causes, needs overwhelmingly strong reasons to compensate for the damage done and for the danger of drawing the rest of the world into the conflict. In these days it is hard to conceive of any past grievance that could compensate for breaking an existing peace. Another reason is the existence of international tribunals and the United Nations. To bypass them at this critical juncture of their struggling existence by direct appeal to the sword would postpone indefinitely man's only hope of a peaceful world.

2. *A defensive war to preserve a nation's rights and freedom by the use of effective means is morally admissible.* There is no peace without justice, law, and order. Free field cannot be given to brutal violence and lack of conscience. A nation's defense is not restricted to conventional weapons, since to be adequate, its weapons must match the weapons of the attackers. Nuclear warfare of a limited character may be used morally under the following conditions:

First, the war must be imposed on the nation by the enemy's obvious and grave injustice. Defensive war is not defined in terms of declaring war or crossing borders or dropping the first bombs, but the war must be thrust on the nation by an enemy's unjust act that can be met and stopped.

Second, nuclear weapons, if used, must be indispensable for defense. The enemy must either already have resorted to nuclear weapons, or there must be moral certainty that he will do so.

---

*This material is taken from John Courtney Murray, "Remarks on the Moral Problem of War," *Theological Studies,* March, 1959, reprinted in *We Hold These Truths,* ch. 11, and in *Morality and Modern Warfare,* ch. 5.

Third, the proportion of good to evil, including the prospect of success, must be maintained. This proportion is not to be estimated only in terms of deaths and physical damage but takes in such values as a nation's liberty and independence, which have always been thought a valid cause for war.

Fourth, a new principle of limitation is introduced. Conventional warfare is naturally limited by the limited destructiveness of the weapons used. Now that the new weapons have almost unlimited destructiveness, limitation in war must be voluntarily imposed by man. This principle of limitation bans a war of extermination and the unloosing of an evil that wholly escapes man's control.

TOTAL WAR

It may be said that the foregoing discussion is unrealistic, for the next world war is not going to be a limited war. Thus we are led to the concept of total war. It is supposed to be the ultimate in absolute horror and, among its other totalities, totally immoral. If this is what the term means to most people, we had better not try to make it respectable. However, we can distinguish some levels of totality. "Total" means "all," but all of what?

1. A totally total war would involve the extinction of all mankind, an apocalyptic Armageddon that would wipe out vanquished, victor, and everybody else, whether by an explosion that would shatter the earth itself, or by a radioactive pollution of the earth's whole atmosphere, or by a bacterial epidemic that would rage wholly out of control. Obviously, such a war could not be defensive and could accomplish no good.

2. Total war might mean a war of extermination and obliteration of the enemy, the systematic wiping out of a whole people with all their cities and goods. Some such wars may have occurred in history, but it is difficult in these days to imagine the rest of the world standing by and letting it happen. Even so, it would be utterly immoral. No whole people can be so vicious as to deserve such a fate.

3. Total war might mean a war waged for the purpose of imposing absolute defeat on the enemy by the use of any and every means available and with no consideration of humanity or morality. It is probably this meaning of total war that has given the term its execrable reputation. No wonder! It has immorality built into its definition.

4. A fourth meaning might be only this, that the nation has mobilized all its personnel and all its resources for the war effort and will use them all if need be. Such a war need not be total in its aims but only in its means, and even the means, though all of them may be used, may be restricted in their use to what is morally allowable. This kind of war is total only in a very restrained sense, and it is better not to call it by that name. An aggressive war of this kind would be immoral, not from the fact that it is total in this modified sense but from the fact that it is aggression. On the other hand, a nation unjustly attacked by these methods would have difficulty defending itself except by the adoption of the same technique, by the mobilization and use of all its personnel and resources for defense.

If it is to preserve some semblance of morality, a thermonuclear war of defense would have to fit under this last heading. The abandonment of the theory of massive retaliation, the development of cleaner bombs, the greater accuracy of the means of delivery, the "no cities rule," and the confining of attacks to definite military targets all indicate a better understanding of what the consciences of people can tolerate.

Still, there is danger of escalation. The moralist who bases the morality of war on the principle of legitimate defense must fix the place beyond which war cannot go and remain moral, and he should find it in the very notion of defense itself. Just as a nation that causes a war to begin with, that is responsible for changing peace into war, is the aggressor, so the nation that causes the escalation of a war henceforth becomes the aggressor to that extent, even if it began as the defender. A war can turn from moral to immoral by the later adoption of an immoral mode of fighting. This is not to say that a nation may never escalate a war for the sake of getting it over more quickly, but the decision to do so must be based on an estimation of the total proportion of good to evil as it affects oneself, the enemy, and the rest of the world.

BOMBING OF CITIES

What if a war does actually escalate through the enemy's initiative to the point where it threatens to become a mutual thermonuclear bombing of cities? Must the defender give up, or may he respond in kind? Many, and not only nuclear pacifists, consider such bombing to be absolutely wrong because it is a direct attack on the civilian population, and they warn that the good end of self-defense may not be obtained by the use of morally evil means. The disadvantage to the defenders will have to be made up in some other way— by more adequate preparation, by greater cleverness of strategy, by better use of resources, by building up an indefectible morale. If the conditions of limited war do not prevail, it is our business to create such conditions and impose them on any potential enemy. The task is enormous, but the stakes are high enough to call forth the ultimate in human ingenuity.

Yet not all are satisfied that this position is realistic enough. Limited nuclear defense may be adequate for the present danger and the next world conflict, if there is one, but is it a universal principle for all time? It is an indubitable moral principle

that we may not use evil means to accomplish an end, however good, but on the other hand we cannot admit that evil is inevitably destined to triumph because we are forbidden the only means that could oppose it. Are these means necessarily immoral in the situation we are considering? Five arguments for the affirmative have already been given.[*] Five arguments for the negative are tentatively suggested here for what they are worth. They should at least stimulate discussion:

1. It is said that the distinction between combatant and noncombatant must still be maintained in modern war but that the class of noncombatants has been diminishing until in all-out war it becomes a null class. More and more civilians are engaged in war work until one whole nation in arms is facing another whole nation in arms. Thus they all become legitimate targets and may be attacked directly. The only exceptions are children, the aged, and the sick, and it is the enemy's responsibility to evacuate them from all potential danger spots.

2. Another way of arguing is to question the distinction between combatant and noncombatant. How absolute is it? Does it come from the nature of things or rest on convention? Does it really correspond to the older writers' distinction between the guilty and the innocent, or is it only a relic of hand-to-hand fighting inapplicable to modern conditions? Then the battlefield was a nicely marked-off spot that civilians could avoid, but now there are no battlefields. Is there any absolute reason why a nation must commit its defense to a specified group of its population designated as combatants and must respect a similar distinction among its attackers, when the enemy refuses to respect any such distinction and exploits its immunity? Then, who is the combatant in a push-button

---

[*]See p. 414.

war? The one who fires the intercontinental missile, the one who commands him to fire it, the few who constructed the instrument, or the scientists who developed it? In this kind of war the conscripted foot soldier, despite his uniform, is hardly more of a combatant than anyone else.

3. A third argument looks at the city itself as the modern equivalent of the ancient fortress. Siege has always been considered a legitimate form of warfare, even though it caused more suffering to the besieged civilians than to the military. The whole city could be burned or starved into submission, the harm to any civilians present being an indirect consequence, according to the principle of double effect. *Who* are the direct object of attack is determined not by their number but by their function, and if the place absolutely must be taken, the proportion of good to evil can still be observed. A fortress commanded the whole countryside and had to be reduced if the war was to be successful. Today the metropolitan centers of population are the nerve ganglia of the whole country, the centers for railroads, highways, shipping, communication, manufacturing, fuel storage, food processing, and distribution of all materials on which a modern mechanized army relies completely. Such centers of the enemy's fighting potential must be put out of commission.

4. Another mode of argument looks for the overriding moral principle in this clash between defense and the proper use of means. Some things are only conditionally evil. Under normal conditions they must not be done, but in a desperate situation they cease to be evil because of some other and prevailing principle. A common example is that of marriage between brother and sister, which is normally prohibited because it is harmful to the family and the proper continuance of the race, but which would be allowed if these were the only two people left on earth, because in this extreme case it would be the only possible

family and the only way of continuing the race. Likewise, the killing of enemy noncombatants is normally evil but may not be so in the desperate situation in which the very survival of the nation is at stake. The whole question of war is one of survival, and in this case the survival of enemy noncombatants against the survival of the defender's whole state. If the enemy has started to bomb our cities indiscriminately and the only way of stopping a second and a third strike is by massive retaliation, why should our non-combatants have to continue to die because we are forbidden to kill theirs?

5. For all evils nature supplies a remedy: for fire there is water, for hunger there is food, for darkness there are lamps, for poisons there are antidotes. Nature's remedy for force is counterforce. Against the wrong use of force there is the right use of it. This right use is the only moral justification for any war, nuclear or conventional, just as it is the only moral justification for self-defense, but nature cannot be so constructed that evil must necessarily triumph because of a moral prohibition to use the remedy nature has provided. When the wrong use of force escalates, so must the counteracting right use of force if it is to be more than an empty gesture.

These arguments have been expressed, not to defend a "hawkish" position, but to stimulate the citizen of a nuclear nation to make up his mind what he will do if some foreign power starts dropping nuclear bombs on his country. He knows that it will not sit still and take it. How does he adjust himself morally to such a situation?

DISARMAMENT

All of the foregoing is only an interim solution, an adjustment to an imperfect world, which is the world we have to live in, and live in morally. The ultimate goal has to be the banishment of all war. It will take much time and effort, including a changeover from excessively nationalistic to internationalistic thinking, but the very survival of man on this planet makes that goal an imperative.

In the meantime every effort at disarmament must be made. But no nation can be expected to disarm while its potential enemies remain armed. So long as some are unwilling to submit to a system of international inspection and control, mutual disarmament is an empty illusion. The only interim solution is to match arms for arms in the hope that neither side would dare to use them first, knowing the price of retaliation. This is the perpetuation of an irrational condition, but those who thrust it on the world by their refusal to cooperate must bear the responsibility. Unilateral disarmament would be a government's abdication of its moral duty to protect its people.

Hence it is not wrong to conduct nuclear tests and to stockpile nuclear weapons in peacetime, at least until disarmament can actually be effected. Some say that it is allowable to have such weapons for deterrence, so long as they will never be used, but there is some incoherence in this thinking. Is it allowed to threaten to do to another what you think it would be immoral to do in actual fact? You can hardly tell the enemy that you will not use these weapons, if they are to have a deterrent effect, nor can you tell your own people without informing the enemy. Hence they have to go on the assumption that the weapons will be used, if deterrence fails to deter, and have to adjust their consciences to this possibility.

CONCLUSION

War is one of the most regrettable things that has come to deface our fair world, a useless, wasteful, man-made evil. But we must live with the breed of men we find in this world, and if they make war on us, we must defend ourselves. Otherwise the good must live as slaves of the wicked, who will then be free for every kind of violence and tyranny. In such a world there could be no peace. War is therefore an evil, but sometimes an unavoidable one. In a just war it is the duty of every citizen to support his country at the expense of fortune, liberty, and even of life itself if necessary, and his country has the right to call on him for such support. How to steer his country through the tangles of international complications without recourse to war's horrors is the virtue of the statesman.

SUMMARY

Militarism glorifies war; *pacifism* condemns it, either absolutely or relatively. Most think that war can sometimes be morally justified. It may be the only means a state has to protect or recover its lawful rights or even to preserve itself in being; it has a natural right to the means necessary to this end.

The just war theory has *three conditions for a just war:*

1. *Lawful authority.* War is an act of the state as such and must be properly authorized. This authorization gives the soldier his right to kill and use force. So long as there is hope, guerrilla fighting and underground resistance movements are lawful, even when the government that authorized them has fallen.

2. *Just cause.* This condition can be the result of either the attempted or the accomplished violation of a nation's strict rights. There must be *sufficient proportion* between the good intended and the evil permitted. War must be the *last resort* after the breakdown of all feasible forms of negotiation. There must be *fair hope of success,* or there can be no proportion.

3. *Right intention.* Objective grounds for war may exist, and yet the nation may fight it for the wrong motives. The cause must be *known to be just;* if it is doubtful, subordinates can form their consciences

420

and trust to the wisdom of their leaders. Nations must make proper provisions for *conscientious objectors,* even for those who object against a particular war only, and those who are firmly convinced of the wrongness of the war must refuse to fight in it. The punishment of war criminals can be defended as an act of natural justice.

There is one added condition for a *morally allowable* war:

4. *Right use of means.* A war otherwise justifiable can become wrong by the way it is fought. The right way is the putting of the enemy's effective war machine out of commission. The treatment of prisoners, spies, and hostages; the use of siege and blockade; and the handling of enemy property and respect for the rights of neutrals—these and similar matters are only vaguely indicated by natural morality and are determined by custom and international agreement. Such contracts must be kept unless they are substantially broken by the other side, but no nation may do what is inherently immoral because the other side does so.

Defensive war is *just* when fought to repel an unjust aggressor, even when the defense takes the appearance of attack. *Offensive* war is *just* when fought to vindicate seriously violated rights; otherwise it is *unjust* aggression.

Nuclear warfare can be limited and can thus be made to conform to the accepted principles. Some would add two new qualifications: that any war of aggression, even a just offensive war, is morally forbidden; and that the limitation of warfare, formerly automatic because of the small weapons used, must now be voluntarily imposed.

Total war may mean the extermination of the human race, or of a whole people, or the use of any means, however immoral. In all these senses it is utterly immoral. The mobilization of a nation's whole manpower and resources for its own defense is not immoral. Is it allowed to bomb enemy cities in massive retaliation as defense against further bombings? Both a yes and a no answer have their difficulties.

Disarmament is to be promoted, but unilateral disarmament is unrealistic.

QUESTIONS FOR DISCUSSION

1 Does it not seem that even the attempt to justify so irrational and inhuman a thing as war must itself be an immoral undertaking? If war could be made moral by a verbal listing of conditions, what cannot be made moral?

2 Even granting that a purely defensive war could be just, how in actual practice can defense and offense be distinguished, since the causes leading up to a war are so complex? How many wars of history verify the conditions of a just war?

3 What is your view on the status of combatant and noncombatant? Is this a natural law distinction, a *jus gentium* distinction, one based on historical convention, or one resting on treaty only? Is the distinction still valid in nuclear war?

4 What do you think of total war? Is a defensive total war as a response to an aggressive total war possible? If it is possible, is it

also moral? Is limited nuclear war the only kind of nuclear war that could be moral? Is it possible?

5 Have the nations of the world a moral obligation to tend toward disarmament? Is any nation morally obliged or morally allowed to disarm unilaterally? If no nation starts to disarm, how can disarmament begin? If any nation starts first, does it not fail in its obligation to defend its people?

READINGS

The older writers who formed the theory of the just war, though they had no notion of modern war, still have something valuable to tell us. Read St. Augustine, *City of God*, bk. XIX, ch. 5-17; St. Thomas, *Summa Theologica*, II-II, qq. 40-42; Francis de Vitoria, *De Jure Belli* (On the Right of War) and *De Bello* (On War), both translated in J. B. Scott, *Francisco de Vitoria and His Law of Nations;* St. Robert Bellarmine, *De Laicis, or the Treatise on Civil Government*, ch. 14-15; Francis Suarez, *The Three Theological Virtues: On Charity*, disp. XIII (On War), translated in J. B. Scott, *Classics of International Law: Suarez*, vol. II, pp. 797-865; and Hugo Grotius, *Rights of War and Peace*, especially bk. I and III.

The following modern works on war in general will be useful: John K. Ryan, *Modern War and Basic Ethics;* John Eppstein, *Code of International Ethics* and *The Catholic Tradition of the Law of Nations;* and Heinrich Rommen, *The State in Catholic Thought*, ch. 19.

On pacifism: M. K. Gandhi, *Non-Violence in Peace and War*, reprints his numerous papers and authoritatively describes his position. Franziskus Stratmann, *War and Christianity Today*, is among the most forceful of pacifist literature. Roland Bainton, *Christian Attitudes Toward War and Peace*, is moderately pacifist with a good historical survey. John C. Ford's article, "The Morality of Obliteration Bombing," in *Theo-logical Studies*, vol. V (1944), is an outspoken criticism of this phase of World War II.

James Finn edits *A Conflict of Loyalties: the Case for Selective Conscientious Objection.*

On nuclear war: Herman Kahn, *On Thermonuclear War* and *Thinking about the Unthinkable*, though not treating of ethics, set the stage by analyzing what to expect in future wars. Peter Hodgson, *Nuclear Physics in Peace and War*, is a very clear short summary. The pacifist case is presented in Charles S. Thompson (ed.), *Morals and Missiles;* Walter Stein (ed.), *Nuclear Weapons, a Catholic Response;* and Justus Lawler, *Nuclear War, the Ethic, the Rhetoric, the Reality.* Bertrand Russell, *Common Sense and Nuclear Warfare*, continues as a redoubtable champion of pacifism.

William Nagle (ed.), *Morality and Modern Warfare*, is a good symposium. Paul Ramsey, *War and the Christian Conscience*, is an excellent, well-balanced study. Thomas E. Murray, *Nuclear Policy for War and Peace*, argues for limited war only, as does John Courtney Murray, "Remarks on the Moral Problems of War," in *Theological Studies*, vol. XX (1959), reprinted in his own book, *We Hold These Truths*, ch. 11, and in Nagle's symposium, ch. 5. A very pertinent short study is William V. O'Brien, *Nuclear War, Deterrence and Morality.*

Austin Fagothey, *Right and Reason—an Anthology*, contains John Courtney Murray's article "War as a Moral Problem," ch. 11 of his book, *We Hold These Truths.*

422

CHAPTER 37

PEACE

PROBLEM

If war is an irrational condition of mankind, and if wars are not made by the common people but by the leaders of nations, and if the reason that nations have been unable to settle their differences without war is that there is no higher authority to which they can appeal and whose decisions they will respect, the question that immediately comes to mind is: Why do not nations establish such an authority?

The logic of the situation seems so reasonable that we may forget that human beings do not act on logic alone. Individuals often see very clearly what they ought to do, but they do not do it. It is harder to get a group moving than an individual, and the larger and more complex the group, the harder it is. To move the whole human race, already caught up in a vast network of interlocking societies, has so far been an unsuccessful task. But the point has been reached where, unless this problem is solved, the very survival of man is at stake. We ask these questions:

1. What is man's normal condition, peace or war?
2. What has been done toward international organization?
3. Is international organization possible?
4. Is international organization necessary?
5. How do nationalism and internationalism argue their case?
6. Can sovereignty be limited?

MAN'S NORMAL CONDITION

We must face the fact that in the history of mankind wars have been almost continual. Thomas Hobbes wrote:

Hereby it is manifest that during the time men live without a common power to keep them all in awe, they are in that condition which is called war; and such a war as is of every man against every man. For war consisteth not in battle only, or the act of fighting, but in a tract of time wherein the will to contend by battle is sufficiently known, and therefore the notion of time is to be considered in the nature of war, as it is in the nature of weather. For as the nature of foul weather lieth not in a shower or two of rain, but in an inclination thereto of many days together; so the nature of war consisteth not in actual fighting, but in the known disposition thereto, during all the time there is no assurance to the contrary. All other time is peace.[*]

If Hobbes could write thus in the seventeenth century, what would he say of our modern nations, which are permanently organized on a military basis? Each nation must live in constant fear of its neighbors, while the armament race, war of nerves, cold war, economic blockade, espionage, propaganda, and ideological warfare fill the interval between open hostilities. By Hobbes' definition there has been no peace within the memory of any man now alive.

Despite the grain of truth in Hobbes' statement, we cannot accept his view that war is the normal and natural condition of man, that war is the positive reality and

---

[*]Hobbes, *Leviathan*, ch. 13.

peace is only its negation. Which is the normal condition is not to be judged by the amount of time a nation spends in peace or war but by an analysis of the nature of each. The normal does not mean the most frequent, but the standard by which things are measured. There are probably only a few perfectly healthy persons in the world, but disease cannot be regarded as the normal thing. International society is a chronic invalid indeed, but it is a fallacy to make its disease the very substance of its life.

St. Augustine's oft-quoted words containing his two famous definitions of peace as "well-ordered concord" and "tranquility of order" deserve to be read and pondered:

Whoever gives even moderate attention to human affairs and to our common nature, will recognize that if there is no man who does not wish to be joyful, neither is there any one who does not wish to have peace. For even they who make war desire nothing but victory—desire, that is to say, to attain peace with glory. For what else is victory than the conquest of those who resist us? and when this is done there is peace. It is therefore with the desire for peace that wars are waged, even by those who take pleasure in exercising their warlike nature in command and battle. And hence it is obvious that peace is the end sought for by war. For every man seeks peace by waging war, but no man seeks war by making peace. For even they who intentionally interrupt the peace in which they are living have no hatred of peace, but only wish it changed into a peace that suits them better. They do not, therefore, wish to have no peace, but only one more to their mind. . . .*

The peace of the body then consists in the duly proportioned arrangement of the parts. The peace of the irrational soul is the harmonious repose of the appetites, and that of the rational soul the harmony of knowledge and action. The peace of body and soul is the well-ordered and harmonious life and health of the living creature. Peace between man and God is the well-ordered obedience of faith to eternal law. Domestic peace is the well-ordered concord between those of the family who rule and those who obey. Civil peace is a similar concord among the citizens. The peace of the

celestial city is the perfectly ordered and harmonious enjoyment of God, and of one another in God. The peace of all things is the tranquility of order. . . . As, then, there may be life without pain, while there cannot be pain without some kind of life, so there may be peace without war, but there cannot be war without some kind of peace, because war supposes the existence of some natures to wage it, and these natures cannot exist without peace of one kind or another.*

The common philosophical tradition is that peace is the positive reality because it is the good, whereas war is the evil that consists in the privation of this good. The state exists for the sake of preserving and promoting peace, both within itself and with other states; war is the result of some state's failure as a political and social entity. A state does not exist for the sake of waging war and of using peace only as a breathing space to prepare for more war; rather, it is supposed to go to war only for the sake of achieving a just and honorable peace. No cynical observations on how nations really do act can destroy the moral obligation placed on every nation, and on every citizen of every nation, to work for peace.

HISTORY OF PEACE EFFORTS

The idea of a worldwide society embracing all nations is not new but has been prevalent throughout the ages. As imaginative writers have put forth innumerable utopias portraying what they thought the ideal structure of a single state, so there have been many idealistic schemes of world union. The difference is that, although the ideal state has never existed, there do exist real states that function despite their defects; world union, on the other hand, has never yet even come near real accomplishment. However, there have been some more or less promising endeavors in that direction, roughly

---

*St. Augustine, *City of God*, bk. XIX, ch. 12.

Ibid., ch. 13.

paralleling the development of international law.

In ancient times the Roman Empire took on itself the task of governing the then known world. Without consciously facing the problem, it solved it by the method of *one dominant nation,* and the solution was remarkably successful so long as the Empire preserved its vigor. Three main defects are apparent in this solution: the Empire itself had to be built up by war and conquest before it could maintain world peace; it never did include the whole world, and its overextension contributed much to its downfall; and the solution was satisfactory to the dominant Romans but galling and irksome to their subjugated peoples. Militant dictatorships have tried this sort of solution in our time; free peoples will have none of it.

Medieval society naturally turned to the Church as a model of international organization. Why could not nations produce in the political sphere what the Church had successfully accomplished in the religious sphere? Feudalism, with its hierarchical arrangement of overlord and vassal, its limitation and subordination of powers, supplied the means for effecting this organization and logically tended toward a union of the whole world. Dante in his *De Monarchia* envisions the Pope and the Emperor side by side, one supreme in the spiritual and the other in temporal matters, with all other rulers owing them fealty. This arrangement never got far beyond the stage of an ideal, and as a political venture the Holy Roman Empire was among the less successful, but the ideal colored the whole of medieval political thinking. This concept is past all hope of revival.

When the decline of feudalism and the breakup of united Christendom made the medieval ideal impossible, Renaissance writers such as Grotius turned to international law as the means for keeping the peace. Nations might retain full sovereignty yet cooperate by voluntary agreement. The Congress of Vienna, which assembled after the French Revolution and the Napoleonic Wars, the Geneva Convention and the Court of Arbitration at The Hague, the League of Nations after the first World War, and the United Nations of today are various attempts to mitigate or outlaw war and to maintain the peace of the world. They have had a moderate success in mediating small disputes but none at all in preventing the two world wars that have wracked our century. If we succeed in avoiding a third world war, the credit for doing so will hardly go to the United Nations as constituted at present.

The difficulty seems to be that, so long as each nation is unwilling to part with any of its sovereignty, there is no way of making any international organization authoritative and effective. World wars are not caused by small countries, which can easily be kept in line by threat of intervention, but by the great powers. If each sovereign great power can veto any decision it does not like, the only decisions that are of value are unanimous ones, and if there is unanimity, there is no dispute to settle. Hence a world organization along these lines seems to be either inadequate or superfluous, except as the expression of a hope that it will some day develop into an effective instrument.

POSSIBILITY OF INTERNATIONAL ORGANIZATION

Can we say that because efforts toward a really working international organization in the past have been unsuccessful, they must necessarily be so throughout all the future? Surely this conclusion would be unwarranted. Here a distinction must be made between the absolute perfectionists and those who are willing to limit themselves to human possibilities. The ideal of the absolute perfectionist can never be realized, for all human works are imperfect, and utopia in this world can never be more than a dream. This limitation affects single states as well as international organizations. We cannot hope that all threat of war will forever be abolished from the earth, any more than we can hope to see our own government functioning without the slightest snarl or hitch. But approximations to the ideal are possible, and man is able by his own efforts, aided by social cooperation, to improve his condition. That is how he advanced this far, and who is to tell him he must stop? There is a midpoint between a foolish optimism and a paralyzing pessimism.

This problem is the concern of the moral philosopher and of the practical statesman. It can be phrased in two questions:

1. Is mankind today morally obliged to work toward the establishment of an effective world organization?
2. How can a world organization be set up that will have authority and will be effective of world peace?

The first question alone concerns the moral philosopher; the second is for the practical statesman and outside our province. When we examined the theory of the state we did not try to draw up a constitution for any country, and when we studied industrial relations we merely suggested a few of the practical means of bringing management and labor into accord; so now we merely point out to men politically organized into separate nations with occasionally conflicting interests their international obligations and leave to their ingenuity the construction of the instruments.

One may immediately object that there can be no obligation to do the impossible, and thus until the second question is answered the first cannot be. This objection would be valid if we could prove that no effectual world organization is possible, neither now nor at any future time. But how can this be proved? If a man has an obligation to fulfill, but the means he is now using are futile, he is not thereby freed from the duty of seeking better means. We are not yet certain that better means can never be devised. If the refusal of even one great power to cooperate with the rest of the world makes useless all present effort toward international organization, we have no certainty that this situation must be perpetual. Does not that nation brand itself as guilty of immoral conduct, thus confirming the existence of the moral obligation?

Hence the first question can be answered independently of the second. If a thing can be proved impossible, there is no sense in trying to accomplish it. But if it cannot be proved possible except by actually doing it, we cannot wait for proof of possibility before starting to work at it. An international organization cannot be proved impossible, and positive proof of its possibility can come only from success in the effort.

NECESSITY OF INTERNATIONAL ORGANIZATION

The argument here is only a logical extension of the proof used to show that man is morally obliged to organize himself into political society. There it was said that the state is the natural outgrowth of the family; that when a number of families in a region find it impossible to defend themselves or to supply their needs singly, they are morally obliged to cooperate for their common good; that when a simple tribal organization becomes inadequate, they are further obliged to form themselves into the society called the state and to set up governmental machinery with authority to carry on political functions. The formerly autonomous family was obliged to surrender part of its independence to create the sovereignty of the newly fashioned state.

Because of the diffusion of the human race across geographical barriers and the lack of contact between isolated sections, a number of political states sprang up in different parts of the world. It was formerly quite possible for each state to be wholly or nearly self-sufficient. It could defend itself against aggression from without and maintain law and order within, besides supplying its people with their comparatively simple needs. There were wars, all too fierce and frequent, but they were mostly localized. As yet there was no call for an international organization; travel was too difficult, and much of the world's surface was undiscovered.

Today advancing civilization and scientific discovery have broken through all geographical barriers and brought every part of the world into closest contact with every other part. No longer can any nation live in isolation, no matter how hard it tries. National economy is geared to world economy, and national peace is dependent on world peace. Overnight any nation can find its livelihood throttled or its territory the battleground of a world war through no action of its own. The self-sufficiency of the individual state has all but disappeared. Small states, though still technically sovereign, are caught up in the orbits of a few great powers, and these powers are at loggerheads, threatening to embroil the whole world in their clash. There is plainly a need of something larger than the state itself to curb international lawlessness.

As human society outgrew the family and, without destroying the family, required the formation of a larger organization, the state, so today human society is outgrowing the state and, without destroying it, is beginning to demand the formation of a still more extensive organization, a world society. Within each state the civil law can do efficiently enough its work of keeping order and making human life livable, but between states we find fear, suspicion, insecurity, deceit, disorder, and lawlessness, and the only court of appeal is force. Man is morally obliged to do his best to eliminate such evils from his international life. As now conducted, man's international life does not square with the norm of morality, for it is not rational.

NATIONALISM AND INTERNATIONALISM

In the debate between nationalism and internationalism, the nationalists argue that the dreams of the internationalists, as contained in the foregoing and similar arguments, are unrealistic. For example:

1. The nations of the world are viable entities, for despite their imperfections they actually exist. But a union of all nations is unworkable. They are too diverse in location, race, resources, needs, language, and culture. They may communicate in words, but they do not understand each other. They cannot be made to agree or cooperate even for their mutual benefit.

2. A federation of nations on the analogy of the United States of America is impracticable. The thirteen colonies were alike in language and culture, and occupied a single contiguous region. Even the union they created was unable to avoid a disastrous civil war. Thus a federation is not the answer to the problem of war nor an assurance of lasting peace between nations.

3. Our international efforts have succeeded in establishing only an international debating society. Hardly any accomplishment matches the enormous flood of words. No nation is willing to sacrifice even the least advantage and refuses to accept the decision of the majority. Votes of censure are cynically disregarded.

4. Every nation deserves representation in any international body, but the

nations are so unequal in size and power that it is impossible to organize them equitably. Why should two tiny backward states have twice the vote of one large progressive state with twenty times their combined population? The large nations' veto power, designed to counterbalance this anomaly, is the most abused feature of the United Nations.

5. We see that no sooner are all nations united in one organization than they begin jockeying for position. Power blocs and splits are formed among them, negating the purpose for which they are united. What advantage is this over the alignment of nations by treaties and the workings of the balance of power?

6. To equip the world organization with legislative, executive, and judicial power is to make of it a superstate, whatever we call it. The tendency of a supergovernment is to absorb more and more power to itself, even if it is constituted on federal or confederated lines. The encroachment of the federal government in the United States should be a salutary warning. Ultimately the nations of the world, if they form a superstate, will have bartered away their sovereignty, and independence.

7. There is the greater danger, not only of the world organization dominating the nations under it, but of one powerful nation seizing control of the world organization and using it as a means of making itself the world ruler. Thus a world organization could be perverted from its whole purpose. From being a protector of the rights of peoples it would become their destroyer.

8. Contrary to its intent, the argument actually proves, not that nations can be organized to preserve peace among them, but that there can be no peace so long as there are nations. It would follow that the state is not a natural society but only a transitory one that history is outgrowing. By proving too much, it proves nothing.

The internationalists think they can meet objections of this sort. For instance:

1. Would a project such as the Roman Empire have seemed viable to anyone undertaking explicitly to organize it? True, it came into being on imperial lines and not on democratic lines, but it was so successful because it allowed much local autonomy to its constituent nations. We have now learned representative democracy and a better way of combining local autonomy with central control. No democratic body achieves full agreement, but it can come to a practical settling of differences without war.

2. It would certainly be a much more difficult task to organize the nations of the world than to unite the American colonies, but there is more contact between even the remotest nations today than there was between neighboring colonies two centuries ago. Simultaneous translations make language no longer a barrier, and we know more about each other's customs and culture than ever before. We engage in international trade without difficulty; why should we think politics a region of irresolvable conflict? The American Civil War was a disaster indeed, but no one thinks that it could be repeated.

3. The United Nations is ineffective precisely because nations are unwilling to sacrifice the least advantage and refuse to accept the decision of the majority. The organization has no teeth, no power to enforce its decisions. No nation will take the lead in applying sanctions. The organization itself must have power above the separate nations.

4. Each nation deserves representation, but there should be some way of making the representation proportional. Why should there be more difficulty in doing this between nations than within a single nation made up of unequal regions and groups? Much ingenuity would be needed to devise the best scheme, but where is there a better use for human ingenuity?

5. Jockeying for position, blocs and alignments, lobbying and horsetrading, characterize all human assemblies and should be expected in an assembly of nations. Let nations try to gain what advantage they can by talk, if only they will refrain from war, the sort of war that will destroy us all. Balance of power is one of the ways to curb power, especially if there is a superpower to keep it from getting out of balance.

6. There are those who find nothing repulsive in a worldwide superstate. If hundreds of millions of people can be united in one state, why not the several billion that make up the whole planet? Others prefer a federation or a confederacy, some with more, some with less national autonomy. Tendency toward encroachment by the world organization would have to be resisted, but would that be harder to cope with than the encroachment of nation against nation, as we have had to face in several world wars?

7. The ambition of one nation to dominate the world organization and use it as a means of world domination would have to be curbed by the other nations. They have to do this anyway, world organization or not. They would find in a world organization a ready-made means for acting together with a united front against encroachment, instead of being obliged to oppose it piecemeal, as now. Every effort should be made to build into the world organization checks and balances that would make the chance of a take-over as remote as possible. It would not be perfect, but it can be better than anything we have now.

8. If unlimited sovereignty is an absolute requirement for a state, then it would be impossible to organize states into any effective world organization without eliminating the states as distinct entities. But many challenge this concept of sovereignty, thinking it not only unnecessary but the very thing that will destroy all states

if each one persists in claiming this fiction. The next section examines this point more fully.

LIMITATION OF SOVEREIGNTY

To be authoritative the world society, whatever form it may take at the dictation of political prudence, must have legislative, executive, and judicial power. To provide it with these powers individual states will have to consent to some limitation of their sovereignty. Any suggestion of this sort raises an agonized protest from outraged nationalism and a vigorous waving of the flag. But such protest is beside the point. Limitation of sovereignty is not in any way contrary to true patriotism, but only to that vicious sort of nationalism which is akin to racial and religious prejudice or is committed to a program of militaristic imperialism. Exaggerated nationalism has never been a virtue but a vice, the very vice from which most of our international chaos springs.

Limitation of sovereignty is only a recognition of the ethical fact that no human right can be absolutely unlimited. National freedom and independence must be maintained, but what right have we to make national *sovereignty* into such a fetish that we must wreck the world in order to preserve it? Sovereignty is only a means to an end, the common good; when it swells to such a size that it blocks the path to the end, it must be trimmed down to its proper proportions. As the rights of the individual are limited by the rights of other individuals, as the rights of the family are limited by the rights of other families, so the rights of the state are limited by the rights of other states and of mankind in general.

Some say that the very concept of sovereignty requires that it be unlimited, that the notion of limited sovereignty is a contradiction in terms. There is good historical

429

background for this interpretation, since the idea of sovereignty was developed to fit the claims of the newly emerged absolutist and autocratic monarchies of the sixteenth century. Jean Bodin,* originator of this concept, defines sovereignty as "the absolute and perpetual power of the commonwealth," and says that it "is not limited either in power, charge, or time," that the sovereign prince is "divided from the people," "is the image of God," and "need give account only to God." Democratic and other nonabsolutist states use the word *sovereignty* even in such a phrase as *sovereignty of the people,* but for them it can mean no more than independence, autonomy, nonsubjection to another state. There still remains about it some aura of its former meaning, some connotation of irresponsibility. If sovereignty must mean absolute and unlimited power it can belong to God alone, and never was or could be a real attribute of any state or prince. We have long ago repudiated any such fantastic claims of states and princes, and if the word *sovereignty* still has this meaning for us, we had better drop it.

Each state has the right to autonomy and independence, to full control over its domestic affairs, to *internal* sovereignty (if we wish to use that word). There is no reason why it must continue to insist on absolute *external* sovereignty, why it should not accept the guidance and submit to the authority of a world organization in the control of such of its international affairs as have worldwide repercussions and can lead to a worldwide disaster, engulfing that very state itself. Small states today, though clinging to the fiction of unlimited sovereignty, are practically obliged to accept the guidance of the great powers in their international behavior. The great powers are the ones that need curbing, and if this is not to be done by the system of the *one*

dominant nation, it must be done by some organization superior to them all. Limitation of sovereignty is merely the acknowledgment of an existing fact, anyway. It would not destroy a nation's dignity but only its lawless irresponsibility. An individual does not lose his dignity by becoming a citizen, nor should a state by becoming a member of an efficiently organized family of nations.

CONCLUSION

The very survival of the human race depends on man's ability to solve this question of worldwide peace. The condition of international bumbling, with a world war breaking out every generation, never was a tolerable condition, and now that we have the ability to destroy ourselves and ruin our planet as a place to live in, the prospect of another world war is altogether too ghastly to face. If the human race succeeds in destroying itself, it will not be nobody's fault; it will be our fault. We see the condition facing us and have the moral obligation to do something about it. World apathy in the presence of such destructive forces is an unreasonable attitude and not excusable because, by refusing to look at it, we foster a present moment of illusory safety. Will we continue sunk in the morass of unreason, or will we have the vision and courage to rise to the next step logically indicated in the social organization of humanity?

This is undoubtedly the main moral problem before the world today. We may never see it solved in our lifetime, but we cannot shirk the responsibility of seeking some solution and trying to lay the first stones in the edifice. The answer just suggested has been dismissed as visionary by tradition-directed minds still relying on a vanished isolation. Those who think so are invited either to devise a solution of their own or to justify the present world disorder by what ethical reasons they can find.

---

*Bodin, *De la république,* bk. I, ch. 8. See Maritain, *Man and the State,* ch. 2.

Meanwhile the world rolls on. Man does not have to wait, in fact he cannot wait, for the solution of the social and international problems to live his personal life. Whatever be the social conditions in which his lot is cast and whatever be his opportunity for contributing to the common betterment of mankind, the individual has his own life to live and his own personal character to develop in its distinctive uniqueness. He can always freely guide his life in such a way as to discharge his moral duty, fulfill his moral aspirations, and thus arrive at the possession of the highest good.

SUMMARY

Despite its frequency, war is the disease of man's political life, peace its normal condition. Wars should be fought to secure peace, peace should not be only a preparation for more war. Peace is the positive good, war the evil that is its privation.

Attempts to organize the nations of the world in the interest of international harmony have all been futile. This does not prove that the nations never can be organized, but only that we have not yet found successful means to this end. It is not for ethics to find these means, but to point out our obligation to search for them.

That an *international organization is necessary* is but a logical continuation of the argument that the state is necessary. The individual is insufficient and forms the family, the family is insufficient and forms the tribe, the tribe becomes insufficient and organizes itself into the political state. Today, because of the surmounting of geographical barriers, the state is no longer self-sufficient and must band with the other states of the world for their mutual safety and benefit.

Nationalists claim that a world organization is impossible because of the diversity of nations, the complexity of the organization, the wordy debates, the inequity of representation, the blocs and splits among the constituents, the tendency toward centralization, the danger of domination by a strong power, and the extinction of the states in a superstate.

Internationalists acknowledge the difficulties but think that they can be overcome. If the organization can offer some hope of eliminating world wars, it will be worth all the effort and will certainly be better than our present condition, which offers no such hope.

To be *authoritative and effective* a world society needs legislative, executive, and judicial power, so that states will have to consent to some *limitation of sovereignty.* Sovereignty cannot be absolute anyway but is limited by the rights of other states. A transfer of political sovereignty in matters that concern the peace of the world, provided all other states did the same, would not compromise a nation's dignity or independent equality with all other nations; it would only curb the lawless irresponsibility with which the great powers have pursued their selfish ambitions.

The present international chaos is immoral. If the foregoing solution be unacceptable, right reason demands that some better one be sought.

QUESTIONS FOR DISCUSSION

1 What seems to be the chief failure in the various peace ventures of the past? Can practical politicians be expected to bother about

the ethical theories of philosophers? Is speculation on these matters doomed to futility?

2 What hope is there in the United Nations? Is there a moral obligation to support the United Nations, or is that optional? Should it be supported until something better can be devised?

3 What is your theory on national sovereignty? Must it be supreme, absolute? Can it be divided? Is the notion of limited sovereignty a contradiction? Has a nation the moral right to hand over part of its sovereignty to a more inclusive organization?

4 Is a world state inevitable? Would the formation of a world federation or confederation with real power tend to greater and greater centralization until it forms in effect one world empire? Is this too great a price to pay for peace? Is it the only price?

5 Is it moral for a man to concentrate solely on the living of his own individual moral life and to wash his hands of social, national, and international problems as something he can do nothing about? Is he involved in these matters by the mere fact that he is human?

READINGS

Read Immanuel Kant's famous little essay, *Perpetual Peace,* which is perhaps the first articulate call for world peace through world organization.

Two popes, Benedict XV in the first World War and Pius XII in the second, have expressed themselves on world organization, John XXIII in his encyclical letter, *Pacem in terris* (Peace on earth), and Paul VI in his address to the United Nations reinforce their statements. Though speaking as religious leaders, they base their views on the dictates of reason and political philosophy.

Robert M. Hutchins' lecture, *St. Thomas and the World State,* has some interesting speculations;

so also has Mortimer Adler's *How to Think about War and Peace.* Read Jacques Maritain, *Man and the State,* ch. 1-2, 7, and Heinrich Rommen, *The State in Catholic Thought,* ch. 31-32.

Don Luigi Sturzo, *Nationalism and Internationalism,* ch. 8-9, has pertinent material.

William Ebenstein, *Modern Political Thought,* reprints some provocative articles from prominent writers on the passage from nationalism to world order.

Austin Fagothey, *Right and Reason—an Anthology,* contains Kant's essay, *Perpetual Peace,* and St. Augustine's passages from *The City of God,* bk. XIX, ch. 12-14, 17.

BIBLIOGRAPHY

Revised and updated by Milton Gonsalves, S.J.

CLASSICAL PHILOSOPHERS AND MORALISTS

Plato, *Dialogues*. In Benjamin Jowett, *The Dialogues of Plato*, 5 vols., London, Oxford University Press, Inc., 1892. Other translations and editions.

Aristotle, *Nicomachean Ethics, Politics, Metaphysics, Categories, Posterior Analytics, Rhetoric, On the Generation of Animals*. In W. D. Ross (ed.), *The Works of Aristotle Translated into English*, 12 vols., Oxford, The Clarendon Press, 1908-1952. Other translations and editions.

Lucretius, *On the Nature of Things*, translated by Cyril Bailey, Oxford, The Clarendon Press, 1910. Other translations and editions.

Cicero, *Tusculan Disputations, On Duties, On the Republic, On Laws, Academics, Paradoxes of the Stoics, For Milo*. Loeb Classical Library, Cambridge, Mass., Harvard University Press. Other translations and editions.

Seneca, *Letters* (Epistolae Morales), 3 vols., *Moral Essays* (Dialogi Morales), 3 vols., Loeb Classical Library, New York, G. P. Putnam's Sons, 1917-1935.

Epictetus, *Discourses*, 2 vols., Boston, Little, Brown & Co., 1891. Other editions.

Marcus Aurelius, *Meditations*, New York, A. L. Burt Co., Inc., n.d. Other translations and editions.

Diogenes Laertius, *Lives and Opinions of Eminent Philosophers*, 2 vols., Loeb Classical Library, Cambridge, Mass., Harvard University Press, 1925.

St. Augustine, *The City of God, On Free Will, Against Faustus the Manichaean, Questions on the Heptateuch, On Lying, Against Lying, The Happy Life, On the Morals of the Catholic Church, On Christian Doctrine*. English translations in the Fathers of the Church Series, New York, Cima Publishing Co., and in the Ancient Christian Writers Series, Westminster, Md., The Newman Press. The English titles vary in different editions.

Boethius, *The Theological Tractates* and *The Consolation of Philosophy*, Loeb Classical Library, Cambridge, Mass., Harvard University Press, 1918.

St. Isidore of Seville, *Etymologies*. In Migne, *Patres Latini*, vol. 82, Paris, 1850. No English translation available.

Abelard, Peter, *Ethics, or Know Thyself*. In J. R. McCallum, *Abelard's Ethics*, Oxford, Basil Blackwell & Mott, Ltd., 1935.

St. Thomas Aquinas, *Summa Theologica, Summa Contra Gentiles, In Libros Ethicorum, De Veritate, De Regimine Principum*.
Commentary on the Nicomachean Ethics, Chicago, Henry Regnery Co., 1964.
On Kingship to the King of Cyprus (De Regimine Principum), Toronto, Pontifical Institute of Mediaeval Studies, 1949.
Summa Theologica, 3 vols., New York, Benziger Brothers, Inc., 1947. Older edition in 22 vols., Benziger Brothers, Inc., 1911-1929. Blackfriars Edition, Latin with English translation, New York, McGraw-Hill Book Co., 1963-1965.
Truth (De Veritate), 3 vols., Chicago, Henry Regnery Co., 1953.
On the Truth of the Catholic Faith (Summa Contra Gentiles), 6 vols., New

York, Doubleday & Co., Inc., 1954. Older edition in 5 vols., Benziger Brothers, Inc., 1923.

Cajetan, Thomas de Vio, *Commentaries on the Summa Theologica of St. Thomas.* In the Leonine Edition of St. Thomas' works. No English translation.

Machiavelli, Niccolò, *The Prince and Other Works,* New York, Farrar, Straus, & Giroux, Inc., 1941.

Bodin, Jean, *On the Commonwealth* (De la république). An abridged translation by M. J. Tooley, New York, The Macmillan Co., 1955.

James I. In Charles McIlwain (ed.), *The Political Works of James I,* Cambridge, Mass., Harvard University Press, 1918.

Vitoria, Francisco de, *On the Indians, On the Right of War, On War.* In J. B. Scott, *The Spanish Origin of International Law: Francisco de Vitoria and His Law of Nations,* Oxford, The Clarendon Press, 1934.

Bellarmine, St. Robert, *On the Laity.* In *De Laicis, or the Treatise on Civil Government,* New York, Fordham University Press, 1928.

Suarez, Francisco, *On Laws, Defense of the Catholic Faith, On the Theological Virtues: Charity.* In J. B. Scott, *The Classics of International Law: Selections from Three Works of Francisco Suarez,* Oxford, The Clarendon Press, 1944.

Grotius, Hugo, *The Rights of War and Peace,* New York, Universal Classics Library, 1901.

De Lugo, John Cardinal, *On Justice and Right* (De Justitia et Jure), Venice, N. Pezzana, 1751. No English translation.

Hobbes, Thomas, *The Elements of Law, Natural and Politic,* New York, Barnes & Noble Books, 1969.
Leviathan, Oxford, The Clarendon Press, 1909. Many other editions.

Descartes, René, *Meditations, Objections and Replies.* In *The Philosophical Works of Descartes,* London, Cambridge University Press, 1931. Many other editions.

Spinoza, Baruch, *Ethics, Theologico-Political Treatise, Political Treatise.* In *Chief Works of Spinoza,* New York, Dover Publications, Inc., 1951. Many other editions of the *Ethics.*

Leibniz, Gottfried, *Principles of Nature and Grace.* In *Leibniz Selections,* New York, Charles Scribner's Sons, 1951.

Locke, John, *Letter Concerning Toleration,* New York, Appleton-Century-Crofts, 1937.
Two Treatises of Government, New York, Hafner Publishing Co., Inc., 1947. Contains Sir Robert Filmer's *Patriarcha.*

Cudworth, Ralph, *Treatise Concerning Eternal and Immutable Morality.* In Selby-Bigge, in Raphael, and in Rand.

Mandeville, Bernard de, *An Inquiry into the Origin of Moral Virtue.* In *The Fable of the Bees,* etc. In Selby-Bigge, in Raphael, and in Rand.

Shaftesbury, Anthony, Earl of, *Characteristics of Men, Manners, Opinions and Times.* In Selby-Bigge, in Raphael, and in Rand.

Clarke, Samuel, *Discourse upon Natural Religion.* In Selby-Bigge and Raphael.

Hutcheson, Francis, *Illustrations on the Moral Sense,* ed. by Bernard Peach, Cambridge, Mass., Belknap Press of Harvard University Press, 1971.
An Inquiry into the Original of Our Ideas of Beauty and Virtue. In Selby-Bigge, in Raphael, and in Rand.

Butler, Joseph, *The Works of Joseph Butler,* vol. 2, *Sermons,* Oxford, The Clarendon Press, 1874. In Selby-Bigge, in Raphael, and in Rand.

Edwards, Jonathan, *Freedom of the Will,* ed. by Arnold S. Kaufman and William K. Frankena, Indianapolis, The Bobbs-Merrill Co., Inc., 1969.

Hume, David, *Inquiry Concerning Human Understanding,* Indianapolis, The Bobbs-Merrill Co., Inc., 1955.
Inquiry Concerning the Principles of Morals, Indianapolis, The Bobbs-Merrill Co., Inc., 1957.
Treatise of Human Nature, Oxford, The Clarendon Press, 1888.

Malthus, Thomas, *On Population,* ed. by Anthony Flew, Harmondsworth, England, Penguin Books, Ltd., 1971.

Montesquieu, Charles Louis de Secondat, *The Spirit of the Laws,* translated by Thomas Nugent, introd. by Franz Neumann, New York, Hafner Publishing Co., 1949.

Smith, Adam, *The Theory of Moral Sentiments.* In *Smith's Moral and Political Philosophy,* New York, Hafner Publishing Co., Inc., 1948. In Selby-Bigge, in Raphael, and in Rand.
The Theory of Moral Sentiments, New Rochelle, N.Y., Arlington House, Inc., 1969.

Reid, Thomas, *Essays on the Active Powers of Man.* In *The Philosophical Works of Thomas Reid,* vol. II, Edinburgh, James Thin, 1895.

Rousseau, Jean Jacques, *The Social Contract,* New York, Hafner Publishing Co., Inc., 1947.

Kant, Immanuel, *Fundamental Principles of the Metaphysic of Morals, Critique of Practical Reason, The Metaphysic of Morals, Lectures on Ethics, Perpetual Peace.* Numerous translations and editions. All are in the Library of Liberal Arts, Indianapolis, The Bobbs-Merrill Co., Inc., except *Lectures* (New York, Harper & Row, Publishers).
Kant's Political Writings, ed. by Hans Reiss, translated by H. B. Nisbet, Cambridge, Cambridge University Press, 1970.

Hegel, Georg W. F., *Encyclopaedia of the Philosophical Sciences,* Oxford, The Clarendon Press, 1892.
Phenomenology of Mind, translated by J. B. Baillie, New York, The Macmillan Co., 1931.
Philosophy of Right, Oxford, The Clarendon Press, 1949.
Science of Logic, New York, The Macmillan Co., 1929.

Schopenhauer, Arthur, *The World as Will and Idea,* 3 vols., London, Trübner & Co., 1883-1886.
Complete Essays of Schopenhauer, translated by T. B. Saunders, New York, Willey Book Co., 1942.

Kierkegaard, Søren, *Concluding Unscientific Postscript,* London, Oxford University Press, 1941.
Fear and Trembling, Sickness unto Death, Princeton, N.J., Princeton University Press, 1941.
Philosophical Fragments, Princeton, N.J., Princeton University Press, 1941.

Nietzsche, Friedrich, *Thus Spake Zarathustra, Beyond Good and Evil, Genealogy of Morals.* In Collected Works, New York, Russell & Russell Inc., Publishers, 1964.

Comte, Auguste, *The Positive Philosophy of Auguste Comte,* condensed by H. Martineau, 2 vols., London, Trübner & Co., 1853.

Bentham, Jeremy, *An Introduction to the Principles of Morals and Legislation,* New York, Russell & Russell, Inc., Publishers, 1962. Other editions.

Huxley, Thomas H., *Evolution and Ethics,* New York, Kraus Reprint Co., 1969. Reprint of 1897 ed.

Mill, John Stuart, *Essays on Economics and Society,* London, Routledge & Kegan Paul, Ltd., 1967.
Mill's Ethical Writings, ed. by J. B. Schneewind, New York, The Macmillan Co., 1965.
Utilitarianism, On Liberty, Representative Government, London, J. M. Dent & Sons, Ltd., Publishers (Everyman's Library), 1957.

Sidgwick, Henry, *The Methods of Ethics,* London, Macmillan & Co., Ltd., 1901, 1968.

Spencer, Herbert, *The Principles of Ethics,* 2 vols., New York, D. Appleton & Co., 1896.

Marx, Karl, *Capital: a Critique of Political Economy,* New York, The Modern Library, 1936.

Capital: a Critique of Political Economy, ed. by Frederick Engels, translated by Samuel Moore and Edward Aveling, 3 vols., New York, International Publishers Co., Inc., 1967.

A Contribution to the Critique of Political Economy, New York, The International Library Publishing Co., 1904.

Critique of the Gotha Programme, New York, International Publishers Co., Inc., 1938.

Critique of Political Economy, translated by S. W. Ryazanskaya, London, Lawrence & Wishart, Ltd., 1971. (Original, 1859).

Pre-Capitalist Economic Formations, New York, International Publishers Co., Inc., 1965.

Revolution and Counterrevolution, ed. by E. M. Aveling, London, George Allen and Unwin, Ltd., 1971.

Selected Writings in Sociology and Social Philosophy, translated by T. B. Bottomore, ed.; introd. and notes by T. B. Bottomore and Maximilien Rubel; foreword by Erich Fromm, New York, McGraw-Hill Book Co., 1964.

Fromm, Erich (ed.), *Marx's Concept of Man,* New York, Frederick Ungar Publishing Co., Inc., 1961.

Marx, Karl, and Engels, Friedrich, *The German Ideology,* New York, International Publishers Co., Inc., 1947.

The Holy Family, Moscow, Foreign Languages Publishing House, 1956.

Engels, Friedrich, *Anti-Dühring; Herr Eugen Dühring's Revolution in Science,* Moscow, Foreign Languages Publishing House, 1962.

Dialectics of Nature, New York, International Publishers Co., Inc., 1960.

Ludwig Feuerbach and the Outcome of Classical German Philosophy, New York, International Publishers Co., Inc., 1941.

The Origin of the Family, Private Property and the State, Moscow, Foreign Languages Publishing House, 1959.

Selected Writings, ed. by W. O. Henderson, Baltimore, Penguin Books, Inc., 1967.

Socialism, Utopian and Scientific, Moscow, Foreign Languages Publishing House, 1958.

Lenin, Vladimir I., *Imperialism, the Highest Stage of Capitalism,* Moscow, Foreign Languages Publishing House, 1947.

The State and Revolution, Moscow, Foreign Languages Publishing House, 1947; New York, International Publishers Co., Inc., 1954 (copyright 1932).

Possony, Stefan T. (ed.), *Lenin Reader,* Chicago, Henry Regnery, 1966.

Mao Tse-tung, *Papers: Anthology and Bibliography,* ed. by Ch'en Jerome, London, Oxford University Press, 1970.

Selected Works, 5 vols., New York, International Publishers Co., Inc., 1954—.

Newman, John Henry, Cardinal, *Apologia pro Vita Sua,* New York, D. Appleton & Co., 1865.

Grammar of Assent, London, Burns, Oates & Co., 1870.

The Idea of a University, London, Longmans, Green & Co., 1885.

Bradley, Francis Herbert, *Ethical Studies,* London, P. S. King & Son, Ltd., 1876.

Moore, G. E., *Ethics,* 2nd rev. ed., New York, Oxford University Press, 1966.

Principia Ethica, London, Cambridge University Press, 1903.

James, William, *Pragmatism,* New York, Longmans, Green & Co., Inc., 1907.

Principles of Psychology, 2 vols., New York, Henry Holt & Co., 1890.

The Will to Believe, New York, Longmans, Green & Co., Inc., 1932.

Dewey, John, *Human Nature and Conduct,* New York, Henry Holt & Co., 1922.

The Quest for Certainty, New York, Minton, Balch & Co., 1929.

Reconstruction in Philosophy, New York, Henry Holt & Co., 1920.

Theory of Valuation, Chicago, The University of Chicago Press, 1939.

Perry, Ralph Barton, *General Theory of Value,* Cambridge, Mass., Harvard University Press, 1926.

Realms of Value, Cambridge, Mass., Harvard University Press, 1954.

Russell, Bertrand, *Authority and the Individual,* London, George Allen & Unwin, Ltd., 1966.

The Conquest of Happiness, New York, Liveright, 1958 (1930, 1st ed.).

Human Society in Ethics and Politics, New York, Simon & Schuster, Inc., 1955.

Marriage and Morals, New York, Liveright, 1957 (1929, 1st ed.).

Mysticism and Logic, New York, Longmans, Green & Co., Inc., 1918.

Road to Freedom: Socialism, Anarchism and Syndicalism, New York, Barnes & Noble Books, 1966.

Why Men Fight: A Method of Abolishing the International Duel, New York, Garland Publishing, Inc., 1972 (copyright 1916).

Brentano, Franz, *Foundation and Construction of Ethics,* translated by E. H. Schneewind, London, Routledge & Kegan Paul, Ltd., 1972; New York, Humanities Press, 1973.

The Origin of Our Knowledge of Right and Wrong, ed. by Oskar Kraus; Eng. ed. by R. M. Chisholm, translated by R. M. Chisholm and E. H. Schneewind, London, Routledge & Kegan Paul, Ltd.; New York, Humanities Press, Inc., 1969.

Hartmann, Nicolai, *Ethics,* 3 vols., New York, The Macmillan Co., 1932.

Heidegger, Martin, *Being and Time,* translated by J. Macquarrie and E. Robinson, New York, Harper & Row, Publishers, 1962.

Sartre, Jean-Paul, *Being and Nothingness,* New York, Philosophical Library, Inc., 1956.

Existentialism, New York, Philosophical Library, Inc., 1956.

Maritain, Jacques, *Essay on Christian Philosophy,* New York, Philosophical Library, Inc., 1955.

Existence and the Existent, New York, Pantheon Books, Inc., 1948.

Freedom in the Modern World, New York, Charles Scribner's Sons, 1936.

Moral Philosophy: an Historical and Critical Survey of the Great Systems, New York, Charles Scribner's Sons, 1964.

The Person and the Common Good, New York, Charles Scribner's Sons, 1947.

The Range of Reason, New York, Charles Scribner's Sons, 1942.

The Rights of Man and Natural Law, translated by Doris C. Anson, New York, Gordian Press, Inc., 1971.

Science and Wisdom, New York, Charles Scribner's Sons, 1940.

True Humanism, New York, Charles Scribner's Sons, 1938.

Gilson, Étienne, *Moral Values and Moral Life,* Hamden, Conn., The Shoe String Press, Inc., 1961.

The Christian Philosophy of St. Thomas Aquinas, New York, Random House, Inc., 1956.

MODERN BOOKS ON ETHICS

Acton, Henry B., *Kant's Moral Philosophy,* London, Macmillan Publishers, Ltd., 1970.

Adler, Mortimer, *A Dialectic of Morals,* Notre Dame, Ind., The Review of Politics, University of Notre Dame Press, 1941.

The Idea of Freedom, Garden City, N. Y., Doubleday & Co., Inc., 1958.

The Time of Our Lives: the Ethics of Common Sense, New York, Holt, Rinehart & Winston, Inc., 1970.

Aiken, Lillian W., *Bertrand Russell's Philosophy of Morals,* New York, Humanities Press, Inc., 1973.

Aschenbrenner, K., *The Concept of Value, Foundations of Value Theory,* Dordrecht, the Netherlands, D. Reidel Publishing Co., 1971.

Atkinson, R. F., *Conduct: an Introduction to Moral Philosophy,* London, Macmillan Publishers, Ltd., 1969.

Ayer, A. J., *Language, Truth and Logic,* London, Victor Gollancz, Ltd., 1950.

Baier, Kurt, *The Moral Point of View,* Ithaca, N. Y., Cornell University Press, 1958.

Barr, Stringfellow, *The Three Worlds of Man,* Columbia, Mo., University of Missouri Press, 1963.

Barrett, William, *Irrational Man,* Garden City, N. Y., Doubleday & Co., Inc., 1958.

Beardsmore, R. W., *Moral Reasoning,* London, Routledge & Kegan Paul, Ltd., 1969.

Becker, Lawrence C., *On Justifying Moral Judgments,* London, Routledge & Kegan Paul, Ltd., 1973.

Bonhoeffer, Dietrich, *Ethics,* New York, The Macmillan Co., 1955.

Bourke, Vernon J., *Ethics,* ed. 2, New York, The Macmillan Co., 1966.
History of Ethics: a Comprehensive Survey of the History of Ideas from the Early Greeks to the Present Time, New York, Doubleday Publishing Co., 1968.

Broad, C. D., *Five Types of Ethical Theory,* London, Routledge & Kegan Paul, Ltd., 1930.

Brody, Baruch, *Moral Rules and Particular Circumstances,* Englewood Cliffs, N.J., Prentice-Hall, Inc., 1970.

Buber, Martin, *I and Thou,* translated by Walter Kaufmann, New York, Charles Scribner's Sons, 1970.

Campbell, C. A., *In Defense of Free Will,* New York, Humanities Press, Inc., 1967.
On Selfhood and Godhood, New York, The Macmillan Co., 1957.

Camus, Albert, *The Myth of Sisyphus,* New York, Alfred A. Knopf, Inc., 1955.
The Rebel, New York, Alfred A. Knopf, Inc., 1954.

Collins, James, *The Existentialists,* Chicago, Henry Regnery Co., 1952.

Corbett, Patrick, *Ideologies,* London, The Hutchinson Publishing Group, Ltd., 1965.

Cronin, Michael, *The Science of Ethics,* 2 vols., New York, Benziger Brothers, Inc., 1922.

D'Arcy, Eric, *Conscience and its Right to Freedom,* New York, Sheed & Ward, 1962.
Human Acts, Oxford, The Clarendon Press, 1963.

D'Arcy, Martin, *The Mind and Heart of Love,* London, Faber & Faber, Ltd., 1945.

D'Entrèves, A. P., *Natural Law,* London, Hutchinson & Co. (Publishers), Ltd., 1951.

De Rougemont, Denis, *Love in the Western World,* New York, Pantheon Books, Inc., 1956.

Desan, Wilfrid, *The Planetary Man,* 2 vols., New York, The Macmillan Co., 1972.

Dilman, Ilham, and Phillips, D. Z., *Sense and Delusion,* New York, Humanities Press, Inc., 1971.

Dorszynski, Julian A., *The Catholic Teaching about the Morality of Falsehood,* Washington, The Catholic University of America Press, 1949.

Dworkin, Gerald, *Determinism, Free Will, and Moral Responsibility,* Englewood Cliffs, N.J., Prentice-Hall, Inc., 1970.

Edel, Abraham, *Ethical Judgment: the Use of Science in Ethics,* New York, The Free Press, 1964.
Method in Ethical Theory, Indianapolis, The Bobbs-Merrill Co., 1963.

Edgley, Roy, *Reason in Theory and Practice,* London, The Hutchinson Publishing Group, Ltd., 1969.

Ewing, A. C., *The Definition of Good,* new ed., London, Routledge & Kegan Paul, Ltd., 1966.
Ethics, London, English Universities Press, Ltd., 1953.
The Morality of Punishment with some Suggestions for a General Theory of Ethics, Montclair, N.J., Patterson Smith Publishing Corp., 1970 (reprint of 1929 ed., London, Kegan Paul).

438

Farrell, Walter, *Companion to the Summa,* 4 vols., New York, Sheed & Ward, 1938. Volumes II and III on ethical subjects.

Field, G. C., *Moral Theory,* London, Methuen, 1966.

Findlay, J. N., *Axiological Ethics,* London, Macmillan Publishers, Ltd., 1970.

Fingarette, Herbert, *On Responsibility,* New York, Basic Books Inc., Publishers, 1967.

Fletcher, Joseph, *Moral Responsibility,* Philadelphia, The Westminster Press, 1967. *Situation Ethics,* Philadelphia, The Westminster Press, 1966.

Flew, A. G. N., *Evolutionary Ethics,* New York, St. Martin's Press, 1967.

Fotion, N., *Moral Situations,* Yellow Springs, Ohio, Antioch Press, 1968.

Frankena, William K., *Ethics,* new ed., Englewood Cliffs, N.J., Prentice-Hall, Inc., 1974.

Franklin, R. L., *Freewill and Determinism,* New York, Humanities Press, Inc., 1968.

Fried, Charles, *An Anatomy of Values: Problems of Personal and Social Choice,* Cambridge, Mass., Harvard University Press, 1970.

Fromm, Erich, *The Art of Loving,* New York, Harper & Row, Publishers, 1956.

Fuss, Peter, *The Moral Philosophy of Josiah Royce,* Cambridge, Mass., Harvard University Press, 1965.

Garner, Richard T., and Rosen, Bernard, *Moral Philosophy: a Systematic Introduction to Normative Ethics and Meta-ethics,* New York, The Macmillan Co., 1967.

Gauthier, David P., *The Logic of Leviathan: the Moral and Political Theory of Thomas Hobbes,* London, Oxford University Press, 1969. *Morality and Rational Self-Interest,* Englewood Cliffs, N.J., Prentice-Hall, Inc., 1970.

Girvetz, Harry K., *Beyond Right and Wrong,* New York, The Free Press, 1973.

Glass, Bentley, *Science and Ethical Values,* Chapel Hill, N.C., University of North Carolina Press, 1965.

Glover, Jonathan, *Responsibility,* London, Routledge & Kegan Paul, Ltd., 1970.

Gosling, J. C. B., *Pleasure and Desire: the Case for Hedonism Reviewed,* Oxford, The Clarendon Press, 1969.

Gotesky, Rubin, *Personality: the Need for Liberty and Rights,* New York, Libra Publishers, Inc., 1967.

Greene, Norman, *Jean-Paul Sartre: the Existentialist Ethic,* Ann Arbor, Mich., University of Michigan Press, 1960.

Grice, Godfrey Russell, *The Grounds of Moral Judgment,* New York, Cambridge University Press, 1967.

Hampshire, Stuart, *Freedom of the Individual,* New York, Harper & Row, Publishers, 1965. *Morality and Pessimism,* Cambridge, Cambridge University Press, 1972. *Thought and Action,* New York, The Viking Press, Inc., 1960.

Hare, R. M., *Applications of Moral Philosophy,* London, Macmillan Publishers, Ltd.; Berkeley, Calif., University of California Press, 1972. *Essays on Moral Concepts,* London, Macmillan Publishers, Ltd., 1972. *Freedom and Reason,* New York, Oxford University Press, Inc., 1965. *The Language of Morals,* new ed., London, Oxford University Press, 1973.

Harrison, Jonathan, *Our Knowledge of Right and Wrong,* London, George Allen & Unwin, Ltd., 1971.

Hart, H. L. A., *The Morality of the Criminal Law,* London, Magnes Press; London, Oxford University Press, 1965.

Hartman, Robert S., *The Structure of Value: Foundations of Scientific Axiology,* Carbondale, Ill., Southern Illinois University Press, 1967.

Hawkins, D. J. B., *Man and Morals,* New York, Sheed & Ward, 1960.

Hazo, Robert, *The Idea of Love,* New York, Praeger Publishers, Inc., 1967.

Hildebrand, Dietrich von, *Christian Ethics,* New York, David McKay Co., Inc., 1953.

Hodgson, D. H., *Consequences of Utilitarianism: a Study in Normative Ethics and Legal Theory,* Oxford, The Clarendon Press, 1967.

Hook, Sidney, *Education and the Taming of Power,* LaSalle, Ill., Open Court Publishing Co., 1973.

Reason, Social Myths and Democracy, New York, Harper & Row, Publishers, 1965.

Hospers, John, *Human Conduct,* New York, Harcourt, Brace & World, Inc., 1961.

Hudson, W. D., *Ethical Intuitionism,* New York, St. Martin's Press, 1967.

Modern Moral Philosophy, London, Macmillan Publishers, Ltd., 1970.

Johann, Robert O., *The Meaning of Love,* Westminster, Md., The Newman Press, 1955.

Johnson, Oliver, *Moral Knowledge,* The Hague, Martinus Nijhoff, 1966.

The Moral Life, London, George Allen & Unwin, Ltd., 1969.

Jonsen, Albert R., *Responsibility in Modern Religious Ethics,* Washington, Corpus Books, 1968.

Kaplan, Abraham, *American Ethics and Public Policy,* New York, Oxford University Press, 1958, 1963.

Kattsoff, Luis O., *Making Moral Decisions: an Existential Analysis,* The Hague, Martinus Nijhoff, 1965.

Kaufman, A., *The Science of Decision Making: an Introduction to Praxeology,* translated by R. Audley, London, George Weidenfeld & Nicolson, Ltd., 1968.

Kaufmann, Walter, *Without Guilt and Justice, From Decidophobia to Autonomy,* New York, Peter H. Wyden/Publishers, 1973.

Kaye, Michael, *Morals and Commitment,* London, Covent Garden Press, 1971.

Kemp, J., *Ethical Naturalism: Hobbes and Hume,* London, Macmillan Publishers, Ltd., 1970.

Kenner, George C., *The Revolution in Ethical Theory,* London, Oxford University Press, 1966.

Klubertanz, George, *Habits and Virtues,* New York, Appleton-Century-Crofts, 1965.

Philosophy of Human Nature, New York, Appleton-Century-Crofts, 1953.

Knox, Sir Malcolm, *Action,* New York, Humanities Press, Inc., 1968.

Kolenda, Konstantin, *The Freedom of Reason,* San Antonio, Texas, The Princip Press of Trinity University, 1964.

Kovesi, Julius, *Moral Notions,* London, Routledge & Kegan Paul, Ltd., 1967.

Kurtz, Paul, *Decision and the Condition of Man,* Seattle, University of Washington Press, 1965.

Lehmann, Paul, *Ethics in a Christian Context,* New York, Harper & Row, Publishers, 1963.

Lepp, Ignace, *The Authentic Morality,* New York, The Macmillan Co., 1965.

Lewis, C. I., *Analysis of Knowledge and Valuation,* LaSalle, Ill., Open Court Publishing Co., 1946.

Values and Imperatives, Stanford, Calif., Stanford University Press, 1969.

Lewis, C. S., *The Four Loves,* London, Geoffrey Bles, Ltd., Publishers, 1960.

Lewy, Casimir, *G. E. Moore on the Naturalistic Fallacy,* from *Proceedings of British Academy,* vol. L (1964), London, Oxford University Press, 1965.

Loring, L. M., *Two Kinds of Values,* foreword by Karl Popper, London, Routledge & Kegan Paul, Ltd., 1966.

Mabbott, J. D., *An Introduction to Ethics,* London, The Hutchinson Publishing Group, Ltd., 1966; New York, Doubleday Publishing Co., 1969.

McCloskey, H. J., *Meta-Ethics and Normative Ethics,* The Hague, Martinus Nijhoff, 1969.

McGann, Thomas F., *Ethics: Theory and Practice,* Chicago, Loyola University Press, 1971.

McGrath, Patrick, *The Nature of Moral Judgment,* London, Sheed and Ward, Ltd., 1967.

McGill, V. J., *The Idea of Happiness,* New York, Praeger Publishers, Inc., 1967.

Macintyre, Alasdair, *Against the Self-Images of the Age, Essays on Ideology and Philosophy,* London, Gerald Duckworth & Co., Ltd., 1971; New York, Schocken Books, Inc., 1971.

A Short History of Ethics, New York, The Macmillan Co., 1966.

Mackay, Donald, *Freedom of Action in a Mechanistic Universe,* Cambridge, Cambridge University Press, 1967.

Macmurray, John, *Freedom in the Modern World,* London, Faber & Faber, Ltd., 1968.

Persons in Relation, London, Faber & Faber, 1959; New York, Humanities Press, Inc., 1962, 1970.

Reason and Emotion, London, Faber & Faber, Ltd., 1935.

The Self as Agent, London, Faber & Faber, 1957; New York, Humanities Press, Inc., 1969.

Macquarrie, John, *Three Issues in Ethics,* London, SCM Press, Ltd., 1970.

Mandelbaum, Maurice H., *The Phenomenology of Moral Experience,* Baltimore, The Johns Hopkins University Press, 1969.

Margenau, Henry, *Ethics and Science,* Princeton, N.J., D. Van Nostrand Co., Inc., 1964.

Margolis, Joseph, *Psychotherapy and Morality: a Study of Two Concepts,* New York, Random House, Inc., 1966.

Maslow, Abraham H., *Toward a Psychology of Being,* Princeton, N.J., D. Van Nostrand Co., Inc., 1962.

May, Rollo, *Love and Will,* New York, W. W. Norton & Co., Inc., 1969.

Mercer, Philip, *Sympathy and Ethics: a Study of the Relationship between Sympathy and Morality with special reference to Hume's Treatise,* Oxford, The Clarendon Press, 1972.

Messner, Johannes, *Social Ethics,* St. Louis, B. Herder Book Co., 1949.

Miller, K. Bruce, *Ideology and Moral Philosophy,* New York, Humanities Press, Inc., 1971.

Monden, Louis, *Sin, Liberty and Law,* New York, Sheed & Ward, 1965.

Monro, D. H., *Empiricism and Ethics,* Cambridge, Cambridge University Press, 1967.

Morano, Donald V., *Existential Guilt, a Phenomenological Study,* Assen, the Netherlands, Van Gorcum, B. V., 1973.

Mounier, Emmanuel, *Personalism,* London, Routledge & Kegan Paul, Ltd., 1952.

Munz, Peter, *Relationship and Solitude,* Middletown, Conn., Wesleyan University Press, 1965.

Murdoch, Iris, *The Sovereignty of Good,* London, Routledge & Kegan Paul, Ltd., 1970.

The Sovereignty of Good over Other Concepts, Cambridge, Cambridge University Press, 1967.

Nabert, Jean, *Elements for an Ethic,* translated by William J. Petrek, Evanston, Ill., Northwestern University Press, 1969.

Narveson, Jan, *Morality and Utility,* Baltimore, The Johns Hopkins University Press, 1967.

Nédoncelle, Maurice, *Love and the Person,* New York, Sheed & Ward, 1966.

Neville, Robert C., *The Cosmology of Freedom,* New Haven, Conn., Yale University Press, 1974.

Niebuhr, H. Richard, *The Responsible Self,* New York, Harper & Row, Publishers, 1963.

Norman, Richard, *Reasons for Actions: a Critique of Utilitarian Rationality,* Oxford, Basil Blackwell & Mott, Ltd., 1971.

Nowell-Smith, P. H., *Ethics,* Baltimore, Penguin Books, Inc., 1954.

Nygren, Anders, *Agape and Eros,* New York, Harper & Row, Publishers, 1969.

O'Connor, D. J., *Aquinas and Natural Law,* London, Macmillan Publishers, Ltd., 1967.

Free Will, New York, Doubleday Publishing Co., 1971.

441

O'Connor, William R., *The Eternal Quest,* New York, Longmans, Green & Co., Inc., 1947.

Olafson, Frederick A., *Principles and Persons,* Baltimore, The Johns Hopkins University Press, 1967.

Olson, Robert, *The Morality of Self-Interest,* New York, Harcourt, Brace & World, Inc., 1965.

Olthuis, James H., *Facts, Values and Ethics,* Assen, the Netherlands, Van Gorcum, B. V., 1968.

Paton, H. J., *The Categorical Imperative,* Chicago, The University of Chicago Press, 1948.

Pepper, Stephen, *Sources of Value,* Berkeley, University of California Press, 1959.

Perry, David L., *The Concept of Pleasure,* The Hague, Mouton Publishers, 1966.

Peters, Richard S., *Reason and Compassion,* London, Routledge & Kegan Paul, Ltd., 1973.

Pfänder, Alexander, *Phenomenology of Willing and Motivation,* translated by Herbert Spiegelberg, Evanston, Ill., Northwestern University Press, 1967.

Phillips, D. Z., and Mounce, H. O., *Moral Practices,* London, Routledge & Kegan Paul, Ltd., 1970.

Pieper, Josef, *The Four Cardinal Virtues,* Notre Dame, Ind., University of Notre Dame Press, 1967.

Leisure, the Basis of Culture, New York, Pantheon Books, Inc., 1952.

Prichard, H. A., *Moral Obligation,* Oxford, The Clarendon Press, 1949.

Quinton, Anthony, *Utilitarian Ethics,* London, Macmillan Publishers, Ltd., 1973.

Ramsey, Paul, *Deeds and Rules in Christian Ethics,* New York, Charles Scribner's Sons, 1967.

Rand, Ayn, and Branden, Nathaniel, *The Virtue of Selfishness,* New York, The New American Library, Inc., 1964.

Reinhardt, Kurt, *The Existentialist Revolt,* Milwaukee, The Bruce Publishing Co., 1952.

Rickaby, Joseph, *Moral Philosophy,* Stonyhurst Series, London, Longmans, Green & Co., Ltd., 1910.

Ricoeur, Paul, *Fallible Man, Philosophy of the Will,* translated by Charles Kelbley, Chicago, Henry Regnery Co., 1965.

Freedom and Nature: the Voluntary and Involuntary, translated by Erazim V. Kohak, Evanston, Ill., Northwestern University Press, 1966.

Freud and Philosophy: an Essay on Interpretation, translated by Denis Savage, New Haven, Conn., Yale University Press, 1970.

The Symbolism of Evil, translated by Emerson Buchanan, New York, Harper & Row, Publishers, 1967.

Roberts, Moira, *Responsibility and Practical Freedom,* New York, Cambridge University Press, 1965.

Robinson, Bishop John A. T., *Christian Morals Today,* Philadelphia, The Westminster Press, 1964.

Honest to God, Philadelphia, The Westminster Press, 1963.

Rommen, Heinrich, *The Natural Law,* St. Louis, B. Herder Book Co., 1948.

Ross, Stephen David, *The Nature of Moral Responsibility,* Detroit, Wayne State University Press, 1972.

In Pursuit of Moral Value, San Francisco, Freeman, Cooper & Co., 1973.

Ross, W. D., *Foundations of Ethics,* Oxford, The Clarendon Press, 1939.

The Right and the Good, Oxford, The Clarendon Press, 1930.

Rotenstreich, Nathan, *On the Human Subject,* Springfield, Ill., Charles C Thomas, Publisher, 1966.

Roubiczek, Paul, *Ethical Values in the Age of Science,* New York, Cambridge University Press, 1969.

Rubenstein, Richard L., *Morality and Eros*, New York, McGraw-Hill Book Co., 1970.

Ryle, Gilbert, *The Concept of Mind*, New York, Hutchinson's University Library, 1949.

Scheler, Max, *Formalism in Ethics and Non-Formal Ethics of Values*, translated by Manfred S. Frings and Roger L. Funk, 5th rev. ed., Evanston, Ill., Northwestern University Press, 1973.

Schlick, Moritz, *Problems of Ethics*, New York, Dover Publications, Inc., 1939.

Sesonske, Alexander, *Value and Obligation: the Foundations of an Empiricist Ethical Theory*, New York, Oxford University Press, 1964.

Shirk, Evelyn, *The Ethical Dimension: an Approach to the Philosophy of Values and Valuing*, New York, Appleton-Century-Crofts, 1965.

Simon, Yves R., *Freedom of Choice*, ed. by Peter Wolff, New York, Fordham University Press, 1969.

Freedom and Community, ed. by Charles P. O'Donnell, New York, Fordham University Press, 1968.

The Nature and Functions of Authority, Aquinas Lecture, Milwaukee, Marquette University Press, 1940.

The Tradition of Natural Law, New York, Fordham University Press, 1965.

Smart, J. J. C., and Williams, Bernard, *Utilitarianism: For and Against*, Cambridge, Cambridge University Press, 1973.

Spitz, David, *The Liberal Idea of Freedom*, Tucson, Ariz., University of Arizona Press, 1964.

Stern, Alfred, *The Search for Meaning: Philosophical Vistas*, Memphis, Tenn., Memphis State University Press, 1971.

Stern, Axel, *The Science of Freedom: an Essay in Applied Philosophy*, translated by Christopher and Rosalind Strachan, foreword by Raymond Williams, Harlow, England, Longman Group, Ltd., 1969.

Stevenson, C. L., *Ethics and Language*, New Haven, Conn., Yale University Press, 1946.

Stocks, John Leofric, *Morality and Purpose*, ed. by D. Z. Phillips, London, Routledge & Kegan Paul, Ltd., 1969; New York, Schocken Books, Inc., 1969.

Taylor, Richard, *Good and Evil: a New Direction*, New York, The Macmillan Co., 1970.

Toulmin, Stephen, *Examination of the Place of Reason in Ethics*, London, Cambridge University Press, 1950.

Urmson, J. O., *The Emotive Theory of Ethics*, London, The Hutchinson Publishing Group, Ltd., 1968.

Van Melsen, Andrew G., *Science and Responsibility*, translated by Henry J. Koren, Pittsburgh, Duquesne University Press, 1970.

Veatch, Henry, *Rational Man*, Bloomington, Indiana University Press, 1964.

Vivas, Eliseo, *The Moral Life and the Ethical Life*, Chicago, The University of Chicago Press, 1950.

Von Wright, Georg Henrik, *An Essay in Deontic Logic and the General Theory of Action*, with a bibliography of deontic and imperative logic, Amsterdam, North-Holland Publishing Co., 1969.

The Varieties of Goodness, New York, Humanities Press, Inc., 1963.

Walsh, W. H., *Hegelian Ethics*, London, Macmillan Publishers, Ltd., 1969.

Ward, Leo, *Christian Ethics*, St. Louis, B. Herder Book Co., 1952.

Values and Reality, New York, Sheed & Ward, 1935.

Warnock, G. J., *Contemporary Moral Philosophy*, New York, St. Martin's Press, 1967.

The Object of Morality, New York, Barnes & Noble Books, 1971.

Warnock, Mary, *Ethics Since 1900*, 2nd rev. ed., London, Oxford University Press, 1966.

Existentialist Ethics, New York, St. Martin's Press, 1967.

443

Werkmeister, W. H., *Man and His Values,* Lincoln, Neb., University of Nebraska Press, 1967.

    Theories of Ethics, Lincoln, Neb., Johnsen Publishing Co., 1961.

Wertheimer, Roger, *The Significance of Sense: Meaning, Modality and Morality,* Ithaca, N.Y., Cornell University Press, 1972.

Westermarck, Edward, *Ethical Relativity,* New York, Harcourt, Brace & Co., 1932.

    The Origin and Development of Moral Ideas, 2 vols., New York, The Macmillan Co., 1906-1908.

Wild, John, *Plato's Modern Enemies and the Theory of Natural Law,* Chicago, The University of Chicago Press, 1953.

Wilhelmsen, Frederick D., *The Metaphysics of Love,* New York, Sheed & Ward, 1962.

Willey, Basil, *The English Moralists,* London, Chatto and Windus, Ltd., 1964; Methuen in "University Paperback Series," 1965.

Williams, Bernard A. O., *Morality: an Introduction to Ethics,* New York, Harper & Row, Publishers, 1972.

Winch, Peter, *Ethics and Action,* London, Routledge & Kegan Paul, Ltd., 1972.

Zink, Sidney, *The Concepts of Ethics,* New York, St. Martin's Press, 1962.

ANTHOLOGIES AND COLLECTIONS

Abelson, Raziel (ed.), *Ethics and Metaethics,* New York, St. Martin's Press, Inc., 1963.

Anshen, Ruth Nanda, *Moral Principles of Action,* New York, Harper & Row, Publishers, 1952.

Bayles, Michael D. (ed.), *Contemporary Utilitarianism,* New York, Doubleday Publishing Co., 1968.

Berofski, Bernard (ed.), *Free Will and Determinism,* New York, Harper & Row, Publishers, 1966.

Binkley, Robert, Bronaugh, Richard, and Marras, Ausonio (eds.), *Agent, Action, and Reason,* Toronto, University of Toronto Press, 1971.

Bowker, Gordon (ed.), *Freedom: Reason or Revolution?* London, Routledge & Kegan Paul, Ltd., 1970.

Burns, Emile, *Handbook of Marxism,* New York, International Publishers Co., Inc., 1935.

Burtt, Edwin, *The English Philosophers from Bacon to Mill,* New York, Modern Library, Inc., 1939.

Casey, John (ed.), *Morality and Moral Reasoning,* New York, Barnes & Noble Books, 1971.

Castaneda, Hector-Neri, and Nahknikian, George (eds.), *Morality and the Language of Conduct,* Detroit, Wayne State University Press, 1965.

Cheney, David R. (ed.), *Broad's Critical Essays in Moral Philosophy,* preface by C. D. Broad, London, George Allen & Unwin, Ltd.; New York, Humanities Press, Inc., 1971.

Cooke, Robert E. (ed.), *The Terrible Choice: the Abortion Dilemma,* New York, Bantam Books, Inc., 1968.

Cox, Harvey (ed.), *The Situation Ethics Debate,* Philadelphia, The Westminister Press, 1968.

Cunningham, Robert L., *Situationism and the New Morality,* New York, Appleton-Century-Crofts, 1970.

Davies, Hugh Sykes, and Watson, George (eds.), *The English Mind: Studies in the English Moralists Presented to Basil Willey,* New York, Cambridge University Press, 1964.

Davis, John William (ed.), *Value and Valuation: Axiological Studies in Honor of Robert S. Hartman,* Knoxville, Tenn., University of Tennessee Press, 1972.

Donnelly, John, and Lyons, Leonard (eds.), *Conscience,* New York, Alba House, 1973.

Ebenstein, William, *Modern Political Thought,* New York, Holt, Rinehart & Winston, Inc., 1954.

Ekman, Rosalind (ed.), *Readings in the Problems of Ethics,* New York, Charles Scribner's Sons, 1965.

Enteman, Willard F. (ed.), *The Problem of Free Will,* New York, Charles Scribner's Sons, 1967.

Fagothey, Austin, *Right and Reason—an Anthology,* St. Louis, The C. V. Mosby Co., 1972.

Feinberg, Joel (ed.), *Moral Concepts,* London, Oxford University Press, 1969.
  Reason and Responsibility, Belmont, Calif., Dickenson Publishing Co., Inc., 1965.

Finn, James (ed.), *A Conflict of Loyalties: the Case for Selective Conscientious Objection,* New York, Pegasus, 1968.

Foot, Philippa (ed.), *Theories of Ethics,* London, Oxford University Press, 1967.

Honderich, Tod (ed.), *Essays on Freedom of Action,* London, Routledge & Kegan Paul, Ltd., 1972.

Hook, Sidney (ed.), *Determinism and Freedom in the Age of Modern Science,* New York, New York University Press, 1958.
  Law and Philosophy, a Symposium, New York, New York University Press, 1964.

Hudson, W. D. (ed.), *The Is-Ought Question,* New York, St. Martin's Press, 1969.
  New Studies in Ethics, Vol. I: Classical Theories; Vol. II, Modern Theories, London, Macmillan Publishers, Ltd., 1974.

In Quest of Value, Readings in Philosophy and Personal Values Selected by the San Jose State College Associates in Philosophy, San Francisco, Chandler Publishing Co., 1964.

Katope, C. G., and Zolbrod, P. G. (eds.), *Beyond Berkeley: a Source Book in Student Values,* New York, World Publishing Co., 1966.

Klausner, Samuel Z. (ed.), *The Quest for Self-Control, Classical Philosophies and Scientific Research,* New York, The Free Press, 1965.

Körner, Stefan (ed.), *Practical Reason,* Oxford, Basil Blackwell & Mott, Ltd., 1974.

Laslett, P., Runciman, W. G., and Skinner, Q. (eds.), *Philosophy, Politics and Society,* Oxford, Basil Blackwell & Mott, Ltd., 1972.

Lawson, Douglas E., and Lean, Arthur E. (eds.), *John Dewey and the World View,* Carbondale, Ill., Southern Illinois University Press, 1964.

Lepley, Ray (ed.), *The Language of Value,* New York, Columbia University Press, 1957.
  Value, a Cooperative Inquiry, New York, Columbia University Press, 1949.

McKeon, Richard, *Basic Works of Aristotle,* New York, Random House, Inc., 1941.

Mackinnon, Donald M. (ed.), *Making Moral Decisions,* London, S.P.C.K. (The Society for Promoting Christian Knowledge), 1969.

McLean, George F. (ed.), *New Dynamics in Ethical Thinking,* Lancaster, Pa., Concorde Publishing Co., 1974.

Mandelbaum, M., Gramlich, F. W., Anderson, A. R., and Schneewind, J. B., *Philosophic Problems,* ed. 2, New York, The Macmillan Co., 1967.

Mortimore, G. W. (ed.), *Weakness of Will,* London, Macmillan Publishers, Ltd., 1971.

Oates, W. J., *Basic Writings of St. Augustine,* 2 vols., New York, Random House, Inc., 1948.
  The Stoic and Epicurean Philosophers, New York, Random House, Inc., 1940.

Outka, Gene, and Ramsey, Paul (eds.), *Norm and Context in Christian Ethics,* New York, Charles Scribner's Sons, 1968.

Pegis, Anton, *Basic Writings of St. Thomas Aquinas,* 2 vols., New York, Random

House, Inc., 1945. Selections from this in *Introduction to St. Thomas Aquinas,* New York, Modern Library, Inc., 1948.

Quinn, Francis X. (ed.), *The Ethical Aftermath of Automation,* Westminster, Md., The Newman Press, 1962.

Radcliff, P. (ed.), *Limits of Liberty,* Belmont, Calif., Wadsworth Publishing Co., Inc., 1966.

Rand, Benjamin (ed.), *The Classical Moralists,* Boston, Houghton Mifflin Co., 1909.

Raphael, D. D. (ed.), *British Moralists,* 2 vols., Oxford, The Clarendon Press, 1969.

Selby-Bigge, L. A., *British Moralists,* Indianapolis, The Bobbs-Merrill Co., Inc., 1964.

Straus, Erwin W., and Griffith, Richard M. (eds.), *Phenomenology of Will and Action,* Pittsburgh, Duquesne University Press, 1967.

Thomson, J. J., and Dworkin, Gerald (eds.), *Ethics,* New York, Harper & Row, Publishers, 1968.

Todd, Charles, and Blackwood, Russell T. (eds.), *Language and Value,* New York, Greenwood Press, Inc., 1969.

Vesey, G. N. A. (ed.), *The Human Agent.* Royal Institute of Philosophy Lectures, 1966-67, vol. I, New York, St. Martin's Press, 1968.

Wallace, G., and Walker, A. D. M. (eds.), *The Definition of Morality,* New York, Barnes & Noble Books, 1970.

Walsh, James J., and Shapiro, Henry L. (eds.), *Aristotle's Ethics: Issues and Interpretations,* Belmont, Calif., Wadsworth Publishing Co., Inc., 1967.

BOOKS ON APPLIED ETHICS AND ON TOPICS RELATED TO ETHICS

1. LEGAL ETHICS: RIGHTS, LAW, JUSTICE

Acton, H. B. (ed.), *The Philosophy of Punishment: a Collection of Papers,* London, Macmillan Publishers, Ltd., 1969.

Andelson, Robert V., *Imputed Rights,* Athens, Ga., University of Georgia Press, 1972.

Armstrong, R. A., *Primary and Secondary Precepts in Thomistic Natural Law Teaching,* The Hague, Martinus Nijhoff, 1966.

Barry, Brian, *The Liberal Theory of Justice: a Critical Examination of the Principal Doctrines in 'A Theory of Justice' by John Rawls,* Oxford, The Clarendon Press, 1973.

Beccaria, Cesare, *An Essay on Crimes and Punishments,* Philadelphia, P. H. Nicklin, 1819.

Bird, Otto A., *The Idea of Justice,* New York, Frederick A. Praeger, 1967.

Blackstone, William, *Commentaries on the Laws of England,* San Francisco, Bancroft-Whitney Co., 1915.

Bodenheimer, Edgar, *Treatise on Justice,* New York, Philosophical Library, 1967.

Bowie, Norman E., *Towards a New Theory of Distributive Justice,* Amherst, University of Massachusetts Press, 1971.

Brownlie, Ian (ed.), *Basic Documents on Human Rights,* London, Oxford University Press, 1971.

Care, Norman S., and Trelogan, Thomas K. (eds.), *Issues in Law and Morality,* Cleveland, The Press of Case Western Reserve University, 1973.

Davis, Philip E., *Moral Duty and Legal Responsibility,* New York, Appleton-Century-Crofts, 1966.

Flew, Anthony, *Crime or Disease?* London, Macmillan Publishers, Ltd., 1973.

Friedrich, Carl Joachim, *The Philosophy of Law in Historical Perspective,* ed. 2, Chicago, University of Chicago Press, 1963.

Fuller, Lon L., *The Morality of Law,* New Haven, Conn., Yale University Press, 1964.

446

Ginsberg, Morris, *On Justice in Society,* new ed., Harmondsworth, England, Penguin Books, 1971.

Haines, Charles G., *Revival of Natural Law Concepts,* Cambridge, Mass., Harvard University Press, 1930.

Harding, Arthur L. (ed.), *Natural Law and Natural Rights,* Dallas, Southern Methodist University Press, 1955.

Hart, H. L. A., *The Concept of Law,* Oxford, The Clarendon Press, 1961.
  Punishment and Responsibility: Essays in the Philosophy of Law, New York, Oxford University Press, 1968.

Holmes, Oliver Wendell, *Collected Legal Papers,* New York, Harcourt, Brace & World, Inc., 1920.
  Holmes-Pollock Letters, Cambridge, Mass., Harvard University Press, 1941.

Hook, Sidney (ed.), *Law and Philosophy,* New York, New York University Press, 1964.

Kelsen, Hans, *What Is Justice?* Berkeley, University of California Press, 1957.

Kindregan, Charles P., *Quality of Life: Reflections on the Moral Values of American Law,* New York, Macmillan Publishers, Ltd., 1969.

Le Buffe, Francis P., and Hayes, James V., *The American Philosophy of Law,* New York, Jesuit Educational Association, 1953. Formerly entitled *Jurisprudence.*

Leiser, Burton M., *Custom, Law, and Morality: Conflict and Continuity in Social Behavior,* New York, Doubleday Publishing Co., 1969.

Luijpen, Wilhelmus Antonius, *Phenomenology of Natural Law,* translated by Henry J. Koren, Pittsburgh, Duquesne University Press, 1967.

Milne, A. J. M., *Freedom and Rights,* New York, Humanities Press, Inc., 1968.

Mitchell, Basil, *Law, Morality and Religion in a Secular Society,* London, Oxford University Press, 1967.

Moberly, Sir Walter, *The Ethics of Punishment,* London, Faber & Faber, Ltd., 1968.

Natural Law and Modern Society, Center for the Study of Democratic Institutions, Cleveland, World Publishing Co., 1962.

Natural Law Institute Proceedings, College of Law, University of Notre Dame, Indiana, 1947 ff.

Pennock, J. Roland, and Chapman, John W. (eds.), *Equality,* New York, Atherton Press, 1967.

Perelman, Chaim H., *Justice,* New York, Random House, 1967.

Raphael, D. D. (ed.), *Political Theory and the Rights of Man,* London, Macmillan Publishers, Ltd., 1967.

Rawls, John, *A Theory of Justice,* Cambridge, Mass., Belknap Press of Harvard University Press, 1972, copyright 1971.

Ritchie, David G., *Natural Rights,* London, George Allen & Unwin, Ltd., 1952.

St. John-Stevas, Norman, *Law and Morals,* New York, Hawthorn Books, Inc., 1964.
  Life, Death, and the Law, Bloomington, Indiana University Press, 1961.
  The Right to Life, New York, Holt, Rinehart & Winston, Inc., 1963.

Shklar, Judith N., *Legalism,* Cambridge, Mass., Harvard University Press, 1964.

Simpson, A. W. B. (ed.), *Oxford Essays in Jurisprudence,* Oxford, The Clarendon Press, 1972.

Strauss, Leo, *Natural Rights and History,* Chicago, The University of Chicago Press, 1953.

Stumpf, Samuel Enoch, *Morality and the Law,* Nashville, Tenn., Vanderbilt University Press, 1966.

Summers, Robert S. (ed.), *Essays in Legal Philosophy,* Oxford, Basil Blackwell & Mott, Ltd., 1968.
  More Essays in Legal Philosophy, General Assessments of Legal Philosophies, Berkeley, Calif., University of California Press, 1971.

UNESCO (ed.), *Human Rights,* a symposium, Greenford, Middlesex, Allan Wingate (Publishers), Ltd., n.d.

2. MEDICAL ETHICS: LIFE, HEALTH, SAFETY

American Friends Service Committee, *Who Shall Live? Man's Control Over Birth and Death,* New York, Hill & Wang, 1970.

Beecher, Henry K., *Research and the Individual: Human Studies,* Boston, Little, Brown & Co., 1970.

Blum, Richard, and associates, *Utopiates,* New York, Atherton Press, 1964.

Campbell, Alastair, V., *Moral Dilemmas in Medicine,* Baltimore, The Williams & Wilkins Co., 1972.

Clark-Kennedy, A. E., *Man, Medicine, and Morality,* Hamden, Conn., The Shoe String Press, Inc., 1970.

Claxton, Ernest, and McKay, H. A. (eds.), *Medicine, Morals and Man,* New York, International Publications Service, 1969.

Cohen, Sidney, *The Beyond Within,* New York, Atherton Press, 1964.

Cutler, Donald R. (ed.), *Updating Life and Death,* Boston, Beacon Press, 1969.

Day, Stacey B. (ed.), *Ethics in Medicine in a Changing Society,* Minneapolis, University of Minnesota, Bell Museum of Pathology, 1973.

Dedek, John F., *Human Life: Some Moral Issues,* New York, Sheed & Ward, Inc., 1972.

Edmunds, Vincent, and Scorer, C. Gordon, *Ethical Responsibility in Medicine: a Christian Approach,* New York, Longman, Inc., 1967.

Entralgo, P. L., *Doctor and Patient,* New York, McGraw-Hill Book Co., 1969.

Etziony, M. B. (ed.), *The Physician's Creed,* Springfield, Ill., Charles C Thomas, Publisher, 1973.

Ficarra, Bernard, *Newer Ethical Problems in Medicine and Surgery,* Westminster, Md., The Newman Press, 1951.

Fletcher, Joseph, *Morals and Medicine,* Princeton, N. J., Princeton University Press, 1954; Boston, Beacon Press, 1960.

Flood, Peter (ed.), *The Ethics of Brain Surgery,* Chicago, Henry Regnery Co., 1955.
Medical Experimentation on Man, Chicago, Henry Regnery Co., 1955.
New Problems in Medical Ethics, 2 vols., Westminster, Md., The Newman Press, 1953.

Frazier, Claude, *Is it Moral to Modify Man?* Springfield, Ill., Charles C Thomas, Publisher, 1973.

Frazier, Claude A. (ed.), *Should Doctors Play God?* Nashville, Tenn., Broadman Press, 1971.

Freund, Paul A. (ed.), *Experimentation With Human Subjects,* New York, George Braziller, Inc., 1970.

Gelfand, Michael, *Philosophy and Ethics in Medicine,* New York, Longman, Inc., 1968.

Häring, Bernard, *Medical Ethics,* Notre Dame, Ind., Fides Publishers, Inc., 1973.

Healey, Edwin, *Medical Ethics,* Chicago, Loyola University Press, 1956.

Huxley, Aldous, *Doors of Perception,* New York, Harper & Row, Publishers, 1954.

Ingle, Dwight J., *Who Should Have Children? An Environmental and Genetic Approach,* Indianapolis, The Bobbs-Merrill Co., Inc., 1973.

Kantrowitz, Adrian, et al., *Who Shall Live and Who Shall Die: the Ethical Implications of the New Medical Technology,* New York, Union of American Hebrew Congregations, 1968.

Katz, Jay, *Experimentation With Human Beings: the Authority of Investigator, Subject, Professions and State in the Human Experimentation Process,* New York, Russell Sage Foundation, 1972.

Kelly, Gerald, *Medico-Moral Problems,* St. Louis, Catholic Hospital Association, 1958.

Leach, Gerald, *The Biocrats,* Baltimore, Penguin Books, Inc., 1972.

Lyons, Catherine, *Organ Transplants: the Moral Issues,* Philadelphia, The Westminster Press, 1970.

448

McFadden, Charles, *Medical Ethics,* ed. 6, Philadelphia, F. A. Davis Co., 1967.

Mann, Kenneth W., *Deadline for Survival: a Survey of Moral Issues in Science and Medicine,* New York, The Seabury Press, Inc., 1970.

Marshall, John, *Medicine and Morals,* New York, Hawthorn Books, Inc., 1960.

Masters, N. C., and Shapiro, H. A., *Medical Secrecy and the Doctor-Patient Relationship,* New York, International Publications Service, 1966.

Miller, George W., *Moral and Ethical Implications of Human Organ Transplants,* Springfield, Ill., Charles C Thomas, Publisher, 1971.

Nelson, James B., *Human Medicine: Ethical Perspective on New Medical Issues,* Minneapolis, Augsburg Publishing House, 1973.

O'Donnell, Thomas, *Morals in Medicine,* Westminster, Md., The Newman Press, 1956.

Pappworth, Maurice H., *Human Guinea Pigs,* Boston, Beacon Press, 1968.

Ramsey, Paul, *The Ethics of Fetal Research,* New Haven, Conn., Yale University Press, 1975.
> *Fabricated Man: The Ethics of Genetic Control,* New Haven, Conn., Yale University Press, 1970.
> *The Patient as Person: Exploration in Medical Ethics,* New Haven, Conn., Yale University Press, 1974.

Schmeck, Harold M., *Semi-Artificial Man,* New York, Walker & Co., 1965.

Sigerist, Henry E., *Medicine and Human Welfare,* Washington, D.C., McGrath Publishing Co., 1970.

Smith, Harmon L., *Ethics and the New Medicine,* Nashville, Tenn., Abingdon Press, 1970.

Torrey, E. Fuller, *Ethical Issues in Medicine: the Role of the Physician in Today's Society,* Boston, Little, Brown & Co., 1968.

Vaux, Kenneth, *Biomedical Ethics,* New York, Harper & Row, Publishers, 1974.

Visscher, Maurice B. (ed.), *Humanistic Perspectives in Medical Ethics,* Buffalo, N.Y., Prometheus Books, 1972.

Wertz, Richard W. (ed.), *Readings on Ethical and Social Issues in Biomedicine,* Englewood Cliffs, N.J., Prentice-Hall, Inc., 1973.

Williams, Preston, *Ethical Issues in Biology and Medicine,* Morristown, N.J., General Learning Corp., 1973.

A. ABORTION

Arnstein, Helene S., *What Every Woman Needs to Know About Abortion,* New York, Charles Scribner's Sons, 1973.

Bajema, Clifford E., *Abortion and the Meaning of Personhood,* Grand Rapids, Mich., Baker Book House, 1974.

Bird, Lewis, *What You Should Know About Abortion,* ed. by William J. Petersen, New Canaan, Conn., Keats Publishing, Inc., 1974.

Bluford, Robert, Jr., and Petres, Robert E., *Unwanted Pregnancy,* New York, Harper & Row, Publishers, 1973.

Callahan, Daniel, *Abortion: Law, Choice and Morality,* New York, The Macmillan Co., 1970.

Cohen, Marshall, Nagel, Thomas, and Scanlon, Thomas (eds.), *The Rights and Wrongs of Abortion,* Princeton, N.J., Princeton University Press, 1974.

DeMarco, Donald, *Abortion in Perspective,* Cincinnati, Hiltz & Hayes, 1974.

Fleming, Alice, *Contraception, Abortion, Pregnancy,* Nashville, Tenn., Thomas Nelson, Inc., 1974.

Gardner, R. F., *Abortion,* New York, Pyramid Publications, 1974.
> *Abortion: the Personal Dilemma,* Old Tappan, N.J., Fleming H. Revell Co., 1974.

Gardner, R. F. (ed.), *Abortion: the Personal Dilemma,* new ed., Grand Rapids, Mich., Wm. B. Eerdmans Publishing Co., 1972.

Granfield, David, *The Abortion Decision*, New York, Doubleday Publishing Co., 1969; 1971.

Grisez, Germain, *Abortion: the Myths, the Realities, and the Arguments*, New York, Corpus Books, 1970.

Hall, Robert E., *Abortion in a Changing World*, 2 vols., New York, Columbia University Press, 1970.
Doctor's Guide to Having an Abortion, New York, New American Library, Inc., 1971.

Hardin, Garrett, *Stalking the Wild Taboo*, Los Altos, Calif., William Kaufmann, 1973.

Hendin, David, *Everything You Need to Know About Abortion*, New York, Pinnacle Books, 1971.

Hilgers, Thomas, and Horan, Dennis J. (eds.), *Abortion and Social Justice*, New York, Sheed & Ward, Inc., 1973.

Horobin, G. W. (ed.), *Experience With Abortion*, New York, Cambridge University Press, 1973.

Jenness, Linda, Lund, Carolina, and Jaquith, Cindy, *Abortion: Women's Fight for the Right to Choose*, New York, Pathfinder Press, 1973.

Keast, Laury, *The Abortion Controversy*, new ed., ed. by D. Steve Rahmas, Charlotteville, N.Y., Sam Har Press, 1973.

Kohl, Marvin, *The Morality of Killing: Euthanasia, Abortion and Transplants*, New York, Humanities Press, Inc., 1974.

Mace, David R., *Abortion: the Agonizing Decision*, Nashville, Tenn., Abingdon Press, 1972.

Mankekar, Kamia, *Abortion: a Social Dilemma*, Portland, Ore., International Scholarly Book Service, 1974.

McCarthy, John F., *In Defense of Human Life*, Houston, Tex., Lumen Christi Press, 1970.

McEllhenney, John G., *Cutting the Monkey-Rope: Is the Taking of Life Ever Justified?* Valley Forge, Pa., Judson Press, 1973.

Newman, Sidney H., Beck, Mildred B., and Lewit, Sarah (eds.), *Abortion, Obtained and Denied: Research Approaches*, Bridgeport, Conn., Key Book Service, 1971.

Noonan, John T. (ed.), *The Morality of Abortion: Legal and Historical Perspectives*, Cambridge, Mass., Harvard University Press, 1970.

Osofsky, Howard J., and Osofsky, Joy D., *The Abortion Experience*, New York, Harper & Row, Publishers, 1973.

Patterson, Janet, and Patterson, Robert C., *Abortion: the Trojan Horse*, Nashville, Tenn., Thomas Nelson, Inc., 1974.

Perkins, Robert L. (ed.), *Abortion: Pro and Con*, Cambridge, Mass., Schenkman Publishing Co., Inc., 1974.

Reiterman, Carl (ed.), *California Committee on Therapeutic Abortion: Abortion and the Unwanted Child*, New York, Springer Publishing Co., Inc., 1971.

Rudel, Harry W., Kincl, Fred A., and Henzl, Milan R., *Birth Control: Contraception and Abortion*, New York, The Macmillan Co., 1973.

Saltman, Jules, and Zimering, Stanley, *Abortion Today*, Springfield, Ill., Charles C Thomas, Publisher, 1973.

Sarvis, Betty, and Rodman, Hyman, *The Abortion Controversy*, ed. 2, New York, Columbia University Press, 1974.

Shaw, Russell B., *Abortion on Trial*, New York, International Publications Service, 1969.

Sloane, Bruce R. (ed.), *Abortion: Changing Views and Practice*, New York, Grune & Stratton, Inc., 1971.

Storer, Horatio R., and Heard, Franklin F., *Criminal Abortion*, New York, Arno Press, Inc., 1974.

450

B. EUTHANASIA

Downing, A. B., *Euthanasia: Right to Death,* Plainview, N.Y., Nash Publishing Corp., 1970.

Downing, A. B. (ed.), *Euthanasia and the Right to Death: the Case for Voluntary Euthanasia,* New York, Humanities Press, Inc., 1970.

Gould, Jonathan, and Lord Craigmyle (eds.), *Your Death Warrant? The Implications of Euthanasia,* New Rochelle, N.Y., Arlington House, Inc., 1973.

Kohl, Marvin, *Beneficent Euthanasia,* Buffalo, N.Y., Prometheus Books, 1974.

Maguire, Daniel C., *Death by Choice,* New York, Doubleday Publishing Co., 1974.

Mannes, Marya, *Last Rights,* New York, William Morrow & Co., Inc., 1974.

Trubo, Richard, *An Act of Mercy: Euthanasia Today,* Freeport, N.Y., Nash Publishing Co., 1973.

Wertenbaker, Lael T., *Death of a Man,* Boston, Beacon Press, 1974.

3. SOCIOLOGICAL ETHICS: SOCIETY, COMMUNITY, EDUCATION

Arendt, Hannah, *On Violence,* New York, Harcourt, Brace & World, 1970.

Aron, Raymond, *Progress and Disillusion: Dialectics of Modern Society,* new ed., Harmondsworth, England, Penguin Books, Ltd., 1972.

Baier, Kurt, and Rescher, Nicholas (eds.), *Values and the Future: the Impact of Technological Change on American Values,* New York, The Free Press, 1969.

Bay, Christian, *The Structure of Freedom,* New York, Atheneum Publishers, 1965.

Becker, Ernest, *Beyond Alienation: a Philosophy of Education for the Crisis of Democracy,* New York, George Braziller, Inc., 1967.

Benjamin, A. Cornelius, *Science, Technology and Human Values,* Columbia, Mo., University of Missouri Press, 1965.

Brandt, Richard B. (ed.), *Social Justice,* Englewood Cliffs, N.J., Prentice-Hall, Inc., 1962.

Brumbaugh, Robert S., and Lawrence, Nathaniel M., *Philosophers on Education: Six Essays on the Foundations of Western Thought,* Boston, Houghton Mifflin Co., 1963.

Carson, Rachel, *Silent Spring,* Boston, Houghton Mifflin Co., 1962.

Cox, Harvey, *The Secular City,* New York, The Macmillan Co., 1965.

Dewey, John, *Democracy and Education,* New York, The Macmillan Co., 1916.

Downie, R. S., *Roles and Values: an Introduction to Social Ethics,* New York, Barnes & Noble Books, 1971.

Durkheim, Emile, *Suicide,* New York, The Free Press of Glencoe, Inc., 1951.

Ellis, William W., *White Ethics and Black Power,* Chicago, Aldine Publishing Co., 1969.

Emmet, Dorothy, *Rules, Roles and Relations,* New York, St. Martin's Press, 1966.

Feibleman, James K., *Moral Strategy: an Introduction to the Ethics of Confrontation,* The Hague, Martinus Nijhoff, 1967.

Feinberg, Joel, *Social Philosophy,* Englewood Cliffs, N.J., Prentice-Hall, Inc., 1973.

Fromm, Erich (ed.), *Socialist Humanism: an International Symposium,* New York, Doubleday Publishing Co., 1965.

Gotschalk, D. W., *Human Aims in Modern Perspective: Outlines of a General Theory of Value with Special References to Contemporary Social Life and Politics,* Yellow Springs, Ohio, Antioch Press, 1966.

Grimm, Robert H., and Mackay, Alfred F. (eds.), *Society: Revolution and Reform,* Cleveland, The Press of Case Western Reserve University, 1971.

Hill, Brian Victor, *Education and the Endangered Individual,* New York, Teachers College Press, 1974.

Jacobs, P., and Landau, S., *The New Radicals: a Report with Documents,* New York, Random House, Inc., 1966.

Jünger, Friedrich, *The Failure of Technology,* Chicago, Henry Regnery Co., 1956.

Keeling, Michael, *Morals in a Free Society,* London, SCM Press, Ltd., 1967.

Keniston, Kenneth, *The Uncommitted,* New York, Harcourt, Brace & World, Inc., 1965.

> *Young Radicals,* New York, Harcourt, Brace & World, Inc., 1968.

Kiefer, Howard E., and Munitz, Milton K. (eds.), *Ethics and Social Justice,* Albany, N.Y., State University of New York Press, 1970.

Kirk, Russell, *Academic Freedom,* Chicago, Henry Regnery Co., 1955.

Koestler, Arthur, *Insight and Outlook: an Inquiry Into the Common Foundations of Science, Art, and Social Ethics,* Lincoln, Neb., University of Nebraska Press, 1965.

Kurtz, Paul (ed.), *Moral Problems in Contemporary Society: Essays in Humanistic Ethics,* Englewood Cliffs, N.J., Prentice-Hall, Inc., 1969.

Kwant, Remy C., *Phenomenology of Social Existence,* Pittsburgh, Duquesne University Press, 1965.

Laszlo, Ervin, and Stulman, Julius (eds.), *Emergent Man: His Chances, Problems and Potentials,* New York, Gordon & Breach, Science Publishers, Inc., 1973.

Lippmann, Walter, *The Good Society,* Boston, Little, Brown & Co., 1937.

MacIver, Robert, *Academic Freedom in Our Time,* New York, Columbia University Press, 1955.

Marcel, Gabriel, *The Decline of Wisdom,* New York, Philosophical Library, Inc., 1955.

> *Man Against Mass Society,* Chicago, Henry Regnery Co., 1952.

Miller, David, *Individualism: Personal Achievement and the Open Society,* Austin, Texas, University of Texas Press, 1967.

Natanson, Maurice, *The Journeying Self: a Study in Philosophy and Social Role,* Reading, Mass., Addison-Wesley Publishing Co., 1970.

Niebuhr, Reinhold, *Man's Nature and His Communities: Essays on the Dynamics and Enigmas of Man's Personal and Social Existence,* New York, Charles Scribner's Sons, 1965.

> *Moral Man and Immoral Society,* New York, Charles Scribner's Sons, 1949.

Ossowska, Maria, *Social Determinants of Moral Ideas,* Philadelphia, The University of Pennsylvania Press, 1970; London, Routledge & Kegan Paul, Ltd., 1971.

Osterhoudt, Robert G. (ed.), *The Philosophy of Sport: a Collection of Original Essays,* Springfield, Ill., Charles C Thomas, Publisher, 1973.

Passmore, John, *The Perfectibility of Man,* London, Gerald Duckworth & Co., Ltd., 1970.

Peterson, Forrest H., *A Philosophy of Man and Society,* New York, Philosophical Library, 1970.

Riesman, David, *The Lonely Crowd,* New Haven, Conn., Yale University Press, 1950.

Ross, Ralph Gilbert, *Obligation: a Social Theory,* Ann Arbor, University of Michigan Press, 1970.

Schroyer, Trent, *The Critique of Domination,* New York, George Braziller, Inc., 1973.

Sheed, Frank J., *Society and Sanity,* New York, Sheed & Ward, 1953.

Snook, I. A. (ed.), *Concepts of Indoctrination: Philosophical Essays,* London, Routledge & Kegan Paul, Ltd., 1972.

> *Indoctrination and Education,* London, Routledge & Kegan Paul, Ltd., 1972.

Sorokin, Pitirim, *The Crisis of Our Age,* New York, E. P. Dutton & Co., Inc., 1941.

Stone, Julius, *Social Dimensions of Law and Justice,* Stanford, Calif., Stanford University Press, 1966.

Taylor, John F. A., *The Masks of Society: an Inquiry into the Covenants of Civilization,* New York, Appleton-Century-Crofts, 1966.

Teodori, Massimo, *The New Left: a Documentary History,* Indianapolis, The Bobbs-Merrill Co., Inc., 1969.

Thornhill, J., *The Person and the Group,* Milwaukee, The Bruce Publishing Co., 1967.

Weiss, Paul, *Sport: a Philosophic Inquiry,* Carbondale, Ill., Southern Illinois University Press, 1969.

Van Melsen, A. G., *Physical Science and Ethics: a Reflection on the Relationship between Nature and Morality,* Louvain, Belgium, N.V. Uitgeverij Nauwelaerts Edition S. A., 1969.

Wolff, Robert P., Moore, Barrington, Jr., and Marcuse, Herbert, *A Critique of Pure Tolerance,* London, Jonathan Cape, Ltd., 1969.

4. DOMESTIC ETHICS: MARRIAGE, FAMILY, SEX

Atkinson, Ronald, *Sexual Morality,* London, The Hutchinson Publishing Group, Ltd., 1965.

Atkinson, Ronald, et al., *Sexual Latitude: For and Against,* ed. by Harold H. Hart, New York, Hart Publishing Co., Inc., 1971.

Baker, Robert, and Elliston, Frederick (eds.), *Philosophy and Sex,* Buffalo, N.Y., Prometheus Books, 1975.

Bertocci, Peter, *Sex, Love, and the Person,* New York, Sheed & Ward, 1967.

Birmingham, William (ed.), *What Catholics Think About Birth Control,* New York, Signet Book, 1964.

Brenton, Myron, *The American Male,* New York, Coward-McCann, 1966; Fawcett Premier Books, 1970.

Bromley, Dorothy, *Catholics and Birth Control,* New York, The Devin-Adair Co., 1965.

Burgess, Ernest, and Wallin, Paul, *Engagement and Marriage,* Philadelphia, J. B. Lippincott Co., 1953.

Calderone, Mary S. (ed.), *Sexuality and Human Values,* New York, Association Press, 1974.

Cooper, Boyd, *Sex Without Tears: a Guide for the Sexual Revolution,* ed. by Walter Schmidt, Los Angeles, Calif., Charles Publishing Co., 1972; New York, Bantam Books, Inc., 1974.

Dedek, John F., *Contemporary Sexual Morality,* New York, Sheed & Ward, Inc., 1971.

Dupré, Louis, *Contraception and Catholics,* Baltimore, Helicon Press, Inc., 1964.

Duvall, Evelyn Millis, *Why Wait Till Marriage?* New York, Association Press, 1965.

Edwards, John N. (ed.), *Sex and Society,* Chicago, Rand McNally & Co., 1972.

Ford, John, and Kelly, Gerald, *Contemporary Moral Theology,* vol. II, *Marriage Questions,* Westminster, Md., The Newman Press, 1963.

Grisez, Germain, *Contraception and the Natural Law,* Milwaukee, The Bruce Publishing Co., 1964.

Hildebrand, Dietrich von, *In Defense of Purity,* New York, Sheed & Ward, 1938. *Marriage,* New York, Longmans, Green & Co., Inc., 1942.

Hope, Wingfield, *Life Together,* New York, Sheed & Ward, 1944.

Kennedy, Eugene C., *The New Sexuality: Myths, Fables and Hang-Ups,* New York, Doubleday Publishing Co., 1973.

Kirkendall, Lester A., and Whitehurst, Robert N. (eds.), *The New Sexual Revolution,* New York, Prometheus Press, 1974.

Lepp, Ignace, *The Psychology of Loving,* translated by B. B. Gilligan, Baltimore, Helicon Press, Inc., 1963.

Morrison, Eleanor, and Borosage, Vera (eds.), *Human Sexuality: Contemporary Perspectives,* Palo Alto, Calif., Mayfield Publishing Co., 1973.

Nobile, Philip (ed.), *The New Eroticism: Theories, Vogues and Canons,* New York, Random House, 1970.

453

Noonan, John T., *Contraception,* Cambridge, Mass., Harvard University Press, 1965.

Novak, Michael (ed.), *The Experience of Marriage,* London, Darton, Longmans & Todd, Ltd., 1965.

Oakley, Anne, *Sex, Gender and Society,* New York, Harper & Row, Publishers, 1973.

Oraison, Marc, *The Human Mystery of Sexuality,* New York, Sheed & Ward, 1967.

Otto, Herbert A., *New Sexuality,* Palo Alto, Calif., Science and Behavior Books, Inc., 1971.

Paul, Leslie, *Eros Rediscovered: Restoring Sex to Humanity,* New York, Association Press, 1970.

Roberts, Archbishop T. D. (ed.), *Contraception and Holiness,* London, William Collins Sons & Co., Ltd., 1964.

Rock, John, *The Time Has Come,* New York, Alfred A. Knopf, Inc., 1963.

Suenens, Leon Joseph Cardinal, *Love and Control,* Westminster, Md., The Newman Press, 1961.

Thibon, Gustave, *What God Has Joined Together,* Chicago, Henry Regnery Co., 1952.

Thielicke, Helmut, *The Ethics of Sex,* translated by J. W. Doberstein, New York, Harper & Row, Publishers, 1964; Grand Rapids, Mich., Baker Book House, 1975.

Wayne, T. G., *Morals and Marriage,* New York, Longmans, Green & Co., Inc., 1936.

Wilson, John, *Logic and Sexual Morality,* Baltimore, Penguin Books, Inc., 1965.

A. WOMEN'S LIBERATION

Andreas, Carol, *Sex and Caste in America,* Englewood Cliffs, N.J., Prentice-Hall, Inc., 1971.

Armundsen, Kristen, *The Silenced Majority,* Englewood Cliffs, N.J., Prentice-Hall, Inc., 1971.

de Beauvoir, Simone, *The Second Sex,* translated by H. M. Parshley, New York, Alfred A. Knopf, Inc., 1953; Bantam Books, Inc., 1971.

Cooke, Joanne, Bunch-Weeks, Charlotte, and Morgan, Robin (eds.), *The New Women,* Indianapolis, The Bobbs-Merrill Co., Inc., 1970; Fawcett World Library, 1971.

Dahlstrom, Edmund (ed.), *Changing Roles of Men and Women,* rev. ed., Boston, Beacon Press, 1971.

Daly, Mary, *Beyond God the Father: Toward a Philosophy of Women's Liberation,* Boston, Beacon Press, 1973.

Figes, Eva, *Patriarchal Attitudes,* New York, Stein & Day Publishers, 1970; Fawcett World Library, 1971.

Firestone, Shulamith, *The Dialectic of Sex,* New York, William Morrow & Co., Inc., 1970; Bantam Books, Inc., 1971.

Friedan, Betty, *The Feminine Mystique,* new foreword and epilogue, New York, Dell Publishing Co., 1975.

Greer, Germaine, *The Female Eunuch,* New York, McGraw-Hill Book Co., 1971; Bantam Books, Inc., 1972.

Harbeson, Gladys, *Choice and Challenge for the American Woman,* ed. 2, Cambridge, Mass., Schenkman Publishing Co., 1972.

Komisar, Lucy, *The New Feminism,* New York, Franklin Watts, Inc., 1971.

Marine, Gene, *A Male Guide to Women's Liberation,* New York, Avon Books, 1974.

Millet, Kate, *Sexual Politics,* New York, Avon Books, 1973.

Mitchell, Juliet, *Woman's Estate,* New York, Pantheon Books, Inc., 1971.

Morgan, Robin (ed.), *Sisterhood is Powerful,* New York, Random House, Inc., 1970.

O'Neill, William, *Everyone was Brave,* Chicago, Quadrangle Books, 1969.

Roszak, Betty, and Roszak, Theodore (eds.), *Masculine/Feminine,* New York, Harper & Row, Publishers, 1969.

B. HOMOSEXUALITY

Abbott, Sidney, and Love, Barbara, *Sappho Was a Right-On Woman: a Liberated View of Lesbianism,* New York, Stein & Day Publishers, 1972.

Churchill, Wainwright, *Homosexual Behavior Among Males: a Cross Cultural and Cross Species Investigation,* Englewood Cliffs, N.J., Prentice-Hall, Inc., 1971.

Clark, Lige, and Nichols, Jack, *Roommates Can't Always Be Lovers: an Intimate Look at Male-Male Relationships,* New York, St. Martin's Press, 1974.

Drakeford, John, *Forbidden Love: a Homosexual Looks for Understanding and Help,* Waco, Tex., Word, Inc., 1971.

Fisher, Peter, *The Gay Mystique: the Myth and Reality of Male Homosexuality,* New York, Stein & Day Publishers, 1972.

Karlen, Arno, *Sexuality and Homosexuality: a New View,* New York, W. W. Norton & Co., Inc., 1971.

Martin, Del, and Lyon, Phyllis, *Lesbian-Woman,* New York, Bantam Books, Inc., 1972.

McCaffrey, J. (ed.), *Homosexual Dialectic,* Englewood Cliffs, N.J., Prentice-Hall, Inc., 1972.

Oberholtzer, W. Dwight (ed.), *Is Gay Good? Ethics, Theology, and Homosexuality,* Philadelphia, The Westminster Press, 1971.

Ruitenbeek, Hendrik M. (ed.), *Homosexuality a Changing Picture: a Contemporary Study and Interpretation,* New York, Humanities Press, 1974.

Ruitenbeek, Hendrik M., *Problem of Homosexuality in Modern Society,* New York, E. P. Dutton & Co., Inc., 1963.

Saghir, Marcel T., and Robins, Eli, *Male and Female Homosexuality: a Comprehensive Investigation,* Baltimore, The Williams & Wilkins Co., 1975.

Weinberg, Martin S., and Williams, Colin J., *Male Homosexuals: Their Problems and Adaptations,* New York, Oxford University Press, 1974.

Wysor, Bettie, *The Lesbian Myth,* New York, Random House, Inc., 1974.

5. POLITICAL ETHICS: STATE, GOVERNMENT, PROTEST

Barry, Brian, *Political Argument,* London, Routledge & Kegan Paul, Ltd., 1965.

Bedeau, Hugo, *Civil Disobedience: Theory and Practice,* New York, Pegasus, 1969.

Berlin, Sir Isaiah, *Four Essays on Liberty,* London, Oxford University Press, 1969.

Bosanquet, Bernard, *The Philosophical Theory of the State,* London, Macmillan Publishers, Ltd., 1966.

Bottomore, T. B., *Critics of Society: Radical Thought in North America,* 2nd revised ed., London, George Allen & Unwin, Ltd., 1969.

Braybrooke, David, *Three Tests for Democracy: Personal Rights, Human Welfare, Collective Preference,* New York, Random House, Inc., 1968.

Carter, April, *The Political Theory of Anarchism,* London, Routledge & Kegan Paul, Ltd., 1971.

Childress, James F., *Civil Disobedience and Political Obligation: a Study in Christian Ethics,* New Haven, Conn., Yale University Press, 1971.

Cohen, Carl, *Democracy,* Athens, Ga., University of Georgia Press, 1972.

Deininger, Whitaker T., *Problems in Social and Political Thought, a Philosophical Introduction,* New York, The Macmillan Co., 1965.

D'Entrèves, A. P., *Aquinas, Selected Political Writings,* Oxford, Basil Blackwell & Mott, Ltd., 1948.

Douglas, Paul H., *Ethics in Government,* Cambridge, Mass., Harvard University Press, 1952.

Drinan, Robert F., *Democracy, Dissent, and Disorder,* New York, The Seabury Press, Inc., 1969.

Figgis, John, *The Divine Right of Kings,* London, Cambridge University Press, 1914.

Flathman, Richard E., *The Public Interest: an Essay Concerning the Normative Discourse of Politics,* New York, John Wiley & Sons, Inc., 1966.

Frankel, Charles, *The Democratic Prospect,* New York, Harper & Row, Publishers, 1964.

Friedrich, Carl Joachim, *Tradition and Authority,* London, The Pall Mall Press, 1972.

Gewirth, Alan, *Political Philosophy,* New York, The Macmillan Co., 1965.

Ginsberg, Morris, *On Justice and Society,* London, Heinemann Educational Books, Ltd., 1965.

Graham, George A., *Morality in American Politics,* New York, Random House, Inc., 1952.

Green, Thomas H., *Lectures on the Principles of Political Obligation,* introd. by Lord Lindsay of Birker, Ann Arbor, Mich., University of Michigan Press, 1967.

Hall, Robert T., *The Morality of Civil Disobedience,* New York, Harper & Row, Publishers, 1971.

Hamilton, Madison, and Jay, *The Federalist Papers,* New York, The New American Library, 1961. Many other editions.

Hook, Sidney, *The Paradoxes of Freedom,* Berkeley, Calif., University of California Press, 1962.

Humboldt, Wilhelm von, *The Limits of State Action,* ed. by J. W. Burrow, translated by editor and Joseph Coultard, Cambridge, Cambridge University Press, 1969.

King, Martin Luther, Jr., *Why We Can't Wait,* New York, Harper & Row, Publishers, 1964.

Lakoff, Sanford A., *Equality in Political Philosophy,* Cambridge, Mass., Harvard University Press, 1964.

Letwin, Shirley Robin, *The Pursuit of Certainty,* Cambridge, Cambridge University Press, 1965.

Lindblom, Charles E., *The Intelligence of Democracy: Decision Making Through Mutual Adjustment,* New York, The Macmillan Co., 1965.

Lippmann, Walter, *The Public Philosophy,* Boston, Little, Brown & Co., 1955.

Macfarlane, L. J., *Modern Political Theory,* London, Thomas Nelson & Sons, Ltd., 1970.

Malcolm X, *The Autobiography of Malcolm X,* New York, Grove Press, 1964.

Maritain, Jacques, *Man and the State,* Chicago, The University of Chicago Press, 1951.

Scholasticism and Politics, New York, The Macmillan Co., 1940.

Murray, John Courtney, *We Hold These Truths,* New York, Sheed & Ward, 1960.

Oliver, James H., *Demokratia, the Gods, and the Free World,* Baltimore, The Johns Hopkins University Press, 1960.

Parekh, Bhikhu, and Berki, R. N. (eds.), *The Morality of Politics,* London, George Allen & Unwin, Ltd., 1972.

Pincoffs, Edmund L., *The Rationale of Legal Punishment,* New York, The Humanities Press, 1966.

Plamenatz, J. P., *Consent, Freedom and Political Obligation,* ed. 2, London, Oxford University Press, 1968.

Raphael, David Daiches, *Problems of Political Philosophy,* London, The Pall Mall Press, 1970.

Rees, John C., *Equality,* London, The Pall Mall Press, 1971.

Rommen, Heinrich, *The State in Catholic Thought,* St. Louis, B. Herder Book Co., 1945.

Simon, Yves, *Philosophy of Democratic Government,* Chicago, The University of Chicago Press, 1951.

Singer, Peter, *Democracy and Disobedience,* London, Oxford University Press, 1973.

Stevick, Daniel B., *Civil Disobedience and the Christian,* New York, The Seabury Press, Inc., 1969.

Thoreau, Henry David, *Civil Disobedience.* In *The Works of Thoreau,* Boston, Houghton Mifflin Co., 1937.

Vaizey, John, *Social Democracy,* London, George Weidenfeld & Nicolson, Ltd., 1971.

Wickum, Carl, *The Total State: a Philosophical Interpretation of Contemporary and Future Society,* Boston, Forum Publications, 1964.

Willhoite, Fred H., Jr., *Beyond Nihilism: Albert Camus's Contribution to Political Thought,* Baton Rouge, La., Louisiana State University Press, 1968.

Woetzel, Robert, *The Philosophy of Freedom,* Dobbs Ferry, N.Y., Oceana Publications, Inc., 1966.

Wolff, Robert Paul, *In Defense of Anarchism,* New York, Harper & Row, Publishers, 1970.

6. ECONOMIC ETHICS: PROPERTY, BUSINESS, CONTRACTS

Acton, Henry B., *The Morals of Markets: an Ethical Exploration,* London, Longman in association with the Institution of Economic Affairs, 1971.

Barnard, Chester I., *Elementary Conditions of Business Morals,* Berkeley, Calif., University of California Press, 1958.

Bartels, Robert (ed.), *Ethics in Business,* Columbus, Ohio, Ohio State University Press, 1963.

Bensman, Joseph, *Dollars and Sense,* New York, The Macmillan Co., 1967.

Boulding, Kenneth E., *The Organizational Revolution: a Study in the Ethics of Economic Organization,* New York, Harper & Row, Publishers, 1953.

Braun, Carl F., *Fair Thought and Speech,* Alhambra, Calif., C. F. Braun, 1969.

Childs, Marquis, and Cater, Douglass, *Ethics in a Business Society,* New York, Harper & Row, Publishers, 1954.

Christensen, C. Roland, Andrews, Kenneth R., and Bower, Joseph L., *Business Policy: Text and Cases,* ed. 3, Homewood, Ill., Richard D. Irwin, Inc., 1973.

Christian, Portia, and Hicks, Richard (eds.), *Ethics in Business Conduct: Selected References from the Record; Problems, Attempted Solutions, Ethics in Business Education,* Detroit, Gale Research Co., 1971.

Coleman, Bruce P., and Bonge, John W., *Concepts for Corporate Strategy: Readings in Business Policy,* New York, The Macmillan Co., 1972.

Diamond, Sigmund, *The Reputation of the American Businessman,* Gloucester, Mass., Peter Smith, 1970.

Dietze, Gottfried, *In Defense of Property,* Chicago, Henry Regnery Co., 1963.

Eckel, Malcolm W., *Case Studies from the Ethics of Decision Making,* New York, Morehouse-Barlow Co., Inc., 1968.

Elbing, Alvar O., and Elbing, C. J., *Value Issues of Business,* New York, McGraw-Hill Book Co., 1967.

Flubacher, Joseph Francis, *The Concept of Ethics in the History of Economics,* New York, Vantage, 1950.

Fulton, R. B., *Adam Smith Speaks to Our Times; a Study of His Ethical Ideas,* Boston, Christopher Publishing House, 1963.

Garrett, Thomas M., *Ethics in Business,* New York, Sheed & Ward, 1963.
Business Ethics, New York, Appleton-Century-Crofts, 1966.

Garrett, Thomas M., Baumhart, R. C., Purcell, T. V., and Roets, P., *Cases in Business Ethics,* New York, Appleton-Century-Crofts, 1968.

Gelinier, Octave, *The Enterprise Ethic,* Levittown, N.Y., Transatlantic Arts, Inc., n.d.

Hadley, Arthur T., *Standards of Public Morality,* reprint of 1907 ed., New York, Arno Press, 1973.

Healy, James, S.J., *The Just Wage, 1750-1890, A Study of Moralists: From Saint Alphonsus to Leo XIII,* The Hague, Martinus Nijhoff, 1966.

Heilbroner, Robert L., *The Worldly Philosophers,* ed. 4, New York, Simon & Schuster, Inc., 1972.

Heyne, Paul T., *Private Keepers of the Public Interest,* New York, McGraw-Hill Book Co., 1968.

Hodges, Luther, *The Business Conscience,* Englewood Cliffs, N.J., Prentice-Hall, Inc., 1963.

Johnston, Herbert, *Business Ethics,* New York, Pitman Publishing Corp., 1956.

Masterson, Thomas, and Nunan, J. Carlton (eds.), *Ethics in Business,* New York, Pitman Publishing Corp., 1968.

Merrill, Harwood, *Responsibilities of Business Leadership,* Cambridge, Mass., Harvard University Press, 1948.

Milton, Charles R., *Ethics and Expediency in Personnel Management: a Critical History of Personnel Philosophy,* Columbia, S.C., University of South Carolina Press, 1970.

Mulcahy, Richard, *Economics of Heinrich Pesch,* New York, Holt, Rinehart & Winston, Inc., 1952.

Myrdal, Gunnar, *An American Dilemma,* New York, Harper & Row, Publishers, 1944.

Nider, Johannes, *On the Contracts of Merchants,* ed. by R. B. Shuman, translated by C. H. Reeves, Norman, Okla., University of Oklahoma Press, 1966.

Noonan, John T., *The Scholastic Analysis of Usury,* Cambridge, Mass., Harvard University Press, 1957.

Passell, Peter, and Ross, Leonard, *Retreat from Riches: Affluence and Its Enemies,* New York, The Viking Press, Inc., 1974.

Powers, Charles W. (ed.), *People-Profits: the Ethics of Investment,* New York, Council on Religion and International Affairs, 1972.

Preston, Lee E., *Social Issues in Marketing,* Glenview, Ill., Scott, Foresman & Co., 1968.

Proudhon, P. J., *What is Property?,* translated by B. R. Tucker, New York, The Humboldt Publishing Co., n.d.

Russon, Allien R., *Personality Development for Business,* ed. 4, Cincinnati, South-Western Publishing Co., 1973.

Selekman, Benjamin, *A Moral Philosophy for Management,* New York, McGraw-Hill Book Co., 1959.

Sharp, Frank C., and Fox, Philip G., *Business Ethics: Studies in Fair Competition,* New York, Appleton-Century-Crofts, 1969, copyright 1937.

Shenfield, Barbara, *Company Boards: Their Responsibilities to Shareholders, Employees, and the Community,* Mystic, Conn., Lawrence Verry, 1971.

Simon, John G., Powers, Charles W., and Gunnemann, Jon P., *The Ethical Investor: Universities and Corporate Responsibility,* New Haven, Conn., Yale University Press, 1972.

Smith, George A., Jr., and Matthews, John B., Jr., *Business, Society, and the Individual,* rev. ed., Homewood, Ill., Richard D. Irwin, Inc., 1967.

Taeusch, Carl F., *Policy and Ethics in Business,* reprint of 1931 ed., New York, Arno Press, Inc., 1973.

Taylor, O. H., *Economics and Liberalism; Collected Papers,* Cambridge, Mass., Harvard University Press, 1955.

Veblen, Thorstein, *The Theory of the Leisure Class,* New York, The Macmillan Co., 1899.

Walton, Clarence C., *Ethos and the Executive: Values in Managerial Decision Making,* Englewood Cliffs, N.J., Prentice-Hall, Inc., 1969.

Wirtenberger, Henry, *Morality and Business,* Chicago, Loyola University Press, 1962.

7. INDUSTRIAL ETHICS: MANAGEMENT, LABOR, CAPITALISM

Bagrit, Leon, *The Age of Automation,* New York, The New American Library, 1965.

Baldwin, R. W., *Social Justice,* Elmsford, N.Y., Pergamon Press, Inc., 1966.

Bowie, Norman E., *Towards a New Theory of Distributive Justice,* Amherst, Mass., University of Massachusetts Press, 1971.

Buckingham, Walter, *Automation: Its Impact on Business and People,* New York, Harper & Row, Publishers, 1961.

Clark, John Maurice, *Economic Institutions and Human Welfare,* New York, Alfred A. Knopf, Inc., 1957.

Cronin, John F., *Catholic Social Principles,* Milwaukee, The Bruce Publishing Co., 1950.

Diebold, John, *Beyond Automation,* New York, McGraw-Hill Book Co., Inc., 1964.

Drummond, William, *Social Justice,* Milwaukee, The Bruce Publishing Co., 1955.

Dunlop, John T., *Automation and Technological Change,* Englewood Cliffs, N.J., Prentice-Hall, Inc., 1962.

Ellul, Jacques, *The Technological Society,* translated by John Wilkinson, New York, Alfred A. Knopf, Inc., 1970.

Ginzberg, Eli, and Yohalem, Alice M., *Corporate Lib: Women's Challenge to Management,* Baltimore, The Johns Hopkins University Press, 1973.

Nell-Breuning, Oswald von, *Reconstruction of Social Economy,* Milwaukee, The Bruce Publishing Co., 1936.

Rescher, Nicholas, *Distributive Justice: a Constructive Critique of the Utilitarian Theory of Distribution,* Indianapolis, The Bobbs-Merrill Co., Inc., 1966.

Ryan, John A., *Distributive Justice,* New York, The Macmillan Co., 1942.

Smith, William J., *Spotlight on Labor Unions,* New York, Duell, Sloan & Pearce, Inc., 1946.

Smuts, Robert W., *Women and Work in America,* New York, Columbia University Press, 1959.

Tannenbaum, Frank, *A Philosophy of Labor,* New York, Alfred A. Knopf, Inc., 1951.

Tawney, R. H., *Religion and the Rise of Capitalism,* New York, Harcourt, Brace & Co., Inc., 1926.

Toner, Jerome, *The Closed Shop,* Washington, D.C., American Council on Public Affairs, 1944.

Weber, Max, *The Protestant Ethic and the Spirit of Capitalism,* London, George Allen & Unwin, Ltd., 1930.

8. MARXIAN ETHICS: COMMUNISM, SOCIALISM

Acton, H. B., *The Illusion of the Epoch: Marxism-Leninism as a Philosophical Creed,* London, Cohen & West, 1955.

Ash, William, *Marxism and Moral Concepts,* New York, Monthly Review Press, 1964.

Avineri, Shlomo, *The Social and Political Thought of Karl Marx,* Cambridge, Cambridge University Press, 1969.

Barton, William E., *The Moral Challenge of Communism: Some Ethical Aspects of Marxist-Leninist Society,* London, Friends Home Service Committee, 1966.

459

Berdyaev, Nicholas, *The Origin of Russian Communism,* London, Geoffrey, Bles, Ltd., Publishers, 1937.

Cameron, J. M., *A Scrutiny of Marxism,* London, SCM Press, Ltd., 1948.

Cole, G. D. H., *Meaning of Marxism,* London, Victor Gollancz, Ltd., 1948.

Croce, Benedetto, *Historical Materialism and the Economics of Marx,* New York, The Macmillan Co., 1914; London, Frank Cass & Co., Ltd., 1966.

Denno, Theodore, *The Communist Millenium: the Soviet View,* The Hague, Martinus Nijhoff, 1964.

Dunayevskaya, Raya, *Marxism and Freedom: From 1776 until Today,* preface by Herbert Marcuse, New York, Twayne Publishers, Inc., 1964.

Dunn, John, *Modern Revolutions,* Cambridge, Cambridge University Press, 1972.

Dupré, Louis, *Philosophical Foundations of Marxism,* New York, Harcourt, Brace & World, Inc., 1966.

Feuerbach, Ludwig, *The Essence of Christianity,* New York, Harper & Row, Publishers, 1957.

Friedrich, Carl J. (ed.), *Nomos VIII: Revolution,* New York, Atherton Press, 1966.

Hampsch, George H., *The Theory of Communism, an Introduction,* New York, Philosophical Library, Inc., 1965.

Hook, Sidney, *From Hegel to Marx,* New York, Humanities Press, Inc., 1950.

Hunt, R. N. Carew, *Theory and Practice of Communism,* New York, The Macmillan Co., 1951.

Kalin, Martin G., *The Utopian Flight from Unhappiness: Freud against Marx on Social Progress,* Chicago, Nelson-Hall Co., 1974.

Kamenka, Eugene, *The Ethical Foundations of Marxism,* New York, Praeger Publishers, Inc., 1962.
Marxism and Ethics, New York, St. Martin's Press, 1969.

Kautsky, Karl, *Ethics and the Materialist Conception of History,* Chicago, Kerr, 1907.

Kropotkin, Peter A., *Ethics, Origin and Development,* New York, Dial Press, 1924.

Krosch, Karl, *Marxism and Philosophy,* translated by F. Halliday, London, New Left Books, 1972.

Lewis, John, *Marxism and the Open Mind,* London, Routledge & Kegan Paul, Ltd., 1957.

Macintyre, Alasdair, *Herbert Marcuse: an Exposition and a Polemic,* ed. by Frank Kermode, New York, The Viking Press, Inc., 1970.

Marcuse, Herbert, *Counterrevolution and Revolt,* Beacon Press, 1972.
An Essay on Liberation, Boston, Beacon Press, 1969.
One Dimensional Man, Boston, Beacon Press, 1964.
Reason and Revolution: Hegel and the Rise of Social Theory, New York, Humanities Press, Inc., 1954.
Soviet Marxism: a Critical Analysis, New York, Columbia University Press, 1958.

Marek, Franz, *Philosophy of World Revolution,* translated by D. Simon, London, Lawrence & Wishart, Ltd., 1969.

Mayo, H. B., *Democracy and Marxism,* New York, Oxford University Press, Inc., 1955.

McFadden, Charles, *The Philosophy of Communism,* New York, Benziger Brothers, Inc., 1939.

Meyer, Alfred G., *Marxism: the Unity of Theory and Practice,* Cambridge, Mass., Harvard University Press, 1970.

Niebuhr, Reinhold, *Moral Man and Immoral Society,* New York, Charles Scribner's Sons, 1933.

Nivison, David S., *Communist Ethics and Chinese Tradition,* Cambridge, Mass., The M.I.T. Press, 1954.

Parsons, Howard L., *Ethics in the Soviet Union Today,* New York, American Institute for Marxist Studies, 1965.

Humanism and Marx's Thought, Springfield, Ill., Charles C Thomas, Publisher, 1971.

Petrazhitskii, Lev I., *Law and Morality,* Cambridge, Mass., Harvard University Press, 1955.

Plamenatz, John, *Ideology,* London, The Pall Mall Press, 1970.

Sanderson, John B., *An Interpretation of the Political Ideas of Marx and Engels,* London, Longman Group Ltd., 1969.

Schram, S. A., *The Political Thought of Mao-Tse-Tung,* Harmondsworth, England, Penguin Books, Ltd., 1969.

Schumpeter, Joseph, *Capitalism, Socialism, and Democracy,* New York, Harper & Row, Publishers, 1950.

Selsam, Howard, *Ethics and Progress: New Values in a Revolutionary World,* New York, International Publishers Co., Inc., 1965.
Socialism and Ethics, London, Lawrence & Wishart, Ltd., 1949.

Sheed, Frank, *Communism and Man,* New York, Sheed & Ward, 1939.

Somerville, J., *Soviet Philosophy,* New York, Philosophical Library, Inc., 1946.

Stalin, Joseph, *Dialectical and Historical Materialism,* New York, International Publishers Co., Inc., 1940.

Stillman, Edmund O., *Bitter Harvest; the Intellectual Revolt Behind the Iron Curtain,* New York, Praeger Publishers, Inc., 1959.

Sweezy, Paul, *Socialism,* New York, McGraw-Hill Book Co., 1949.

Titarenko, A. H., *Morality and Politics: Critical Essays on Contemporary Views about the Relationship between Morality and Politics in Bourgeois Sociology,* ed. by Jim Riordan, translated by Don Danemanis, London, Central Books, 1972.

Tucker, Robert C., *Philosophy and Myth in Karl Marx,* London, Cambridge University Press, 1961.

Venable, Vernon, *Human Nature: the Marxian View,* New York, The World Publishing Co., 1966.

Von Mises, Ludwig, *Socialism,* New Haven, Conn., Yale University Press, 1951.

Wetter, Gustav A., *Dialectical Materialism,* New York, Frederick A. Praeger, Inc., 1958.
Soviet Ideology Today, translated by Peter Heath, New York, Frederick A. Praeger, 1966.

Wilson, Edmund, *To the Finland Station,* Garden City, N.Y., Doubleday & Co., Inc., 1940.

9. INTERNATIONAL ETHICS: WORLD COMMUNITY, WAR, PEACE

Adler, Mortimer, *How to Think About War and Peace,* New York, Simon & Schuster, Inc., 1944.

Bainton, Roland, *Christian Attitudes Toward War and Peace,* Nashville, Tenn., Abingdon Press, 1960.

Clausewitz, Karl von, *On War,* translated by J. J. Graham, 3 vols., London, Routledge & Kegan Paul, Ltd., 1949.

Crosser, Paul K., *War is Obsolete: the Dialectics of Military Technology and its Consequences,* Amsterdam, B. R. Grünner, 1972.

Delavignette, Robert, *Christianity and Colonialism,* New York, Hawthorn Books, Inc., 1964.

De Soras, Alfred, *International Morality,* New York, Hawthorn Books, Inc., 1963.

Eppstein, John, *The Catholic Tradition of the Law of Nations,* Washington, D.C., Catholic Association for International Peace, 1935.
Code of International Ethics, Westminster, Md., The Newman Press, 1953.

Forsyth, M. G., Keens-Soper, H. M. A., and Savigear, P. (eds.), *The Theory of International Relations. Selected texts from Gentili to Treitschke,* London, George Allen & Unwin, Ltd., 1970.

461

Gandhi, M. K., *Non-Violence in Peace and War*, 2 vols., Ahmedabad, India, Navajivan Publishing House, 1942-1948.

Goldmann, Kjell, *International Norms and War Between States, Three Studies in International Politics*, Stockholm, Läromedelsförlagen, for The Swedish Institute of International Affairs, 1971.

Halévy, Élie, *The Era of Tyrannies: Essays on Socialism and War*, translated by R. K. Webb, note by Fritz Stern, New York, Doubleday and Co., 1965.

Hodgson, Peter, *Nuclear Physics in Peace and War*, New York, Hawthorn Books, Inc., 1961.

Horsburgh, H. J. N., *Non-Violence and Aggression: a Study of Gandhi's Moral Equivalent of War*, London, Oxford University Press, 1968.

Hutchins, Robert M., *St. Thomas and the World State*, Aquinas Lecture, Milwaukee, Marquette University Press, 1949.

Kahn, Herman, *On Thermonuclear War*, Princeton, N.J., Princeton University Press, 1961.
    Thinking about the Unthinkable, New York, Horizon Press, 1962.

Lawler, Justus, *Nuclear War, the Ethic, the Rhetoric, the Reality*, Westminster, Md., The Newman Press, 1965.

Murray, Thomas E., *Nuclear Policy for War and Peace*, Cleveland, World Publishing Co., 1960.

Nagle, William, *Morality and Modern Warfare*, Baltimore, Helicon Press, Inc., 1960.

O'Brien, William V., *Nuclear War, Deterrence and Morality*, Westminster, Md., The Newman Press, 1967.

Ramsey, Paul, *War and the Christian Conscience*, Durham, N.C., Duke University Press, 1961.

Rapoport, Anatol, *Strategy and Conscience*, introd. by Karl W. Deutsch, New York, Harper & Row, Publishers, 1964.

Russell, Bertrand, *Common Sense and Nuclear Warfare*, New York, Simon & Schuster, Inc., 1959.

Ryan, John K., *Modern War and Basic Ethics*, Milwaukee, The Bruce Publishing Co., 1940.

Scott, James B., *The Catholic Conception of International Law*, Washington, D.C., Georgetown University Press, 1934.

Stratmann, F., *War and Christianity Today*, Westminster, Md., The Newman Press, 1956.

Stein, Walter, *Nuclear Weapons, a Catholic Response*, New York, Sheed & Ward, 1961.

Sturzo, Luigi, *Nationalism and Internationalism*, New York, Roy Publishers, Inc., 1946.

Thompson, Charles S. (ed.), *Morals and Missiles*, London, James Clarke & Co., Ltd., Publishers, 1959.

Tooke, Joan D., *The Just War in Aquinas and Grotius*, London, SPCK (The Society for Promoting Christian Knowledge), 1965.

10. EARTH: THE AGED, POLLUTION, POPULATION, POVERTY, RESOURCES

Allsop, Bruce, *The Garden Earth: the Case for Ecological Morality*, New York, William Morrow & Co., Inc., 1972.

Armstrong, Terry R. (ed.), *Why do We Still Have an Ecological Crisis?* Englewood Cliffs, N.J., Prentice-Hall, Inc., 1972.

Barbour, Ian, *Earth Might Be Fair: Reflections on Ethics, Religion and Ecology*, Englewood Cliffs, N.J., Prentice-Hall, Inc., 1972.

Barkley, Paul W., and Seckler, David, *Economic Growth and Environmental Decay: the Solution Becomes the Problem*, New York, Harcourt Brace Jovanovich, 1972.

Baumol, William J., and Oates, Wallace E., *The Theory of Environmental Policy,* Englewood Cliffs, N.J., Prentice-Hall, Inc., 1975.

Beatty, Ralph P., *Senior Citizen,* Springfield, Ill., Charles C Thomas, Publisher, 1962.

Benthall, Jonathan (ed.), *Ecology in Theory and Practice,* New York, The Viking Press, Inc., 1973.

Black, John, *The Dominion of Man: the Search for Ecological Responsibility,* Chicago, Aldine Publishing Co., 1970.

Borgstrom, Georg, *Too Many: an Ecological Overview of Earth's Limitations,* New York, The Macmillan Co., 1971.

Boughey, Arthur S., *Ecology of Populations,* ed. 2, ed. by Charles E. Stewart, New York, The Macmillan Co., 1973.

Brantl, Virginia M., and Brown, Sr. Marie R. (eds.), *Readings in Gerontology,* St. Louis, The C. V. Mosby Co., 1973.

Brubaker, Sterling, *To Live on Earth: Man and His Environment in Perspective,* Baltimore, The Johns Hopkins University Press, 1972.

Carson, Rachel, *Edge of the Sea,* New York, The New American Library, Inc., 1971.

 Silent Spring, Boston, Houghton Mifflin Co., 1962.

Chen, Kan, and Lagler, Kurt (eds.), *Growth Policy: Population, Environment, and Beyond,* Ann Arbor, Mich., University of Michigan Press, 1974.

Cobb, J. B., Jr., *Is It Too Late: a Theology of Ecology,* Milwaukee, Bruce Publishing Co., 1971.

Commoner, Barry, *The Closing Circle,* New York, Alfred A. Knopf, Inc., 1971; Bantam Books, Inc., 1972.

 Science and Survival, New York, Ballantine Books, Inc., 1970.

De Beauvoir, Simone, *The Coming of Age: the Study of the Aging Process,* New York, G. P. Putnam's Sons, 1972.

Deedy, John, and Nobile, Philip (eds.), *The Complete Ecology Fact Book,* New York, Doubleday Publishing Co., 1972.

Degen, Charles, *Age Without Fear: How to Face the Later Years With Confidence,* Jericho, N.Y., Exposition Press, 1972.

Disch, Robert (ed.), *Ecological Conscience: Values for Survival,* Englewood Cliffs, N.J., Prentice-Hall, Inc., 1970.

Douglas, William O., *The Three Hundred Year War: a Chronicle of Ecological Disease,* New York, Random House, Inc., 1972.

Dubos, René, *A God Within,* New York, Charles Scribner's Sons, 1973.

 So Human an Animal, New York, Charles Scribner's Sons, 1968.

Egler, Frank, *Way of Science: a Philosophy of Ecology for the Layman,* Riverside, N.J., Hafner Press, 1970.

Ehrenfeld, David, *Conserving Life on Earth,* New York, Oxford University Press, 1972.

Ehrlich, Paul, *The Population Bomb,* new rev. ed., New York, Ballantine Books, Inc., 1971.

Ehrlich, Paul, and Ehrlich, Anne, *Population, Resources, Environment,* ed. 2, San Francisco, W. H. Freeman & Co., Publishers, 1972.

Emery, F. E., and Trist, E. L., *Towards a Social Ecology: Contextual Appreciation of the Future in the Present,* New York, Plenum Publishing Corp., 1973.

Falk, Richard A., *This Endangered Planet: Prospects and Proposals for Human Survival,* New York, Random House, Inc., 1972.

Foss, Philip O., *Politics and Ecology,* N. Scituate, Mass., Duxbury Press, 1972.

Fraser, Dean, *The People Problem: What You Should Know About Growing Population and Vanishing Resources,* Bloomington, Ind., Indiana University Press, 1973.

Frejka, Tomas, *The Future of Population Growth: Alternate Paths to Equilibrium,* New York, John Wiley & Sons, Inc., 1973.

Hall, Judith, *The Problem That Cannot Be Resolved: Population and World Order,* New York, Grossman Publishers, 1975.

Hardin, Garrett, *Exploring New Ethics for Survival: the Voyage of the Spaceship Beagle,* New York, The Viking Press, Inc., 1972.

Jackson, Barbara Ward, Lady, *A New Creation? Reflections on the Environmental Issue,* Vatican City, Pontifical Commission for Justice and Peace, 1973.

   The Rich Nations and the Poor Nations, New York, W. W. Norton & Co., Inc., 1962.

Jackson, Barbara Ward, Lady and Dubos, René, *Only One Earth: the Care and Maintenance of a Small Planet,* New York, W. W. Norton & Co., Inc., 1972.

Juzck, Charles, and Mehrtens, Susan, *Earthkeeping: Reading in Human Ecology,* Pacific Grove, Calif., The Boxwood Press, 1974.

Kaplan, S. J., and Kivy-Rosenberg, E., *Ecology and the Quality of Life,* Springfield, Ill., Charles C Thomas, Publisher, 1973.

Katz, Robert, *A Giant in the Earth: the Green Revolution and the Future With 100 Billion People,* New York, Stein & Day, Publishers, 1972.

Kozlovsky, Daniel G. (ed.), *An Ecological and Evolutionary Ethic,* Englewood Cliffs, N.J., Prentice-Hall, Inc., 1974.

Liang, Daniel S., *Facts About Aging,* Springfield, Ill., Charles C Thomas, Publisher, 1973.

Lippard, Vernon W. (ed.), *Family Planning, Demography, and Human Sexuality in Medical Education,* New York, Josiah Macy, Jr. Foundation, 1974.

Livingston, John A., *One Cosmic Instant: Man's Fleeting Supremacy,* Boston, Houghton Mifflin Co., 1973.

McHarg, Ian, *Design with Nature,* Garden City, N.Y., Natural History Press, 1971.

Maddox, John, *The Doomsday Syndrome,* New York, McGraw-Hill Book Co., 1973.

Meeker, Joseph W., *The Spheres of Life: an Introduction to World Ecology,* New York, Charles Scribner's Sons, 1974.

Percy, Charles H., and Mangel, Charles, *Growing Old in the Country of the Young,* New York, McGraw-Hill Book Co., 1974.

Scoby, Donald R. (ed.), *Environmental Ethics: Studies of Man's Self-Destruction,* Minneapolis, Burgess Publishing Co., 1971.

Sloan, Irving J., *Environment and the Law,* Dobbs Ferry, N.Y., Oceana Publications, Inc., 1971.

Slusser, Gerald, and Slusser, Dorothy M., *Technology, the God That Failed: the Environmental Catastrophe,* Philadelphia, The Westminster Press, 1971.

Smith, G., and Smyth, J. C., *Biology of Affluence,* New York, Longman, Inc., 1973.

Soleri, Paolo, *The Bridge Between Matter and Spirit is Matter Becoming Spirit,* New York, Doubleday Publishing Co., 1973.

Stanford, Quentin (ed.), *The World's Population: Problems of Growth,* New York, Oxford University Press, 1972.

Stone, Glenn C. (ed.), *A New Ethic for a New Earth,* New York, Friendship Press, 1971.

Strong, Maurice F. (ed.), *Who Speaks for Earth?* New York, W. W. Norton & Co., Inc., 1973.

Vann, Anthony, and Rogers, Paul (eds.), *Human Ecology and World Development,* New York, Plenum Publishing Corp., 1974.

464

11. SPECIALIZED BIBLIOGRAPHIES

Bochenski, Joseph M. (ed.), *Guide to Marxist Philosophy: an Introductory Bibliography,* Chicago, The Swallow Press, Inc., 1972.

Dollen, Charles J., *Abortion in Context: a Select Bibliography,* Metuchen, N.J., Scarecrow Press, Inc., 1970.

Floyd, Mary K. (ed.), *Abortion Bibliography for 1970,* Troy, N.Y., Whitston Publishing Co., 1972.
Abortion Bibliography for 1971, Troy, N.Y., Whitston Publishing Co., 1973.
Abortion Bibliography for 1972, Troy, N.Y., Whitston Publishing Co., 1973.
Abortion Bibliography for 1973, Troy, N.Y., Whitston Publishing Co., 1974.

Israel, Stanley, *The Bibliography on Divorce,* New York, Bloch Publishing Co., Inc., 1973.

McLean, George F. (ed.), *An Annotated Bibliography of Philosophy in Catholic Thought, 1900-1964,* New York, Frederick Ungar Publishing Co., Inc., 1967.
A Bibliography of Christian Philosophy and Contemporary Issues, New York, Frederick Ungar Publishing Co., Inc., 1967.

Matczak, Sebastian A., *Philosophy: a Select, Classified Bibliography of Ethics, Economics, Law, Politics, Sociology,* Louvain, Belgium, N.V. Uitgeverij Nauwelaerts Edition S. A., 1969.

Parker, William, *Homosexuality: a Selective Bibliography of Over Three Thousand Items,* Metuchen, N.J., Scarecrow Press, Inc., 1971.

Sollitto, Sharmon, and Veatch, Robert M. (eds.), *A Selected and Partially Annotated Bibliography of Society, Ethics and the Life Sciences, 1975,* rev. by Dianne Fenner, Hastings-on-Hudson, N.Y., Institute of Society, Ethics and the Life Sciences, 1975.

Weinberg, Martin, and Bell, Alan (eds.), *Homosexuality: an Annotated Bibliography,* New York, Harper & Row, Publishers, 1972.

INDEX